From Myth to Modern Mind

American University Studies

Series V
Philosophy

Vol. 171

PETER LANG
New York • Washington, D.C./Baltimore
Bern • Frankfurt am Main • Berlin • Vienna • Paris

Richard H. Schlagel

From Myth to Modern Mind

A Study of the Origins
and Growth of Scientific Thought

Volume 2
Copernicus through Quantum Mechanics

PETER LANG
New York • Washington, D.C./Baltimore
Bern • Frankfurt am Main • Berlin • Vienna • Paris

Library of Congress Cataloging-in-Publication Data

Schlagel, Richard H.
From myth to modern mind: a study of the origins and growth of scientific
thought/ Richard H. Schlagel.
p.   cm. — (American university studies. Series V, Philosophy; vol. 170-171)
Includes bibliographical references and index.
Contents: v. 1. Theogony through Ptolemy — v. 2. Copernicus through
quantum mechanics.
1. Science—Philosophy—History. 2. Science—History.
I. Title. II. Series.
Q174.8.S335   509—dc20   94-47030
ISBN 0-8204-2672-5 (v.1)
ISBN 0-8204-2699-7 (v.2)
ISSN 0739-6392

Die Deutsche Bibliothek-CIP-Einheitsaufnahme

Schlagel, Richard H.:
From myth to modern mind: a study of the origins and growth of scientific
thought/ Richard H. Schlagel. - New York; Washington, D.C./Baltimore; San
Francisco; Bern; Frankfurt am Main; Berlin; Vienna; Paris: Lang.
Vol. 1. Theogony through Ptolemy.
(American university studies: Ser. 5, Philosophy; Vol. 170)
ISBN 0-8204-2672-5
NE: American university studies/ 05
Vol. 2. Copernicus through quantum mechanics.
(American university studies: Ser. 5, Philosophy; Vol. 171)
ISBN 0-8204-2699-7
NE: American university studies/ 05

Cover design by Nona Reuter.

The paper in this book meets the guidelines for permanence and durability
of the Committee on Production Guidelines for Book Longevity
of the Council of Library Resources.

© 1996 Peter Lang Publishing, Inc., New York

Printed in the United States of America.

DEDICATED TO MY WIFE

IN GRATEFUL APPRECIATION

FOR HER FORTITUDE, ENCOURAGEMENT, AND HELP

TABLE OF CONTENTS

x

ILLUSTRATIONS

PREFACE

I would like to take this opportunity, as I did in the previous Preface, to express my deep gratitude to those who made this endeavor possible. First, thanks are due to the Columbia School of Arts and Sciences of The George Washington University for granting me five sabbatical leaves that permitted the time for the research and writing such an extended project entailed, along with subventions for preparing and supporting the final publication. Second, as someone who regards the computer as a powerful aide but still somewhat alien species, and who was distressed at the prospect of having to submit the manuscripts to the publisher in "camera ready" form, I want to convey my warm gratitude to Mrs. Ann Reese and her husband Paul (Kip) for their dedicated, exacting work in putting the texts in final form to be photoprinted by Peter Lang. Third, I would like to thank Ms. Nona Reuter, the Editor at Peter Lang, for supervising the editing of the two volumes and especially for designing the very attractive book covers.

Finally, although there is no adequate way of stating my appreciation, at least I want to thank my wife again for enabling me to devote all my 'spare time' to this work by relieving me of the financial and other chores that are essential for successfully organizing one's life, but which can be so tedious and time consuming. As a result of her support and encouragement, I have had the privilege of devoting all of my leisure to coming to know the thinking of these outstanding philosophers and scientists, which has been a great joy. In contrast to the usual conception of science as an abstract, arid, personally irrelevant discipline, I have tried to convey some of the adventure, excitement, and romantic significance that accompanies the scientific endeavor to come to a truer conception of the universe. Would that this work conveys to the reader as much understanding and pleasure as I derived from writing it.

October 24, 1995   Richard H. Schlagel

INTRODUCTION

As we approach the end of the second millennium stretching from the beginning of the Christian era, among all the extraordinary changes that have erupted in the twentieth century, none is more striking than the increasingly pervasive influence of science and technology on contemporary life. New discoveries and developments in every field from astronomy to zoology are heralded in our newspapers, journals, and television specials. Hardly any aspect of life is left unaffected. There are rumblings of a resurgence of religion, especially among the fundamentalist Protestants and Muslims, but does anyone expect them to withstand the rationalizing, secularizing impact of modern science? Fundamentalism is a ripple from the past, not a wave of the future. Based on the authority of prophets, belief in revealed texts, worship of savior-gods, and adherence to absolute values and sacred institutions, the conservative nature of religions deeply rooted in the past make them vulnerable to cultural and intellectual transformations, whereas science and technology represent dynamic forces of change—cognitive and cultural, as well as institutional. For this reason an understanding of how mankind—people on this isolated but precious planet—came to develop scientific methods of inquiry and theories of explanation is crucial if we are to understand the challenges of the present and prospects for the future.

In this second volume, *Copernicus through Quantum Mechanics*, the endeavor begun in the first, *Theogony through Ptolemy*, to discern and describe "the origins and growth of scientific thought" will be continued. From the archaic legacy of theogonic or mythopoetic cognition we have seen how the Presocratic tradition of successive critical reflection, beginning in the sixth century B.C. among the Milesians, led to a progressively more objective and rational understanding of the astronomical realm, the terrestrial world, and of man. These early reflections culminating in the remarkable cosmological systems of Democritus, Plato, and Aristotle by the fourth century B.C., then evolved to a prototype of modern scientific inquiry among the Hellenistic scientists of the third century associated with the fabled Museum of Alexandria.

As argued previously, had this scientific tradition continued it undoubtedly would have culminated in the belated scientific achievements of the seventeenth century, the "age of genius" that created modern classical science. For despite the critical analyses of Aristotle's astronomical system along with his explanation of gravitational fall and projectile motion by Scholastics from the fourteenth to the sixteenth centuries, the predecessors explicitly mentioned by Copernicus, Kepler, and Galileo (such as Philolaus, Heraclides, Aristarchus of Samos, Euclid, Archimedes, and Apollonius), were the ancient Greeks. What could have been a natural progression to modern classical science was delayed for nearly two millennia.

In the last two centuries prior to the Christian era, even though Greek remained the prevalent language of scholars, the ascendence of the Roman Republic stifled (with the exception of Hipparchus who lived in Alexandria during the second century) the high level of scientific achievements that adorned the third century. Yet, as if to demonstrate its enduring legacy, Hellenism produced in the second century A.D. two of the greatest scientists of antiquity: Ptolemy and Galen. In fact, it was the rejection of the crucial presuppositions of their scientific systems that unleashed the revolutionary potentialities of modern astronomy and physiology. Ptolemy and Galen represent the coda to Hellenistic science, after which there was to be no comparable performance by the Romans or medieval philosophers.

Instead, the Roman genius expressed itself in military conquests, governing, engineering, architecture, art, and literature, rather than mathematics and theoretical science. Whatever conditions are necessary for the flowering of these latter disciplines were lacking in the Roman Empire. Furthermore, the subsequent cultural movement that would determine the intellectual orientation of the Western and Near Eastern worlds would not be scientific but religious. Emerging from the radically different historical background of Judaism, a new cultural and spiritual manifestation, Christianity, would arise creating a fundamentally different *weltanschauung* in the Occident. The eventual triumph of Christianity and emergence of Islam after the seventh century would radically change mankind's ways of conceiving reality, organizing society, justifying ideals, and seeking emotional fulfillment.

Yet even before the fall of Rome in 476 A.D. the centers of learning and culture had dispersed from the West to the East, especially the metropolis established by Constantine at the ancient city of Byzantium. Constantinople, the crown of a brilliant culture, with the magnificent Hagia Sophia as its finest jewel, became the grandest city in Christendom. For the succeeding thousand years, from the fourth to the thirteenth centuries, whatever discoveries occurred in mathematics and science took place in the Eastern domains of Byzantium and especially Islam (with influences from India and China), while darkness settled over the Latin West. Even the subsequent reawakening in the West of a scientific interest in the world largely was due to the stimulus of Arabic and Greek works reintroduced to Europe as a result of the Moslem conquest of southern Spain in the thirteenth century and the Humanists' recovery of ancient manuscripts after the fall of Constantinople in 1453.

Along with the shift in historical sequence, there is a change in emphasis from the first volume. Attempting to present an overview of the origins and growth of modern science (essentially focused on physics and cosmology) from Copernicus to the present precludes, obviously, describing in detail all the numerous contributors to and facets of this extraordinary history. Indeed, within the confines of a single volume only the main features of this achievement can be sketched. Yet in its own way this is an advantage, in the way that a view from a promontory provides a clearer perspective from that acquired closer by. As indicated in the previous volume, the purpose of this study is to attain an overall view of the essential aspects of the development of scientific rationalism from its origin to the present, rather than a detailed understanding of a particular era in the history of science—to acquire an appreciation and understanding of the growth of science to its present status as the most influential cultural and intellectual enterprise in the world.

While the previous volume utilized anthropological and psychological studies in the attempt to describe the *cognitive processes* (for example, decentering, abstracting, refining diffuse and concrete concepts) underlying the growth of scientific thought, this volume will focus on changes and refinements in the *conceptual frameworks* and *methodologies* of science. Since modern science emerged from a background of previous theories (Atomic, Platonic, Aristotelian, Ptolemaic, etc.), as well as diverse methodologies, the nature of this development can be understood best in relation to the creation, transformation, and replacement of the concepts composing these systems of interpretation. As we now believe, human knowledge consists of an intricate network of interrelated concepts that acquire their objective meanings and reference from diverse experiences: mystical or religious, affective or aesthetic, sensory, intuitive (as in logic and mathematics), and observational or experimental. The diversity of these various epistemic origins can be seen in the different systems of Plato, Aristotle, Epicurus, Plotinus, Augustine, Galileo, Kepler, etc. While the most basic, elementary terms of our ordinary language usually retain some meaning from their original ostensive definitions, most words and concepts have acquired their significance over a long history of gradual modification or refinement within a comprehensive conceptual-linguistic framework. Nowhere is this more apparent than in the development of science with its history of continuous theoretical changes based on improved methodologies.

The importance of flexibility in interpreting empirical data along with the significance of conceptual changes was emphasized by Butterfield in his classic study of "the origins of modern science."

> [Scientific] change is brought about, not by new observations or
> additional evidence in the first instance, but by transpositions that
> were taking place inside the minds of the scientists themselves [. . .]
> of all forms of mental activity, the most difficult [. . .] is the art of
> [. . .] placing [the same bundle of data] in a new system of relations
> with one another by giving them a different framework, all of which
> virtually means putting on a different kind of thinking-cap for the
> mind.[1]

While this emphasis on cognitive transpositions is crucial, Butterfield's
statement seems to minimize the role of new discoveries in initiating
conceptual revolutions. Although the methodology of science, unlike the
dogmatic tradition of religions, is progressive in requiring the testing of
theories and experimental probing of nature to uncover new information,
scientists themselves are usually conservative, preferring accepted theories to
revolutionary changes. Thus the greatest stimulus to conceptual change
usually has been the confrontation with anomalous theoretical consequences
or negative experimental results, which then requires the kind of exciting
restructuring of the theoretical framework and alteration in mental outlook
emphasized by Butterfield. Almost by definition, revolutionary changes
originally are counter-intuitive which accounts for the initial resistance to
them.

Conceptual transformations do involve reconceiving familiar phenomena
within novel contexts of relations or different frameworks of interpretation,
exposing presuppositions too familiar even to be regarded as assumptions,
revising the meanings of concepts to comply with the anomalous
developments, and recognizing that theoretical impasses or crises usually are
harbingers of fascinating unforseen possibilities. Rather than modifying single
concepts, it usually is the implicative relations among the meanings of a
complex network of concepts that have to be readjusted when revisions of
theories are forced by recalcitrant data or disruptive developments within the
theory. These revisions of meanings also imply changes in ontology as the
referents of the theories change, but not in such a wholesale, irrational manner
as advocates of the incommensurable interpretation of theory change suggest.[2]

Although each of these processes will be described throughout the book,
illustrations might be useful at this point to preview the contents. The
Copernican revolution consisted of regarding familiar astronomical data from
an altered, sun-centered perspective. Kepler had to discard the time-honored
assumptions of circular, uniform orbital motions in order to obtain agreement

between his laws and Tycho Brahe's astronomical data. To reduce philosophical objections to his telescopic observations in support of the heliocentric theory, Galileo had to combat the Aristotelian distinctions between celestial and terrestrial bodies and "natural" circular and rectilinear motions, replacing these distinctions with new meanings. Achieving a better explanation of projectile motion required replacing Aristotle's conception that unnatural motion required a continuous mover producing a constant velocity with an interpretation incorporating such new concepts as mass, force, inertia, momentum, and acceleration.

But it was Newton who finally eliminated the ancient distinction between celestial and terrestrial motions by conceiving Galileo's law of free fall and Kepler's three planetary laws as manifestations of a single law of gravitation. Lavoisier brought about a revolution in chemistry by using the balance to prove that oxygen was consumed in combustion rather than phlogiston being expelled. Dalton reinvigorated atomism by claiming that the proportional relations in which gases combine could be attributed to the weights of the atoms composing the gases. Young and Fresnel found that the wave theory of light provided a better explanation of diffraction patterns and the polarization of light when refracted through Iceland Crystal than the corpuscular theory. Faraday and Maxwell emended Newtonian mechanics by conceiving electromagnetic phenomena as waves propagated in fields at the same velocity as light.

Einstein concluded that if the velocity of light were accepted as a constant then the asymmetries in electrodynamics could be eliminated, although this meant rejecting Newton's absolute space and time and the previously inviolable assumption of the invariance of spacial, temporal, and mass dimensions with velocity. Planck reluctantly concluded that the ultra-violet catastrophe could be explained if one discarded the venerable assumption that radiational processes occur in continuous, rather than discrete quantities. C.N. Yang and T.D. Lee predicted the violation of parity or mirror symmetry for radiation produced by the weak force. But while scientists constantly test, revise, and extend their theories with correspondingly more precise, novel, and independent predictions, these changes result in a deeper and more comprehensive understanding of the universe, contrary to the skeptical criticisms of science by many philosophers.

Thus a further consequence of this study will be the obvious divergence between the development of modern philosophy and science. In adopting as their paradigm of inquiry the attempt to ground scientific knowledge on some certain foundation, whether the clear and distinct propositions of Descartes, or the privileged access and indubitability of subjective sensory contents like the simple ideas, impressions, sensory manifold, or sense data of Locke, Berkeley, Hume, Kant, and twentieth century philosophers such as Russell, Moore, Ayer, and Carnap (originally), philosophers successively created an impenetrable screen between themselves and physical reality. Although Locke claimed that physical objects consist of particles and that our ideas of primary qualities "resemble" the actual qualities of the particles composing matter, the other philosophers denied that we could attain any knowledge of the "secret powers" or "inner natures" of physical objects, to use Hume's terminology.

The existence of a cognitive curtain between our minds and an independent reality was reinforced by Kant's distinction between the phenomenal world which, though "objectively real" was "transcendentally ideal", meaning that while it was subject to objective laws and therefore not illusory it nevertheless was mind dependent. And while the phenomenal world was the world of things in themselves as they appear to us, we could never know them as they are in themselves. This belief that we could never acquire knowledge of the natures of physical substances, because that would depend upon transcending observations and accepting theoretical entities as having some reality, was the basic thesis of the positivists who attempted to reduce theoretical concepts to protocol statements referring to indubitable sensory data or ordinary physical objects. This antirealist, skeptical tendency is continued today by those who deny any progress to science[3] or any validity to scientific theories beyond their empirical predictability or "adequacy."[4]

But while the philosophers were becoming enclosed in their subjectivistic or skeptical paradigm, the scientists were progressively discovering more about the universe and physical reality based on their different methods of investigation. Although encountering many obstacles and limitations in their inquiries, they did not succumb to the view that they were shut off from the physical world by an impenetrable cognitive screen. When one compares historically the theoretical and technological achievements of scientists in their various fields with the skeptical position of the philosophers one cannot but marvel at the disparity—at the outstanding achievements of the former and the unwarranted pessimism of the latter.

NOTES

1. Herbert Butterfield, *The Origins of Modern Science* (New York: Collier Books, 1962), p. 13. Brackets added.

2. Cf. Thomas S. Kuhn, *The Structure of Scientific Revolutions*, revised edition enlarged (Chicago: University of Chicago Press, [1962] (1970), ch. X.

3. Cf. Arthur Fine, *The Shaky Game* (Chicago: University of Chicago Press, 1986), ch. 7. For a critique of this position from a realist perspective see Richard H. Schlagel, ''Critical Notice: Fine's 'Shaky Game' (and Why NOA is no Ark for Science)'', *Philosophy of Science*, Vol. 58, No. 2, June, 1991, pp. 307-323.

4. Cf. Bas C. van Fraassen, *The Scientific Image* (Oxford: Clarendon Press, 1980, pp. 72, 197. Again, for a critique of this position from a realist perspective see Richard H. Schlagel, ''Experimental Realism: A Critique of Bas van Fraassen's 'Constructive Empiricism,' ''*Review of Metaphysics*, No. 41, June, 1988, pp. 789-814.

CHAPTER I

THE PRECURSORS OF MODERN SCIENCE

[. . .] anyone who is honestly interested in [. . .] the formation of modern science must examine in detail the germinal concepts of the preceding periods.[1]

Clagett

Although the purpose of this volume is to trace the growth of modern science from its inception in the Copernican Revolution, the study would be incomplete if it did not acknowledge the antecedents of this commencement. In the Chapter on "The Dawn of Scientific Thought" in the previous volume, the first question raised was whether the emerging scientific rationalism burst forth as a spontaneous illumination or appeared like a ray of light gradually dispelling the mythical haze that enveloped primitive mentality. With the unveiling of Presocratic thought it became evident, however, that despite the attempt to supplant mythos by logos and to utilize empirical analogies in the endeavor to attain a more objective and rational explanation of natural phenomena, these early philosophers were still reflecting within the conceptual scheme of the older mythopoetic or theogonic systems. The very questions they posed, such as what was the nature of the primal state from which everything arose, how did the one and the many come to be from this original condition, and what principles govern the coming to be and ceasing to be of phenomena, were abstracted unconsciously from the older frameworks of interpretation. Moreover, explicit residuals of Hesiod's *Theogony* could be discerned in Anaximander's *Apeiron* and conception of retributive justice, along with the explanation of change in terms of the conflict of opposites in Heraclitus and Empedocles' notions of Love and Strife. Surely there are novelties of thought, but these are not without their germinal antecedents. So it is with the creation of modern science. To understand why and how it occurred it is necessary to review developments several centuries earlier.

While the revival of learning in the West accelerated in the twelfth and thirteenth centuries, stimulated by the reintroduction of the Latin translations of the Greek classics from the Arabic and the emergence of the medieval universities of Bologna, Paris, Oxford, Prague, and Heidelberg, critical analysis and restructuring of Aristotle's system occurred mainly in the fourteenth century. Still deprived of the major treatises of Greek science and mathematics, along with the most important works of Aristotle, twelfth-century scholastic inquiry was dominated by Platonic and Neoplatonic influences. By the thirteenth century, however, most of the writings of Aristotle were translated from the Siriac-Arabic editions into Latin making possible the synthesis of Christian doctrine and Aristotelian philosophy, accomplished mainly through the writings of the English Franciscan Alexander of Hales, the Dominican Albertus Magnus (Albert von Bollstädt), and the latter's brilliant student Thomas Aquinas.

Having attracted in the twelfth century such renown teachers as Abelard and Peter Lombard, in the thirteenth century the University of Paris ("the mother of universities") was host to such famous scholars as Roger Bacon from England, Albertus Magnus from Germany, and Aquinas and Dante from Italy. In addition, due to an increased knowledge of the texts of Euclid, Ptolemy, Galen, and Alhazen, the thirteenth century is noteworthy for the optical investigations of Dietrich of Freiberg, Robert Grosseteste (Bishop of London), Roger Bacon, John Peckham, and Witelo. A phenomenon long of great interest because of its mysterious effects, magnetism was studied by Petrus of Maricourt, better known as the eccentric Petrus Peregrinus, probably the person extolled by Roger Bacon as the greatest experimenter of his time. In his *Epistola de Magnete* written in 1269, Petrus advanced the study of magnetism probably more than anyone prior to Gilbert. Fascinated by the occult, the thirteenth century also was a period of intensive research in astrology, alchemy, and magic, symptoms of a deep belief in the mysterious, marvelous, and profoundly secrete operations of nature characteristic of the medieval mind.

Thus despite the revival of interest in scientific matters and methodology, as well as emphasis on experimentation and mathematics so evident in the Scholastics of the thirteenth century, the continued dominance of the medieval outlook precluded scientific inquiry emerging as a discipline independent of theology. It was only after further study of the scientific and mathematical writings of the Greeks and Arabs (such as al-Khwarizmi, al-Battani, Avicenna, and Averroës) that this independence became more established.

Ever since Augustine, Christian doctrine had seemed particularly amenable to interpretation by the philosophical systems of Plato or Plotinus, especially as Aristotle was known only for his logical treatises. Now that the corpus of Aristotle was recovered, a new philosophical synthesis was possible, though not without initial opposition. Because of the long dominance of Aristotelianism from the thirteenth to the seventeenth centuries, it is often not realized that the initial reintroduction of Aristotle met with considerable resistance. As Dijksterhius states:

> The reception of Aristotle into Latin Christendom was not therefore completed without ecclesiastical opposition. Three Popes, namely Honorius III, Gregory IX, and Urban IV, promulgated decrees by which the teaching of Aristotelian metaphysics was either forbidden altogether or considered restricted; a long struggle was necessary to overcome this opposition and establish the conviction that the Church could find no more faithful ally and no stouter supporter than the Stagirite.[2]

The person mainly responsible for overcoming this opposition was Thomas Aquinas who, in the *Summa Theologica*, showed that a harmonious synthesis of Aristotle's organismic cosmology with Christian doctrine was not only possible, but constituted a stronger philosophical foundation for Christianity.

SCIENTIFIC RESEARCH IN THE FOURTEENTH CENTURY

This Aristotelian synthesis of the High Scholasticism of the thirteenth century was its great legacy to the fourteenth. Whereas Plato had extolled attaining knowledge of the intelligible world of Forms by freeing the mind from its dependence on the senses which were directed to the unreal world of appearances, Aristotle had claimed that sensory observations, although not constituting scientific knowledge, were the indispensable origin of such knowledge, thereby encouraging investigations of natural phenomena. What is more important, the Scholastics now possessed a theoretical framework that not only enhanced philosophical interpretation of theological problems, as a comprehensive cosmological system providing explanations of celestial and terrestrial phenomena the framework facilitated a critical examination of Aristotle's treatment of motion and change that previously had been beyond the conceptual purview of the Scholastics. Aware of the revolt of the founders of modern science against Scholasticism, it is difficult perhaps to appreciate the way Aristotle's theoretical framework, in this earlier period, projected intelligibility into nature. Compared to earlier centuries, it was as if a mysterious, unfathomable physical cosmos was made comprehensible by means of Aristotle's conceptual analyses, categories of interpretation, and comprehensive explanations. But, as emphasized elsewhere,[3] making more intelligible some domain of experience by interpreting it within a conceptual framework also increases the likelihood that new empirical data or theoretical discrepancies will appear requiring critical evaluation of the interpretative framework itself.

Owing to the pioneering research of the French physicist and historian of science Pierre Duhem and the meticulous investigations of the German scholar Anneliese Maier, both of whom studied the voluminous scientific manuscripts of the fourteenth century, we now are aware of the extensive criticisms and conceptual innovations that fourteenth-century Scholastics brought to their study of the Stagirite. While not detracting from the originality of the seventeenth-century founders of modern science, it is recognized now that their mathematical treatment of physical problems, their use of certain scientific concepts and terms, as well as some crucial discoveries had their origins in this earlier period. This had been obscured by the prevalent practice in the seventeenth century of not acknowledging the sources of one's ideas, leaving an impression of their exclusive uniqueness and originality. Because of his leading role in the scientific revolution, this has been a singular problem in accessing the originality of Galileo's contributions. As Clavelin asserts, Galileo

> held up the "superhuman genius" of Archimedes against the authority of Aristotle in order to mark his determination that all his own discoveries should be based on mathematics; moreover, by failing to mention any Peripatetic contributions other than those of Aristotle himself and only very occasionally of some of his own contemporaries, he apparently tried to disown any debt he might have owed to the Middle Ages.[4]

Because the emphasis of this study is on the growth of scientific thought in terms of changes in methodology and conceptual revisions of explanatory frameworks, the fourteenth century provides a paradigm case illustrating this constructive revision, especially regarding the explanation of motion. As Butterfield states:

> Of all the intellectual hurdles which the human mind has confronted and has overcome in the last fifteen hundred years, the one which seems to me to have been the most amazing in character and the most stupendous in the scope of its consequences is the one relating to the problem of motion [. . .].[5]

Considering the recent remarkable developments in particle physics, molecular biology and genetics, and discovery of the three basic forces in the universe (weak, strong, and electromagnetic) one can question whether explaining motion has been *the* most important achievement of modern science, but it certainly is one such achievement.

ARISTOTLE'S MECHANICS OF MOTION

Before turning to an examination of the contributions of such fourteenth-century Scholastics as Thomas Bradwardine, Richard Swineshead, Jean Buridan, and Nicole Oresme to the understanding of terrestrial and celestial motions, it is necessary to recall Aristotle's explanations since he was the founder of the science of motion in antiquity, the starting point of all future discussions. As we know from Chapter XIV of the previous volume, Aristotle had divided the cosmos into two qualitatively different realms characterized by different natural motions: (1) the celestial realm consisting of the seven planets with their various spheres revolving on diverse axes plus the eighth outermost orb of the fixed stars, all of which rotated in circular orbits around the center of the universe; and (2) the terrestrial world extending from the center of the universe to the inner concave lunar sphere composed of the four elements earth, water, air, and fire, the earth stationary at the center of the cosmos surrounded by the successively lighter elements. Within this cosmic schema Aristotle provided more detailed explanations of the specific occurrences.

As for celestial phenomena, the heavenly bodies along with their spheres were composed of a weightless, incorruptible substance, the aither. The circular motion of the spheres, whose perfect geometrical configuration ensured their unchanging continuity, was transmitted successively to each succeeding sphere guaranteeing the eternal motion of the celestial world. Yet Aristotle later added to this explanation the empathetic influence of a Prime Mover with lesser Intelligences accounting for the individual motions of the planets. As the culmination of all final, formal, and efficient causes, the immaterial Prime Mover (somehow located in the Empyrean Realm beyond the fixed stars) and the lesser Intelligences constituted a logically primary source of motion of the celestial bodies by exerting an empathetic influence analogous to the way an intelligent being can be 'moved' by an object of knowledge or a beloved person. Supplementing a seemingly self-sufficient, quasi-mechanistic account of celestial motion due to the successive rotary influence of the spheres, this additional explanation apparently had its origin in the pervasive teleological, hylomorphism of Aristotle's organismic cosmology.

Ultimately, for Aristotle, the self-generating motion of a living organism caused by a desire of the soul was the most self-contained form of movement—a legacy of primitive animism!

Regarding terrestrial motions, ideally there would be no motion if each of the four elements were in their natural places, places of rest: 'A body moves naturally to the place where it rests without constraint, and rests without constraint in that place to which it moves.' Aristotle's belief that all *terrestrial* motions naturally come to rest, so that rest is 'unconstrained' or 'natural' while continuous motion is 'constrained' or 'unnatural,' is supported by ordinary experience. When removed from their natural places, each element because of its nature either rises (fire and air) or falls (earth and water) by a rectilinear motion to its natural place, earth at the center of the universe, water surrounding the surface of the earth, air filling the terrestrial cavity, and fire surrounding the innermost concave lunar sphere. *Violent* or *unnatural* motion of the *elements*, such as downward bolts of lightning and driving winds, hurricanes, and tornados, are turbulent effects in the terrestrial world produced by the rotation of the moon and the approach and recession of the sun. The heat from the sun causes evaporation and condensation forming clouds in the air that produce downpours of rain. A physical object displaced from its natural state of rest by being pushed, pulled, rotated (twirled), or thrown exhibits an 'enforced' or 'violent unnatural motion' seeking to return to its natural place. A raised, unsupported physical object falls straight to the earth (because the earth is in the center of the universe), as does a projectile when its propelling motion is exhausted. These motions were a species of change that also include generation and decay, composition and decomposition, substantial and qualitative alterations, as well as modifications of state when water freezes or evaporates, a healthy person becomes ill, or a student learns.

As a general description of the most obvious occurrences of natural phenomena Aristotle's system fits reasonably well, far more exactly than Plato's, for example. Only when we examine closely the phenomena described and interpreted within his framework does its weaknesses or limitations become apparent, as they did to the fourteenth-century Scholastics. The problem that had the most significance for later developments in mechanics was Aristotle's treatment of 'natural' and 'unnatural violent motions.' In the case of the 'enforced violent motions' of pushing, pulling, and rotating (as with the potter's wheel), because the mover remains for the most part in contact with what is moved, it is not as difficult to understand how the force of a continuous motion can counteract the object's natural tendency to come to rest. Moreover, it is apparent that the more effort expended in pushing, pulling, and throwing the greater the object will be moved, while heavier objects require additional effort to move them. As Aristotle expressed this, twice the force will move the same object twice as far, while doubling the weight of the object will cause it to be moved half as far with the same effort. He was aware, however, that doubling the weight does not always lead to halving the distance if the weight is so great that the same effort will be insufficient to move it at all.[6]

ARISTOTLE'S EXPLANATION OF ENFORCED UNNATURAL MOTION

Aristotle's explanation of enforced unnatural motion included three fundamental principles that were the main obstacles later in developing a more adequate theory of dynamics: (1) that an inanimate object requires a mover external to it to move it, (2) that unnatural motions require that a mover be in *continuous contact* with the object, and (3) that a constant mover (or force) acting on a body will produce a constant or uniform motion.

As became clear later, no adequate theory of dynamics could be based on these commonsense principles. The first principle is not always necessary while the second conflicts with the law of inertia that in *the absence of external influences* continuous motion is as natural as continuous rest. As the following quotation indicates, Aristotle knew of inertial motion but rejected it because it was contrary to everyday experience.

> Further, no one could say why a thing once set in motion [in a void] should stop anywhere [there being no resistance of the air]; for why should it stop *here* rather than *[t]here*? So that a thing will either be at rest or must be moved *ad infinitum*, unless something more powerful get in its way.[7]

The law of inertia applies in the abstract or idealized situation where no forces act on an object, not the case in ordinary experience. But while idealized conditions will play an essential role in Newtonian mechanics their importance was not recognized by Aristotle. His third principle that a constant force produces a constant velocity conflicts with Newton's law that a constant force (F) acting on a mass (M) produces a constant acceleration (A), not a constant velocity: $F = MA$, not $F = WV$, where (W) equals weight and (V) equals velocity. This was the crucial principle that had to be replaced in the transition to Newtonian mechanics.

ARISTOTLE'S EXPLANATION OF FREE FALL

Aristotle's explanation of free fall, although a natural motion, raised similar problems. An unsupported material object falls, but what exactly produces the observed increase in motion as the object descends to the earth? Without the now familiar concepts of mass, gravitational force, and acceleration, how is free fall to be accurately described and explained? Aristotle's account depends particularly on weight being an inherent quality, fire and air naturally rising while earth and water naturally fall: 'this is precisely what it means for them to be light or heavy, namely, that they tend upward or downward respectively.' Yet many questions remain. What produces this 'natural' motion, a 'tendency' in the object, weight as a 'form' or 'attribute' of the object, the 'attraction' of its natural place, or what? Denser objects are heavier and thus usually fall more rapidly, as indicated by the different velocities with which a heavy rock, a piece of light wood, or a ball of wool fall. This difference is explained by the various amounts of air mixed with the matter of the object, the levity of air counteracting the natural downward motion of the object. Does earth, then, which is devoid of air have an absolute velocity, as some passages suggest? Moreover, because objects have different weights or fall with different velocities depending on the density of the medium, a heavy object falling more slowly in water than in air, is weight an absolute attribute or relative to the medium?

Whatever the answer to these questions, Aristotle formulated what can be called a law of free fall: namely, that the velocity of a freely falling object is directly proportional to its weight and inversely proportional to the resistance of the medium. As we would express the ratio today in an equation: $V = W \backslash R$, where (V) equals the velocity, (W) equals weight, and (R) equals the resistance of the medium.[8] Because a light object like a piece of wood floats in water rather then descends, for (V) to have a positive value W must be greater than (R). An obvious consequence of this law, which Galileo assumed Aristotle realized, is that if the medium is constant the velocity of fall is directly proportional to the weight, so that an object weighing ten times more than another will fall ten times as fast. There is some evidence Aristotle drew this conclusion, although it is not unequivocal. Because in Aristotle's system both (W) and (R) could change as an object falls, (V) either could be constant or could change uniformly or nonuniformly. While it was too early for Aristotle to confront this problem, it became an important issue in the fourteenth century.

ARISTOTLE'S EXPLANATION OF PROJECTILE MOTION

Even less satisfactory than his treatment of enforced unnatural motion and natural free fall was his attempt to explain projectile motion. According to his first principle of motion, for an object to continue to move it must be continuously acted upon by a moving agent in contact with it: 'we can define motion as *the fulfillment of the movable* qua *movable*, the cause of the attribute *being contact with what can move*. . . .'[9] While the enforced unnatural motions of pushing, pulling, and rotating do not raise a problem as long as the mover is in contact with the moved, 'how is it that some things, e.g., things thrown, continue to be in motion when their movement is no longer in contact with them?' What produces the continuous motion of a projectile when the mover, a person's hand, the string of a bow, or a sling ceases to be in contact with the spear, arrow, or stone? Why does a miller's stone or potter's wheel continue to rotate when the action of the mover ceases? Because the natural tendency of the object where possible is to fall to the center of the universe (or to the surface of the earth because the earth lies at the center) and come to rest, what causes it to continue to move and how does the cause operate when the object ceases to be in contact with it?

Since antiquity there have been attempts to explain this, none very satisfactory. One proposed answer ('*antiperistasis*') attributed to Plato is that as the object is put in motion by the mover it leaves a void behind it, and because nature opposes a vacuum the air rushing in to fill the void propels the object forward.[10] Counteracted by the resistance of the air and the natural tendency to fall and come to rest, the object's forward motion gradually diminishes. Rejecting this explanation, Aristotle attributed the motion of the projectile to the compressed air behind it produced by the motion of the original mover, the decompressing air successively propelling the object, which in turn is resisted by the air and tendency to fall. According to this account, when the original mover ceases to be in contact with the adjacent air its effect of having compressed the air leaves the latter as a mover propelling the object through a series of transmitted pressures:

> [. . .] the original movent gives the power of being a movent either to air or to water [. . .] naturally adapted for imparting and undergoing motion [. . .] [which] ceases to be in motion at the moment when its movent ceases to move it, but it still remains a movent, and so it causes something else consecutive with it to be in motion, and of this again the same may be said. The motion begins to cease when the

motive force produced in one member of the consecutive series is at
each stage less than that possessed by the preceding member [. . .].[11]

The phrase 'naturally adapted for imparting and undergoing motion' expresses
Aristotle's conviction that air and water, being lighter than the object, can be
moved more rapidly than the latter's natural downward motion, thus pushing
it forward despite its tendency to fall: 'the air that has been pushed pushes
[. . .] with a movement quicker than the natural locomotion [. . .] to its proper
place.' Applying to an anterior cause, this hardly would explain the motion of
a discus or javelin caused by the thrower's hand being in contact with the
object.

BURIDAN'S THEORY OF IMPETUS

As we shall find, there were many objections to this explanation that
awakened the Scholastics of the fourteenth century from their "dogmatic
slumber": that is, from the belief that "the philosopher" had provided final
explanations of these occurrences. The most systematic criticism was that of
Jean Buridan who was the rector of the University of Paris and founder of the
school of the dynamics of motion at Paris.[12] Regarding both the explanations
of Plato and Aristotle which depended upon the pressure of air, he raised the
following cogent objections. (1) When a smith's grinding mill is revolved it
continues to move after the source of motion is withdrawn, even though it does
not leave its original place (as a projectile does) allowing air to press against
it. (2) 'A lance having a conical posterior as sharp as its anterior would be
moved after projection just as swiftly as it would be without a sharp conical
posterior. But surely the air following could not push a sharp end in this way,
because the air would be easily divided by the sharpness.' (p. 533). (3) A boat
under sail will continue to glide forward even after the sails are drawn and in
opposition to the current of water and flow of air, thus its motion cannot be
due to the push of air from behind. (4) 'Also a ship drawn swiftly is moved
a long time after the haulers have stopped pulling it' (p. 534), so its motion is
not caused by the posterior pressure of air. (5) 'Again, the air, regardless of
how fast it moves, is easily divisible. Hence it is not evident as to how it
would sustain a stone of weight of one thousand pounds projected in a sling
or a machine.' (p. 534) (6) Moreover, if it were the pressure of the air
produced by the motion of one's hand that impels the projectile, one would
expect that the same motion would propel a feather farther than a stone, the

first being lighter, which decidedly is not the case.

Based on these objections, Buridan concluded that it was not the force of air behind the object that impelled it, but a 'motive force' or 'impetus' conveyed directly to the projectile by the mover which persists after contact has been severed.

> Therefore, it seems to me that it ought to be said that the motor in moving a moving body impresses (*imprimit*) in it a certain impetus (*impetus*) or a certain motive force (*vis motiva*) [. . .] in the direction toward which the mover was moving the moving body, either up or down, or laterally, or circularly. (p. 534)

This explanation could be applied as well to a discus and javelin removing the objection indicated previously.

In addition to stating that the direction of the impressed impetus changes with, and therefore depends upon, the direction of the motive force, Buridan attempts to quantify the relation between the two. Because it is evident the greater the initial force the more the object will be moved (in terms of distance, swiftness, or force of impact), if the movement is due to an impressed impetus then the amount of the impetus must be proportional to the originating force: '*And by the amount the motor moves that moving body more swiftly, by the same amount it will impress in it a stronger impetus.*' (p. 535)

However, as the movement of a feather and a stone illustrates, the extent of the motion does not depend solely on the magnitude of the original force but also on the compactness or density of the material composing what is moved: the same force propelling a stone farther than a feather or a leaf.

> Hence by the amount more there is of matter, by that amount can the body receive more of that impetus and more intensely (intensius).
> Now in a dense and heavy body, other things being equal, there is more of prime matter [Aristotle's concept] than in a rare and light one. Hence a dense and heavy body receives more of that impetus and more intensely, just as [. . .] a feather receives such an impetus so weakly (remisse) that such an impetus is immediately destroyed by the resisting air. (p. 535; brackets added)

Despite the lack of explanation as to how the motor 'impresses' a 'motor force' or 'impetus' on the moving object, this concept is far superior to the 'vacuum' or 'compressed air' explanations of Plato and Aristotle. Moreover, there is some similarity between Buridan's idea of impetus and the later concept of kinetic motion as well as between his definition of an object's density and the concept of mass.

This is not to imply, however, that these concepts originated entirely with Buridan. In the sixth century John Philoponus in his *Commentaria* on Aristotle had used the term 'impetus' in describing how the impressed air in Aristotle's explanation could have received its motive power: 'the air which is pushed in the first instance [. . .] receives an impetus to motion [. . .] thus pushing the missile on while remaining always in contact with it [. . .].' (pp. 508-509) But Philoponus rejected this explanation in favor of one closer to that of Buridan: '*Rather is it necessary to assume that some incorporeal motive force is imparted by the projector to the projectile*' (p. 509), a force that Clagett describes as an "incorporeal kinetic force [. . .] impressed in the body (not the medium) and this impressed force continues the movement of the body until it is spent by the resistance [. . .]." (p. 509)

Then in the eleventh century Avicenna, in his famous *Book of Healing of the Soul* (a commentary on the works of Aristotle), apparently influenced by Philoponus, also rejected the theories of Plato and Aristotle, along with the concepts of an 'engendering' and 'propension of influence,' in favor of an explanation in which the moved object receives an 'inclination' from the mover:

> But when we verified the matter we found the most valid opinion to
> be that of those who hold that the moved receives an inclination (*mail*)
> from the mover. The inclination is that which is perceived by the
> senses to be resisting a forceful effort to bring natural motion to rest
> or to change one violent motion into another. (pp. 511-512)

This Arabic idea of '*mail*' would appear to antedate the concept of 'impetus' since, like the later, it is not equated with the moving force but is considered an *instrument* of that force. In addition, Avicenna attempted to explain free fall as caused by gravity acting on the 'natural *mail*' in the object, again predating the conception of impetus. Finally, unlike Aristotle who denied the possibility of a vacuum because he believed it would imply instantaneous motion because successive motion depends on the resistance of the medium, which would not occur in a vacuum, Avicenna defended the possibility of such motion. Perhaps again owing to the influence of Philoponus who also held such a view, Avicenna argued that since the '*mail*' producing the motion of a projectile is not diminished except by the resistance of the air and natural tendency to fall, in a vacuum devoid of resistance the projectile should persist in motion until the *mail* is overcome by gravity. (cf. pp. 512-513) Buridan, too, conceived of the impressed force or impetus as not self-expending but negated by external resistance: "'the impetus would last indefinitely (*in infinitum*) if it were not diminished by a contrary resistance or by an inclination to a contrary motion. . . .'" (p. 524) Because of its similarity to inertia, this explanation has raised considerable controversy, to be discussed later, as to whether the theory of impetus antedates, rather than merely anticipates, the theory of inertia.

There was further discussion of the *mail* or impressed forces theory in the twelfth and thirteenth centuries, but the notion of an impelling force conveyed directly from the projector to the projectile was rejected by both Thomas Aquinas and Roger Bacon who clung to Aristotle's position that in violent motion an external mover must be in continuous contact with the moved. However, in the early part of the fourteenth century Franciscus de Marchia, after an extensive discussion of the possible explanations of projectile motion, concluded that the original mover when it ceases to be in contact with the moved object leaves behind 'a residual force,' either in the medium or in the object or both, which causes the continued motion. This residual force is of a temporary, self-expending nature. (cf. 519)

When considering the alternative of the residual force residing either in the medium or in the object he supports the latter: 'It seems preferable that a force of this kind resides (*sit*) in the body which is moved rather than in the medium, regardless of what the Philosopher and the Commentator have said on this matter.' (p. 529) ("The philosopher" of course is Aristotle and "the Commentator" Averroës.) Franciscus apparently favored this position as the simpler of the two and also because it could explain the motion of a potter's wheel, eliminating the need for Aristotle's intelligences since God could have conveyed an original impetus to celestial bodies directly. (cf. pp. 529-530)

But it was primarily Buridan's exposition and defence of the impetus theory, also in the first half of the fourteenth century, that led to its being taken up by his successors in Paris in the second half of the century, namely, by Nicole Oresme, Albert of Saxony, and Marsilius of Inghen. (cf. p. 522). Just as the Moslems, particularly Avicenna and Abu' l-Barakat, had used the *mail* theory to account for free fall, Buridan utilized his impetus concept to explain both terrestrial fall and celestial motions. But before discussing Buridan's explanation we again have to consider why it was proposed in light of the weaknesses in Aristotle's account.

DEFICIENCIES IN ARISTOTLE'S DYNAMICS

Beginning with gravitational fall, like his theory of projectile motion Aristotle's explanation was admirable as a first approximation but left many unanswered questions: first, the *dynamic* question of what causes the free fall and how it produces the effect; second, the *kinematic* question of the precise description of the magnitude of the fall, such as the rate of its incremental increase or acceleration (uniform or nonuniform).   Consistent with his emphasis on causes, Aristotle concentrated on the dynamic question in contrast to Galileo who, in his demonstrated solution to the kinematic problem, dismissed as inappropriate at the time the question of the possible causes of gravitational fall.[13]   The most succinct statement of Aristotle's conception of the natural rising and falling of objects is the following:

> [. . .] how can we account for the motion of light things and heavy
> things to their proper situations? The reason for it is that they have
> a natural tendency respectively towards a certain position: and this
> constitutes the essence of lightness and heaviness, the former being
> determined by a upward, the latter by a downward, tendency.[14]

The 'reason' things are light or heavy, then, is that they have a 'natural tendency respectively towards a certain position,' which 'constitutes the essence of lightness and heaviness.' Moreover, since the 'earth moves more quickly the nearer it is to the centre, and fire the nearer it is to the upper place,'[15] this would imply that lightness and heaviness are *relational* qualities that vary with the object's speed as it rises or descends to its natural place. Indeed, he does affirm this: 'superior speed in downward movement implies superior weight [. . . .]'[16] Yet the usual interpretation of Aristotle is that it is the *nature* of the elements as fire and air or earth and water that *produces the tendency* to rise or fall, the rate of the rising and falling depending upon the purity of the element. This latter interpretation, moreover, seems to be reinforced in his definition of absolute lightness (*levitas*) and heaviness (*gravitas*): 'there is an absolutely light and an absolutely heavy body. And by absolutely light I mean one which of its *own nature* always moves upward, by absolutely heavy one which of its *own nature* always moves downward, if no obstacle is in the way.'[17] Despite the fact that only animate bodies are supposed to be self-moving, Aristotle even says the 'nature' of weight or lightness 'means a source of movement within the thing itself. . . .'[18] This position complements his conception that the eternal circular motion of the heavens requires a fifth element, the aither, which has this motion as an essential attribute.[19]

Furthermore, he accounts for the relative lightness or heaviness of bodies in terms of their 'endowed weights,' objects of equal bulk or size but of less endowed weight falling more slowly: 'By lighter or relatively light we mean that one, of two bodies endowed with weight and equal in bulk, which is exceeded by the other in the speed of its natural downward movement.' [20] The purest of these ascending or descending bodies is identified with fire or earth: 'Fire, then, has no weight. Neither has earth any lightness [. . .].' [21] Thus it is ambiguous as to whether the tendency to rise or fall constitutes a functional definition of lightness and heaviness, or whether fire and earth as natural elements having these absolute properties explains the tendency to rise or fall! One does not know whether to attribute these diverse interpretations to the uncertain source of Aristotle's writings or to the fact that he may not have clearly separated the issues in his thinking, another example perhaps of the thesis maintained in Volume I that the development of thought depends upon distinguishing concepts that are indeterminate at an earlier stage of syncretic consciousness.

There are additional complications or ambiguities in Aristotle's conception of the interrelation between potentiality and actuality and form and natural place. He had defined motion as '*the fulfillment of what exists potentially, in so far as it exists potentially,*' [22] and maintained that this fulfillment is motion of a body to its 'own place and form.'

> Now, that which produces upward and downward movement is that which produces weight and lightness, and that which is moved is that which is potentially heavy or light, and the movement of each body to its own place is motion toward its own form.[23]

This statement implies that since rest is the natural state of the elements, as they rise or fall to their place of rest they actualize their forms, the motion being the transition from potentiality to actuality. But how do the natural places exert this attractive influence and actualize the form? Simplicius in his *Commentary* on Aristotle in the sixth century restates the problem without answering it.

> Aristotle holds that as bodies approach the whole mass of their own element, they acquire a greater force therefrom and recover their form more perfectly; that thus it is by reason of an increase of weight that

earth moves more swiftly when it is near the center. [24]

Finally, commentators introduced further complications in Aristotle's explanation of free fall related to the resistance of the medium as the object descends.   According to Simplicius, since as the body falls there is less air below than above it, its approach to the earth should cause it to increase in speed.[25]   Alternatively, since it was known that motion produces heat, does the downward movement of the object heat the air causing it to become more rarified and therefore less resistant?   These questions indicate how thoroughly the Scholastics explored the various alternatives.

That the density of the medium affects the swiftness of movement is true both of projectile motion and free fall, giving rise to the generalizations that the velocity (V) is proportional to the weight (W) and the resistance of the medium (R), or to the motive force (F) and the resistance (R) of the medium. As we would express the ratio today: $V = W/R$ (in free fall) or $V = F/R$ (in projectile motion).   Again, however, while this generalization seems to hold for immediate experience it is not a correct expression of a law of nature and raised many problems for the Scholastics. For example, Aristotle inferred that if the resistance were zero as in a void, then there would be nothing to retard the movement of objects so that their motions would be the same regardless of their relative weights.   Although we now know that this conclusion is correct for freely falling objects in a void, Aristotle rejected it, as stated earlier, because he thought it implied instantaneous motion: 'by so much as the medium is more incorporeal and less resistant and more easily divided, the faster will be the movement.' [26]   Thus in a void with no resistance the movement would be instantaneous which Aristotle rejected as physically impossible.   Yet his inference is not necessary because the fall of objects in a vacuum could still be successive and increasing, although the same for all objects, despite the absence of the resistance of the air.   Nevertheless, this conclusion is so counter-intuitive that one can see why Aristotle rejected it.

But Philoponus (a contemporary of Simplicius) in his *Commentary* on Aristotle's *Physics* argued that the rapidity of an object's fall is not dependent upon the medium but solely on the object's weight: 'if bodies possess a greater or a lesser downward tendency in and of themselves, clearly they will possess this difference [. . .] even if they move through a void.' (Clagett, p. 433) At first he drew what must have seemed the obvious conclusion, even though false:

'The same space will consequently be traversed by the heavier body in shorter time and by the lighter body in longer time, even though the space be void [. . .] due [. . .] to the natural weight of the bodies in question. . . .' (p. 433)

Yet, like Galileo, when he actually dropped bodies of different weights and observed their rates of fall he realized that the above conclusion was false.

But this is completely erroneous, and our view may be corroborated by actual observation more effectively than by any sort of verbal argument. For if you let fall from the same height two weights of which one is many times as heavy as the other, you will see that the ratio of the times required for the motion does not depend on the ratio of the weights, but that the difference in time is a very small one. And so, if the difference in the weights is [. . .] considerable, that is, if one is, let us say, double the other, there will be no difference, or else an imperceptible difference, in time [. . .]. (p. 546)

Although there might have been earlier instances, this is the first record of anyone having performed such an experiment, predating by nearly a millennium those of Stevin and Galileo. It was Einstein who was struck by the fact that the gravitational force exerted on an object is proportional to the object's mass, accounting for the constant acceleration (if air resistance is eliminated) of all objects, one of the considerations that led to the general theory of relativity. Apparently based on his experiments of dropping objects of different weights, Philoponus antedated the conclusion stated by Galileo:

[. . .] I greatly doubt that Aristotle ever tested by experiment whether it be true that two stones, one weighing ten times as much as the other, if allowed to fall, at the same instant, from a height of, say, 100 cubits, would so differ in speed that when the heavier had reached the ground, the other would not have fallen more than ten cubits [. . . .] But I, Simplicio, who have made the test can assure you that a cannon ball weighing one or two hundred pounds, or even more, will not reach the ground by as much as a span ahead of a musket ball weighing only half a pound, provided both are dropped from a height of 200 cubits.[27]

BURIDAN'S CRITICISM OF AVERROËS

Returning to the solution of Buridan, like his predecessors he too considers various emendations of Aristotle's explanations, especially as formulated by "the Commentator" (Averroës), which he rejects before presenting his own position.[28] If the acceleration of falling bodies depends upon the motion heating the air making it more rarified and thus less resistant as the body falls to the earth, then why do not objects fall more swiftly in summer than in winter when the air is warmer?—yet no such effect is observed. Moreover, a person moving their hand downward at the same speed initially as a falling object feels the air becoming cooler rather than warmer. In addition, if it is argued that the greater the height of air the more resistance it should offer (because there is more of it beneath the object), then one would expect that an object dropped from a great height would begin its descent more slowly than an object dropped closer to the earth, which is not the case.

Rather than the air, perhaps it is the place that exerts an attractive force on the object, 'as a magnet draws iron,' causing it to descend more swiftly the closer it approaches the earth. But if that were true, then it should be more difficult to lift a heavy stone near the earth than on a mountain top, a difference not detectable. Furthermore, if closeness to the earth is the primary cause of the acceleration, then a stone dropped near the earth should fall as rapidly as one dropped from a tower, which is not true. These explanations having been rejected, Buridan proposes his own.

Analogous to Avicenna's argument involving the '*mail*,' Buridan asserts that the initial descent of the object is caused by its permanent 'natural gravity' (not an external force but an inner tendency of the object to fall) which, as the object begins its fall, produces an additional impetus that, when conjoined with the original gravity, results in an added increase in motion that causes even more impetus, further accelerating the motion throughout the fall. The increase in motion, therefore, is due to the impetus caused by the gravity combining with the latter to impress even more impetus on the object in a continuously accelerating descent. By this explanation Buridan was able to circumvent those inadequate conjectures based on the influence of the medium or the natural place of the object, as he states.

> With the [foregoing] methods of solving this question set aside [. . .]
> it follows that one must imagine that a heavy body not only acquires
> motion unto itself from its principle mover, i.e., its gravity, but that it
> also acquires unto itself a certain impetus with that motion. This

impetus has the power of moving the heavy body in conjunction with the permanent natural gravity. And because that impetus is acquired in common with motion, hence the swifter the motion is, the greater and stronger the impetus is [. . . .] and thus it will always and continually be accelerated to the end. (pp. 560-561)

The fact that the impetus grows with the increase in motion means that it also decreases (even though it is a permanent attribute) when the natural resistances to the motion, produced by the air or the attaining of its natural place, overcomes the original gravity or motive force. Whereas neither the explanations of Plato nor Aristotle could account for the continued rotation of a smith's mill or potter's wheel in terms of air pressure, Buridan's impressed impetus theory does account for it. In fact, it leads to the conclusion, mentioned earlier, that suggests he could have anticipated the theory of inertia.

If you cause a large and very heavy smith's mill to rotate and you then cease to move it, it will still move a while longer by this impetus it has acquired. Nay, you cannot immediately bring it to rest, but on account of the resistance from the gravity of the mill, the impetus would be continually diminished until the mill would cease to move. And if [. . .] there were no resistance corrupting the impetus, *perhaps* the mill would be moved perpetually by that impetus. (p. 561; brackets and italics added)

This is one of those dramatic instances in history when a person comes so close to grasping a fundamental scientific principle that would have constituted an immortal breakthrough, only to allow it to slip by. While Buridan seized on the possibility of his impetus theory replacing Aristotle's intelligences as an eternal mover of the *celestial* bodies, he still was too much committed to the latter's general framework to accept the possibility of an impetus induced, inertial motion in the *terrestrial* world:

[. . .] one could imagine that it is unnecessary to posit intelligences as the movers of celestial bodies since the Holy Scriptures do not inform us that intelligences must be posited. For it could be said that when God created the celestial spheres, He began to move each of them as He wished, and they are still moved by the impetus which He gave to them because, there being no resistance, the impetus is neither corrupted nor diminished. (p. 561)

Believing that this is never true in the terrestrial world, we are left with the
'perhaps' in the previous statement, rather than with the acknowledgement of
a real possibility.   Moreover, Buridan is consoled by the idea that if his
impetus is considered an 'accidental gravity,' then it is consistent with the
doctrines of both Aristotle and Averroës: 'Whence this [impetus or 'accidental
gravity'] appears to be harmonious with Aristotle and the Commentator [. . .].
(p. 561; brackets added)

Earlier it was stated that an adequate theory of motion involves two
fundamental questions: (1) the dynamic question concerning an explanation
of the *cause* of the motion, and (2) the kinematic question regarding a correct
mathematical representation of the nature and dimensions of the rate of fall.
So far we have discussed the dynamic question.   But, as we shall discover
later, it was the solution to the kinematic question (in terms of Kepler's three
astromonical laws and Galileo's law of free fall) that led to the final resolution
of the problem of celestial and terrestrial mechanics, with Newton's universal
law of gravitation.   Buridan had attributed the acceleration to an incremental
addition of impetus to the permanent gravity in the object causing the original
descent.   While he had described this increase in motion as a constant
acceleration, he had not stated explicitly whether the acceleration was a
function of the distance through which the object fell or the time.   In fact, as
one would expect at this early attempt at an explanation, since there are
passages in which he refers to one or the other of the alternatives they
apparently were not clearly distinguished in his thinking—a further example
of syncretic or diffuse thought.   Clagett believes that "he made no clear
distinction between the mathematical difference involved in saying that the
velocity increases directly as the distance of fall and saying that it increases
directly as the time of fall." (p. 563)

One of the followers of Buridan, Albert of Saxony, in his *Questions on the
Books on the Heavens and the World of Aristotle*, attempted to quantify the
rate of descent and in so doing did consider the alternatives of the rate varying
with the time or the space.   But after considering two mathematical
expressions for the increase in speed depending upon either the duration or the
distance of the fall, he seemed to prefer the latter, erroneous conclusion.   His
mathematical formulation states that the increase in motion is proportional to
the units of space (or time) so that the motion is doubled in double the space
(or time) interval, triple in triple the space (or time) interval, and so forth. (cf.
p. 565)   Galileo also initially considered space to be the essential factor, but
subsequently rejected the idea on the grounds that if an object's acceleration
were directly proportional to the units of space, so that its speed at the end of

the second unit of space were double that of the first unit, its speed at the end of the third triple that of the first, and so on, then the object would travel through any unit of space in the same time as one unit. But, as Galileo pointed out, for an object to travel any distance whatsoever in the same time would be possible only if the motion were not successive but instantaneous, a conclusion he rejected as empirically implausible.[29]

Buridan also rejects this mathematic proportion, but on the basis of a different *reductio ad absurdum* argument. As he interpreted it, if the rate of increase were a direct multiple of the temporal or spatial units, then in any fractional division of the spatial or temporal units, *regardless of how small*, one would expect the same rate of increase during that interval, which, if added together, would produce an infinitely large velocity: 'it would follow that any natural motion at all, which would last through any time as small as you like or traverse any space as small as you wish, would attain before the end any degree at all of velocity.' (p. 566) 'If the increase of speed took place in this first way then it would become infinite' (p. 565), a conclusion he naturally rejected as false.

Unlike the first mathematical ratio which was 'divergent,' the second is 'convergent.' If one considers the increase in velocity as beginning at zero and ending with a final magnitude, Albert attempts to describe the mathematical convergence from zero to the terminal velocity: 'in the first place there is a certain speed, and then in the second place there is added to it some degree of velocity, then in the third place there is added half of that degree of velocity, in the fourth place one-fourth that degree, and so on.' (p. 565) As formalized by Clagett, the converging series would be stated as follows:

> [. . .] it is converging from the initial velocity V_0 toward a final velocity V_f, where $V_f = V_0 + 2a$, where a is the first given increment of speed; and furthermore any velocity (V_n) after V_0 is given as follows: $V_n = V_0 + a + a/2 + a/4 + \ldots + a/2^{n-1}$. (p. 567)

While none of these mathematical functions is correct, still they are important as attempts to quantify the phenomena. Moreover, when Albert considers Buridan's impetus explanation, he does arrive at the correct qualitative conclusion that the increase in motion varies with the time of descent, but he does not attempt to quantity this:

> [. . .] it is to be imagined that a heavy body in its motion acquires unto itself beyond its natural gravity a certain impetus or accidental

gravity, which helps the natural gravity to move the heavy body more
quickly . . . . and according as that natural body is moved a longer and
longer *time*, so accordingly more and more impetus is acquired unto
itself [. . .]. (p. 566; italics added)

The exact relationship was represented correctly in graphic form by
Oresme, another follower of Buridan. When discussing Aristotle's theory of
lightness and heaviness, it was pointed out that there was an ambiguity in his
account between light and heavy being defined as the *tendency* to move
upward and downward (which implied that these qualities increased with the
movement of the respective element to its natural place), and their *inherent
formal qualities* characteristic of a particular element, such as fire and earth.
This ambiguity also was noted by Oresme in his *On the Book of the Heavens
and the World of Aristotle*.

And when he [Aristotle] says that the weight is greater just as the
velocity is greater, we are not to understand by 'weight' a natural
quality which inclines downward [because then it would increase with
the descent]. For if a stone of one pound should descend from a high
place so that the movement was swifter in the end than at the
beginning, the stone still would have no more natural weight at the
one time than at the other. But we ought understand by this 'weight'
which increases in descent an accidental quality which is caused by
the compulsion of the increase in the velocity [. . .]. And this quality
can be called 'impetuosity.' (p. 570; brackets added)

Earlier we noted that the attempt to formulate a correct theory of motion
was impeded by the lack of such concepts as inertia, of the distinction between
weight and mass, and of whether the acceleration of objects is proportional to
the units of space or of time. Here we find an explicit recognition of the
distinction between the concepts of weight and momentum, although the latter
term had yet to be introduced. What Oresme has recognized is that as a heavy
object falls its weight does not increase (as one of Aristotle's statements
implied), but that something increases as a function of the constant weight and
increasing velocity, namely, the momentum: $M = WV$, where (M) stands for
momentum, (W) stands for weight (not mass as we would express this today),
and (V) stands for velocity. Thus another indispensable concept for the final
explanation of motion was identified. That Oresme did explicitly recognize
the significance of what we call momentum is illustrated in a famous example.

According to Aristotle, a heavy object such as a boulder descending to the center of the universe comes to rest there. In contrast, Oresme asks us to imagine a passage extending to the earth's core and then continuing to the opposite side. If we dropped a heavy object down the passage would it stop at the center, its natural place of rest, even if unimpeded by the earth, as Aristotle implied, or would its 'impetuosity' compel it to move beyond the center until the impetuosity became expended, after which it would fall back towards the center again continuing a short distance beyond because of its lesser 'impetuosity,' and so on. In this way an oscillatory motion about the center of the earth would be created until the impetuosity was exhausted.

According to Oresme, if the object has more than just a tendency to rise or fall to its natural place, but acquires an 'impetuosity' (or momentum) as a function of its weight and velocity, then we would expect this momentum to carry the object beyond the center until exhausted.

> And this [. . .] 'impetuosity' [. . .] is not weight properly [speaking] because if a passage were pierced from here to the center of the earth or still further, and something heavy were to descend in this passage or hole, when it arrived at the center it would pass on further and ascend by means of this accidental and acquired quality, and then it would descend again, going and coming several times in the way that a weight which hangs from a beam by a long cord [swings back and forth]. And so [this impetuosity] is not properly weight, since it causes ascent. And such a quality exists in every movement—natural and violent—as long as the velocity increases, the movement of the heavens being excepted. (p. 570; brackets in the original)

This concept of 'impetuosity' might simply be equated with Buridan's notion of 'impetus,' but the fact that Oresme introduced a new term with the example of the oscillating object indicates that he recognized that a new concept, 'impetuosity' (or momentum), was required by the example. But before considering further Oresme's additional contributions, we shall discuss the development of the science of kinematics in the fourteenth century.

ORIGIN AND DEVELOPMENT OF KINEMATICS

Because of the opposition in the seventeenth century of the Scholastic Aristotelians to the heliocentric theory of the universe, while the major proponents of the theory (Copernicus, Kepler, and Galileo) were strongly influenced by the ancient Pythagoreans and/or Neoplatonists, there often is some confusion as to whether Plato or Aristotle had the greatest influence on the development of the science of kinematics, a description of motion in terms of distance, time, and speed. The evidence is diverse: Copernicus justified his defense of the heliocentric view by citing the early Pythagoreans, Kepler was inspired in his search for planetary laws by Neoplatonism and the five Platonic or Pythagorean solids, while Galileo had the utmost praise for Archimedes for his mathematical gifts and for the Pythagoreans because of their daring in accepting a mathematical model of the universe over the testimony of their senses.[30] The latter's assertion that "the great book of nature is written in the language of mathematics" sounds very Platonic; however, it should not be overlooked that Plato criticized the Pythagorean Archytas along with Eudoxus for attempting to apply mathematics to empirical problems, even those in astronomy. For Plato the purpose of learning mathematics was not to facilitate empirical investigations, but to free reason from its dependence on sensory images so that it could attain knowledge of the Forms (this will be discussed more fully in Chapter IV).

Indeed, as we learned previously, it was not Plato but Aristotle who, in his distinction between the investigation of the causes and effects of motion, implied that the study of motion should be divided into the two sciences of dynamics and kinematics. Furthermore, Aristotle's classification of the different kinds of motion along with his three principles that (1) an inanimate terrestrial object must have an external cause as its source of motion, (2) that this external cause must be in continuous contact with the moving object to cause motion, and (3) that a continuous mover produces a constant motion was the theoretical basis of all subsequent inquiry of motion in the succeeding centuries. Finally, his attempt at quantifying motion in terms of the ratio of different forces or weights to the distances and durations of movement, his definition of velocity as proportional to the force and inversely proportional to the resistance, and his law of gravitational fall as a constant increase in motion proportional to the weight of the falling body encouraged further mathematical investigation of these phenomena.

As one would expect of the earliest attempt to deal with these problems, Aristotle's explanations were somewhat confused, limited, and invariably erroneous. He denied instantaneous and inertial motions, did not distinguish between mass and weight, and though he recognized variations in motions he lacked a precise conception of acceleration. His belief that the motion of inanimate terrestrial objects requires a continuous mover resulting in a constant motion was false, as were his mathematical descriptions of velocity and free fall. His definition of motion as a transition from potentiality to actuality owing to a mover being in contact with the object actualizing motion in it (analogous to a teacher actualizing learning in a pupil by instructing him), shows how elementary were his conceptions. Motion, in fact, was merely a species of change. Thus the fourteenth-century Scholastics encountered a formidable task when attempting to introduce greater conceptual clarity and mathematical precision in this theoretical morass.

Even *their* attempts to clarify and quantify motions led to peculiar questions based on strange analogies, such as whether certain categorizations of phenomena can themselves be categorized in the same way: that is, is a change in quality itself a quality or a change in quantity also a quantity? Could changes in velocity be conceptualized like changes in quality, as when objects become hotter or change color? Drawing on theology, they conjectured whether changes in motion should be considered modifications within the object analogous to changes of states in the soul, as when a person becomes more or less pious. While the swiftness or slowness of the motion of objects was described in terms of spatial and temporal magnitudes, could motion as an abstract concept be quantified as speed or velocity? Though we are accustomed to using general concepts like force, mass, and acceleration in functional equations (for example, $F = MA$ or $a = \frac{1}{2}gt^2$) made empirically significant by interpreting the variables in terms of measurable magnitudes, this mathematical procedure had yet to be developed.

Without ever really rejecting Aristotle's general conceptual framework, the fourteenth-century Scholastics tried to revise, refine, or reconstruct the conceptual interrelation of meanings to attain a more precise mathematical description of motions. This was the accomplishment mainly of two groups of scholars, the Mertonians at Oxford and the Parisians at the University of Paris. Since it was the Mertonians, Thomas Bradwardine, William Heytesbury, Richard Swineshead, and John Dumbleton, who first gave kinematics a mathematical foundation by representing degrees of heat or amounts of motion by letters, by introducing some of the basic terminology, and by discovering the 'mean speed' and 'distance maxims,' our discussion will begin with them. For example, while Aristotle had differentiated the causes of motion from their effects, implying a different mode of inquiry for each,

Bradwardine distinguished expressly between the study of motion *sub specie causae motivae* (that is, dynamics) and that of motion *sub specie effectus* (that is, kinematics) and noted that the proportions obtaining between speeds may be determined by reference to either causes or effects.[31]

In place of describing motions as swifter or slower depending upon whether they covered the same distance in less time or a shorter distance in the same time, the Mertonians introduced the distinction between 'extensive' and 'intensive' magnitudes, the former designating the extent of the distances, durations, and weights, while the latter referred to increases ('*intension*') and decreases ('*remission*') in the intensity of motions. As Clavelin states, this "new conception of speed as an intensive magnitude" was a significant innovation enabling physicists to study speed directly as "the effects of a motion depend[ing] on the value which its intensity assumes from one moment to the next." (p. 70; brackets added). The model for this approach was changes in quality, such as an object growing hotter or colder or a person becoming more or less devout. But this way of posing the question raised its own problems as to how the latter changes could be explained. Do such changes occur by an addition to or subtraction from the qualities, by altering the qualities, by the replacement of the qualities, or in what way? A heated object has a fixed temperature at any moment and yet its changes of temperature seem to occur as a continuous process, so do the degrees supersede each other from one moment to another or undergo some kind of transformation?

Despite the complexity of the problem, by 1320 the Mertonians had succeeded in distinguishing "the quality of a motion (that is, its velocity) from its quantity (that is, the distance traversed)." (p. 65) Moreover, "once velocity was treated as an intensive magnitude, it became *coextensive* with motion, which could therefore be analyzed in its very process." (p. 66) Making it possible to treat changes of motion or velocity directly, the concept of intensive motion ('*intensio motus*') also led to consideration of uniform and nonuniform motions, acceleration and deceleration, along with instantaneous changes in velocity. The mathematical treatment of these problems would not be exact until Newton's introduction of the concepts of differentiation, limits, and integration in the infinitesimal calculus, but that the approach of the Oxfordians presupposed that kind of mathematics itself attests to a tremendous achievement.

Just as Aristotle had made an important contribution to the formalization of logic by introducing letters to stand for noun and predicate phrases, the Mertonians "were the first to express physical magnitudes systematically by means of literal and numerical symbols, for instance referring to fixed amounts of heat or speed as *a* or *b*." (p. 72) They also classified changes in speed by orders of magnitude ranging, for example, from 0 to 8, enabling them to augment or reduce as well as contrast the magnitudes in precise numerical proportions. Because of their attempts to express changes in velocity as mathematical functions and their discovery of the mean speed and distance maxims the Mertonians were known as the *Calculatores*.

Bradwardine, for example, in his *Tractatus Proportionum* which dates from 1328, redefined Aristotle's fundamental principle of motion that velocity varies directly with the force (F) and inversely with the resistance (R). He objected to Aristotle's formulation "firstly on the ground that it cannot be inferred from it what happens when F and R change simultaneously," and "secondly because it would follow that any indefinitely small force can set in motion any indefinitely heavy body,"[32] which is contradicted by experience (although Aristotle was aware of this). To circumvent these problems Bradwardine maintained that it was not merely the ratio of (F) to (R) that was important, but "that the proportion in which the velocity changes 'follows' the manner in which the proportion between force and resistance changes [. . .]." [33] If the degree of change is not sufficient no velocity occurs. In addition, he reformulated the relation between the change in the ratio F/R and the velocity that 'follows' this change. Because the 'summing' of ratios at this time was not a function of adding but of multiplying the fractions (the 'addition' of the ratios a/b and c/d resulting in ac/bd), Bradwardine concluded that if the ratio F/R becomes n times as great, so does the velocity: "in order to get n times the velocity, the ratio F/R has to be raised to the nth power. In modern notation this is equivalent to the relation $V = c \times \log F/R$, $F>R$."[34] For Bradwardine, the advantage of this formulation is that it was possible for the velocity to take on any value if the ratio changed as indicated, so that it would approach zero as the ratio F/R approaches one. While this formula still is not valid, its importance lies in the attempt to devise a more precise mathematical expression for a discoverable functional relation in nature.

Pursuing these kinds of inquiries, the Mertonians did arrive at two correct mathematical formulations of changes in motion which, although they may seem simple to us, were the basis for further progress in the mathematical investigations of changes in motion: the 'mean speed and distance maxims.' The mean speed maxim, which was known also as the "Merton Theorem," states that in the case of uniformly *variable* motions the distance traversed in a specified time is equal to what would be traversed in the same time by a *uniform* motion with a velocity equal to the uniformly variable motion at its mid-point. In modern notation, $S = 1/V_o + V_f/2(t)$, where S equals distance,

V_o the initial velocity, V_f the final velocity, and t the time.   William Heytesbury stated this maxim at Oxford about 1330 as follows: "With respect [. . .] to the distance traversed in a uniformly accelerated motion [. . .] terminating at some finite degree [. . .], the motion as a whole [. . .] will correspond to its mean degree [of velocity]."[35]   Unfortunately, when Heytesbury derived a distance law from the mean speed law he fell into error, stating that

> when the acceleration of a motion takes place uniformly from zero degree to some degree [of velocity], the distance it will traverse in the first half of the time will be exactly one-third of that which it will traverse in the second half of the time. (p. 272)

The correct proportion stated later by Swineshead and Oresme, and reaffirmed by Galileo, is one-quarter to three-quarters.

There were many attempts to prove the mean speed law, but the one by Richard Swineshead, ("the calculator") is the best known.   His proof in *The Book of Calculations: Rules on Local Motion* is based on the symmetry between two identical uniformly accelerating motions, one increasing to a maximum degree in a certain time and the second decreasing from that degree at the same rate in the same time.   Because both motions are equivalent, although in different 'directions' (one ascending and the other descending), the total distance covered will correspond to what would be covered if each motion moved with an average uniform velocity during both time periods. Otherwise stated, if e is the mean velocity of both motions, the sum of their velocities will be 2e: if 'e is the mean degree,' then 'the velocities of a and b together continually will be equal to a degree twice that of e [. . .].' (p. 290)

Unlike Heytesbury, Swineshead arrived at the correct ratio of the distances traversed during the first and second halves of the duration of the acceleration: 'whenever a power accelerates uniformly from zero degree, it will traverse three times as much space in the second half of the time as in the first.' (p. 291) Since the acceleration is constant during the two intervals of time, today the proof would be expressed as: $s = \frac{1}{2}at^2(t)$, if one lets (at) stand for the acceleration from V_o to V_t.

While the mean speed and distance theorems were the most significant contribution of the Mertonians to kinematics, they also were responsible for defining such crucial concepts as uniform and nonuniform motions (or accelerations) used in the expressions of the maxims.   They introduced the term 'difform motion' to designate motions that vary, but such difform motions could be uniform or nonuniform. If motions undergo a steady increase in velocity they were called 'uniformly difform,' whereas if the increase were irregular they were called 'difformly difform.' Further distinctions were introduced between changes in velocity "subject to uniform variations (uniformly difformly difform motions) and those in which no law could be assigned to the changes (nonuniformly difformly difform motions)."[36]

Heytesbury also defined 'instantaneous velocity' verbally, although he did not give it a precise mathematical expression:

[. . .] a nonuniform or instantaneous velocity (*velocitas instantanea*) is not measured by the distance traversed, but by the distance which *would* be traversed by such a point, *if* it were moved uniformly over such or such a period of time at that degree of velocity with which it is moved in that assigned instant. (p. 236)

Lacking the necessary mathematical notation, the fourteenth-century Scholastics could not give a precise mathematical representation of either constant acceleration or instantaneous velocity. The first awaited Galileo and the latter Newton's calculus. As Clavelin states:

In modern mechanics, the speed of a point at any given moment is the differential coefficient of space with respect to time, and the quotient expressing it, namely ds/dt is simply the limit of the ratio of the finite space s to the finite time t, as t approaches zero [. . .].[37]

In addition to their other innovations, the Mertonians introduced the concept of 'latitude' to represent an 'increment' of motion when measuring acceleration. As defined by Swineshead:

Hence just as in the use of uniform local motion where the velocity is measured by the maximum line described by some point [in some given time], so in acceleration the rate of acceleration is measured by the maximum increment (*latitudo*) of velocity acquired in some given time. (p. 244)

Thus the 'intensity' of motion or velocity was conceived as a 'quality' of motion at some moment, while the 'quantity' of motion was the total velocity attained during a definite time period. The 'degree' of motion designated the magnitude of the quality or 'intensity' of motion which was constant in uniform motion and changed in instantaneous increments in nonuniform (difform) motions.

The 'latitude' of motion, in a positive or negative acceleration, represented either the positive or negative incremental increase or decrease in velocity. According to Swineshead, it was used to represent "the 'distance' between two degrees of quality or velocity." (pp. 210-211). As Bradwardine expressed this:

> [. . .] every alteration is intension or remission, and because every intension or remission is in quality, it follows that every alteration is in quality [. . .] Some qualities are uniform. Some are difform. [. . .] A quality uniformly difform is, or is called, that latitude itself [. . .].
> (p. 449)

The distance between degrees of latitude is designated the 'latitude of quality,' and since distances and times contain infinite points, as Aristotle held, there are 'infinite degrees in every latitude.'

Having produced the basic vocabulary, two crucial mathematical theorems, and the initial conceptual framework of kinematics, these contributions of the Oxford Mertonians were transmitted to Italy and France about the middle of the fourteenth century. In Italy the Franciscan Giovanni di Casali in his treatise *On the Velocity of the Motion of Alteration*, published in 1345, may have been the first to represent the quality and quantity of motion by a graph. But it was the Parisian Nicole Oresme about mid-century who, after writing a book on *Questions on Euclid's Elements*, published his *Tractatus de configurationibus qualitatum* which contained a much more fully developed graphical representation of motion and therefore had the greatest influence on the succeeding three centuries.

The precedent of representing magnitudes by lines had a long tradition, extending back to Aristotle who employed lines to depict durations of time and lengths of distances. Roger Bacon had referred to a 'line of intension and remission' (p. 334), while the Mertonians used lines to designate motions. John Dumbleton represented degrees of velocity along a single line and Swineshead even used "a two-dimensional geometrical *analogy* to explain intension and extension and their relationships [. . .] compar[ing] geometrical length and breadth in an area with extension and intension." (p. 335) But it was Oresme who first represented the *variability* of the intensity of a quality (the velocity of motion) graphically, using geometrical figures as images of *different variations* in motions and their magnitudes. This use of geometrical figures not just to represent fixed spacial configurations and areas, but to depict functional relations between the time and the intensity (latitude) of motions marks a significant transition to a higher level of abstraction. Today we take for granted the representation of nonspatial variables by lines and curves in the study of analytic geometry and especially calculus, but its original expression by Oresme was a remarkable development!

The rationale for this abstract geometrical representation of velocity, as Oresme states, is that it is a continuous quantity and all magnitudes can be represented by points, lines, and planes.

> Every measurable thing except numbers is conceived in the manner of continuous quantity. Hence it is necessary for the measure of such things to imagine points, lines, and surfaces—or their properties—in which, as Aristotle wishes, measure or proportion is originally found . . . . Hence every intension which can be acquired successively is to be imagined by means of a straight line erected perpendicularly on some point or points of the [extensible] space or subject of the intensible thing. (p. 347)

Having asserted that intension can be represented by perpendicular straight lines drawn on a plane representing points of space, Oresme circumvents the ancient Greek obstacle to comparing different kinds of quantities, such as temporal and spacial dimensions, by declaring that 'although time and a linear magnitude are not [strictly] comparable in quantity, yet there is no ratio found between one time [interval] and another that is not also found between lines [. . .].' (p. 356) Since this is true also of *various* intensions of velocities, 'we can arrive at a knowledge of the difformities of velocities by the imagination of lines and also figures.' (p. 356)

The graphic representation of motion consisted of plotting the successive intensities (*qualitas successiva*) of motion during a time internal. What we now call the abscissa of a graph he designated the 'longitude,' representing the duration of the motion, while the ordinate, a line drawn perpendicular to the longitude, was called the 'latitude,' its length designating the 'intensity' of the motion or velocity. Because the longitude can be divided into successive instants, there can be drawn on each of these instants a latitude designating the intensity of the velocity at that moment. A line connecting these different latitudes provides a visual image (shape) of the progression of the velocity, while the geometrical figure between this line and the corresponding longitude conveys a graphic representation of uniform or difform motions.

Every velocity endures in time. And so the time or duration of that velocity will be a longitude. The intension of the velocity will be its latitude. [. . .] Let [. . .] body D be moved through time [. . .] over line *AB* [. . .]. And let perpendicular lines be erected upon the whole of line *AB* to form a surface. Let this surface or figure have an altitude proportional to the intension in velocity *D*. I say, therefore, that the velocity of the moving body *D* can be assimilated to that surface or figure, and [hence] can be suitably imagined ('*ymaginari*') by means of it [. . .]. (pp. 356-357)

Thus a rectangle (Fig. 1) whose latitudes (intensities of motion) are identical represents a uniform motion while a right triangle (Fig. 2) depicts a constantly accelerated motion from zero to some intensity. A triangle on a rectangular figure (Fig. 3) designates a constantly accelerated motion from some original intensity of motion. Motions which do not have a constant acceleration but change uniformly can be represented by a convex (Fig. 4) or concave (Fig. 5) 'summit line' constituting the hypotenuse of a triangle, depending upon whether the change increases or decreases in a constant manner.[38]

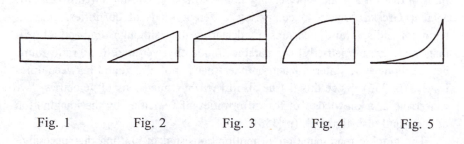

Fig. 1   Fig. 2   Fig. 3   Fig. 4   Fig. 5

As Clavelin asserts, "Oresme believed that a large enough number of latitudes would allow one to correlate every type of variation to a geometrical construction, serving to *transpose its particular process of intension or remission in the order of extension.*"[39]

Because time, instantaneous velocities, and the amount of speed (*quantitas velocitatis*) were crucial ingredients of Oresme's '*configurationes*,' as they will be in Galileo's demonstration of the law of free fall, he was close to discovering Galileo's law. In fact, one of his graphical representations does precede an aspect of Galileo's discovery, namely, that a body accelerating uniformly from zero to some fixed duration of time will transgress units of space corresponding to a series of odd numbers.

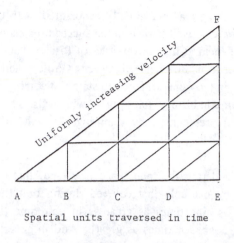

Spatial units traversed in time

Spaces traversed in successive times:	0	1	3	5	7
Total distances:	0	1	4	9	16

Fig. 6. A - E: equal units of time
A - F: uniformly increasing velocity

Since Oresme believed that the total area (the sum of the individual triangular areas) in the triangle represents the total velocity and thus the total distance traversed during successive units of time, it can be seen (by counting the triangles) that during the progressive time intervals from A to B, B to C, C to D, and D to E that the unit distances covered are 1, 3, 5, and 7.[40] Moreover, the diagram clearly illustrates the distance law discovered by the Mertonians, that during the first half of the time of fall (A to C) only 1/4th the distance will be traversed (a total of 4 units) while during the second half (C to F) 3/4ths of the distance will be covered (a total of 12 units).

Although Clagett asserts that "Galileo was in all probability not acquainted with Oresme's *De configurationibus*" (p. 346), these proportions figured strongly in his derivation of the law of gravitational fall for which he is justly famous:

It is thus evident by simple computation that a moving body starting from rest and acquiring velocity at a rate proportional to the time, will, during equal intervals of time, traverse distances which are related to each other as the odd numbers beginning with unity, 1, 3, 5, [7];[41]

Even if Galileo was not directly acquainted with Oresme's work, the latter's writings were so well known in the succeeding centuries that Galileo probably learned of them at the Universities of Pisa or Padua.

The crucial difference between Galileo and Oresme is that Galileo continued in the same sentence to state the correct law of gravitational fall for the first time in history, the truth of which also can be seen from the previous triangular representation by summing the units of space in successive time intervals:

> or considering the total space traversed, that covered in double time will be quadruple that covered during unit time; in triple time, the space is nine times as great as in unit time [in quadruple time, the space is sixteen times as great]. And in general the spaces traversed are in the duplicate ratio of the squares of the times. (*Ibid.*, brackets added)

Galileo's conclusion seems so obvious that one is left wondering why Oresme, who had carried the argument so far, did not take the final, crucial step? The most plausible answer, a consensus of the scholars, is that while he thought of his '*configurations*' as representing *possible* motions, he did not, as Galileo, have confidence that they represented existing motions in nature. Despite the subtlety of his arguments, there is not a single reference to objects actually falling with a certain velocity as one finds in Galileo. The Scholastic manner of treating changes in motion hypothetically was apparently too instilled in Oresme to consider these changes descriptions of actual occurrences in nature. As Clagett states:

> The object of Oresme's *On the Configurations of Qualities* is, as the title suggests, to represent by figures, that is geometrically, variations in qualities. It must be understood immediately, however, that Oresme's representations are entirely 'ymaginationes,' as he calls them. They are concerned with a figurative presentation of hypothetical quality variations and thus are totally unrelated to any empirical investigations of actual quality variations. (p. 340)

Yet it is important to remember that prior to the research of Duhem, Maier, and more recent scholars, it was believed that the discoveries of Galileo were unprecedented. We now know, however, that the investigations of the Mertonians and the Parisians were "a preparation for the mechanics of the sixteenth and seventeenth centuries [. . .]."[42] In fact, the terminology along with the representation of changes in velocity and acceleration geometrically will recur in the writings of Galileo due to their transmission to the scholars of the Renaissance. It does not denigrate from the striking originality of Galileo to recognize once again that anticipations and derivations are more characteristic of the development of science than discontinuities and abrupt novelties.

NOTES

1. Marshall Clagett, *The Science of Mechanics in the Middle Ages* (Wisconsin: University of Wisconsin Press, 1959), p. xix. I am especially indebted to this work both for the translations and for the commentaries on the original texts.

2. E.J. Dijksterhuis, *The Mechanization of the World Picture*, translated by C. Dikshoorn (Princeton: Princeton University Press, 1986), p.128.

3. Richard H. Schlagel, *Contextual Realism: A Meta-physical Framework for Modern Science* (New York: Paragon House, 1986), p. 268.

4. Maurice Clavelin, *The Natural Philosophy of Galileo*, translated by A.J. Pomerans (Cambridge: The MIT Press, 1974), p. 61.

5. Herbert Butterfield, *The Origins of Modern Science* (New York: Collier Books, 1962), p. 15.

6. Cf. Aristotle, *Physica*, Bk. VII, Ch. 5. Translated by R.P. Hardie and P.K. Gaye. The following references to the *Physica* are from this translation.

7. *Ibid.*, Bk. IV, Ch. 8, 215a, 19-22. Brackets added.

8. Cf. Dijkstertuis, *op. cit.*, pp. 24-32; Clavelin, *op. cit.*, pp. 48-60.

9. Aristotle, *op. cit.*, Bk. III, Ch. 2, 202a, 6-8.

10. Cf. Clavelin, *op. cit.*, p. 54; also Clagett, *op. cit.*, pp. 507-509.

11. Aristotle, *op. cit.*, Bk. VIII, Ch. 10, 267a, 4-8. Brackets added.

12. Cf. Jean Buridan, *Questions on the Eight Books of the Physics of Aristotle*, translated by Marshall Clagett, *op. cit.*, pp. 532-562. Unless otherwise indicated, the page references in the text are to Clagett's book.

13. Cf. Galileo Galilei, *Dialogues Concerning Two New Sciences*, translated by H. Crew and A. de Salvio (New York: McGraw-Hill Book Company, 1963), p. 160.

14. Aristotle, *op. cit.*, Bk. VIII, Ch. 4, 255b, 14-18.

15. ————, *De Caelo*, Bk. I, Ch. 1, 277a, 29-30. Translated by J. L. Stocks. All following quotations from the *De Caelo* are from this translation.

16. *Ibid.*, 277a, 32-33.

17. *Ibid.*, Bk. IV, Ch. 4, 311b, 15-19. Italics added.

18. *Ibid.*, Bk. III, Ch. 2, 301b, 18-19.

19. Cf. *ibid.*, Bk. I, Ch. 3, 270b, 21-26.

20. *Ibid.*, Bk. IV, Ch. 1, 308a, 31-33.

21. *Ibid.*, Bk. IV, Ch. 4, 311b, 28-29.

22. ————, *Physics*, Bk. III, Ch. 1, 201a, 10-11.

23. ————, *De Caelo*, Bk. IV, Ch. 2, 310a, 31-35.

24. Clagett, *op. cit.*, p. 543.

25. Cf. Clagett, *op. cit.*, p. 543.

26. Aristotle, *Physics*, Bk. IV, Ch. 8, 215b, 9-11.

27. Galileo, *op. cit.*, p. 60.

28. This summary of some of Buridan's arguments is based on *Questions on the Four Books on the Heavens and the World of Aristotle*, translated by E.A. Moody, in Clagett, *op. cit.*, pp. 557-562.

29. Cf. Galileo, *op. cit.*, p. 161.

30. Cf. Galileo Galilei, *Dialogue Concerning the Two Chief World Systems—Ptolemaic and Copernican*, translated by Stillman Drake, second edition (Berkeley: University of California Press, 1970), pp. 327-328.

31. Clavelin, *op. cit.*, p. 63. Until otherwise indicated, the following page references in the text are to this work.

32. Dijksterhuis, *op. cit.*, pp. 189-190.

33. *Ibid.*, p. 190.

34. *Ibid.*, pp. 190-191.

35. Clagett, *op. cit.*, p. 272. Unless otherwise indicated, the following page references in the text are to this work.

36. Clavelin, *op. cit.*, p. 68.

37. *Ibid.*, p. 71 and f.n. 27.

38. Cf. Clagett, *op. cit.*, pp. 351-359; Clavelin, *op. cit.*, p. 77.

39. Clavelin, *op. cit.*, p. 76.

40. Cf. Stephen Toulmin and June Goodfield, *The Fabric of the Heavens* (New York: Harper & Row, 1961), p. 216; also Clagett, *op. cit.*, pp. 341-345.

41. Galileo, *op. cit.*, p. 170. Brackets added.

42. Dijksterhuis, *op. cit.*, p. 189.

CHAPTER II

THE RISE OF MODERN SCIENCE

[. . .] it is the ultimate picture which an age forms of the nature of its world that is its most fundamental possession. [1]

Burtt

In retrospect the transition from the ancient cosmos to the heliocentric universe marks a shift in perspective nearly as profound as the first awakening of scientific rationalism. Though Copernicus' innovation was neither original nor especially revolutionary, it nonetheless had world-shattering consequences. As Thomas Kuhn states, "a revolution-making work is at once the culmination of a past tradition and a source of a novel future tradition." [2] It is no mistake that the "Copernican Revolution" has been viewed as one of the great turning points in the intellectual development of mankind opening up an endless vista of exploration pursued more vigorously today than at any time in the past.

NICOLAUS COPERNICUS

It would be difficult to find a more unlikely person than Copernicus to initiate a conceptual revolution that would change forever man's view of the universe and his place in it. As an individual Copernicus was a reclusive, dour, and timorous person who arouses little sympathy for his character. Yet it is not for his character that history venerates him, but for his scientific achievement. Arthur Koestler was so repulsed by Copernicus' personality that he was unable to appreciate his revolutionary contribution to astronomy, [3] but if we were to denigrate the accomplishments of gifted persons because of their weaknesses of character how many would be left to celebrate?

Thus it will not be for his personality that we will evaluate Copernicus but for his role in the development of astronomy. Moreover, the tendency of scholars such as Kuhn to belittle Copernicus's contribution because of the conservative aspects of his thought overlooks two strong impediments to conceptual change: (1) the near impossibility of intellectually freeing oneself from more than a few entrenched presuppositions (this is why the young Einstein is so remarkable), and (2) the natural reluctance to face the hostility that one inevitably encounters from challenging even those few assumptions. The effect of both those constraints are clearly evident in Copernicus. Yet a thinker as gifted as Kepler apparently suffered a nervous breakdown following a strenuous eight year effort to replace the venerated concepts of uniform circular motion with non-uniform elliptical orbits, while even as combative a person as Galileo put off announcing his commitment to Copernicanism for a number of years owing to a fear of being ridiculed.

Apprehensive that he would be derided or "hooted off the stage" for advocating what "seemed an absurd opinion"[4] that the earth moves, Copernicus justified his treatise on "the revolution of the spheres" by claiming that he was just following the precedent of the ancient Pythagoreans.

> I found in Cicero that Nicetus [in fact the Pythagorean Hicetas] had supposed that the Earth moved. After that I discovered in Plutarch also that certain others held the same opinion, and I decided to quote his words here, so they are generally accessible: 'Some say that the earth is at rest, but Philolaos the Pythagorean says that it is carried in a circle round the heavenly fire, slantwise, in the same way as the Sun and Moon. Heraclides of Pontus and Ecphantus the Pythagorean give the Earth motion, not indeed translation, but like a wheel on its axis, from west to east, about its own centre.'[5]

While he does not mention Aristarchus in the Preface (there are several references later), the Hellenistic astronomer who most nearly anticipated his own position and thus is called the "Copernican of antiquity," he did refer to him in the original manuscript at the end of Book I ("some say that Aristarchus of Samos was of the same belief [in the mobility of the earth]"[6]), but deleted the reference in the final printing.

Born in 1473 in Torun in the center of northern Poland then a diocese of Prussia which had previously been ruled by the Teutonic Knights, this has given the Germans some claim to share in his fame. Copernicus' father who was a prosperous merchant died when he was ten, whereupon his family came under the custody of his maternal uncle, Lucus Waczenrode, who became Bishop of Ermland and thus in effect ruler of the region in 1489. Following in the academic footsteps of his uncle, at age eighteen Copernicus began his studies at the University of Cracow, then in the capital of Poland, where he remained for four years taking the usual courses along with studying astronomy under Brudzewski. He left Cracow without earning a degree to continue his education for ten years at the universities of Northern Italy whose city-states were the hub of the Renaissance. Like his uncle earlier, he enrolled at the University of Bologna in 1496 for a degree in canon law, but took the occasion to study with Domenico Maria da Novara, the well-known professor of astronomy, and made some observations of the moon later recorded in his major work. The fact that Novara was critical of the Ptolemaic system because of its undue complexity and lack of coherence undoubtedly had some influence on Copernicus, as did the writings of Cusa, Peurbach, and Regiomontanus which were studied and discussed. Peurbach in his textbook had emphasized that the orbital motions of the planets are governed by the Sun, while Regiomontanus indicated a strong interest in the heliocentric system of Aristarchus. [7]

Owing to his uncle's influence, Copernicus was elected a canon of the Cathedral of Frauenburg which brought him a substantial prebend for life though he never became a priest. He benefited from a second absentee prebend, a "Scholasticus of the Collegiate Church of the Holy Cross in Breslau," despite never having visited Breslau nor preformed any functions connected with his title. After a visit to Ermland to be installed in the Cathedral's chapter, he returned to Italy to continue his education at the University of Padua where Galileo later was to teach. But before matriculating at Padua he spent a year in Rome, the jubilee year 1500, where he claimed to have lectured on mathematics. Yet it was from the University of Ferrara that he earned his degree of Doctor of Canon Law in 1503. For the following two years he studied medicine and though he did not seek a degree he later practiced as a physician at Heibsberg Castle, the residence of his uncle. He chose wisely to continue his studies in Italy because it was the Italian Universities that produced most of the initiators of the impending scientific revolution: Vesalius (1514-64), Fabricius (1537-1619), Galileo (1564-1642), Harvey (1578-1657), as well as Copernicus himself.

Owing to the Humanists and the flowering of the Renaissance in Italy, he encountered the leading theories of the day along with the latest research techniques and discoveries. Intent on reviving ancient Greek and recovering original manuscripts that could be translated directly into Latin, thereby providing a more accurate basis of interpretation, the Humanists contributed greatly to the Renaissance. The recovery of the writings of the Presocratics, especially, diverted attention from "the philosopher" (Aristotle) and "the commentator" (Averroës) to the more mathematical writings of the Pythagoreans. Because the Humanists championed Plato over Aristotle and were bitter opponents of what they considered to be the logic-chopping, hair-splitting, sterile methods of argumentation of the Scholastics, who occupied the main positions at the leading universities, they shared some of the critical beliefs and attitudes of the more independently minded scientists of the

Renaissance.   Yet as Dijksterhuis has warned:

> One must, however, beware of the illusion that a common enemy presupposes harmonious agreement and that on this account figures like Marsilio Ficino and Erasmus might be expected to have furthered natural science to some extent, because the former combated the Paduan Schoolmen and the latter ridiculed those in Paris. [8]

Dedicated primarily to the revival of classical literature and art by recovering and translating original Greek manuscripts and usually knowing very little science and mathematics, the Humanists often expressed the opinion that, compared to literature and the arts, science did not have much significance for life.   Yet their dedication to discovering any Greek manuscripts and devotion to preserving the original meaning by translating them directly into Latin, thereby eliminating the distortions due to the Seriac-Arabic translations and interpretations, produced more reliable scientific texts. Thus, as several dramatic examples cited by Marie Boas confirm, the Humanists' preference for original works in literature and art did not preclude their recovering manuscripts in the sciences.

> In 1417 the Italian humanist Poggio Bracciolini was as pleased with his discovery in a "distant monastery" of a manuscript of Lucretius [. . .] as he was with the manuscripts of Cicero that he found at the monastery of St. Gall.   Guarino of Verona, hot in pursuit of Latin literature, was happy in finding the medical work of Celsus (in 1426) unknown for over 500 years.   When Jacopo Angelo returned from Constantinople with manuscripts for baggage, only to be shipwrecked off Naples, one of the treasures he managed to pull to shore was Ptolemy's *Geography*, mysteriously unknown to the Christian West that had revered Ptolemy's work on astronomy for three centuries; he had already translated it into Latin (1406) so that it was ready for the public. [9]

Returning to Ermland probably in 1505 at the age of thirty-one after completing his formal studies, Copernicus became an assistant to his uncle, Bishop of Ermland.   Despite his administrative responsibilities, in true humanist fashion he translated into Latin the Epistles of Theophylactus Simocatta, a Byzantine Christian of the seventh century.   Following the death of his uncle in 1512 he settled in Frauenburg where, despite unfavorable climatic conditions, he made the few observations that he used in support of his new astronomical system. Not fond of star-gazing, he made between sixty and seventy observations during his lifetime, twenty-seven of which were recorded in the *De Revolutionibus*.

During this time he wrote the *Commentariolus* (Little Commentary), an unpublished preliminary sketch of his new astronomical theory that he circulated in manuscript form among a select group of friends. Perhaps owing to the positive reception of this work he was invited by Bernhard Sculteti, a friend and chaplain to the Pope, to come to Rome to help in a proposed reform of the calendar. Realizing, however, that without more accurate knowledge of the orbital periods of the Sun and the Moon no exact calendar could be devised, he declined—later in 1582 the Gregorian calendar was introduced based on his revised tables. Despite his reluctance to publish his views because of fear of ridicule, the favorable interest aroused by the *Commentariolus* led several friends, especially Tiedemann Giese, Bishop of Kulm, and Nicolaus von Schönberg, Cardinal of Capua, whose entreating letter is included between Osiander's preface and the dedication to Pope Paul III (the Pope who commissioned Michelangelo to paint the "Last Judgment" on the ceiling of the Sistine Chapel), to press for publication of a full account of his system.

But the person most responsible for its publication was Rheticus, a young German Lutheran who was professor of mathematics and astronomy at the University of Wittenberg (the school attended by Shakespeare's *Hamlet*) who, having heard of Copernicus' revolutionary ideas, requested a leave of absence in the spring of 1539 to visit him in Frauenburg to convince him to publish the manuscript and help prepare it for printing. However, because Copernicus could not be persuaded,

> Rheticus published in 1540 a short work, *Narratio Prima* (First Account), on the Copernican theory of astronomy, and in 1542 [the year preceding Copernicus' death and the publication of his great work] a separate edition of the trigonometrical chapters which later formed the last section of Book I of *The Revolutions*. [10]

Refusing to be deterred, Rheticus returned to stay with Copernicus from the summer of 1540 to September of 1541 helping prepare the manuscript for printing, finally convincing his *Domine Praeceptor* ("my teacher" as he referred to Copernicus) to agree to publication. Rheticus read the entire manuscript checking the figures and tables for accuracy, copying it by hand to prepare it for the printer, and arranging for the printing itself, taking the manuscript to Nüremberg for that purpose. But to avoid a scandal related to his sexual orientation, Rheticus accepted a position at the University of Leipzig and therefore was unable to remain in Nüremberg to supervise the final printed which was entrusted to another protestant professor at Wittenberg named Osiander. [11]

It was the latter who inserted the Preface, "To the Reader on the Hypotheses in this Work," which proved so contentious because there was no indication that Copernicus had not written it himself, thus misleading the reader into believing that he was the author. Giese was aware of the deception as was Kepler, but most readers assumed that it had been written by Copernicus. According to Duncan, "[o]nly the rediscovery of the original manuscript in the middle of the nineteenth century put the authorship of the preface beyond doubt." (p. 13) The reason that Osiander introduced it was to deflect criticism by Catholics and Protestants who might have objected to the theory if taken as factually true. Asserting that "it is proper for an astronomer to establish a record of the motions of the heavens with diligent and skillful observations, and then to think out and construct laws for them or rather hypotheses," he added that it is not "necessary that these hypotheses should be true, nor indeed even probable, but it is sufficient if they merely produce calculations which agree with the observations." (p. 22)

While presenting hypotheses for the correct prediction of phenomena, according to Osiander's disarming statement the work "does not do so in any way with the aim of persuading anyone that they are valid [. . .]. (p. 22) This, of course, was directly contrary to the intention of Copernicus and hence was a misleading if not dishonest representation of his position, despite Osiander's well-intentioned effort to reduce the possibility of the work being rejected as absurd. That this fear was justifiable is indicated by a statement made by Luther in 1539, four years even before publication of *De Revolutionibus*:

> People give ear to an upstart astrologer [the term was used for astronomers at the time, but here it may be intentionally derogatory] who strove to show that the earth revolves, not the heavens or the firmament, the sun and the moon. . . . This fool wishes to revise the entire science of astronomy; but sacred Scripture tells us [Joshua 10:13] that Joshua commanded the sun to stand still, and not the earth. [12]

Considering Copernicus' own deeply expressed fears and that Osiander (who was a colleague of Rheticus, Luther, and Melanchton at the University of Wittenberg, the cradle of the Reformation) as a Protestant was especially aware of the threat from that quarter, perhaps we should be more understanding of his motivation for inserting the Preface and even for leading the reader to believe that it was written by Copernicus himself, since that would make it more effective than if written by someone else. Yet the preface itself is somewhat ambiguous in that although Osiander asserts that astronomical laws should be interpreted hypothetically and instrumentally, rather than as literally true, he begins his assertion with what appears to be a strong declaration of the truth of the Copernican system (although the exact wording varies with the translation).

> I have no doubt that certain learned men, now that the novelty of the hypothesis in this work has been widely reported—*for it establishes that the Earth moves, and indeed that the Sun is motionless in the middle of the universe* [italics added]—are extremely shocked, and think that the scholarly disciplines, rightly established once and for all, should not be upset. (p. 22)

One would expect that he would have used the term 'assumes' or 'postulates,' rather than 'establishes,' if indeed he intended to minimize the truth of the system. We do not know what Copernicus' reaction to the insertion was because he suffered a stroke in 1542 and died the following year. The accounts differ as to whether he knew about the insertion and his response to it, but according to tradition he was presented a copy of his book as he lay stricken on his deathbed.

The episode is interesting also for foreshadowing the controversy between Galileo and his Aristotelian opponents in the Catholic Church and even for the present realist-antirealist interpretation of scientific theories. Galileo was granted permission by Pope Urban VIII to publish his *Dialogue Concerning the Two Chief World Systems* provided he did not include the tides in the title nor imply that physical arguments (such as the twofold motion of the earth causing the tides) proved the Copernican system, did not enter into any theological or Scriptural disputes, and treated both the geocentric and heliocentric theories impartially, although he could present "mathematical arguments" in support of the Copernican system as "hypotheses to save the appearances." [13] But just as Copernicus believed the heliocentric theory to be true, not just a convenient model for calculating astronomical data to save the phenomena, Galileo, by the time he wrote the *Dialogue*, was also convinced of its truth, as is clearly evident to anyone who reads it. For most scientists, belief that scientific theories actually represent physical reality to some degree of exactitude, and thus are approximately true, has been indispensable for their pursuit of scientific knowledge, as the examples of Copernicus, Kepler, Galileo, and Einstein confirm. Kepler was so disturbed by Osiander's preface that he wrote the following in the prefatory material of the *Astronomia*:

> "It is a most absurd fiction, I admit, that the phenomena of nature can be explained by false causes. But this fiction is not in Copernicus. He thought that his hypotheses were true [. . .]. And he did not merely think so, but he proves that they are true. As evidence I offer this work."[14]

Like Descartes (who, during his lifetime, sent away his *Traité du Monde* lest he be tempted to publish it and bring on himself, as did Galileo, the condemnation of the Inquisition), Copernicus was cautious by temperament (he kept the *De Revolutionibus* "suppressed and hidden [. . .] for almost four times nine years"), but this personal timidity should not be confused with intellectual timidity. Both he and Descartes were revolutionary thinkers despite their cautious natures and the fact that their systems display a much greater dependence on the past than they were aware. Copernicus' dedicatory preface to the Pope justifying final publication of his great book and appealing to the latter's "authority" and "influence and judgment" to "restrain the stings of false accusers," clearly indicates how apprehensive he was of being slandered for his publication. Nor was such fear unjustified, as a letter from Galileo to Kepler, written about fifty years later (1597) thanking him for sending him a copy of the *Mysterium Cosmographicum*, indicates:

> I have written many arguments in support of him [Copernicus] and in refutation of the opposite view—which, however, so far I have not dared to bring into public light, frightened by the fate of Copernicus himself, our teacher, who, though he acquired immortal fame with some, is yet to an infinite multitude of others (for such is the number of fools) an object of ridicule and derision. [15]

The reasons Copernicus gives for considering alternative hypotheses for "calculating the motions of the spheres of the universe" are, first, "that the mathematicians themselves are inconsistent in investigating them" (p. 25), for they have not been able to describe coherently or accurately the orbits of the

Sun and the Moon or the length of the sidereal year. Second, in depicting the motions of the other five planets "they do not use the same principles or assumptions, or explanations of their apparent revolutions and motions"(p. 25), the Aristotelians and Averroësts relying on homocentric circles while the followers of Ptolemy utilize eccentric circles, epicycles, and equants. Third, even with those artifices they were not able to "extract" the phenomena with numerical accuracy. Fourth, and chiefly, "they have not been able to discover or deduce from them [. . .] the form of the universe and the clear symmetry of its parts." (p. 25) The fact that after all these centuries the supporters of the geocentric system had been able to produce only an astronomical "monster" consisting of disconnected, unsymmetrical components is what disturbed him the most.

> Therefore on long pondering this uncertainty of mathematical traditions on the deduction of the motions of the system of the spheres, I began to feel disgusted that no more certain theory of the motions of the mechanisms of the universe, which has been established for us by the best and most systematic craftsman of all, was agreed by the philosophers, who otherwise theorized so minutely with most careful attention to the details of this system. (p. 25)

Thus it was the theoretical and predictable inadequacies of the usual systems of interpretation that "disgusted" Copernicus. As in his earlier years, he continued to be upset by the fact that even as regards the most prominent planets, the Sun and Moon, no exact representations of their motions, and hence of the sidereal month and year, could be devised, obviating the construction of an exact calendar. Following the previously quoted statement, he says that because of the indicated reasons he was impelled to read "the books of all other philosophers that were available" to see if he could find a better explanation. As claimed by Kuhn, he does not include among "all other philosophers" any Neoplatonist, even though the prominent Florentine Neoplatonist, Marsilio Ficino, who probably was a friend of his teacher Novara, was still alive when Copernicus began his studies in Italy. The evidence cited for the Neoplatonic (as opposed to simply Platonic) influence is the following lavish description of the Sun by Copernicus in Chapter X of Book I.

> In the middle of all is the seat of the sun. For who in this most beautiful of temples would put this lamp in any other or better place

than the one from which it can illuminate everything at the same time? Apply indeed is he named by some the lantern of the universe, by others the mind, by others the ruler. Trismegistus called him the visible God, Sophocles Electra, the watcher over all things. Thus indeed the sun as if seated on a royal throne governs his household of Stars as they circle round him. (p. 50)

Yet even in this passage he does not refer to a Neoplatonist but to the legendary figure Hermes Trismegistus. [16] It was the Pythagoreans who had replaced the earth by a central fire (not the Sun), calling it the ''Hearth of the World'' and the ''Throne of Zeus,'' while Plato had compared the Good to the illuminating and life-sustaining power of the Sun (*Republic*, Part III, Ch. XXIII, vi, 509a). There are numerous passages in *De Revolutionibus* to confirm the influence of the Pythagoreans and Plato, but not of the Neoplatonists.

Although Copernicus' dedication to devising a more harmonious astronomical system can be explained best in terms of the problems internal to mathematical astronomy, this does not mean outside influences had no effect at all. That his professor Novara was critical of the Ptolemaic system must have influenced Copernicus, along with the fact that greater emphasis was being placed on the technical problems growing out of the mathematical tradition of astronomy from the Pythagoreans to Ptolemy, than on the cosmological concerns of the Aristotelians or the speculative metaphysics of such Neoplatonists as Nicolas of Cusa. While there is no reference to Cusa in Copernicus' work, he does refer to Philolaus, Heraclides, Plato, Callippus, Euclid, Hipparchus, Ptolemy, Al-Battani, Peurbach, and Johannes Muller (Regiomontanus). The latter two Humanists who lived in the fifteenth century were greatly responsible for the detailed study and spread of knowledge of Ptolemy by their clarifying exegesis and explanation of his system, although they also demonstrated by their own observations that it contained many errors. Thus they were important in emphasizing the crucial significance of the *Almagest* for astronomical research, while also drawing attention to the empirical discrepancies in it.

Peurbach was asked in 1460 by Cardinal Bessarian to write a commentary on the *Almagest*, but died in 1461 at age thirty-eight before he could complete the work. The project was taken over by his pupil Regiomontanus who devoted many years before his own death at forty to interpreting the *Almagest*, as well as discovering and translating works by Hellenic authors. In addition, as Dijksterhuis states, as a pioneer of printing, at his private Nüremberg printing-office he made generally accessible in book-form, besides other astronomical works, the *Theoricae novae Planetarium* of his teacher Peurbach, which embodied the latter's Viennese lectures, and thus gave to Greek astronomy a more prominent place in Western scientific thought than it had occupied before. To this extent his work ran parallel to that of the numerous philosophers and men of letters [mainly Humanists] who in the fifteenth and sixteenth centuries helped to introduce Hellenic wisdom and beauty into Western culture. [17]

As advocates of a sun centered universe, Peurbach and Regiomontanus were not just admirers of Ptolemy, but exhorted astronomers to go beyond previous investigations.

This change of attitude marked a crucial difference between the critical approach of the fourteenth-century Scholastics and the astronomers of the fifteenth and sixteenth centuries. As was apparent in the previous chapter, while the Mertonian and Parisian Scholastics were acutely critical of Aristotle's dynamic explanations and kinematic descriptions of motions, they drew back from accepting the consequences of their critical analyses when it meant challenging Aristotle's system. In the succeeding two centuries, however, the intellectual outlook toward the study of mathematical astronomy had changed, so that scientists were not just engaged in the philosophical exercise of finding hypothetical points of criticism in previous systems, they were actively seeking better alternatives. This altered viewpoint is reflected in Copernicus' search among the early Pythagoreans for a possible replacement for the geocentric system of Aristotle and Ptolemy. Other factors undoubtedly stimulated this critical attitude, such as the greater availability of accurate translations of ancient manuscripts, the dramatic spread of knowledge caused by the greater accessibility of printed texts due to the newly developed printing press, the increased demand for better astronomical charts used in global navigation, the much needed calendar reform, but dissatisfaction with previous astronomical systems and belief that a better solution could be found were the primary influences leading to Copernicus' revolutionary program.

In what, then, did this revolutionary work consist? Obviously it is not possible to examine fully the extensive astronomical data, detailed geometrical diagrams, complex technical arguments, and numerous comparisons of stellar positions as they had been recorded by astronomers throughout the centuries that comprise the major part of the *De Revolutionibus*. Instead, the focus will be on the main reasons that Copernicus presents for advancing his heliocentric system. While there was no significant overall reduction in the complexity of Copernicus' theory over Ptolemy's, it is clearly evident throughout the Six Books of the treatise that for Copernicus the Sun centered system had an interlocking coherence and harmony lacking to the geocentric model. Moreover, even though as an astronomer he made relatively few observations, he did present a detailed description of the astronomical instruments he used. And though relying too much on the observations of the ancients, his comparative evaluation of their data presented in his astronomical charts was the reason for their being the basis for Reinhold's and Kepler's improved tables and the reformed Gregorian calendar.

Perhaps as early as Plato's *Timaeus* but certainly since Heraclides of Pontus, the ancient astronomers realized that a major astronomical simplification could be achieved by explaining the observed diurnal westward revolution of the whole celestial realm as an apparent movement due to the daily eastward rotation on its axis of the much smaller earth. In addition, believing that a 'heavenly fire' occupied the center of the universe, Philolaus had claimed that the earth revolved in a circular orbit along with the Sun and the Moon around this central fire. Later, according to the fragment in Archimedes' *Sand-Reckoner*, Aristarchus placed the Sun in the center of the universe attributing to the earth both a diurnal axial rotation and an orbital revolution around the Sun. This way of "saving the astronomical phenomena," however, was rejected by Hipparchus, Ptolemy, and the followers of Aristotle for a variety of reasons based on the apparent immobility of the earth and the seemingly disconfirming consequences if the earth moved with the assigned rotation and revolution.

Throughout the Middle Ages the geocentric system was so well established that there was little speculation about its validity, even though the alternative theories never had been entirely forgotten. Then in the fourteenth century, the very same Scholastics, particularly Buridan and Oresme who had been so critical of Aristotle's dynamic and kinematic treatment of motion, also acutely examined the evidence and arguments used to *refute* the mobility of the earth. Their rebuttals set forth in scholastic precision are so similar that they can be treated together.

First, as regards the observed daily revolution of the celestial realm around the stationary earth, they both argued that such motion is entirely relative. Because the detection of *uniform* motion depends upon some reference system, an object moving uniformly will appear the same whether it is moving relative to an observer or the observer is moving in relation to it. On a smoothly sailing ship, for example, it can appear that the shore is receding or another ship is passing when in fact the perceived motion is due to one's own movement. This is so, Buridan argued, because the person's "eye would be completely in the same relationship to the other ship regardless of whether his own ship is at rest and the other moved, or the contrary situation prevailed."[18] This relativity of terrestrial motions, he concluded, could also apply to celestial revolutions, as Oresme states:

> [. . .] if the upper of the two parts of the universe [. . .] should today move with a diurnal movement, just as it is, and the lower part should not, and tomorrow the contrary should prevail [. . .] we could not perceive this change in any way, but everything would seem to be the same today and tomorrow. [19]

The identical argument from the relativity of motion is stated by Copernicus even more explicitly.

> For every apparent change in respect of position is due to motion of the object observed, or of the observer [. . .]. Now the earth is the point from which the rotation of the heavens is observed [. . .]. If therefore some motion is imputed to the Earth, the same motion will appear in all that is external to the Earth, but in the opposite direction, as if it were passing by. The first example of this is the diurnal rotation. This seems to whirl round the whole universe, except the Earth and the things on it. But if you grant that the heaven has no part in this motion, but that the Earth revolves from west to east, as far as the apparent rising and setting of the Sun, Moon and stars is concerned, if you consider the point seriously, you will find that this is the way of it. [20]

Because experience itself cannot establish whether the heavens or the earth revolves, the resolution must be found on other grounds, namely, simplicity. Thus declaring that "it is better to save the appearances [. . .] by an easier way than by a more difficult one," Buridan concluded that because "it is easier to move a small thing than a large one [. . .] it is better to say that the [smaller] earth [. . .] is moved most swiftly and the highest sphere is at rest than to say the opposite."[21] Copernicus is more emphatic: "Indeed we should be even surprised if the universe, vast as it is, revolves in the space of twenty-four hours rather than the tiny part of it which is the Earth." (p. 42)

By itself, however, the argument from simplicity was insufficient to settle the issue because there were other physical objections derived from a rotating earth. If, for example, the earth spins from west to east rapidly enough to complete its rotation in twenty-four hours, should we not see the clouds drift by from east to west and feel the rush of air as we speed through it? Not so, Buridan argues, if the atmospheric air and everything in it were carried along by the earth's motion.

> If anyone were moving very swiftly on horseback, he would feel the air resisting him. Therefore, similarly, with the very swift motion of the earth [. . .] we ought to feel the air noticeably resisting us. But [. . .] [if] the earth, the water, and the air in the lower region are moved simultaneously with diurnal motion [. . .] there [would be] no air resisting us. [22]

Again Copernicus argues similarly that "the air which is nearest to the Earth will appear still, and objects suspended in it will be set in motion only by wind or some other impulse [. . .]." (pp. 44-45)

Moreover, as Aristotle had claimed, if the earth rotated from west to east swiftly enough to complete its daily journey in twenty-four hours, then an object projected vertically in the air should not fall back to the same position on the earth, because during the time of its ascent and descent the earth would have revolved eastward (at a rate of a thousand miles per hour), so that the object should fall to the west of its original launching position. The rebuttal provided by Buridan, and even more explicitly by Oresme, is that the reason the object returns in its original trajectory is that it partakes of two motions, the vertical projectile motion and the rotary motion of the earth. Just as we do not feel or observe the earth's rotation which we also participate in, so we do not observe the rotary motion of the projectile, only its vertical trajectory. Yet, as Oresme argues, its trajectory is a "compound" or "mixture" of both motions:

> [. . .] concerning the arrow or stone projected upward etc., one would say that the arrow is trajected upwards and [simultaneously] with this trajection it is moved eastward very swiftly with the air [. . .] and with all the mass of the lower part of the universe [. . .], it all being moved with a diurnal movement. For this reason the arrow returns to the place on the earth from which it left. [23]

Thus the motions of both the arrow and the stone consist of a "composition or mixture of movements'' (*ibid.*, p. 603), even though only one is observed. Copernicus again maintains the same conclusion when accounting for similar phenomena: "We have indeed to admit that the motion of falling and rising bodies is a dual motion [. . .] a compound of straight and circular motion." (p. 45) This, of course, was contrary to Aristotle's mechanics which precluded compounding contrasting motions.

Extending the analogy between being on the earth and on a ship, Oresme again not only antedates another of Galileo's famous arguments countering objections to the earth's mobility, he anticipates his discovery of inertial systems. Inertial systems are those at rest or moving uniformly which have the unexpected feature that the physical occurrences or laws in such systems are indistinguishable. As Oresme states: "If air were enclosed [in a cabin] in a moving ship, it would seem to the person situated in the [still] air that it was not moved."[24] As the example implies, and Galileo inferred, since the laws of nature are the same in all inertial systems nothing can be concluded from occurrences within such systems as to whether they are at rest or in motion! And since the earth is an inertial system the conclusion applies to it. Thus both Buridan and Oresme admit, in the latter's words, "that one could not by any experience whatsoever demonstrate that the heavens and not the earth are moved with diurnal movement." (*Ibid.*, p. 603) While not reproducing this argument, Copernicus certainly acquiesces in its conclusion.

However, unlike Copernicus who accepted both the argument from simplicity and the counter-arguments rebutting objections to the earth's diurnal rotation, Buridan and Oresme declined to take the decisive step. Strangely enough, after refuting the objection that the earth's motion would contradict Biblical passages asserting that the Sun "turns" around an immobile earth, by arguing that "the Holy Scripture which says that the sun revolves [. . .] is [. . .] [simply] conforming to the manner of common human speech" (*ibid.*, p. 604); (again Galileo will use a similar argument), Oresme reinvokes the authority of Scripture to affirm that it is the heavens rather than the earth that moves.

> Yet, nevertheless, everyone holds, *and I believe* [italics added], that they (the heavens), and not the earth, are so moved, for "God created the orb of the earth, which will not be moved" (Ps. 92: I), not withstanding the argument to the contrary. (*Ibid.*, p. 606)

As indicated earlier, the crucial difference underlying the negative conclusion of Buridan and Oresme in contrast to the positive affirmation of

Copernicus, is that they were evaluating the evidence and arguments from a hypothetical point of view while remaining committed to the Aristotelian framework, whereas he was earnestly seeking an alternative to the Ptolemaic system to accommodate better the astronomical data. Yet it hardly can be denied that their arguments, so clearly reproduced by Copernicus and then by Galileo, prepared the way for the later revolutionary developments. As Clagett asserts:

> That the Parisian mechanics spread to Cracow and throughout Eastern Europe, as well as to Italy is abundantly clear from manuscript evidence, and it is certainly possible, if not probable, that Copernicus knew of this Parisian question of the earth's rotation during his student days at Cracow." (*Ibid.*, pp. 588-589).

While Copernicus had predecessors who at least defended the possibility of a diurnal rotation of the Earth, when it came to supporting the earth's annual rotation around the center of the universe, he had to devise new arguments. There were three kinds of astronomical phenomena that he believed could be explained more simply if one posited this second motion: (1) the retrograde motions of the inferior and superior planets, (2) the variations in brightness of the planets as they complete their orbital revolutions, and (3) the more accurate calculation of their orbital distances and periods. As for the first simplification, if it could be shown that the perceived retrograde motions were not actual motions but an apparent effect projected on the planets as a result of assuming the earth to be stationary, then he could eliminate five deferents and epicycles to explain such motions.

> If then the Earth also performs other motions [than the diurnal rotation], as for example the one about the centre ["so that it can be regarded as one of the wandering stars" or planets] [. . .] the stations, retrogressions and progressions of the wandering stars will be seen not as their own motion but as the Earth's, which they transform into their apparent motions. (p. 46; brackets added)

Secondly, the observed variations in brightness of the planets as they revolved in their orbits had been interpreted since antiquity as implying that they must approach and recede from the earth. Because this would be impossible if they revolved in circular orbits with the earth at the center, various geometrical devices such as epicycles, eccentrics and equants (the latter particularly repugnant to Copernicus because it violated the principle of uniform circular motion), had been introduced to explain the appearances. But if the earth revolved with the other planets along the zodiac, then their positions relative to the earth during their various orbital revolutions (for example, oppositions and conjunctions) would make them appear brighter (nearer) or dimmer (distant), especially if their light was due to the reflection of the sun as Copernicus believed. "For the fact that the wandering stars are observed to be sometimes nearer to the Earth and sometimes further away from it necessarily shows that the centre of the Earth is not the centre of their orbits." (p. 40)

Thirdly, Copernicus showed that both the sequential distances of the planets as well as their orbital periods could be calculated more precisely from a sun centered rather than an earth centered perspective (actually this is not quite true since his calculations were based on the center of the earth's orbit rather than the position of the sun which was slightly removed from the latter, hence the designation 'heliostatic' is more accurate than 'heliocentirc' to describe his system). He also attributed a third motion to the earth, an annual conical rotation of its axes, or 'trepidation' as he called it, to explain the cyclical variation in the precession of the equinoxes and inequality of the days and nights. (cf. pp. 51-52) However, this rotation was not necessary since it was based on inaccurate observations by Hipparchus, Ptolemy, and Al-Battani, another example of Copernicus' unfortunate reliance on ancient authorities.

As was true of axial rotation, there were numerous objections to attributing to the terrestrial earth an annual revolution in the celestial realm while claiming that the Sun, a celestial body, resides motionless in the terrestrial world. But the fact that Copernicus does not bother to address the horrendous disparity of displacing a stellar body, whose ethereal nature required an eternal circular motion in the translunar world, with a terrestrial globe, whose earthly nature is to be at rest in the center of the sublunar world, shows how little he was concerned with those kinds of qualitative cosmological objections. Unlike the Aristotelians for whom these questions were primary, Copernicus was mainly concerned with accommodating the astronomical data. This is a vivid illustration of the way "rational arguments" are transformed during scientific revolutions when previous premises are revised or discarded. The opposing deductions are contradictory, but since they are derived from different premises, each are valid.

For an Aristotelian the earth cannot have a continuous circular motion because such a motion would be unnatural for a terrestrial object, and unnatural motion (it was believed) leads to disintegration of the object. The conclusion follows logically from the premises, but if one denies the premise that circular motion is "unnatural" to the earth and replaces it by another, then a different logical deduction follows. This is precisely what Copernicus does; he simply replies that circular motion is natural to a sphere, and since the earth is a sphere there is nothing unnatural or destructive in its having that motion.

> Yet if anyone should hold the opinion that the Earth revolves, he will surely assert that its motion is natural, not violent. What is natural produces contrary effects to what is violent [. . .]. There is therefore no need for Ptolemy to fear the scattering of the Earth and of all terrestrial objects in a revolution brought about by the working of nature [. . .]. (p. 43)

As for the Sun being at rest in the terrestrial world, he merely reiterates the Pythagorean conviction that for a luminous body dispensing its beneficent radiation throughout the universe no more suitable position could be found than a central location.

Most arguments are of this kind. It is not that the disputants are being irrational, but that they derive opposing conclusions from different premises reflecting diverse background beliefs or knowledge. This explains why arguments that are perfectly convincing at one time can become irrelevant at a later time: for example, Aristotle's argument that a vacuum cannot exist because its lack of resistance to motion would imply instantaneous velocity; Aquinas' argument that because everything in the universe is contingent and nothing contingent is necessary, the universe must be grounded in a necessary being; the argument that just as artifacts (like clocks) are created by intelligent beings the world machine must have been created by a divine mechanic; or the claim that the origin of human beings and lower organisms presupposes a special creation, rather than a natural evolutionary process. In none of these cases has the argument been disproved or invalidated, it merely has become obsolete or irrelevant in terms of later developments in knowledge (for those who accept the knowledge).

The superiority of the heliocentric system for Copernicus consisted in its harmonious interconnectedness. Outstanding scientists usually have the ability to discern, in what to others appear as an amorphous or disjointed array of data, an intrinsic structure and unifying symmetry. Such visionaries will 'see' the data as fitting a new pattern of organization according to unusual principles of interpretation. As Robert Small, in his classic study of Kepler's astronomical discoveries, says:

It was the celebrated Copernicus [. . .] to whom the exclusive honour belongs, of substituting for the Ptolemaic a new and more beautiful system, representing the celestial motions with much more simplicity, and, after its principles were fully understood, with incomparably greater accuracy. [25]

Because these new principles of interpretation challenging previous assumptions often appear counterintuitive or "absurd" to others committed to the traditional view, demanding ingenious supporting arguments, the underlying reasoning has been described by critics such as Kuhn[26] and Feyerabend[27] as "irrational." But rather than being irrational, such thinkers were originating and authenticating new inferences or arguments involving novel conceptual implications derived from different premises or principles. Rationality is not just an abstract logical feature of arguments, but a function of semantic implications based on the meanings of certain concepts and presuppositions: what is a rational inference in one system is not in another. As Copernicus illustrates in his prefatory letter to the Pope:

Thus assuming the motions I attribute to the Earth in the following work I eventually found by long and intensive study that if the motions of the wandering stars are referred to the circular motion of the Earth and calculated according to the revolution of each star, not only do the phenomena agree with the result, but also *it links together* the *arrangement* of all the stars and spheres, and their sizes, and the very heaven, so that *nothing can be moved in any part of it without upsetting the other parts* and the whole universe. (p. 26; italics added)

The deficiencies of Ptolemy's system as seen by Copernicus were aptly described by Small a century and a half later:

Its suppositions were often dissimilar, and even inconsistent with one another; and instead of answering to the title of a system, it was an assemblage of parts connected by no general principle of union, and between which there subsisted no known mutual relations [. . .].[28]

In contrast to this "monstrous system," by calculating the dimensions of the various orbital periods from the center of the earth's orbit, Copernicus found that the results were so interrelated that he could not modify one without disrupting the whole arrangement. [29]

In particular, the perplexing problem since ancient times of deciding the position of the orbits of Mercury and Venus in relation to those of the Moon and the Sun could be settled. Here was an interlocking harmony, not a disconnected, *ad hoc* arrangement of spheres. Like beauty, even if part of this symmetry lay in the eye of the beholder, another part reflected an objective order.

> The first and highest of all is the sphere of the fixed stars, which contains itself all things, and is therefore motionless. It is the location of the universe [. . . .] There follows Saturn, the first of the wandering stars, which completes its circuit in thirty years. After it comes Jupiter which moves in a twelve-year long revolution. Next is Mars, which goes around biannually. An annual revolution holds the fourth place, in which [. . .] is contained the Earth along with the lunar sphere which is like an epicycle. In fifth place Venus returns every nine months. Lastly, Mercury holds the sixth place, making a circuit in the space of eighty days. In the middle of all is the seat of the Sun. (pp. 49-50)

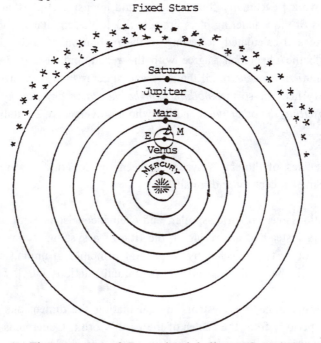

Fig. 1. The structure of Copernicus' heliocentric universe.

As Kuhn has pointed out, in the final analysis "Copernicus' system is neither simpler nor more accurate than Ptolemy's,"[30] both requiring over thirty circles. In fact, he found it necessary to increase the number of circles used by Ptolemy from forty to forty-eight. Yet Copernicus could find in the arrangement of the heliocentric system a "marvelous symmetry of the universe, and a sure linking together in harmony of the motion and size of the spheres, such as could be perceived in no other way." (p. 50) The Aristotelian philosophers would not find it so, but other like-minded astronomers such as Kepler and Galileo would agree.

In characterizing Copernicus as a "visionary," I have disagreed with those commentators who emphasize the conservative aspect of his thinking: retention of the traditional finite spherical universe, use of eccentrics, deferents, and epicycles, and acceptance of the crystalline spheres. As Kuhn justly states:

> In every respect except the earth's motion the *De Revolutionibus* seems more closely akin to the works of ancient and medieval astronomers and cosmologists than to the writings of the succeeding generations [. . .]. (*Ibid.*, p. 137)

This implies that Copernicus should have rejected more of Ptolemy's system in constructing his own model, but there are sound reasons, beyond a conservative nature, for his not doing so.

Copernicus was in the direct tradition of Hellenistic astronomers, so much so that the plan of *De Revolutionibus* follows very closely Ptolemy's *Almagest*. The reason is that Ptolemy's geocentric model (or current variations of it), despite Copernicus' criticisms, contained up to then the most accurate representation of astronomical observations available. Unlike Aristotelians who relied solely on concentric circles and thus could offer only a very general, qualitative sketch of the motions of the planets, Ptolemy's use of eccentrics, epicycles, and equants (despite their *ad hoc* introduction) enabled him to derive mathematical descriptions of the declensions, periods, and distances of the planet's orbits, along with accounting for such phenomena as the precession of the equinoxes and solstices. These descriptions and explanations at the time could be derived only by using the geometrical configurations and basic assumptions of his model.

Copernicus was acutely aware that if he were to succeed in opposing the entrenched geocentric system, then he had to be able to show that his heliocentric (in fact heliostatic) hypothesis, in addition to appearing simpler and more coherent, would lead to more accurate descriptions of the same phenomena, as he attempted to demonstrate in the remaining five books of his treatise. If he could not show that his system was superior to Ptolemy's, as Ptolemy's had been to Hipparchus', and Hipparchus' had been to Apollonius', then no astronomer would be attracted to his theory. To lure mathematical astronomer's away from Ptolemy, he had to show that his calculations and tables were preferable, but to do this he inevitably had to accept most of Ptolemy's framework, otherwise he could not have derived comparable observations and computations.

Thus to succeed in his astronomical reconstruction Copernicus had to submit to the exacting constraints of a mathematical astronomer. As he was aware, were he to indulge in the cosmological speculations of Nicolas Cusa (Cusanus) regarding an infinite universe with no testable observations or predictions, professional astronomers would not have taken him any more seriously than they did the Cardinal. So when his heliocentrism (like that of Aristarchus) implied that "the Earth is relatively to the sky as a point is to a body, or as finite to infinite in size" (p. 42), he refrained from speculating further; or, when confronted by Aristotelians arguing that the finitude of the universe is dependent on its motion, he replied: "let us leave the question whether the universe is finite or infinite for the natural philosophers to argue." (p. 44) That he submitted to the constraints of his discipline, making whatever revisions in Ptolemy's model seemed necessary to achieve what to him appeared to be a simpler, more coherent and accurate astronomical system is the reason his theory, not that of Cusa or Bruno,[31] initiated modern astronomy and inaugurated a new era, the modern world.

In relating an historical development, especially one that was to have revolutionary consequences, it is impossible not to assume in the description the knowledge one has of its outcome. Thus in our account of Copernicus' heliocentric system we did not describe it as a possible failure, but as if its success were a foregone conclusion. Yet nothing could be further from the truth at the time. Even astronomers who accepted the simplicity and computational superiority of the Copernican system over Ptolemy's did not necessarily embrace his conception of a mobile earth orbiting a central, stationary sun. They could, after all, accept the suggestion of Osiander that even if Copernicus' hypotheses led to measurements that could more systematically "save the phenomena," this does not prove that they are true or that his conjectured motions are real. Moreover, there was Tycho Brahe's compromise position as we shall see.

As conservative as Copernicus' revisions were, just interchanging the roles of the sun and earth was tremendously disturbing cognitively, psychologically, and religiously. Rejecting the time-honored qualitative distinction between the celestial and terrestrial worlds, it undermined confidence in ordinary sensory observations and commonsense beliefs that attest to a central, stationary earth, along with challenging the Scriptural passages supporting the geocentric theory. While the belief that he was defending a truer conception of the universe could be his compensation for these unsettling consequences, they were of no satisfaction to those who held the traditional conception of the homocentric universe.

It is not surprising, then, that in Protestant countries, where there was a reform movement to return to the simple, primary truths of Scripture, religious leaders such as Luther, his disciple Melanchthon, and Calvin ridiculed Copernicus' hypotheses as "absurd" and "impious." Even as respected an astronomer as Erasmus Reinhold, who relied on Copernicus' system and techniques of computation for bringing out a new book of astronomical tables in 1551, called the *Prutenic Tables* after his patron the Duke of Prussia, refused to take a position regarding the truth of heliocentrism, perhaps bowing to the official opposition of the University of Wittenberg. Although initially the Catholic Church was not antagonistic, it became progressively more so in the first half of the seventeenth century as proponents of the heliocentric theory, especially Galileo, were seen as undermining Catholic doctrine and challenging the authority of the church.

TYCHO BRAHE

Opposition to the 'heliocentric' position was not based solely on commonsense prejudices and religious hostility. The greatest astronomer of the second half of the sixteenth century was Tycho Brahe who opposed Copernicus' system for astronomical reasons. Born in 1546 to an aristocratic Danish family, Tycho's father had been Governor of Helsingborg Castle across from Elsinor while his uncle, who adopted him to acquire an heir, was a landed gentry and vice-admiral to King Ferdinand II. Despite this privileged background, the event that made the most impression on his life was the observation of a partial eclipse of the moon when he was fourteen. For those persons potentially gifted in the sciences, witnessing some striking physical phenomena can serve as a window on their future careers. Einstein recalled that shown a pocket compass at age five he was deeply impressed by the fact that the needle always pointed in the same direction, as if responding to some mysterious power. The observation of a forecasted lunar eclipse similarly left a lasting impression on Tycho of the predictability of astronomical events. Despite the opposition of his uncle who had expected that he would prefer the life of a country squire, from then on Tycho was determined to become a star-gazer, rather than succumb to a life of "horses, dogs and luxury."

Sent to the University of Copenhagen when he was thirteen years old, he studied there for three years. From there he went to the University of Leipzig for one year and then divided his time for the next ten years among the Universities of Wittenberg, Rostock, Basle, and Augsburg. During this decade he was mainly involved in procuring and improving the instruments then available for measuring astronomical phenomena, becoming renown for their expense and gargantuan size. Determined as he was to surpass ancient astronomers in accuracy and continuity of observations, he utilized these large devices to enhance precise measurements and initiated continuous observations of the planets for more complete data. One night at the early age of seventeen he had observed that Saturn and Jupiter were in conjunction, yet when he consulted the Alphonsine tables he found the listing off by an entire month and the Copernican tables mistaken by several days.[32] He resolved then that there could be no more important endeavor for him than improving the accuracy and completeness of past astronomical data by continuous observations. As a result he became, as Kuhn states, "the best of all naked-eye observers."

The event that provided him with the opportunity to demonstrate his skill occurred when he was twenty-six years old on the evening of November 11, 1572. Returning home one evening he was startled to observe a luminous body brighter than Venus in a position in the sky where there should be no planet. After confirming his observation, he resolved to establish what kind of celestial entity it could be. Because of the common belief since Aristotle that what distinguished the celestial from the terrestrial world was the "changeless," "incorruptible" nature of the former, any new occurrence in the skies aroused considerable excitement and apprehension. Given the prevalent belief in astrology, these unexpected events could presage either fortuitous or disastrous occurrences. Like most people of his time, Tycho's attitude toward astrology was ambiguous. According to Koestler, "he became a court astrologer and had to waste much of his time with the casting of horoscopes," although "he did it with his tongue in cheek" and "despised all other astrologers as quacks," yet he had a kind of superstitious belief "that the stars influenced man's character and destiny though nobody quite knew how." (p. 287) In the Bayeaux tapestry of 1066 a comet is prominently displayed which was interpreted as a bad omen by Harold, the English King, and a good omen by William the Conqueror which, as it happened, turned out to be correct. As early as 125 B.C. Hipparchus records seeing a new star, but given the prohibition of celestial novelties, such unusual occurrences were interpreted as taking place within the sublunar world, attributed to the igniting of gases.

What differentiated the terrestrial from the celestial world was the atmospheric changes that occurred in the former, such a lightning and thunder storms, in contrast to the incorruptible, eternal nature of the latter. Because the planets or 'wanderers' were distinguished from the fixed stars owing to their orbital revolutions, the status of the brilliant new arrival could be inferred from its position among the celestial bodies. As it remained visible for eighteen months in the exact same location, astronomers from Maestlin in Tübingen to Digges in England inferred that it must belong to the realm of the fixed stars. But while Maestlin used pieces of string to arrive at his conclusion, Tycho employed a new instrument, "a sextant with arms five and a half feet long, joined by a bronze hinge, with a metallic arc scale graduated to single minutes and, as a novelty, a table of figures designed to correct the errors of the instrument" (p. 289), to demonstrate unequivocally that the stellar apparition remained fixed. The following year he published a book, *De Nova Stella*, containing such precise astronomical measurements that from then until his death in 1601 he was the unrivalled authority, superceding Hipparachus, Ptolemy, and Copernicus, for the accuracy and reliability of his observations. Then five years following his observation of the Nova there appeared a brilliant comet which he demonstrated must be "at least six times" as distant in space as the moon." So by proving that the heavens contained new occurrences he inadvertently contributed to the growing success of Copernicus, or at least to the decline of Aristotelianism.

Yet, as indicated earlier, Tycho never was converted to Copernicanism (despite the contrary conviction of his brilliant research assistant, Kepler) for two main reasons. First, revising the ancient objection of Aristotle that if the earth moved a projectile launched vertically would not return to its original position, Tycho introduced the modified argument that if the earth rotated on its axis from west to east then a cannon ball shot westward would have a longer range than one shot eastward, because in the former case the earth's rotation would carry the canon away from the trajectory adding to its range, while in the latter case it would move toward its trajectory decreasing the range. Second, the primary and more serious objection pertained to the lack of an observed parallax predicted from the earth's annual orbital revolution. Just as when we turn our heads objects in our visual field are displaced in the opposite direction, it was inferred that a stellar body selected as a reference point would have its position shifted when observed from opposite positions on the earth's orbit.

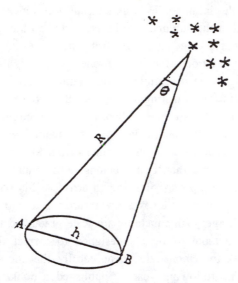

Fig. 2.   The formula for calculating the angle of parallax is: $\theta = \dfrac{2.1 \times 10^{5''} h}{R}$.
It can be seen, therefore, that the angle of parallax decreases either as R increases or the orbital distance h decreases between A and B.

Because the extent of the displacement as measured by the angle of parallax is a function both of the distance of the earth from the stars and the size of the earth's orbit, the predicted effect diminishes as the earth's distance from the stars increases and its orbital size decreases. As Aristarchus and Copernicus had argued, the absence of an observed parallax could be explained if the size of the earth's orbit shrank to a point in proportion to its distance from the fixed stars. Presupposing an enormously enlarged universe, it was this along with religious scruples that prevented Tycho from accepting Copernicus' theory. Adopting a compromise position based on Heraclides' model, he held that the Moon and the Sun revolve around the Earth as in the geocentric system, but that the five remaining planets (Mercury, Venus, Mars, Jupiter, and Saturn) revolve around the sun as in Copernicus' theory.

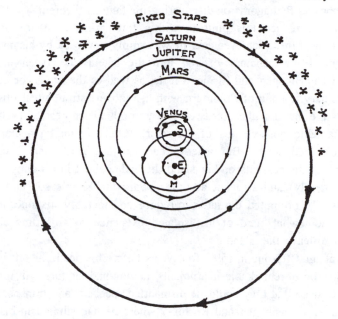

Fig. 3. Tycho Brahe's conception of the universe.

In addition to being very unsymmetrical, Tycho's system reverts to the traditional position that the whole universe is carried around daily by the sphere of the fixed stars, a particular disadvantage to those seeking a simpler explanation of diurnal motion.

Unlike Ptolemy and Copernicus, he did not derive a book of tables based on his system, so it remained merely a descriptive model, yet as a compromise between Ptolemy and Copernicus he believed that it was correct, attempting on his deathbed to persuade Kepler to adopt it. Even though grossly unbalanced along with presenting unusual computational difficulties in that the orbits of five of the planets were considerably removed from the center of the universe and had to be computed not from a stationary but from an orbiting Sun, it nonetheless appealed to astronomers who were convinced of the immobility of the earth and yet believed that the position of the Sun was a determining factor in the orbital revolutions of the inferior and superior planets.

In any event, Tycho's reputation as the outstanding astronomer of his time was not based on his theoretical model, but on the extraordinary accuracy and continuity of his observations. While Copernicus remarked to Rheticus that "if he were able to reduce observational errors to ten minutes of arc, he would be as happy as Pythagoras on discovering his famous theorem"(p. 123), Tycho was able to reduce this limit to within four minutes of arc or less. In recognition of these achievements he was amply rewarded by his patron. King Ferdinand II of Denmark offered him the island off Hveen in the Sund between Copenhagen and Elsinor Castle, as well as the funds for building the extraordinary domain of Uraniburg with its renown astronomical observatories and massive instruments. For twenty years on his island estate Tycho pursued his remarkable observations of the solar system, including a mapping of a thousand fixed stars. But when Frederick the Great died Tycho's cruel treatment of the peasants on his island (he had chained in his dungeon a tenant and his family) and arrogant attitude toward the King's son and successor, Christian IV, prompted the latter to reduce considerably his sinecure. Having become somewhat tired of his isolated existence by this time anyway, he decided to leave the island.

So at age fifty-one in 1597, four years before his death, he left Hveen with his collection of remarkable instruments, having had the foresight to have them constructed so that they could be dismantled, packed, and transported. After traveling to Copenhagen and Rostock, where he had studied in his youth, he continued to Hamburg, Dresden, and Wittenberg. Again he was fortunate in attracting another benefactor, this time Emperor Rudolph II who resided in Prague. Offered a choice of castles, a salary of three thousand florins a year, and income from his property of additional thousands, he settled in the town and castle of Benatky, twenty-two miles north-east of Prague, in 1599. It was here that he received Kepler six months later as his research assistant. As brief as their association was because of Tycho's untimely death, it would prove to be a most significant scientific collaboration.

JOHANNES KEPLER

Kepler's family history and background, physical appearance and health, and first marriage were so wretched and depressing that they are better passed over in silence.[33] Often on the brink of dying or of some personal or financial disaster, few individuals have paid for their gifts of genius and rhapsodic moments of creative insight with such a depressing personal life. Unlike the ancient Greeks who cloaked their discoveries in mystery, Kepler leads us through all the tortuous paths of his creative process, the false starts, crooked turns, agonizing failures, as well as the exhilarating successes. No one has been more unguarded, unsparing, or relentless in sharing with the reader their innermost thoughts and feelings.

Born in the medieval town of Weil der Stadt in Swabia in 1571, five years later his parents moved to Leonberg in the duchy of Württemberg which was fortunate because during the reformation the Dukes of Württemberg established numerous Latin schools (in addition to the inferior German schools) to provide a sounder educational background for those intended for the clergy or the civil service. Sent initially to a German school, the precocious intelligence of Kepler led to his transfer to a Latin school to prepare for his entrance to the university. Like Tycho, whose observation of a lunar eclipse at an early age redirected his life, the sight of the great comet in 1577 when he was only six, and of a lunar eclipse when he was nine, left a lasting impression on Kepler. Completing his studies at the Latin school he entered the convent school of Adelberg at thirteen and two years later the seminary at the Cistercian monastary, Maulbroon. An outstanding student, his teachers praised him not only for his intellectual ability but also for his ardent introspective self-criticism and fervent religious disposition and beliefs.

After passing the baccalaureate examination in 1588 he matriculated in the "Stift," a seminary at the prestigious University of Tübingen. The spartan schedule required students to arise at 4:30 a.m. maintaining religious discipline throughout the day while pursuing a rigorous course of studies. Although his curriculum was directed mainly to theological studies, it also included lectures on ethics, dialectics, rhetoric, Greek, Hebrew, astronomy, mathematics, and physics. Graduated from the Faculty of Arts at age twenty he advanced to the Theological Faculty where he studied for nearly four years. In 1591 he passed the Master's Examination placing second among fourteen candidates. His professors had a high regard for him, as their comments approving a renewal of fellowship aid indicates: "[b]ecause [. . .] Kepler has such a superior and magnificent mind that something special may be expected of him, we wish, on our part, to continue [. . .] his stipend, as he requests [. . .]."[34]

At the university he read the *Analytica Posteriora* and the *Physica* of Aristotle in the Greek, but found the *Meteorologica* the most stimulating. Declaring that he "loved mathematics above all other studies," he was particularly attracted to the philosophies of Pythagoras, Plato, and the Neoplatonist, Nicholas of Cusa. The *Exercitationes exotericae* by Julius Caesar Scaliger aroused in the young scholar all kinds of questions pertaining to philosophy, theology, and physics. Recognizing Kepler's unusual ability, his Greek teacher, Martin Crusius, the well-known Hellenist, took such an interest in him that he tried, unsuccessfully, to enlist his collaboration on a commentary on Homer. Although at this time Kepler did not display the enthusiasm for astronomy that later was to consume his life, he did study under Magister Michael Maestlin, professor of mathematics and astronomy, one of the notable astronomers of the day. In his lectures on mathematics Maestlin discussed Euclid, Archimedes, and Apollonius along with more recent developments in trigonometry, while for his lectures on astronomy he wrote a textbook called *Epitome Astronomie*. It was during these lectures that Kepler was introduced to the Copernican system, though perhaps for reasons of prudence Maestlin always declared his allegiance to Ptolemy's geocentrism. In contrast, when Kepler committed himself to the Copernican system he did so with his usual fervor and without the inhibitions of his teacher. Yet despite their different temperaments they became close friends, carried on an active correspondence throughout most of Kepler's life (although twenty years his senior, Maestlin outlived him), and though Maestlin did not always respond to Kepler's frequent requests, he was instrumental in securing Kepler's first appointment while his approval of Kepler's first book was critical for its publication.

The same apparent simplicity and symmetry of the heliostatic system that had drawn Copernicus also attracted Kepler. The centrality of the Sun especially appealed to him "on physical, or, if one prefers, metaphysical, grounds," along with the mathematical advantages stressed by Copernicus (although at this time Kepler's knowledge of mathematics was still meager). Along with his growing interest in astronomy, he maintained his interest in astrology. Since a young man he had cast horoscopes of himself and members of his family, as if to understand or explain the distressing circumstances of his life. Even as a student he established a reputation for the excellence of his horoscopes.

Despite these interests, however, at this time he did not intend to become either an astronomer or a mathematician, but a theologian. The event that was to redirect his career was the offer of a position of mathematics professor at the Protestant seminary in Graz, in the provence of Styria, Austria. Asked to nominate someone for the position, the Senate at Tübingen recommended Kepler, much to the latter's astonishment. But after some doubts and hesitation he decided to accept and left for Graz in 1594 at age twenty-three.

There was little interest in advanced mathematics among the students at the Siftsschule of Graz, only a few of which took his courses the first year and none the second, so Kepler compensated by teaching other subjects, such as arithmetic, rhetoric, history, and ethics.

He was more successful, fortunately, at another chore required of the District Mathematician, that of issuing calendars. The calendars were like later almanacs containing all kinds of useful information pertaining to the weather, harvests, favorable times for bleeding, forecasts of pestilence or plagues, prospects for war or peace, predictions of auspicious days for ceremonial and religious occasions, and so forth. Because the success or failure of these astrological prophesies could have dire consequences, a certain skill was involved in making the predictions amenable to various outcomes or interpretations. Like Tycho, Kepler seems to have been ambivalent about astrology, condemning "the customary rules and prophecies as horrible superstition, as 'necromantic monkeyshines,' yet on the other hand held just as positively to the conviction of an influence of the stars on earthly events and human fate"[35] as Tycho. He did enhance both his reputation and income (by an extra twenty gulden) with his first calendar by prophesying a harsh winter and the invasion of the Turks, both of which turned out to be true, although it is not known on what basis he made these predictions.

But these pursuits were incidental to his main studies. As indicated previously, Maestlin's lectures on Copernicus had aroused the enthusiasm of Kepler to the extent that he staunchly defended the Heliostatic system. Two features of the system that particularly appealed to him were first, the sun's more central position in the universe which fitted in with his Pythagorean and Neoplatonic beliefs that it should play a determining role in the cosmic scheme; secondly, the fact emphasized by Copernicus, that in his system the planetary orbits were so interconnected that one could not be altered without disturbing the whole arrangement. This interrelated symmetry raised in Kepler's mind the question as to why this was so? Why are there just six planets: Mercury, Venus, earth (with the Moon as its satellite), Mars, Jupiter, and Saturn? Why do they occupy their specific distances from the Sun? Why, as one proceeds outward from the Sun, does it take a disproportionately longer time for the more distant planets to complete their orbits? —Saturn taking thirty years rather than twenty-four as one might expect since its distance is twice that of Jupiter whose period is twelve years. This questioning is typical of the way scientific thought develops, each advance leading to further questions. Having discovered what he believed to be an objective order in nature, Copernicus accepted this pattern as given; Kepler, being presented with the pattern, wanted to explain it.

Two major influences seemed to have directed his approach to the problem. First, as a devoutly religious person Kepler believed that God had created the universe according to the most elegant plan. But what was the key to this plan? There is only one philosopher in the past who, even though he presented it as "a likely story," tried to show how the Divine Craftsman or Demiurge constructed the world from geometrical proportions. In addition, this philosopher in the same treatise tried to depict the geometric structure of the four elements and shape of the universe in terms of the five Pythagorean figures, explaining the interactions, decompositions, and recombinations of the elements in terms of the triangles composing these Pythagorean or Platonic solids. (cf. Vol. I, ch. 12) The philosopher, of course, was Plato and the treatise the *Timaeus*.

But the key insight into the structure of the universe did not come directly from reading Plato; it occurred indirectly when Kepler was drawing a geometrical figure for his class on July 9, 1595, as he later wrote. The figure, consisting of an equilateral triangle set within two circles, suggested to him that the ratios of the dimensions of the circles could represent the orbits of the two furthest planets.

Fig. 4. Kepler's diagrammatic inspiration.

According to Koestler:

> As he looked at the two circles, it suddenly struck him that their ratios were the same as those of the orbits of Saturn and Jupiter. The rest of the inspiration came in a flash. Saturn and Jupiter are the 'first' (i.e., the two outermost) planets, and 'the triangle is the first figure in geometry. Immediately I tried to inscribe into the next interval between Jupiter and Mars a square, between Mars and Earth a pentagon, between Earth and Venus a Hexagon. . .' (p. 249)

He later wrote "[w]hat delight I have found in this discovery I shall never be able to describe in words."[36]

His geometrical shapes being plane figures, he soon realized they were inadequate to account for the three-dimensional structure of the universe: "[w]hy should there be plane figures between solid spheres?" (p. 67) Remembering that Euclid had proven that in a three-dimensional space only five polyhedra could be constructed, so that if inserted in a sphere with a common center each of their edges met the inner surface of the sphere, or if enveloping a sphere the inner faces touched the sphere, Kepler concluded that because the six planets had exactly five spatial intervals, God must have allowed only five solids for the express purpose of separating the six planets.

> It is my intention, reader, to show in this little book that the most great and good Creator, in the creation of this moving universe, and the arrangement of the heavens, looked [. . .] to those five regular solids, which have been so celebrated from the time of Pythagoras and Plato down to our own, and that he fitted to the nature of those solids, the number of the heavens, their proportions, and the law of their motions. (p. 63)

Fig. 5.   The five polyhedra or regular solids are the
               tetrahedron (pyramid), octahedron,
               icosahedron, cube, and dodecahedron.

If this were true, then there would be an *a priori* connection between the *three* dimensions of space, the *five* perfect solids, and the *six* planets. For a Christian Platonist this could not be accidental because the geometric order of the universe preexisted in God's mind before the creation. Thus Kepler could combine the Biblical story of creation with Plato's vision of the Divine Craftsman. As he exclaimed later: "Geometry existed before the Creation, is co-eternal with the mind of God [. . .] provid[ing] God with a model for the Creation [. . .]."[37] This also conformed to the Neoplatonic belief that human thought could replicate Divine thought by deducing the structure of the universe, one of the most ancient aspirations (or illusions) of man.

For Kepler this consisted of deducing which Platonic solid should be inserted between each of the planets to account for the order and sizes of the orbits Copernicus had assigned to them.

> The Earth is the circle which is the measure of all. Construct a dodechahedron [a polyhedron composed of twelve pentagons] round it. The circle surrounding that will be Mars. Round Mars construct a tetrahedron [a pyramid consisting of four equilateral triangles]. The circle surrounding that will be Jupiter. Round Jupiter construct a cube. The circle surrounding that will be Saturn. Now construct an icosahedron [composed of twenty equilateral triangles] inside the earth. The circle inscribed within will be Venus. Inside Venus inscribe an octahedron [consisting of eight equilateral triangles]. The circle inscribed within that will be Mercury. There you have an explanation of the number of Planets. (p. 69; brackets added)

In the center was the sun and surrounding the solar system was the sphere of the fixed stars. As the English title suggests, "The Secret of the Universe" had been revealed in this little book. This is an excellent example of how false presuppositions eventually can lead to true discoveries, as we shall see.

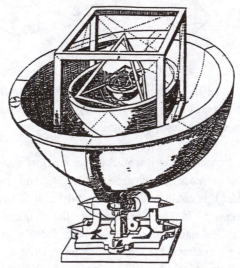

Fig. 6. Johannes Kepler's drawing of the interposition of the Platonic solids among the planets in the *Mysterium Cosmographicus*, copper engraving from the first edition (Tübingen, 1596).

Although Kepler was enraptured with the results, they were of course completely mistaken. Even he realized that neither the spheres nor the five perfect solids could be taken as literally true or actually existing. While initially he declared that the five Platonic solids represented the orbital intervals "perfectly," later when he compared their dimensions with those of Copernicus he realized that they did not agree, especially Mercury and Jupiter. Nonetheless, this fanciful construction led him to a significant conclusion that would prove crucial for his later investigations, namely, that the Sun rather than the center of the earth's orbit was the actual center of the cosmos. At long last a truly heliocentric universe replaced the heliostatic universe of Copernicus. Once having made this decision, Kepler began searching for a mathematical correlation between the planets' distances from the Sun and their orbital periods or rotational speeds because there is no apparent ratio between the two, except that the further the planet is from the Sun the slower it appears to revolve: Mercury's period is about eighty days, Venus' seven and a half months, Mars' two years, Jupiter's twelve years, and Saturn's thirty. That Kepler looked for a pattern among these variations, as well as a possible explanation, marked a crucial advance astronomically, a fulfillment of Copernicus' expectations.

The Pythagorean or Neoplatonic presuppositions of his thought may have been the decisive influence. Having decided that the Sun was in the center of the universe, it seemed natural to assume that its position must signify a functional role. Thus Kepler began asking whether the mystery of the planets' orbits might not depend upon some influence or force emanating from the sun, analogous to light, a major change in outlook. As Koestler states:

> It would be difficult to over-estimate the revolutionary significance of this proposal. For the first time since antiquity, an attempt was made not only to *describe* heavenly motions in geometrical terms, but to assign them a *physical cause*. We have arrived at the point where astronomy and physics meet again, after a divorce which lasted for two thousand years. This reunion [. . .] led to Kepler's three laws, the pillars on which Newton built the modern universe. (p. 258)

Fortunately, Kepler shares with the reader the process of his reasoning. Recall that for Aristotle and during the middle ages it was believed that "intelligences" or "angels" guide the planets' revolutions in their orbits. Since the outer or superior planets move more slowly than the inner or inferior, does this mean that their guiding spirits are less active, or is it more reasonable to assume it is the sun's influence that diminishes with the distance: that it is this decrease in strength that is the cause?

> But if [. . .] we wish to make an even more exact approach to the truth, and to hope for any regularity in the ratios [between the distances and the velocities of the planets], one of two conclusions must be reached: either [1] the moving souls are weaker the further they are from the Sun; or, there is [2] a single moving soul in the center of all the spheres, that is, in the Sun, and it impels each body more strongly in proportion to how near it is. In the more distant ones on account of their remoteness and the weakening of its power, it becomes faint, so to speak. Thus, just as the source of light is in the Sun [. . .] so [. . .] the motion and the soul of the universe are assigned to that same Sun [. . .]. (p. 199; brackets added)

As one would expect in this initial formulation, the 'force' is still conceived as vitalistic or animistic, called the 'soul' or '*anima motrix*.' Although at this time Kepler could give only a qualitative description of how the *anima motrix* functioned, claiming that it consisted of rays like light that emanated from the sun in the plane of the ecliptic (rather than in all directions) that decrease in density with the distance, in the *Astronomia Nova* he will describe this functional correlation precisely in his first two laws. Here he naturally assumed that as the *anima motrix* dispersed it became less concentrated so that with increased distance fewer rays impinge on the planets, hence their motion is slower. At this stage his religious convictions were so prominent that he believed this cosmic arrangement could be symbolized by the Trinity: the Sun represented by God the Father, the Heavens by Christ the Son, and the motive force of the *anima motrix* by the Holy Spirit. (cf. p. 63)

When the *Mysterium* appeared in the spring of 1597 Kepler sent copies to all the prominent astronomers, including Tycho and Galileo. Although Maestlin's reaction was enthusiastic, not all the responses were favorable. Galileo acknowledged receipt of the book after reading the Preface, welcoming Kepler as a supporter of Copernicus and promising to write later—not satisfied, Kepler urged him to reply more fully, even if critically. Some astronomers, like Praetorius, objected to Kepler's *a priori* method and therefore rejected the book without realizing it contained the germinal ideas for a mathematical description of the cosmos. As Kepler states in the "Dedicatory Epistle" to the second edition of the *Mysterium*, published twenty-five years later in 1621, "almost every book on astronomy which I have published since that time could be referred to one or another of the important chapters set out in this little book, and would contain either an illustration or completion of it.'' (p. 39)   Probably the most consequential reply came from Tycho who graciously praised the originality of the book, although in a private letter to Maestlin he was more critical, expressing his misgivings at an attempt to explain the positions of the planetary orbits based on *a priori* reasoning rather than observation. But he recognized the brilliance of the author which led, three years later, to their historic collaboration.

During the intervening three years Kepler studied mathematics, attempted to measure the earth's parallax, and tried to ascertain more precisely the eccentric orbits of the planets. He realized, however, there was only one person, Tycho Brahe, who possessed the accurate and continuous astronomical data he needed, and Tycho was jealously guarding his observational measurements for his own use in constructing his compromise astronomical model. At one point Tycho had written expressing the hope that Kepler could ''some day'' visit him at his observatory. In the meantime, Kepler tried to make the best of the situation in Graz, a Protestant seminary, situated in Catholic Austria where the Archduke Ferdinand of Hapsburg intended to rid Austria of the Lutheran heresy. The seminary was finally closed in 1599 requiring a desperate Kepler to seek a new position. In the kind of extraordinary coincidence that lead people to believe in a controlling destiny, Tycho, while on his wanderings after leaving the Island of Hveen, was offered the position of Imperial Mathematicus by Rudolph II which he gladly accepted. After setting up residence at Benatky Castle near Prague, he wrote Kepler in December of 1599 asking him to join him in their ''common study.'' Being able to fulfill his two pressing needs, that of immediate employment and access to Tycho's precious data, Kepler joined him in February of the new century.

As Koestler vividly describes the encounter, it would be difficult to find two persons less compatible for a collaboration.

Tycho was fifty-three, Kepler twenty-nine. Tycho was an aristocrat, Kepler a plebeian; Tycho a Croesus, Kepler a church-mouse; Tycho a Great Dane, Kepler a mangy mongrel. They were opposite in every respect but one: the irritable, choleric disposition which they shared. The result was constant friction, flared into heated quarrels, followed by half-hearted reconciliations. [38]

Even this personal incompatibility was exacerbated by the jealousy and rivalry that erupted between Kepler and Tycho's co-workers and son who resented the arrival of the more gifted research assistant. Nonetheless, accommodations were made and Kepler was given the most difficult assignment, that of determining the orbit of Mars, which would prove the *pièce de resistance* in his architectonic scheme. Bragging and betting that he would solve the problem in eight days, it actually took him almost eight years and perhaps a nervous breakdown, but in the end he had "solved the problem of the planets" that had tormented astronomers for over two millennia. Tycho, unfortunately, died unexpectedly a year and a half later (Kepler was often away during that period), as if his main mission in life, to provide Kepler with the crucial data, had been accomplished. For although Tycho's former senior assistant and son-in-law inherited his fabulous instruments, Kepler managed to retrieve his precious observations. Two days after Tycho's death in 1601, Kepler was appointed Imperial Mathematicus as his successor.

Kepler held this position in Prague for eleven years until 1612 when Rudolph II died. More secure in his new appointment (although his salary was continuously in arrears) and finally in possession of Tycho's astronomical records, this was the most productive period of his life. The longer he worked with Tycho's figures of the eccentrics and mean distances of the planetary orbits, the more the (spurious) question of the positions of the five solids receded into the background and the larger the (genuine) problem of the exact planetary speeds and orbital distances emerged in the foreground. Because of its great eccentricity, it was the orbit of Mars especially that held the clue to the solution. It will be recalled that to explain the observed differences in brightness and variations in orbital speeds on the assumption that the planets revolved uniformly in circular orbits, Ptolemy had utilized eccentrics and equants (*punctum aequans*) to demonstrate that while the planets' orbital motions seemed to approach and recede from a central point, they were uniform from another position eccentric to it. Copernicus had hoped that by replacing the earth by the Sun and calculating from the center of the earth's orbit he could describe the orbital motions of the planets in a more coherent and interconnected manner. But no combination of circular uniform motion fit the observations.

As Kepler struggled with the data prescribing the orbit of Mars, the configuration that kept emerging was egg-shaped or oval, with the more constricted end (perihelion) nearer the Sun and the broader (aphelion) further away. While this conformed to his causal explanation in the *Mysterium*, that the planets would move more rapidly when nearer the sun because of the greater density of the rays and thus would make a tighter loop, this did not agree with the assumptions of uniform circular motion. Discarding his former *a priori* approach, Kepler searched for an explanation that agreed with the data. "Those speculations may not *a priori* run counter to obvious empirical knowledge, rather they must be brought into agreement with it.'"[39] At one point he rejected several year's work because of a discrepancy of 8' arc between his computations and Tycho's, a match that in the past would have been welcomed. Having altered Copernicus' system by accepting the Sun rather than the center of the earth's orbit as the center of the universe, he now revised it further. Copernicus had postulated that the plane of the orbit of Mars oscillated due to the influence of the earth.[40] Declaring that "this was no business of the earth," Kepler surmised that the planes of all the planetary orbits have the Sun as their center. In addition, owing to Tycho's observations of the continuous positions of the planets and his own causal explanation, he now was willing to accept a *nonuniform* motion.

Rejecting the cumbersome epicycles and returning to the single equant of Ptolemy, since an oval configuration cannot be constructed from a central point, Kepler inferred that if the Sun's influence determined the configuration of the orbit then it must coincide with the position of the equant. But since the precise dimensions had to be plotted from the earth, it was necessary to determine the earth's orbit. To accomplish this another reference system was required, so Kepler imagined his position of observation "as from a watchtower" located on Mars. As he suspected, this showed that the earth also revolved eccentrically with a nonuniform motion, faster at its perihelion and slower at its aphelion. Apparently suggesting the possibility of a causal explanation, the astronomical argument is interrupted to search for a physical explanation of the eccentric orbit.

In the *Mysterium* Kepler had posited an animate force emanating from the sun as the cause of the planet's motion. But working with the exact data supplied by Tycho seemed to have had a sobering effect on his youthful animism. In place of the soul or *anima motrix*, whose rays converging on the planets propelled them in their orbits, Kepler now thought in terms of a 'force' (*vis.*) As he describes the transition in the second edition of the *Mysterium* published after the *Nova*:

If for the word "soul" you substitute the word "force," you have the very same principle on which the Celestial Physics is established [. . .] For once I believed that the cause which moves the planets was precisely a soul [. . .] [b]ut when I pondered that this moving cause grows weaker with distance, and that the Sun's light also grows thinner with distance from the Sun, from that I concluded, that this force is something corporeal, that is, an emanation which a body emits, but an immaterial one. (p. 203, note 3)

This replacement of a more natural 'force' for the earlier 'soul' as a moving cause was an extraordinary advancement, almost as important as Kepler's replacement of the five perfect solids by his planetary laws. We can see in Kepler's intellectual development a recapitulation of mankind's cognitive evolution from a subjective, animistic, concrete point of view to a more objective, naturalistic, abstract explanation illustrative of the essential thesis of this study. As Koestler remarks:

As we watch the working of the mind of Kepler [. . .] we find no abrupt break with the past, but a gradual transformation of the symbols of [. . .] cosmic experience—from *anima motrix* into *vis motrix*, moving spirit into moving force, mythological imagery into mathematical hieroglyphics [. . .].[41]

But Kepler's transition to 'an immaterial force' emanating from the Sun as the cause of planetary motion was not the only advance in his search for a physical explanation in the *Astronomia Nova*. Realizing that if only a single force impinged on the planets this would not explain their ovoid orbits, Kepler added a second force to account for the planets' continuous ovally sweep around the sun. In 1600 the English physician William Gilbert had published a widely read book, *On the Magnet*, in which he had declared that the earth was a huge magnet with a north and south pole. Assuming that all planets, including the sun, were polar magnets, Kepler conjectured that if the south pole of the sun were embedded in its center so that the magnetic effect of the north pole circumscribed its surface, and as the planets revolved in their orbits their polarity reversed direction relative to the Sun, then as the south poles approached the Sun they would be progressively attracted, whereas when their north poles were closer they would be gradually repelled. Accordingly, the force emanating from the sun would tend to propel the planet tangentially while the mutual magnetic attraction and repulsion would cause the planet to approach and recede from the Sun in an oval orbit.[42] In addition, Kepler surmised that the bulk of the planets produce a certain 'inertia' inclining them to rest, further explaining their deviation from a circular motion.

Although the correct explanation of the nature and function of these forces had to await the formulation of the concepts of inertia and gravity, Kepler correctly saw that the planets' orbits are a function of two counterbalancing forces. Newton would provide the final explanation, but Kepler certainly paved the way. In addition, realizing that the strength of the propelling force emanating from the sun decreases with the distance, Kepler formulated the inverse speed law, "that the force from the sun varies inversely with the distance." This law, along with the solar propelling force, magnetic attraction or repulsion, and inertia approximately accounts for each planet's particular orbit and speed. Even though the inverse speed law was incorrect, its approximate truth provided a partial explanation of why the planets increase in speed as they approach the Sun (perihelion) and decrease as they recede from it (aphelion).

It was these explanations, apparently, that led Kepler to a precise formulation of the relation between a planet's speed and its orbital distance from the Sun: a radius vector joining the planet to the sun sweeps out equal areas in equal times (in the figure below, area a = b). This was Kepler's famous second law, a law in which the *areas* vary uniformly with the time, not the orbital *speed*, as in the ancient uniform speed law.

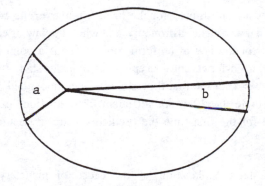

Fig. 7. Illustration of Kepler's second law.

Although this law correlates the speed of the planet with its distance from the sun in its orbit, it does not specify the shape of the orbit. By now, however, Kepler was convinced that the orbital shape was oval.

The conclusion is quite simply that the planet's path is not a circle— it curves inward on both sides and outward again at opposite ends. Such a curve is called oval. The orbit is not a circle, but an oval figure. [43]

Yet still he failed to see that the oval shape, which was too vague to be given precise geometrical dimensions, was an ellipse. He had studied Apollonius' work on conic sections so he knew that an ellipse, a variation of a circle, was formed by a diagonal slice through a cone, but he persisted in failing to identify the oval as an ellipse, even writing to a friend at one point that "if only the shape were a perfect ellipse all the answers could be found in Archimedes' and Apollonius' work."[44] It is this kind of trance-like groping in a forward direction that led Koestler to describe the founders of modern science as "sleepwalkers."

Finally, after measuring the exact extent of the "inner curve" of Mars' orbit (.00429 of the radius [45]) Kepler recognized at last that its shape was an ellipse. Thus he arrived at his first law, that the planetary orbits are elliptical with the Sun at one foci, after he had formulated the second. Everything now fell into place with his two laws eliminating in one fell swoop the artifacts of epicycles, eccentrics, and equants used by his predecessors. As Kuhn states:

> When ellipses are substituted for the basic circular orbits common to Ptolemy's and Copernicus' astronomy and when the law of equal areas is substituted for the law of uniform motion about a point at or near the center, all need for eccentrics, epicycles, equants and other *ad hoc* devices vanishes. For the first time a single uncompounded geometric curve and a single speed law are sufficient for predictions of planetary position, and for the first time the predictions are as accurate as the observations. [46]

Although Kepler's explanation of the cause of planetary motion and discovery of the two astronomical laws had been anticipated in the *Commentaries on the Movements of Mars*, his *magnus opus* was the *Astronomia Nova* published in 1609 by Ernest Vogelin in Heidelberg. Dedicated to his patron Rudolph II, the full English title is:

NEW ASTRONOMY Based on Causation
or A PHYSICS OF THE SKY
derived from the Investigations of the
MOTIONS OF THE STAR MARS
Founded on the Observations of THE NOBLE TYCHO BRAHE

It was customary at the time for book titles to contain flowery descriptions of their contents and purpose. Justly acclaimed as the first treatise of modern astronomy for presenting the first two planetary laws ever discovered, along with the first modern attempt to explain planetary motions by physical causes, the *Nova* also proposed a new astronomical framework, celestial mechanics. Rejecting the prevalent Aristotelian view that heaviness and lightness are inherent tendencies in objects to descend or ascend, Kepler argued that gravity was analogous to magnetism, a natural attractive force exerted by objects proportional to their masses independent of their location in space.

> Gravity is the mutual bodily tendency between cognate bodies towards unity or contact [. . .], so that [. . .] [i]f two stones were placed anywhere in space near to each other, and outside the reach of force of a third cognate body, then they would come together, after the manner of magnetic bodies, at an intermediate point, each approaching the other in proportion to the other's mass.[47]

A striking example of his prescience, Kepler anticipated the modern law of gravitation according to which two bodies attract proportional to their masses and inversely proportional to the square of the distances. Having foreseen the first part of the law, he came very close to foretelling the second because in the *Optics* (1604) he had shown that the strength of light *decreased inversely with the square of the distance,* and since he now compared gravity with light this implied a similar effect for gravity! Moreover, as Koestler points out, he suggested that rather than being propagated in space, gravity resembled a kind of Einsteinian field, a structure of space that causes the motion of bodies within in it. This force ''cannot be regarded as something which expands into the space between its source and the movable body, but as something which the movable body receives out of space which it occupies [. . .].''[48]

Based on this conception of gravity, he correctly explained the cause of the tides as due to the combined gravitational forces of the moon and the earth: ''[i]f the earth ceased to attract the waters of the sea, the seas would rise and flow in to the moon [. . .].[49] Had Galileo read Kepler's books he might have reconsidered his explanation in the *Dialogue Concerning the Two Chief World Systems,* that the tides were caused by the two contrasting motions of the earth, even though he believed that explaining the tides by gravity acting at a distance invoked occult qualities.

Drawing the correct inferences from these conclusions, Kepler even conceived of the cosmos as a "heavenly machine" that runs like "clockwork" according to purely "physical forces," anticipating the celestial mechanics of Newton. As he states in a letter to a friend:

> My aim [in the *Nova*] is to show that the heavenly machine is not a kind of divine, live being, but a kind of clockwork [. . .] insofar as nearly all the manifold motions are caused by a most simple, magnetic, and material force, just as all motions of the clock are caused by a simple weight. And I also show how these physical causes are to be given numerical and geometrical expressions. [50]

In the previous Volume (ch. II) it was pointed out that an individual's thought can function on several different levels and nowhere is this more evident than in the mind of Kepler. While in the *Mysterium* his thinking was guided by images of the five Platonic solids and the primitive notion of an animate force, in the *Nova* he discards all animism envisioning a celestial mechanics based on natural forces described mathematically and operating mechanistically like clockwork. This capacity for an abstract, purely mechanistic form of thought was exemplified also in the earlier *Optics* and especially in the *Dioptrics* published a year after the *Nova*.

In the former work he had demonstrated how light refracted through the lens to the interior of the eye produces an inverted image on the retinae, along with explaining the function of the *camera obscura* and of the lenses in spectacles, while in the latter book (in response to Galileo's use of the telescope) he provided the first optical explanation for the use of refractive lenses in the new telescopic instrument. Both works justify his being named the father of modern optics, as the *Astronomia Nova* earned him the title of the father of modern astronomy. Yet in two of his later major works, the *Harmonice Mundi* published in 1619 and the *Epitome Astronomiae Copernicanae* in 1621, the earlier modes of imagistic, Neoplatonic, teleological thought again become dominant. He seemed to function on whatever level of thought was demanded by the task at hand or prompted by the immediate inspiration.

The death of Rudolph II in 1612 forced Kepler to search for a new position. After considering a number of alternatives, he accepted the post at Linz of Provincial Mathematicus to the new Emperor, Matthias, believing that it would be the most beneficial for his wife who was recovering from a prolonged illness. But a life so devoted to the celestial bodies seemed star-crossed: first his adored six-year-old son died and then shortly after his wife succumbed to what he described as "melancholy despondency." So at age forty-one before moving to Linz, Kepler was left a widower with the responsibility of two young children. Once he arrived at Linz, a provincial city he never really preferred nor came to like, he began searching for a wife to manage his household as was the custom of the day. Presented with eleven possibilities, after much coaching from friends, indecision, and comic relief he choose a woman seventeen years younger who had been orphaned as a child and who worked in a nobleman's household. Judging her to be "modest, thrifty, and diligent," as well as a person who would love his children, her more stable disposition contributed to a much happier marriage than Kepler's earlier one. They had seven children of whom three died in infancy. Considering how many of Kepler's children died, reaching adulthood in some families must have been something of an exception at that time.

Once settled in Linz he returned to his work. Although the two laws presented in the *Nova* are now regarded as Kepler's major achievements, they were not considered as such either by Kepler or by his contemporaries, neither of whom knew quite what to make of elliptical orbits and nonuniform motions. The full import of new ideas is difficult to assimilate and access, so that what we think should have been clearly understood at the time often is opaque. It is the following generation, usually, that comprehends the significance of these revolutionary developments and has little difficulty in accepting them.

As we have seen, when writing the *Nova* he appeared to be fully aware that he was introducing a radically new conceptual framework, a veritable celestial *mechanics*, but once it was finished he lapsed back into his former modes of thought. Ever since writing the *Mysterium*, he had dreamed of discovering a mathematical correlation relating the durations of the planets' periods to their distances from the Sun. In the earlier work he was convinced the five perfect solids were God's geometric solution to the structure of the universe, even though they did not quite fit. Never having forsaken this dream, in the *Harmonice Mundi* he returned to his *a priori* approach supplemented by the ancient Pythagorean vision of a mathematical musical harmony orchestrating the celestial movements. It is as if he had completely forgotten (or another hemisphere of his brain had repressed) the ellipses, physical forces, and clockwork mechanism of the *Nova* for an explanation of planetary motion again using the five Platonic solids, along with such musical notation as notes, pitches, octaves, and harmonies, all graphically depicted throughout the book).[51]

Yet despite these whimsical notions and flights of fantasy, Kepler's unfailing scientific or mathematical intuition led him to discover the correct law. By comparing Tycho's figures for the periods of pairs of planets and their respective mean distances from the Sun, he discovered that the squares of the former are equal to the cubes of the latter: $(P^1/P^2)^2 = (D^1/D^2)^3$; or, expressed differently, the (planetary period)$^2 \propto$ the (distance from the sun)^3, so that the periods of the revolutions vary with the 3/2th power of their distances. As Kepler states in Chapter 3 of Book V of *The Harmonies of the World*: "it is absolutely certain and exact that *the ratio which exists between the periodic times of any two planets is precisely the ratio of the 3/2th power of the mean distances,* i.e., *of the spheres themselves* [. . .]."[52] Thus Kepler fulfilled Copernicus' great ambition, which became his own obsession, of finding an exact mathematical correlation between the distances of the planets and their periods. At last he had discovered the archetypical law in God's mind. It is the above ratio, repeated by Newton, that was the clue to his formulation of the university law of gravitation.

Perhaps the illusory pursuits in this book as well as its everlasting achievement were escapes for what was one of the most humiliating and depressing periods in Kepler's life. As he worked to finish the *Harmonice Mundi* his aged, and in truth wretched, mother was accused of being a witch and proceedings brought against her. When one reads of the bizarre charges, ghastly proceedings, incredible beliefs, and depraved natures of the people involved, one almost believes that only a demonic force could have produced the grotesque drama. It is only because Kepler's mother, even when shown the execution chamber with its horrible instruments of torture, in the hope of frightening her into confessing, steadfastly maintained her innocence, and that Kepler himself helped prepare the defense and sought help from his most influential friends at court, that the unfortunate woman was spared the rack and possibly being burned at the stake. After having been imprisoned for fourteen months, much of the time in chains, it was decided that her fortitude in maintaining her innocence despite her terror had invalidated the preposterous charges against her, allowing the Duke to set her Free. About six months later she died at age seventy-three.

Even the depressing absurdity of this occurrence could not stifle Kepler's creativity. Having long contemplated writing a book in honor of Copernicus, after this appalling episode he completed in 1621 a text describing the order and motions of the planets based on Copernicus' theory and his own original causal explanations. Entitled *Epitome Astronomiae Copernicanae*, in homage to Copernicus, it succeeds Ptolemy's *Almagest* and Copernicus' *Revolutionibus* as one of the great astronomical treatises of the past. Gone are the circular spheres, uniform motions, orbital oscillations, and spurious centers of the universe and in their place are Kepler's discoveries of elliptical orbits, nonuniform motions, and the causal influence of the Sun, the new monarch in the heavenly state. It goes beyond the *Nova* in that his two laws are not just limited to the orbit of Mars but applied to all the planets, even to the Moon and the satellites of Jupiter (Kepler introduced the term "satellite" to designate the moons of Jupiter discovered by Galileo [53]). Yet even in this work his discoveries are merged with his earlier preconceptions, as Casper states.

> Thus old and new, mechanistic and animistic considerations, causal and teleological principles, Platonic speculations and scholastic abstractions are interwoven into a fascinating picture that [. . .] announces a new scientific style. [54]

Following his numerous publications, not all of which have been mentioned (he was even the author of a work on science fiction, *Somnium*, a dream of a journey to the moon and its inhabitants, published posthumously), in a lifetime hung over with adversity, Kepler had one major project to complete, the *Rudolphine Tables*, that he had been promising to publish for many years. A tedious, time consuming task, he finally settled down to compiling it. In 1614 the Englishman John Napier had published a famous book, *Merifici Logarithmorum Canonis Descriptio*, containing the logarithmic tables that would considerably simplify astronomical calculations. However, Napier had just presented the numerical tables without explaining how they had been derived or computed, leaving mathematicians suspicious of their value. Kepler, however, understood their significance, so in the years 1621-22 he wrote a book explaining how the logarithms were derived and why they were so valuable. After the book was published in 1623, Kepler decided to include it in the *Rudolphine Tables*. This task of publication was beset with the usual tribulations: petty disputes with Tycho's heirs over the rights and dedication, the costs of printing, the difficulty of selecting or purchasing a suitable press and type, finding a competent but affordable printer, and purchasing the required paper, all of which he had to arrange himself. After the usual delays everything was accomplished so that the *Tabula Rudolphinae* was published in 1627, named for his patron, Emperor Rudolph II. Along with the new logarithmic table and the accompanying rules and instructions for their use, as well as the standard planetary data, it contained a star catalogue of over a thousand fixed stars and even a voluminous listing of the cities throughout the world with their longitudes and latitudes. The joint product of the greatest astronomical observer up to that time and the most brilliant theoretician, the

Rudolphine Tables provided the basis for all astronomical calculations for over a century.

Having left Linz to supervise the publication of the *Tables* at Ulm, Kepler avoided returning to the city that he so disliked. Once again he was seeking to find a reliable and generous patron; in fact, he had offers from England, Italy, and from his friend Bernegger in Strassburg (the latter two in the form of teaching positions), but he decided to enter the service (mainly as astrologer) of the Emperor's victorious General, Wallenstein. So the last years of his life were spent in the General's Duchy of Sagan, which turned out to be even more inhospitable than Linz. But after one more journey death would put an end finally to his travails. Fearful of the future of his patronage when Wallenstein was dismissed as the Emperor's General, Kepler set out for Leipzig and then for Ratisbon [55] where the Emperor was presiding over the Diet, to attempt one last time to collect the Crown's debt to him of 11,817 florins. Three days after arriving in Ratisbon he was bedridden with a fever from which he never recovered. He died on November 15, 1630, slightly more than a month before his sixtieth birthday and separated from his family. He was buried "outside the town" of Ratisbon in the cemetery of St. Peter, but due to numerous battles the burial grounds were demolished so that his precise resting place is unknown. In death as in life, Kepler suffered mortification and abasement.

In the years separating the publication of Copernicus' *De Revolutionibus* in 1543 and Kepler's *Epitome* in 1621, a little over three-quarters of a century, the conception of the solar system, for those astronomers who accepted the heliocentric universe, was drastically changed. In place of uniform circular motions, crystalline spheres, and Divine Movers, along with Ptolemy's epicycles, eccentrics, and equants, there now was Kepler's three planetary laws. For the first time in history it was possible to predict each planet's orbital rotation with considerable accuracy, along with the ratio between their distances from the sun and their orbital periods. In place of souls, intelligences, or angels as causes of the planets' movements, Kepler in his more sober moments had conceived of the possibility of a celestial mechanics based on physical forces. Much work was necessary before the precise structure of this theoretical framework would be articulated, but there is no doubt that the ancient Greek and medieval cosmos was being replaced by a more modern universe. Unlike Cusa, Bruno, Digges (as well as poets like Donne and Milton), the most prominent astronomers in the drama, Copernicus, Brahe, Kepler, and Galileo, shrank from drawing the inevitable conclusion that the ancient, finite, spherical cosmos was too constricted for the newly expanded universe, but that would be corrected very soon. The finite, homocentric universe of antiquity was destined for obliteration.

NOTES

1. E.A. Burtt, *The Metaphysical Foundations of Modern Science* (Garden City, N.Y.: Doubleday & Co., 1954), p. 17.

2. Thomas S. Kuhn, *The Copernican Revolution* (Cambridge: Harvard University Press, 1957), p. 134.

3. Cf. Arthur Koestler, *The Sleepwalkers* (New York: Grosset's Universal Library, 1959). Despite Koestler's extreme psychological reactions and biased interpretations, his treatment of Kepler is extensive and very carefully documented. All further references to Koeslter are to this book.

4. A.M. Duncan, *Copernicus: On the Revolution of the Heavenly Spheres*, a new translation from the Latin (Newton Abbot: David & Charles Limited, 1976), pp. 23 and 26 respectively. All further references to Duncan's translation of the *De Revolutionibus* are to this work.

5. *Ibid.*, pp. 25-26. Brackets added.

6. *Ibid.*, p. 53.

7. Cf. Koestler, pp. 209-210.

8. E.J. Dijksterhuis, *The Mechanization of the World Picture*, translated by C. Dikshoorn (New Jersey: Princeton University Press, 1986), p. 224.

9. Marie Boas, *The Scientific Renaissance* 1450-1630 (New York: Harper & Row, 1962), p. 23-24.

10. Duncan, p. 13.

11. Upon receiving the offer of a Chair in Mathematics from the University of Leipzig and turning over to Osiander the supervision of the printing of the manuscript, Rheticus immediately left Nüremberg. From that time on he had nothing further to do either with the book or with Copernicus. This undoubtedly is due to the fact that while in his Preface to the Pope Copernicus named Cardinal Schönberg and his old friend Bishop Giese as

the two people who persuaded him to have the manuscript published, he nowhere acknowledges the crucial help and influence of Rheticus, the prime mover in the project! This must have hurt Rheticus deeply considering all he had done for Copernicus: he went to Frauenburg despite the fact that the new Bishop of Ermland, Dantiscus, ordered Lutherans to leave Ermland, threatening them with loss of life and property should they return. Even though Rheticus was a Lutheran and protege of Melanchton and therefore not the best endorsement for a book dedicated to the Pope, it was inexcusable for Copernicus not to have acknowledged his devoted help in seeing to its publication. Rheticus had written a biography of Copernicus, now lost, that Giese and others urged him to publish, but he refused to do so.

12. Translated and quoted by Andrew D. White, *A History of the Warfare of Science with Theology in Christendom* (New York: Appleton, 1896), I, p. 126. Quoted from Kuhn, p. 191. The first set of brackets added.

13. Cf. Stillman Drake, *Galileo At Work: His Scientific Biography* (Chicago: The University of Chicago Press, 1978), p. 320.

14. Johannes Kepler, *Astronomia Nova*, Prefatory matter, *Gesammelte Werke*, Vol. III, Rosen's English translation. Quoted from Koestler, p. 169.

15. Koestler, p. 356. Brackets added.

16. Hermes Trismegistus (meaning thrice blessed Hermes), although never existing was believed at the time to be the author of numerous treatises ("the Hermetic writings") attributed to the Egyptians during the time of Moses. According to Hugh Kearney the "treatises first became available to the West after the fall of Constantinople (1453) and they were translated from the Greek by Marsilio Ficino (1433-95) as a matter of urgency by order of Cosimo de Medici [. . .]." Following this legend, the Egyptians were thought to have received a divine revelation of knowledge of the physical world as God had revealed to Moses the ten commandments, which cast the Egyptians as the source of secular wisdom, antedating the Hellenic philosophers, while the Jews were considered the source of sacred wisdom. The motive was to attribute all knowledge to a divine source rather than the speculations of the "pagan philosophers." According to the Hermetic writings the sun, symbolic of God and situated in the center of the universe, radiated light as the source of life-giving power around which the universe revolved. Incorporating the Pythagorean doctrine that numbers constitute the *archē* of the universe displayed in the musical

harmonies of the spheres, the Hermetic treatises claimed that the "secrets of the cosmos had been written by God in a mathematical language [. . .]." See Hugh Kearney, *Science and Change* 1500-1700 (New York: McGraw-Hill Book Co., 1971), pp. 38-39. A picture of a mosaic of Trismegistus from the Cathedral of Sienna, dating from 1480, can be found on page 36 of Kearney's book.

17. Dijksterhuis, *op. cit.*, p. 274. Brackets added.

18. John Buridan, *Questions on the Four Books on the Heavens and the World of Aristotle*, in Marshall Clagett, *The Science of Mechanics in the Middle Ages* (Wisconsin: The University of Wisconsin Press, 1959), p. 595.

19. Nicole Oresme, *On the Book of the Heavens and the World of Aristotle*, in Clagett, *op. cit.*, p. 602.

20. Duncan, p. 40. The following page references in the text are to this work.

21. Buridan, *op. cit.*, p. 596. Brackets added.

22. *Ibid.* Brackets added.

23. Oresme, *op. cit.*, p. 602.

24. *Ibid.*, p. 602. Brackets added.

25. Robert Small, *An Account of the Astronomical Discoveries of Kepler*, a reprinting of the 1804 text (Madison: The University of Wisconsin Press, 1963), p. 82.

26. Thomas S. Kuhn, *The Structure of Scientific Revolutions*, second edition, enlarged (Chicago: The University of Chicago Press, 1970), pp. 148-152.

27. Paul Feyerabend, *Against Method* (London: Verso, 1975), ch. 12.

28. Small, *op. cit.*, p. 79. Brackets added.

29. In describing how Copernicus calculated the planetary motions, Kuhn gives an excellent account of what Copernicus meant by their "being linked together in harmony." Cf. Kuhn, *The Copernican Revolution*, pp. 171-176.

30. *Ibid.*, p. 170.

31. Giordano Bruno, an apostate from the Dominican Order (the Order of St. Thomas), was burned at the stake in 1600 for refusing to renounce heretical beliefs. He also was criticized for maintaining that there are many inhabited worlds like ours in the universe.

32. Cf. Koestler, p. 287. The immediately following references in the text are to Koestler's book.

33. For those interested, see the excellent biography, *Kepler*, by Max Casper, translated and edited by C. Doris Hellman (London: Abelard-Schuman, 1959); also Koestler, Part IV. All further references to Casper are to the above book.

34. *Ibid.*, p. 44.

35. *Ibid.*, p 58.

36. Johannes Kepler, *Mysterium Cosmographicum*, translated by A.M. Duncan (New York: Abaris Books, 1981), p. 69. The immediately following page references in the text are to this work.

37. Kepler, *Harmonice Mundi*, Lib. IV, Ch. I, *Gesammelte Werke*, Vol. VI. Quoted from Koestler, p. 262. Brackets added.

38. Koestler, p. 302. Casper gives a more detailed comparison, pp. 100-101.

39. Quoted by Casper, p. 127.

40. As the *Nova* is not available in English, in this recapitulation of Kepler's reasoning I am guided by Koestler's excellent discussion as he obviously read the *Astronomia Nova* thoroughly in reconstructing the argument. This interpretation agrees with Casper's summary, pp. 123-142.

41. Koestler, p. 259.

42. Cf. Kuhn, p. 246; also Casper, p. 138.

43. Kepler's statement in the *Nova* quoted by Koestler, p. 329.

44. Letter to D. Fabricius, 4.7.1603, *Gesemmelte Werke*, Vol. XIV, p. 409. Quoted from Koestler, p. 330.

45. Cf. Koestler, p. 331.

46. Kuhn, p. 212.

47. Kepler, *Astronomia*, Introduction. Quoted from Koestler, p. 337.

48. *Ibid.*, Vol. III, Ch. 33. *Ibid.*, p. 341.

49. *Ibid.*, Introduction. *Ibid.*, p. 338.

50. Kepler, *Gesammelte Werke*, Vol. XV, p. 145. Quoted from Koestler, p. 340.

51. Cf. *Great Books Of The Western World*, edited by R.M. Hutchins, vol. 16 (Chicago: The University of Chicago, 1952), p. 10009.

52. *Ibid.*, p. 1020.

53. Cf. Koestler, p. 378.

54. Casper, p. 297.

55. Koestler gives the name of the city as Ratisbon while Casper lists it as Regensburg. I believe the former is the original name.

CHAPTER III

GALILEO GALILEI: THE FATHER OF MODERN SCIENCE

THE PREPARATORY YEARS OF INVESTIGATION

Galileo [. . .] was a unique intellect—mathematician, physicist, astronomer;
he is often referred to as the father of modern scientific thought.[1]
Kaplan

According to Hegel the *"weltgeist"* (world spirit) manifests itself most directly in great men bestriding the stage of history. While Hegel had in mind particularly legendary conquerors such as Alexander, Caesar, and his own contemporary, Napoleon, on whom societies foolishly lavish their highest laurels, one could hardly find a more suitable example than Galileo. Despite such outstanding contemporaries as Bacon, Kepler, Descartes, Fermat, Gassendi, and Mersenne, Galileo was the archetypal renaissance figure looming high above the others. Owing to his revolutionary contributions to science in the areas of statics and hydrostatics, telescopic astronomy, theoretical cosmology, and kinematic physics (dynamics was the achievement of Newton), he established the *new* science of motion, the central problem of mechanics. In his emphasis on observation, mathematical demonstration, and the experimental testing of hypotheses, Galileo successfully challenged the scientific methodology of Aristotle consisting of logical deductions from inductive premises comprising essential classifications based on generic distinctions. Opposing the latter's conception of scientific knowledge as a closed theoretical framework grounded on direct observation as interpreted within a fixed system of categories, Galileo championed an open science based on experimental inquiry utilizing geometrical demonstrations.

Explicitly following the example of such Hellenistic thinkers as Euclid, Archimedes, and Apollonius, he reinstated the Pythagorean procedure of applying geometry to problems of nature in contrast to Plato's idealistic view of mathematics as relating solely to the unchanging Realm of Forms subsisting independently of the world of appearances. In Galileo's conception of abstract idealized conditions and mathematical approximations, along with the attempt to establish exact units of measurements, he was far ahead of his time. In his comparison of the "Two Chief World Systems" Galileo administered the *coup de grâce* to Aristotle's cosmology with its qualitative division between the celestial and terrestrial realms, while in his traumatic confrontation with the

Aristotelians and Catholic Church, despite the humiliation of being forced to abjure his belief in Copernicanism, he ultimately succeeded in his crusade to free scientific inquiry from the shackles of the Aristotelian orthodoxy and Church authority. More than any other individual, it was Galileo who insisted that the modern conception of the world must be based on observations, experimental tests, and mathematical demonstrations.

He was born in 1564 in the countryside of Pisa of a somewhat distinguished Florentine family whose ancestral paternal origins can be traced to a prominent physician of the fifteenth century, Galileo Bonaiuti, from whom the family name of Galilei was derived.[2] Although his mother Giulia Ammannati of Pescia was an intelligent and well educated woman, she did not arouse much affection either in Galileo or his brother, Michelangelo. Closer to his father, Vincenzio, who was an accomplished lutenist, music critic, and author of a *Dialogue on Ancient and Modern Music*, it was he who instilled in Galileo a lifelong love and interest in music (in the *Dialogue Concerning the Two Chief World Systems* Galileo devotes the last ten pages of the first day's dialogue to an analysis of the various tones produced by vibrating strings) and literature. His earliest education entrusted to a tutor, he then was sent to a monastery in Vallombroso where he studied grammar, logic, and rhetoric, even becoming a Novice in the Order. Wishing, however, to revive the family's distinguished heritage in medicine, his father had him withdrawn from the Order and transferred to another monastery in Florence until he could be enrolled as a medical student in the University of Pisa in 1581.

As was true also of Tycho and Kepler, there then occurred an event in his life that completely changed his career, despite his father's intentions. Owing to the annual transfer of the Court at Florence to Pisa from Christmas to Easter, during his second year at the University Galileo accidentally overheard Ostilio Ricci, mathematician to the Grand Duke, lecturing to the court pages on Euclid. Intrigued by the rigor of the demonstrations (as would be true also of Einstein), he discretely attended further lectures and began to read Euclid by himself. Although only members of the court were permitted to attend Ricci's lectures, having met him socially Galileo felt free to address questions to him in private about his studies. Immediately recognizing Galileo's natural aptitude for mathematics, Ricci encouraged him and assisted him in his research. Eventually, Galileo enlisted Ricci's help in persuading his father to allow him to pursue a career in mathematics and natural philosophy, rather than medicine.

Although as a medical student he was compelled to study Aristotle's treatises on natural philosophy and Galen's medical works, he was more intrigued by Eudoxus' theory of proportions and Archimedes' treatises *On Plane Equilibrium* and *On Bodies in Water*, introduced to him by Ricci. It was from these works that Galileo acquired his interest in statics and hydrostatics, the subjects of his earliest writings in mathematical physics. Perhaps influenced by his father's polemical discourses on music, even at this early age Galileo developed a reputation for his contentiousness and criticism of Aristotle, especially the latter's law that falling objects acquire a speed proportional to their bulks, a fact which he believed was refuted by hailstones which appeared to descend with the same speed regardless of their sizes. (p. 2)

Learning that Galileo was neglecting his medical assignments to pursue other interests, Vincenzio declared that unless he discontinued these pursuits and devoted his efforts to his medical studies he would cease his financial support. This Galileo refused to do but succeeded in persuading his father to continue his support for another year after which he would be on his own. Since there were more positions available teaching Aristotelian philosophy than mathematics, Galileo set himself in the summer of 1584 to preparing lectures on Aristotle's natural philosophy and methodology which appear in his collected works under the title of *Juvenilia*. Discontinuing his studies at the University in the spring of 1585 without a degree, he supported himself by giving private lectures on mathematics at Florence and Siena, while also doing some public teaching at Siena.

In 1586 he began his scientific publications with a book written in Italian entitled *La Bilancetta* (The Little Balance) prescribing refinements in the Westphal balance for determining specific gravities and improvements in Archimedes theory for calculating specific weights. He then started composing in Latin a dialogue on motion that he never finished, but which provided the basis for the *De Motu* of 1590.[3] The unfinished dialogue shows "Galileo's early challenge to Aristotelian authority, his Archimedean application of mathematics to physics, and his interest in scientific questions raised by practical men." (p. 7) This is the first evidence, which we shall discuss more fully later, refuting Alexandre Koyré's view that in "struggling against Aristotle's philosophy Galileo does so from the vantage point [. . .] of the philosophy of Plato [. . .].[4] While Galileo occasionally applauds Plato for emphasizing the importance of geometry in the study of philosophy, he was anything but a Platonist in his conception of scientific inquiry. Indicative of his lifelong interests, the *De Motu* addresses questions about motion, especially free fall, projectiles, impetus, and movement in the void, that will be given final expression in his last and most important scientific work, *Dialogues Concerning Two New Sciences* (hereafter referred to as "Two New Sciences" to distinguish it from the earlier *Dialogue*). This youthful monograph shows that even in his early twenties Galileo was concerned with the kind of kinematic problems that would preoccupy him throughout his life, but especially in his last years. Of less importance was a manuscript "Treatise on the Sphere, or Cosmography," written a little later containing a standard discussion of "climatic geography and spherical astronomy" that may have been the basis of his early lectures on astronomy given at Pisa and Padua. (cf. p. 12)

In 1587 Galileo sought support for a vacated chair of mathematics at the University of Bologna. While he had acquired some acclaim due to having derived several theorems pertaining to "the centers of gravity of parabolic solids of revolution" inspired by Archimedes' treatise *On Plane Equilibrium*, the position went to G.A. Magini, a Paduan astronomer who had more published works to his credit. But when the chair of mathematics at the University of Pisa was vacated in 1589, Galileo's reputation was such that he succeeded in obtaining a three year appointment. He was just twenty-five years old when he began teaching at the University of Pisa at an annual salary of 60 florins, half that of his predecessor. Given his financial needs at the time that salary was adequate, but the death of his father in 1591 left him with additional financial responsibilities as head of the family, particularly the necessity of providing dowries for his two sisters, so he was soon in search of a more highly paid position.

The most well-known anecdote about Galileo takes place during his tenure at Pisa. In 1637 toward the end of his long life Galileo recalled to Vincenzio Viviani, then his student assistant who later became his first biographer, a public demonstration while he was at Pisa disproving Aristotle's law that free falling bodies acquire speeds proportional to their weights. According to his account, as part of the demonstration he dropped objects made of the same material but of various sizes from the Leaning Tower of Pisa to show that their times of fall were the same or their differences negligible. However, there being no record of a public demonstration witnessed by students and faculty along with discrepancies in the story that developed over the years, scholars have tended to dismiss the account as legendary, despite Galileo's later reference to it. Drake, however, has given a very reasonable justification for believing the event authentic consistent with what we know about Galileo's early criticism of Aristotle's law and his penchant for dramatic public demonstrations. (cf. pp. 19-21) During his appointment at Pisa his most important research consisted of revising and extending the *De Motu*. Of particular interest is the fact that although he had read Copernicus' *De*

Revolutionibus, he still clung to the geocentric position while continuing to criticize Aristotle's explanation of motion, particularly the division between natural and forced motions. He argued that in addition to the distinction being arbitrary, in some cases there were "neutral motions" that did not fit into either category, a position central to his attack on Aristotle's view that it was impossible for a vertical projectile at the peak of its trajectory to come to rest before its descent because during the time of transition it would have to be both at rest and in motion, a contradiction. Arguing that although *at* the time of the transition the projectile's upward propulsion and downward tendency balanced, this did not mean that the body remained at rest *for* some time. (cf. p. 30)

These attacks on Aristotle's theories obviously did not endear him to the Peripatetic philosophers who were predominant at the University of Pisa so, realizing that his contract probably would not be renewed after its expiration in the spring of 1592, he began looking for another position offering a better salary. As it happened, a chair in mathematics at the more prestigious University of Padua had been vacant since 1588. Although Magini, who had bestead him in his earlier attempt to obtain the position of mathematician at Bologna, also sought this appointment in his native city, this time Galileo's reputation and support were sufficient to win him the post at a salary of 180 florins, three times more than he had earned at Pisa.

Located only twenty-five miles from Venice, one of the greatest seaports, international crossroads, munitions center, and artisanal capitals of the world at the time, the University of Padua was well situated to provide Galileo the opportunity of meeting some of the distinguished visitors, renown scholars, and accomplished artisans that frequented the city. His books abound with examples of compasses, sextants, pulleys, sailing ships, cannons, levers, lenses, beams, and so forth that reflect the busy nautical and technological activities around him. Although his method was more Archimedean, his interests in natural phenomena were Aristotelian in their scope and diversity, again belying Koyré's thesis that he was a Platonist. Few scientists have been as inherently curious and multi-sided as Galileo whose investigations included not only balances and machines, magnets and music, insects and optics, but comets and planets. He even constructed a number of instruments, including a calculator, a mechanism for raising water by horsepower, a refined quadrant for use in aiming and elevating cannons, various measuring devices or calibrators, a military compass, and of course the famous "spyglass" or "telescope," along with a microscope. His need of an artisan was so great that in 1599 he invited Marcantonio Mazzoleni and his family to live with him as his personal instrument maker. According to Drake, "[a]ll the documents from his early years at Padua indicate his interest in technological rather than philosophical questions." (p. 33)

While in his first years at Padua his activities were mainly directed to these more practical concerns, he did compose a treatise on *Mechanics* influenced by his reading of the ancient pseudo-Aristotelian *Questions of Mechanics*, as well as "the first modern treatise on mechanics. . .published in Latin by Guidobaldo del Monte in 1577 and translated into Italian in 1581." (p. 35) Of more significance was his increasing adherence to the Copernican system, especially as the twofold motion attributed to the earth by Copernicus suggested the possibility of a mechanical explanation of the tides. Suspicious of the ancient lunar theory which he believed to be based on hidden or occult forces, he thought that just as the agitation of water in barges is caused by conflicting motions (sudden accelerations, abrupt stops, and lateral dips and churning caused by waves), so the contrast between the axial diurnal rotation and the annual orbital revolution of the earth could produce oscillations in the earth's ocean-basins explaining the tides. (cf. pp. 36-44)[5] His complete theory is presented in the discussion of the fourth day in the *Dialogue*. Convinced that his tidal explanation was the most direct confirmation of the Copernican theory, it will play an important role in his controversy with the Church. The first definitive expression of his allegiance to the Copernican system occurred in a letter thanking Kepler for sending him his first published book, the *Mysterium Cosmographicum*. Congratulating Kepler for his public defense of the Copernican system which Galileo says he also had supported in silence for some years, he wrote:

> [. . .] as from that position [the Copernican] I have discovered the causes of many physical effects [an allusion probably to his tidal theory] which are perhaps inexplicable on the common [lunar] hypothesis. I have written many reasons and refutations of contrary arguments [of the Copernican position] which up to now I have preferred not to publish, intimidated by the fortune of our teacher Copernicus, who though he will be of immortal fame to some, is yet by an infinite number (for such is the multitude of fools) laughed at and rejected. [6]

This indication of the scorn with which Copernicus was regarded even then by the majority of philosophers is further confirmation that his original fear of being ridiculed was by no means unfounded.

Apparently Galileo's academic performance and technological achievements were appreciated because, despite some opposition, he was reappointed to the chair of mathematics at Padua for four years at a salary of 320 florins, considerably more than previously. The additional income was especially welcome because of the obligation he and his brother incurred of providing a large dowry for his sister Livia and also because he was entering into a permanent, though non-marital, relationship with a Venetian woman named Marina Gamba. She bore him three children, two daughters named Virginia and Livia, both of whom entered the convent of San Matteo in Arcetri, and a son Vincenzio II, who was legitimized at Florence and later married.[7] Because Galileo's personal life was not as interwoven with his professional accomplishments as was that of Kepler, little more will be said about it.

Following his reappointment Galileo pursued his earlier interests in mechanical problems, completing his book on *Mechanics* about 1602. Among the notable inquiries were his investigations of the ratios of planetary speeds and distances, a resumption of his inclined plane experiments begun in the *De Motu*, and especially his discovery of the law of free fall. Unlike Kepler, he was unable to formulate the exact laws relating the dimensions of the various planetary orbits and speeds from their distances from the sun, but comparing each planet's orbit to Saturn's he arrived at the conclusion that "the speed of any planet was to Saturn's speed as the distance of Saturn is to the mean proportional between that distance and the distance of the planet."[8] (p. 65)

At the same time his experiments with pendulums led to his discovery that the times or periods of their swings were uniform or isochronal, the speed depending not on the weight of the bob but on its length. This discovery that in the same medium bobs of different weights have (nearly) identical periods of swing apparently suggested to him that in a vacuum all objects would descend with the same velocity regardless of their weights, in contrast to Aristotle's law.[9] About 1603 he renewed his experiments with inclined planes, and by 1604 he ascertained experimentally that accelerating from rest the distances traversed in equal times were as the odd numbers beginning with unity, as Oresme previously had stated. Like Oresme, he illustrated the results with diagrams but there is no evidence of a direct influence by the fourteenth century Parisian on Galileo, though his works were generally known at the time.

As important as was the discovery of the odd-number rule, it still did not relate the speed to the time. However, it was evident from the data that if the distances increased successively as the odd numbers beginning with unity and starting from rest, then the cumulative distances or speeds would vary with the squares of the times. As he wrote, the "contraries of speeds are *times*—and indeed I do get the times by taking the square roots of the distances from rest, the same distances whose squares are as the speeds from rest."[10] Thus he seemed to have arrived at the odd-number rule first, then by reasoning backward inferred that the square roots of the distances gave the times which, when squared, provided the increases in speed or acceleration. On 16 October he wrote to Sarpi that "he had found a proof for the square law, the odd-number rule, and other things [. . .]." (p. 100) This law would be the keystone of his "creation of a new science of motion" presented in the *Two New Sciences*.

Until 1604 Galileo had not shown a great interest in astronomy nor had he made any astronomical observations, but then the appearance of a brilliant nova like the one sighted in 1572 by Tycho aroused great curiosity. Any novelty in the heavens generated intense interest among astrologers because of its significance as an omen, as well as considerable controversy among the astronomers and Aristotelian philosophers regarding its location because the Aristotelian conception of the heavens as unalterable precluded any new occurrences. Just as Tycho had collected data from astronomers throughout Europe that had confirmed his own observations that no parallactic effect was discernible, implying that the supernova of 1572 existed at least as far as the translunar world, so Galileo obtained information from neighboring cities that substantiated his own observations that no parallax or evidence of motion of the new star was apparent. The interest was so intense that Galileo gave three lectures, attracting thousands of people,

> to explain the nature and application of parallactic reasoning to
> measurement of distances and to refute the Aristotelian theory that
> new stars and comets were sublunar phenomena in the supposed
> region of fire above the air and below the moon. (p. 106)

While the Copernican system was not mentioned, the criticism of Aristotle's views inevitably drew a response from the Peripatetics. The essential question concerned the reliability of the application of mathematics in astronomy, in contrast to physical principles derived from more direct observations. Aristotle had utilized mathematical ratios in describing terrestrial motions, but he held that the remoteness of astronomical phenomena precluded a precise mathematical description of celestial motions, as well as an exact knowledge of the composition of celestial bodies. For Aristotle, precision of knowledge varied considerably with the nature of the subject-matter. Thus the Peripatetics claimed that while astronomers could use ingenious geometrical constructions "to save the phenomena," these artifices should not be considered real, as Osiander also wrote in his Preface to Copernicus' *De Revolutionibus*.

However, astronomers such as Copernicus, Tycho, and Kepler began to have greater confidence in their ability (especially after Tycho's improved observations) to describe accurately the orbital sizes, distances, and speeds of the planets. Although Galileo's early conjectures about the orbital dimensions of the planets in relation to the sphere of Saturn did not qualify him as a mathematical astronomer, his remarkable mathematical ability and genius for applying geometry to numerous physical inquiries instilled in him a respect for mathematical demonstrations based on exact measurements. This confidence that experimentally acquired measurements provided a secure foundation for *astronomical* as well as *physical* inquiry is what distinguished Galileo's methodology from that of the Aristotelian philosophers.

When it was a question of accepting the evidence of parallax derived from astronomical calculations or interpreting the evidence to fit a preconceived cosmological system based on philosophical principles, there could be no doubt where Galileo stood. As Drake asserts, he believed that "whenever it is possible to find a mathematical rule which is exemplified by things accessible to sensory verification and which is not contradicted by further experience, we may be certain the rule holds wherever applied." (p. 107) Thus parallactic displacement which is confirmed in the terrestrial world can be predicted reliably also of the celestial world. While such an inference seems reasonable enough today, it repudiated the time-honored conviction that the qualitative difference between the terrestrial and celestial worlds presupposes diverse modes of reasoning based on different principles of explanation. It was the rejection of this assumption that enabled Galileo systematically to dismantle the Aristotelian cosmology in his first *Dialogue*.

Although the controversy over the nova aroused strong opposition among his Aristotelian opponents, Galileo succeeded in having his appointment renewed at a salary of 520 florins. The next several years were devoted to investigating problems in hydrostatics, strength of metals, and parabolic projectile trajectories. By 1609 he arrived at the conclusion that projectile motion consisted of two components, the horizontal projection and the vertical descent, each of which could be depicted by two sides of a right angle so that the hypotenuse joining the two lines constituted the combined impetus of the two motions. Thus he arrived at the important conception of the vector addition of motions which he called "equality in the square." (p. 135) This represented a significant advance because it subverted the Aristotelian principle that two contrary motions could not be combined into a single motion, thereby allowing Galileo to attain a correct description of parabolic trajectories.

Furthermore, overcoming the ancient conceptual opposition to instantaneous motion based on the supposition that because all motions take some time instantaneous motion is contradictory and therefore impossible, Galileo simply considered acceleration as a continuous series of increases in instantaneous motion until the resistance balanced the gravitational increase producing a constant speed.   Unlike the fourteenth century Scholastics' conception of impetus as a change produced and occurring *within* the object, for Galileo impetus came to mean simply the motion of the object regardless of its cause.   This change in meaning in turn shifted emphasis from a search for an adequate explanation of the *cause* of motion to its precise mathematical *description*.   *These transitions of meaning and alterations in conceptual implications are precisely what constitute modifications in the conceptual framework integral to the development of thought.*

Galileo was forty-five years old in the summer of 1609 with a growing reputation for his inventions and original research in mechanics but who, when compared to Kepler whose astronomical laws were published in the same year, was a relatively unknown scientist.   Then, during a trip to Venice, he learned of a new instrument that would provide him with the opportunity not only of being propelled to stellar status as a scientist, but also of transforming the ancient discipline of astronomy and along with it the conception of the universe.   The instrument was a Dutch invention then called a "spyglass" because it magnified distant objects in such a way that they were seen as much closer.   Rather common in northern Europe, an instrument was brought to Venice with the purpose of selling it to the Venetian Republic.   On learning of this Galileo returned to Padua where he received a letter from Paris from a French nobleman, Jacques Badovere, confirming the existence of such instruments, whereupon he began thinking about its possibilities and how it might be constructed.   As he later recalled in the *Sidereus Nuncius* or *Starry Messenger*:

This finally caused me to apply myself totally to investigating the principles and figuring out the means by which I might arrive at the invention of a similar instrument [. . .].   And first I prepared a lead tube in whose ends I fitted two glasses, both plane on one side while the other side of one was spherically convex and of the other concave.

Then, applying one eye to the concave glass, I saw objects satisfactorily large and close [. . . .] Finally, sparing no labor or expense, I progressed so far that I constructed for myself an instrument so excellent that things seen through it appear about a thousand times larger and more than thirty times closer than when observed with the natural faculty only.[11]

Always alert to the opportunity of improving his financial situation, as soon as Galileo had perfected the nine-power "spyglass" he took the instrument to Venice where he exhibited its use from the highest point, the campanile in St. Mark's square, first to the general populace and then to the Senate of the Venetian Republic. Pointing out its nautical and military potential (it made distant vessels under full sail visible two hours prior to their arrival at the Venetian port) in a letter accompanying a gift of the spyglass to the Doge, the authorities reciprocated by renewing Galileo's appointment at the University of Padua for life at a salary of 1,000 florins per year. But the true significance of the telescope lay in other uses.

Although he was not the first to use the telescope for astronomical observations, his skill in increasing the telescope's power and resolution along with his proficiency in its use, soon made him preeminent in the new discipline of telescopic observations. While he may have begun his observations of the moon as early as October of 1609, by the end of November he had constructed a twenty-power telescope with which "his first carefully recorded lunar observation with this instrument was made on December 1, 1609 [. . .]." (p. 143) From this observation he made a sketch of the crescent shape of the moon, the first in a series that depicted the moon's irregular surface, then went on to make his momentous discovery of the satellites of Jupiter.

Anxious to establish his priority in these observations, he began to compose the book, *Sidereus Nuncius*, in January. Completed and printed at Venice in March, the book was dedicated to Cosimo de' Medici, his former student and now the ruler of Tuscany, in whose honor he christened the four satellites of Jupiter the "Medicean Stars" for the four Medicean princes. Projecting Galileo to immediate international fame, the book is remarkable for its modernity. While not as theoretically comprehensive and lacking the star charts of the works of Ptolemy, Copernicus, Tycho, and Kepler, the new astronomical data revealed by the telescope were so strikingly superior to naked eye observations that their impact was much more dramatic.

Moreover, in contrast to the works of Kepler which are largely unintelligible because of their mystical obscurity, Galileo writes as if he were living today. Unlike those whose commitment to the Aristotelian framework made it difficult to observe the new discoveries even when pointed out to them, Galileo's open-mindedness immediately enabled him to grasp the phenomena with their full significance. The style of the *Sidereus Nuncius* is so persuasive that when Kepler received his copy he was completely convinced of its truth even before he could confirm the observations himself. As he immediately wrote to Galileo: "I may perhaps seem rash in accepting your claims so readily with no support of my own experience. But why should I not believe a most learned mathematician, whose very style attests the soundness of his judgment?"[12]

Beginning with his observations of the moon supported by diagrams, the book is striking for Galileo's willingness to recognize "a similarity between the Moon and the Earth." Supporting Anaxagoras' conjecture two millennia earlier, Galileo describes the surface of the moon based on comparisons with the earth. The boldness of his reasoning can be appreciated if we recall that at that time the planets were considered to be perfectly smooth spherical bodies composed of an entirely different material from that of the earth. As he says:

> By oft-repeated observations [. . .] we have been led to the conclusion that we certainly see the surface of the Moon to be not smooth, even, and perfectly spherical, as the great crowd of philosophers have believed about this and other heavenly bodies, but, on the contrary, to be uneven, rough, and crowded with depressions and bulges. And it is like the face of the Earth itself, which is marked here and there with chains of mountains and depths of valleys. (p. 40)

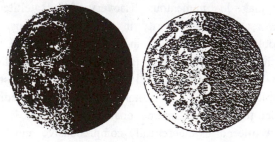

Figure. 1. An example of Galileo's diagram of the surface of the moon, Drake, p. 145. The Moon as seen through a high power telescope (left, Lick Observatory Photograph) and as drawn by Galileo (right, from his Messenger). (Photo by University of Toronto Photographic Services). With kind permission from the University of Toronto Press.

Observing the contrast in illumination of the numerous lunar depressions depending on whether they were opposite to or facing the Sun, as well as their glistening ridges, he says "we have an almost entirely similar sight on Earth, around sunrise, when the valleys are not yet bathed in light but the surrounding mountains facing the Sun are already seen shining with light." (p. 41) A particularly large cavity near the center of the Moon he describes as offering "the same aspect to shadow and illumination as a region similar to Bohemia would offer on Earth, if it were enclosed on all sides by very high mountains, placed around the periphery in a perfect circle." (p. 47) Based on the lengths of the shadows cast by the Moon's largest mountains he calculated their height, estimating some to be thirty times higher than those on the earth. Finally, he explained the ashen light that bathes the dark side of the Moon just preceding and following its new appearance, asserting that it is caused by the sun's light reflected from the earth.

Turning next to his observation of the stars and of the satellites of Jupiter, he notes and attempts to explain why the fixed stars, along with the planets other than the Moon, are not as greatly enlarged as other objects when seen through the telescope. So many more stars came into view when he directed his observations to constellations such as Orion, the Pleiades, and Praecepe that he was "overwhelmed by the enormous multitude of stars [. . .]." (p. 59) Observing the Milky Way, he wrote that it "may be observed so well that all the disputes that for so many generations have vexed philosophers are destroyed by visible certainty [. . .] [f]or the Galaxy is nothing else than a congeries of innumerable stars distributed in clusters." (p. 62) Thus he confirmed the ancient conjecture of Democritus that the Milky Way is "like densely sprinkled salt."

The final portion of the *Nuncius* is devoted to his unexpected discovery and continuous observations of the satellites or moons of Jupiter, with diagrams depicting their various positions on successive nights. Observing Jupiter on 7 January with a more powerful instrument, he recorded his initial reaction:

[. . .] that three little stars were positioned near him[13]—small but very bright. Although I believed them to be among the number of fixed stars, they nevertheless intrigued me because they appeared to be arranged exactly along a straight line and parallel to the ecliptic, and to be brighter than others of equal size. (p. 64)

Then, as his successive drawings show, he was startled to find "a very different arrangement'' on the succeeding night which continued to change with his observations.   Believing the new appearances to be fixed stars, he attributed the variation in the positions to the motion of Jupiter, but "moving from doubt to astonishment, I found that the observed change was not in Jupiter but in the said stars.'' (p. 66) From this he inferred "that in the heavens there are three stars wandering around Jupiter like Venus and Mercury around the sun." (p. 66) Then, on 14 January, the fourth star that had previously lain outside his telescopic field emerged into view. Closely noting their respective variations in positions and motion in relation to Jupiter, he subsequently concluded that "they whirl [. . .] in unequal circles" around Jupiter with those "describing smaller circles" moving faster. (p. 84) He began calculating their periods, although he did not publish the figures until 1612 with results "not very different from findings three centuries later [. . .].''[14] Despite only oblique references to the Copernican system, the astronomical implications were glaringly evident.   According to Copernicus the earth, accompanied by its satellite the moon, revolves in its orbit around the center of the universe near which rests the stationary sun. But how could a terrestrial body exist in the celestial realm? Yet if the surface of a celestial body like the moon resembled that of the earth, as Galileo's observations disclosed, then the argument based on their qualitative differences loses much of it force. Since "[a]ny challenge to perfect sphericity of the perfect heavenly bodies constituted the worst threat of all in the eyes of philosophers,''[15] Galileo's description and drawings of the irregular surface of the moon drew immediate rebuttal from the Aristotelians.   It being difficult to deny his observations outright, some argued that the mountains and craters were submerged within the smooth crystalline surface of the moon, but that their transparency allowed light to be reflected from the peaks and depressions. Needless to say, the *ad hoc* implausible nature of this explanation drew only ridicule from Galileo.

Furthermore, proponents of the geocentric system had argued that their model was more symmetrical since all the planets revolve around the centrally located earth, while in the heliocentric view the moon revolved around the earth.   In a symmetrical universe, why should there by only one orbiting satellite? Now, however, Galileo could argue that "our vision offers us four stars wandering around Jupiter like the Moon around the Earth while all together with Jupiter traverse a great circle around the Sun [. . .]." (pp. 84-85) Not only affirming a similarity between the earth's moon and the satellites of Jupiter, he adds that Jupiter revolves around the sun as he believed was true of the earth.

Finally, the tremendous increase in the number of the observed stars along with their minute size in comparison to the planets, implying a vastly larger and more distant stellar sphere, could remove the major *astronomical* obstacle to accepting the Copernican system, the absence of stellar parallax. Although Galileo never acknowledged an infinite universe, his telescopic observations led to a foreshortening of the planetary system in relation to a greatly expanded stellar sphere.

As was to be expected, despite the compelling observational evidence reinforced by his drawings and carefully reasoned conclusions, rather than these new revelations of the heavens being welcomed, Galileo's adversaries immediately took to the offensive. But it must be remembered that at that time it was believed that God had created human beings with a visual acuity commensurate with their position in the universe, so unlike today one did not expect an optical instrument to disclose hidden celestial bodies too remote and therefore too small to be observed by the naked eye. Furthermore, while the reliability of the telescope could be confirmed by sightings on the earth, there was a reluctance to believe that this also was true of the celestial world considering the qualitative difference between the two. Finally, lacking a comprehensive optical theory that could explain how the lenses functioned in the telescope, it is understandable that those who opposed the new observations on philosophical grounds would be skeptical of its dependability. Some, like Cremonini, refused to look through the telescope on the grounds that if such novelties existed Aristotle would have reported them. Others attributed the observations to "illusions of the lens," while even more sympathetic astronomers had problems duplicating and confirming Galileo's observations because of the difficulty in using the telescope.

It was typical of Galileo's genius that he immediately foresaw the potential of the spyglass, had the technical skill to perfect it, and quickly learned to use it properly. Even in Venice, which was a center of glass making and known for its proficiency in grinding lenses for spectacles, producing proper lenses for the telescope was not an easy task because they had to be ground and polished to different specifications. Galileo admitted that of the sixty instruments he had made only a few were actually suitable for astronomical use. (cf. p. 92) Although Kepler had a deeper knowledge of optics, he impatiently waited for the opportunity to use one of Galileo's telescopes before attempting to confirm his observations, hence constructing the instrument could not have been easy or he would have had one made for his own use. Once in possession of a suitable instrument, learning to use it effectively was itself difficult as his instruction implies:

[. . .] the instrument must be held firm, and hence it is good, to escape the shaking of the hand that arises from motion of the arteries and from breathing, to fix the tube in some stable place. The glasses should be kept clean and polished by a cloth, or else cloud is generated there by the breath, humid or foggy air, or vapor which evaporates from the eye itself, especially when warm. It is best that the tube be capable of being lengthened a bit [. . .]. It is good that the convex glass, which is the one far from the eye, should be partly covered and that the opening left should be oval in shape, since thus are objects seen much more distinctly.[16]

Even when guided by Galileo himself the results were not always successful, especially when the observers were hostile. When Galileo visited Bologna in April of 1610 to demonstrate his telescope to Magini and other leading astronomers, the results were extremely disappointing, as Magini's assistant Horky gloatingly reported in a letter to Kepler.

Galileo Galilei, the mathematician of Padua, came to us in Bologna and he brought with him that spyglass through which he sees four *fictitious* planets. On the twenty-fourth and twenty-fifth of April I never slept, day and night, but tested that instrument of Galileo's in innumerable ways, in these lower [earthly] as well as the higher [realms]. On Earth it works miracles; in the heavens it *deceives*, for other fixed stars appear double [. . . .] I have as witnesses most excellent men and most noble doctors [. . .] who [. . .] all acknowledged that the instrument *deceived*. And Galileo became silent, and on the twenty-sixth, a Monday, dejected, he took his leave from Mr. Magini very early in the morning.[17]

Despite this disappointment Galileo was successful in a more important objective, that of changing his position from mathematics professor at Padua to mathematician and philosopher to the Grand Duke of Tuscany. In addition to preferring to live in the capital of his birthplace under the patronage of close and powerful friends, he wanted to be relieved of his teaching duties so that he could devote himself full-time to the numerous research projects listed in his formal application, for despite the title of the ''Chief Mathematician of the University of Pisa'' the position did not require any formal teaching. On July 10, 1610, just a few months after his lifetime appointment at Padua by the Venetian Republic, he was delighted to accept at Florence the position of

"Chief Mathematician of the University of Pisa and Philosopher to the Grand Duke" (the latter title an added designation that he requested) at a salary of 1,000 florins a year, the same as his Paduan salary. Moreover, the Grand Duke having assented to Galileo's observations took it upon himself to further the cause, making the issue one of state.

> The Tuscan ambassadors at the courts in Prague, London, Paris, and Madrid were alerted that Galileo would send them copies of his book and perhaps spyglasses as well, and they were instructed to use their good offices to promote Galileo's discoveries. The expenses that Galileo incurred [. . .] were born by the Tuscan treasury. (p. 100)

Furthermore, by the end of the year 1610 Galileo's confidence in the reliability and accuracy of the telescope was completely vindicated. Late in September his Venetian friend Antonio Santini had observed the satellites of Jupiter, as had Kepler in Prague who published a brief tract reporting his observations. Moreover, Thomas Harriot in England and several observers in France added their confirmations. By then Galileo had increased his own discoveries, first observing what are now called the rings of Saturn which to him looked like two protuberants or "ears" on each side of Saturn and, more importantly, the phases of Venus.

He had already begun observing the latter when his former pupil Benedetto Castelli wrote on 5 December asking if he would confirm the prediction of Copernicus that as Venus revolves around the Sun in the heliocentric system she should display phases analogous to the Moon, while on the Ptolemaic or earth-centered view she would exhibit only variously sized crescent shapes. Realizing that this presented an unusual opportunity to test the validity of either position, Galileo continuously observed Venus until he could write on 11 December "to Giuliano de' Medici, the Tuscan ambassador in Prague, that he had observed a phenomenon that was a strong argument for the Copernican Theory." (p. 107) Hiding his discovery in an anagram, he revealed its meaning by the end of the month as "'the mother of love [Venus] emulates the figures of Cynthia [the Moon].'" (p. 107) That Venus undergoes phases similar to the Moon as predicted by Copernicus was a decisive factor in convincing Galileo, along with others, of the truth of the Copernican system. Constituting a disconfirmation of the geocentric model, it did not confirm the Copernican theory because the phases of Venus also were consistent with the Tychonic model, but since Galileo (along with Kepler) always rejected the latter theory, he was justified in interpreting his observations as strong evidence for the Copernican alternative.

After a triumphal visit to Rome where he was honored by the distinguished members of the Collegio Romano who testified to Cardinal Bellarmine regarding the authenticity of his observations and where he was initiated into the prestigious *Accademia dei Lyncei* (it was during the latter initiation banquet in his honor that the name *"telescopium"* was proposed for his *"occhilai"* or *"spyglass"*[18]), he again became involved in a number of disputes.   In the first concerning floating bodies, Galileo opposed the Aristotelian interpretation that what enabled an object to float or sink in water was its shape, taking the Archimedean position that the crucial factor was the specific weights (or gravities). In addition, he maintained that ice was rarified water and therefore less dense so that it descends to the extent that it displaces its own weight in water, while the Aristotelians argued that ice was condensed water which, though heavier, floated because of its broad flat shape. At the urging of the Grand Duke (who advised that written arguments were a more suitable genre for scholarly debates than heated discourse), he presented his views in an essay which became the basis for his *Discourse on Bodies On or In Water* which he brought out in three revised editions.

At about the same time he became involved in another dispute over "sunspots."   A series of letters were published under the pseudonym "Apelles")[19] which explained the observed sunspots as due to tiny stars moving near the sun's surface, analogous to Jupiter. In a letter in May, 1613, Galileo wrote that he could demonstrate mathematically that the changing position of the spots indicated that they were not stars but solar phenomena that were formed and dispersed like clouds on the earth. Perhaps on the basis of this new evidence and that of the phases of Venus, in his third letter on sunspots written the following November, Galileo unequivocally expressed his support for the Copernican system.

Furthermore, in the same letter he conveys one of his most explicit conceptions of the objectives and limitations of scientific inquiry written up to that time, a conception that may be one of the sources of the modern antirealist, anti-Aristotelian notion that scientists can attain knowledge only of the *external* attributes of objects, not of their *inner* states.   While the Peripatetics claimed that we could know the essential natures of terrestrial substances but not of celestial bodies, Galileo argued that actually we do not know the essences of *any natural substances*, whether terrestrial or celestial, and therefore should be content with attaining knowledge of some of their properties. This position, developed later by Boyle and Locke and drawn to its skeptical conclusion by Hume and Kant, is probably one of the sources of the antirealistic attitude toward science of many modern philosophers.

> For in our speculating we either seek to penetrate the true and internal essence of natural substances or content ourselves with a knowledge of some of their properties. The former I hold to be as impossible an undertaking with regard to the closest elemental substances as with more remote celestial things [. . . .] But if what we wish to fix in our minds is the apprehension of some properties of things, then it seems to me that we need not despair of our ability to acquire this respecting distant [celestial] bodies just as well as those close at hand—and perhaps in some cases even more precisely in the former than in the latter.[20]

Having constantly avowed that mathematical demonstration and experimental testing, not reliance on authority, were the actual sources of truth, Galileo makes this very explicit in his criticism of "the Peripatetics:"

> So far as I can see, their education consisted in being nourished from infancy on the opinion that philosophizing is and can be nothing but to make a comprehensive survey of the texts of Aristotle so that from diverse passages they may quickly collect and throw together a great number of solutions to any proposed problem. They wish never to raise their eyes from those pages—as if this great book of the universe had been written to be read by nobody but Aristotle, and his eyes had been destined to see all for posterity.[21]

As someone who had observed for the first time in history astronomical phenomena previously inaccessible to anyone, we can appreciate Galileo's last statement. Yet his criticism was not directed to Aristotle, but to the Peripatetics who "go about defending the inalterability of the sky, a view which perhaps Aristotle himself would abandon in our age."[22]

The question of the warrant of authority pertained not only to the writings of Aristotle but also to Holy Scripture. Replying to another letter from Costelli, Galileo wrote that in "articles concerning salvation and the establishment of Faith" there could be no higher authority than Scripture, but when it came to questions of physics and astronomy, any Scriptural pronouncements that contradict scientific demonstrations should be attributed to the common modes of speech and interpreted accordingly, especially as God had endowed man with the capacity to interpret nature a well as Scripture. In fact, Galileo maintained that in those instances when scientists acquire a demonstrable knowledge of nature this is equivalent to divine knowledge, one of the textual doctrines that the Church found offensive. Regarding the conflict of assertions between Scripture and science, he wrote:

> [. . .] it being moreover manifest that two truths can never contradict each other, it is the office of wise expositors to work to find the true senses of passages in the Bible that accord with those physical conclusions of which we have first become sure and certain by manifest sense or necessary demonstrations. Indeed [. . .] as we are unable to assert with certainty that all interpreters speak with divine inspiration, I should think it would be prudent if no one were permitted to oblige Scripture and compel it in a certain way to sustain as true some physical conclusions of which sense and demonstrative and necessary reasons may show the contrary. And who wants to set bounds to the human mind? Who wants to assert that everything is known that can be known to the world?[23]

To appreciate the novelty of Galileo's conception it must be remembered that it was a legacy of the Middle Ages that authority, whether vested in Aristotle's writings or in Scripture as the revealed word of God, still was considered the final repository of truth. In contrast, Galileo was advocating a conception of knowledge accepted today but unorthodox at the time, that of continuous discoveries requiring new interpretations that should not be constrained by appeals to authority, especially as man's senses and intellect also were endowed by God:

> [. . .] I do not think it is necessary to believe that the same God who has given us our senses, reason, and intelligence wished us to abandon their use, giving us by some other means [such as Scripture] the information we could gain through them [. . .].[24]

This ''Letter to Castelli''was the ''forerunner of Galileo's famed Letter to the Grand Duchess Christina [. . .].'' (p. 492, f.n. 15).

Based on his triumphal visit to Rome and the success of his publications on *Bodies in Water* and *Sunspot Letters,* Galileo concluded that the surge of resistance toward the Copernican doctrine had waned, but in this he was sadly mistaken. The more his publications succeeded in convincing some people and in enhancing his reputation, the greater the resentment of his adversaries toward him personally and the stronger their determination to fight back. It is the nature of an authoritarian system that it cannot make any concessions without fearing the collapse of the entire system, hence it must be defended at all costs. As Father Grienberger, a member of the Jesuit Collegio Romano, reported to a friend of Galileo, "had not Aristotle been involved, the Jesuits would have agreed with everything, but that by order of the General of the Jesuits they could not oppose Aristotle in anything [.. .]." (p. 236) The pressure of this resentment finally erupted in Florence when, on December 21, 1614, Tommaso Caccini, a fiery young Dominican, "denounced from the pulpit of Santa Maria Novella the Galileists, and all mathematicians along with them, as practitioners of diabolical arts and enemies of true religion." (p. 238) While many of the priests in Florence and Rome, especially among the Dominicans, were embarrassed and dismayed by Caccini's bombastic attack, it ignited a potentially explosive series of events that would eventuate in Galileo's trial and condemnation by the Inquisition.

Concerned for Galileo's health which was always precarious, friends like Sagredo and Prince Cesi urged him to remain calm and not enter the fray. But this was difficult, especially as the cardinals of the Inquisition had decided to examine Galileo's "Letter to Castelli" (in which he had presented his views on the conflict between Scriptural assertions and Copernicus' heliocentric position) to see if it contained objectionable material. It also was rumored that Copernicus' *De Revolutionibus* could be declared heretical. Although difficult to believe, some of his opponents were so ignorant and poorly read that they believed that Galileo was the author of Copernicus' work. Thus one detractor, Monsignor Gherardini, Bishop of Fiesole, had to be "tactfully advised that the author of this [heliocentric] doctrine is not at all a living Florentine, but a dead German [*sic*], who printed it 70 years ago and dedicated his book to the Supreme Pontiff." (p. 243; brackets added) However, when a Carmelite Father, P.A. Foscarini of Naples, published a book reconciling all the scriptural passages with the position of Copernicus, Galileo decided to publish openly his own support of Copernicus in a expanded version of his "Letter to Castelli," known as the "Letter to the Grand Duchess Christine."

Furthermore, when Galileo had recovered his health toward the end of 1615 he decided to go to Rome to clear himself of any allegations of heresy and to try to persuade the Church authorities not to condemn the Copernican theory. In contrast to his previously successful visit of 1611, this venture was a tragic failure. As Drake summarizes the proceedings:

In view of all the documents I believe that though the pope

probably wanted the Holy Office to proceed against Galileo personally, Cardinal Bellarmine counseled a less personal procedure. First a technically independent panel of theologians would find against the notions that the earth moved and the sun stood still, and then Galileo would be informed of this and asked to abandon those views. Bellarmine had no doubt that he would agree; a decree of general scope could then be published and the matter would be resolved without alienating either the Medici or the several cardinals who remained favorable to Galileo. The finding of the panel was handed in on 24 February; on the 25th, at the weekly meeting of the cardinals of the Inquisition, the pope instructed Bellarmine in their presence to inform Galileo of it and require him to abandon these opinions. If he resisted, then the commissary of the Inquisition was to instruct Galileo in the presence of a notary and witnesses that if he did not obey he would be jailed. (p. 253)

The meeting between Galileo and Bellarmine took place in the latter's home on 26 February in the presence of a notary, witnesses, and other officials. Although unsigned, the document states that Bellarmine "told Galileo of the official findings against the motion of the earth and stability of the sun," while both he and the commissary of the Inquisition "admonished Galileo in the name of the pope that he must not hold, defend, or teach in any way, orally or in writing, the said propositions on pain of imprisonment," to which Galileo agreed! (p. 253) [25]

In connection with his later trial and condemnation, the important fact is that at this time Galileo agreed not to "hold, defend, or teach in any way, orally or in writing, the said doctrines" of the motion of the earth and stability of the sun. There then followed the edict of 1616 prohibiting all books (such as Foscarini's) attempting to reconcile the Copernican heliocentric system with statements in the Bible, and suspending until corrected Copernicus' *De Revolutionibus* and Diego de Zuñiga's commentary on the Book of Job. No books of Galileo's were mentioned and he did not understand the decree as banning Copernicus' work, but merely suspending it until corrected. (cf. pp. 255-256)

Concerned that his enemies would use this incident to discredit him, Galileo sought an extended audience with the pope to present his case. During the meeting the pope assured him "that he knew Galileo's integrity and sincerity, told him not to worry, said that not only he but the entire Congregation of the Holy Office knew about his unjust persecution, and added the unusual remark that so long as he, Paul V, lived, Galileo remained secure.'' (p. 256) This assurance was remarkable considering that the pope was not known for favoring intellectuals, particularly independent thinkers like Galileo.

When Galileo expressed similar concerns to Bellarmine, the Cardinal also took steps to reassure him, the nature of which would prove significant in the later trial: ''he wrote out a signed statement [it was this statement probably that Galileo believed would exonerate him in the later trial] that Galileo had neither adjured nor done penance, but had merely been informed of the general edict governing all Catholics.'' (p. 256; brackets added) Thus while failing in his primary objective of preventing the Church authorities from taking any action against the Copernican theory, Galileo did succeed in safeguarding his own reputation.

Meanwhile, in the fall of 1618 three comets were sighted that generated considerable interest in Rome, provoking a public lecture by Orazio Grassi, professor of mathematics at the Collegio Romano (known today as the Pontifical Gregorean University), which was later printed and widely read. Although Aristotle had believed that comets were fiery vapors in the air just below the lunar sphere ignited by its rotational motion, a theory generally supported by the Aristotelians, Grassi followed Tycho in interpreting comets as ''imitation planets'' orbiting around the sun close to Venus. The basis for placing the comets in the translunar rather than sublunar world, contrary to Aristotle, was the lack of parallax, that they did not appear enlarged when seen through the telescope (a characteristic of more remote objects), and that they occurred in the vicinity of Venus. Grassi's essay was unpolemical in tone and based on exact observations with an interpretation essentially correct, but it contained some inferences and arguments that were unacceptable to Galileo, especially one claiming (for some obscure reason) that the existence of the comets refuted the Copernican theory. Thus Galileo felt compelled to reply despite the edict of 1616 preventing him from discussing the Copernican hypothesis.

Because Galileo was bedridden at the time, it was decided that his reply would be presented in the form of a series of lectures given to the Florentine Academy by Mario Guiducci who had become Galileo's assistant and who had just been elected Consul of the Academy. Although Guiducci delivered the lectures, he did not disguise the actual author, stating in the published version of his address, ''Discourse on Comets,'' that ''I shall bring before you—not positively but merely probably and with reservations, as I think should be done in so obscure and difficult a matter—those conjectures which have taken shape in the mind of your Academician Galileo.''[26] Moreover, when reading the essay no one could doubt its authorship considering the numerous inferences to celestial phenomena drawn from analogies with ordinary terrestrial experiences, a kind of reasoning almost uniquely characteristic of Galileo.

Considering the unpolemical content of Grassi's essay, the *Discourse* seems unnecessarily caustic and sarcastic. In a period notorious for its vicious polemical attacks, it has to be said that Galileo often excelled in his zeal for disputation, one of the reasons he aroused such heated and determined opposition to his views. In addition, the essay displays his usual disdain of authorities. Criticizing Aristotle's explanation of the generation of heat, he accused him of "relying more upon false and fanciful concepts than upon sensible experiences [. . .]." (pp. 30-31) Strongly opposed to Tycho's unsymmetrical cosmological system, Galileo severely criticized Grassi's Tychonic belief that the comets orbit the sun near Venus, arguing that neither the absence of parallax (which would not apply to comets if they were vapors and not physical bodies) nor the lack of telescopic magnification were reliable indicators of the location of the comets. Furthermore, he maintained that the evidence did not support the idea that the motion of the comets was regular and sustained in a great circle as Tycho had held, (erroneously) concluding that "[w]e are certain, then, of the invalidity of Tycho's reasoning." (p. 59) Claiming that he never had acceded "to the vain distinction (or rather contradiction) between the [terrestrial] elements and the heavens" (p. 53; brackets added), Galileo lightly dismissed the distinction between the celestial and the terrestrial realms so dear to the Aristotelians. Yet it undoubtedly was because of this that he was free to draw conclusions about celestial phenomena based on analogies with terrestrial occurrences. Finally, instead of limiting his rebuttal to Grassi, he unnecessarily criticized the mathematicians of the Collegio Romano who earlier had graciously entertained and honored him.

The predictable result was that Grassi not only was provoked into replying in kind under the guise of a student named "Lothario Sarsi" of Siguenza, but the Jesuits henceforth were galvanized into an opposition determined to thwart Galileo's growing influence. Thus even those, like the present author, who have a tremendous admiration for Galileo's endless curiosity, marvelous intelligence, courageous independence of thought, and unsurpassed dialectical skills must admit that his haughty, contentious character was a major factor in his eventual humiliation by the Church. The one mitigating element is that at that time vitriolic disputes were so common that it is difficult to decide how much to attribute to Galileo's natural vanity and belligerency, and how much to the prevalent style of disputation. In any case, Grassi's response to the *Discourse* claiming to weigh the arguments of Galileo in a "*Libra*

Astronomia" or "*Astronomical Balance*" led to the latter's composing the *Il Saggiatore* or *Assayer*, another play on words signifying a "precise scale" in which he in turn would measure the arguments of Grassi.

Though exceedingly critical of Grassi's explanation of comets, Galileo was uncertain about the correct interpretation. Admitting that he was "vanquished and almost totally blind when it comes to penetrating the secrets of nature" (p. 260), and that he "cannot determine precisely the manner in which comets are produced" (p. 236), he seemed to believe they were a kind of "simulacrum" or "image" created in a diaphanous material similar to vapors by reflecting and refracting the sun's light. (cf. pp. 190, 231, 245). As for their location, the evidence appeared too inconclusive for a confident determination. However, the *Il Saggiatore* is especially important as Galileo's "scientific manifesto" because it contains some of his most explicit statements regarding his philosophy of science.

Concerning heat or fire, he follows the ancient atomists in distinguishing between the sensation of heat as experienced by the person and its inherent physical nature consisting of "a multitude of minute particles having certain shapes and moving with certain velocities." (p. 312) The burning of materials is explained as caused by "fire-corpuscles" (*ignicoli*) or "particles" which, by virtue of their minuteness and velocity, can penetrate materials decomposing them with a rapidity depending upon their density or rarity. (cf. p. 312) This same argument will be used later by atomists like Robert Boyle.

Thus in contrast to the Aristotelians who believed that sensation or perception does not produce, but reproduces or represents sensory qualities and substantial forms in the sensorium of the individual as they exist independently in objects, like the ancient atomists Galileo located sensations solely in the person due to the effects on the various sense organs of the insensible particles that possess the primary qualities of shape, size, solidity, and motion. As he says in a famous passage:

Therefore I say that upon conceiving of a material or corporeal substance, I immediately feel the need to conceive simultaneously that it is bounded and has this or that shape; that it is in this place or that at any given time; that it moves or stays still [. . .]. I cannot separate it from these conditions by any stretch of my imagination. But that it must be white or red, bitter or sweet, noisy or silent, of sweet or foul odor, my mind feels no compulsion to understand as necessary accompaniments [. . .]. For that reason I think that tastes, odors, colors, and so forth are no more than mere names so far as pertains to

the subject wherein they reside, and they have their habitation only in
the sensorium. Thus, if the living creature (*l'animale*) were removed,
all these qualities would be removed and annihilated. (p. 309)

While odors, tastes, sounds, and other sensations or sensory qualities do not
exist in the world independently of the sensing organism, the primary qualities
do. It was Galileo, therefore, prior to Boyle, Locke, Gassendi, or Newton who
(like the ancient atomists) adopted the modern scientific explanation of sensory
qualities as being caused by the impact on the senses of insensible particles
defined in terms of primary qualities. He thus had a nominalistic conception
of sensory qualities and a realistic conception of primary qualities as they exist
in objects.

Despite having antagonized the Jesuits by his essays on the comets,
ironically (in connection with his later trial) the most prominent catholic of all
was very favorably disposed to *Il Saggiatore*. Shortly before completion of
the printing of the essay, Pope Gregory XV (who had succeeded Paul V who
had assured Galileo of his protection) died and was succeeded by Cardinal
Maffeo Barberini who took the name of Urban VIII. This was the occasion
for much rejoicing by Galileo and the members of the Lincean Academy
because the new pope, a learned person, was an ardent admirer of Galileo who
previously had written a poem in his honor and who was well disposed toward
the Lincean Academy. The Linceans, who were sponsoring publication of *Il
Saggiatore*, thus decided to dedicate it to the new pope, redesigning the title
page to show his armorial bearings, three bees. So in addition to Gregory
XV's censor including into the imprimatur a written eulogy of Galileo, the
new pope was so pleased by the essay that "he had portions of it read to him
at table." (p. xix)

Once the *Il Saggiatore* was finished, Galileo resumed work on a tract on
the tides that he had written for Cardinal Alessandro Orsini during his
unsuccessful 1616 visit to Rome. Attempting to account for the ocean tides
in terms of a periodic agitation produced by the two motions of the earth
postulated by Copernicus, this would be the crucial argument in his support of
the Copernican system in the later *Dialogue Concerning the Two Chief World
Systems*. In addition, at this time (1623) he seems to have perfected a
compound microscope (*occhialino*) which he used to observe insects, his
descriptions indicating his usual enthusiastic interest in natural phenomena.
After stating how the instrument was used, he says

I have observed many tiny animals with great admiration, among which the flea is quite horrible, the gnat and the moth very beautiful; and with great satisfaction I have seen how flies and other little animals can walk attached to mirrors, upside down . . . .[27]

Given the enthusiastic reception of his *Essay* by the pope, Galileo considered the moment auspicious for another visit to Rome to seek permission to write his long contemplated work on the relative merits of the Aristotelian or Ptolemaic and Copernican systems. Arriving in Rome in April 1624, he was granted six audiences with the pope "who presented to him silver and gold medals and promised a pension to his son Vincenzio" (p. 289), while also obtaining his primary objective of permission to write on the two cosmological systems. The pope, in fact, expressed the opinion (in Drake's works) "that the Holy Church had never condemned Copernicus as heretical, and never would, holding it only to be rash, there being no fear that anyone would prove it true." (p. 291) Recall, however, that during Galileo's earlier visit to Rome in 1616 he had been told by Cardinal Bellarmine "not to hold, defend, or teach in any way whatsoever, verbally or in writing, the Copernican system." Apparently the new pope was not aware of this prohibition and Galileo, either inadvertently or intentionally neglected to tell him, a decision that would have dire consequences. As Drake states, Galileo

left Rome with assurances from Urban that he was free to write on the two systems of the world provided that he treated them impartially and did not go beyond the astronomical and mathematical arguments on both sides. But because Bellarmine had instructed Galileo in 1616 to regard the admonition given him by the Commissary of the Inquisition as having no official existence, so long as Bellarmine's own words to him were heeded, Galileo never told Urban VIII what had actually taken place on that occasion. In the end that omission on his part turned out to have been a fatal error. (p. 291)

Thus despite Bellarmine's restrictions, now that he had the permission of the pope Galileo felt free to write on the relative merits of the two systems.

In June Guiducci wrote to Galileo about a treatise criticizing the Copernican system written in 1616 by Francesco Ingoli, urging him to reply —perhaps even the pope might have mentioned the treatise during one of their discussions and suggested that he respond. Although somewhat dated, the treatise offered Galileo the opportunity of resuming discussion of the Copernican system, so he composed a lengthy critique known as the "Reply to Ingoli" that anticipated some of the arguments in the later *Dialogue*. Limiting himself to the astronomical and philosophical contents, ignoring the theological arguments, his rationale for replying was to show that catholics were not ignorant of the arguments relating to the Copernican hypothesis—the same justification he would present in the *Dialogue*.

There were two items in the *Reply* that are of special interest: first, his criticism of Ingoli's verbal argument that the earth as the heaviest body belongs in the center or 'lowest' part of the universe, while the ethereal element belonged to the circumference or 'highest' part: "I reply that those ['lowest' and 'highest'] are words and names, proving nothing and having nothing to do with calling anything into existence."[28] This nominalist response is indicative of Galileo's belief that the traditional Aristotelian classifications should not be allowed to settle physical disputes, because often the real issue concerned the validity of the distinctions themselves. Secondly, Galileo indicated, regarding the reference to dropping objects from the masthead of a ship at rest and then in motion, that he had "made the experiment" despite the fact that he had been persuaded by "physical reasoning [. . .] that the effect must turn out as it indeed does."[29] As Drake points out, this statement refutes the erroneous inference, based on a similar assertion in the *Dialogue*, that because he was already convinced of the conclusion he had never performed the experiment on ships. Although Descartes and Mersenne (as well as Koyré) accused Galileo of claiming that he had performed experiments when he had not, I have not found this to be true in terms of the textual evidence, as we shall find. Though only circulated in manuscript form, the *Reply* was widely read and much praised, even by the pope.

A reference by Galileo to his "Dialogue on the Tides" indicates that about this time his 1616 essay on the tides was now taking on the form of his later *Dialogue*. However, ill health and caution led him to postpone work on the *Dialogue* for some time, turning instead to the problem of indivisibles or continuous quantities, along with experiments on magnetism stimulated by his reading of Gilbert's *De Magnete*. Then, after a lapse of three years and at the urging of his friends, he resumed work on the *Dialogue* which he finished by the end of 1629. Clearly the greatest literary and philosophic polemic in the history of science, the *Dialogue* establishes Galileo along with Plato as the foremost dialectician of all time. By critically examining the crucial presuppositions, definitions, and principles of Aristotle's conceptual framework Galileo systematically demolished his venerable cosmology. Following the publication of the *Dialogue* in 1632, the Aristotelian organismic, geocentric cosmology was for all essential purposes destroyed.

NOTES

1. Morton F. Kaplan, ed., *Homage to Galileo* (Cambridge: The MIT Press, 1965), p. ix.

2. The following biographical sketch is based on Stillman Drake, *Galileo At Work* (Chicago: University of Chicago Press, 1978). Like other scholars, I am deeply indebted to Professor Drake's excellent translations of Galileo's works and lifelong devotion to documenting the chronological development of Galileo's investigations and writings, as well as clarifying their origins, meaning, and significance. Unless otherwise indicated, the immediately following textual page references are to this work.

3. Both the unpublished first manuscript and the *De Motu* are reprinted in Stillman Drake and I.E. Drabkin, *Mechanics in Sixteenth-Century Italy* (Madison: The University of Wisconsin Press, 1969), pp. 329-387.

4. Alexandre Koyré, *Galileo Studies*, translated by John Mepham (New Jersey: Humanities Press, 1978), p. 159.

5. Drake (pp. 36-44) provides an excellent account of why Galileo believed that his mechanical theory offered a more concrete and comprehensive explanation of the tides than Kepler's theory.

6. Antonio Favaro, *Le Opere di Galileo Galilei* (Florence, 1890-1909), Vol. 10, p. 68. Quoted from Drake, p. 41. Brackets added.

7. I believe that Galileo did not do the same for his daughters, instead placing them in convents, because of the necessity of providing dowries for them if they had wished to be married. His burden of providing dowries for his sisters left him financially strained in the early years. This is just conjecture, however.

8. For a detailed account see Stillman Drake, *Galileo: Pioneer Scientist* (Toronto: University of Toronto Press, 1990), ch. 1.

9. These calculations became the basis for his Platonic conjecture, in the first day's discussion in the *Dialogue* (p. 29), as to how the "Divine Architect" in creating the universe endowed each planet with their "assigned

tendencies of motion,'' and then allowed them to descend to their preordained orbits with their respective velocities. This probably is the strongest evidence of a Platonic influence on Galileo.

10. Folio, 189r, Vol. 72, Galilean manuscripts. Quoted from Drake, p. 102.

11. Galileo Galilei, *Sidereus Nuncius*, trans. by Albert Van Helden (Chicago: The University of Chicago Press, 1989), pp. 37-38. Unless otherwise indicated, the immediately following textual references are to this work.

12. E. Rosen, *Kepler's Conversation with Galileo's Sideral Messenger* (New York: Johnson Reprint Corp., 1965), pp. 12-13. Quoted from Van Helden, *op. cit.*, p. 94.

13. As Van Helden states: "While in recent times it has become customary in the English language to refer to heavenly bodies with the personal pronoun *it*, until the nineteenth century the Sun, Mercury, Mars, Jupiter, and Saturn were referred to as *he* and the Moon and Venus as *she*."(p. 31, f.n. 10). It also was customary to capitalize the names.

14. Drake, *op. cit.*, p. 168.

15. *Ibid.*, p. 184.

16. Favaro, *Opere*, Vol. 10, pp. 277-278. Quoted from Drake, p. 147.

17. Quoted from Van Helden, pp. 92-93. Italics and brackets added. As an indication of how unscrupulous Horky was, he added a sentence in German (probably to prevent Magini from reading it): "'Unknown to anyone, I have made an impression of the spyglass in wax, and when God aids me in returning home, I want to make a much better spyglass than Galileo's.'" There is no evidence that he was capable of doing so and Magini dismissed him shortly afterwards on other grounds. *Ibid.*, p. 93.

18. Cf. Edward Rosen, *The Naming of the Telescope* (New York: Henry Shuman, 1947), p. 31.

19. The author of "Appeles" was Christopher Scheiner, a mathematician of the Jesuit order who was told by his superior not to publish the book under his own name lest he bring discredit to the order. Cf. Drake, p. 489, f.n. 4. Unless otherwise indicated, the references in the text again will be to Drake's book.

20. Favaro, *Opere*, Vol. 5, pp. 186-188. Quoted from Drake, p. 199. Brackets added.

21. *Ibid.*, pp. 190-191. Drake, p. 200.

22. *Ibid.*, pp. 231-234. Drake, p. 201.

23. *Ibid.*, pp. 281-288. Drake, p. 226.

24. *Ibid.* Brackets added.

25. The procedure is more complicated than described here, although what actually took place is a matter of some conjecture. Drake gives his reconstructed account on pp. 253-256. Another excellent account is that of Giorgio de Santillana, *The Crime of Galileo* (Chicago: University of Chicago Press, 1955).

26. *The Controversy On The Comets Of 1618*, translated by Stillman Drake and C.D. O'Malley (Philadelphia: University of Pennsylvania Press, 1960), p. 24. This volume contains the two essays by Horatio Grassi, the rejoinder by Guiducci (representing Galileo's views), Galileo's *Il Saggiatore* (*The Assayer*), and a brief tract by Kepler, Appendix to the *Hyperaspistes*. The immediately following page references in the text are to this work.

27. *Opere*, Vol. 13, p. 208. Drake, p. 286. On page 290 Drake has reproduced exact drawings of bees made in Rome in 1624 with one of Galileo's microscopes.

28. *Opere*, Vol. 6, p. 535. Drake, p. 293. Brackets added.

29. *Ibid.*, p. 545. Drake, p. 294.

CHAPTER IV

GALILEO GALILEI: FATHER OF MODERN SCIENCE
THE MOMENTOUS YEARS OF ACHIEVEMENT

Philosophy is written in this grand book—I mean the universe—which stands continually open to our gaze, but [. . .] written in the language of mathematics [. . .].[1]

Galileo

As indicated in the previous chapter, Galileo's justification (or pretext) for writing the *Dialogue* was to inform the world beyond the *"transalpine"* boarders of Italy that, despite the edict of 1616 prohibiting catholics from "holding, defending, or teaching" the heliocentric or Copernican theory, Italians (*"particularly those in Rome"*) are as well informed of the issues as anyone else. Moreover, despite Urban VIII's consent that he could write on the two world systems "provided that he dealt with them impartially," Galileo admits that

> *I have taken the Copernican side in the discourse, proceeding as with a pure mathematical hypothesis and striving by every artifice to represent it as superior to supposing the earth motionless—not, indeed, absolutely, but as against the arguments of some professed Peripatetics.*[2]

If he thought that by saying he was treating the Copernican theory as a "hypothesis" and not "absolutely," and that he could count on the pope's avowed admiration of him and his close friendship with the pope's nephew Cardinal Barberini to override the transgressions, he was sadly mistaken as events will show.

THE FIRST DAY

Divided into four days of dialogue, "The First Day" is devoted to refuting the distinction (already rejected in *Il Saggiatore*) between the celestial and the terrestrial worlds, thereby permitting the earth to move in the heavens with the motions attributed to it by Copernicus. The Aristotelian system consisting of a theoretical network of contrasting qualitative concepts such as perfect circular versus imperfect rectilinear motion, natural or simple as opposed to unnatural or violent motions, and the unchanging perfection of the celestial realm in opposition to the contingent transitions in the terrestrial world, Galileo's strategy is to demonstrate the nominal nature or arbitrariness of these concepts and hence the overall weakness of the framework.

While Aristotle defines circular motion as around a center and rectilinear motion as to and from a center, as if these were absolute distinctions, Galileo replies "that in the real universe there are thousands of circular motions" as well as "thousands of motions upward and downward." (p. 16) In addition, why should straight line motion *to and from the center* be called simple and natural when it could be "made in any direction whatever." Furthermore, he accuses Simplicius,[3] who represents the views of the Aristotelians, of circularity in his distinction between simple and mixed motions and simple and compound bodies, thereby bringing out the inadequacy of the distinctions.

> A little while ago you would have it that simple and mixed motions would reveal to me which bodies were compound and which simple. Now you want to use simple and compound bodies to find out which motion is simple, and which is mixed—an excellent rule for never understanding either motions or bodies. (p. 17)

But it is especially Aristotle's classification of perfect circular motion as being essential to the celestial realm, in contrast to the imperfect rectilinear motion of the terrestrial world, that is the focus of Galileo's attack.

> This is the cornerstone, basis, and foundation of the entire structure of the Aristotelian universe, upon which are superimposed all other celestial properties—freedom from gravity and levity, ingenerability, incorruptibility [. . .]. All these properties he attributes to a simple body with circular motion. The contrary qualities of gravity or levity, corruptibility, etc., he assigns to bodies movable in a straight line. (p. 18)

Despite the apparent plausibility of Aristotle's definitions and first principles, Galileo maintains that his position "does present many and grave difficulties" and that "whenever defects are seen in the foundations, it is reasonable to doubt everything else that is built upon them." (p. 18)

To further undermine Aristotle's distinction between the celestial and terrestrial worlds based on the contrast between perfect circular and imperfect rectilinear motions, Galileo argues that because "only circular motion can naturally suit bodies which are integral parts of the universe as constituted in the best arrangement" (p. 32), *this motion is primary also of the terrestrial world.* That terrestrial elements exhibit rectilinear motion is due to their being "found outside their proper places, arranged badly, and are therefore in need of being restored to their natural state by the shortest path." (p. 32) Even then, however, it is false to assume that they "move in a straight line and not in a circular or mixed one." (p. 33)

Although he omits the explanation at this point, he seems to be assuming his later contention that terrestrial objects do not fall simply in a straight line but also partake in the two circular motions of the earth. (cf. p. 139) Furthermore, he denies that motion to and from the center of the universe is natural, arguing that "parts of the earth do not move so as to go toward the center of the universe, but so as to unite with the whole earth" (p. 33), which explains the spherical shape of the earth. Anticipating his heliocentric conclusion, he says

> I might add that neither Aristotle nor you [Simplicius] can ever prove that the earth is *de facto* the center of the universe; if any center may be assigned to the universe, we shall rather find the sun to be placed there, as you will understand in due course. (p. 33; brackets added)

Having denied that circular motion is particular to celestial bodies and therefore cannot be used to distinguish the celestial from the terrestrial world, the argument turns to the "difference Aristotle establishes between celestial and elemental bodies by making the former ingenerable, incorruptible, inalterable, etc., and the latter corruptible, alterable, etc." (p. 38) Once again drawing on the distinction between circular and rectilinear motions, Simplicius argues that since generation and corruption presuppose a contrary (the opposite), and since rectilinear motion has opposites (a beginning and an end) while circular motion being continuous does not, generation and corruption can be true only of the terrestrial world. Galileo counters with a number of arguments, but the essential one is this:

> [. . .] if one denies Aristotle's statement that circular motion does not belong to the earth as it does to celestial bodies, then it follows that whatever is true of the earth as to its being generable, alterable, and so forth, is true of the heavens. (pp. 40-41)

This is reinforced by the claim that if lightness and heaviness are considered contrary qualities of the terrestrial elements, then this contrariety should be attributed to the celestial world also in consequence of its rarity and density (the celestial bodies being denser than the aether of the orbs). (cf. 43)

Simplicius, of course, remains unpersuaded: "[t]his way of philosophizing tends to subvert all natural philosophy, and to disorder and set in confusion heaven and earth." (p. 37) Salviati therefore suggests that they put aside the general question of what motions are proper to specific bodies and "proceed to demonstrations, observations, and particular experiments" (p. 44), by which he means the new evidence provided by the telescope. For example, the surface of the moon as described in the *Sidereus Nuncius* being similar to that of the earth, if the existence of mountains and caverns on the earth were produced by violent eruptions, then perhaps such "mutations" occurred on the moon as well. Furthermore, "[e]xcellent astronomers have observed many comets generated and dissipated in places above the lunar orbit, besides the two new stars of 1572 and 1604, which were indisputably beyond all the planets." (p. 51) Then there is evidence of sunspots the size of the Mediterranean Sea or of Africa that have been observed to have condensed and dissolved "on the face of the sun [. . .] like the clouds on the earth [. . .]." (p. 51)

While ancient astronomers might have been justified in believing that the heavens were immutable and perfect, the new evidence suggests that these convictions have to be revised. Moreover, why should a uniformly unalterable system be deemed more perfect than a variegated changing one, especially since the manifold splendors of the earth depend upon the diversity, multiplicity, and interaction of its elements? Here again we find Galileo challenging the basic presuppositions of Aristotle's system by questioning the soundness of its primary distinctions. Though more diverse and complex than described here, this summary of the arguments of "The First Day" illustrates Galileo's purpose of undermining the qualitative distinctions essential to Aristotle's cosmological framework which, as he was well aware, requires nothing less than "the reform of the human mind [. . .]." (p. 57)

THE SECOND DAY

After declaring that the purpose of the first day's discussion was to remove the "disparity" between the universe's two domains so that the earth can "enjoy the same perfection" as the other celestial bodies and thus imitate them in its motions, he attempts to deflect any criticism of his direct support of the Copernican system by having Salviati declare that he had not "concluded in favor of the opinion that the earth is endowed with the same properties as the heavenly bodies," but merely presented the relevant arguments, leaving "the decision to the judgment of others." (p. 107) He then satirizes the reliance on authority in terms of two stories, the more interesting of which refers to a contemporary philosopher who, when told of the new discoveries using the telescope, maintained that the invention had been anticipated by Aristotle who described being able to see stars during the daytime if observed from the bottom of a deep well.

> Here you have the well, which represents the tube; here the gross vapors, from whence the invention of glass lenses is taken; and finally here is the strengthening of the sight by the rays passing through a diaphanous medium which is denser and darker. (p. 109)

This illustrates the extent to which Peripatetics would go to preserve the priority and perpetual authority of Aristotle.

Being now accustomed to continuous scientific discoveries often with startling consequences, it perhaps is difficult to accept that at the time scholars could have believed that all knowledge was contained in the works of Aristotle. Yet, as Simplicius says: "[t]here is no doubt that whoever has the skill will be able to draw from his books demonstrations of all that can be known; for every single thing is in them." (p. 108) In reply Salviati states that while it is admirable to read and study the works of Aristotle, "I reproach [. . .] those who give themselves up as slaves to him in such a way as to subscribe blindly to everything he says [. . .]." (p. 112) In contrast to relying on authority, Galileo was extolling the continuous development of scientific knowledge based on "observations, demonstrations, and experiments," while also emphasizing the extreme limits of human knowledge:

> [. . .] there is not a single effect in nature, even the least that exists, such that the most ingenious theorists can arrive at a complete understanding of it. This vain presumption of understanding everything can have no other basis than never understanding anything. (p. 101)

In recounting the story of Socrates who was declared by the Delphic Oracle to be the wisest of men because he alone knew the limits of his knowledge, Galileo is identifying his own Socratic role in exposing the tenuousness of

Aristotle's teachings. (cf. p. 101)

But the second day's dialogue is concerned mainly with the diurnal axial rotation attributed to the earth by Copernicus to account for the daily rising and setting of the celestial bodies, and the terrestrial and celestial arguments opposed to it by the Peripatetics. Observing that "whatever motion comes to be attributed to the earth must necessarily remain imperceptible to us"(p. 114) because we also participate in it, the evidence for the motion must be indirect. But, then, as Oresme and Copernicus argued, it is simpler to explain the (apparent) diurnal revolving of the stellar sphere as due to the axial rotation of the much smaller earth than to the spinning of the whole celestial world:

> [. . .] let us consider only the immense bulk of the starry sphere in contrast with the smallness of the terrestrial globe [. . .]. Now if we think of the velocity of motion required to make a complete rotation in a single day and night, I cannot persuade myself that anyone could be found who would think it the more reasonable and credible thing that it was the celestial sphere which did the turning, and the terrestrial globe which remained fixed. (p. 115)

Furthermore, as it was well known that the orbital speeds of the planets become disproportionately slower the further they are from the center, the superior planets moving much more slowly than the inferior (Mercury taking eighty days to complete its orbit while Saturn requires thirty years although their orbital sizes are not in that ratio), a tremendous discontinuity would result if it were necessary "to pass on beyond to another incomparably larger sphere [the stellar], and make this one finish an entire revolution in twenty-four hours."(p. 119; brackets added) In addition, were the whole stellar sphere to revolve this would result in an "immense disparity between the motions of the stars, some of which would be moving very rapidly in vast circles, and others very slowly in little circles, according as they are located farther or closer to the poles."(p. 119) Finally, this daily westward rotation of the entire heavens would be contrary in direction to the common eastward revolution of the planets along the ecliptic, adding an additional asymmetry and improper contrariety to the heavens. Yet all these difficulties could be removed and the appearances saved if, instead of the whole universe rotating westward, an eastward spin were attributed to the earth.

> Make the earth the *primum mobile*; that is, make it revolve upon itself in twenty-four hours in the same way as all the other spheres. Then,

without its imparting such a motion to any other planet or star, all of them will have their risings, settings, and in a word all their other appearances. (p. 122)

But while this solution would save the celestial phenomena, it presented difficulties from a terrestrial standpoint. Particularly, after considering several secondary objections, Galileo turns to the crucial terrestrial argument against the earth's motion, the rebuttal of which brought out an unexpected feature of scientific discoveries, namely, *that often they are counterintuitive.* Aristotle's argument (and its various exemplifications) is perfectly reasonable and yet it does not correctly represent the actual conditions in nature. As recounted by Salviati:

> Aristotle says, then, that a most certain proof of the earth's being motionless is that things projected perpendicularly upward are seen to return by the same line to the same place from which they were thrown, even though the movement is extremely high. This, he argues, would not happen if the earth moved, since in the time during which the projectile is moving upward and then downward it is separated from the earth, and the place from which the projectile began its motion would go a long way toward the east, thanks to the [eastward] revolving of the earth, and the falling projectile would strike the earth that distance away from the place in question. (p. 139; brackets added)

Also discussed is a variant of this argument introduced by Tycho involving two cannon balls shot with the same force from an identical position and elevation but in opposite directions, one to the east and the other to the west. During the time that the projectiles are in flight the independent rotation of the earth would carry the cannon eastward so that the range of the missiles measured from the cannon would be either lengthened or shortened depending on the direction.

> For when the ball goes toward the west, and the cannon, carried by the earth, goes east, the ball ought to strike the earth at a distance from the cannon equal to the sum of the two motions, one made by itself to the west, and the other by the gun, carried by the earth, toward the east. On the other hand, from the trip made by the ball shot toward the east it would be necessary to subtract that which was

made by the cannon following it. (p. 126)

A third "experiment" involved shooting a crossbow in opposite directions from an open carriage drawn by galloping horses. In this example, especially, it would seem that the arrow shot in the direction opposite the motion of the carriage would travel farther (as measured from the position of the carriage when both arrows strike the ground) than that shot in the same direction because of the forward velocity of the carriage. (cf. pp. 168-169)

While the conclusion from these arguments that the distance (or in the case of the vertically falling object the path) of the projectiles would be affected by their motion in relation to the changing position of the earth seems perfectly reasonable, it depends upon the assumption that the two motions are *independent*. However, while satisfying the Aristotelian principle that an object cannot participate in two motions at the same time, it does not conform to physical reality. As Oresme and Copernicus had argued earlier and Galileo reiterates, if in the above examples the motion of the projectile is not considered independently of the motion of its origin but seen as a function of *two motions*, the *specific* motion conveyed to it along with the *shared* motion of the vehicle (earth or carriage) of projection, then the argument fails. It is because everything on the earth participates in the common motion of the earth, that this motion cancels out leaving only the specific motion conveyed to the projectile which, since its magnitude is the same regardless of the direction, will alone determine the form or length of the trajectory.

Consider a stone descending perpendicularly to the surface of the earth. Because it is impossible to test experimentally whether a vertically falling stone would exhibit a different trajectory if the earth moved than if it were stationary, an analogous situation is considered, that of dropping a stone from the masthead of a ship at rest and under sail. According to Aristotle, when the ship is at rest the stone will fall parallel to the mast striking the deck the same distance from the mast as it began because its trajectory is a function of one motion. In contrast, if the ship were under sail as the stone fell, then during the descent the ship would move forward so the trajectory would not be a straight drop but an oblique descent reflecting *the two independent motions* of the vertical path of the stone and the forward movement of the ship.

According to Galileo, however, because the falling stone (and the observer) would participate in the forward motion of the ship, the only motion that would be apparent would be the vertical descent of the object parallel to the masthead. Thus the common movement is as if it did not exist; it remains insensible, imperceptible, and without any effect whatever. All that remains observable is the motion which we lack, and that is the grazing drop to the base of the 'mast'. (p. 171)

When Simplicius continues to support the Aristotelian interpretation he is asked whether he had ever seen the experiment performed, whereupon he replies that he had not but that he was certain that "the authorities" who adduced the former conclusion must have, whereupon Salviati states:

You yourself are sufficient evidence that those authorities may have offered it without having performed it [. . . .] For anyone who does will find that the experiment shows exactly the opposite of what is written; that is, it will show that the stone always falls in the same place on the ship, whether the ship is standing still or moving with any speed you please. (p. 144)

Because the example of the earth is analogous to that of the ship, from the fact that the stone falls straight down regardless of whether the ship is in uniform motion or at rest and thus not indicative of either motion, "nothing can be inferred about the earth's motion or rest from the stone falling always perpendicularly" to the earth. (pp. 144-145) It is at this point in the *Dialogue* that Simplicius elicits from Galileo the response that even "[w]ithout experiment, I am sure that the effect will happen as I tell you, because it must happen that way" (p. 145), leading some commentators to the erroneous conclusion that he had never performed the experiment.[4]

The example of the arrows being shot from a crossbow in opposite directions in a rapidly drawn open carriage is somewhat more complex. It certainly seems that while the two arrows were in flight the carriage would have moved away from the one fired in the opposite direction and toward the one in the same direction, thus the distances measured from the carriage at the instant the arrows landed could not be the same. Here again, however, the argument overlooks a crucial factor, namely, that the motion of the arrows *is not independent of the motion of the carriage.*

Specifically, when the motion of the carriage is *added* to the speed of the arrow when it is in the same direction but *subtracted* when it is in the opposite direction, just compensating for the difference in distance due to the forward movement of the carriage, the changing position of the carriage is eliminated as a factor, thus the arrows strike the ground the same distance apart. In fact, this illustrates an alternative way of explaining the above examples, namely, that the motion of the ship, earth, or carriage conveys to the projectile an "impetus" which is the source of the second, though unobserved, motion: "the impetus of the ship's motion remains indelibly impressed on the stone after it has separated from the mast [. . .]." (p. 154) The conclusion appears counterintuitive only if one fails to realize that the trajectories of the arrows incorporate the two causes, the *similar cause* of the crossbow and the *opposite motion* of the carriage. As Salviati states, "the course of the carriage itself regulates the flights" (p. 170), so that they are equal.

The other objections to the earth's motion are easily disposed of. If the earth moved with the two motions (in today's figures, an axial diurnal rotation of 1000 miles per hour and an orbital revolution of about 20 miles per second), then why do not birds have difficulty keeping up with the earth's motion? The answer is that "the air [. . .] following naturally the whirling of the earth, takes along the birds and everything else that is suspended in it, just as it carries the clouds." (p. 183) For the same reason, we do not feel a rush of air as the earth rotates because the air "participates" in the earth's rotation.

Again presenting an example used by Oresme and Copernicus, Galileo says that if we observe the behavior of any object (flying birds, thrown balls, or dripping water) in a ship's cabin below the deck, "so long as the motion is uniform" you "will discover not the least change in all the effects named, nor could you tell from any of them whether the ship was moving or standing still." (p. 187) Nonetheless, would not the combined motions result in objects on the earth being "hurled into the sky by such precipitous whirling?" (p. 132) The answer is "no" if the assumption is discarded that only straight line motion is natural to earthly objects with the consequence that the combined circular movements being forced or unnatural are destructive; if circular motion is natural to earthly bodies, as Galileo is attempting to demonstrate, then the "parts [of the earth] would also be moved circularly" without any destructive affect. (p. 133; brackets added)

While this reply is formulated in Aristotelian terms, it does not reflect our current explanation that the reason objects are not thrown from the whirling earth is that the gravitational pull downward is stronger than the centrifugal force extending outward. Yet even though he lacked the concept of a gravitational force generated by the mass of the earth, and the terms 'centrifugal' and centripetal,'[5] Galileo provided an additional explanation that approximated these forces. Arguing that the force of projection is proportional to the speed of the spinning surface but decreases as the diameter of the surface increases, he concluded that an object would not be projected from a revolving surface if the natural gravitational tendency downward were greater than the outward propelling force caused by the speed of rotation relative to the circumference of the spinning surface. Thus Salviati concludes that to "have projection occur, it is required that the impetus along the tangent prevail over the tendency along the secant" (p. 196), while "it is obvious that the larger the wheel becomes, the more the cause for projection is diminished." (p. 217) In addition to these arguments there are numerous "digressions," but the strategy is the same: to expose the presuppositions in the arguments opposing the diurnal rotation of the earth that make them appear valid, and then show how the axial rotation follows naturally if these presuppositions are rejected.

Given the persuasiveness of his arguments despite the obligation to treat both positions impartially, Galileo apparently thought it prudent to have Salviati state that in his role of defending Copernicus he was merely play acting:

> Before going further I must tell Sagredo that I act the part of Copernicus in our arguments and wear his mask. As to the internal effects upon me of the arguments which I produce in his favor, I want you to be guided not by what I say when we are in the heat of acting out our play, but after I have put off the costume, for perhaps then you shall find me different from what you saw of me on the stage. (p. 131)

Not withstanding such disclaimers attempting to show that he was complying with the pope's instruction to treat both systems impartially, he avows his admiration for the Copernicans and his disdain of the Peripatetics and Ptolemaics because the former had carefully studied their adversaries arguments, while the latter had seldom examined the reasons supporting the Copernican position:

> [. . .] considering that everyone who followed the opinion of Copernicus had at first held the opposite, and was very well informed concerning the arguments of Aristotle and Ptolemy, and that on the other hand none of the followers of Ptolemy and Aristotle had been formerly of the Copernican opinion and had left that to come round to Aristotle's view—considering these things, I say, I commenced to believe that one who forsakes an opinion which he imbibed with his milk and which is supported by multitudes, to take up another that has few followers and is rejected by all the schools and that truly seems

to be a gigantic paradox, must of necessity be moved, *not to say compelled*, by the most effective arguments. (pp. 128-129; italics added)

This was another passage in Galileo's book that the Church commission cited as offensive: "[t]hat he represented it to be an argument for the truth that Ptolemaics became Copernicans, but not vice versa." (p. 474, note 103) But his harshest criticism is reserved for those who rely on authority rather than experimental inquiry as a criterion of truth, as Salviati's biting rebuke of Simplicius indicates:

I see that you have hitherto been one of that herd who, in order to learn how matters [. . .] take place, and in order to acquire a knowledge of natural effects, do not betake themselves to ships or crossbows or cannons, but retire into their studies and glance through an index and a table of contents to see whether Aristotle has said anything about them; and, being assured of the true sense of his text, consider that nothing else can be known. (p. 185)

Having accomplished the primary purpose of the discourse of the second day, that of showing that attributing a diurnal rotation to the earth is not as absurd as the Aristotelians claimed, the rest of the *Dialogue* is devoted to more general considerations. Although there is insufficient space to examine these various arguments, one problem of interpretation arising in these discussions is of special interest. Ever since Alexandre Koyré published his very influential *Galileo Studies*, the question of the role of mathematics in scientific investigations and *whose conception most influenced Galileo* has been much discussed. The various contenders for this honor are the Pythagoreans, Plato, Aristotle, and Archimedes.

THE INFLUENCES ON GALILEO'S THOUGHT

It would seem, perhaps, that at least Aristotle could be *eliminated* since Galileo constantly opposed the authority of Aristotle (along with his negligence in not testing ordinary observations, his excessive reliance on qualitative distinctions and definitions, and his preference for logic over mathematics in scientific demonstrations) with his own emphasis on experimentally controlled observations and the use of mathematics in empirical inquiry. As Simplicius asserts, if one rejects the "senses and experience" as "our guide in philosophizing," then "'the criterion of science itself will be badly shaken if not completely overturned.'"(p. 248) In another passage he states even more explicitly the Peripatetic philosopher's conception of the aim of scientific inquiry in contrast to that of "mathematicians" such as Copernicus, Kepler, and Galileo.

> Philosophers occupy themselves principally about universals. They find definitions and criteria, leaving to the mathematicians certain fragments and subtleties [. . .]. Aristotle contented himself with defining excellently what motion in general is, and showing the main attributes of local motion [. . .] and for the accelerated motions he was content to supply the causes of acceleration, leaving to mechanics or other low artisans the investigation of the ratios of such accelerations and other more detailed features. (pp. 163-164)

But before taking this statement as eliminating Aristotle, it must be remembered that Aristotle's classifications and definitions were an essential preliminary stage in the attempt to understand motion. Moreover, despite Simplicius' derisive reference to "the investigation of ratios" as belonging to "mechanics or other low artisans," Aristotle himself attempted to find ratios wherever possible, as his definition of uniform motion and law that objects fall with an acceleration proportional to their weights and inversely proportional to the medium, testify. That these early efforts were necessarily simplistic does not negate the fact that it was Aristotle, not Plato, who initiated these inquiries. Galileo's admiration for Aristotle is indicated in his description of him as "a man of brilliant intellect [. . .]." (p. 321)

As we noted in Chapter I, when the fourteenth century Mertonians and Parisians attempted to explain and mathematize motion, they were motivated by and working within Aristotle's theoretical framework. Similarly, when the founders of modern science tried to find alternative explanations as well as a more satisfactory mechanical theory, they usually began by criticizing the conceptions and arguments of Aristotle. If imitation is the highest form of flattery, then criticism is the strongest sign of recognition. Simplicius' statement does reveal, however, a fundamental difference between the approaches of Aristotle and Galileo, namely, the former's emphasis on causal explanations in contrast to Galileo's belief that it was fruitless at that time to seek causes of natural phenomena, in contrast to discovering measurable correlations in phenomena, such as the law of free fall. Further evidence of

Galileo's respect for Aristotle—but not for the Peripatetics—occurs in an exchange of letters two years before his death with the Aristotelian Fortunio Liceti. In one letter Galileo says "I claim (and surely believe) that I observe more religiously the [. . .] Aristotelian teachings than do many who wrongfully put me down as averse from good Peripatetic philosophy [. . .]."[6] These "teachings" of Aristotle, as Galileo goes on to elaborate in a succeeding letter, comprise

> our taking care to avoid fallacies in reasoning [. . .] and using it adroitly to syllogize and to deduce from the conceded premises the necessary conclusion; and [. . .] the putting of experience before any reasoning, [. . .] it not being possible that a sensible experience is contrary to truth [. . .] a precept much esteemed by Aristotle and placed far in front of the value and force of the authority of everybody in the world.[7]

In this passage Galileo acknowledges Aristotle's contribution to the principles of valid inference in logical deductions and to the significance of being guided by "sensible experience" in one's reasoning, rather than just following fanciful *a priori* conjectures (as tended to be true of Parmenides and the Pythagoreans), but he realized that Aristotle's method was still inadequate. Emphasizing that direct observations, although initially necessary, are not a sufficient basis of philosophizing as the geocentric perspective illustrates, Galileo criticized the Peripatetics for blindly adhering to Aristotle's arguments despite the new telescopic evidence. He also stressed the importance of mathematical demonstrations over logical inferences. Nonetheless, he concluded by saying "I am sure that if Aristotle should return to earth he would accept me among his followers [. . .]."[8] This hardly constitutes a repudiation of Aristotle for Plato!

While the question of influence initially may have *seemed* to *preclude* Aristotle, an exchange between Simplicius and Salviati at the very beginning of the *Dialogue* might appear to *proclaim* Plato. Following a discussion as to whether the three dimensions of the cosmos are a sign of its perfection, as Aristotle claimed, Salviati replies that he has "no compulsion to grant that the number three is a perfect number" (p. 111), whereupon he is rebuked by Simplicius: "You, who are a mathematician, and who believe many Pythagorean philosophical opinions, now seem to scorn their mysteries." (p. 11) To this Salviati gives the significant reply:

That the Pythagoreans held the science of numbers in high esteem, and that Plato himself admired the human understanding and believed it to partake of divinity simply because it understood the nature of number, I know very well; nor am I far from being of the same opinion. (p. 11)

This statement, along with the fact that Salviati invokes the image of Socrates and uses the Socratic method of questioning, led Koyré to affirm that the "allusions to Plato" and "references to the Socratic method" are not to be interpreted as merely "stylistic ornaments" but "must be taken absolutely seriously [. . .]."[9] Moreover, because Plato's view that "understanding numbers partakes of divinity" conformed to Galileo's repeated assertion that although "*extensively*" the scope of human knowledge comes to nothing, "*intensively*" our knowledge of some mathematical and geometrical propositions "equals the Divine in objective certainty" (p. 103), Koyré concluded "that Galileo is a Platonist."[10]

I believe Koyré became convinced of this, despite conclusive evidence to the contrary, because he overlooked the difference between Plato's conception of the role of mathematics in scientific inquiry and that of the Pythagoreans, Archimedes, and Galileo. Koyré quotes with approval Jacopo Mazzoni's description of the contrasting conceptions of mathematics held by Plato and Aristotle:

'Plato believed that mathematics is particularly well suited to physical speculations. This is why on several occasions he made use of it in resolving questions in physics. But Aristotle's view was diametrically opposed to this, and he attributed Plato's errors to his love of mathematics.' [11]

But Koyré should have known that Mazzoni's characterization of the difference between Platonism and Aristotelianism was false. Even at that time anyone who had read Plato carefully would see that he did not believe that mathematics was "well suited to physical speculations" nor to "resolving questions in physics." On the contrary, Plato was severely critical of mathematicians who saw any value in applying mathematics to physical investigations:

[. . .] no one who has even a slight acquaintance with geometry will deny that the nature of this science is in flat contradiction with the absurd language used by mathematicians [Pythagoreans like Archytas,

Eudoxus, and Menaechmus] [. . .] [who] constantly talk of 'operations' like 'squaring,' 'applying,' 'adding,' and so on, as if the object were to *do* something, whereas the true purpose of the whole subject is knowledge—knowledge, moreover, of what eternally exists, not of anything that comes to be this or that at some time and ceases to be.[12]

For Plato, only that which was infallible and had the real as its object could be called knowledge (*episteme*), hence only belief (*doxa*) could be attained of physical objects in the imperfect domain of becoming and perishing. The value of mathematics and geometry was to direct the mind away from the sensory world of appearances to the eternal, ideal realm of Forms: "[g]eometry will be suitable or not, according as it makes us contemplate reality or the world of change."[13] Dialectics as the search for the essential meaning of terms as exemplified in the archetypical Forms was the highest method of inquiry, not mathematics.[14]

On Plato's view of knowledge there could be no natural science as advocated by Galileo, one consisting of observation, experimentation, and mathematical demonstrations based on empirical measurements and discovered correlations. Like geometry, arithmetic or "the science of numbers" derived its value from "leading the mind upwards and forcing it to reason about pure numbers, refusing to discuss collections of material things which can be seen and touched."[15] In fact, the highest or purest form of knowledge could be attained best by a disembodied soul. It was this very idealistic conception of mathematics along with Speucippus' attempt, as Plato's successor as head of the Academy, "to turn philosophy into mathematics" that Aristotle was objecting to, not the application of mathematics to physical problems.

The contrast between Plato's view of mathematics and that of the Pythagoreans is particularly striking, as illustrated in a statement by Archytas, a contemporary of Plato:

Mathematicians seem to have excellent discernment, and it is no way strange that they should think correctly concerning the nature of particular existences [. . .]. Indeed, they have handed on to us a clear judgment on the speed of constellations and their rising and settings, as well as on geometry and numbers and solid geometry, and not least on music; for these mathematical studies appear to be related.[16]

It was because they believed that mathematics could be fruitfully applied in such sciences as astronomy and physics, as well as music, that the Pythagorean tradition produced Philolaus, Heraclides, Aristarchus, Apollonius, Archimedes, and Ptolemy—all referred to as "Pythagoreans" by both Copernicus and Galileo.

Even in astronomy Plato did not believe that mathematicians could discern precise laws of motion based on observation:

> These intricate traceries in the sky are, no doubt, the loveliest and most perfect of material things, but still part of the visible world, and therefore they fall far short of the true realities—the real relative velocities, in the world of pure numbers and all perfect geometrical figures, of the movements which carry round the bodies involved in them.[17]

Unlike Copernicus who believed that calendar reform was possible if based on exact astronomical observations interpreted within the correct (heliocentric) theory, Plato claimed that the "genuine astronomer [. . .] will think it absurd to believe that these visible material things" could provide precise enough information to "find exact truth in them."[18] Yet despite this contrary evidence, Koyré claims that "the mathematisation of physics *is* Platonism"[19] and that Archimedes—although his genius lay in solving both theoretical and practical mathematical problems—was "the greatest of the Platonists [. . .]."[20] But the person who initiated investigations into statics, hydrostatics, and mechanics that was so fruitfully pursued by Archimedes (and Galileo) was Aristotle, not Plato.

Significantly, Galileo directly addresses the problem raised by Plato, as to whether such a precise, abstract, formal discipline as mathematics can be effectively applied to the imperfect, concrete, physical world, and then has the Aristotelian Simplicius present the Platonic objection to this: "it is the imperfection of matter which prevents things taken concretely from corresponding to those considered in the abstract." (p. 207) Sounding exactly like Plato, Simplicius adds that "[w]hat I mean about these angles [. . .] and ratios is that they all go by the board for material and sensible things."(p. 203) In contrast, Salviati presents Galileo's view that mathematics can be applied to the natural world if the scientist eliminates the irrelevant data:

> [. . .] the mathematical scientist (*filosofo geometra*), when he wants to recognize in the concrete the effects which he has proved in the abstract, must deduct the material hindrances, and if he is able to do

so, I assure you that things are in no less agreement than arithmetical computations.   The errors, then, lie not in the abstractness or concreteness, not in geometry or physics, but in a calculator who does not know how to make a true accounting. (pp. 207-208)

As Galileo has Sagreto state, in direct opposition to Plato, "trying to deal with physical problems without geometry is attempting the impossible." (p. 203)

The final refutation of Koyré's argument that Galileo was a Platonist occurs in Galileo's famous statement about the book of nature being written in the language of mathematics. While Plato held that arithmetic and geometry referred to the independently subsisting mathematical objects in the Realm of Forms, and thus could *not* be applied to the natural world, Galileo argued that the *only* language by which nature could be understood *was* mathematics:

> Philosophy is written in this grand book—I mean the universe—which stands continually open to our gaze, but it cannot be understood unless one first learns to comprehend the language and interpret the characters in which it is written. It is written in the language of mathematics, and its characters are triangles, circles, and other geometrical figures, without which it is impossible to understand a single word of it; without these, one is wandering about in a dark labyrinth.[21]

That Galileo was not a Platonist regarding the role of mathematics in scientific inquiry does not mean, of course, that he did not admire Plato nor at times favor Plato over Aristotle in his disputations with the Peripatetics. Since the Platonists extolled mathematics over sensory knowledge, it was natural for Galileo to align himself with them when it benefited his arguments, even though his conception of the applied function of mathematics was opposed to theirs. But his highest praise was reserved for Archimedes whose inquiries in statics and hydrostatics were the model for his own investigations. As was true of Archimedes, mathematical demonstrations were the crucial element in Galileo's scientific method, along with his special emphasis on observation and experimentation. In the *La Bilancetta* he extols "'the writings of that divine man (which moreover are extremely easy to understand so that all other geniuses are inferior to that of Archimedes [. . .].'''(p. 479, f.n. 204). Thus in answer to whose influence was strongest, I believe the evidence clearly indicates that the impact of the Pythagoreans was foremost in astronomy and that of Archimedes in mechanics, although neither the influence of Aristotle especially nor that of Plato can be discounted.

THE THIRD DAY

Turning now to the discussion of the third day, this is concerned mainly with refuting arguments opposed to attributing an annual orbital revolution to the earth. Following a long rebuttal of Chiaramonti's attempt to prove that the nova of 1572 was in the sublunar realm contrary to the calculations of Tycho and most other astronomers, Galileo addresses the problem of the annual revolution assigned the earth by Aristarchus and Copernicus. When Simplicius identifies the greatest difficulty in accepting such a motion, that of removing the earth from its natural stationary position in the center of the universe and conferring on it a revolution along the circumference of a circle, Salviati initially replies that the concept of a center presupposes a finite spherical universe, whereas it has not been "proved whether the universe is finite and has a shape, or whether it is infinite and unbounded." (p. 319) However, as this was one of the theses that led to Bruno's martyrdom, it is quickly dropped in favor of the supposition that the universe is spherically finite. Salviati then confronts Simplicius with the question whether, if forced to choose, Aristotle would prefer that the earth be in the middle of the universe (even if it were not the center of the spheres) or that the middle be the common center of the celestial spheres, though located apart from the earth. Simplicius agrees that it would be preferable if the celestial orbs had a common center, but wonders why the earth cannot be located there.

This sets the stage for the following discussion because Galileo (like Copernicus) is going to show that based on the astronomical evidence a harmoniously integrated system of planetary orbits can be constructed only by placing the sun, not the earth, at the center. The primary evidence is the fact that during their orbital revolutions the planets are found to vary markedly in their distances from the earth, an impossibility if their circular orbits were centered on the earth. When Simplicius objects that even if true, this does not show that the sun is the center, Salviati replies:

This is reasoned out from finding the three outer planets—Mars, Jupiter, and Saturn—always quite close to the earth when they are in opposition to the sun, and very distant when they are in conjunction with it. This approach and recession is of such moment that Mars when close looks sixty times as large as when it is most distant. Next,

it is certain that Venus and Mercury must revolve around the sun,
because of their never moving far away from it, and because of their
being seen now beyond it and now on this side of it, as Venus'
changes of shape conclusively prove. (p. 322)

Thus unlike the daily cycle that could be explained either by the Earth's
rotation or by the turning of the heavens in the opposite direction, "this annual
motion, mixing with the individual motions of all the planets, produces a great
many oddities which in the past have baffled all the greatest men in the
world." (p. 322)

Given the evidence of the oppositions and conjunctions of the planets to
the sun as seen from the earth, Salviati shows why the inferior planets must
have their orbits below that of the earth and the superior above it. Similar
reasoning shows the moon's orbit circles the earth. As for the fixed stars,
rather than distribute them in an infinite space, they are placed within an orb
at different altitudes between "two spherical surfaces—a very distant concave
one, and another closer [. . .]." (p. 326) Thus based on the astronomical
evidence, the system of planetary orbits conforms to that described by
Aristarchus and Copernicus leading Sagredo to ask why, if "this very ancient
arrangement of the Pythagoreans is so well accommodated to the appearances
[. . .] it has found so few followers in the course of centuries [. . .]." (p. 327)
To this Salviati gives Galileo's famous reply:

> No, Sagredo, my surprise is very different from yours. You wonder
> that there are so few followers of the Pythagorean opinion, whereas I
> am astonished that there have been any up to this day who have
> embraced and followed it. Nor can I ever sufficiently admire the
> outstanding acumen of those who have [. . .] through sheer force of
> intellect done such violence to their own senses as to prefer what
> reason told them over that which sensible experience plainly showed
> them to the contrary [. . .] that Aristarchus and Copernicus were able
> to make reason so conquer sense that, in defiance of the latter, the
> former became mistress of their belief. (pp. 327-328)

After dismissing several common sense objections to the rotation of the
earth, that mountains stretching upwards during half of its rotation would
extend downward during the second half or that someone in the depths of a
well could never observe the sky because the rim of the well would pass by
too quickly, Salviati takes up the more serious difficulties of the enormous

variations predicted in the sizes of Mars and Venus when they approach and recede from the earth which are not observed by the naked eye. After expressing his admiration for Copernicus who was able to disregard these objections owing to the other advantages of the heliocentric system, Salviati says that because the invention of the telescope removes many of the limitations of ordinary observation these calculated variations in size have been confirmed, vindicating Copernicus' earlier judgment. (cf. 335-339) He then takes up the objection previously answered in *Sidereus Nuncius*, that it is peculiar that the Moon circles the Earth while all the other planets revolve around the sun. Here again the telescope has provided new evidence, the "Jovian Moons," whose revolutions around Jupiter "removes this apparent anomaly of the earth and moon moving conjointly." (p. 340) Having eliminated these objections, Salviati reaffirms Galileo's commitment to scientific realism by emphasizing that "saving the phenomena" by various artifices, though it may pacify the astronomer as a *calculator*, will not satisfy the astronomer as *scientist*. Acknowledging that Copernicus in his early studies could have

> rectified astronomical science upon the old Ptolemaic assumptions [. . .] this was still taking them separately planet by planet. He goes on to say that when he wanted to put together the whole fabric from all individual constructions, there resulted a monstrous chimera composed of mutually disproportionate members, incompatible as a whole. Thus however well the astronomer might be satisfied merely as a calculator, there was no satisfaction and peace for the astronomer as a scientist. And since he very well understood that although the celestial appearances might be saved by means of assumptions essentially false in nature, it would be very much better if he could derive them from true suppositions [. . .].[22] (p. 341; italics added)

With this the disputants go on to consider three more issues, sunspots, the absence of parallax, and retrograde motion, the latter explained in the diagram below.

Fig. 1. In the diagram below from the *Dialogue*, Galileo shows how the various positions (regressions and advances) of Jupiter in the second circle beyond the sun 'O' changes in relation to points on the stellar sphere (the furthest sphere) as seen from various positions on the earth (the first sphere), as it revolves in its orbit from B to M.

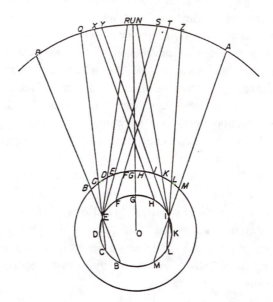

With regard to retrograde motion, Galileo used Copernicus' argument to show that when a planet's movement, as seen from the earth against the background of the fixed stars, appears to pause, regress, then advance again, this actually is caused by the unnoticed change in position of the observer relative to the planet as the earth revolves in its orbit. With this explanation a number of the epicycles introduced by Ptolemy to account for retrograde motion could be eliminated. As for the contentious sunspots, repeating the argument used previously in his "Letters to Mark Welser" in reply to Scheiner's claim that they were stars circulating the sun analogous to the satellites of Jupiter, Galileo points out that their shapes, location, and duration were inconsistent with rotating stars, suggesting a formation similar to clouds on the earth which appear to revolve on the sun's surface due to the latter's rotation on its axis. (cf. p. 345) From this Galileo deduced that the "sun, being located at the center of the ecliptic, rotated upon an axis that was not perpendicular but tilted to the plane of the ecliptic." (cf. pp. 351-352)

Regarding the lack of an observed parallax, the critics of Copernicus argued that if the annual revolution of the earth produces such apparent changes in the orbital motions of the planets as their retrogressions along with their approaches and recessions, then analogous displacements should be observed among the fixed stars. As Simplicius asserts, "the earth's orbit would necessarily cause changes and variations in the stellar sphere,"but since no such changes are observed "the annual movement of the earth is rendered untenable and is overthrown." (pp. 364-365) If, to avoid this conclusion, one assumes that the stellar sphere must be extremely distant and enormously large, then it was inferred that "in order for a fixed star to look as large as it does, it would actually have to be so immense in bulk as to exceed the earth's orbit—a thing [. . .] entirely unbelievable." (p. 372) To this Salviati replies that since the objectors have never determined precisely what changes should occur, it is difficult to know what to look for and what to conclude if no alterations are apparent.

> Not having heard anyone go on to say what, in particular, these visible changes ought to be, and in what stars, I think it quite reasonable to suppose that those who say generally that the fixed stars remain unchanged have not understood (and perhaps have not even tried to find out) the nature of these alternations, or what it is that [. . .] ought to be seen. (p. 378)

Furthermore, since it is in relation to the background of the fixed stars that the annual revolution of the earth can be detected as indicated in the movements of the planets, the fact that there is no additional sphere that could serve as a background for noting the reflected revolution of the earth in relation to the sphere of the fixed stars, one does not know what to expect. (cf. p. 382) Nonetheless, the fact that most astronomical observations support the heliocentric theory leads Salviati to conclude, like Copernicus, that it is clearly the most probable of the two systems.

> See, then, how two simple noncontradictory motions assigned to the earth, performed in periods well suited to their sizes, and also conducted from west to east as in the case of all movable world bodies, supply adequate causes for all the visible phenomena. These phenomena can be reconciled with a fixed earth only by renouncing all the symmetry that is seen among the speeds and sizes of moving bodies, and attributing an inconceivable velocity to an enormous sphere beyond all the others, while lesser spheres move very slowly. Besides, one must make the motion of the former contrary to that of the latter, and to increase the improbability, must have the highest sphere transport all the lower ones opposite to their own inclination. I leave to your judgment which has the more likelihood in it. (p. 396)

The dialogue of the third day concludes with references to Gilbert's magnetic theory which does not add significantly to the discussion. While Galileo says he has "the highest praise, admiration, and envy" for Gilbert, he wished Gilbert were "a little more of the mathematician" and had "especially a thorough grounding in geometry" which would have rendered his proofs and reasons more "rigorous." (p. 406)

THE FOURTH DAY

Turning finally to the dialogue of the fourth and last day, this contains the greatest irony in what surely was a most ironic life, in every sense of that word. Acknowledging that from an astronomical point of view the relativity of motions leaves it inconclusive as to whether the heavens revolve around a central stationary earth or that the two motions attributed to the earth produce some of the apparent motions of the celestial bodies, Galileo sought in the ebb and flow of the tides a more concrete proof of the earth's motion. He was so convinced that the variation in velocity produced by the combined daily rotation and annual revolution of the earth caused the tides, thereby confirming the reality of these motions, that he had intended to include in the title of the *Dialogue* a reference to the tides, had not this been prohibited by the pope.

What creates the irony is that despite the climactic nature of the argument based on his detailed investigations and knowledge of the various kinds of tides and the reasonableness of his conclusions supporting his conviction, it was false. The correlation between the periodic rhythm of the tides and the cyclical motion of the moon was so striking that most astronomers throughout the past had attributed the tides to a mysterious effect of the moon. Kepler had argued in the *Astronomia Nova* of 1609 that since all bodies exert a mutually attractive force on each other proportional to their respective masses, the moon must attract the waters on the earth so that if this force were not counteracted by the earth's own pull on the oceans they would rise to the moon. Convinced that this explanation depended on the ancient belief in mysterious hidden forces or occult causes, Galileo rejected it for a "mechanical explanation" (probably reinforced by his opposition to Kepler's mystical, Neoplatonic tendencies) that remained "within the bounds of nature." (cf. pp. 416-419, 445, 462)

Noting that the ebb and flow of the oceans manifest three periods, the daily tide, a monthly phase, and an annual cycle, Galileo attempts to explain each of these. The primary effect is the conspicuous rising and lowering of the tides in six hour intervals, roughly twice a day. Drawing an analogy with barges carrying fresh water to Venice, wherein the water is seen to rush back and forth either as the barge dips into the sea so that the prow and stern are alternately lowered or raised or with sudden halts or accelerations in the forward motion of the barge, Galileo argues similarly that the tides are caused by shifting motions of the basins containing the oceans and seas. Such alterations in motion are produced when the axial rotation of the earth coincides with or is in opposition to the annual revolution. Alluding to ''a mechanical model in which the effects of these marvelous compositions of movements may be observed in detail'' (pp. 430-431), he describes how the two motions of the earth could produce the desired effect:

> [. . .] just as it is true that the motion of the whole globe and of each of its parts would be equable and uniform if it were moved with a single motion, whether this happened to be the annual or the diurnal, so it is necessary that upon these two motions being mixed together there results in the parts of the globe this uneven motion, now accelerated and now retarded by the additions and subtractions of the diurnal rotation upon the annual revolution. (p. 427)

Thus he concludes:

> [. . .] if the terrestrial globe were immovable, the ebb and flow of the oceans could not occur naturally; and that when we confer upon the globe the movements just assigned to it, the seas are necessarily subjected to an ebb and flow agreeing in all respects with what is to be observed in them. (p. 417)

Even though his conclusion is false, Galileo's reasoning displays the usual astuteness. In particular, in his thought experiments imaginatively altering the magnitudes of the additions and subtractions to the annual motion due to the diurnal rotation which results in variations in the ''concomitant causes'' of the tides (p. 428), and in supposing one or the other deleted so as to deduce the effects (cf. p. 448), Galileo was explicitly using the methods of inductive reasoning that John Stuart Mill classified as the ''methods of agreement, difference, and concomitant variation.''[23] Furthermore, he rejects Hume's subsequent famous critique of induction that causes and effects are so disconnected that an inference from one to the other can be based only on habit or custom, not on a necessary connection, in favor of a stronger inferential relation. Even though we do not know the underlying causes, "a fixed and constant connection" (which Hume denies while maintaining a constant conjunction) between causes and effect justifies an inference from one to the other.

> Thus I say that if it is true that one effect can have only one basic cause, and if between the cause and the effect there is a fixed and constant connection, then whenever a fixed and constant alteration is seen in the effect, there must be a fixed and constant variation in the cause. (p. 445)

In contrast to Hume's later position, Galileo believed that these "constant connections" were evidence of underlying causal connections that could, in time, be discovered.

Having dealt with the diurnal period of the tides of which he says "the primary and universal cause has [. . .] been proven"(p. 444), Salviati turns to "the secondary and concomitant causes" affecting their monthly and annual variations. Asserting that the same principles of explanation apply in these cases as in the daily tides, the monthly and annual variations must be produced either "by altering the annual motion and keeping fixed the magnitudes of the additions, or by changing the size of these and keeping the annual motion uniform"(p. 453), or by "a combination of these two [. . .]." (p. 448) In fact, he argues that the correlation between the monthly alteration of the tides and the revolution of the moon, inferred by Kepler and other astronomers, is not due to a direct effect of the moon on the oceans and seas, but produced by a variation in the earth's orbital motion caused by the moon's rotation around the earth which results in the earth moving faster when the moon is between the earth and the sun and slower when it is beyond the earth (thus affirming with Kepler a nonuniform motion of the earth as one of the planets).

> From this it may be clear that the annual movement of the earth in its orbit along the ecliptic is not uniform, and that its irregularity derives from the moon and has its periods and restorations monthly. (p. 453)

Accordingly, the moon does play a role "without having anything to do with oceans and waters." (p. 454)

Similarly, the annual variation in the tides is caused by changes in the magnitudes of the additions and subtractions to the earth's annual motion produced by its diurnal rotation and "the tilting of its axis to the plane of the

[. . .] ecliptic."(p. 457) "This,"he says, "is the whole story, but it is wrapped in the obscurity which you perceive." (p. 457) Yet Galileo believed that these physical variations were sufficient to demonstrate that the tides were produced by mechanical motions rather than "occult"influences from the moon. To the very end, he chides Kepler for having "lent his ear and his assent to the moon's dominion over the waters, to occult properties, and to such puerilities." (p. 462) One can only regret that because of his markedly different temperament and scientific outlook, Galileo was unwilling to take Kepler's explanation more seriously.

Thus ends the greatest dialectical work in the history of science. As Sagredo concludes:

> In the conversations of these four days we have, then, strong evidences in favor of the Copernican system, among which three have been shown to be very convincing—those taken from the stoppings and retrograde motions of the planets, and their approaches toward and recessions from the earth; second, from the revolution of the sun upon itself, and from what is to be observed in the sunspots; and third, from the ebbing and flowing of the ocean tides. (p. 462)

Despite all his pretexts, caveats, and disclaimers, it is eminently clear that Galileo believed that in accounting for the tides the two essential motions attributed to the earth by Copernicus were demonstrated to exist. That his arguments went beyond treating the two world systems "mathematically, hypothetically, and impartially" was evident to his enemies and to the church authorities, whatever his deepest convictions and what he thought he had maintained in the *Dialogue*. Even at the very end he appears dissembling in having Simplicius, rather than Salviati who speaks *for him*, state the admonition expressed *to him* by the pope:[24]

> As to the discourses we have held, and especially this last one concerning the reasons for the ebbing and flowing of the ocean, I am really not entirely convinced [. . .] indeed, keeping always before my mind's eye a most solid doctrine that I once heard from a most eminent and learned person [Pope Urban VIII], and before which one must fall silent, I know if asked whether God in His infinite power and wisdom could have conferred upon the watery element its observed reciprocating motion using some other means than moving its containing vessels, both of you would reply that He could have,

and that He would have known how to do this in many ways which are unthinkable to our minds. From this I forthwith conclude that, this being so, it would be excessive boldness for anyone to limit and restrict the Divine power and wisdom to some particular fancy of his own. (p. 464; brackets added)

In choosing the Aristotelian Simplicius to express the pope's doctrine, was Galileo following "the only possible course" as Drake claims (p. 491, f.n. 464), or was he consciously or unconsciously distancing himself from it? There are passages, as we have seen, in which he sincerely and emphatically upholds the limits of human knowledge, yet at times he writes as if the evidence for the Copernican system, if not conclusive, certainly was compelling. Even Salviati's immediate rejoinder to Simplicius is somewhat enigmatic:

An admirable and angelic doctrine, and well in accord with another one, also Divine, which, while it grants to us the right to argue about the constitution of the universe (perhaps in order that the working of the human mind shall not be curtailed or made lazy) adds that we cannot discover the work of His hands. Let us, then, exercise these activities permitted to us and ordained by God, that we may recognize and thereby so much the more admire His greatness, however much less fit we may find ourselves to penetrate the profound depths of His infinite wisdom. (P. 464)

Is God, as this statement implies, merely goading or teasing humans to inquire into his creation to enhance their admiration of him, knowing that any depth of understanding is ultimately futile? Perhaps this is what Galileo, and all inquirers, finally come to believe: that while it is man's right and duty to pursue knowledge of the universe, its ultimate attainment always will be illusive. Or is Einstein's position less skeptical: "Subtle is the Lord, but malicious he is not."

THE TRAVAILS OF PUBLICATION

Completed by the end of 1629, Galileo had intended, at the urging of Prince Cesi, that the *Dialogue* be published in Rome under the auspices of the Lincean Academy. Initially, the prospects seemed most favorable despite the usual opposition of his opponents. The pope himself, along with his nephew Cardinal Barberini, were considered strong supporters of Galileo. Urban VIII declared, regarding the repressive edict of 1616 (without knowing then of Galileo's involvement), that "if it had been up to me that decree would never have been issued."[25] Giovanni Ciampoli, the pope's personal confidential secretary, worked with Riccardi who was in charge of licensing books printed in Rome to ensure the approval of the *Dialogue*. Then, however, the situation began to unravel. Cesi died unexpectedly preventing the Linceans from printing the manuscript. Because changes in the title page, preface, and conclusion were required, Riccardi expected Galileo to come to Rome to assist in the revisions, but the outbreak of the plague prevented this. So instead Riccardi suggested that Galileo send the manuscript to Rome where he and Ciampoli would make the necessary adjustments. However, Galileo decided that he would prefer to have the book printed in Florence where he could supervise the process, so he obtained permission to have only the sections requiring revision sent to Rome.

But then there remained the problem of who in Florence would serve as censor for the complete book. The procedure was finally resolved with the following instruction sent by Riccardi to the Florentine Inquisitor:

> [. . .] your Reverence may use your authority and approve or not approve the book independently of my revision, but keeping it in mind that it is his Holiness' view that *the title and subject may not propose the tides*, but absolutely [only] mathematical considerations of the Copernican positions about the motion of the earth, with the purpose of proving that, excluding divine revelation and holy doctrine, the appearances could be saved in this position, resolving all the contrary arguments that might be adduced from experience and the Peripatetic philosophy, *so that this position is never conceded absolute but only hypothetical truth*, and apart from the Scriptures. It must also be shown that this work was done only to show that all the arguments that this side can adduce are known, and that it was not from lack of their knowledge at Rome that this opinion was here abandoned, conformably with the beginning and the end of the book that will be sent from here corrected. With the above caution the book will have no obstacle here in Rome, and your Reverence may pacify the author and serve his Highness, who shows much pressure in the matter. (p. 320; italics added)

At least in a literal sense, one can understand why Galileo might have believed that he had complied with the pope's demands when granted permission to write the *Dialogue*: using various literary techniques throughout the discourse, he has Salviati state that he never pretended to an "absolute truth" in the discussion, however persuasively he might have argued in favor of the Copernican system, and that his justification for writing the book was to show that among Italians, even Romans, the edict of 1616 was not based on a lack of understanding of the arguments for the heliocentric position.

RECRIMINATIONS AND TRIAL

The printing of the *Dialogue* finally accomplished by February 21, 1632, Galileo's friends, such as Castelli, Cavalieri, and Campanella, were enthralled by it. Castelli wrote that "'I still have it by me, having read it from cover to cover to my infinite amazement and delight [. . .].'" (p. 336) Meanwhile, a storm of opposition was gathering with the Jesuits agitating to have the book prohibited. Unexpectedly, the fiercest reaction came from the pope himself. Angered that Galileo had included at the end of the Dialogue only one of the three arguments that he had requested and even had that one stated by Simplicius, the most inept of the three disputants, he was furious when he learned of the edict of 1616 instructing Galileo not to "hold, defend, or teach in any way, orally or in writing" the motion of the earth and the stability of the sun, "on pain of imprisonment." Because Galileo had not informed him of this during their meeting in 1624 when he had granted him permission to write the *Dialogue*, the pope saw this as a deliberate deception, a betrayal of his trust in Galileo and a personal insult. As Drake says, "[n]o other explanation of the pope's sudden and implacable anger seem's adequate." (p. 339)

As a consequence, in September the Inquisitor at Florence sent the original manuscript to Rome for examination, while all sales of the book were prohibited[26] and Galileo ordered to appear before the Roman Inquisition the following month. Although requests were made through Niccolini, the Tuscan Ambassador, to spare Galileo the arduous trip to Rome, the pope was adamant. As an indication of his aroused feelings, believing that he had been "imposed upon" by Riccardi and especially Ciampoli in facilitating licensing of the *Dialogue*, he dismissed Ciampoli "as papal secretary and sent him to a distant city." (p. 432) Yet despite the urgency, Galileo's precarious health, which forced him to be bedridden as attested by three doctors, resulted in the Florentine Inquisitor granting him a month's delay. Finally, the Roman

Inquisition, implying that he was using his illness as a subterfuge, decreed that "if he did not proceed to Rome at once, or as soon as his life was not thereby endangered, he would be carried there in chains and charged for the expense of all doctors and transportation." (p. 342) Provided a litter and an attendant by the grand duke to make his journey as comfortable as possible, Galileo arrived in Rome on 13 February 1633, two days before his seventieth birthday. Rather than being imprisoned as was the custom, the pope permitted him initially to reside at the Tuscan embassy as a favor to the grand duke.

Despite the seriousness of the situation, Galileo apparently believed that the affidavit of assurance given him in 1616 by Cardinal Bellarmine (of which none of his accusers were aware) would exonerate him, especially if he also were allowed to defend his book (retaining his usual confidence in his persuasive ability). He confided to Niccolini what he believed was the crucial accusation against him, a charge he thought he could refute. As Niccolini wrote shortly after, this was the fact that

> in 1616 Galileo had been ordered "not to dispute or discuss this [Copernican] opinion; nevertheless he says that the command was not given in this form, but rather that he should not hold or defend it, he believing that he has a way of justifying himself. . . [and] that all other things seem to be of less importance or easier to get out of." (p. 343)

Notwithstanding my tremendous admiration for Galileo and contempt for the deplorable censorship of the Catholic Church and the vileness of the Inquisition, it is difficult to understand how Galileo could have "justified himself." With a deep feeling of disappointment and sadness, I have concluded that he was guilty of bad faith or self-deception. Even if the unsigned edict of 1616 did not have the proper legal standing and even though Bellarmine's affidavit did not (as the edict did) contain the words "or teach in any way, orally or in writing, the said propositions" regarding the motion of the earth and stability of the sun, Galileo did agree to abide by Bellarmine's affidavit stating that the Copernican opinion, which is contrary to Sacred Scripture, "may not be defended or held." (p. 348) It was this letter that Galileo intended to use as a defence against the accusations. But how, in all honesty, could he have done so?

Was he prepared to say that he did not "hold" the Copernican system to be more probable than the Aristotelian or Ptolemaic, contradicting what he had written to Kepler and expressed on a number of occasions verbally and in writing? Could he sincerely maintain that in composing the *Dialogue*, despite the frequent disclaimers, that he had not intended to "defend" the two movements of the earth? It belies credulity to think that Galileo could have written with such critical insight, deep conviction, and caustic humor had he not believed in the overwhelming superiority, if not absolute truth, of the Copernican system, especially as he believed that the tides were "proof" (as he said) of the earth's motion. The latter argument, a physical demonstration rather than a mathematical hypothesis to save the phenomenon, was expressly prohibited by the pope, not just in the title but also in the "subject." Furthermore, it is beyond dispute that he did not treat the two systems "hypothetically and impartially," as instructed by the pope. Thus it seems likely that Galileo *deliberately* did not tell the pope of the edict of 1616 and the letter given him by Bellarmine because, if he had done so, it would have been impossible for him to write the *Dialogue* with the intended purpose. He was such an ardent partisan for certain views (such as his explanation of the tides), that he would not have found it of interest to write about the two chief world systems hypothetically and impartially—it being entirely contrary to his nature. This interpretation, I believe, is born out by his own statements during the trial.

Initially the pope had appointed a special commission to handle the inquest, but as a result of their findings it was turned over to the Inquisition. On 12 April Galileo was transferred from the Tuscan embassy "to the offices of the Inquisition, where he was received in a friendly way by the commissary and housed in a comfortable apartment there, with his own attendant lodged with him." (p. 344) The interrogation began the following day and is reproduced by Drake. (cf. pp. 344-347) Questioned about the events leading to the hearing, he subsequently was asked about the edict and affidavit of 1616. What is of special import is that after saying that Bellarmine's affidavit stated "that the opinion of Copernicus cannot be held or defended, because of its being against the Holy Scriptures" (p. 346), Galileo shortly thereafter (in answer to another question) said "I claim not to have contravened in any way the precept [of 1616], that is not to have held or defended the said opinion of the motion of the earth and stability of the sun on any account." (p. 347; brackets added)

As Drake states, "the only real issue was whether or not he had received and disobeyed a specific personal order." (p. 348) Legally, because there was no "signed original of the notarial document on which the Inquisition had relied in bringing charges" (p. 349), the case against Galileo was equivocal. Still, the Inquisition could not admit to a false charge of heresy and realizing that Galileo's statement denying that he had not "contravened in any way the precept [. . .] not to have held or defended the said opinion of the motion of the earth and stability of the sun"was contradicted by his book, the objective was to get him to see this and confess his error. As Vincenzo Maculano, Commissary General of the Inquisition, wrote at the close of the initial hearing:

> [. . .] because Galileo denied at his hearing what is evident in the book he wrote, there would have to be greater rigor in the proceedings and less regard for niceties in this affair. Finally I proposed a means: that the Holy Congregation grant me power to deal extra-judicially with Galileo to the end of convincing him of his error and bringing him to the point of confessing it when he understood. (p. 349)

This "extra-judicial"procedure consisted of meeting with Galileo privately to persuade him "that he was clearly wrong and that in his book he had gone too far." (p. 349) Admitting this, Galileo "agreed to confess this judicially," requesting time to compose his confession. On the last day of April he appeared at a second hearing during which he said he had reconsidered his earlier replies and having been given the opportunity he had reexamined the arguments in his book. He then went on to say, in Drake's works, that

> having reread it he realized that in many places a reader ignorant of his intention might think the arguments earned the day *for the position he meant to confute,* especially the arguments from sunspots and from the tides. He could only excuse himself on grounds of vanity and ambition, every man liking to show himself cleverer than others in his own subtleties. He had not meant any disobedience but confessed vain ambition, ignorance, and inadvertence. (p. 350; italics added)

After signing this confession he was released to the custody of Ambassador Niccolini.

This confession, I believe, provides additional evidence of Galileo's bad faith or self-deception. How could he sincerely maintain that his *real intention* had been to "confute"(disprove) the Copernican system, but that this had been misconstrued owing to his arguments about the sunspots and tides? In fairness I should add that I do not know what other position he might have taken, but confessing that he actually had intended to "confute"or refute the Copernican view was certainly dishonest. Had the effects of the proceedings, the possibility of torture and imprisonment, the implacable opposition of the pope, and the final humiliation (a process well known today as "brainwashing") so affected the ailing, aged warrior that he actually believed at the time that this had been his purpose?   Or was the whole episode evidence of a deep self-deception in that if he had not been brought to account he would have accepted the accolades due to his incisive arguments showing the superiority of the Copernican system, while once challenged he could rationalize that this had not been his intended purpose at all, never having really believed in the Copernican system? [27]

It would appear that during the trial he underwent some kind of ideological conversion, conceding to the "masters in theology" the right to decide the truth of the Copernican system.   At least this is what he maintained in a letter to Francesco Rinuccini written less than ten months before he died:

> The falsity of the Copernican system must not on any account be doubted, especially by us Catholics, who have the irrefragable authority of Holy Scripture interpreted by the greatest masters in theology, whose agreement renders us certain of the stability of the earth and the mobility of the sun around it.   The conjectures of Copernicus and his followers offered to the contrary are all removed by that most sound argument, taken from the omnipotence of God [the argument of Urban VIII introduced at the end of the *Dialogue*].   He being able to do in many, or rather infinite ways, that which to our view and observation seems to be done in one particular way, we must not pretend to hamper God's hand and tenaciously maintain that in which we may be mistaken.   And just as I deem inadequate the Copernican observations and conjectures, so I judge equally, and more, fallacious and erroneous those of Ptolemy, Aristotle, and their followers, when without going beyond the bounds of human reasoning their inconclusiveness can be very easily discovered. (p. 417; brackets added)

In contrast to the position he held prior to his abjuring the Copernican system, this statement is "astonishing" as Drake says, indicating the extent to which his mental outlook regarding *this question* (not generally, because he wrote *Two Chief Sciences* after the trial) had been affected by the proceedings.

While previously he had argued that when there is a conflict between Holy Scripture and astronomical conclusions based on new observational evidence, the biblical assertions should be interpreted in terms of the limitations of common beliefs and ordinary expressions at the time the Bible was written, now he maintained that their authority transcends any astronomical evidence. Moreover, this applies to the "fallacious and erroneous" observations and conjectures of Ptolemy and Aristotle, even though their geocentric system agrees with the scriptural passages. In astronomical matters he now defers to the theologians, a position he never would have conceded earlier, especially as he had argued that God had endowed man with the capacity for scientific reasoning as well as faith and revelation. While previously he had admitted that the authority of Holy Scripture was to be accepted in questions of faith and morality, he had excluded astronomy, but now was willing to concede that also. I hope this attempt at an honest appraisal of his state of mind will be seen as paying due respect to a very great man who, like everyone, had his weaknesses.

As to his penalty, this was decided by the pope himself who

on 16 June ordered Galileo's examination on intention, to be followed (if he sustained this) by imprisonment for an indefinite term at the pleasure of the Holy Office, confiscation of the *Dialogue*, and mandatory public reading of the sentence to professors of mathematics throughout Italy and elsewhere. (p. 351)

When on 21 June Galileo was examined on intention, he maintained that prior to 1616 he had considered discussion of the two world systems to be allowed but thereafter, in Drake's words,

he had adhered to the fixed earth and movable sun; in his book he had considered no argument as conclusive and the decision of "sublime authority" as binding. Asked whether he spoke truly, on pain of torture, he replied: "I am here to obey, and have not held this opinion after the determination made, as I said." (p. 351)

"Iam here to obey" could mean that the alternative being imprisonment and torture, he felt compelled to abjure his previous beliefs. But in my opinion his statements suggest not that he had made a conscious decision to confess to avoid torture, but that he was so disoriented that he really believed that after the edict of 1616 he truly had never intended to hold or defend the Copernican view.

Finally, on the following day "the sentence of life imprisonment was read to Galileo at a formal ceremony in the presence of the cardinals of the

Inquisition and witnesses, after which he had to abjure on his knees before them.'' (p. 351) Thus ends what justly has been described as ''the disgrace of the century,'' and I would add, the permanent debasement of the Catholic Church.[28] Francesco Barberini, the pope's nephew, who throughout the trial had acted as mediator between the pope, Riccardi, Niccolini, and the Holy Congregation in the best interests of Galileo, was one of three Cardinals who refused to sign the final document containing the sentence. He also arranged that Galileo's imprisonment be commuted to the Tuscan embassy after which he was permitted to be placed in the custody of Archbishop Piccolomini of Siena, who had invited Galileo to reside with him if permitted after the trial.

A well-known anecdote attributes the words *Eppur si muove* (''still it moves'') to Galileo at the end of the proceedings. Drake is certainly correct when he says that ''popular version is preposterous, since no sympathetic ear could have been there to hear him, nor could Galileo have escaped the most dire consequences for any such foolish act.'' (p. 356) Moreover, if Galileo underwent an ideological conversion as the quotation mentioned earlier seems to indicate, such as assertion would have been completely out of character at the time. Drake traces the origin of the utterance to a statement by Giuseppe Baretti published in *The Italian Library* in 1757. (cf. p. 357) In addition, a painting has been discovered dated around 1643 in which Galileo is pictured in the dungeons of the Inquisition (which of course is false) pointing to a wall on which appear the words, *Eppur si muove*. Thus the account probably originated at that time.

As soon as the trial was over in July, Galileo left for Siena where he remained in the warm hospitality of Ascania Piccolomini until December. The Archbishop, who came from a distinguished cultured family and who had studied mathematics under Cavalieri, had a tremendous respect for Galileo and did everything possible to help him regain his health and mental stability. At first distraught at the punishment which he considered especially harsh considering he had agreed to an extra-judicial confession, Galileo spent many fitful nights when ''he did not sleep, but went through the night crying out and rambling so crazily that it was seriously considered whether his arms should be bound'' (p. 353) to prevent any injury. Gradually, under the affectionate care of his host, he regained his physical strength and mental composure and even began writing his great book, *Two New Sciences*. At the request of Ambassador Niccolini and with the intercession of Cardinal Barberini,[29] on the first of December ''the pope recommended to the Holy Office that Galileo be permitted to return to his villa at Arcetri, in the hills beyond Florence, provided he receive few visitors and refrain from teaching.'' (p. 356) Thus, by mid-December he was installed in his own home close to the convent of his beloved daughter, Sister Maria Celeste. But even this precious consolation soon was to be denied him by a malicious fate that caused her sudden death in April of the following year.

THE TWO NEW SCIENCES

Given his mental anguish at the time, it is a mark of Galileo's extraordinary intellectual strength that during his five month's confinement at Siena he was able to conceive the contents of and begin writing sections of *Two New Sciences*. Then in 1634 he wrote to Elia Diodati in Paris of his intention to publish the book that would bring to culmination his research in the sciences of motion and percussion, begun during his eighteen year tenure at the University of Padua. By 1637 the manuscript was nearing completion, but the problem was to find a publisher. An especially close friend during this period was the Venetian Fulgenzio Micanzio who, when he inquired about the possibility of the publication of the manuscript in Venice or Florence, was told by the Inquisitor that "there was an express order prohibiting the printing or reprinting of any work of Galileo, either in Venice or any other place, *nullo excepto*."[30] The severity of the Holy Office is indicated further in the response of the Inquisitor to Galileo's request to visit Florence to have a painful hernia treated by doctors there (none being available in Arcetri) who not only denied his request, but personally informed him that "any more petitions from him would result in imprisonment." (p. 360) Obviously if his manuscript were to be published, it would have to be at a place beyond the long reach of the Court of the Holy Office.

Several possibilities were explored, including the attempt by the grand duke to have Prince Mathia de' Medici arrange the publication in Germany under the auspices of The Holy Roman Emperor through the influence of Giovanni Pieroni, a friend and admirer of Galileo who served as military engineer to the Emperor. Finally, however, it was Galileo's correspondence with Diodati that led to a visit in 1636 to Arcetri by Louis Elzevir, founder of the famous publishing firm in Amsterdam still bearing his name, that resulted in the book being printed in 1637, with the index, title-page, and dedication added in the completed edition in 1638.

Even the latter had its peculiar history. The dedication was offered to the Count of Noailles (a former student of Galileo at Padua who, as ambassador of France to Rome since 1634, had attempted unsuccessfully to obtain a pardon for Galileo from the Holy Office), who gratefully accepted. But even in the dedicatory letter Galileo committed a further deception (perhaps warranted by the precariousness of the situation), pretending that he had given a copy of his manuscript to the Count which, unknown to Galileo, was "suddenly and unexpectedly" printed by the Elzevirs. (cf. p. xviii)

Although the earlier *Dialogue* is unsurpassed as an example of sheer dialectical skill, Galileo considered his later book, as he wrote to Diodati, "superior to everything else of mine hitherto published [. . .] contain[ing] results which I consider the most important of all my studies [. . .]"[31] Indeed, from the standpoint of the development of a scientific framework and rationale for explaining motion (the primary task of physics from Aristotle to Newton), the *Two New Sciences* represents Galileo's greatest achievement. Thus his contributions to the origins of modern science may be summarized as follows: (1) the demonstration in the *Dialogues* that the fundamental presuppositions along with the conceptual distinctions and explanations underlying the defence of the Aristotelian-Ptolemaic worldview were incompatible with the new astronomical observations; (2) the justification begun by Copernicus that a simpler, more coherent description of astronomical motions could be achieved from a heliocentric perspective utilizing the new principles of mechanical motion; and (3) the demonstration in *Two New Sciences* of the fundamental theorems and conceptual innovations underlying Galileo's new geometrical mechanics of motion.

Ideally, in conformity with the objectives of this study, a complete account of Galileo's achievement in the latter work would include a description of how his explanatory framework and conceptual system depended on, borrowed from, and improved upon the earlier investigations of the fourteenth century Mertonians and Parisians who were the first to attempt to formulate the principles and concepts necessary for the mathematization of motion, and then indicate the extent to which Galileo's geometrical kinematics anticipated, laid the foundations for, but fell short of Newtonian mechanics. Although limitations of space prevent such a comprehensive review, especially considering the extent to which Galileo already has been discussed, it fortunately is unnecessary because such a study previously has been made by Maurice Clavelin in his remarkable book, *The Natural Philosophy of Galileo*,[32] to which the reader is referred.

The present objective, therefore, will be to describe succinctly Galileo's major contributions to the development of the science of kinematics in the *Two New Sciences* which, according to Elzevir's Preface to the Reader, comprises the science of motion and the science that "deals with the resistance which solid bodies offer to fracture by external forces [. . .]."(p.xx) Not knowing the causes of motion nor the internal structure of solids that account for their resistance to external pressures, Galileo was restricted to demonstrating geometrically the magnitudes of the controlling parameters. Surprisingly, it is not until the beginning of the dialogue of the third day that Galileo presents the famous passages in which he declares his purpose, along with his expectation of the consequences for the future development of science.

> My purpose is to set forth a very new science dealing with a very ancient subject. There is, in nature, perhaps nothing older than motion, concerning which the books written by philosophers are neither few nor small; nevertheless I have discovered by experiment some properties of it which are worth knowing and which have not hitherto been either observed or demonstrated. Some superficial observations have been made, as for instance, that the free motion of a heavy falling body is continuously accelerated; but to just what extent this acceleration occurs has not yet been announced; for so far as I know, no one has yet pointed out that the distances traversed during equal intervals of time, by a body falling from rest, stand to me another in the same ratio as the odd numbers beginning with unity.[33]
> (p. 147)

The law of free fall constituting Galileo's first and greatest discovery, he then refers to his second along with his expectations of the future of such investigations.

> It has been observed that missiles and projectiles describe a curved path of some sort; however no one has pointed out the fact that this path is a parabola. But this and other facts, not few in number or less worth knowing, I have succeeded in proving; and what I consider more important, there have been opened up to this vast and most excellent science, of which my work is merely the beginning, ways and means by which other minds more acute than mine will explore its remote corners. (pp. 147-148)

As indicated, Galileo is going to deal with the ancient problem of motion but in such as a way as to create an entirely new approach to that phenomenon. This new science breaks with the Peripatetic tradition in describing motion not as an effect of a motive cause, but as due to an inner state (*impetus*) or momentum (*velocitas*) that can be quantified as ratios between two basic magnitudes, space and time. This allowed him to deal with motion abstracted from physical manifestations whose two essential properties could be represented spatially and therefore analyzed geometrically. Thus by depicting the spatial and temporal parameters of motion in geometrical diagrams, geometry could be used to analyze and demonstrate its properties so that the science of motion could be reduced to a deductive mathematical system.

Intending to establish this new science as a rigorous discipline, he followed Euclid and Archimedes in presenting it as a deductive system consisting of original definitions, axioms, and derived theorems (the form Newton also would adopt for the *Principia*). Although an enormous undertaking, this kinematic approach appealed to Galileo because he did not believe that he knew enough about the causes of phenomena to introduce them effectively in his explanations. That it was a limited approach requiring completion by Newtonian dynamics does not detract from its tremendous originality and effectiveness.

Galileo begins his treatment of motion by defining uniform motion as "one in which the distances traversed by the moving particle during any equal intervals of time, are themselves equal." (p. 148) From this he derives his first theorem: "[i]f a moving particle, carried uniformly at a constant speed, traverses two distances the time-intervals required are to each other in the ratio of these distances." (p. 149) He then demonstrates this with two segmented lines, the divisions standing for the spatial and temporal intervals, whose ratios constitute the proof. This is typical of his approach throughout the book.

From uniform motion he advances to naturally accelerated motion. First exclaiming that he is not seeking merely a *possible* geometrical representation of motion but "a definition best fitting natural phenomena [. . .] such as actually occurs in nature," he then affirms that he has arrived at a "demonstration" of the essential properties of observed accelerated motions such that "experimental results are seen to agree with and exactly correspond with those properties [. . .]." (p. 154) He adds that in investigating nature one should follow her example in employing "only those means that are most common, simple and easy."

Applying his definition of uniform motion to uniformly accelerated motion, he says "we may picture to our mind a motion as uniformly and continuously accelerated when during any equal intervals of time whatever, equal increments of speed are given to it." (p. 155) In modern terminology, Galileo discovered that constantly accelerating motion involves *a uniform change in the rate of motion* proportional to the times of descent. Not having the benefit of differential and integral calculus (developed later independently by Newton and Leibniz) he could not use the differential function to express instantaneous increases in velocity between successive instants when these intervals tend toward zero (dv/dt), and then integrate (or sum) these constant increases from the beginning of the descent:

$$v_t = \int_{t_0}^{t} (\frac{dv}{dt}) dt.^{34}$$

Or, even more precisely, he could not express acceleration as a "second derivative" designating the increase in velocity undergone at each instant by the falling object. As stated by Priogonine and Stengers:

> At each instant the state of a moving body can be defined by its position r, by its velocity v, which expresses its "instantaneous tendency" to modify this position, and by its acceleration a, again its "instantaneous tendency," but now to modify its velocity. Instantaneous velocities and accelerations are limiting quantities: the variation of r (or v) during a temporal interval Δt, and this interval Δt when Δt tends to zero. Such quantities are "derivatives with respect to time," and since Leibniz they have been written as v = dr/dt and a = dv/dt. Therefore, acceleration, the derivative of a derivative, a = d^2r/dt^2, becomes a "second derivative" [. . .] of the acceleration undergone at each instant by the points that form a system. The motion of each of these points over a finite interval of time can then be calculated by *integration*, by adding up the infinitesimal velocity changes occurring during this interval.[35]

Lacking the infinitesimal calculus, Galileo had to base his demonstration of this law on two theorems which were proven by geometrical demonstrations in which the magnitudes of the spaces, times, and uniform accelerations were represented spatially by the lengths of lines. The first theorem was the old "mean speed law" while the second was the new law that the "spaces described by a body falling from rest with a uniformly accelerated motion are to each other as the squares of the time-intervals employed in traversing these distances." (p. 167) Or, as he summarizes this conclusion:

> It is thus evident by simple computation that a moving body starting from rest and acquiring velocity at a rate proportional to the time, will,

during equal intervals of time, traverse distances which are related to each other as the odd numbers beginning with unity, 1, 3, 5; or considering the total space traversed, that covered in double time will be quadruple that covered during unit time; in triple time, the space is nine times as great as in unit time. And in general the spaces traversed are in the duplicate ratio of the times, i.e., in the ratio of the squares of the times. (p. 170)

Called upon by Simplicius to provide an experimental proof of this law, Galileo illustrates his conviction that however convincing a mathematical demonstration of a particular phenomena may be, it should be confirmed by experimental evidence. Incredibly, given the detailed description of this experimental test, Mersenne doubted whether Galileo had actually performed the experiment while Descartes "'denied' all of Galileo's experiments!"[36] and even Koyré expressed reservations about whether "there could be such exact agreement between the experiment and the predictions!"[37]

Responding to Simplicius' request, Salviati states that the demand is a reasonable one especially in those sciences "where the principles, once established by well-chosen experiments, become the foundations of the entire superstructure." (p. 171)

So far as experiments go they have not been neglected by the author; and often, in his company, I have attempted in the following manner to assure myself that the acceleration actually experienced by falling bodies is that above described.

A piece of wooden moulding or scantling, about 12 cubits long, half a cubit wide, and three finger-breadths thick, was taken; on its edge was cut a channel a little more than one finger in breadth; having made this groove very straight, smooth, and polished, and having lined it with parchment, also as smooth and polished as possible, we rolled along it a hard, smooth, and very round bronze ball. Having placed this board in a sloping position, by lifting one end some one or two cubits above the other, we rolled the ball, as I was saying, along the channel, noting, in a manner presently to be described, the time required to make the descent. We repeated this experiment more than once in order to measure the time with an accuracy such that the deviation between two observations never exceeded one-tenth of a pulse-beat. (p. 171)

Is it likely that such a detailed account of the experimental equipment and procedure, as witnessed by Salviati, would have been presented had not Galileo performed the experiment? If Mersenne was not able to duplicate the results of the experiment, then this should be taken as indicating that he was not as skilled an experimenter as Galileo—not that Galileo had not performed the experiments, especially as there is such an inclined plane in the *Instituto E Museo Di Storia Della Scienza* in Florence.

He then describes the measured ratios of the times and distances of fall, namely, that the rolling ball fell through only ¼ the distance during the first half of the descent and ¾ (owing to its acceleration) during the second half, the spaces traversed being in the ratio of the squares of the times.

> Having performed this operation and having assured ourselves of its reliability, we now rolled the ball only one-quarter the length of the channel; and having measured the time of its descent, we found it precisely one-half of the former. Next we tried other distances, comparing the time for the whole length with that for the half, or with that for two-thirds, or three-fourths, or indeed for any fraction; in such experiments, repeated a full hundred times, we always found that the spaces traversed were to each other as the squares of the times, and this was true for all inclinations of the plane, i.e., of the channel, along which we rolled the ball. (pp. 171-172)

Because the accelerated velocity of a free falling body is too fast to be measured directly (less than three seconds from a ten story building), Galileo devised the incline plane experiment as a test of his law "that the spaces traversed were to each other as the squares of the times." But how did he know that the measured ratios on the inclined plane would be true also of free fall? Galileo's last statement addresses this problem asserting that if the ratio holds for "all [angles] of inclinations of the plane," then it should hold in the extreme case where the angle equals 90°, as in free fall. Finally, Galileo describes how the times were determined by measuring the differences and ratios of the water that accumulated during the descent "with such accuracy that although the operation was repeated many, many times, there was no appreciable discrepancy in the results." (p. 172) Unlike Koyré, I do not see any difficulty in accepting this conclusion.

In addition to proving the law of free fall, Galileo devised arguments and demonstrations to show that in a vacuum objects would fall with the same velocity regardless of their weights (as the Epicureans also had believed), not instantaneously as Aristotle had argued. Based on much earlier experiments in hydrostatics in which he compared the descent of objects of the same weight in media of different densities (air and water), of objects of different weights in media of the same density, and finally of objects of different weights in media of different densities, he concluded that the variations in speed were not due to the various (specific) weights of the objects, but to the differences in the densities of the medium.

> Our problem is to find out what happens to bodies of different weight moving in a medium devoid of resistance, so [. . .] we shall observe what happens in the rarest and least resistant media as compared with what happens in denser and more resistant media. Because if we find as a fact that the variation of speed among bodies of different specific gravities is less and less according as the medium becomes more and more yielding, and if finally in a medium of extreme tenuity, though not a perfect vacuum, we find that, in spite of great diversity of specific gravity, the difference in speed is very small and almost inappreciable, then we are justified in believing it highly probable that in a vacuum all bodies would fall with the same speed. (pp. 69-70)

While that is the argument, the demonstration is based on the isochronal periods of pendular swings which he had investigated as a young man observing the movements of the suspended lanterns in the cathedral of Pisa. Since ascertaining "whether two bodies differing greatly in weight will fall from a given height with the same speed offers some difficulty" (p. 80), he turned to pendular motion where the speed could be reduced to the slowest possible, thereby diminishing the effect of the resistance of the medium which increases with speed. Suspending a ball of cork and a ball of lead that was "a hundred times heavier" from equally fine threads of the same length, he was able to show that when drawn in an arc from the vertical position and released at the same moment, each completes its periodic swings in the same time, indicating that their speeds are equal: "if these same bodies traverse equal areas in equal times we may rest assured that their speeds are equal." (p. 82) The speeds do vary with the size of the arcs, becoming slower as the arcs become smaller (just as the accelerations of falling bodies are less for shorter distances of fall), but "this does not contradict the fact that they maintain equal speeds in equal arcs" (p. 83), regardless of their weights. Thus objects of different weights, such as "a bird-shot and a cannon ball," falling in a vacuum with no resistance of a medium, would fall with the same velocities!

Furthermore, his investigation of pendulums also confirmed his earlier discovery that free falling objects accelerate proportional to the squares of the times or to the *square roots* of the distances.

> As to the times of vibration of bodies suspended by threads of different lengths, they bear to each other the same proportion as the square roots of the lengths of the thread; or one might say the lengths are to each other as the squares of the times [. . .]. (p. 92)

After two thousand years of investigation Galileo's demonstration of the correct law of free fall, like Kepler's discovery of the three laws of planetary motion, marks one of the great milestones in mankind's attempt of arrive at an exact description of the two basic motions in nature. It was left for Newton to formulate the law and the causal theory uniting and explaining both of these motions.

Galileo's second major discovery pertains to projectile motion, the correct description of which also proved illusive from the time of Plato and Aristotle. What enabled Galileo to solve this problem was his rejection of Aristotle's belief that two motions could not be combined; instead, Galileo argued that projectile motion was a compound of a uniform horizontal motion and a naturally accelerated vertical motion, the combined trajectory describing a parabola. As Salviati states:

> Our Author next undertakes to explain what happens when a body is urged to a motion compounded of one which is horizontal and uniform and of another which is vertical but naturally accelerated; from these two components results the path of a projectile, which is a parabola. The problem is to determine the speed [*impeto*] of the projectile at each point [or moment]. (p. 248; second brackets added)

Here again without recourse to the formalism of the infinitesimal calculus Galileo had to demonstrate his theorems with intersecting line segments whose lengths depicted the relevant magnitudes. Nonetheless, he was able to prove that the hypotenuse of a right angled triangle represents the combined motions of the accelerated vertical descent and (approximately) uniform horizontal projection. (cf. pp. 246-247) Thus his kinematic description of projectile motion, like his law of the constant acceleration of free fall, while not providing a *causal* explanation of these motions, were the first convincing *mathematical demonstrations* of their exact magnitudes. Reversing Aristotle's conviction that in seeking an accurate account of motions causal explanations should take precedence, Galileo showed that any causal explanation first requires discovering the exact law expressing the functional magnitudes involved. (cf. 160) Like his other innovations, this procedure has become so commonplace that we forget its revolutionary origins.

It is in the context of this discussion of projectile motion that Galileo describes the possibility of a "perpetual" horizontal motion of a ball propelled along a frictionless surface which has generated considerable controversy regarding the extent to which he had formulated and accepted the principle of inertia, the keystone in the construction of Newtonian mechanics. As usual the problem can be traced to Greek antiquity when Democritus (while lacking the term 'inertia') endowed the atoms, prior to the creation of individual worlds, with an inertial motion in that they moved in a random direction in an isotropic space with a rectilinear speed until interacting with other atoms. Possessing mass they also exhibit momentum, but since they lacked weight they would not naturally descend until forced to do so (by vortical pressure) within individual worlds. (cf. Volume I, Ch. X) Because weight was so important in Aristotle's explanation of terrestrial motions and since objects are not seen to continue in motion indefinitely but invariably come to rest, Aristotle denied inertial motion after explicitly describing it.[38]

Both in the *Dialogue* and in *Two New Sciences* Galileo mentions "perpetual" motion, the most explicit description being the following:

> Imagine any particle projected along a horizontal plane without friction; then we know [. . .] that this particle will move along this same plane with a motion that is uniform and perpetual, provided the plane has no limits. But if the plane is limited and elevated, then the moving particle, which we imagine to be a heavy one, will on passing over the edge of the plane acquire, in addition to its previous uniform and perpetual motion, a downward propensity due to its own weight [. . .]. (p. 324)

This example, while maintaining the conservation of motion (when all resistance has been removed) does not affirm the principle of inertia because without the support of the horizontal plane the weighted ball would naturally fall toward the center of the earth. Thus Galileo does not consider how the ball would move independently of the influence of *gravitas* or weight.

In the *Dialogue* he presented the example of a ship circumnavigating the earth which "if all external and accidental obstacles were removed [. . .]

would thus be disposed to move incessantly and uniformly [in a circle around the globe] from an impulse once received." (p. 287; brackets added) Like the previous example, this illustrates the conservation of motion but not the principle of inertia. In none of his examples does Galileo ever describe the motion of an object free from any gravitational impetus, thus he does not distinguish mass from weight nor formulate the principle of inertia as a natural *state* of a body to remain at rest or continue in motion in a straight line unless acted upon by some other influence. Given his impatience with abstract or nonempirical speculation, he probably thought such conjectures fruitless. It was Descartes, for reasons similar to Democritus, who explicitly formulated the principle of inertia which became the first axiom or law of motion in Newton's *Principia*. As Koyré states:

> Descartes-the-physicist's greatest claim to fame is certainly that he gave a 'clear and distinct' formulation to the principle of inertia, and that he realized its importance. Of course it could be argued that by the time he did this, i.e., by the time his *Principles* was published (twelve years after Galileo's *Dialogue* and six years after his *Discourses*) it was no longer a particularly notable achievement nor a very difficult one. For by 1644 the law of inertia was no longer an unheard-of or novel idea. On the contrary, thanks to the work and writings of Gassendi, Torricelli and Cavalieri [both disciples of Galileo] it was beginning to have the status of a generally accepted truth.[39] Brackets added.

Although Galileo's investigations in the *Two New Sciences* were more extensive than reported (including attempts to measure the velocity of light, experiments in the fracture of beams and marble columns, and investigations of sound), his major contributions to the advancement of physics have been described. As previously indicated, these consist primarily of an exact mathematical description of the constant acceleration of free fall and projectile motion, ending over two thousand years of speculation regarding their proper conceptualization and precise mathematical expression. While unable to provide causal explanations of their occurrence, he did succeed in submitting them to geometrical demonstrations, illustrating his thesis that the proper language of nature is mathematics. This mathematization of motion, along with his demolition of Aristotle's cosmology, are his everlasting achievements. While Aristotle had relied on untested observations, logical demonstrations, and qualitative causal explanations in his philosophy, by introducing instrumentally enhanced observations, the experimental testing of hypotheses, and mathematical demonstrations of laws Galileo moved natural philosophy much closer to the image of modern science. As Clavelin states:

> The reason, therefore, why no scientific problem was ever the same again as it had been before Galileo tackled it lay largely in his redefinition of scientific intelligibility and in the means by which he achieved it: only a new explanatory ideal and an unprecedented skill in combining reason with observation would have changed natural philosophy in so radical a way. No wonder then that, as we read his works, we are struck above all by the remarkable way in which he impressed the features of classical science upon a 2000-year-old picture of scientific rationality.[40]

The world and man's place in it was never the same after Galileo. Bringing about a revolutionary transformation in our thinking about the universe, he initiated the modern scientific worldview.

The "Two New Sciences" was published in 1638, four years before his death. Although blind and physically exhausted, he still continued his scientific inquiries until the end on January 9, 1642, at Arcetri, less than a month before his seventy-eighth birthday. Interred in the church of Santa Croce in Florence, the region of his birthplace, the grand duke "wished to erect [. . .] a sumptuous tomb across from that of Michelangelo," but the church "forbad any honors to a man who had died under vehement suspicion of heresy."[41] Yet this injunction must have been circumvented eventually because there exists today in Santa Croce a monument honoring Galileo just as grand as that paying tribute to Michelangelo.

NOTES

1. Galileo Galilei, *The Assayer*. Reprinted in *The Controversy On The Comets Of 1618*, translated by Stillman Drake and C.D. O'Malley (Philadelphia: Univ. of Pennsylvania Press, 1960), pp. 183-184.

2. Galileo Galilei, *Dialogue Concerning the Two Chief World Systems—Ptolemaic and Copernican*, second revised edition, translated by Stillman Drake (Berkeley: Univ. of California Press, 1967), pp. 5-6. The

following page references in the text are to this work unless otherwise indicated.

3. The name is derived from the sixth century scholastic who, after Aristotle and Theophrastus, is one of our main sources of knowledge about the Presocratics, and was often quoted by the Aristotelians. The other two participants, Sagredo and Salviati, were lifelong friends and benefactors of Galileo who had died before he finished the *Dialogue* and whom he wanted to honor. Sagredo, a Venetian nobleman and diplomat, represents the intelligent arbiter in the discourse while Salviati, a wealthy Florentine aristocrat, speaks for Galileo who is usually referred to as "the Academician."

4. The example does present an interesting contrast, however. The followers of Aristotle were so certain on deductive grounds that a stone dropped from the masthead of a ship could not fall parallel to the mast if the ship were moving, that they never performed the experiment. Also on deductive grounds, Galileo was convinced that it would and actually performed the experiment as he indicated in *Il Saggiatore*. Einstein offers a similar example of the confidence he had in his theoretical deductions. When he showed Ilse Rosenthal-Schneider the telegram from Eddington declaring that the latter's 1919 eclipse expedition in Principe, West Africa, had confirmed his prediction of the bending of light in the gravitational field of the sun, his casual manner led Ilse to ask what he would have thought had the results of the expedition not confirmed his predictions. Einstein replied: "'Then I would have been sorry for the dear Lord—the theory is correct.'" Ronald W. Clark, *Einstein: The Life and Times* (New York: The World Publishing Co., 1971), p. 230.

5. The term 'centrifugal' was introduced by Christian Huygens and 'centripetal' by Newton, although both forces were recognized by the Presocratics, Anaxagoras and Empedocles respectively.

6. Drake, *Galileo At Work, op. cit.,* ch. III, pp. 408-409.

7. *Ibid.*

8. *Ibid.,* p. 409.

9. Alexandre Koyré, *Galileo Studies,* trans. by John Mepham (New Jersey: Humanities Press, 1978), p. 207.

10. *Ibid.*, p. 205.

11. *Ibid.*, p. 201.

12. Plato, *Republic*, Part III, Ch. XXVI, Sec. vii, 527c. Cornford translation. Brackets added.

13. *Ibid.*

14. *Ibid.*, Ch. XXVII, Sec. vii, 531C-535A.

15. *Ibid.*, Ch. XXVI, Sec. vii, 525c. In the *Timaeus* Plato does attempt to explain the imposition of geometrical order on the heavens in mathematical proportions and to describe the four elements and their interactions in terms of the triangles making up the four Platonic solids, but this endeavor is completely *a priori*, not at all what Galileo meant by mathematical demonstration based on observation and experimentation.

16. Archytas fragments, Diels 44B1. Quoted from S. Sambursky, *The Physical World of the Greeks*, translated by Merton Dagut (New York: Collier Books, [1956] 1962), p. 55.

17. Plato, *op. cit.*, Ch. XXVI, Sec. vii, 529a.

18. *Ibid.*

19. Koyré, *op. cit.*, p. 202.

20. *Ibid.*, p. 208.

21. Galileo Galilei, "The Essayer," translated by Stillman Drake, *The Controversy On The Comets of 1618* (Philadelphia: University of Pennsylvania Press, 1960), pp. 183-184.

22. This should provide food for thought for anti- or nonrealists like Paul Feyerabend, Thomas Kuhn, Arthur Fine, and Bas van Fraassen.

23. John Stuart Mill, *A System of Logic*, Bk. I, Ch. VIII: "Of the Four Methods of Experimental Inquiry."

24. The inclusion of this argument of the pope regarding divine omnipotence was required (probably at the direction of the pope himself) by Niccoló Riccardi, the licensing censor at Rome, and by the Inquisitor at Florence, along with a revised title page and preface.

25. Drake, *Galileo at Work*, *op. cit.*, p. 312. Again, the immediately following quotations cited in the text will be to this work unless otherwise indicated.

26. Despite the prohibition, copies reached Paris and other countries. Pierre Fermat had a copy and Descartes was lent a copy by Isaac Beeckman in 1634. (cf. p. 361) Bernegger's Latin translation of the *Dialogue* was printed 1635. (cf. p. 368) Thomas Hobbes, who visited Galileo in 1635 (Milton was another famous visiter), informed him that an English translation had been made, although it never was published. (cf. p. 502, f.n. 23) The well-known English translation by Thomas Salusbury appeared in London in 1661.

27. As late as 1641, a year before he died, in a letter to Liceti he wrote that "this earth is not only not the center of their [the planets] circular movements but [. . .] [o]ne place that could almost be put as the center for all planets but the moon would be the sun, better than any other [. . .]." (pp. 411-412; italics added)

28. In October, 1992, the Polish pope, John Paul II, attempted to amend the error of the Church in condemning Galileo by restoring and honoring his standing as a good Christian. According to the pope, the theologians of the Church had been wrong in the seventeenth century in not distinguishing between belief in the Bible and the correct interpretation of it. As our knowledge changes, the meaning of the Bible has to be reinterpreted as Galileo argued. He subsequently was exonerated.

29. This again is Cardinal Francesco Barberini, nephew of the pope, who refused to sign the judgment against Galileo and who did so much to serve his cause during the trial. He should not be confused with Cardinal Antonio Barberini, brother of the pope, who was not a friend of Galileo and who "ordered that Galileo's sentence and abjuration be read to all mathematicians in every university city throughout Catholic Europe." (p. 502, f.n. 1). Being held accountable historically for their actions perhaps redresses to some extend the harm done by individuals during their lifetimes.

30. Galileo, *Dialogues Concerning Two New Science*, *op. cit.*, p. xi.

31. *Ibid.*, p. ix. The following references in the text are to this work unless otherwise indicated.

32. Maurice Clavelin, *The Natural Philosophy of Galileo*, translated by A. J. Pomerans (Cambridge: The MIT Press, 1974). Where the following references to this book in the text are unambiguous (in contrast to references from *Two New Sciences*), they will be cited in the text.

33. This odd number law had, of course, been discovered by Oresme in the fourteenth century, but whether Galileo was aware of it is not known.

34. Clavelin, p. 296.

35. Ilya Prigogine and Isabelle Stengers, *Order Out Of Chaos* (New York: Bantam Books, 1984), p. 84. Originally published in 1979 as *La nouvelle alliance*.

36. Mersenne states "I doubt whether Galileo actually performed the experiments of fall down inclined planes, since he does not speak of them, and since the ratio he gives is often contradicted by experiment [. . .]."(*L' Harmonie Universelle*, Vol. I, p. 112) Descartes' skepticism is expressed in a letter to Mersenne (*Oeuvres de Descartes*, Vol. I, p. 287). Both references are from Koyré, *op. cit.*, p. 126, f.n. 177 and 176.

37. Koyré, *ibid.*, p. 107.

38. Aristotle, *Physics*, Bk. IV, Ch. 8:19-22.

39. Koyré, *op. cit.*, p. 129.

40. Clavelin, *op. cit.*, p. 383.

41. Drake, *op. cit.*, p. 436.

CHAPTER V

CREATION OF THE CORPUSCULAR-MECHANISTIC WORLD VIEW

[. . .] the genius of the seventeenth century.[1]
Whitehead

The astronomical advancements recounted in the previous three chapters are frequently cited as constituting one of the greatest revolutions in the history of science, a cosmological transformation so radical that the two contending systems, the geocentric and heliocentric, were cognitively incommensurable. On this interpretation, the ancient classification of the universe into the celestial aethereal realm with its eternal circular motion and the terrestrial domain of the four elements with their terminal rectilinear motions, all woven into a fabric of conceptual implications and semantic designations, precluded any rational comparison and evaluation between it and the heliocentric universe. But this depiction of the controversy is greatly exaggerated.[2]

As radically disparate as were the two cosmologies, the crucial issue involved primarily an interchange of the positions of the earth and the sun, leaving the orbits of the other planets only slightly rearranged. As acutely aware as they were of the inadequacies of geocentric astronomy, given the new telescopic evidence the ancient Greek astronomers probably would have embraced the heliocentric model. Even in the sixteenth century it was not the astronomical revision that had such revolutionary consequences, but its threat to the metaphysical distinctions inherent in the Aristotelian system defended by the Peripatetics, the theological implications guarded by the Christian theologians, and the traumatic displacement of mankind from the center of the universe.[3]

In contrast, the formation of the corpuscular-mechanistic world view required rejecting in *toto* Aristotle's conception of an organismic universe and teleological explanatory schema. Rather than merely revising a previously accepted cosmology, it required laying on nature a completely new theoretical framework of interpretation and network of conceptual implications. While Galileo was primarily responsible for dismantling the Aristotelian-Ptolemaic cosmology, the creation of the corpuscular-mechanistic worldview was the achievement of a number of investigators—although it too owed its final culmination to Newton. Despite the fact that Aristotelianism was the official natural philosophy taught in the universities throughout Europe during most of the seventeenth century, at the beginning of the century the most creative scholars in the major countries, Italy, France, Germany, England, and the Netherlands, were rebelling against the Peripatetic system of thought and education. They all found the Aristotelian methodology sterile and stultifying, the conceptual framework limiting and outmoded, the explanations abstract and verbal, and the appeal to authority dogmatic and repressive. After four centuries of fruitful development, the Aristotelian legacy was spent and ripe for replacement.

One of the first to launch the attack in 1585 was the gifted Dutch mathematician and physicist Simon Stevin whose mathematical work, *L'Arithmétique*, introduced decimal fractions along with significant advances in algebra, followed a year later by his *Beghinselen des Waterwichts* (*Elements of Hydrostatics*) which rejected Aristotle's treatment of hydrostatics in favor of Archimedes' principle of specific gravity and axiomatic method. The year 1600 proved particularly significant, an *anni merabiles*, a truly extraordinary century of new beginnings. Though martyred in that year for his heretical religious teachings rather than his audacious scientific conjectures, Giordano Bruno rebelled against the closed Aristotelian system, advocating in its place the ancient atomistic doctrine that our sun with its planets was merely one among an innumerable number of universes.[4] Furthermore, he proposed the conservation of mass and energy and "the principle of the survival of the 'best-adapted' being," while also extolling science as the wave of the future (yet adhering to a Neoplatonic interpretation of the universe and equating science with magic).[5] But probably the work that most exemplified the new spirit of philosophical emancipation and renewed confidence in independent empirical research was *De Magnete* of William Gilbert.[6]

WILLIAM GILBERT

After earning an M.D. in 1569 from St. John's College, Cambridge, practicing medicine "with great success and applause," elected a Fellow of the Royal College of Physicians in 1573, appointed by Elizabeth I as her court "physician-in-ordinary," Gilbert (1544-1603) began an eighteen year study of the phenomena of magnetism and electricity, that culminated in his great book of 1600.[7] Like other subsequent works whose titles announced their novelty (for example, Kepler's *Astronomia Nova*, Bacon's *Novum Organum*, and Galileo's *Two New Sciences*), the full title of Gilbert's work (in English: *Concerning the Magnet, Magnetic Bodies, and the Great Magnet of the Earth*;

a New Physiology Demonstrated both by Many Arguments and by Many Experiments) contains the words "*physiologia nova*," proclaiming a new physics of the magnet (at the time Physiology meant Physics).

Beginning with an exhaustive history (he points out that Plato says that Euripides originated the name "magnet") and comprehensive critical review of previous theories of magnetism, he then discusses the origins of the loadstone and of iron and steel, the properties of electricity, the construction of the compass, the role of the polar orientation and verticle dip of its magnetic needle in determining longitudes, latitudes, and meridians, and even attempts to explain the diurnal rotation of the earth and precession of the equinoxes as due to the magnetic force of the earth's poles.

Contemptuous of previous investigators who "not being practical in the research of objects in nature, being acquainted only with books, being led astray by certain erroneous physical systems, and having made no magnetical experiments" (pp. 5-6), he declares that "in the discovery of secret things and in the investigation of hidden causes, stronger reasons are obtained from sure experiments and demonstrated arguments than from probable conjectures and the opinions of philosophical speculators [. . . .]" (p. xlvii) True to his convictions, the work is surprisingly modern in its dependence on a multitude of observations and imaginative experiments to test hypotheses, along with numerous diagrams to demonstrate the properties of magnetic (and electrical) phenomena. Relying mainly on the "*terrella*" ("little earth"), a spherical magnet, in his experimental demonstrations, he investigates such phenomena as "*verticity*" (the innate polar strength or "energy" of a magnet), "*magnetic coition*" (the mutuality of magnetic attractions and movements), "sphere of influence" (the space in which the magnetic force extends), "excited magnetic bodies" (such as iron or steel that are magnetized by a loadstone), "*magnetized versorium*" (the suspended iron or steel needle whose orientation depends upon the direction and strength of the magnetic fields), and "*declinatorium*" (the degree to which the needle dips from the horizon due to the magnetic force, an indicator of latitude). (cf. p. liv) He rhapsodizes the magnetic needle, "that soul of the mariner's compass, that wonderful director in sea-voyages, the finger of God [. . . .]" (p. 223)

Whereas previously the poles of the magnetic needle were identified by the direction in which it pointed, he is proud of correcting this error. The magnetized needle

> moves and revolves until one of its poles, being impelled toward the
> north, comes to rest in its predetermined point on the horizon; the pole

that comes to a stand looking north is (as appears from the foregoing rules and demonstrations) southern, not northern, though till now every one has supposed it to be northern because it turns to the north. (p. 278)

For this to be true the polarity of the needle has to be preestablished by a magnet, not by the direction it points, the southern pole pointing north and the northern pole pointing south. Contrary to the Aristotelians who thought that discovering the causes of phenomena was the primary aim of any investigation, Gilbert (like Galileo) considered the search for causal explanations subordinate to accurate descriptions of the phenomenon's behavior: "[a]s for the causes of magnetic movements, referred to in the schools of philosophers to the four elements and to prime qualities, these we leave for roaches and moths to prey upon." (p. 104) Nonetheless, he does reflect on the causes of magnetism and electricity. Rejecting the "*causa formalis*," "*secunda forma*," and "*causa corporum*" of Aristotle, he attributes magnetic movements to an "astral form" that inheres in each celestial globe constituting its primary cohesive energy ("*vigor*"). (cf. 105) Like the terrella, the earth is a huge magnetic with opposite poles and "*verticity*" originating not from a point but from "all of the parts of the whole" which becomes stronger as one approaches the poles and weaker near the equator. Finally, however, like Thales and the ancient Egyptians and Caldeans, Gilbert attributes the magnetic properties of the terrella, earth, and heavenly globes to their being animate or endowed with a soul. This soul is identical in the "homogenic parts" of each globe, although it varies in "superiority" or "nobility" among the celestial globes. (cf. p. 308)

Not a very advanced explanation, Gilbert nonetheless does describe the properties and movements of magnetic (and electrified) bodies and forces in exact qualitative terms, although not quantitatively, for which he was chided by Galileo. Moreover, while previously magnetic and electric forces (particularly static electricity) were often confused, Gilbert distinguished them by their origins and operations: electrical attraction generated in electrical *substances* like amber by rubbing, causing them to attract bits of straw and chaff due to an invisible "effluvia" acting "in a right line toward the centre of electricity." Magnetic forces, in contrast, are incorporeal, originating from the *form* of lodestones which mutually attract "on a line perpendicular to the circumference only at the poles, elsewhere obliquely and transversely [. . . .]" (p. 97) In addition, whereas magnetic forces are transferred to the attracted body without loss of power and are not impeded by material bodies, electric forces do not electrify the attracted body and are obstructed by intervening materials.

In Book VI of *De Magnete*, the final book, Gilbert describes the magnetic properties of the earth and their astronomical significance. Scornfully rejecting Aristotle's prime mover, "this fiction, this something not comprehensible by any reasoning" (p. 322), he accepts Copernicus' argument that it is simpler to account for the apparent diurnal rotation of the whole universe by the revolution of the earth "because it is more accordant to reason that the one small body, the earth, should make a daily revolution than that the whole universe should be whirled around it." (cf. p. 327) As in his discussion of magnetism, he shows a comprehensive and detailed knowledge of the writings of ancient astronomers (such as Philolaus, Heraclides, and Ptolemy), as well as more recent authors such as Copernicus and Tycho. Galileo, who devoted fifteen pages in the *Dialogue* to a discussion of Gilbert, might have been influenced by his arguments supporting Copernicanism.

Having accepted one of the motions attributed to the earth by Copernicus, the diurnal rotation, did Gilbert also believe that the earth revolved around the sun in a circular orbit? Some scholars such as Dijksterhuis deny this, asserting that "Gilbert [. . .] accepts the diurnal motion of the earth, but without committing himself with regard to the annual motion,"[8] but I think the evidence clearly shows the contrary. The basis of the uncertainty is that his primary arguments were aimed at proving the diurnal rotation of the earth (not its annual revolution) and the inclination of its axis toward the ecliptic, which he believed is caused by the magnetic poles in order to ensure the change of seasons and variation in temperature necessary for sustaining life on the earth.

> The earth then revolves [. . .] and this movement brings growth and decay, gives occasion for the generation of animated things [. . . .] The motion of the whole earth, therefore, is primary, astral, circular about its poles, whose verticity rises on both sides from the plane of the equator, and the energy is infused into opposite ends, so that the globe by a definite rotation might move to the good [of man], sun and stars inciting. (pp. 334-335; brackets added)

Thus the earth "rotates in virtue of her magnetic and primary energy" with its poles inclined from the ecliptic, otherwise "there would be no change of seasons [. . .] but the face of things would persist forever unchanged" in relation to the sun. "Hence (for the everlasting good of man) the earth's axis declined from the pole of the zodiac just enough to suffice for generation and diversification." (p. 347) All of this, naturally, was arranged by God. Thus

Gilbert subscribed to the ancient argument that life on this planet is evidence of the fact that God created the conditions to make it possible, not the modern belief that life was possible because these conditions existed.

Regarding Gilbert's belief in the annual revolution of the earth in its orbit, there are two passages that support this. In one he implies that the planets have the sun, not the earth, as the center of their orbits: "For all planets have a like movement to the east [. . .] whether it be Mercury or Venus within the sun's orbit [that is, below it], or whether they revolve round the sun [that is, above it]." (p. 330; brackets added). In the second passage he distinguishes the fact that the earth not only "rotates" on its axis but "revolves in a circle towards the sun."

> The earth therefore *rotates*, and [. . .] by an energy that is innate, manifest, conspicuous, *revolves* in a circle toward the sun; through this motion it shares in the solar energies and influences; and its verticity holds it in this motion lest it stray into every region of the sky. The sun (chief inciter of action in nature), as *he causes the planets to advance in their courses*, so, too, doth *bring about the revolution of the globe* by sending forth the energies of his spheres—his light being effused. (p. 333; italics added)

While there would be no uncertainty had Gilbert stated that the earth revolves *around* the sun rather than *toward* it, the fact that he uses the term "revolve" when he is referring to a circular orbital motion in contrast to an axial rotation, indicates that he was distinguishing in the passage the one motion from the other. Furthermore, since it is only within the Copernican heliocentric system that the sun is interpreted as causing the motion of the planets, this would also support the view that the sun causes the "revolution" (not rotation) of the earth. Finally, it is the earth's verticity in relation to the sun's "energies and influences" (the sun also having a magnetic field) that keeps the earth in its circular revolution "lest it stray into every region of the sky." Perhaps the reason Gilbert used the phrase "revolves in a circle toward the sun" is that since magnetic influences are mutual and the sun is the more massive body, the earth would revolve "toward the sun." What would keep it from eventually joining the sun is not explained. Newton would substitute reciprocal gravitational forces for Gilbert's mutual magnetic forces, explaining the reason the planets do not come together as due to the counteracting inertial forces.

This conception of a mutually attractive magnetic force as one component of the cause of a planet's orbital motion, which influenced Kepler's attempt at a dynamic explanation, was not elaborated in the *De Magnete*, but was described in the later *De Mundo*.

> The force which emanates from the moon reaches to the earth, and, in like manner, the magnetic virtue of the earth pervades the region of the moon: both correspond and conspire by the joint action of both, according to a proportion and conformity of motions, but the earth has more effect in consequence of its superior mass; the earth attracts and repels the moon, and the moon, within certain limits, the earth; not so as to make the bodies come together, as magnetic bodies do, but so that they go on in a continuous course.[9]

Although he does not indicate what the "repelling" force is, Gilbert clearly recognizes in a general way, perhaps for the first time in history, that two opposing forces are necessary to account for the planet's orbital revolution. That in itself is a significant achievement. In any case, the *De Magnete* along with the *De Revolutionibus* constitutes one of the germinal works in the history of modern classical science. Although Copernicus' work was essentially theoretical advancing a new astronomical system, Gilbert's is mainly empirical exemplifying how the new method of experimental scientific inquiry should be pursued. Perhaps the best evaluation of his contribution is that of Galileo, who has Salviati say of Gilbert:

> I have the highest praise, admiration, and envy for this author, who framed such a stupendous concept regarding an object which innumerable men of splendid intellect had handled without paying attention to it. He seems to me worthy of great acclaim also for the many new and sound observations which he made [. . .]. What I might have wished for in Gilbert would be a little more of the mathematician, and especially a thorough grounding in geometry, a discipline which would have rendered him less rash about accepting as rigorous proofs those reasons which he puts forward as *verae causae* for the correct conclusions he himself had observed. His reasons, candidly speaking, are not rigorous, and lack that force which must unquestionably be present in those adduced as necessary and eternal scientific conclusions.[10]

Yet Salviati adds that while with the course of time he expects "further observations'' and even more ''conclusive demonstrations,'' yet ''this need not diminish the glory of the first observer.''

RENÉ DESCARTES

Credited with being the father of the mechanistic worldview (along with modern philosophy), one hardly could find a more striking contrast to Gilbert than Descartes. Whereas for Gilbert knowledge was *a posteriori*, comprising an accumulation of empirical evidence based on controlled observations and experiments, for Descartes it was *a priori*, consisting of a deductive system derived from self-evidence principles analogous to mathematics. It is not that Descartes was unacquainted with experimentation or opposed to observations: on the contrary, in his various writings in *Dioptrics* (1637), *Météores* (1637), and *Passions of the Soul* (1649), he showed considerable skill in conducting a number of experiments on the optics of vision, the refraction of light (anticipating Snell's sine law), the function of the heart and circulation of the blood, and the transmission of ''animal spirits'' through the nerves to the brain, along with innumerable acute anatomical, physiological (the ''phantom limb''), optical, and meteorological observations. But while Descartes realized that knowledge of empirical phenomena required observation and experiment, he believed that a theoretical system for interpreting physical reality had to be rooted in metaphysics, the source of the self-evident principles of knowledge: ''[p]hilosophy as a whole is like a tree; of which the roots are Metaphysics, the trunk is Physics, and the branches emerging from this trunk are all the other brands of knowledge.''[11]

Educated at what he called the ''celebrated'' Jesuit School of La Flèche, Descartes (1696-1650) vividly recounts his disillusionment at the conclusion of his courses because of the unresolved conflict of views and the uncertainty of conclusions. As he states in the *Discourse on Méthode* (1637), upon completing his studies he found himself ''embarrassed with so many doubts and errors that it seemed to me that the effort to instruct myself had no effect other than the increasing discovery of my own ignorance.''[12] Furthermore, he had learned from his ''College days that there is nothing imaginable so strange or so little credible that it has not been maintained by one philosopher or another [. . . .]'' (p. 90) Like all the other *savants* of the seventeenth century, Descartes did not find the scholastic education he received at the hands of Jesuits relevant or convincing. The one subject that was not disappointing was mathematics in which he was ''delighted [. . .] because of

the certainty of its demonstrations and the evidence of its reasoning [. . . .]''
(p. 85) Yet mathematics by itself conveys no knowledge of the external world
and even its demonstrations were not immune to error.

But it was especially empirical, sensory knowledge that Descartes (like
Plato) found untrustworthy. In addition to the usual illusions, limitations, and
defects of the senses, as a convinced Copernican Descartes must have been
tremendously influenced by the realization that if the heliocentric view were
true, then throughout the past mankind has been fundamentally deceived by
his/her senses. Furthermore, the phenomenon of dreams was particularly
disturbing because if we believe that what we experience in waking life is
dependent upon—and therefore evidence of—an external world, then how is
it possible to have such lifelike experiences in dreams when the usual external
causes are absent? As he says in the sixth *Méditation* (1641),

> I never have believed myself to feel anything in waking moments
> which I cannot also sometimes believe myself to feel when I sleep,
> and as I do not think that these things which I seem to feel in sleep,
> proceed from objects outside of me, I do not see any reason why I
> should have this belief regarding objects which I seem to perceive
> while awake. (p. 189)

Given these uncertainties, Descartes turned to the "method of doubt" to
revolve them. Deciding to "put aside" any beliefs that could possibly be
questioned, he enquired whether any assertion was impervious to doubt,
especially if an "evil genius" set out to deceive him: "I shall consider that the
heavens, the earth, colours, figures, sound, and all other external things are
nought but the illusions and dreams of which this genius has availed himself
in order to lay traps for my credulity [. . . .]'' (p. 148) Nonetheless, even as
he doubted all his beliefs there was one he could not doubt, since the very fact
of his doubting presupposed its truth; namely, the *"cogito ergo sum,"* "I think
(or doubt), therefore I am." Be there

> some deceiver or other, very powerful and very cunning, who ever
> employs his ingenuity in deceiving me. Then without doubt I exist
> also if he deceives me, and let him deceive me as much as he will, he
> can never cause me to be nothing so long as I think [. . .]. So that
> after having reflected well and carefully examined all things, we must
> come to the definite conclusion that this proposition: I am, I exist, is
> necessarily true each time I pronounce it, or that I mentally conceive

it. (p. 150)

In these brief "meditations" Descartes had the incredible effect of inverting the whole previous tradition of Aristotelianism, which had claimed a direct veridical knowledge of the external world, proclaiming instead that what we indubitably know is that we exist as conscious beings with the particular contents of consciousness that we experience having. For though we can doubt that any of our perceptions or beliefs are true representations of an independent reality, that we have such conscious experiences is itself incontrovertible. Regarding our presumed authentic experiences of the physical world,

> it will be said that these phenomena are false and that I am dreaming. Let it be so; still it is at least quite certain that it seems to me that I see light, that I hear noise and that I feel heat. That cannot be false [. . .]. (p. 153)

Furthermore, because we are certain that we exist as conscious beings while being doubtful of the existence of any physical entities such as our bodies, our consciousness cannot depend on our bodies: "it is very certain that the knowledge of my existence [. . .] does not depend on things whose existence is not yet known to me," namely, "corporeal things." (p. 152) Descartes thereby introduced two new paradigms that redirected all subsequent philosophical inquiry and had a profound effect on science as well: (1) the epistemic and ontological priority of consciousness over physical reality, and (2) the Cartesian dualism of mind and matter. Combined, these paradigms injected the notorious subjective-turn in western thought that persisted well into the twentieth century.

This primacy of consciousness and dubitable existence of the external world posed the problem of knowledge. Since what we directly know is the contents of our consciousness rather than an external world, whatever knowledge of physical reality is attainable must be derived, for Descartes, like mathematics, from self-evident principles and deductive inferences originating in the mind. The criteria of self-evidence are clearness and distinctness, the very features that enabled him to infer that he must exist if he doubts, and affirm such propositions as "what is past cannot be undone" and "something cannot both exist and not exist at the same time." This belief that he could derive a true theory of reality based on his own thought was influenced by a dream he had on November 10, 1619, at age twenty-three. In that dream an "angel of truth" appeared to him announcing that the structure of physical reality was mathematical and that the means of understanding this structure was geometry. Overwhelmed, he vowed and subsequently completed a pilgrimage to Loretto in gratitude. This inspiration led to the publication of his *La Géométrie* (1637), in which he combined the recent developments in mathematical analysis using algebraic functions and notation with classical geometry, creating the new discipline of analytic geometry. One of the great achievements in mathematics, it represented a rejection of the dependence on classical geometry and a search for new techniques and notation for dealing with the novel problems in mechanics.[13]

His success in solving mathematical problems with these new methods was so remarkable that he resolved to follow the same general procedures in dealing with scientific questions. The famous "Rules of Reasoning" in the "Discourse on the Method of Rightly Conducting the Reason and Seeking for Truth in the Sciences" (1637) are precisely those used in solving mathematical problems. (cf. 92) However, there is a crucial difference between a mathematical system and a physical theory: whereas the *validity* of a mathematical system depends solely on valid deductive inferences or internal consistency, the *truth* of a cosmological theory requires its (approximate) conformity to the structure of physical reality. But with the doctrine of the primacy of consciousness precluding any experiential access to this reality, how was the truth of the scientific framework to be determined?

Herein lies the crucial weakness of Descartes' philosophy. Because material truths derived from the mind are not self-confirming as in mathematics, their justification had to be sought elsewhere. In brief, Descartes' argument consists in proving the existence of God, acknowledging God's perfection, and concluding that since deception is inconsistent with God's perfect nature (ignoring the agelong deception of geocentrism) we can be confident that our perceptions and reasoning (which ultimately depend on God), if kept within proper limits, are trustworthy. Thus Descartes' philosophy is based on the

> Metaphysical foundation that God is supremely good and by no means deceitful, and that, accordingly, the faculty which He gave us to distinguish the true from the false cannot err when we use it correctly and perceive something clearly with its help. Such are Mathematical demonstrations; such is the knowledge that material things exist; and such are all evident demonstrations which are made concerning material things.[14]

In this reliance on "the light of reason" as the source of knowledge and God's veracity as the guarantor of truth, Descartes forsakes the Aristotelian tradition for Platonic-Augustinianism.

Turning to Descartes' conception of the physical universe presented in the *Principia Philosophaie*,[15] for geometry to serve as the method for understanding physical reality there must be a congruence between the two. This in fact is the case since he distinguishes between mind and matter, or more precisely soul and physical substances, in terms of the essential properties of thought and extension. Having introduced these definitions in the sixth Meditation, he repeats them in the *Principles*:

> [. . .] each substance has only one principal property which constitutes its nature and essence, and to which all the other properties are related. Thus, extension in length, breadth, and depth constitutes the nature of corporeal substance; and thought constitutes the nature of thinking substance. (p. 23)

Abstracting all the sensory qualities and corporeal properties such as visual shapes, colors, hardness, textures, and generic kinds (for example, metals, stones, liquids, organic objects) from physical objects, Descartes defined matter by the sole geometric property of extension, thereby (like Parmenides and Plato) reducing it to spatiality: "the same extension which constitutes the nature of body also constitutes the nature of space [. . .]." (p. 44) All other characteristics were relegated to the mind. Rejecting atomism on the grounds that all extension is infinitely divisible, like Aristotle he also denies the existence of a vacuum or of the void, maintaining that the universe is an "indefinitely extended plenum." Physical objects are distinguished from homogeneous space by their three-dimensional configurations and their motions, although completely contiguous. It is their effects on the senses, producing pressures in the "animal spirits" in the nerves which are transmitted to the cavities of the brain, that in turn agitate the pineal gland containing the soul which results in physical objects appearing to us to have the qualities and properties they do.[16]

Along with their three-dimensional sizes and shapes, material bodies are differentiated by the places they occupy. Because the universe is a plenum, when any body is modified in size or shape or changes its position, whatever space remains is instantaneously filled by adjacent matter. As in any completely mechanical system, all alteration is due to motion and impact: "all the variation in matter, or all the diversity of forms, depends on motion."

(p. 50) Thus Descartes is the founder of a completely mechanistic universe. Because the position of a static entity or the trajectory of a moving body appears quite different to observers moving relative to each other (as in Einstein's theory of relativity), all motion and rest are relative, hence their designation depends upon a frame of reference, a Cartesian coordinate system. Movement is *"the transference of one part of matter or of one body, from the vicinity of those bodies immediately contiguous to it and considered as at rest, into the vicinity of others."* (p. 51)

This extreme relativity of motion was adopted by Huygens but rejected by Newton because it would not allow for a definite velocity and trajectory of a particle and, according to Newton, would lend support to atheism. As Westfall states, Newton "vehemently rejected the relativism of Cartesian mechanics for an absolutistic dynamics founded on the principle that force is the distinguishing characteristic of true motion."[17] The followers of Descartes, such as Huygens and Leibniz, accepted Descartes' conception of mechanism as based solely on motion and impact, rejecting Newton's conception of forces (such as gravity and cohesion) acting at a distance.

Although Descartes often uses the term 'force,' this effect is not due to any influence other than impact or the pressure of adjacent bodies, though God is the original source of all motion: "God is the primary cause of motion; and [. . .] He always maintains an equal quantity of it in the universe." (p. 57) Descartes thus embraces the law fundamental to any mechanistic system, the conservation of matter and motion. He then introduces three laws regulating these motions, the first of which maintains that objects at rest or in motion always persist in the same state unless affected by some external cause.

> The first law of nature: that each thing, as far as in its power, always remains in the same state; and that consequently, when it is once moved, it continues to move. (p. 59)

Rejecting Aristotle's explanation that certain substances have an inner tendency to rise or fall to their natural places, Descartes maintains that rest and motion are persistent states which, because they are not subject to inner influences, always require external causes for any change in these states:

> [. . .] each thing, provided it is simple and undivided, always remains in the same state as far as is in its power, and never changes except by external causes. Thus, if some part of matter is square, we are easily convinced that it will always remain square unless some

external intervention changes its shape. (p. 59)

This is true also if the object is at rest or in motion. He points out that
although objects thrown on the earth come to rest as Aristotle noted, it is the
resistance of the air or of some medium that causes the slowing down. Hence
without resistance, a moving body will "continue to move at the same speed
in the same direction." (p. 63) Thus Descartes was the first to accurately state,
in its full generality, the principle of inertia.

The second law rejects the Aristotelian distinction between circular
celestial and rectilinear terrestrial motions, maintaining that straight line motion
is primary.

> The second law of nature: that all movement is, of itself, along
> straight lines; and consequently, bodies which are moving in a circle
> always tend to move away from the center of the circle which they are
> describing. (p. 60)

Although the original "parts of matter," as we shall learn, were "endowed by
God" with circular motion causing the fluid revolution of the heavens and the
vortical rotation of the individual celestial bodies, to avoid contradiction
Descartes seems to maintain that despite the necessary circular motion of
"collective" bodies, "individual" particles once in motion tend to move
inertially in a straight line, or linearly away from the center in rotary motions
(which Huygens will call "centrifugal motion"):

> [. . .] each part of matter, considered individually, tends to continue its
> movement only along straight lines, and never along curved ones;
> even though [. . .] in any movement, a circle of matter which moves
> together [collectively] is always in some way formed. (p. 60; brackets
> added)

While Descartes states the principle of inertia in a more correct form than
Galileo, who restricted inertial motion to bodies moving along a frictionless
plane surface or otherwise to circular motion, Descartes' conception was not
as free from ambiguity as Koyré would have us believe.[18] In particular, how
does one explain the fact that while circular motion is typical of *collective*
bodies, inertial and what Huygens named centrifugal linear motion are
characteristic of *individual* particles? How do these motions convert into one
another?

While the first two laws specify the states of individual bodies, the third describes the results of their interaction when in motion.

> The third law: that a body, upon coming in contact with a stronger one, loses none of its motion; but that, upon coming in contact with a weaker one, it loses as much as it transfers to that weaker body. (p. 61)

He adds that "[a]ll the individual causes of the changes which occur in [the motion of] bodies are included under this third law [. . . .]" (p. 62). While Descartes clearly conceives of momentum as the product of a body's density and velocity which is conserved in impact with a "stronger" or weaker" object, the main flaw in his third law is that he denies any exchange of momentum when a moving body meets an "unyielding" object—in contrast to Newton's third law which states that "to every action there is always opposed an equal reaction."

Serving the same function (although derived *a priori*), these laws anticipate Newton's famous three laws of motion stated in the *Principia*. Descartes' first two laws are roughly equivalent to Newton's first law of inertia, while his third law approximates Newton's second two laws. The crucial difference is that Newton's second law depends upon forces and all three laws are fundamental to modern classical mechanics. Descartes adds seven additional laws "to determine, from the preceding laws, how individual bodies increase or decrease their movements or turn aside in different directions because of encounters with other bodies" (p. 64), but none of these have been retained in classical mechanics. It is one of the peculiarities of Descartes' program that while he was the father of the modern mechanistic conception of the universe, intending to reduce physical reality to a geometric system, and therefore establish mechanics on a purely mathematical basis, he was unable to formulate a single mathematical law or formula, with the exception of the (nonquantitative) law of inertia and an approximation to Snell's law of refraction.

Undoubtedly this was a consequence of his methodology. Believing that the clearness and distinctness of his principles were a sign of divine validation, he did not think it necessary to test them, either by observation or experiment, against empirical evidence, as required by Gilbert, Kepler, and Galileo, as well as all succeeding scientists. As he says, "[w]e have discovered certain principles concerning material things; and there can be no doubt about the truth of these principles, since we sought them by the light of reason and not through the prejudices of the senses.'' (p. 84) Thus mathematical demonstration, which was only one of Galileo's principle methods (the others being observation and experimentation), was his sole source of knowledge:

> [. . .] I do not accept or desire in Physics any other principles than in Geometry or abstract Mathematics; because all the phenomena of nature are explained thereby; and certain demonstrations concerning them can be given. (p. 76)

It is as if Descartes applied Plato's conception of geometry to the empirical world while retaining the notion that the truth of applied geometry was not dependent upon empirical measurements.

After a lengthy discussion of astronomical phenomena along with an evaluation of the hypotheses of Ptolemy, Copernicus, and Tycho (further illustrating Descartes' extraordinary range of knowledge), he presents his own cosmological theory, a reintroduction of the ancient vortical model of the universe. Dismissing Aristotle's distinction between celestial and terrestrial substances, he beings by claiming that ''all bodies which compose the universe are formed of one [sort of] matter [. . .] divisible into all sorts of parts [. . .] the motions of which *are in some way circular* [. . .].'' (p. 106; italics added)

Then, despite his earlier repudiation of sensory experience, he says that ''seeing that these parts could have been regulated by God in an infinity of diverse ways; experience alone should teach us which of all these ways He chose.'' (p. 106) Although experience is not a reliable *source* of knowledge, it must be appealed to in deciding which among the innumerable theoretical possibilities open to God is the one He selected. In what way experience shows this he does not say. In any case, how one imagines the exact arrangement of the original parts of matter is unimportant because he believed that his laws inevitably would lead to the same effect: ''given that these laws cause matter to assume successively all the forms it is capable of assuming [. . .] we shall finally be able to reach the form which is that of this world.'' (p. 108)

Nonetheless, he supposes

> that God, in the beginning, divided all the matter of which He formed the visible world into parts as equal as possible and of medium size [. . .] the average of all the various sizes of the parts which now compose the heavens and the stars. And let us suppose that He endowed them collectively with exactly that amount of motion which

is still in the world at present. (p. 106)

He then caused them all in one group to revolve separately with the same force around a common center forming the fluid heavens, while others rotated around various centers "equidistant from each other, arranged in the universe as we see the centers of the fixed Stars to be now; and also around other somewhat more numerous points, equal in number to the Planets (and the Comets)."(pp. 106-107) The various interactions of the motions of these latter vortices at their poles and meridians produce the individual orbits and speeds of the fixed stars, planets, and comets. Descartes refers to a number of plates to illustrate how this occurs.

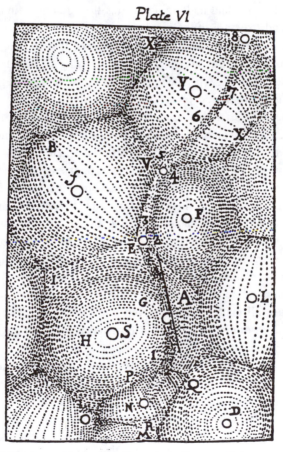

Plate VI

Fig 1. This is a representation of the sun's vortex surrounded by other vortices, the letters designating

their various positions and meridian rotations. As
these are all in contact as required by his plenum,
their combined interactions account for the stellar
and solar movements in the universe. This diagram
was taken from an old leather bound edition of *Les
Principles De La Philosophie de René Descartes,
Ecrits en Latins, Et traduit en Francais par un de
ses Amis*. (Rouen: *Chez* Jean-Baptiste Besogne,
1698), p. 224.

Beginning with this description of the initial possible organization of the
matter of the universe and its laws, Descartes then describes in more detail the
composition and structure of the present universe as we observe it. Originally
the parts of matter were of diverse irregular shapes that completely filled void
space, but which "became spherical with the passing of time because of their
various circular motions." (p. 108) These spherical bodies or globules (as he
later calls them) are referred to as "the second kind of matter" owing to their
circular shapes. The friction caused by the movement of these globules
produce "scrapings" which are dust-like particles so tiny and mobile that they
easily are reduced to even more minute particles which "fill all the angles (or
spaces) into which the other parts of matter cannot enter." (p. 109) Although
produced later by the rubbing of the circular bodies, they are called the first
kind of matter because of their mobility and "indefinite smallness" and
because they constitute the matter of stellar bodies and the sun. There is a
third kind of matter "which is composed of parts which are either much
bulkier or have shapes less suited to movement" (p. 110), and it is this matter
that makes up the planets, earth, and comets, those bodies which do not radiate
light. Although he refers to the three bodies as "very different kinds of
matter," because all matter is qualitatively the same these distinctions depend
solely on the three-dimensional sizes and shapes along with the motility of the
particles (as in ancient atomism).

Again, all of this is rather obscure. How does space as an undifferentiated
continuum devoid of any particularizing physical properties become
fragmented into innumerable discrete "bodies," "particles," and "elements,"
and how do the original spherical bodies or globules as purely mobile spatial
configurations by their rubbings produce "scrapings" that are the first matter
filling all the orifices and composing the matter of the fixed stars and the sun?
Even Descartes had to admit that his account was incomprehensible, declaring
that "matter [which is nothing but extension] is divisible into an indefinite

number of parts, even though this is beyond our comprehension.'' (p. 56; brackets added) While in the development of science there are always some things which are left inexplicable as the basis of other explanations, this admission is particularly damaging for someone who derives his system from clear and distinct ideas. In any event,

> all the bodies of this visible world are composed of these three elements: the Sun and the fixed Stars of the first, the Heavens of the second, and the Earth, the Planets, and the Comets of the third. (p. 110)

The general picture is that of an immense expanse of the heavens composed of the second matter of globules revolving around the vortex of the sun, since Descartes is a Copernican. At furthest remove from the sun are the fixed stars composed (as the sun) of the finer particles of the first matter and located at the centers of their vortices which in turn are distributed equally throughout their particular heaven. Situated serially in the heavens below in the center of their vortices are the planets and the earth with their respective orbits and velocities, along with the comets, composed of the bulkier, less mobile third element. Mindful of Galileo's condemnation by the Inquisition, Descartes complies with the prohibition against attributing motion to the earth by claiming that while it is carried by the annual revolution of the heavens and the diurnal rotation of its vortex, insofar as it does not move in relation to the vortical matter adjacent to it, it can be considered to be at rest:

> [. . .] no movement, in the strict sense, is found in the Earth or even in the other Planets; because they are not transported from the vicinity of the parts of the heaven immediately contiguous to them, inasmuch as we consider these parts of the heaven to be at rest. (p. 94)

Thus he claims to have been able to ''deny the motion of the Earth more carefully than Copernicus and more truthfully than Tycho.'' (p. 91)

An outward linear tendency away from the center produced by vortical motions plays a crucial role in this system. It is this tendency that propels the larger particles of the second matter outward, forcing the finer particles inward forming the centers of the vortices of the fixed stars and the sun. The latter vortical motions create an outward pressure throughout the transparent heavens that is light. Because a vacuum cannot exist in a plenum, the displacement of the particles occurs simultaneously producing the instantaneous transmission of light.

> The force of light [which he also calls "rays"], insofar as it spreads to
> all parts of the heaven from the Sun and stars [. . .] considered in
> itself, is nothing other than a certain pressure [among the heavenly
> globular particles] which occurs along straight lines drawn from the
> Sun to the Earth [. . . .]" (p. 194; brackets added)

Nothing further that he says makes this any clearer. According to the
translators, "light is simply the pressure, or tendency to centrifugal motion, of
the parts of transparent bodies [in the heavens]; it does not involve the motion
of anything physical [like waves or particles] from the sun or stars to the eye."
(p. 117; f.n. 68; brackets added)

Analogous to light, gravitational fall or weight is caused by the pressure
of particles, in somewhat the reverse manner in which the material of the stars
and sun are formed. In the case of gravity, the tendency of the lighter particles
(composing the air surrounding the earth) to recede from the circumference of
the earth forces denser bodies suspended in the air to fall in order to occupy
the space vacated by the ascending particles:

> [. . .] the force which the individual parts of the heavenly matter have
> to recede from {the center of} the Earth cannot produce its effect
> unless, while those parts are ascending, they press down and drive
> below themselves some terrestrial parts into whose places they rise
> [. . .]. (p. 191)

It is this downward pressure (as in the system of Democritus) of objects that
we call weight. Because of his emphasis on spatial displacement Descartes
was led to the erroneous conclusion that freely falling objects accelerate
according to the spaces traversed, not according to the squares of the times as
Galileo demonstrated.

Before concluding this discussion we should mention Descartes'
conception of "grooved" particles because of its novelty and its use in
explaining such diverse phenomena as the formation of the third kind of matter
and the occurrence of sunspots, rainbows, and magnetism. Their
configurations determined by the necessity of the parts of the first matter to
penetrate the triangular openings left by the congruence of the bodies of the
second matter (which because of their spherical shapes cannot be contiguous
at every point), these grooved particles are "triangular in cross-section" and

shaped "as small {fluted} cylinders with three grooves {or channels} which are twisted like the shell of a snail." (p. 134) "This enables them to pass in a twisting motion through the little spaces which have the form of the curvilinear triangle [. . .] always found between three contiguous globes of the second element." (p. 134) The shapes of the grooves of these oblong particles are determined by the passages they penetrate, "the particles coming from opposite poles [. . .] twisted in opposite directions." (p. 134) When discussing magnetism he will describe these grooved cylinders as "twisted like the thread of a screw." (p. 243)

Though shaped very differently from the other particles of the first element, they are included among them because of their size and of their primary function to fill the interstices among the other parts of matter. The "inequality of their shapes" causing them to adhere produce extensive spots near the surface of the equator of the sun whose rotation gives the appearance of revolving sunspots. (cf. 136) It is the thinning of the edges of these spots caused by the friction of the circulating heavens that produce rainbows: "the extremities of their circumference, growing thinner, allow the Sun's light to pass through" becoming "tinted by the colors of the rainbow [. . . .]" (p. 137) This also accounts for the formation of the third matter comprising the planets and the earth. Although the earth originally might have been a star like the sun though smaller, it was transformed into the earth by the adhering of the grooved particles along with other tiny bodies into "the matter of the third element." (p. 181)

But the most imaginative use of these fluted particles occurs in his explanation of magnetism. While he does not mention Gilbert, the detailed discussion of magnetic phenomena leaves no doubt that he read *De Magnete* very carefully and thoroughly. Like Gilbert, he describes the earth as a vast spherical magnet with opposite poles toward which contrasting ('magnetic') particles are attracted. Following a detailed "enumeration of the properties of magnetic force" (cf. pp. 250-252), he attempts to explain these properties by the features and motions of his fluted particles whose grooves twisted in opposite directions (right and left) account for the opposition in magnetic forces and polar attractions. Magnetic circulation occurs through "pores" with correspondingly opposite grooves cut through the center of the earth connecting the poles. These particles passing through their appropriate pores emerge from the poles and then circulate through the air surrounding the earth to the opposite pole in a continuous rotation.

In order to understand the causes of these properties, let us consider the Earth AB, of which A is the South pole, and B the North; and let us note that the grooved particles {represented by those little twisted bodies which have been drawn around it} coming from the Southern part E of the heaven are twisted in a completely different way from those coming from the Northern part F [see Fig. 2]: as a result, it is absolutely impossible for those of one group to enter the other group's pores.   Let us note also that the Southern particles proceed in a straight line from A to B through the middle of the Earth, and then return from B to A through the air surrounding the Earth; and at the same time, the Northern ones proceed from B to A through the middle of the Earth, and then return from A to B through the surrounding Air: because the pores through which the grooved particles passed from one side of the earth to the other are such that the particles cannot return through them. (pp. 252-253)

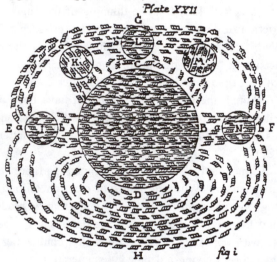

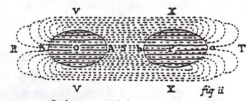

Fig. 2. This diagram of these particles occurs in Descartes' *Les Principles De La Philosophie, op. cit.,* pp. 514, 523.

The grooved particles are constantly being "crushed" by their motion through the medium around the earth, but are replenished by particles arriving from the heavens. Using similar arrangements of particles and pores, Descartes explains the properties of magnets, their orientation and declination, along with their attractions and repulsions. But the general nature of his explanation should be evident without going into further detail.

As is evident, Descartes' contribution to the history of science is somewhat anomalous. Unlike his contemporary Galileo who confronted Aristotelianism directly with new telescopic data along with experimental evidence, and then attacked the Stagirite's theoretical assumptions, conceptual interpretations, and linguistic implications supporting the geocentric-organismic world view, or unlike Kepler who derived accurate, astronomical laws from the new heliocentric perspective, Descartes summarily dismissed the Ptolemaic-Aristotelian cosmology for an *a priori* theory of vortices based on clear and distinct ideas. After having read Galileo's *Two New Sciences* shortly after its publication, he wrote a long letter on October 11, 1638, to Mersenne extensively criticizing the *Dialogue*, including the statement, "I see nothing in his books to make me envious, and hardly anything I should wish to avow mine."[19]

Beginning from an entirely different conception of scientific knowledge, Descartes attempted to construct a theory of the universe based exclusively on geometrical principles and the mechanical concepts of matter in motion and impact. As if trying to surmise and replicate the theoretical possibilities confronting God at the moment of creation, Descartes appealed to sensory perception only in deciding which among the various alternatives open to God seemed to be exemplified in the observable universe. Only a multifaceted genius such as Descartes would have had the temerity to attempt such an undertaking—but then most people are not inspired by an "angel of truth." Yet as ingenious as his theory of vortices was and though it introduced in one imaginative leap a mechanistic conception of the universe, nothing but the principle of inertia (whose time in any case had arrived) has been retained in modern classical science, unlike the contributions of Galileo, Kepler, Huygens, and Newton. Perhaps the best assessment of Descartes' system is given by Huygens whose father was a close friend of Descartes, thus he knew him as a respected family friend:

M. des Cartes had found the way to make his conjectures and fictions pass for truths. And those who read his Principles of Philosophy experienced somewhat the same as do the readers of Romances, which

give pleasure and make the same impression as veritable histories. . .
It seemed to me when I first read this book of the Principles that
everything in it was as good as could be, and I believed, when I found
some difficulty there, that it was my fault for not correctly
understanding his thought. I was only 15 or 16 years old. But having
since then discovered there from time to time things visibly false, and
others highly improbable, I have retreated far from the predilection I
then had, and at the present hour I find almost nothing that I can
approve as true in all his physics, or metaphysics, or meteors.[20]

Thus while Descartes introduced the modern mechanistic world view, its
actual construction and development was due to others. Yet as a tribute to his
brilliant imagination, in a recent lecture on "Space Physics, Planetary Science,
and Astrophysics" it was impossible not to think of Descartes during the
description of the interacting magnetospheric-ionospheric convections and
currents composed of a plethora of electromagnetic particles surrounding the
planets, the sun, and the stellar bodies, as well as occupying the space of our
solar system. The fundamental features of the explanation were not unlike
those of Descartes'.

FRANCIS BACON

Francis Bacon (1561-1626), who became Lord Verulum in 1618, occupies
a peculiar but deserved niche in the history of modern science. Not trained as
a research scientist like Gilbert, Kepler, and Galileo, nor as an experimentalist
and speculative cosmologist like Descartes, all of whom at various periods
were his contemporaries, he nonetheless perceived the need for an entirely new
approach to the investigation of nature. Though he made some pretense to
original research, his essential contribution consists of his plea for a new
scientific method and of his urging the possible benefits of this for the
improvement of mankind. Despite his model of science being natural history
rather than astronomy, optics, or physics, his trenchant depiction of the foibles
of human nature and incisive criticism of the outmoded Peripatetic philosophy,
along with his eloquent advocacy of a new scientific methodology, had a
marked influence on succeeding thinkers. Kant, for example, precedes his
Critique of Pure Reason with a dedicatory reference to Baco De Verulamio.
    In his opposition to the traditional philosophy taught in the universities and
demand for a "reconstruction of the sciences on a new foundation," as well as

his emphasis on the "operative" consequences of experimental inquiry for the control of nature, Bacon reminds one of John Dewey. Unlike Locke, who later provided an epistemological interpretation of the new corpuscularian-mechanistic science, Bacon was preeminent in extolling the practical benefits of a new method of investigation and in attempting to elucidate those aspects of the method in which he believed the fruitful consequences depended.

Entering Cambridge University in 1573 at the early age of twelve, he was submitted to the usual Peripatetic education, along with considerable grounding in the ancient Greeks and Augustine. Three years later he enrolled in Grey's Inn intending that his legal studies prepare him for a lucrative and illustrious life in the affairs of state. In this he proved eminently successful, his native ambition and exceptional intelligence and administrative skills propelling him to a succession of higher positions culminating in his becoming "Lord Chancellor, Baron Verulam of Verulam, and Viscount St. Albans."[21] Despite the arduous demands of his high positions (for example, Soliciter-General, Attorney-General, and Lord Keeper of the Great Seal), he retained an abiding interest in "The Great Instauration" of science. His first major philosophical work, *The Advancement of Learning*, was published in 1605, while his best known book, the *Novum Organum* was published in 1620, a few years before he was forced to resign the office of Chancellor on charges of bribery. The *Organon* was preceded by at least twelve unpublished copies.

Like each of the major contributors to the nascent science, Bacon too rebelled against the Aristotelian philosophy he was forced to study at Cambridge because of its preoccupation with syllogistic disputation and lack of practical benefits. As he says at the beginning of the Preface to the *Organon*, it was written because

> *the state of knowledge is not prosperous nor greatly advancing, and that a way must be opened for human understanding entirely different from any hitherto known, and other helps provided, in order that the mind may exercise over the nature of things the authority which properly belongs to it.*

Like the other great books of the period, Bacon added the adjective "New" to the title of his treatise, in direct reference to the *Organon* of Aristotle, intending to contrast his logic of inquiry with Aristotle's conception of scientific method consisting of deductive demonstrations based on syllogistic reasoning. As he states, his work differs from Aristotle's "in three points especially—viz., in the end aimed at, in the order of demonstration, and in the starting point of the inquiry." (p. 19)

Rather than serving disputation, the purpose of Bacon's logic is to guide scientific research. Reversing Aristotle's starting point of inquiry and the order of demonstration, his method does not consist of syllogistic demonstrations from first principles, but emphasizes "educing" general axioms or laws of scientific explanation based on the method of induction. Of course Aristotle also derived his first principles from induction and Bacon's axioms sound like Aristotle's first principles, but his conceptions of induction and axioms are very different from Aristotle's, conforming more to the procedures of his scientific contemporaries.

Bacon's conception of induction is fundamental to his new logic of inquiry: "what the sciences stand in need of is a form of induction which shall analyze experience [. . .] and by a due process of exclusion and rejection lead to an inevitable conclusion." (p. 20)   He rejects Aristotle's view of induction which he says "proceeds by simple enumeration [. . .], concludes at hazard, is always liable to be upset by a contradictory instance, takes into account only what is known and ordinary, and leads to no result." (p. 20)   In contrast, Bacon's conception anticipates Mill's methods of agreement, difference, and concomitant variation.[22]   Like Aristotle's, Bacon's method purports to reveal the essential "forms" of objects, but again he means something different by the concept: "when I speak of forms, I mean nothing more than those laws and determinations of absolute actuality which govern and constitute any simple nature, as heat, light, weight, in every kind of matter [. . .] that is susceptible of them." (Bk. II, XVII)   Again this could be interpreted as similar to Aristotle except that Bacon does not mean by "absolute actuality" Aristotle's analysis of objects into substances and qualities or classifications into genus and species.

As for the initial stage of induction, which Mill called "the method of agreement," Bacon labels it the *"Table of Essence and Presence."*

> The investigation of forms proceeds thus: a nature being given, we must first of all have a muster or presentation before the understanding of all known instances which agree in the same nature, though in substances the most unlike [. . .] without premature speculation [. . .].
> (Bk. II, XI)

As an example he lists twenty-seven different substances, from fiery meteors to hot vapors and boiling liquids, isolating their common form.

Next, he emphasizes the importance of noting exceptions and differences in which the form is absent, which Mill designated "the method of difference" and Bacon calls "The Table of Deviation or of Absence in Proximity."

> Secondly, we must make a presentation to the understanding of instances in which the given nature is wanting; because the form, as stated above, ought no less to be absent when the given nature is absent, than present when it is present. (Bk. II, XII)

Recognizing that listing all the negative instances would be impractical, he suggests inquiring into "those subjects only that are most akin to the others in which it is present and forthcoming." (*Ibid.*) The instances in which the form is absent, especially when they resemble those in which it is present, serve as a check on false comparisons and invalid inductions.

The third method, named by Mill "the method of concomitant variation" and called by Bacon the "*Table of Degrees* or the *Table of Comparison*," consists in detecting different amounts of the form in variations of the same subject or in comparisons of different subjects manifesting the identical form but in various intensities.

> Thirdly, we must make a presentation to the understanding of instances in which the nature under inquiry is found in different degrees, more or less; which must be done by making a comparison either of its increase and decrease in the same subject, or of its amount in different subjects, as compared one with another. (Bk. II, XIII)

In contrast to Aristotle's induction wherein the procedure "has been to fly at once from the sense and particulars up to the most general propositions [. . .] and from these to derive the rest by middle terms" (p. 20), Bacon believes his is "the true method [. . .] commencing as it does with experience duly ordered and digested, not bungling or erratic, and from it educing axioms, and from established axioms again new experiments [. . .]." (Bk. I, LXXXII)

This inclusion of experiments derived from established axioms marks a radical departure from Aristotle's method which is based on demonstrating that a particular fact exhibits the qualities or functions it does because it belongs to a higher class or genus which possesses those features due to its essential nature. As evidence for the superiority of Bacon's method from the modern point of view, he is not led, as Aristotle was, to classify heat as an essential quality or form of a body, but to interpret it as motion: "the nature of heat [. . .] appears to be motion. [. . .] displayed most conspicuously in flame

[. . .] and in boiling or simmering liquids, which also are in perpetual motion.'' (Bk. II, XX)

Although the expression of this necessarily is obscure and rudimentary, the true goal of science in benefiting mankind can be realized only by gaining knowledge of an object's ''engendering nature'' in order to change it's form into a new nature to realize some purpose.

> On a given body, to generate and superinduce a new nature or new natures is the work and aim of human power. Of a given nature to discover the form, or true specific difference, or nature-engendering nature, or source of emanation [. . .] is the work and aim of human knowledge. (Bk. II, I)

This knowledge in turn depends upon

> the discovery, in every case of generation and motion, of the *latent process* carried on from the manifest efficient and the manifest material to the form which is engendered; and in like manner the discovery of the *latent configuration* of bodies at rest and not in motion. (*Ibid.*)

These references to a *''latent process''* of bodies in motion and a *''latent configuration''* of bodies at rest ''engendering'' forms, when conjoined to experimentation, seem to depict the necessary conditions of experimental inquiry. But it is difficult to tell whether Bacon meant the kinds of experiment exemplified by Gilbert and Galileo, or those associated with alchemy and magic. While he says that when one looks ''closely into the works of the alchemists or the magicians, he will be in doubt perhaps whether to laugh over them or to weep''(Bk. I, LXXXV), his own conception of gaining control over objects consists in the ''transformation'' of their forms, a notion very close to the alchemical dream of ''transmuting'' the elements into gold, an example Bacon himself uses. Furthermore, after attributing to metaphysics (like Aristotle) the investigation of the highest forms and axioms, he calls this knowledge ''magic,'' in contrast to the more mechanical, practical knowledge of physics.

> Thus, let the investigation of forms, which are [. . .] eternal and immutable, constitute *Metaphysics*; and let the investigation of the efficient cause, and of matter, and of the latent process, and the latent

configuration (all of which have reference to the common and ordinary course of nature, not to her eternal and fundamental laws) constitute *Physics*. And to these let there be subordinate two practical divisions: to Physics, *Mechanics*; to Metaphysics, what (in a purer sense of the word) I call *Magic*, on account of the broadness of the ways it moves in, and its greater command over nature. (Bk. II, IX)

As for exercising power over bodies by the transformation of forms, he illustrates this by the alchemical example of gold.

The rule or axiom for the transmutation of bodies is of two kinds. The first regards a body as a [. . .] collection of simple natures [. . . .] This kind of axiom, therefore, deduces the thing from the forms of simple natures. For he who knows the forms of yellow, weight, ductility, fixity, fluidity, solution, and so on, and the methods for superinducing them and their gradations and modes, will make it his care to have them joined together in some body, whence may follow the transformation of that body into gold. (Bk. II, V)

This conception of converting bodies into one another by "superinducing" their forms seems remote from the Boyle-Lockean notion of objects consisting of inherent particles possessing primary qualities with powers having the capability of producing changes in other objects. But Boyle and Locke lived several generations later and in their clarification of these concepts Boyle had the benefit of his own experiments on gases while Locke was informed not only by Boyle's research but also by the investigations of Newton.

The second kind of axiom mentioned above pertains to compound bodies, investigating "from what beginnings, and by what method and by what process, gold or any other metal or stone is generated" and "the process of development in the generation of animals [. . .] and in like manner of other bodies." (Bk. II, V) Despite the crudity of these statements, Bacon is dimly aware of what is required in order to understand and gain control over nature, as the following statement more clearly indicates.

Therefore a separation [analysis] and solution [synthesis] of bodies must be effected [. . .] by reasoning and true induction, with experiments to aid [. . .] if we intend to bring to light the true textures and configurations of bodies on which all the [. . .] specific properties and virtues in things depend, and from which, too, the rule of every

powerful alteration and transformation is derived.   (Bk. II, VII;
brackets added)

Bacon uses the terms "textures and configurations" that Locke later will use
in describing the source of the powers inherent in things to produce their
various effects. The application of this method is what will grant mankind
control over objects and render the sciences useful. While he maintains that
"whatever deserves to exist deserves also to be known, for knowledge is the
image of existence" (Bk. I, CXX), he does not just support knowledge for its
own sake, because "the true and lawful goal of the sciences is none other than
this: that human life be endowed with new discoveries and powers." (Bk. I,
LXXXI)

Thus Bacon is not, as often portrayed, a devout empiricist who advocated
"immaculate perception."   While he does assert such seemingly naive
empiricist statements as "all depends on keeping the eye steadily fixed upon
the facts of nature and so receiving their images simply as they are" (p. 29),
he also says that "by far the greatest hindrance [. . .] of the human
understanding proceeds from the dullness, incompetency, and deceptions of the
senses [. . .]." (Bk. I, L) Very much aware of the fallibility and limitations
of sensory observations, he neither extolled nor rejected then, astutely
declaring that "certain it is that the senses deceive; but then at the same time
they supply the means of discovering their own error [. . .]." (p. 21)

One would think that he had in mind the Copernican Revolution but, alas,
he rejected the earth's motion. Instead he had in mind microscopes "which
disclose the latent and invisible minutiae of bodies and their hidden
configurations and motions by greatly increasing their apparent size," so "that
if Democritus had seen one, he would perhaps have leaped for joy, thinking
a way was now discovered of discerning the atom, which he had declared to
be altogether invisible." (Bk. II, XXXIX) Yet it is difficult to judge how
much significance to give to this because he also claims that "the
incompetency [. . .] of such glasses, except for minutiae alone [. . .] destroys
the use of the invention." (*Ibid.*) Apparently he read Galileo's *Sidereus
Nuncius* carefully because he accurately describes the telescopic observations
reported by Galileo in that book.

Yet even more important than instruments in aiding the senses are
experiments, since the correction of the senses is accomplished

not so much by instruments as by experiments. For the subtlety of
experiments is far greater than that of the sense itself, even when

assisted by exquisite instruments—such experiments, I mean, as are skillfully [. . .] devised for the express purpose of determining the point in question. To the immediate and proper perception of the sense, therefore, I do not give much weight; but I contrive that the office of the sense shall be only to judge of the experiment, and that the experiment itself shall judge of the thing. (p. 22)

Even granting that experiment at that time did not have the current meaning of probing nature to uncover new data beyond the reach of the senses, signifying mainly the technique of testing hypotheses, this still shows an exact understanding of its role in scientific inquiry. As he says in a famous Aphorism, "Nature to be commanded must be obeyed [. . .]." (Bk. I, III)

However, it is not just the weakness of the senses that leads to distorted knowledge but the fact that sensory evidence itself is usually misinterpreted. Thus he distinguishes between "*Anticipations of Nature* (as a thing rash or premature)" and eliciting "facts by a just and methodical process," which he calls the "*Interpretation of Nature.*" (Bk. I, XXVI) The precise relation between theorizing and gathering empirical data he describes in the famous simile of the ant, the spider, and the bee.

Those who have handled sciences have been either men of experiment or men of dogmas. The men of experiment are like the ant, they only collect and use; the reasoners resemble spiders, who make cobwebs out of their own substance. But the bee takes a middle course: it gathers its material from the flowers of the garden and of the field, but transforms and digests it by a power of its own. Not unlike this is the true business of philosophy; for it neither relies solely or chiefly on the powers of the mind, nor does it take the matter which it gathers from natural history and mechanical experiments and lay it up in the memory whole, as it finds it, but lays it up in the understanding altered and digested. Therefore from a closer and purer league between these two faculties, the experimental and the rational (such as has never yet been made), much may be hoped. (Bk. I, XCV)

Here Bacon displays a very sophisticated understanding of the interdependence of empirical data and their interpretation, now expressed in the familiar notion that "all data are theory-laden."

Although he occasionally mentions the role of mathematics in the physical sciences, as in the acknowledgement that "inquiries into nature have the best result when they begin with physics and end in mathematics'' (Bk. II, VIII), the main weakness of his scientific programme lies in the omission of any serious discussion of the crucial functions of scientific measurement and of the mathematical formalism in scientific inquiry. He was, however, obsessed with the project of a natural history, in vain imploring the British government, universities, and prominent individuals to contribute to such an undertaking. He sought the help of Queen Elizabeth and evoked the precedent of Alexander's generous contributions to Aristotle's museum of natural history to entice James I to support such an endeavor, but to no avail. As Fulton Alexander states: ''[a] generation was to elapse before scientists, at home and abroad, hailing Bacon as a 'new Aristotle' and 'nature's secretary,' undertook at his bidding and according to his directions the collecting of myriad natural histories.'' (pp. xxviii-xxix)

Indeed, Bacon's model of science was not mathematical physics but natural history, as he says: ''[g]ood hopes may therefore be conceived of natural philosophy, when natural history, which is the basis and foundation of it, has been drawn up on a better plan; but not till then.'' (Bk. I, XCVIII) He described this plan in his publication of 1622, *Natural and Experimental History for the Foundation of Philosophy: Or Phenomena of the Universe; Which is the Third Part of the Great Instauration.*

Even more famous than his simile of the ant, spider, and the bee are Bacon's ''Idols'' of the mind, depicting the mental weaknesses, pitfalls, and entrapments that beset all people in their attempts to attain truth and acquire knowledge of nature.

> The idols and false notions which are now in possession of the human understanding, and have taken deep root therein, not only so beset men's minds that truth can hardly find entrance, but even after entrance is obtained, they will again in the very instauration of the sciences meet and trouble us, unless men being forewarned of the danger fortify themselves as far as may be against their assaults. (Bk. I, XXXVIII)

These universal failings of the human intellect are listed under four headings: Idols of the Tribe, Idols of the Cave, Idols of the Market Place, and Idols of the Theater. Idols of the Tribe originate in the common weaknesses of human nature, especially in the limitations of the senses and the deficiencies of human understanding which do not represent the universe as it is, but as reflected through their distorted apprehensions. Idols of the Cave refer to individual weaknesses, a person's peculiar preferences, biases, and capacities that deform what each individual learns. Idols of the Market Place designate those misconceptions acquired through communication with others, involving the misuse of words along with imprecise definitions and inadequate explanations, resulting in unnecessary confusions, fruitless controversies, and foolish fancies. Finally, there are Idols of the Theater, so-called because they include deceptive myths, fanciful systems, and artificial productions created by individuals to explain nature and social institutions. These Idols represent all the deficiencies of perception and contortions of thought that prevent a true understanding of nature.

It was to rid humanity of these that Bacon proposed *The Great Instauration*, the "formation of ideas and axioms by true induction" that was to serve as "the remedy to be applied for the keeping off and clearing away of idols." (Bk. I, XL) Furthermore, Bacon believed that riding mankind of these Idols would not only eliminate ignorance and superstition, but also support religious faith:

> [. . .] if the matter be truly considered, natural philosophy is, after the word of God, at once the surest medicine against superstition and the most approved nourishment for faith, and therefore she is rightly given to religion as her most faithful handmaid, since the one displays the will of God, the other his power. (Bk. I, LXXXIX)

Thus despite Bacon's aspirations for his new science, he still retained the medieval conception that natural philosophy (science) ultimately is a "handmaid" of religion.

ROBERT BOYLE

Although Descartes was the originator on a purely speculative or *a priori* basis of the modern mechanistic world view, his conception of physical reality as a plenum filled with a material continuum of vortices that denied the void along with the atomic structure of matter (despite describing matter as differentiated into "globules"), set him apart from the major creators of modern classical science: Galileo, Boyle, and Newton. The impending demise of the Peripatetic philosophy incorporating prime matter, substantial forms, and the explanation of change and motion in terms of the actualization of potentiality called for a new theory of physical reality; however, the adoption of a mechanistic framework of matter in motion did not itself specify how this was to be conceived. Prior to Aristotle Leucippus and Democritus had introduced such a materialistic interpretation which later was embellished by Epicurus and Lucretius, but atomism was eclipsed by Stoicism and Neoplatonism during the Hellenistic period and all but disappeared during the Middle Ages and early Renaissance. Yet it was this ancient atomism that was revived in the seventeenth century by Pierre Gassendi on the continent and Robert Boyle in England as the ontological foundation of mechanism. Because Boyle's contribution to the development of the corpuscular-mechanistic system was more direct and lasting, his will be discussed.

The Honorable Robert Boyle, later made Earl of Cork by James I, was born at Lismore, Ireland, in 1627. Educated at Eton, he spent several years in Geneva under the tutelage of a learned French gentleman, and then (like Bacon a precocious student) traveled to Florence where he was reading Galileo at the time of the latter's death in 1642. After residing in France for several years, he returned to his estates in Ireland where he became known as "The Great Earl of Cork," eventually settling in Oxford and then in London. One of the founders of the Royal Society, he also served for a time as President. Famous as the discover of the gas law named after him, his book *The Sceptical Chymist* published in 1661 is generally considered the beginning of modern chemistry. It was his investigation of gases and chemical reactions that led to his defense of mechanism and to his becoming the father of the corpuscularian philosophy. A major figure in the "century of genius" that included John Locke, Robert Hooke, Christian Huygens, Gottfried Leibniz, and especially Isaac Newton, he was duly honored by being buried in Westminster Abbey in 1691.

Written in the more popular dialogue form that suggests the influence of Galileo, *The Sceptical Chymist* presented Boyle's corpuscular-mechanistic system as an alternative to the two leading schools of the day: (1) the peripatetic philosophy claiming that matter consists of the four elements fire, earth, air, and water with change explained in terms of substantial forms and occult qualities; and (2) the alchemist doctrine supported by the followers of Paracelsus (1493-1541) and van Helmont (1577-1644) that the "*tria prima*" elements or "hypostatical principles" responsible for both chemical and physiological (meaning physical) reactions were salt, sulphur, and mercury. In addition, van Helmont discovered that alkalis and acids neutralize each other, but little experimental information was derived from this discovery. Since modern chemistry had yet to be established, these alchemists were considered experimentalists in contrast to the Peripatetics. As we shall learn later,

Newton devoted considerable effort and resources for nearly thirty years to alchemical experiments.

The research programme of the alchemists or "spagyrists" included the following peculiar beliefs: (1) that the diversity and complexity of nature masked a simple unity so that the secrets of nature could be shown to depend upon a few elements from which gold and other substances could be transmuted in a quasi-magical manner; (2) that a strong analogy exists between humans and external nature leading to a sexual classification of reagents and reactions into male and female and attributing to natural substances human attributes, affinities, and moral qualities; (3) the animistic view that substances have souls and that physical phenomena possess a vital spirit, the "Archeus," accounting for physical and chemical reactions; (4) the attribution of an especially prominent role to fire which was believed to have the unique power of reducing complex mixtures or substances to simple constituents or elements; (5) the consequent investigation of all kinds of exotic substances to determine their properties and reactive characteristics; and (6) the production of furnaces and instruments eventually useful to the founders of the emerging discipline of chemistry.

Referring to the alchemists as "vulgar spagyrists," Boyle was particularly critical of their fanciful assumptions and conceptions, their loosely defined terminology, their lack of a disciplined method of inquiry, and the fact that there were no objective or even agreed upon results. "A considering man," he says in *The Sceptical Chymist*,

> may very well question the truth of those very suppositions which chymists as well as peripateticks, without proving, take for granted; and upon which depends the validity of the inferences they draw from their experiments.[23]

At other times he is even more critical, quoting with approval the statement of someone who, after observing the experiments of the chymists, declared *"that he had often seen detected many tricks and impostures of cheating alchymists."* (Part III, p. 101).

He begins with a critical examination of the main tenet of the peripatetics and chymists that the number of elements composing matter is limited respectively to four or three, and that each is qualitatively different and homogeneous:

> [. . .] the experiments [. . .] whether by the common peripateticks, or by

the vulgar chymists, to demonstrate, that all mixt bodies are made up precisely either of the four elements, or the three hypostatical principles, do not evince what they are alleged to prove. (Part V, p. 184).

Indeed, as he goes on to say, such experiments "are commonly grounded upon such unreasonable or precarious suppositions, that 'tis altogether as easie and as just for any man to reject them, as for those that take them for granted to assert them [. . .]."(*Ibid.*) Basically, the peripatetics and the chymists failed to realize the "great variety there is in the textures and consistences of compound bodies" (Part V, p. 160), and how difficult it is to define an element.

Having rejected the notion that the variety of compounds can be reduced to three or four simple components, he then attacks the chymists belief that fire, because of some mysterious power, can be relied upon to resolve mixed or compound bodies into the pure and elementary elements from which they are composed.

> Since, in the first place, it may justly be doubted whether or no the fire be, as chymists suppose it, the genuine and universal resolver of mixt bodies;
>
> Since we may doubt, in the next place, whether or no all the distinct substances that may be obtained from a mixt body by the fire were pre-existent there in the formes in which they were separated from it;
>
> Since also, though we should grant the substances separable from mixt bodies by the fire to have been their component ingredients, yet the number of such substances does not appear the same in all mixt bodies [. . . .];
>
> And since, lastly, those very substances that are thus separated are not for the most part pure and elementary bodies, but new kinds of mixts [. . .]. (Part V, p. 161)

Unlike the alchemists, Boyle raises the crucial questions which a theory like theirs would have to answer to be accepted.

He does not deny that fire can be used to break down compounds, but his conception of what constitutes fire that makes this possible is different, consisting of the motion of minute particles that by penetrating substances decomposes them or in mingling with then forms new substances:

[. . .] if that be true which was the opinion of Leucippus, Democritus, and [. . .] in our dayes revived by no mean philosophers; namely, that our culinary fire, such as chymists use, consists of swarmes of little bodies swiftly moving, which by their smallness and motion are able to permeate the sollidest and compactest bodies [. . .] it will not be irrational to conjecture, that multitudes of these fiery corpuscles [. . .] may associate themselves with the parts of the mixt body whereupon they work, and with them constitute new kinds of compound bodies, according as the shape, size, and other affections of the parts of the dissipated body happen to dispose them [. . .]. (Part IV, p. 119)

It is not some mysterious power of fire that enables it to penetrate bodies and subdivide them, but the swift motion or action of the particles composing it:

[. . .] for it rather seems, that the true and genuine property of heat is, to set a moving, and thereby to dissociate the parts of bodies, and subdivide them into minute particles [. . .] as is apparent in the boyling of water [. . .]. (Part I, p. 54)

This conjecture of the possible manner in which fire decomposes and forms new substances raises the essential questions that will have to be faced by the founders of modern chemistry, such as Priestly, Lavoisier, Dalton, and Avogadro: namely, what is the meaning of 'element,' 'mixture,' and 'compound'? How do elements enter into chemical reactions and constitute such mixed substances? Are there a simple number of such elements and can they be recovered by decomposing the compounds or are they irretrievably changed in mixing with them? In what proportions do they interact and does this proportion stay constant for particular substances?

This is an excellent illustration of the way the introduction of a new framework consisting of novel concepts with different semantic implications raises all kinds of original questions that would not have been asked in the older system! While Boyle only hints at most of these questions, he does attempt to answer the first by suggesting the rationale for introducing the concept of element and providing a possible definition:

Now the considerations that induce men to think, that there are elements, may be conveniently enough referred to two heads. Namely, the one, that it is necessary that nature make use of elements to constitute the bodies that are reputed mixt. And the other, that the resolution of such bodies manifests that nature had compounded them of elementary ones. (Part VI, p. 188)

As for the meaning of 'element,' he offers the following definition, apparently without being convinced that such elements truly exist:

> [. . .] I now mean by elements [. . .] certain primitive and simple, or perfectly unmingled bodies; which not being made of any other bodies, or of one another, are the ingredients of which all those called perfectly mixt bodies are immediately compounded, and into which they are ultimately resolved: now whether there be any one such body to be constantly met with in all, and each, of those that are said to be elemental bodies, is the thing I now question. (Part VI, p. 187)

Despite this reservation, *The Sceptical Chymist* contains the early arguments for Boyle's corpuscular theory.

> It seems not absurd to conceive that at the first production of mixt bodies, *the universal matter whereof* [. . .] *the universe consisted, was actually divided into little particles of several sizes and shapes variously moved.* (Part I, p. 30)

In place of the traditional conception of matter as consisting of a limited number of qualitatively different elements with change explained as a transmutation of these elements, Boyle is proposing the now familiar corpuscularian view that matter consists of innumerable homogeneous elements defined in terms of the primary properties of sizes and shapes, and that the diversity and transformations of phenomena can be explained by the contact and interaction of these ''corpuscles.''

> For if we assign to the corpuscles, wereof each element consists, a peculiar size and shape, it may easily enough be manifested, that such differingly figured corpuscles may be mingled in such various proportions, and may be connected so many several ways, that an almost incredible number of variously qualified concretes may be composed of them. (Part I, p. 32).

Boyle concludes by stating that he ''suspected the principles of the world [. . .] to be three, *matter, motion,* and *rest,*'' and ''that colours, odours, tastes, fluidness and solidity, and those other qualities that diversifie and denominate bodies may intelligibly be deduced from these three [. . .].'' (Part VI, p. 200) Therein is contained the crux of the corpuscular view, although considerable precise reflection will be required by both Boyle and Locke before this ''deduction'' is accomplished.

Thirteen years following publication of *The Sceptical Chymist*, there appeared as an appendix to a book on theology an essay entitled ''The Excellency and Grounds of the Corpuscular or Mechanical Philosophy'' containing the clearest, most succinct expression of Boyle's conceptual system and its justification.[24] Its appearance at the end of a theological work was not capricious because Boyle, like most of the scientists of his age, believed that the universe could not have arisen by chance or necessity, but only as the result of the conscious intention of a wise Creator. Wishing to eliminate the traditional association of atheism with atomism, he begins the essay by claiming that ''embracing the corpuscular or mechanical philosophy'' does not commit one to the belief that the world arose from an accidental meeting of atoms in the infinite void, nor that when God created the world he so disposed matter that everything followed of necessity thereafter.

> The philosophy I plead for [. . .] distinguishing between the first origin of things and the subsequent course of nature, teaches that God indeed gave motion to matter; but that, in the beginning, he so guided the various motion of the parts of it as to contrive them into the world he designed they should compose; and established those rules of motion, and that order amongst things corporeal, which we call the laws of nature. (p. 111)

Though the universe was ''framed by God,'' as a mechanist Boyle maintains ''that the phenomena of the world are physically produced by the mechanical properties of the parts of matter, and, that they operate upon one another according to mechanical laws. 'Tis of this kind of corpuscular philosophy that I speak.'' (*Ibid.*) This perhaps was one of the sources of eighteenth century Deism, the belief that God created the universe so that it functioned as a self-contained system thereafter.

Having denied that one should object to this philosophy on theological grounds, he then maintains its superiority over the accepted peripatetic and chymist systems. Pointing out that ''there are many intricate disputes about matter, privation, [and] substantial forms'' among the peripatetics, he then chides the chymists with being ''puzzled to give such definitions, and

accounts, of their hypostatical principles as are consistent with one another,"
concluding that "if the principles of the Aristotelians and chymists are thus
obscure, it is not to be expected that the explications made by the help of such
principles only should be intelligible." (p. 112) In contrast, he argues that
explanations in terms of the corpuscular properties of matter and mechanical
laws of motion recommend themselves because of their "intelligibleness or
clearness," indicative of the extraordinary transformation taking place in the
thinking of the natural philosophers of the seventeenth century, since Aristotle
surely would not have agreed regarding the "intelligibleness or clearness" of
atomism.

> But, as to the corpuscular philosophy, men do so easily understand
> one another's meaning, when they talk of local motion, rest,
> magnitude, shape, order, situation, and contexture, of material
> substances; and these principles afford such clear accounts of those
> things, that are rightly deduced from them alone; that, even such
> peripatetics or chymists, as maintain other principles, acquiesce in the
> explications made by these, when they can be had [. . .]. (*Ibid.*)

Yet such an assertion raises the perplexing question as to why different
theoretical explanations appear clearer and more intelligible to different people,
since obviously Descartes who invoked the criteria of clearness and
distinctness (or intelligibility) did not accept atomism by these criteria nor did
Boyle find that Descartes' vortical theory satisfied those criteria for him,
resembling instead the vague "universal spirit"of the chymists or "the world
soul of the Platonists."

> Though the Cartesians are mechanical philosophers, yet their subtle
> [vortical] matter, which the very name declares to be a corporeal
> substance, is, for ought I know, little less diffused through the
> universe, or less active in it, then the universal spirit of some
> chymists; not to say the world soul of the Platonists. (p. 117; brackets
> added)

Ultimately, of course, it is future developments that determine the truth of
theories, the ancient atomism of Leucippus and Democritus eventually proving
more successful than Aristotle's organismic philosophy or Descartes' theory
of vortices.

Whatever the answer to the above question, Boyle believed that the two principles of matter and motion, the former conceived as basic particles and the latter as local impact,[25] offered the possibility of the most intelligible explanation of physical phenomena, from the motion of the planets to the composition and decomposition of compounds. As he says, "[t]here cannot be any physical principles more simple than matter and motion; neither of them being resoluble into any other thing."(p. 113) Thus the three principles of "matter, motion, and rest" that he invoked in *The Sceptical Chymist* are now reduced to two. Even in cases where it appears that the properties of mixed bodies can be explained in terms of the three principles of the chymists, Boyle maintains that a more basic explanation can be achieved in terms of mechanical principles.

> And when the chymists shall show that mixed bodies owe their qualities to the predominance of any one of their three grand ingredients, the corpuscularians will show that the very qualities of this or that ingredient flow from its peculiar texture, and the mechanical properties of the corpuscles that compose it. (p. 122)

Boyle's importance, however, does not consist just in his selection of the two principles (and their correct interpretation) for a sound mechanistic explanation; he also attempts to redirect the emphasis in scientific inquiry from the influence of the causal "agent" to the processes occurring in the "patient" or substance, for until one has acquired a precise understanding of the changes taking place in the entity itself, it is unlikely that one will arrive at the proper cause (as Galileo had argued).

> Now, the chief thing that a philosopher should look after, in explaining difficult phenomena, is not so much what the agent is or does, as what changes are made in the patient, to bring it to exhibit the phenomena proposed; and by what means, and after what manner, those changes are effected. (p. 117)

Boyle therefore realized that future progress in science would depend upon discovering the "peculiar texture"and "mechanical properties"of the elements composing substances. While the alchemists concentrated on the changes induced in substances due to agents like fire, it was by weighing the ingredients that enter into or are extracted from chemical reactions and trying to understand how they combine, that modern chemistry got its start with Lavoisier about a century later. Moreover, when Dalton attempted to determine the relative weights of the minute particles of bodies, he too was following the direction indicated, if only vaguely, by Boyle.

Accordingly, one of the major presuppositions of modern science, that the complexity of phenomena can be understood best by "reducing" it to a mechanistic interaction of clearly defined physical elements, was explicitly affirmed by Boyle. For natural phenomena to be intelligible,

> it will be *reducible* to matter and some or other of its universal properties. And the indefinite divisibility of matter, the wonderful efficacy of motion, and the almost infinite variety of coalitions and structures that may be made of minute and insensible corpuscles [. . .] [enable us] to make out, by their help, the mechanical possibility of any corporeal agent, how subtle, diffused, or active soever, that can be solidly proved to have a real existence in nature [. . .]. (p. 117; italics and brackets added)

Thus, by his incisive criticism of the two prevalent schools of philosophy, identification of the crucial questions and proper directions guiding inquiry, clear definition of the essential features of a mechanistic system and corpuscular theory, and dismissal of any conceptual barriers to integrating chemistry with the rest of natural philosophy, Boyle contributed greatly to the formulation and eventual acceptance of the theoretical framework that would serve as the ontological interpretation of the new science. For it was the corpuscular-mechanistic conception that by the end of the seventeenth century would replace the ancient cosmological system of Aristotle, lasting until the dawn of the twentieth century.

Owing to his close association and exchanges with Boyle, Locke was able to formulate his influential conception of matter as composed of "insensible particles" defined in terms of primary qualities such as extension, solidity, size, shape, position, and motion. It is the motion and texture of these insensible particles which have the "power" or "secondary qualities" of causing sensations or simple ideas in sentient organisms (by stimulating the sense organs), along with the "third qualities" or "powers" to receive alterations or produce changes in other objects. Although our ideas of primary qualities truly resemble them (especially as these qualities are manifested in macroscopic as well as microscopic bodies), our simple ideas of sensation such as colors, tastes, and sounds or of physical properties such as magnetism, do not resemble those qualities as they exist in objects, attesting only to the *powers* in objects to cause simple ideas of them in us. As Locke summarizes this:

> The ideas that make our complex ones of corporeal substances are of these three sorts. First, the ideas of the primary qualities of things which are discovered by our senses, and are in them even when we perceive them not: such as the bulk, figure, number, situation, and motion of the parts of bodies, which are really in them, whether we take notice of them or no. Secondly, the sensible secondary qualities which, depending on these, are nothing but the powers those substances have to produce several ideas in us by our senses; which ideas are not in the things themselves otherwise than as anything is in its cause. Thirdly, the aptness we consider in any substance to give or receive such alterations of primary qualities as that the substance so altered should produce in us different ideas from what it did before; these are called active and passive powers: all which powers, as far as we have any notice or notion of them, terminate only in sensible simple ideas.[26]

This distinction between primary qualities and powers existing in the insensible particles and their assemblages in the independent physical world, and their sensory effects or qualities as they occur in and for a sentient organism, raised the epistemic problem of its justification, especially as what human beings experience were said to be sensations or ideas, not the independently existing physical reality. While Locke claimed that our ideas of primary qualities (as they exist in macroscopic objects) truly resemble them, and thus should be representative also of the properties of insensible particles (because it is the aggregation of these that compose and produce macroscopic objects), we can only infer the second and third kinds of powers, not directly sense them.

Although this inference seemed reasonable enough to the scientists since telescopes and microscopes disclose phenomena inaccessible to the senses and was based on inductive inference, in that motes of dust, smoke particles, and sugar dissolved in water retain the power to cause us to see, smell, and taste them, it was challenged by Berkeley's rejection of abstract ideas and material reality, Hume's critique of causality and denial of rationally justified inductive inferences, and Kant's distinction between nature knowable as the world of appearances, and reality or noumena unknowable as things in themselves. Thus while scientists went on to investigate the optical causes of perception, the physiological processes of sensation, and the physical or chemical composition of material substances, the philosophers were led to a progressively more subjective conception of knowledge giving rise to absolute idealism and phenomenology.   The latter, although claiming a more certain form of knowledge, has produced nothing than can compare with scientific inquiry.

It was this subjectivistic, epistemic turn in philosophy that has been severely criticized in the twentieth century by such philosophers as Wittgenstein, Dewey, Quine, and Rorty.   But while one can criticize the excessive mentalistic interpretations of Berkeley, Hume, Kant, Hegel, and Husserl, the kinds of theoretical considerations that gave rise to the distinction between an independently existing physical reality and the qualitative world as it appears to man—a distinction held by Galileo, Boyle, Locke, and Newton—seem to be as valid today as they were in the seventeenth century. Investigations in neurophysiology, cognitive psychology, and artificial intelligence, as well as disputes among scientists (such as Einstein and Bohr) and philosophers of science regarding a realist or antirealist (phenomenalist) interpretation of scientific theories, all eventually face the question of the nature and status of sensory qualia in relation to the conception of the physical world disclosed by scientific inquiry.   The earlier attempts by positivists, pragmatists, and ordinary language philosophers to dismiss these questions as misleading or artificial, because they arise from linguistic confusions, have merely shown the superficiality of these approaches.   The problems are not due to causes as superficial as the misuses of language, category mistakes, or conceptual muddles, but are grounded fundamentally in scientific inquiry and the condition of man, especially the change in theoretical framework from the direct realism of Aristotle to the critical realism of modern science.[27]

NOTES

1. Alfred North Whitehead, *Science and the Modern World* (New York: A Mentor Book, 1925), p. 42.

2. In his earlier book, *The Copernican Revolution* (Cambridge: Harvard University Press, 1959), Thomas Kuhn described the astronomical modification initiated by Copernicus as a somewhat conservative transition like "a bend in the road" (p. 181), rather than a discontinuous, incommensurate process so that "[a]s science progresses, its concepts are repeatedly destroyed and replaced." (p. 265).   It was in his later, extraordinarily influential book, *The Structure of Scientific Revolutions* (Vol. II, No. 2 of the *International Encyclopedia of the Unified Sciences*

[Chicago: Univ. of Chicago Press, 1962]), that he introduced the latter more radical conception of scientific revolutions as essentially irrational Gestalt shifts where the opposed scientists find themselves in two disconnected worlds. (cf. ch. X)

3. Kuhn stresses this in his first book, *The Copernican Revolution, op. cit.*, ch. 6.

4. Which has recently been confirmed (1994).

5. Giordano Bruno, *Cause, Principle, and Unity*, translated by Jack Lindsey (New York: International Pub. Inc., 1962), pp. 33-44.

6. Cf. William Gilbert, *De Magnete*, translated by P. Fleury Motteley in 1893 (New York: Dover Pub. Inc., 1958). The immediately following page references in the text are to this work.

7. The *De Magnete* went through a number of well-known succeeding editions. Furthermore, a posthumous work was published in 1651, *De Mundo Nostro Sublunari Philosophia Nova*, which was even more critical of the current schools of philosophy and attempted "to establish a new system of natural philosophy upon the ruins of Aristotelian doctrine." *De Magnete*, p. XXV.

8. E.J. Dihksterhuis, *The Mechanization of the World Picture*, translated by C. Dikshoorn (Princeton: Princeton University Press, 1986), p. 393.

9. The quotation appears in *De Magnete*, p. 346, f.n. 1.

10. Galileo Galilei, *Dialogue Concerning the Two Chief World Systems*, translated by Stillman Drake (California: University of California Press, 1967), p. 406.

11. René Descartes, *Principles of Philosophy*, translated by V.R. Miller and R.P. Miller (Dordrecht: D. Reidel Pub. Co., 1983), p. XXIV.

12. René Descartes, *The Philosophical Works*, Vol. I, translated by Haldane and Ross (Cambridge: At the University Press, 1967), p. 83. The immediately following page references in the text are to this work.

13. The *Geometry* initially had an important effect on Newton who read it carefully, encouraging his study of modern mathematics, although later he disparaged it for more traditional mathematics.

14. Descartes, *Principles of Philosophy*, *op. cit.*, p. 287.

15. Earlier he had written a book entitled *Traité du monde* presenting an entirely new philosophy of nature to replace that of Aristotle. However, when he learned of the judgment by the Inquisition against Galileo in 1633, he sent his treatise away "lest he be tempted to publish it." As a result, the *Traité* was published posthumously in 1664. Thus it is the *Principles of Philosophy* (1644) that contains his cosmological theory. Unless otherwise indicated, the following page references in the text are to this work.

16. Cf. Article XXXIV of *The Passions of the Soul*.

17. Richard S. Westfall, *Never at Rest* (Cambridge: Cambridge University Press, 1980), p. 410.

18. Cf. Alexander Koyré, *Galileo Studies*, translated by John Mepham (New Jersey: Humanities Press, 1978), p. 91.

19. Stillman Drake, *Galileo At Work* (Chicago: University of Chicago Press, 1978), p. 392.

20. Christiaan Huygens, *Oeuvres complètes de Christiaan Huygens*, Société hollandaise des Sciences, Vol. I (La Haye: Martinus Nijhoff, 1888), p.125. Quoted from Howard Stein, "On Locke, 'the Great Huygenius, and the incomparable Mr. Newton,'" Ch. 2, Phillip Bricker and R.I.G. Hughes, *Philosophical Perspectives on Newtonian Science* (Cambridge: The MIT Press, 1990), p. 18.

21. Francis Bacon, *The New Organon*, edited with introduction by Fulton H. Anderson (Indianapolis: The Bobbs-Merrill Co., 1960), p. xi. The following page references are to this work, except that where possible the Book and numbered Aphorism contained in *The New Organon* will be cited so that the reader may refer to other editions.

22. Cf. John Stuart Mill, *A System Of Logic*, Ch. VIII.

23. Robert Boyle, *The Sceptical Chymist* (London: J.M. Dent & Sons, Ltd., no date.), Part III, p. 94. The following references are to this work until otherwise indicated.

24. The most accessible publication of the work is in *The Scientific Background to Modern Philosophy*, edited by Michael R. Matthews (Indianapolis: Hackett Pub. Co., 1989), pp. 111-123. The following page references are to this source.

25. It is this question of 'locality'' of causal effects that is so crucial in the discussion between Einstein and Bohr in the EPR controversy and Bell's theorem.

26. John Locke, *An Essay Concerning Human Understanding*, Bk. II, Ch. 23, Sec. 9.

27. Cf. Richard H. Schlagel, *Contextual Realism: A Meta-physical Framework for Modern Science* (New York: Paragon House, 1986), Introduction.

CHAPTER VI

A BIOGRAPHICAL SKETCH OF NEWTON

Nature and Nature's Laws lay hid in Night:
God said, Let Newton be! and all was light.[1]

Pope

I think it safely may be said that Newton was the greatest scientist that ever lived. While most scientists are either theoreticians or experimentalists, Newton exemplified to the highest degree three forms of genius: mathematical, theoretical, and experimental. His contributions to any one of these disciplines —inventing the calculus (before and independently of Leibniz), demonstrating the universal law of gravitation thereby finally explaining planetary motion, and optical experiments—would have secured his reputation as one of the greatest creative minds in the history of mankind. To have combined all three of these capacities was incomparable. As Halley wrote at the end of the "Ode to Newton" preceding the *Principia*:[2]

> Come celebrate with me in song the name Of Newton, to the Muses dear; for he Unlocked the hidden treasures of Truth: [. . .] Nearer to the gods no mortal may approach.

As with all achievements, Newton's were built on the foundations laid by others as he acknowledged in a famous statement in a letter to Hooke: "If I have seen further it is by standing on ye sholder's of Giants."[3] Nevertheless, it was Newton's vision of the corpuscular-mechanistic universe based on various forces that finally displaced Aristotle's organismic cosmology, providing the general theoretical framework for physical investigations until the end of the nineteenth or beginning of the twentieth century.

Unlike Galileo whose tremendous inner creativity played itself out on the dramatic stage of history, Newton's personal life is largely minuscule in comparison to his colossal intellectual accomplishments. If genius endows some individuals with extraordinary capacities at the expense of more common aptitudes, this certainly was true of Newton. Gifted with exceptional powers of concentration that enabled him to immerse himself totally in theoretical problems, he often neglected to eat or sleep to the detriment of his health (which would be true also of the young Einstein). Accounts of Newton's absentmindedness were legendary, as when he was ascending a hill on returning to his family's home in Woolsthorpe and dismounted his horse so as not to tire it, then forgetting to mount again, leading the horse home. William Stuckley, a younger contemporary, vividly recounted stories of Newton's distracted behavior at Cambridge:

> As when he had been in the hall at dinner, he has quite neglected to help himself, and the cloth has been taken away before he has eaten anything. That sometime, when on surplice days, he would goe toward S. Mary's church, instead of college chapel, or perhaps has gone in his surplice to dinner in the hall. That when he had friends to entertain at his chamber, if he stept in to his study for a bottle of wine, and a thought came into his head, he would sit down to paper and forget his friends.[4]

An extremely sensitive, suspicious, and guarded person who was easily offended, during his younger years he was afflicted by a fear of criticism and dread of controversy. Revered and eulogized during his lifetime for his mathematical and scientific accomplishments as much as anyone who ever lived, as a young man he had an aversion even to entering into correspondence with scholars who were anxious to communicate with him, and perhaps for one or two exceptions, lived a celibate life. As he grew older and was universally venerated, especially after the publication of the *Principia* and his election to Parliament as a representative of Cambridge University, he found personal relationships less difficult and even had an active social life in London when his niece, Catherine Barton, very much admired for her beauty, intelligence, and charm, managed his household. Furthermore, his extraordinary intellect, conscientiousness, and meticulous devotion to detail made him a superb administrator, manifested in his long presidency of the Royal Society and appointment as Master of the Mint.

Never having been attracted to women except for a slight adolescent romance in grammar school, there is strong evidence, though inconclusive because of the sensitivity of the situation and the unusual secrecy with which he screened his life, that Newton had an intimate relation with a much younger Swiss mathematician named Nicolas Fatio de Duillier. It seems more than coincidental that in 1693 when Newton was fifty-one years old he suffered a nervous breakdown (apparently one of several) at the time when his relationship with Fatio was terminated. Other reasons have been offered to explain his severe depression, such as nervous exhaustion from the strain of writing the *Principia* or mercury poisoning incurred as a result of his alchemical experiments (some of the symptoms of which coincided with Newton's but others did not), but the rupture with Fatio would seem to be the more likely explanation. As an expression of his deep affection for Newton Fatio wrote "I could wish Sir to live all my life, or the greatest part of it, with you, if it was possible [. . .]." (p. 533) Given Newton's deep religious convictions, if his affection for Fatio was more than Platonic (and they met often in London), that itself could have caused severe problems. As Westfall states:

> Newton was not the only one who was in turmoil. Fatio was also going through a period of acute personal and religious tension. The sense of approaching crisis became almost palpable in their correspondence in early 1693. It is unlikely that we will ever learn what passed between them in London. Their relation ended abruptly, however, never to be resumed. The primary focus of Newton's attention for four years, from the time they met in 1689, Fatio simply dropped out of Newton's life. The rupture had a shattering affect on both men. Newton rebounded from his breakdown, but Fatio effectively disappeared from the philosophic scene forever. (p. 538)

There is evidence of a previous breakdown in the late 1670s related to the agitated dispute over his theory of colors, the loss perhaps by fire of the papers describing his optical experiments and correspondence, and possibly to the fact that his chamber-fellow, John Wickins, decided to spend considerable less time at Trinity. They had been roommates and close friends since Newton entered the college in 1661, Wickins putting up with his eccentric habits, helping him with his scientific and alchemical experiments, and serving as his anamuensis. As Westfall states, the "crisis in his relations with Fatio de Duillier at that time had its counterpart in Wickins's decision to leave Trinity." (p. 278) Wickins finally resigned from the college in 1684.

In one of the great historical sequences (due in part to the fact that the English protestant calendar was ten days advanced on the continental Gregorian one, otherwise Newton's birth would have been registered later on January 4, 1643), Newton entered the world the year Galileo left it in 1642. Born on Christmas day in the family manor house at Woolsthorpe in Lincolnshire, Newton was named for his father who had died three months previously. The only child of Isaac and Hannah Newton, apparently he was born premature and was so tiny that he was not expected to live. Beginning life precariously and fatherless, Newton soon was to be deprived of the presence of his mother who remarried three years later and whose new husband, a prosperous clergyman named Barnabas Smith, insisted that she join him in his rectory in North Withan, leaving Newton to be raised by his grandmother at Woolsthorpe. Sixty-three years of age when they married, The Reverend Mr. Smith died eight years later but not before having had a son and two daughters with Hannah. Following the death of her second husband, Newton's mother and half-brother and sisters returned to Woolsthorpe in 1653 to live with him. We can surmise that the loss of his father and the removal of his mother until he was ten must have left a marked effect on Newton, especially as he did not seem to be fond of his grandmother.

Two years later when he turned twelve, as was the custom of the time for those who could afford it, he was sent to the Free Grammar School of King Edward VI in Grantham. Some three centuries old and run by a capable Master, Newton received an excellent religious education as well as a good classical background in Greek and Latin, but probably little training in mathematics and none in natural philosophy. At that time he was described as "a sober, silent, thinking lad," who "never was known scarce to play with the boys abroad." (p. 59) Praised for "his strange inventions and extraordinary inclination for mechanical works," one episode especially reveals something of his inner resolution and strength of character. Viciously kicked in the stomach by one of his classmates on the way to school, Newton challenged the boy to a fight after classes with the following result:

> [. . .] as soon as the school was over [. . .] & they went out together into the Church yard, the schoolmaster's son came to them whilst they were fighting & clapped one on the back & winked at the other to encourage them both. Tho Sr Isaac was not so lusty as his antagonist he had so much more spirit & resolution that he beat him till he declared he would fight no more, upon wch the schoolmaster's son bad him use him like a Coward, & rub his nose against the wall & accordingly Sr Isaac pulled him along by the ears & thrust his face against the side of the Church.[5]

As Westfall goes on to recount, although Newton up till then had been a poor student, not satisfied with beating the other boy physically, "he insisted on worsting him academically as well; once on his way, he rose to be first in the school." (p. 60) This strength of character will be manifested years later when Newton will lead the opposition at Cambridge to the attempt by the Catholic

King, James II, to confer a fellowship on a Catholic priest in violation of the regulations at Cambridge that demanded an oath of obedience to Anglican doctrine.

Nothing further would have been heard of Newton if the usual course of events had ensued and he, as the eldest son, had assumed the responsibility at the proper age for managing the affairs at Woolsthorpe. Fortunately for the future of science, however, chance or destiny intervened (as it will thrice again) by interposing a number of impediments: (1) when he returned home for any extended period of time he did not get along well with his family; (2) he had little interest in overseeing a country estate and showed even less aptitude when the servants attempted to instruct him in his duties; and (3) as he progressed in his studies his intellectual gifts became so apparent that they attracted the attention of the headmaster of the school, as well as his maternal uncle who prevailed over his mother to let him pursue a course of studies that would prepare him for the university. Thus as fortune would have it, Newton was admitted in the summer of 1661 to Trinity College, Cambridge, where the same uncle had studied thirty years earlier and which in the early seventeenth century "had been the leading academic institution in England" (p. 189) and was known by some as "the famousest College in the University." (p. 70) Intending to receive a degree, he also matriculated in Cambridge University as was required.

More than four hundred years old at the time, Cambridge was a respected institution but had not yet achieved the reputation for scientific scholarship that it would acquire as a result of Newton's occupying, after the retirement of Isaac Barrow, the Chair of Lucasian Professor, and of a succession of distinguished scientists such as Maxwell, Lord Rayleigh, J.J. Thomson, and Rutherford, along with Dirac and Stephen Hawking who have occupied the Lucasian Professorship in the twentieth century. For Newton, however, who had escaped what Marx would refer to as the "idiocy of the countryside," Cambridge must have seemed the promised land of learning where he would pass the longest period of his life. Although his immediate family's estate was not especially grand, neither was it poor, yet Newton entered Trinity in the humble position of subsizar—even beneath the sizars who earned their keep by working as servants for the Masters and Fellows, but who at least received their lectures and board from the College, while the subsizars had to pay for theirs. Domestic lackeys, both the sizars and the subsizars "functioned as valets to fellows and to other students, rousing them for morning chapel, cleaning their boots, dressing their hair [. . .], carrying their orders from the buttery," (p. 71) and even emptying their chamber pots. To earn their food they waited on tables in the dining hall and were fed afterwards on whatever was left. Being inept at domestic chores but possessing a certain pride, one wonders how Newton adapted to these indignities, although at nineteen one expects a certain resiliency.

The curriculum at Cambridge was traditional, emphasizing religious studies along with a command of Latin and Greek, plus a strong dose of Aristotle, particularly his logic, ethics, and rhetoric. While the emphasis was on acquiring agility in formal disputation using syllogistic logic, Newton also studied Aristotle's mechanics, physics, and cosmology, a necessity for anyone interested in natural philosophy. Soon dissatisfied with the traditional curriculum, Newton began studying the works of more recent authors, such as Descartes, Gassendi, Galileo, Boyle, Hobbes, Digby, Glanville, and Henry More. Surprisingly, more than Galileo's it was Descartes' writings that were being discussed in Cambridge, so Newton set about reading Descartes thoroughly, especially his optical investigations and theory of vortices. In fact, due partly to the laxity of the curriculum, Newton became an autodidact pursuing on his own those subjects that interested him the most. By 1664 these inquiries were listed under the title of "Quaestiones," specific problems pertaining to mechanics and optics forecasting rather closely his later areas of research. As Westfall states, "if the essence of experimental procedure is active questioning whereby consequences that ought to follow from a theory are put to the test, Newton the experimental scientist was born with the "Quaestiones." (p. 93) Always fascinated by machines, he also left sketches of possible perpetual-motion machines driven by the flux of gravitational and magnetic forces.

Furthermore, as the "Quaestiones" record Newton's assessment of the authors he was studying, they disclose especially his criticism of Descartes' treatment of light and theory of colors, his explanation of gravity and the tides, and the difficulty of the vortical theory in accounting for such astronomical phenomena as eclipses and Kepler's three laws. Led to investigating the effects of light on vision, Newton performed experiments on his eyes that temporarily injured his vision and that could have left him blind. (cf. pp. 93-94) Along with his dissatisfaction with the views of Descartes, his studies of Gassendi, Boyle, and perhaps More were drawing him toward atomism and a non-Cartesian but mechanistic interpretation of nature. Equally important, at this time Newton began studying mathematics with the same diligence, independence, and brilliance he displayed in his pursuit of natural philosophy.

While mathematics at the time was no more a part of the curriculum at Cambridge than natural philosophy, Newton's initial encounter with Euclid and continued study of geometry in Franz van Schooten's popular second Latin edition of Descartes' *Géométrie* (which appeared in 1661 with a long commentary as well as several ancillary treatises), led to further reading of Viete's works, Oughtred's algebra, and Wallis' *Arithmetica infinitorum*. As Westfall states, with no previous background in mathematics, in "roughly a year, without benefit of instruction, he mastered the entire achievement of seventeenth-century analysis and began to break new ground." (p. 100) The recent developments in mathematics applying algebra to geometry, such as Descartes' analytic geometry prescribing methods for drawing tangents and finding the equations of curves, along with investigations of areas and limits as well as new techniques for computing instantaneous velocities and infinitesimal quantities, were described as "analysis" in contrast to the traditional Greek methods designated as "synthesis."

Yet despite Newton's remarkable intellectual awakening and progressive studies, there was no assurance of an academic future at Cambridge. Academic advancement at the time did not depend at all on intellectual ability or scholarship, but on social position and connections, patronage, and seniority. As in his narrow escape from exile to Woolsthorpe and successful admission to Trinity College, the obstacles to Newton's progression to the necessary academic sinecures were so formidable that there seemed almost no hope of success. First, in order to become a Fellow of Trinity, which was a prerequisite for obtaining a permanent appointment at the University, he had to obtain a scholarship but for various reasons the conditions for election were anything but favorable to Newton. As Trinity College held elections only every three or four years, there was just one opportunity of being elected; sizars had less chance of being chosen and Newton, because of his unorthodox studies in mathematics and natural philosophy, had not attained the usual academic distinctions that usually were prerequisites for selection to a scholarship; finally, the allotment of scholarships further reduced Newton's chances unless he had an important sponsor, which did not appear to be the case, because his intellectual development was self-propelled and anonymous. Newton's future thus seemed to weigh upon an untoward fate since any expectation of a permanent career in Cambridge would vanish if he were not elected. Again, however, something or someone intervened in his favor, although scholars are not sure what, and in 1664 he was elected to a fellowship, thus nudging him another notch upward in his career. (cf. pp. 100-104)

While the ordeal of being elected to a scholarship had a depressing effect on Newton who was given to "disorders," he soon recovered, devoting the next two years to intense mathematical and scientific studies. Whereas usually the kind of intuition that enables a creative mathematician to solve abstract mathematical problems cannot be applied as successfully to the resolution of physical problems that requires a different kind of insight, Newton's genius encompassed both of these abilities. Thus he was able to pursue natural philosophy with the same extraordinary ingenuity that he displayed in his inquiries in pure mathematics. The years 1665-1666 were a period of such intensive development, culminating in three papers in which he applied his newly acquired mathematical skills to the problem of motion. As described by Westfall:

> Taken all in all, the tract of October 1666 on resolving problems by motion was a virtuoso performance that would have left the mathematicians of Europe breathless with admiration, envy, and awe. As it happened, only one other mathematician in Europe, Isaac Barrow, even knew that Newton existed, and it is unlikely that in 1666 Barrow had any inkling of his accomplishment. The fact that he was unknown does not alter the other fact that the young man not yet twenty-four, without benefit of formal instruction, had become the leading mathematician of Europe. And the only one who really mattered, Newton himself, understood his position clearly enough. He had studied the acknowledged masters. He knew the limits they could not surpass. He had outstripped them all, and by far. (pp. 137-138)

According to Newton's own account, while he would return to mathematical studies in the years to come when dealing with problems of mechanics, it was never with the same fervor as in these two years.

These years between 1664 and 1666 are sometimes referred to as "*anni mirabiles*" because of the extraordinary self-development and ground-breaking achievements of Newton in the areas both of mathematics and natural philosophy. Although his initial mathematical studies and original contributions would seem to have been more than sufficient to fill this brief period, such is not the case. During this same time, as with his study of mathematics, he not only mastered the leading systems of mechanics, but by his critical inquiries raised questions and brought the level of investigation beyond anything he had studied. Stimulated by his reading of Descartes, he began inquiring into the mechanics of motion and conducting the optical experiments that led to his theory of colors.

From both Galileo and Descartes he learned of inertia, one of the key concepts in the explanation of the orbital motion of the planets, for the law of inertia attributes to objects an inherent force to remain in the same motive state unless acted upon by some other force: if at rest to remain at rest or if in motion to continue in motion in a straight or rectilinear direction. This is the reverse of Aristotle's law that because terrestrial objects naturally move to their places of rest, a body in motion to remain in motion requires an active mover continuously in contact with it. Descartes had used the example of a stone twirled in a sling in his *Principles of Philosophy* (which was repeated by nearly everyone) to illustrate the tendency of an object to fly off in a straight line tangential to its circular motion unless constrained by the sling. When twirled the sling keeps the stone moving in a circle until released, whereupon the stone describes a tangential rectilinear motion—a motion different from Huygens' 'centrifugal force' which refers to the tendency of objects to recede from the center of a rotating body or motion.

If the law of inertia applies to planets, then an additional force (functioning like the sling) is necessary at each point of their orbits to keep them from flying off in a tangential straight line. Since the earth attracts objects to its surface by a gravitational force, it could be conjectured that if this force extended to the moon then it could cause the continuous deflection or fall of the moon towards the earth counteracting its inertial motion, thereby explaining its curvilinear orbital trajectory. But though such a conjecture seems reasonable to us after more than three hundred years of familiarity, it took a soaring imagination to surmount the millennia old obstacle to attributing a terrestrial cause to a celestial body.

In the year 1665-66 there occurred the great plague forcing Cambridge to close its colleges and disperse its students. With nowhere else to go Newton returned to his home in Woolsthorpe. According to a well attested tradition, it was during this time when he was in one of the orchards at Woolsthorpe and saw an apple fall that it occurred to him that the same force of attraction exerted on the apple by the earth causing it to descend would, if it reached the moon with sufficient strength, explain how it is kept in orbit around the earth (and if the forces were reciprocal, explain how the moon's attractive pull on the oceans and seas produced the tides). As recorded by John Conduitt, the husband of Newton's niece Catherine and his first biographer:

> In the year 1666 he retired again from Cambridge. . .to his mother in Lincolnshire & whilst he was musing in a garden it came into his thought that the power of gravity (wch brought an apple from the tree to the ground) was not limited to a certain distance from the earth but

that this power must extend much farther than was usually thought. Why not as high as the moon said he to himself & if so that must influence her motion & perhaps retain her in her orbit, whereupon he fell a calculating what would be the effect of that supposition [. . .].[6]

Conduitt goes on to say that Newton's calculations did not agree exactly with his theory because he did not have an accurate figure for the earth's circumference, therefore his computations based on the latitudes were incorrect.

Although he does not mention Woolsthorpe, Newton himself wrote that it was during the plague years of 1665-66, when he was forced to leave Cambridge, that the idea of the earth's gravity extending to the moon occurred to him—confirming part of Conduitt's statement—and that he attempted to compute what the strength of the gravitational force extending to the moon would have to be, comparing it with the gravitational force on the earth. Because such a calculation would have to take into account how the strength of gravity varied with the distance, even this early Newton had inferred from Kepler's third law (the size of a planet's orbit is proportional to the 3/2th power of its averaged distance from the center of its orbit) that the strength of the gravitational force diminishes inversely with the square of the distance. He says that by 1666

I began to think of gravity extending to ye orb of the Moon & [. . .] from Kepler's rule of the periodical times of the Planets being in sesquialterate proportion [3/2nd power] of their distances from the center of their Orbs, I deduced that the forces wch keep the Planets in their Orbs must [be] reciprocally as the squares of their distances from the centers about wch they revolve: & thereby compared the force requisite to keep the Moon in her Orb with the force of gravity at the surface of the earth, & found them answer pretty nearly. All this was in the two plague years of 1665-1666.[7]

The phrase "pretty nearly" supports Conduitt's statement that Newton was not able to arrive at an exact value at that time. In recognition of Huygens' introduction of the term "centrifugal force" to designate the force causing objects to recede from the center of rotary motions, Newton later (1684) would name this attractive force to the center a "centripetal force."

Two other theoretical developments during this period helped to lay the foundation for Newton's later theory of dynamics presented in the *Principia*.

In studying Descartes' account of motion Newton corrected his laws of impact described in the previous chapter, maintaining that bodies act on each other with mutually reciprocating forces. In addition, as a variation on the principle of inertia he asserted "the principle of the conservation of angular momentum for the first time in the history of Mechanics: 'Every body keepes the same reall quantity of circular motion and velocity so long as tis not opposed by other bodys.'" (p. 153) After recording these discoveries in a paper entitled "The Laws of Motion," he turned to what he called the "celebrated Phenomena of Colours."

Whereas Newton's concern with the laws of motion described in the *Principia*, but began in this early period, attest to his genius as a mathematician and theoretical physicist, it is his investigation of colors during this same period but finally presented in the *Opticks* that displays his unusual gifts as an experimentalist. Only one other scientist comes to mind who accomplished so much in such a brief time at such an early age. In 1905, at age twenty-six, Einstein published four articles in *Nature*, three of which had tremendous effects on early twentieth-century physics: an article announcing his special theory of relativity, one on Brownian motion, another on the photoelectric effect, and a less influential article on statistics.

The phenomena of colors have always been fascinating due to their beauty and mystery, as in the case of rainbows. Moreover, the occurrence of what is now called chromatic aberration, which distorted and colored the images seen in the best telescopes, had been a problem since Galileo. Again due to his reading of Descartes, Newton knew of the latter's experiments on colors using a prism described in his *Météores*, as well as Boyle's *Experiments and Considerations Touching Colors* published in 1664, and Hooke's *Micrographia* that appeared in the following year. The prevailing theory was that the light that strikes the retinae and produces the experience of ordinary 'white' or luminous light is homogeneous, so that the sensation of colors is due to the modification or distortion of this homogeneous light by reflection or refraction which, when it strikes the retinae, produces the perception of colors. Thus the two dominant colors, red and blue, were believed to be caused by stronger or weaker impulses of ordinary light striking the retinae, not by a separate light ray corresponding to each color. Not satisfied with the prevalent explanations, Newton decided to perform his own prismatic experiments which, even this early, display his exceptional ingenuity in teasing and testing results by modifying the experimental conditions, along with showing his meticulous attention to detail. Even the diagrams of the experiments and calculations illustrate his seemingly infinite patience with detail and obsession with accuracy. (cf. pp. 160-168) In contrast to the accepted theory, Newton came to the opposite conclusion that light is heterogeneous rather than homogeneous, composed of a mixture of individual rays which the prism "analyses" or "separates" because of their different refractive powers, and that it is these individual homogeneous rays striking the retinae that produce colors. One experiment in particular seemed decisive in drawing him to this conclusion.

> That ye rays wch make blew are refracted more y^n ye rays wch make red appears from this expirem^{nt}. If one hafe [one end] of ye thred *abc* be blew & ye other red & a shade [. . .] be put behind it y^n lookeing on ye thred through a prism one half of ye thred shall appear higher y^n ye other & not both in one direct line, by reason of unequal refractions in ye 2 differing colours.[8]

It was the higher and lower appearance of the two colors owing to their different refractions that was the key.

Then when he directed a beam of light from a pinhole through a prism onto "a wall twenty-two feet aways," he observed "a spectrum five times as long as it was wide." (p. 164) Other investigators, such as Descartes and Hooke, had missed this because they had kept the screen on which the beam of light fell after passing through the prism too close to the prism, not allowing enough distance for the spread to occur. The fact that Newton placed the prism so far from the wall suggests that he had anticipated or foreseen the effect based on the previous evidence of refraction. Realizing that the elongated effect could be attributed to a number of other causes, he devised various clever experiments to eliminate these possibilities. Furthermore, having demonstrated that the elongated spectrum was caused by the prism's analyses of white light into its component rays, he then showed that white light could be reconstituted from these separate rays by reversing the effect with an additional prism. Accordingly, rather than white light being homogeneous, simple, and pure, with colors derived from its modification, Newton's experiments seemed to demonstrate the reverse: that it is the rays that are irreducible and simple and that these produce the experience of color while white light is a heterogeneous mixture of these rays. All his experiments reinforced the conclusion that the rays were not created from something else but were themselves basic. These results were summarized in an essay "Of Colours" written in 1666. As Westfall states: "No other investigation of the seventeenth century better reveals the powers of experimental inquiry animated by a powerful imagination and controlled by rigorous logic." (p. 164)

Despite the significance of these results overturning a theory that went back thousands of years, as one should expect Newton was not at first fully aware of the implications of his discovery. Even after he had listed the dispersion of colors in the spectrum ranging from red, yellow, green, blue, and purple, he did not think of each of these colors as caused by a separate ray, attributing the intermediate colors to a blending of other rays, green being a blend of blue and yellow while purple was a mixture of red and blue, apparently still assuming that the rays causing red and blue were primary. Turning to an explanation of why perceived objects appear having the colors they do, he asserted that reflection as well as refraction can analyze light into its separate rays, an object appearing the color it does because the predominant rays reflected from it (presumably due to some inherent structural properties) produce that color sensation in the observer. (cf. p. 172) Amplifying experiments described by Hooke in his *Micrographia*, Newton attempted to measure the dimensions of different colors caused in a variety of ways by thin transparent films. He also observed the color rings produced by circular lenses which have come to be known as "Newton rings."

Already attracted to the corpuscular-mechanistic framework because of its greater explanatory potential, Newton attempted to explain light on the corpuscular model supported, he believed, by the fact that light forms shadows with straight, sharp boundaries which is consistent with the linear propagation of corpuscles but not of waves. Just as sound and water waves bend around obstacles becoming dispersed, if light were propagated as waves then it should curve around obstructions with a diffused luminosity. Moreover, his original conception of red and blue colors correlated with strong or weak rays could be interpreted mechanistically, in terms of the sizes (or velocities) of the corpuscles. Although later Newton will enter into bitter controversies with Hooke and Huygens because of their support of the wave theory, eventually he realized that the corpuscular interpretation could not account for all of the characteristics of light, such as interference and reinforcement, and therefore considered a pulsational interpretation along with his corpuscular one. Such was his prestige, however, that his advocacy of the corpuscular theory all but eliminated consideration of the wave interpretation until the early nineteenth century when Young and Fresnel discovered diffraction patterns and developed a more precise conceptual framework and mathematical theory of waves. The wave theory then displaced the corpuscular model throughout the nineteenth century until Einstein's explanation of the photoelectric effect, in terms of quanta of energy and subsequent photon theory (confirmed by the scattering experiments of Compton), led to a dualistic interpretation of radiation in terms of both wave and particle properties, as manifested under different experimental conditions.

By the time Newton completed these optical experiments in 1666, along with his mathematical studies and inquiries in natural philosophy, he had received his Bachelor's degree. He immediately faced another formidable obstacle if he were to attain a permanent position at Cambridge, that of being elected to a fellowship at Trinity College: "[a]s with the scholarship three years earlier, Newton's whole future hung in the balance of this election." (p. 176) Again his chances were remote, depending upon the choice of the master and eight senior fellows. Unlike the anxiety over the election to a scholarship, however, that contributed to Newton's earlier "disorder," nothing in his behavior at the time indicates the slightest concern about the outcome. This suggests that he must have known of a strong advocate among the senior fellows, and Humphrey Babington (who may have been the person behind his earlier election to a scholarship) seems the likely candidate, according to Westfall. (cf. p. 177) Whatever the reason, he was elected a fellow on October 1, 1667. At first elected a minor fellow, he automatically became a major fellow when he was created Master of Arts nine months later. With two exceptions, at that time "the sixty fellows of the college were required to take holy orders in the Anglican church within seven years of incepting M.A." (p. 179), and were required to remain celibate. While the latter restriction obviously posed no problems for Newton, he avoided complying with the first because of his opposition to trinitarianism, thus requiring a Royal dispensation for him to remain at Trinity College for twenty-nine years after becoming a fellow.

When Newton was elected to a fellowship Isaac Barrow occupied the Lucasian professorship of mathematics, a chair established in 1664 by the bequest of Henry Lucas. Earlier Barrow had been asked by Newton's tutor to examine him on Euclid in connection with his election to a scholarship, and though Newton succeeded in being elected, he nonetheless believed Barrow had formed an indifferent opinion of him because at the time he was studying Descartes' geometry to the neglect of Euclid, which out of reticence he failed to point out to Barrow. (cf. p. 206) But several years later Newton informed Barrow of his method for calculating infinite series which was to have a profound effect on his career, since soon after when John Collins sent a copy of Nicholas Mercator's *Logarithmotechnia* to Barrow, the latter realized that Mercator's logarithmic investigations were related to Newton's study of infinite series. Thus Barrow wrote to Collins abut Newton's research, promising to send him a copy of Newton's latest paper. Collins of course had never heard of Newton but was very impressed by the paper, "*De analysi per aequationes numero terminorum infinitas*" (*On Analysis by Infinite Series*), which he received from Barrow with the following description of the author: "His name is Mr Newton; a fellow of our College, & very young [. . .] but of an extraordinary genius & proficiency in these things."[9] So if Newton's assessment of Barrow's previous impression of him were correct, this had dramatically changed since their earlier encounter.

Despite Newton's reluctance to allow Barrow to send a copy of *De analysi* to Collins and insistence that it be returned—indicative of his early reticence to exposing his work to public scrutiny—once Collins received it he was so favorably impressed that he sent copies to prominent mathematicians in England, Scotland, and Europe. In addition, he and Barrow "wanted to publish it as an appendix to Barrow's forthcoming lectures on optics" (p. 206), but Newton refused to give his permission. Nonetheless, the paper did serve to introduce Newton to a number of the leading mathematicians of the day and had a positive effect on Newton's life in that it probably contributed to Barrow's decision to resign as Lucasian professor and recommend Newton as his successor.

While Barrow had higher aspirations than occupying a chair in mathematics, attaining appointment "within a year of his resignation [. . .] chaplain to the king" and "within three years master of the college" (p. 207), there was no necessity of his resigning the Lucasian chair prior to seeking these positions or even opposition to his holding the latter two at the same time. Yet Barrow's recognition of Newton's genius, and decisive influence in his selection as his successor, would suggest that he intentionally resigned to Newton's advantage. Whatever the reasons, Newton succeeded at the early age of twenty-seven to the chair of Lucasian professor with its generous endowment, as Westfall indicates:

> By existing standards, Lucas endowed it magnificently; with its stipend of £100, more or less, from the income of lands purchased in Bedfordshire, it ranked behind the masterships of the great colleges and the two chairs in divinity (which were usually occupied by college masters) as the ripest plum of patronage in an institution much concerned with patronage. On 27 October, 1669, this plum fell into the lap of an obscure young fellow of peculiar habits, apparently without connections, in Trinity College—to wit, Isaac Newton. (p. 206)

Considering his deserts, this unexpected beneficence certainly compensated Newton for the previous years of uncertainty and anxiety concerning his academic future. Although he always would remain unduly and unnecessarily apprehensive about the reception of his publications and persist in his abhorrence of controversy, at least now he could be more secure (except for the question of ordination) in his position at the university.

Barrow's perceptive sponsorship of the youthful, unknown, and unpublished Fellow of Trinity College would be vindicated over the next few years as Newton began to demonstrate the several facets of his genius. Underlying this, however, was a deep tension between Newton's initial receptive response to praise and desire to please, and his subsequent aversion to any notoriety and protective withdrawal of his works. Initially he allowed several essays to be published but without his name, as if testing the waters of reception before emerging. Although the teaching obligations of a professor were anything but onerous, Newton was obliged to give a series of lectures during at least one term, and he chose optics as his first topic. These lectures, based on additional experiments, expanded and refined his earlier investigations described in the unpublished essay "Of Colours." Probably composed in 1669-1670, these "*Lectiones opticae*" indicate that he had abandoned his earlier belief that red and blue were caused by two primary rays while the intermediate colors were produced by a blend of these, concluding that there were an indefinite range of colors corresponding to the infinite degrees of refraction. He performed what he called his "*experimentum crusis*" in 1672 to refute definitely the view that colors arise from modifications of white light, leaving his own theory as the only plausible explanation.

His inquiries measuring the diameters of colored rings to within one-hundredth of an inch display his remarkable originality in designing experiments, along with his unrivaled mathematical powers and patience for meticulous measurements. In an essay on "Discourse of Observations" written in 1672, he introduced "pulses" to explain circular rings, although these pulses were not light waves but vibrations in the aether between glasses produced by the impact of the light corpuscles. Not satisfied as Hooke and Huygens had been with noting the periodicity of colors in thin films, he attempted to measure the thickness of the colored circles. Amplifying his explanation of colored bodies, he claimed that it was the thickness of the transparent particles composing bodies that determined the rays they reflect and thus the colors they appear to have. (cf. p. 221) Even as partially summarized here, these investigations (as yet totally unknown to the world) surpassed those of the acknowledged authority of optics at the time, Christian Huygens, and brilliantly reflect just one facet of Newton's genius. They would provide the background for his great work, *Opticks*, an exposition of the experimental work undertaken at this early period but not published until 1704.

At the time of these optical researches Newton also was being inveigled into investigating certain mathematical problems by Collins. Rather than being put off by Newton's refusal to allow him to publish *De analysi*, like Barrow Collins recognized Newton's outstanding mathematical ability and when he had the opportunity received him in London. During the meeting Collins posed several mathematical problems to Newton, such as the method of computing harmonic progressions, the answers to which Newton conveyed several months later. In his reply to Newton, Collins posed a new problem concerning the computation of "the rate of interest N on an annuity of B pounds for thirty-one years purchased for A pounds." (p. 223) Again Newton solved the problem, but only enclosed the formula for computing the interest, not a general procedure for dealing with such problems. Earlier Barrow, apparently aware of Newton's studies of the new developments in mathematical analysis, had suggested to him that he consider putting out a new edition of Gerard Kinckhuysen's *Algebra*, with revisions and annotations, that Collins had recently translated from the Dutch into Latin. So along with the letter to Collins containing his solution of the interest problem, Newton included his annotations to Kinckhuysen showing his usual skill in simplifying the procedures and generalizing the methods. Furthermore, when requested by Collins

> he added significant portions on extracting the roots of cubic equations, including the identification of imaginary roots, and he wrote a masterful exposition of how to reduce problems to equations, in which he treated algebra as a language akin to other languages and the construction of equations as an exercise in translation. (p. 224)

Collins' admiration of Newton's mathematical virtuosity increased with each exchange and not prepared for his strange reserve, he urged him to publish his discoveries and expected to draw him into his circle of prominent mathematicians. When he offered to publish Newton's formula for calculating annuities Newton agreed, but his ungracious reply reveals his aversion both to public recognition and to enlarging his sphere of acquaintances:

> soe it bee wthout my name to it. For I see not what there is desirable in publick esteeme, were I able to acquire & maintaine it. It would

perhaps increase my acquaintance, ye thing wch I cheifly study to decline. (p. 224)

When Collins also offered to publish his "Observations on Kinckhuysen," Newton initially gave his consent as long as his name was not included, suggesting that the phrase "enriched by another author" be used, but even that proved too much because eventually he requested that the annotations be returned without their being published. Observing "a wariness in him to impart," Collins finally decided to "desist, and doe not trouble him any more . . ."[10] Even when Collins generously sent Newton copies of several of the latest important publications in mathematics, he was rebuffed with the request not to send any more books. But the prodding of Barrow and Collins was not without effect, leading to his *Tractatus de methodis serierum et fluxionum* (*A Treatise of the Methods of Series and Fluxions*) based on his earlier *De Analysi* and his latest mathematical investigations, the most extended development yet of his fluxional calculus. Although the *De methodis* was never finished nor ever published, it does reflect Newton's genius, as well as his tendency at this earlier period not to complete a project.

Although so much in Newton's life is exceptional and unexpected, it still is surprising that what first brought him the greatest notoriety was neither his contributions to mathematics nor to optics, but his mechanical inventiveness. Ever since his school days at Grantham, he had been intrigued by various mechanical devices and had shown his usual ingenuity in constructing or drawing plans of various mechanisms. Convinced by his optical investigations that chromatic aberration was unavoidable in refracting telescopes, he decided to build a reflecting telescope to avoid this distortion. Like Galileo who constructed the first truly successful telescope (although Galileo probably built his with the help of an artisan and using purchased lenses), Newton "cast and ground the mirror from an alloy of his own invention," "built the tube and the mount" (p. 233), and boasted to Conduitt many years later that he had even made the tools he used in constructing it. About half a foot long with the eye piece close to the exterior lens, it "magnified nearly forty times in diameter," and eliminated entirely all coloring of the image as Newton had intended. When the Royal Society learned of the telescope they asked to see it, so Barrow who was a member of the Society, took it to London at the end of 1671.

Delighted with the instrument, the Society was particularly concerned that its inventor, an Englishman, be given due credit and therefore thought "it necessary to use some meanes to secure this Invention from ye Usurpation of forreiners,''[11] as Henry Oldenburg, the secretary of the society, wrote to Newton. To this end a detailed diagram of the telescope was made along with a request to Newton to provide the exact specifications which would be sent "in a solemme letter to Paris to M. Hugens, thereby to prevent the arrogation of such strangers [. . . .]''(*Ibid.*) As the outstanding scientist on the continent, especially in the field of optics, it was natural that the Royal Society would inform Huygens of the invention which he admiringly called the "marvellous telescope of Mr. Newton." In recognition of his accomplishment Newton was "proposed Candidate" of the Royal Society, as Oldenburg so informed him in the same letter. Duly elected on January 11, 1672, this was the first of many honors to be bestowed on Newton who, despite his disavowal of "publick esteeme," subsequently would be honored and revered during his lifetime more than any other scientist, with the possible exception of Einstein.

In his letter thanking Oldenburg for the nomination to the Royal Society, Newton concluded by writing that to show his gratitude he soon would convey to the society something of even more scholarly interest than the telescope. Apparently encouraged by the enthusiastic response to his invention and believing that he had a receptive audience (as he later wrote to Oldenburg), Newton was able to overcome his inherent antipathy to possible public criticism and sent in early February a paper on his theory of colors, which the faithful Wickins copied. Almost immediately he received a letter from Oldenburg praising his paper and stating that when read at the Royal Society it "mett both with a singular attention and an uncommon applause" (p. 239), so the Society decided to print it in the *Philosophical Transactions* if Newton agreed. This time Newton did not object. But if he expected complete acquiescence in the conclusions of his paper, he was mistaken. Within two weeks the paper received a lengthy critique from Robert Hooke who considered himself the authority on the subject of colors in England, and did not welcome a theory (especially by a young and still relatively unknown author) that denied the established view. There were other critical replies, for example by the French Jesuit Ignace Gaston Pardies and then by Huygens whose initial reaction was that "the new Theory. . .appears very ingeneous to me"(p. 240), but who later began to raise a number of objections, yet it was Hooke's response that particularly aroused Newton's ire.

To understand the bitter dispute that followed, it is important to take into account the frailties of human nature on the part of both Newton and Hooke. As Westfall states, "[g]enius of Newton's order exacts a toll"(p. 239), as we have seen in his highly sensitive and defensive nature given to extremes of exaltation and "disorders," suggesting a manic-depressive personality. In addition, however, it is understandable that someone as brilliant as Newton, who already knew that he was at least the equal of the foremost mathematicians and optical investigators in England and Europe, would assume that his judgment would be regarded with the utmost respect. For eight years he had performed the most exacting experiments and made meticulous measurements in optics before gradually concluding that white light is a heterogeneous mixture of rays of colors. For those who had not confronted the same experimental evidence and gone through a similar process of reasoning, and who for psychological and intellectual reasons clung to the traditional view, it was natural to be more disposed to look for objections to Newton's theory than to accept it. Yet when his detractors based their criticisms, as was evident to Newton, on poorly designed experiments, imprecise measurements, and faulty logic it was just as natural for him to become impatient and irritated. It was not that he expected others to accept his conclusions uncritically, but that if they offered objections and wanted to be taken seriously, then their reasoning should be on the same high level as his own. Yet if it is difficult for geniuses to suffer fools lightly, it is even more difficult for the foolish to take themselves as such.

The discussions with Hooke and others involved most of these factors. While Hooke conceded the validity of Newton's experiments, he rejected "the hypotheses by which he explained them," reasserting the traditional view that colors are produced by modification of white light without coming to grips with Newton's analysis. He also criticized Newton's explanation of light in terms of corpuscles, stressing his own pulsatory view. (cf. 243-247) Newton was particularly annoyed by Hooke's (and Pardies') references to his theory of colors as a "hypothesis." Aware that his corpuscular interpretation of light was a hypothesis (since it could not be demonstrated experimentally), he subsequently separated this interpretation from the explanation of light as a mixture of rays, which he believed was demonstrated by his experiments. The distinction between experimentally demonstrated results, which Newton regarded as proven or factual, and the introduction of hypotheses which could not (at least up to that time) be demonstrated experimentally, would prove to be a crucial difference in all his writings from this point on. As indicated in his reply to Pardies, his methodology is similar to that of Galileo and Boyle:

> [. . .] it is to observed that the doctrine which I explained concerning refraction and colours, consists only in certain properties of light, without regarding any hypotheses by which those properties might be explained. For the best and safest method of philosophizing seems to

be, first to inquire deligently into the properties of things, and to establish those properties by experiments and then to proceed more slowly to hypotheses for the explanation of them. For hypotheses should be employed only in explaining the properties of things, but not assumed in determining them; unless so far as they may furnish experiments. For if the possibility of hypotheses is to be the test of the truth and reality of things, I see not how certainty can be obtained in any science, since numerous hypotheses may be devised, which shall seem to overcome new difficulties.[12]

This is such a crucial statement of Newton's method that it requires elucidation. There can be little doubt that when Newton contrasts "experimentally established properties" with the "hypotheses" introduced for the explanation of them, and firmly maintains that while hypotheses "should be employed" in *explaining* physical properties they should not be "assumed in *determining* them," he had in mind Descartes' theory of vortices which he had rejected for the reasons indicated. Descartes did not begin with experimentally (or as in astronomy, observationally) determinable results and then infer his explanatory hypotheses from them, as Newton advocates; on the contrary, he began with his theory of vortices based on *a priori* self-evident definitions and then deduced from it the motions that matter must have to conform to his theory, with the result that these deduced motions did not agree with the empirical data (they were inconsistent with Kepler's laws and could not explain eclipses). Given these erroneous consequences (cited also by Huygens), Newton concluded that "if the possibility of hypotheses is to be the test of the truth and reality of things, I see not how certainty can be obtained in any science, since numerous hypotheses may be devised, which shall seem to overcome new difficulties."

Despite Newton's use of the term "certainty," the evidence does not indicate that he was advocating either the positivist's absolute distinction between theory and empirical data or their claim that the empirical data is indubitable. Newton was very much aware that the distinction between experimentally established properties and the hypotheses introduced to explain them is neither absolute nor unchanging, but depends upon the available technology along with the progress of science (e.g., Newton used the concept 'rays' in accounting for the mixture of white light, but he would not have considered rays hypothetical in the way he considered 'corpuscles' hypothetical, and by his day the sine law for the refraction of light would not have been designated a hypothesis as it would have been earlier). Moreover, there is no evidence that he considered the properties established by experiments as indubitable or certain, but rather as the best available evidence for theory construction. In my opinion, Newton was arguing that because hypotheses can be constructed to accommodate any experimental results, if interpretations are to lead to definite (certain) conclusions, then more is required than hypotheses to settle the dispute.

Oldenburg had sent a copy of Hooke's critique to Newton, but out of respect for Newton the critique was not published in the *Philosophical Transactions* (allowing Hooke to read only a brief summary at a meeting of the Royal Society), but Newton's reply was published, indicating how quickly the relative status of the two men had changed. The following quotation indicates the general tenor of Newton's reply, showing that he believed Hooke had misconstrued the issues.

> And those consist in ascribing an Hypothesis to me wch is not mine; in asserting an Hypothesis wch as to ye principall parts of it is not against me; in granting the greatest part of my discourse if explicated by that Hypothesis; & in denying some things the truth of wch would have appeared by an experimentall examination. (p. 247)

Huygens also wrote four successive comments on Newton's paper, each one less favorable. In the first he suggested that a two color explanation (like the one Newton originally had entertained) seemed more promising than one based on an indefinite number of colors (or rays), and that until Newton could provide a mechanical hypothesis explaining how these colors are caused "he hath not taught us [. . .] wherein consists the nature and difference of Colours, but only this accident (which certainly is very considerable,) of their different Refrangibility."[13] This was a more serious objection coming from the European authority on optics and Newton treated it as such. Essentially his reply was that the experimental results show that all the colors are equally primary and cannot be derived from two. Here again Newton was appealing to experimental results over conjectures. Despite having introduced corpuscles as an explanatory hypothesis in his original paper, he now claimed that he .

> never intended to show wherein consists the nature and difference of colours, but onely to show that *de facto* they are originall & immutable qualities of rays wch exhibit them, & to leave it to others to explicate by Mechanical Hypotheses the nature & difference of those qualities; wch I take to be no very difficult matter.[14]

While not strictly true, by this time Newton had decided to focus on the narrower claim to avoid further controversy.

Recalling Galileo's vitriolic encounters with other natural philosophers and his eventual condemnation by the Church, one would not be remiss in thinking that Newton overreached to these criticisms. But such was his character that he could not take any criticism impersonally or lightly. Exasperated by the exchanges, he even threatened to resign from the Royal Society to avoid having to reply further to these objections. Calmed by Oldenburg, Newton did not resign but he did withdraw temporarily from further communication as his reply to the secretary indicates:

> But I must [. . .] signify to you, y^t I intend to be no further sollicitous about matters of Philosophy. And therefore I hope you will not take it ill if you find me ever refusing doing any thing more in y^t kind, or rather y^t you will favour me in my determination by preventing so far as you can conveniently any objections or other philosophicall letters that may concern me.[15]

Newton did not write to Oldenburg again for eighteen months.

Several years later, however, Oldenburg received an additional letter criticizing Newton's original paper on optics from an English Jesuit named Francis Hall, or Linus, according to the Latinization. Rejecting Newton's description of the spectrum based on experiments Linus claimed to have performed thirty years earlier, his criticism hardly warranted an answer, yet as much as Newton abhorred contention he felt compelled to defend his reputation when his experimental results were challenged. To settle the dispute, the Royal Society offered to reproduce Newton's prismatic experiments before the membership which it did finally on April 27, 1676, confirming his observations.

Then, responding to Linus' request that his critical replies be published by the Royal Society, Newton decided to write two papers presenting a comprehensive description of his optical investigations and interpretations. The two papers, "Discourse of Observations" which would comprise much of Book II of the *Opticks,* and "Hypothesis of Light" that included a corpuscular-mechanistic interpretation of light along with the description of an experiment on static-electricity, were read and discussed at meetings at the Royal Society from December 1675 to February 1676. The Society offered to publish the papers in the *Philosophical Transactions,* but Newton declined. Arousing considerable excitement and acclaim, the lectures also brought about a temporary reconciliation between Newton and Hooke at the latter's initiative. Writing to Newton directly, Hooke said he deplored contention, was eager to embrace the truth regardless of who discovered it, and especially respected Newton for his "excellent Disguistions" which he acknowledged went beyond his own inquiries. (cf. p. 273) Newton responded in a similarly manner, declaring his own aversion to disputes and praising Hooke as "a true Philosophical spirit." (p. 273)   While this dispelled the recent clouds of animosity that darkened their relationship, Hooke's later charge of plagiarism regarding the inverse square law of gravitational attraction would renew the hostility with even more intensity.

Although these optical disputes were very irritating to Newton, leading at times to acute mental disorder, they were complemented by increasing acclaim. In February 1675 he attended for the first time a meeting of the Royal Society becoming "a full-fledged member by signing the register" (p. 268) and went to two other meetings during his stay in London.   Greeted with enthusiastic admiration, it was during one of these meetings that he met Robert Boyle whose writings had considerable influence on his formulation of the corpuscular-mechanistic theory. He also entered into correspondence in 1675 with John Smith who "planned to prepare a table of square, cube, and fourth roots of all numbers from 1 to 10,000" (p. 258), and who appealed to Newton for a way of simplifying the computation.   Although Smith never completed the project, he did stimulate Newton into developing a method of interpolation that became the basis of the modern theory. In 1676 Newton dealt with the subject briefly in a paper entitled *Regula differentiarum* and then more extensively in a second paper called *Methodus differentialis* eventually published in 1711. "In the latter paper [. . .] Newton derived what are now referred to as the Newton-Stirling and Newton-Bessel formulas." (p. 259) Newton's insights were so acute that a recent scholar, Duncan Fraser, has written that modern researchers are striving to attain his level of achievement.

It was at this time also that he became acquainted with Leibniz, the co-discoverer of the calculus. Leibniz was a mathematical genius like Newton, as well as a highly original philosopher, but not a theoretical physicist or experimentalist, although at the time the distinction between a metaphysician and natural philosopher was not as sharp as it is today. He had studied mathematics under Huygens' tutelage and then had progressed, like Newton, into a first rate mathematician on his own. He visited London where he became a member of the Royal Society in 1673 (a year after Newton) and entered into an extended correspondence in mathematics with Oldenburg and Collins. Believing that the British were more advanced in dealing with infinite series than continental mathematicians, he pressed Oldenburg and Collins to describe the British achievements. The latter in turn urged Newton (whose contributions along with those of James Gregory were prominently mentioned in the correspondence) to reply which eventually led to his writing two letters to Leibniz describing his work—although as customary, he did not write Leibniz directly but through the mediation of Oldenburg.

Written in 1676 and referred to later as the *Epistola prior* and the *Epistola posterior*, the first letter (based on his earlier *De analysi* and *De methodis*) described his treatment of infinite series and their use in computing curves, areas, and volumes. Furthermore, it "assumed and employed his algorithms for differentiation and integration without expounding them" (p. 263), thus hinting at Newton's invention of the fluxional calculus (the method for computing the ratio of the increment of change of a variable, such as acceleration, as a function of the increment of change of a constant, such as time or gravity). In his reply to Oldenburg thanking him for the *Epistola prior*, Leibniz lavished praise on Newton:

> Your letter contains more numerous and more remarkable ideas about analysis than many thick volumes published on these matters . . . Newton's discoveries are worthy of his genius, which is so abundantly made manifest by his optical experiments and by his catadioptrical tube [the reflecting telescope].[16]

He also visited Collins in London and made such a striking impression on him that the latter indiscreetly allowed him to read Newton's *De analysi* and Gregory's *Historiola*. By 1675 Leibniz had "achieved the fundamental insights of his differential calculus" (p. 261), which though very similar to Newton's fluxional method was arrived at independently, yet the fact the Collins imprudently showed Leibniz the *De Analysi* unfortunately would contribute to the later priority dispute. Although written in 1666, Leibniz did not receive the second letter, *Epistola Posterior* until 1667. This letter described Newton's discovery of the binomial theorem, his fluxional method, and went more deeply into his treatment of infinite series while concealing the crucial aspects of the method in anagrams, customary at the time to avoid plagiarism. As in the case of the prior letter, Leibniz recognized its importance and replied to Oldenburg again with enthusiastic praise of Newton's mathematical achievement, even giving some account of his own differential calculus and exhorting Newton to reply further. He wrote a second letter a month later and since Oldenburg had died shortly afterwards the two letters were forwarded to Newton. Despite the significance of the correspondence in which both men tentatively were disclosing their separate invention of the calculus which could have led to an early acknowledgment of their independent contributions and perhaps to a collaboration, thereby avoiding the unfortunate priority dispute, Newton deigned not to reply to Leibniz thereby terminating the correspondence. Besides having become disinterested in mathematics he was involved in the distasteful disputes in optics and was turning to other areas of inquiry as a consolation. In any event, he wanted to avoid any further contention as he wrote to Oldenburg in connection with the dispute with Linus:

> I see I have made my self a slave to Philosophy, but if I get free of M^r
> Linus's business I will resolutely bid adew to it eternally, excepting
> what I do for my privat satisfaction or leave to come out after me.
> For I see a man must either resolve to put out nothing new or to
> become a slave to defend it.[17]

Although Newton would not "bid adew" to (natural) philosophy eternally, true to his word he temporarily put aside his mathematical and optical investigations along with related correspondence until the late '70s and early '80s. In the interim, a mind as acutely active as Newton's could not just lie idle but turned to subjects of greater interest, namely chemistry or alchemy and doctrinal problems arising in early church history. As alchemical investigations proceeded under the cloak of a secret society in pursuit of an occult knowledge, Newton's notebooks during this period contain references to furtive trips to London to purchase alchemical treatises and materials, along with clandestine visits from mysterious individuals. He applied his exceptional mechanical skills to the construction of sophisticated ovens used in his experiments and enlisted the help of Wickins until his departure and then Humphrey Newton (a distant relative who replaced Wickins) in his investigations. By 1675 he had acquired a vast collection of alchemical literature which at the time of his death included "one hundred and seventy-five books" plus additional pamphlets comprising "about one-tenth of his total library." (p. 292) Despite Boyle's criticism of alchemy described in the previous chapter, he was one of the few people Newton continued to correspond with often on the subject of alchemy.

These alchemical experiments followed by Biblical research were a "rebellion," according to Westfall, against the speculative confines of a mechanistic philosophy that interpreted all phenomena (like ancient atomism) as due solely to the necessary interactions and impact of material particles in motion. Unlike this clockwork framework that tended to exclude, or at least limit, the roles of spirit, forces, dynamic transformation, and God, alchemy embraced the agencies of souls, chemical spirits, mysterious transmutations, and animistic affinities. Thus it seemed to have had a liberating and inspiring influence on Newton, with both a religious and practical significance, despite its nefarious reputation:

> This Philosophy [alchemy] is not of that kind wch tendeth to vanity & deceit but rather to profit & to edification inducing first ye knowledg of God & secondly ye way to find out true medicines [. . .] so y^t ye scope is to glorify God in his wonderful works, to teach a man how to live well, & to be charitably affected helping o^r neighbors.[18]

It was partially due to this liberating influence that Newton, unlike the other natural philosophers of his day, was willing to include in his mechanistic system such nonmechanical active forces as gravity and the attractive and repulsive forces of minute particles. In "The System of the World" ending the *Principia*, he entertained the possibility of "a certain most subtle spirit" which, pervading all bodies, might account for the affinity and cohering of particles, the attraction and repulsion of electrical and magnetic bodies, and even explain sensation and nerve transmissions.[19] Furthermore, his famous conjectures in Query 32 of the *Opticks* regarding heat, light, and chemical reactions, along with his rejection of the common explanation of the cohesion of atoms because of their hooked shapes or occult affinities in favor of mutually attractive forces acting at a distance, were motivated by his alchemical investigations.[20]

Newton was not, however, so bewitched by alchemy that his critical powers were numbed by its beguiling influence, bringing to his inquiries the same gifts for critical evaluation and mathematical analysis as he had displayed in his optical experiments. That his alchemical investigations did not lead to comparably significant results was not the fault of Newton, but of the nature of alchemy. As Westfall states:

> Newton came to the Art with unique intellectual equipment such as no other alchemist ever possessed, and though it appears [. . .] that he entered into the fantastic world of alchemy, he did not leave his special gifts at the door. Indeed, he could not. He brought with him standards of intellectual rigor born of mathematics, which he applied to his own experimentation [. . .] [and] the mechanical philosophers

sense that nature is quantitative [. . .] [so that] his alchemical experimentation revealed an overriding concern for quantitative measurement such as cannot be found in the many tomes he read. He brought with him as well experimental skill [. . .] recently honed to a fine edge in his optical work. (pp. 294-5; brackets added)

As Newton's interest in alchemy began to wane in the '70s he turned to an intensive study of early church history and the origins of Christian doctrine, perhaps to resolve the pressing issue as to whether in good conscience he could accept ordination into the Anglican clergy as required by the regulations of Trinity College. In his fourth year (1672) as a fellow at Trinity, he either would have to be ordained by 1675 or confront expulsion from Cambridge. The sticking point was the doctrine of the Trinity, whether God the Father, Christ the Son, and the Holy Ghost existed as one person in the Godhead, as held by the Anglican (and Catholic) church, or whether Christ and the Holy Ghost were created by God and therefore under His dominion. With his usual concentration and scholarly rigor, Newton devoted years to studying the writings of the patristic fathers along with early church history, focusing on the fourth century when the Council of Nicaea accepted the trinitarian position of Athanasius over the creation view of Arius. While Arius had argued that Scripture stated that God had created Christ to be the mediator between God and man and therefore was subordinate to God the Father, Athanasius claimed they comprised the same Divine Substance.

Based on extensive study, Newton concluded, in the words of Westfall, "that a massive fraud, which began in the fourth and fifth centuries, had perverted the legacy of the early church" (p. 313) assisted by the Pope of Rome, the archenemy of the Anglicans. Believing that the Anglican church also was guilty of idolatry in identifying Christ with God, Newton could not submit to ordination, despite his previous avowals of belief.

Four times within the previous decade Newton had been willing to assert his orthodoxy under oath. When he signed for his degrees in 1665 and 1668, he affirmed his belief in the Thirty-nine Articles of the church. When he became a fellow in 1668, he swore to embrace the true religion of Christ with all his soul, in a context that clearly implied the Anglican definition of true religion. Finally, in 1669, when he took up the Lucasian professorship, he swore that he would conform to the liturgy of the Church of England. To remain a fellow of the College of the Holy and Undivided Trinity, he would need to affirm his orthodoxy one last time, in ordination. By 1675, however, the holy and undivided Trinity itself stood in the way. (pp. 330-331)

As in his earlier crises of collegiate advancement and tenure, it was as if some invisible hand directed the outcome. This time it was in the form of a special dispensation conferred solely on the Lucasian professorship. Since Arianism was considered a heresy, it was necessary to proceed cautiously lest the true motive of Newton's avoidance of ordination was discovered. Had he been found out, not only would he have been expelled from Trinity, he would have been exorcised from society and for someone as sensitive as Newton, this would have been intolerable. There were two possibilities open: either attaining one of the few exempted fellowships or receiving a royal dispensation that would excuse him from ordination. There is some evidence that Newton unsuccessfully pursued the former and then for reasons that are unclear succeeded in the later. Whether it was due again to the propitious intervention of Barrow or to someone else, on "27 April, the dispensation became official. By its terms, the Lucasian professor was exempted from taking holy orders unless "he himself desires to [. . .]." (p. 333) Worded "to give all just encouragement to learned men who are & shall be elected to ye said Professorship" (p. 333), the dispensation was not granted to Newton personally, but to "the Lucasian professorship in perpetuity." So once again and for the final time Newton precariously succeeded in obtaining a favorable decision that would ensure his tenure at Trinity College, Cambridge, as long as he wished.

While it may seem curious that ordination in the clergy (even though one was not required to perform the duties of a cleric) was a necessary condition for a mathematics professor to maintain his fellowship at Trinity, and that Newton despite his obligations as Lucasian professor of mathematics was so exercised by a doctrinal question pertaining to the trinity that he devoted years to the study of Christian doctrine to the neglect of his scientific interests, it should not be forgotten how extremely pervasive religious beliefs and institutions were at that time. Each of the founding fathers of the new science was deeply religious, though not necessarily mystical. While unquestionably committed to a rational understanding of the universe based on observation, experimentation, and mathematical demonstration, sustaining this conviction was the belief that they were investigating the rational laws of the universe imposed by God. Recall Galileo's famous argument that while the Bible contains the revealed word of God, the universe also is a "grand book [. . .] which stands continuously open to our gaze"[21] which, to be intelligible, must be deciphered by the language in which it is written, the language of mathematics. Hence not only theologians but natural philosophers can discern the handiwork of God in his creation. Boyle had argued that there was incomparably more artful design exhibited in the intricate structure of a dog's foot than in the famous clock in Strasburg. Believing that God had created the universe less than 6,000 years ago, Newton held that the perpetuating movements of the planets could not have occurred by chance or necessity, but must have been installed by God in the original creation. It is easy to overlook the lingering influence of the medieval outlook on these creators of modern science, despite their vision of an autonomous science of nature.

Although alchemy and church history dominated Newton's inquiries during the decade of the 1670s, as Lucasian professor he was required to give occasional lectures on mathematics so his involvement in that subject had not entirely lapsed. As mentioned earlier, it was modern analysis presented in Descartes' *Geometry* that had first nurtured Newton's interest in mathematics. Now three publications appeared by Pierre Fermat, Phillipe de la Hire, and Pappus that renewed Newton's mathematical inquiries, especially the "investigation of the classical loci problems, the pinnacles of Greek geometry." (p. 378) This led him to study Euclid and other Greek mathematicians with the consequence that his former admiration for Descartes declined in proportion as his appreciation of the ancient Greeks ascended.

But of considerable more importance than his investigation of the ancient loci problem were the new techniques he developed in clarifying these problems, methods later incorporated in his theory of fluxions or calculus: in particular the calculation of the rate of change of a quantity (called the "fluxion of the quantity") and the conception of "limits" in which the increment of change in the dependent variable is seen as a function of the incremental change in the independent variable as the latter approaches the limiting quantity of zero. Called differentiation, it is the calculation leading from a function to its derivative would prove invaluable in calculating either instantaneous or continuous changes in motion as a function of the ratio of two variable magnitudes, as one approaches zero.

In the same year 1679 as his renewed mathematical investigations, Newton received a letter from Hooke that reawakened his previous interest in natural philosophy. In his letter Hooke proposed a theory of celestial mechanics that could have preempted Newton's discovery of the universal law of gravitation. Having succeeded to the presidency of the Royal Society upon Oldenburg's death, Hooke was one of the leading natural philosophers of that century of remarkable savants. He might even have been considered the foremost British investigator, as Huygens was considered the outstanding European scientist, had he not been overshadowed by the colossal presence of the Lucasian professor. Writing to invite Newton to renew their correspondence, Hooke specifically asked him to comment on Hooke's attempt to prove that the earth moved and that all planetary motions consisted of a tangential (inertial) rectilinear motion that was deflected into a curved orbit by the mutual gravitational attraction of all the planets. The request was based on an early essay (1674), "*Attempt to Prove the Motion of the Earth,*" republished in 1679 as *Lectiones Cutlerianae*, which includes the following remarkable description of the conceptual components essential to a theory of planetary motions or "System of the World."

[At a future date] I shall explain a System of the World differing in many particulars from any yet known, [and] answering in all things to the common rules of mechanical motions. This depends upon three suppositions: first, that all celestial bodies whatever have an attraction or gravitating power towards their own centers, whereby they attract not only their own parts, and keep them from flying from them, as we may observe the earth to do, but that they do also attract all the other celestial bodies that are within the sphere of their activity; and consequently that not only the sun and moon have an influence upon the body and motion of the earth, and the earth upon them, but that Mercury, also Venus, Mars, Jupiter, and Saturn, by their attractive powers, have a considerable influence upon its motion as in the same manner the corresponding attractive power of the earth hath a considerable influence upon every one of their motions also. The second supposition is this: that all bodies whatsoever that are put into a direct and simple motion, will so continue to move forward in a straight line, till they are by some other effectual powers deflected and bent into a motion, describing a circle, ellipse, or some other more compounded curve line. The third supposition is: that these attractive powers are so much the more powerful in operating, by how much the nearer the body wrought upon is to their own centers. Now what these several degrees are I have not yet experimentally verified; but it is a notion, which if fully prosecuted as it ought to be will mightly assist the astronomer to reduce all the celestial motions to a certain rule, which I doubt will never be done true without it.[22]

The fact that Hooke clearly had identified the essential components of an explanation of planetary motions—the crucial role of inertia, the fact that all the planets exert mutual attractive or gravitational forces toward their centers, and that this force increases with the approach to the center—even though he could not give mathematical precision to them, was the basis of his later charge of plagiary concerning Newton's formulation of the universal law of gravitation.   Of particular significance was Hooke's replacement of a propelling force emanating from the sun to explain planetary motion with Descartes' conception of an inertial tangential motion, so that the curvilinear orbital trajectory requires a centrally attractive force continually deflecting the planet from its straight line motion. Prior to Hooke's latter, Newton had referred to the central or gravitating force as counteracting what Huygens would call a "centrifugal force" rather than an inertial force.

Furthermore, in a later letter replying to Newton's response concerning evidence for the earth's motion (in which Newton erroneously describes the path of a body falling from a tower to the rotating earth as a spiral terminating in the center of the earth), Hooke seems to have arrived at the inverse square law of gravitational attraction (if "in duplicate proportion" meant "as the square of"):

> [. . .] my supposition is that the Attraction always is in duplicate proportion to the Distance from the Center Reciprocall, and Consequently that the Velocity will be in a subduplicate proportion to the Attraction and Consequently as Kepler Supposes Reciprocall to the Distance.[23]

However, while Hooke's derivation was based on a fallacious inference from Galileo's law of gravitational acceleration and Kepler's erroneous inverse force law, Newton had derived the correct "inverse-square relation more than ten years earlier by substituting the values from Kepler's third law into his formula for centrifugal force [. . .]." (p. 387)

Thus while Hooke might have influenced Newton to the extent that he replaced the concept of centrifugal force by an inertial force and now considered gravitational attraction as a mutual force among all the planets, Hooke could not claim priority in the formulation of an exact mathematical law of universal gravitation. In fact, in a further letter to Newton Hooke again admitted his failure to demonstrate mathematically how the gravitational force produces an elliptical motion, and what the physical nature of this force is, appealing to Newton for a solution: "I doubt not but that by your excellent method you will easily find out what that Curve must be, and its proprietys, and suggest a physical Reason of this proportion."[24]

As Westfall points out, even if Hooke had possessed the mathematical ability to derive the inverse square law from the continuous deflection of the planets into their elliptical orbits, it is unlikely that he would have done so because of his erroneous approach to the problem. While Hooke seemed to follow Kepler in attempting to deduce the elliptical orbits from the strength of the gravitational field, Newton reversed the problem in realizing that the strength of the attractive force emanating from the sun must diminish so as to account for Kepler's three laws: the elliptical orbits of the planets, the variations in speed at the planet's perihelion and aphelion satisfying the equal areas law, and the correlation of the planet's distance from the sun with the size of its orbit. For the force necessary to counter-balance the planet's inertial tangential motion had to be of such a magnitude as to produce its orbital speed and curvature, thereby explaining Kepler's first two laws.

But it as Kepler's third law, that the lengths of the planetary *periods* increase as their *distances* from the sun increase, not in direct proportion but to the 3/2th power of their distance (so that increasing the distance four times $(2)^2$ augments the planetary year eight times $(2)^3$, that enabled Newton to derive his inverse square law. But even if Newton owed little to Hooke in the mathematical derivation of his inverse square law, he acknowledged that it was Hooke's letters and probing questions that drove him to find a solution. As Westfall indicates, given Kepler's third law and Hooke's description of the two dynamic forces (inertial and attractive) producing orbital motion, Newton had to demonstrate mathematically that the attractive gravitational force must vary "inversely as the square of the distance at the two apsides [extremes] of an ellipse, and then that the same relation holds for every point on the ellipse"(p. 387; brackets added), a task requiring Newton's unique mathematical ability. This was one of the two components necessary in a complete law of universal gravitation (the other being the relation of the force to the masses).

Before concluding this biographical introduction to Newton and turning to an analysis of the major scientific achievements of his life, two additional contributions of this earlier period should be mentioned. Toward the end of 1680 two comets were sighted, one in early November and then in mid-December another was observed moving away from the sun and growing in length, until by late December it had attained an enormous size "with a tail four times as broad as the moon and more than seventy degrees long."(p. 391) As had happened previously at the time of Tycho, Kepler, and Galileo, these citings proved immensely interesting and aroused considerable controversy as to the nature of comets. John Flamsteed, the Royal Astronomer, believed that the two comets were actually one which had reversed its direction after approaching the sun. We will recall that comets still were something of a mystery at this time. Tycho had disproved the Aristotelian explanation that they were ignited vapors in the sublunar world by demonstrating that they existed in the celestial world. Still, they continued to be distinguished from the planets which described curvilinear orbits around the sun, while they were believed to move erratically in straight paths and were thought to be composed of some ephemeral substance.

Having met Newton in 1674 in Cambridge, Flamsteed, like Hooke, appealed to Newton for help in finding an explanation. But Newton's interest already had been aroused to the extent that he first observed the comet through a concave lens, proceeding to a three-foot then seven-foot telescope, and finally considered further improving his observations by constructing a four-foot reflecting telescope based on his earlier model, although he never completed it. (cf. p. 392) Like others, when Newton began reflecting on the occurrence of the comets he did not think of including them within his recently formulated theory of celestial dynamics, adhering to the view that they were strange phenomena outside the laws of the solar system. Gradually, however, as he acquired more precise data from Flamsteed and others regarding the exact position and movement of the comets he revised his view. When what we now call Halley's comet appeared in 1682, Newton added his observations of it to the other data he had acquired, concluding that the comets do not describe rectilinear paths according to some independent laws, but have curved orbits (as Flamsteed had suggested) somewhat analogous to the planets and therefore might be explainable by the same dynamic principles. (cf. 397) Thus another astronomical distinction, a legacy of the Aristotelian system, was dissolved in the newly emerging unified system of celestial mechanics.

Newton's other contributions were in the area of mathematics, and while they are not equivalent to his earlier work or to his theory of fluxions, they did enhance his reputation. The first consisted of a series of lectures on algebra to fulfill the college regulations. Compiled in 1683-84, they were not published until 1707 under the title, *Arithmetica universalis*, which became Newton's "most popular mathematical work" during the eighteenth century. In an anonymous review in the *Acta eruditorum*, Leibniz declared that the *Universal Arithmetick* contained "certain extraordinary features which you will seek in vain in vast volumes of Analysis." (p. 398) As Westfall states: "It is a further measure of Newton's mathematical genius that a contribution to duty, flung off in a spare moment, could merit such praise." (p. 398)

The second work entitled "*Matheseos universalis specimina*" (*Specimens of a Universal System of Mathematics*) was a response initially to a treatise sent to him in 1684 by David Gregory, nephew of the famous Scottish mathematician, James Gregory, expounding his uncle's treatment of infinite series applied to geometrical configurations like quadratures and volumes. As the title suggests, the *"Matheseos"* was an ambitious work that was conceived more as a potential response to his earlier exchange with Leibniz regarding the calculus than as a reply to Gregory. Never completed, it was intended to expound Newton's work on infinite series and compare his method of fluxions with Leibniz'a differential calculus. (cf. 401) But an unexpected visit by Edmund Halley in August of 1684 was to redirect Newton's career and revise henceforth mankind's conception of the universe.

NOTES

1. Alexander Pope's "Epitaph to Newton."

2. Edmund Halley, "The Ode Dedicated to Newton," in Isaac Newton, *Mathematical Principles*, Vol. I, translated by Florian Cajori, revised by Andrew Motte (Berkeley: University of California Press, 1962), p. xv.

3. Newton to Hooke, February 5, 1676; *Corres*. 1, p. 416. Quoted from Richard S. Westfall, *Never at Rest* (Cambridge: Cambridge University Press, 1980), p. 274. As above, I shall include in the footnote the reference cited by Westfall followed by the page in Westfall from which the quotation was derived. Citations in the text are to Westfall unless otherwise indicated. Considerably more demanding than the usual biography because of the necessity of explicating Newton's exacting mathematical and scientific development, along with his esoteric publications in these areas, covering his wide ranging interests and writings on biblical scholarship and theology, along with alchemy, astronomy, optics, and mechanics, describing his extended correspondence and disputes with the scholars of the period, depicting his place in the academic, intellectual, and political life of the era, and researching the extensive archives and voluminous biographical material extant on Newton to convey a full and accurate account of his life, Professor Westfall has presented us with a superbly written, definitive biography which itself is a tribute to the greatest of scientists. The following resumé of Newton's life has been distilled from this monumental account which the page references in the text acknowledge.

4. *Stukeley*, p. 61. Westfall, p. 191.

5. This is quoted by Westfall from Conduitt's (the husband later of Newton's niece Catherine) original version in Keynes MS 130.2, pp. 17-18. Westfall, pp. 59-60; brackets added)

6. Keynes, MS, 130.4, pp. 10-12. Westfall, p. 154.

7. *Add* MS, 3968.41, f. 85. Westfall, p. 143; brackets added.

8. *Add* MS, 3996, f. 122ᵛ. Westfall, p. 160.

9. In correspondence of Barrow to Newton, 20 August 1669. Westfall, p. 202.

10. *Corres.* l, 53-55. Westfall, p. 226.

11. *Corres.* 1, 73. Westfall, p. 234.

12. I. Bernard Cohen (ed.), *Isaac Newton's Papers & Letters on Natural Philosophy* (Cambridge Mass., 1958), p. 106. Westfall, pp. 242-243.

13. *Corres.* 1, 255-6. Westfall, p. 249.

14. *Corres.* 1, 264. Westfall, p. 250.

15. *Corres.* l, 294-5. Westfall, p. 251.

16. *Corres.* 2, 65-71. Westfall, p. 263.

17. *Corres.* 2, 182-3. Westfall, pp. 275-6.

18. Keynes, MS, 33, f. 5ᵛ. Westfall, p. 298; brackets added. For a complete description of Newton's alchemical investigations see Westfall, ch. 8.

19. Cf. Newton, *Principia, op. cit.*, Vol. 2, Part III, p. 547.

20. Cf. Newton, *Opticks, op. cit.*, pp. 388-389.

21. Galileo Galilei, *The Assayer*, translated by Stillman Drake in *The Controversy On The Comets of 1618* (Philadelphia: University of Pennsylvania Press), pp. 183-4.

22. Quoted from Thomas S. Kuhn, *The Copernican Revolution* (Cambridge: Harvard University Press, 1957), p. 254.

23. Hooke to Newton, January 6, 1680; *Corres.* 2, 309. Westfall, p. 386.

24. Hooke to Newton, January 17, 1680; *Corres.* 2, p. 313. Westfall, p. 387.

CHAPTER VII

NEWTON'S REVOLUTION

Nearer the gods no mortal may approach.[1]
Halley

By 1684 the essential dynamic components for a final resolution of the motion of the planets were known to the leading natural philosophers of the day, such as Borelli,[2] Wren,[3] Hooke,[4] Halley,[5] and Huygens.[6] Kepler had proposed two contrary dynamic forces to explain the orbital motion of the planets, an *anima motrix* or natural force (as he later conceived it) emanating from the sun producing the planets' *continuous* motion and a mutual magnetic attraction between the planets and the sun causing the constant *deviation* of the planets' motion into an elliptical orbit. The principle of inertia as formulated by Descartes allowed the substitution of an 'inertial force' for Kepler's *anima motrix* and the general acceptance of an 'attractive force' between the sun and the planets (that diminished with the square of the distance to satisfy Kepler's third law) replaced his magnetic attraction. The problem, as Hooke indicated in his 1679 letter to Newton requesting his mathematical assistance, was to compute how such an attractive force, originating in the major foci of the planet's orbit transformed a succession of instantaneous deviations from an inertial tangential motion into a continuous elliptical orbit, deriving the precise change in velocities as the planet swung through its perihelion and aphelion.

WHAT HALLEY WROUGHT

Although Edmund Halley is popularly known for the comet observed in 1682 named for him, the achievement for which he will be everlastingly remembered is his role as instigator and publisher of the *Principia*. Having met Newton in 1682 and discussed comets with him, after Wren's prize challenge to derive the elliptical orbits of the planets from the inverse square law Halley decided in August of 1684 to visit Newton in Cambridge to seek his opinion. As reported later by Abraham De Moivre, Newton recalled this pregnant meeting with Halley as follows:

> In 1684 Dr Halley came to visit him in Cambridge, after they had been some time together, the D^r asked him what he thought the Curve

would be that would be described by the Planets supposing the force
of attraction towards the Sun to be reciprocal to the square of their
distance from it. Sr Isaac replied immediately that it would be an
Ellipsis, the Doctor struck with joy and amazement asked him how he
knew it, why saith he I have calculated it, whereupon Dr Halley asked
him for his calculation without any farther delay. Sr Isaac looked
among his papers but could not find it, but he promised him to review
it, & then to send it him . . .[7]

Once aroused to the challenge, Newton could not stop with merely
demonstrating how he had derived Kepler's elliptical orbits from a force of
attraction that decreased with the square of the distance, but was impelled to
think out the basic conceptual framework and mathematical formalism of a
system of celestial dynamics based on the astronomical observations available.
By the following November Halley received a short treatise of nine pages
entitled *De Motu corporum in gyrum* (*On the Motion of Bodies in an Orbit*)
that not only derived elliptical orbits from the inverse square law but
conversely demonstrated "that an elliptical orbit entails an inverse-square force
to one focus" (p. 404), while also proving Kepler's other two laws from
additional dynamic principles. Immediately recognizing the extraordinary
originality of the work, Halley reported Newton's achievements to the Royal
Society on 10 December, but already Newton was working on the first of three
successive revisions.

Enlarging his investigations beyond that of the attractive force of the sun
on the planets, he began inquiring about the orbits of the satellites of Jupiter
and Saturn (the 'horns' of Saturn were interpreted as satellites), the attraction
between the earth and the moon producing the latter's orbital deviations, the
causes of the tides, and how and why the comets move as they do. Admitting
to Flamsteed, the Royal Astronomer, that he had not kept informed of the
latest astronomical reports, Newton plied him with requests for information
since his calculations had to be based on and checked by exact astronomical
observations. It is apparent from his questions that as his investigations
proceeded he began to envision the diverse astronomical phenomena fitting
into a unified system of explanation, and thus started inquiring into the precise
operation and magnitude of the forces that could produce the more specific
celestial interactions. The task was enormous because he was creating the
network of celestial dynamics from bare strands. As Westfall states, "while
the seventeenth century had taken giant strides in mechanics, it had yet to
crown its effort with a science of dynamics." (p. 409) All of the natural

philosophers were suspicious of the concept of forces if that implied action at a distance, the crucial *modus operandi* of Newton's dynamics, relying instead on Descartes' mechanistic theory of vortices or at least the notion of direct impact. But Newton's earlier studies of Descartes had convinced him that the theory of vortices was unable to explain the actual astronomical motions while his alchemical inquiries led him to be receptive to the efficacy and necessity of forces, whether they acted at a distance or through the efficacy of some medium.

As the revisions of *De Motu* progressed one sees a gradual clarification of the basic concepts, a fuller description of the laws of motion, and a more precise formulation of the mathematical methods that soon would be presented in a systematic form in the *Principia*. Distinguishing between the "inherent force" of inertia and the "impressed force" of attraction, Newton originally used Galileo's parallelogram diagram to derive the conjoint force produced by these different "species" of motion since the "crux of his dynamics lay in the relation of inherent force and impressed force, what he later called [. . .] 'the inherent, innate and essential force of a body' and 'the force brought to bear or impressed on a body." (pp. 414-5). Eventually realizing that acceleration involved either a change in speed or in direction, he concluded that uniform circular motion was dynamically identical to straight line motion that accelerated uniformly. While the inherent inertial force of a moving body causes it to move forward with a continuous *uniform* velocity, when a constant impressed force is added this produces a continuous *change* in velocity proportional to the two forces: in "this proportionality lay the possibility of a quantitative science of dynamics that would cap and complete Galileo's kinematics." (p. 417) Newton coined the term "centripetal force" to designate this impressed attraction to the center "in conscious parallel to Huygens's word 'centrifugal,' fleeing the center." (p. 411)

Although he employed geometrical demonstrations to show how a series of instantaneous deviations at equal intervals of time due to discrete "impulses" of forces can produce continuous elliptical trajectories, the fact that he created the method of fluxions to compute instantaneous changes of ratios in continuous flux suggests that he used this method in his derivations despite the absence of any explicit reference to them in his publications. (cf. p. 424) Since only Leibniz was familiar with the new techniques of calculation developed in his method of fluxions, this would have been reasonable if he expected others to follow his derivations.

Using the segments of arcs from curved orbits to represent time, Newton was able to demonstrate that "the deviation from the tangent, proportional to the square of the time, corresponds to Galileo's formula for uniformly accelerated motion''(p. 418), as well as Huygens' versed sign ratio computing the deviation from the tangent proportional to the centrifugal force. One can imagine his delight when he realized that these formula agreed, thereby reinforcing his calculations. He defined mass as proportional to density and size, distinguishing it from weight despite their evident equivalence on the earth's surface. Dissatisfied with his earlier use of the parallelogram of forces to compute the combined effect of inertial and impressed forces, he replaced this with what we now know as his third law, that the force impressed on two interacting bodies is opposite in direction but equal in magnitude. By the following November 1685 the revisions of *De Motu* had eventuated in the creation of the foundations of a science of dynamics nearly as it would be presented in the *Principia*. The nine-page treatise that he had sent to Halley a year earlier had been expanded into ''two books of well over ten times that length''(p. 423), to which he gave the title *De motu corporum* (*On the Motion of Bodies*). Because Book I was presented to the University in fulfillment of his lecture requirements in 1684-85 it often is referred to as "*Lectiones de motu*," while Book II was translated into English from the Latin in 1729, two years after Newton's death, by Andrew Motte under the title "The System of the World," and published as Book III, Volume II of the *Principia*.

Now that he had available the rudiments of a celestial dynamics he began applying it to specific problems. In 1665-6 when the idea occurred to him that the same gravitational force that causes an apple to fall if extended to the moon could explain the latter's orbital motion, he attempted to compare the required magnitude of such a force with the gravitational law for free fall at the surface of the earth. Having based these calculations on latitudes derived from inaccurate dimensions of the circumference of the earth, he only obtained an approximate agreement with the inverse square law. Learning of Jean Picard's new measurement of the earth's circumference, he found his calculations based on the corrected value produced the right agreement.

Furthermore, his experiments on the oscillations of pendulums of different weights convinced him that the attractive force of a body is the sum of the attractive force of its constituent particles, measured not from the surface of the body but from its center. This was an enormous simplification that enabled him to calculate the universal gravitational attraction among the sun and the planets along with the various satellites as originating from their centers rather than their surfaces, thus eliminating the necessity of determining the exact magnitude of each celestial body's circumference in order to compute the exact attractive force. As Westfall states, ''a homogeneous spherical shell composed of particles that attract inversely as the square of the distance, attracts a particle external to it, no matter at what distance, inversely as the square of its distance from the center of the sphere.'' (p. 427) For purposes of calculation, Newton could treat the whole planetary system as a congeries of mass-points whose motions, determined by the mutual gravitational forces among all the bodies, varied inversely as the square of the distance from the these mass-points.

Moreover, an additional simplification could be made by treating the sun as the primary source of the gravitational force on the planets (because as we now know, based on Einstein's equation $E=mc^2$, the sun contains 98 percent of the mass of our solar system), while the earth is the primary source of the gravitational force of the moon and Jupiter of its satellites. ''With the demonstration of a sphere's attraction, and with the exact correlation of the moon's motion with the measured acceleration of gravity,'' as Westfall says, ''the logical foundation of the concept of universal gravitation became secure.'' (p. 429) The concept of a universal mutual attraction among all the celestial bodies led Newton to attempt to explain the perturbations in the moon's orbit as due to additional gravitational effects beyond that of the earth, but the complexity of the problem allowed for little success. He tried to calculate the forces producing the tides and the motions of the comets, concluding that the latter move in oval orbits due to the gravitational force of the sun, thus finally drawing these strange phenomena into his explanatory system.

The two books of *De motu corporum* which essentially contained the content of Books I and III of the *Principia* were nearing completion by the autumn of 1686, despite Newton's continuous revisions. Book I, which contained his laws of motion and numerous geometrical demonstrations of the celestial motions, was expanded to include the effects of the medium on moving bodies, but was so enlarged that he separated the latter discussion which became Book II of the *Principia*. When the books were completed he had them copied by Humphrey Newton and sent to the Royal Society. According to his own account, ''The Book of Principles [the *Principia*] was writ in about 17 or 18 months, whereof about two months were taken up with journeys, & the MS was sent to ye R.S. in spring 1686; & the shortness of the time in which I wrote it, makes me not ashamed of having committed some faults.''[8] Perhaps never before or after has such a monumental work been written in such a short time, another testimony to Newton's genius. At the end of April Dr. Vincent, a colleague at Cambridge and fellow of the Royal Society, ''presented to the Society a manuscript entitled *Philosophiae Naturalis principia mathematica*, and dedicated to the Society by Mr. Isaac Newton

[. . .]."[9]

The Society ordered that a letter of thanks be written to Newton and that the book be given to Halley, clerk to the Society and liaison with Newton, who would make a report to the council. When three weeks passed without any action by the council Halley raised the issue of its publication before a meeting of the society on 19 May, whereupon it was voted

> That Mr. Newton's *Philosophiae naturalis principia mathematic* be printed forthwith in quarto in fair letter; and that a letter be written to him to signify the Society's resolution, and to desire his opinion as to the print, volume, cuts, &c.[10]

Having originally incited Newton to write the *Principia*, goaded the Royal Society into assuming responsibility for its publication, Halley also put himself in charge of the printing. The task completed on July 5, 1687, Halley wrote the following note to Newton:

Honoured S[r]

> I have at length brought your book to an end, and hope it will please you. The last errata came just in time to be inserted. I will present from you the books you desire to the R. Society, M[r] Boyle, M[r] Pagit, M[r] Flamsteed and if there by any elce in town that you design to gratifie that way; and I have sent you to bestow on your friends in the University 20 Copies, which I entreat you to accept.[11]

Unlike Copernicus who never acknowledged Rheticus' crucial role in urging him to write the *De Revolutionibus* and arranging the printing, Newton graciously thanked Halley (along with the Royal Society) for his dedicated contribution to the realization of the *Principia*:

> In the publication of this work the most acute and universally learned *Mr. Edmund Halley* not only assisted me in correcting the errors of the press and preparing the geometrical figures, but it was through his solicitations that it came to be published; for when he had obtained of me my demonstrations of the figure of the celestial orbits, he continually pressed me to communicate the same to the *Royal Society*, who afterwards, by their kind encouragement and entreaties, engaged

me to think of publishing them.[12]

Having acted as midwife to the *Principia*, Halley also wrote the beautiful, revered "Ode to Newton," concluding with the immortal line, "Nearer the gods no mortal may approach."

COTES' PREFACE

Roger Cotes, also a Fellow of Trinity and Plumian Professor of Astronomy and Experimental Philosophy, prepared the "greatly amended and increased" second edition published in 1713. At the suggestion of the Reverend Richard Bentley, Master of Trinity College and a great friend and admirer of Newton, Cotes wrote a Preface

> "to add something more particularly concerning the manner of
> Philosophizing made use of and wherein it differs from that of
> Descartes and Others [. . .] by a short deduction of the Principle of
> Gravity from the Phenomena of Nature in a popular way that it may
> be understood by ordinary readers and may serve at ye same time as
> a specimen to them of the Method of ye whole Book."[13]

Although Descartes is singled out in this statement as the primary antagonist of Newton, in the Preface itself Cotes mentions the Peripatetics as also subscribing to a false system of natural philosophy based on occult powers and verbal explanations, extolling Newton's method of analysis and synthesis: that is, his method of deducing from nature the forces and the simple laws manifested by these forces, and then explaining the other phenomena according to these same principles. (cf. XXI) The primary force, of course, is the universal attractive, centripetal or gravitational force extending mutually among all bodies, and the principle law is that due to this force bodies attract in the ratio of the product of their masses and inversely proportional to the square of the distance, as measured from their centers. The great merit of Newton's force-law is that from it one can derive Galileo's gravitational law, Kepler's three laws of planetary motion, and Huygens' versed sine law of centrifugal force.

Moreover, by this same force-law an accurate description is finally possible of all the celestial motions that have perplexed mankind from early times: the revolutions of the planets and satellites like the moon, the movements of the comets, and the periodicity of the tides. These generalized conclusions are based on the maxim of the uniformity of nature, "that effects of the same kind, whose known properties are the same, take their rise from the same causes and have the same unknown properties also." (p. XXVI) It is not from conjectured hypotheses, but by observations and experiments that these effects, properties, and causes are known. Declaring that "gravity must have a place among the primary qualities of all bodies" (p. XXVI), implying that it is an inherent property of matter, Cotes, responding to criticism by Samuel Clarke, adopts Newton's position declaring that his intention "was not to assert Gravity to be essential to Matter" but to accept it as like primary qualities despite the fact that "we are ignorant of the Essential propertys of Matter [. . .]."[14] Being ignorant of the nature and origin of gravity is no justification for either rejecting it or declaring it to be an "occult quality," since of the most basic and simple causes of natural phenomena, one cannot expect a more fundamental explanation.

> For causes usually proceed in a continued chain from those that are more compounded to those that are more simple; when we are arrived at the most simple cause we can go no further. Therefore no mechanical account or explanation of the most simple cause is to be expected or given; for if it could be given, the cause were not the most simple. These most simple causes will you then call occult, and reject them? Then you must reject those that immediately depend upon them, and those which depend upon these last, till philosophy is quite cleared and disencumbered of all causes. (p. XXVII)

Antirealists who often argue that the conditional and approximate nature of scientific explanations preclude their being taken realistically should ponder this reply, as valid now as it was in Newton's day. All explanations eventually must terminate in something being given or assumed, otherwise one would have to know everything to know something. What justifies accepting such causes is that they are supported by observation and experiment, not just conjecture or imagination. Thus unlike Descartes who was satisfied if his laws *could* have been those chosen by God in the original creation, Cotes claims like Newton that the

> business of true philosophy is to derive the natures of things from causes truly existent, and to inquire after those laws on which the Great Creator actually chose to found this most beautiful Frame of the

World, not those by which he might have done the same, had he so pleased. (p. XXVIII)

With Newton's method the gates of inquiry are now spread wide so that "we may freely enter into the knowledge of the hidden secrets and wonders of natural things" (p. XXXII) which is "the safest protection against the attacks of atheists [. . .], the band of godless men." (p. XXXIII) Cotes' Preface is still one of the most succinct and accessible introductions to the *Principia.* A third edition on which the present translation from the Latin was based, was prepared, as Newton acknowledged in the Preface to that Edition, "with much care by Henry Pemberton, M.D., a man of the greatest skill in these matters [. . .]."

NEWTON'S PREFACE

Even more succinctly than Cotes, Newton states in well-known passages in the Preface to the First Edition of the *Principia* the essential purpose of the work. Unlike Plato whose theory of Forms included perfect geometrical figures intended to guarantee the truth of geometry or Descartes who grounded geometry on self-evident ideas illuminated by the natural light of reason, Newton declared that "geometry is founded in mechanical practice" (p. XVII) since it is from mechanics that geometrical figures such as straight lines and circles are derived. Given these figures geometry teaches the "use of them" when applied to measurement. Thus geometry which is founded in mechanical practice "is nothing but that part of universal mechanics which accurately proposes and demonstrates the art of measuring." (*Ibid.*) And since mechanics is concerned essentially with the motions and interactions of physical bodies as they move in space and time according to the intensity of various forces, geometry is the discipline that enables one to rationalize the magnitudes of these motions and forces.

In this sense rational mechanics will be the science of motions resulting from any forces whatsoever, and of the forces required to produce any motions, accurately proposed and demonstrated [. . .] therefore I offer this work as the mathematical principles of philosophy, for the whole burden of philosophy seems to consist in this—from the phenomena of motions to investigate the forces of nature, and then from these forces to demonstrate the other phenomena

[. . .]. (pp. XVII-XVIII)

In so many words Newton created the modern science of mechanics. While Descartes had considered causes and neglected mathematics in his mechanics and Galileo had included mathematics but omitted causes in his, Newton incorporated both. Moreover, he was the only natural philosopher of his time to foresee the role of forces, so crucial to the development of science in the twentieth century. As he says,

> from these forces, by other propositions which are also mathematical, I deduce the motions of the planets, the comets, the moon, and the sea. I wish we could derive the rest of the phenomena of Nature by the same kind of reasoning from mechanical principles, for I am induced by many reasons to suspect that they may all depend upon certain forces by which the particles of bodies, by some causes hitherto unknown, are either mutually impelled towards one another, and cohere in regular figures, or are repelled and recede from one another. These forces being unknown philosophers have hitherto attempted the search of Nature in vain; but I hope the principles here laid down will afford some light either to this or some truer method of philosophy. (p. XVIII)

Natural philosophy would have to await the discovery of atomic or subatomic particles along with various forces before Newton's program would be realized. But he alone of all the natural philosophers foresaw their necessity for explaining natural phenomena.

DEFINITIONS AND LAWS OF MOTION

Turning to the third edition of the *Principia* as now printed in English, it is divided into three books: the first presents the underlying definitions, laws of motion, and mathematical demonstrations of these motions, the second extends these demonstrations to bodies moving in resisting media, and the third contains his more accessible and well-known description of "The System of the World." The first two books occur as Volume I and the second as Volume II. Needless to say, it is neither possible nor necessary to give a full or detailed description of the *Principia*, our task being to describe its essential contents, novelty, methodology, and significance. Emulating the rigorous geometric style of the ancient Greeks such as Euclid and Archimedes, Newton begins with precise definitions of those concepts integral to his system: mass, momentum (without using the term), inertia (*vis inertiae*), external or impressed forces causing a body to change its state of rest or motion, and centripetal forces (such as magnetism and gravity) attracting bodies to a central point proportional to the magnitude of the cause (an "absolute" force), the distance to which it extends (an "accelerative" force), and the velocity it generates (a "motive" force). At this time he does not attempt to explain the nature or origin of such forces, intending "only to give a mathematical notion of those forces, without considering their physical causes or seats." (p. 5)

These definitions are followed by a famous Scholium (remarks) presenting Newton's justification of the absolute frames (ontological coordinate systems) of the universe. As he wrote to Reverend Bentley, "[w]hen I wrote my treatise about our Systeme I had an eye upon such Principles as might work wth considering men for beliefe of a Deity . . ."[15] Having concluded years earlier that Descartes' relativistic conception of motion encouraged atheism because it denied the absolutism of God's creation of and immanence in the world,[16] Newton carefully distinguished between absolute and relative space, place, time, and motion. The common designations and measurements of these extensive, positional, and durational magnitudes depend upon conventional frames of reference and standards of measurements: days, months, and years based on the most obvious regularities of our solar system as expressed in sexagesimal units, positions specified ultimately in terms of the longitudes and latitudes of the earth or in reference to some celestial body, and magnitudes and dimensions expressed in the metric or English measurement systems. However, underlying these standardized conventional units accounting for their approximate accuracy are the absolute magnitudes themselves of space, place, and time.

Thus while "[r]elative space is some movable dimension or measure of the absolute spaces [. . .] [a]bsolute space, in its own nature, without relation to anything external, remains always similar and immovable." (p. 6) Similarly, while "relative, apparent, and common time is some sensible and external [. . .] measure of duration by means of motion [. . .] such as an hour, a day, a month, a year [. . .] [a]bsolute, true, and mathematical time, of itself, and from its own nature, flows equably without relation to anything external [. . .]." (p. 6) A certain intuitive justification underlies these absolute designations in that a universe of interacting material particles would seem to presuppose an independent spatial locus while all the diverse motions in the universe would appear to take place against a background of an invariable flow of time: "[a]ll things are placed in time as to order of succession; and in space as to order of situation." (p. 8) Confronted with the same problem of explaining the status of space and time and of justifying our knowledge of geometry, arithmetic, and mechanics, Kant also will defend the absoluteness of space and time, although not as independently existing realities but as "transcendental forms" or *a priori* conditions of sensibility. Calling his philosophy a "*transcendental idealism*," he contrasts it with a "*transcendental realism*" like Newton's.

> By *transcendental idealism* I mean the doctrine that appearances are [. . .] representations only, not things in themselves, and that time and space are therefore only sensible forms of our intuition, not determinations given as existing by themselves, nor conditions of objects viewed as things in themselves. To this idealism there is opposed a *transcendental realism* which regards time and space as something given in themselves, independent of our sensibility.[17]

In words similar to Newton, Kant says that "[t]ime has only one dimension: different times are not simultaneous but successive (just as different spaces are not successive but simultaneous)."[18]

These pure *a priori* intuitions as preconditions of all experience explain for Kant the *apodictic* certainty but synthetic nature of geometric, arithmetic, and mechanistic principles because such knowledge is limited to the phenomenal world or things in themselves as they appear to man, but not as they are in themselves.

> Geometry is based upon the pure intuition of space. Arithmetic attains its concepts of numbers by the successive addition of units in time, and pure mechanics especially can attain its concepts of motion only by employing the representation of time. Both representations, however, are merely intuitions; for if we omit from the empirical intuitions of bodies and their alterations (motion) everything empirical, i.e., belonging to sensation, space and time will remain, and are therefore pure intuitions that lie *a priori* at the basis of the empirical.[19]

In contrast to Kant, absolute space and time for Newton are not transcendental forms of sensory intuition but ontologically necessary frames of the universe. If they are ultimately grounded in consciousness, it is not the finite consciousness of human beings but the eternal and omnipresent consciousness of God, the *sensorium die*. As he says in the *Opticks*, where he permits such speculation,

> does it not appear from Phaenomena that there is a Being incorporeal, living, intelligent, omnipresent, who in infinite Space [and time], as it were in his Sensory [*Sensorium*], sees the things themselves intimately, and thoroughly perceives them, and comprehends them wholly by their immediate presence to himself [. . .].[20]

Could this reference to a Being comprehending "things themselves" be the basis of Kant's belief that things in themselves only could be known by a direct intellectual intuition, such as God might possess? Newton here refers to an "omnipresent Being" who "sees" as well as "comprehends" things themselves "in his Sensory," but the statement is so similar to Kant's assertion of a nonsensory, intellectual intuition of noumena, that it is difficult not to infer some direct influence.

> If by 'noumenon' we mean [. . .] an *object* of a *non-sensible intuition*, we thereby presuppose a special mode of intuition, namely, the intellectual, which is not that which we possess, and of which we cannot comprehend even the possibility. (CPR, B 307)

By asserting that we cannot comprehend even the possibility of such an intuition Kant is not denying that such an intuition could exist, claiming instead that it would be so unlike anything we can experience and conceptualize that it would transcend our comprehension.

Although important as ultimate frames of the universe, absolute space, place, and time are especially significant for Newton as privileged reference systems for absolute motion which he defines as "the translation of a body from one absolute place into another" and absolute rest as "the continuance of the body in the same part of [. . .] immovable space [. . .]." (p. 7) While his definitions were precise, the justifying evidence proved more illusive.

> It is indeed a matter of great difficulty to discover, and effectively to distinguish, the true motions of particular bodies from the apparent; because the parts of that immovable space, in which those motions are performed, do by no means come under the observation

of our senses. (p. 12)

Not being directly observed, the evidence for the existence of absolute space, motion, and time had to be indirectly inferred. The best evidence Newton could provide pertained to the well-known example of the surface of water in a rotating vessel or bucket. As long as the surface remained flat the water is in a state relative to the vessel, but once the vessel communicates its circular motion to the water this "impressed force" causes the water to recede from the axis of motion and ascend the sides of the vessel, indicative of an absolute circular motion.

> This ascent of the water shows its endeavor to recede from the axis of its motion; and the true and absolute circular motion of the water, which is here directly contrary to the relative, becomes known, and may be measured by this endeavor. (p. 10)

While Newton assumed that the circular motion of the water as a "translation [. . .] from one absolute place into another" (p. 7) produced the centrifugal force of receding, Berkeley (and later Mach) argued that it was not motion in absolute space that produced the centrifugal force, but motion with respect to the stellar masses of the universe.[21]

Given the difficulty of resolving the issue by mechanical means, A.A. Michelson and E.W. Morely in the last decades of the nineteenth century attempted to verify the existence of such a privileged coordinate system as absolute space or rest by optical means. Believing that an ether necessary for the propagation of light waves pervaded absolute space, it was inferred that as the earth orbited it would revolve through the stationary ether producing a counter ether wind, an "ether drift." Then, if two light beams were split and sent in equal perpendicular distances via an interferometer, one radiated to-and-fro the ether and the other traversing it, the light beams reflected back to the interferometer would not be in phase because the beam traversing the ether would take less time to return than the other.

To their consternation, however, even though the experiment was performed under the most exacting conditions in different places in the earth's orbit to eliminate any fortuitous influences, the light beams always returned in phase. Given this null result, it was difficult to decide which of the presuppositions on which the experiment was based had to be discarded: the motion of the earth, the existence of the ether, the variant velocity of light, or what? In one of his famous four articles, "On The Electrodynamics Of

Moving Bodies,'' published in *Annalen der Physik* in 1905, Einstein suggested that the asymmetries in Maxwell's electrodynamics

> together with the unsuccessful attempt to discover any motion of the earth relative to the ''light medium'' [the ether], suggest that the phenomena of electrodynamics as well as of mechanics possess no properties corresponding to the idea of absolute rest [or motion].[22]

The denial of a ''light medium'' or ether at ''absolute rest'' led to a rejection of Newton's absolute frames of the universe, space and time. While Michelson and Morely had predicted a change in the velocity of light as an effect of the ether drift, Einstein drew the opposite conclusion. Accepting the invariant or constant velocity of light, he deduced that space and time were not absolute or privileged coordinate systems underwriting absolute positions and motions, but that all measurements were relative to a particular frame of reference. Furthermore, the magnitudes of space (length), time (duration), and mass were not velocity-invariant, but radically modified as physical systems approached the velocity of light or entered dense gravitational fields: space contracting, time dilating, and mass increasing. Surprisingly, Newton appears to have been aware that it was at least possible that changes in motion could affect the rate of the flow of time or interval of duration, but rejected the idea.

> All motions may be accelerated and retarded, but the flowing of absolute time is not liable to any change. The duration or perseverance of the existence of things remains the same, whether the motions are swift or slow, or none at all [. . .]. (p. 8)

If one included in the ''perseverance of the existence of things'' the physical properties of extension and mass, then these along with duration would be unaffected by motion (as they appear to be due to ordinary slow velocities). Not until Einstein's special theory of relativity would these conclusions be challenged.

Following this first Scholium, Newton presents his three Axioms or Laws of Motion and their Corollaries before his intricate, extensive mathematical demonstrations of the motions of the bodies themselves in Book I. The first is the law of inertia (without introducing the term), the key concept in the mechanistic explanation of planetary motions: *''Every body continues in its state of rest, or of uniform motion in a right [straight] line, unless it is compelled to change that state by forces impressed on it.''* (p. 13; brackets added) First clearly formulated by Descartes, the concept of inertial motion was a crucial break with Aristotle's law that for a physical body to continue to move a contiguous cause must be present throughout the motion. Newton's law states that apart from air resistance and counteracting forces, a body in motion or at rest would continue in that state (in the absence of a continuing cause) unless acted upon by some external influence.

The second law describes the change in inertial motion produced by an external influence: *"The change of motion is proportional to the motive force impressed; and is made in the direction of the right line in which that force is impressed."* (p. 13)   This too represents a fundamental break with Aristotelian mechanics which maintained that a continuous motion requires a continuous cause, while Newton's law states that an *additional force* results in *a change in motion* proportional to the force or magnitude of the cause. Although the equation is not given, this law is more familiar in the form F = MA indicating that additional forces (following the initial force) result in an accelerated motion, involving a change in velocity, direction, or both. In modern notation the equation of motion is expressed as s = s(t) (the distance function) or v = v(t) the velocity function. The derivative of the distance function ds(t)/dt gives the instantaneous velocity at time t, while differentiating the latter velocity function gives a second derivative of the distance function which is the acceleration: $a(t) = dv(t)/dt = d/dt \times ds(t)/dt = d^2s(t)/dt^2$. [23] Both equations express the ratio of the change in velocity and acceleration as a function of the time. With this force law Kepler's and Galileo's kinematic laws were given a dynamic interpretation.

Newton then indicates his agreement with Huygens regarding the reciprocal impacts of moving bodies and the mutual equality of the gravitational attraction between interacting masses. These symmetries are expressed in his third law: *To every action there is always opposed an equal reaction: or, the mutual actions of two parts."* (Despite its novelty and late formulation, Kant included Newton's third law under his category of "Community [reciprocity between agent and patient]," as one of the "pure concepts of synthesis that understanding contains within itself *a priori*.)"[24] This law had theological implications because if the physical universe consists of a system of mutually interacting bodies whose effects are always opposed and equal, then this would seem to exclude any external influence due to a deity. Yet Newton was criticized by Leibniz for admitting the possibility of God injecting energy into the world system or interacting with it after the initial creation. Theoretically, this should have been precluded by Newton's third law unless the physical universe could in turn react on God, but in the

General Scholium to Book III he denies this: "God suffers nothing from the motion of bodies; bodies find no resistance from the omnipresence of God." (p. 545)

From these laws Newton derives a number of "Corollaries," such as the parallelogram of forces, the common center of gravity among interacting bodies to be constantly at rest or to move in a straight line (cf. p. 19), and the fact that the "motions of bodies included in a given space" are the same whether the space be at rest or moving uniformly in a straight line. (p. 20) In the Scholium he asserts that with these laws and corollaries "Galileo discovered that the descent of bodies varied as the square of the time [. . .] and that the motion of projectiles was in the curve of a parabola [. . .]." (p. 21)

BOOK I

Based on these definitions and laws of motion, Newton then presents in Book I his exact mathematical demonstrations of "The Motions of Bodies." It is this book that displays Newton's extraordinary virtuosity as a mathematical physicist, while avoiding any speculation about the nature of the forces or mechanisms producing the motions of bodies.

> I here use the word *attraction* in general for any endeavor whatever, made by bodies to approach to each other, whether that endeavor arise from the action of the bodies themselves, as tending to each other or agitating each other by spirits emitted; or whether it arises from the action of the ether or of the air, or of any medium whatever, whether corporeal or incorporeal, in any manner impelling bodies placed therein towards each other. In the same general sense I use the world *impulse,* not defining in this treatise the species or physical qualities of forces, but investigating the qualities and mathematical proportions of them [. . .]. (p. 192)

Like Galileo, Newton used geometrical diagrams and computations to elucidate his demonstrations but occasionally reveals the role of his theory of fluxions or of calculus on his thinking, as when he deals with "evanescent" quantities and ratios as they approach their "vanishing" limits. By these means he resolves the ancient paradox of Aristotle as to how an object thrown vertically upward can reverse its direction of motion while coming momentarily to rest, which Aristotle believed involved the contradictory implication that at the summit the object would have to be both moving and at rest to change its direction of motion. Analogously, Aristotle denied instantaneous velocity because it would imply motion in a durationless instant, a contradiction in Aristotle's view which lacked the conception of infinitesimal units.

Differential calculus was developed precisely to deal with such perplexing problems as how the rate of a dependent variable changes as the independent variable approaches the (vanishing) limit of zero. Thus the differential ratio ds/dt allows the calculation of infinitesimal magnitudes, such as instantaneous velocities. As Newton says in his reply to an objection such as Aristotle's,

> it may be alleged that a body arriving at a certain place, and there stopping, has no ultimate velocity; because the velocity, before the body comes to the place, is not its ultimate velocity; when it has arrived, there is none. But the answer is easy; for by the ultimate velocity is meant that with which the body is moved, neither before it arrives at its last place and the motion ceases, nor after, but at the very instant it arrives; that is, that velocity with which the body arrives at its last place, and with which the motion ceases. And in like manner, by the ultimate ratio of evanescent quantities is to be understood the ratio of the quantities not before they vanish, nor afterwards, but with which they vanish. (pp. 38-39)

This analysis involves the concept of limit on which differential calculus is based.

> There is a limit which the velocity at the end of the motion may attain, but not exceed. This is the ultimate velocity. And there is the like limit in all quantities and proportions that begin and cease to be [. . . .] For those ultimate ratios with which quantities vanish are not truly the ratios of ultimate quantities, but limits towards which the ratios of quantities decreasing without limit do always converge; and to which they approach nearer than by any given difference, but never go beyond, nor in effect attain to, till the quantities are diminished *in infinitum*. (p. 39)

While Aristotle initially would have found the concept of limit strange and perplexing, it is likely that he soon would have marveled at its mathematical power. It is because the mathematical formalism provides the scientist with the means of dealing with such physical relations and problems that it has proved indispensable to the growth of modern science, as Newton well knew.

> In mathematics we are to investigate the quantities of forces with their proportions consequent upon any conditions supposed; then, when we enter upon physics, we compare those proportions with the phenomena of Nature, that we may know what conditions of those forces answer to the several kinds of attractive bodies. And this preparation being made, we argue more safely concerning the physical species, causes, and proportions of the forces. (p. 192)

Book I is filled with such investigations of "the quantities of forces," the resultant "attractions" or "impulses," and the consequent "motions of bodies." He describes how rotating bodies are continuously deflected from a rectilinear motion due to a centripetal or gravitating force, deriving the exact magnitudes of distances, velocities, forces, and deflections to produce Kepler's first two laws. He shows that if the centripetal or gravitational force of the central body decreases with the square of the distance then "*the periodic times in ellipses are as the 3/2th power [. . .] of their greater axes*," as implied in Kepler's third law. (p. 62) In what was a major simplification, he demonstrates that the centripetal force can be calculated from the center of the sphere (cf. p. 193) and that the magnitude of the attractive force is the sum of the forces of all the particles composing the spherical body. (cf. p. 216) Based on these principles, Newton was able to solve the two-body problem of motion in terms of their mutual attractions around a common center of gravity, calculating their periods and major axes. (cf. pp. 164-171) However, even the orbits of two planets such as the earth and the moon, as well as those of the other planets, are the product of the mutual attraction of all the planetary bodies, as Newton realized. Thus he proceeded to the three-body problem and then to the many-body problem without finding a solution, which has since been shown to be impossible.[25] Fortunately, except for satellites like the moon and those of Jupiter, because the sun constitutes about 98 per cent of the mass of our solar system the gravitational influence of the other planets can be ignored as a safe approximation.

At the close of Book I Newton briefly discusses the reflection and refraction of light, indicating the contributions of Descartes and Snell. Without mentioning Roemer, he states that astronomical observations of the reflection of light from the satellites of Jupiter (when at different distances from the earth) has proven "that light is propagated in succession, and requires about seven or eight minutes to travel from the sun to the earth." (p. 229) While only a minuscule sketch of the contents of Book I, this still should provide an idea of the scope of this seminal work that transformed mankind's conception of the structure and mechanics of the universe, unifying terrestrial and celestial motions into one system of laws and dynamic principles. Not since Archimedes has there been such a mathematical tour de force.

BOOK II

Book II consists of nine sections dealing with such problems as the effects of resisting mediums (tenacity, attrition, and density) on the motion of bodies, the degree of the resistance being in the ratio of the bodies velocity, as measured by the decreasing increments of space traversed. (cf. p. 235) As in Book I, the various Propositions are stated as mathematical problems to which Newton provides a geometrical solution; for example, Proposition XVII, Problem IV states: *"To find the centripetal force and the resisting force of the medium, by which a body, the law of the velocity* [in the ratio of the bodies motion] *being given, shall revolve in a given spiral."* (p. 288; brackets added) The solution to this problem being found, a succeeding problem is posed and solved: *"The law of centripetal force being given, to find the density of the medium in each of the places thereof, by which a body may describe a given spiral."* (p. 289) It is thus clear why Newton entitled his treatise *Philosophiae Naturalis Principia Mathematica* (*Mathematical Principles of Natural Philosophy*) because he is concerned primarily with providing mathematical demonstrations of the motions of bodies, rather than philosophical or physical explanations.

In addition to calculating the ratios of resisting mediums to the velocities of bodies, Newton discusses the compression and density of fluid substances, the motion and resistance of pendulous bodies, the properties of particles in liquids affecting their fluidity, diffusion, and resistance, the manner in which "tremulous" (oscillating) bodies propagate their motions in an elastic medium, and an attempt "to find the velocity of waves" (p, 374) and "the distances of the pulses." (p. 382) He concludes Book II with a critical examination of Descartes' system of vortices preferred by Huygens and Leibniz over his own theory of centripetal or gravitational forces. Arguing that the properties of vortices are in general incompatible with the motions of the planets, he specifically shows that having "found the periodic times of the parts of the vortex to be as the square of the distances from the center of motion" (p. 393), the vortex theory is incompatible with Kepler's third law that the periodic times of the planets are as the 3/2th power (not the square) of their distances from the sun. He concludes "that the hypothesis of vortices is utterly irreconcilable with astronomical phenomena, and rather serves to perplex than explain the heavenly motions." (p. 396)

Yet despite Newton's incisive criticisms, Descartes' theory of vortices "displayed wonderful vitality, even in Cambridge. For about forty years after the first publication of Newton's *Principia* the French system maintained a foothold in England."[26] Undoubtedly this was due to its easier accessibility as a theoretical system along with the fact that it was based on purely mechanical principles, in contrast to Newton's reliance on forces. On the continent Cartesianism had prominent adherents with "Huygens, Perrault, Johann II Bernoulli and others [attempting] to remove some of the glaring defects in the original theory of vortices [. . .]."[27] Even at the time of Voltaire's visit to England toward the end of the seventeenth century to inform himself of the Newtonian system he could write:

A Frenchman who arrives in London finds a great alteration in philosophy, as in other things. He left the world full, he finds it empty [because of the atomic theory]. At Paris you see the universe composed of vortices and subtle matter, in London we see nothing of the kind.[28]

BOOK III

Book III of the *Principia* contains Newton's more concise and readable "System of the World," although still reinforced by mathematical demonstrations as the subtitle (In Mathematical Treatment) indicates. Originally intended as a popular non-mathematical presentation of his World System, he later decided to recast it in more mathematically rigorous form to preclude controversy, as he states at the beginning of Book III:

IN THE PRECEDING BOOKS I have laid down the principles of philosophy; principles not philosophical but mathematical: such, namely, as we may build our reasonings upon in philosophical inquiries [. . . .] It remains that, from the same principles, I now demonstrate the frame of the System of the World. Upon this subject I had, indeed, composed the third Book in a popular method, that it might be read by many; but afterwards, considering that such as had not sufficiently entered into the principles could not easily discern the strength of the consequences, nor lay aside the prejudices to which they had been many years accustomed, therefore, to prevent the disputes which might be raised upon such accounts, I chose to reduce the substance of this Book into the form of Propositions (in the mathematical way) [. . .]. (p. 397)

Before proceeding to the Propositions as such, he describes the underlying rules of reasoning constituting the foundation of his cosmological system. Although empirically based, they are by no means positivistic and since Newton have become the basic principles guiding scientific inquiry. Rule I is an affirmation of Occam's razor that causes should not be multiplied beyond necessity: "*We are to admit no more causes of natural things than such as are both true and sufficient to explain their appearances.*" (p. 398) Based on the conviction that "nature does nothing in vain,"in the eighteenth century this rule was called "the principle of least action"when Pierre-Louis de Maupertuis and Joseph Louis Lagrange claimed that an object moves through paths so as to minimize the action, based on calculations of the body's mass, velocity, and spatial trajectory.

Whereas Rule I affirms the simplicity of Nature, Rule II asserts the uniformity of nature maintaining that (under the usual conditions) similar effects have similar causes: "*Therefore to the same natural effects we must, as far as possible, assign the same causes.*" (*Ibid.*) As examples he says that respiration in man and beasts, the effects of gravity in England and America, the light produced by the fire on the earth and the sun, and the reflection of light on the earth and by the planets may be considered as having similar causes.

While the first two rules are familiar, Rule III is the first justification of a mode of inference crucial to those in the seventeenth century, such as Galileo, Gassendi, Boyle, and Locke, as well as Newton, who were invoking the ancient atomic theory of Democritus and Epicurus as the "metaphysical foundations" of their mechanistic world view.[29] While each used this mode of inference to distinguish between the independently existing primary qualities inherent in microscopic particles from the sensory qualities characteristic of macroscopic objects produced in the organism by the effects of insensible particles (for example, light corpuscles or sound waves) striking the senses, and thus depend upon the organism for their existence, Newton was the only one to support this inference by an explicit rule: "*The qualities of bodies, which admit neither intensification nor remission of degrees, and which are found to belong to all bodies within the reach of our experiments, are to esteemed the universal qualities of all bodies whatsoever.''* (p. 398)

The refinement and compounding of lenses used in telescopes in the first half of the seventeenth century, that had resulted in Galileo's remarkable astronomical discoveries, led to the development of microscopes in the latter half of the century disclosing an additional domain of physical reality, the microscopic. Moreover, Boyle's law describing the relation between the compression, expansion, and pressure of gases, the interpretation of heat as the kinetic motion of the inherent particles, and the forces of attraction and repulsion attributed to these particles by Newton required a specification of the properties of these minute, unobservable entities. Notwithstanding Berkeley's later objection that primary and secondary or sensory qualities are *experienced* as inseparable, it was natural to distinguish between those that seemed *essential* to the very existence of a physical body (extension, size, shape, mass, hardness, position, and motion), and those that characterize macroscopic objects due to the stimulation and intervention of the senses (color, odor, taste, solidity, sound, and tactual qualities), which therefore are merely relational or conditional qualities. Thus those properties "found to belong to all bodies within the reach of our experiments" (based on empirical verification) and not admitting to "intensification nor remission of degree" (which I interpret as meaning they are inseparable from the object), must belong to all bodies whatsoever, even those insensible particles called atoms or corpuscles.

Furthermore, Newton attributes whatever similarity exists between the primary qualities of macroscopic objects and those of microscopic particles as arising from the composition of the latter in the former. Newton's rule thus could be considered an inverted expression of Niels Bohr's "correspondence principle," namely, that the primary qualities of macroscopic objects *correspond* to those of microscopic particles in the limiting case where macroscopic dimensions approach those of the microworld.[30]

> We no other way know the extension of bodies than by our senses, nor do these reach it in all bodies; but because we perceive extension in all that are sensible, therefore we ascribe it universally to all others also. That abundance of bodies are hard, we learn by experience; and because the hardness of the whole arises from the hardness of the parts, we therefore justly infer the hardness of the undivided particles not only of the bodies we feel but of all others. That all bodies are impenetrable, we gather not from reason, but from sensation [. . .].

That all bodies are movable, and endowed with certain powers (which we call the inertia) of persevering in their motion, or in their rest, we only infer from the like properties observed in the bodies which we have seen. The extension, hardness, impenetrability, mobility, and inertia of the whole, result from the extension, hardness, impenetrability, mobility, and inertia of the parts; and hence we conclude the least particles of all bodies to be also extended, and hard and impenetrable, and movable, and endowed with their proper inertia. (p. 399)

This, he contends, "is the foundation of all philosophy." (*Ibid.*)

Finally, this generalization enabled him to dismiss the ancient qualitative distinction between the celestial and terrestrial worlds and apply the same gravitational attraction to both domains because "we must, in consequence of this rule, universally allow that all bodies whatsoever are endowed with a universal principle of mutual gravitation." (*Ibid.*)

The final rule, Rule IV, states Newton's avowed conception of the relation between hypotheses and observations based on inductive inference:

In experimental philosophy we are to look upon propositions inferred by general induction from phenomena as accurately or very nearly true, notwithstanding any contrary hypotheses that may be imagined, till such time as other phenomena occur, by which they may either be made more accurate, or liable to exceptions. (p. 400)

The significance and intent of this rule seems clear enough, yet there have been considerable differences of opinion as to Newton's exact conception of the role of hypotheses because of the conflict between his oft repeated aversion to "framing" or "feigning" hypotheses, particularly as regards the cause and nature of gravity, and his occasional references to "a subtle spirit" as a possible explanation of the underlying causes of physical interactions. Ignoring these latter assertions, the positivists claimed Newton as one of their own based on his frequent condemnation of hypotheses.

But Newton's objection to the introduction of hypotheses to explain physical processes is invariably directed to Descartes' "hypothesis of vortices," a speculative hypothesis based on "clear and distinct ideas" (as Descartes admitted), rather than deduced from phenomena, as Newton specified. As Newton says in the famous "General Scholium," added to Book III twenty-six years later in 1713 when the second edition of the *Principia* was brought out and he was seventy-one years old:

> [. . .] hitherto I have not been able to discover the cause of those properties of gravity from phenomena, and I frame no hypotheses; for whatever is not deduced from the phenomena is to be called an hypothesis; and hypotheses, whether metaphysical or physical, whether of occult qualities or mechanical, have no place in experimental philosophy. In this philosophy particular propositions are inferred from the phenomena, and afterwards rendered general by induction. (p. 547)

While the above statement forcefully expresses Newton's objection to a certain type of hypothesis, it is in his letter to Oldenburg (in reply to objections by Pardies mentioned previously), that he states most fully his conception of the justification versus the improper use of hypotheses.

> For the best and safest method of philosophizing seems to be, first diligently to investigate the properties of things and establish them by experiment, and then to seek hypotheses to explain them. For hypotheses ought to be fitted merely to explain the properties of things and not attempt to predetermine them except in so far as they can be an aid to experiments. [31]

In this passage Newton indicates that he does not object to the use of hypotheses to explain the properties of things *after* they have been "established" by experiments, but to the attempt to "predetermine" them before they have been discovered experimentally. It was the claim by Descartes to have predetermined *a priori* the vortical motions of the planets from clear and distinct ideas independently of observational or experimental evidence that Newton strongly rejected.

Descartes himself had asserted that he was not perturbed if specifics of his explanation of planetary motion could not be shown to be true, as long as they were possible causes of the phenomena that God might have used in his creation. But Newton did not believe that science could advance very far based on the "mere possibility of hypotheses," as he says in a continuation of the quotation in the letter to Oldenburg:

> If any one offers conjectures about the truth of things from the mere possibility of hypotheses, I do not see how any thing certain can be

determined in any science; for it is always possible to contrive hypotheses, one after another, which are found rich in new tribulations. Wherefore I judged that one should abstain from considering hypotheses as from a fallacious argument, and that the force of their opposition must be removed, that one may arrive at a maturer and more general explanation.[32]

It was in another letter, a later one to Cotes, that Newton presented his clearest statement about hypotheses, especially in relation to the organization of his arguments in the *Principia*:

[. . .] the world 'hypothesis' [. . .] in experimental philosophy [. . .] is not to be taken in so large a sense as to include the first principles or axioms, which I call the laws of motions. These principles are deduced from phenomena and made general by induction, which is the highest evidence that a proposition can have in this philosophy. And the word 'hypothesis' is here used by me to signify only such a proposition as is not a phenomenon nor deduced from any phenomena, but assumed or supposed—without any experimental proof.[33]

Although it is evident that Newton was opposed to conjectured hypotheses that were not based on deductions from phenomena, it still is not clear what he meant by the latter and how restrictive he intended it to be. In fact, "deducibility from phenomena" as a criterion of an acceptable hypothesis was not very restrictive, and it is this that has contributed to the different interpretations of exactly what Newton meant.[34] For example, in the same General Scholium in which he adamantly had declared that he would "frame no hypothesis" about "the cause of the property of gravity" because "whatever is not deduced from the phenomena [. . .] has no place in experimental philosophy," he claims that "[t]his most beautiful system of the sun, planets, and comets, could only proceed from the council and dominion of an intelligent and powerful Being." (p. 544) He then proceeds to a detailed discussion of the nature and attributes of God which one would have thought was the province of theology, again declaring (as Aristotle had):

Blind metaphysical necessity, which is certainly the same always and everywhere, could produce no variety of things. All that diversity of natural things which we find suited to different times and places could arise from nothing but the ideas and will of a Being necessarily existing. (p. 546)

Newton thus believed that "much concerning God" could be learned from nature "to discourse of whom from the appearances of things, does certainly belong to Natural Philosophy." (*Ibid.*) If he permitted propositions about God to be deduced from appearances of things or phenomena, then on what grounds could he object to conjectures about vortices as possible causes of what he called centripetal or gravitational forces? If not Descartes himself, his continental followers such as Huygens could maintain that the vortex theory was deduced from phenomena, namely, the phenomena of vortical motions from which Huygens deduced his law of centripetal motions.

Furthermore, in the paragraph in the General Scholium immediately following his disavowal of "framing hypotheses" (*Hypotheses non Fingo*), he unleashes his own imaginative speculation regarding the possible causes of phenomena.

> And now we might add something concerning a certain most subtle spirit which pervades and lies hid in all gross bodies; by the force and action of which spirit the particles of bodies attract one another at near distances, and cohere, if contiguous; and electric bodies operate to greater distances, as well repelling as attracting the neighboring corpuscles; and light is emitted, reflected, refracted, inflected, and heats bodies; and all sensation is excited, and the members of animal bodies move at the command of the will, namely, by the vibrations of this spirit [. . .]. But these are things that cannot be explained in a view words, nor are we furnished with that sufficiency of experiments which is required to an accurate determination and demonstration of the laws by which this electric and elastic spirit operates. (p. 547; brackets added)

This is a remarkable passage in which Newton anticipates the current search in particle physics for a grand unified theory (GUTS). If one substitutes for his term "a most subtle spirit" an "electromagnetic" or "electrodynamic field," there would be no way of knowing that the passage was not written by a contemporary physicist, for even the propagation of nerve discharges is described today in terms of changes in electrical potential among the ions composing the outer membranes of the neurons. Moreover, at the end of the statement Newton does reiterate his claim that such speculations, to be convincing, must be based on experiments which have accurately determined and demonstrated the laws on which these various interactions and their causes depend. Thus the correct interpretation of Newton's conception of the role of hypotheses seems to be that if the axioms and laws of motion are deduced from phenomena and the properties of the causes (usually in terms of particles or corpuscles and their attractive and repulsive forces along with gravity) established by experiments, then one is permitted to introduce hypotheses as possible explanations of these principles of motion, but not before. If one reverses the procedure and begins with "predetermined hypotheses" that are not deduced from phenomena or established by experiments, then no certain progress in science can be expected.

Following the General Scholium at the end of the System of the World in Book III is another recapitulation of the world system which basically is a repetition of the previous one. It is this version of "The System of the World" that he intended to be more accessible to non-mathematicians because it contains fewer geometrical demonstrations and is written in a less technical style. Moreover, he is more concerned in this account to show systematically how the orbits of the superior and inferior planets and their satellites follow from Kepler's laws of motions, along with the action of mutual centripetal forces, and that they are in agreement with the observations of Flamsteed, the Royal Astronomer, along with those of Huygens, Halley, Hooke, and others. Furthermore, he argues that this planetary system requires the sun as the central attracting body or focus of Kepler's elliptical orbits, not the earth, thus finally and conclusively vindicating the supporters of the Copernican system. He demonstrates that all the planets and the sun have a common center of gravity which is at rest, the sun rotating around this center in a slow motion, the last vestige of the geocentric system. The cause of the tides and exact nature and motion of the comets again are explained. With these expositions he terminates the *Principia*, generally acknowledged to be the greatest scientific work ever written.

Once published, the *Principia* took the international community of natural philosophers by storm. Given Newton's already extensive reputation and a superlative unsigned preview of the work in the *Philosophical Transactions* (presumably by Halley), the expectations among the mathematicians and natural philosophers surged like a high tide as news of its publication spread. Nor were they disappointed. Newton's rigorous formal presentation, extensive use of meticulously constructed geometrical demonstrations at times revealing an entirely new mathematical technique, intricate tables of figures, tightly formulated arguments, as well as the sweep of his imagination and integration of knowledge was astonishing—so much so that some wondered whether it could have been written by an ordinary mortal.   When the Marquis de l'Hopital, a French mathematician of some reputation, was shown the *Principia*

> he cried out with admiration Good god what a fund of knowledge there is in that book? he then asked [. . .] every particular about S'I. even to the colour of his hair said does he eat & drink & sleep. is he like other men? & was surprised when [. . .] told him he conversed chearfully with his friends assumed nothing & put himself upon a level with all mankind.[35]

A more humorous but equally incredulous comment was made by a Cambridge student who, on seeing Newton in the street, remarked "there goes the man that writt a book that neither he nor any body else understands."[36]

NEWTON'S MORAL COURAGE AND
LATER NERVOUS BREAKDOWN

As consuming as was his involvement with the *Principia*, it was not the only important activity of Newton during this period. At the very time when Newton was completing his masterpiece there occurred a dangerous political crises at Cambridge that provides further evidence of Newton's steadfast and courageous character, despite his neurotic aversion to controversy. The Puritan Revolt of Oliver Cromwell was followed by the restoration of Charles II (the son of Charles I who had been beheaded) to the throne of England. Although Charles II was probably at heart a Roman Catholic, he became a popular king who tolerated religious and political freedom. His death in 1685 brought James II, an avowed Roman Catholic, to the throne who was determined to reconvert England to Catholicism. Realizing that this could be accomplished best by permitting Catholics to attain positions of influence in the universities, he attempted to use the traditional "letters of mandate" to confer upon Catholics higher degrees with the intent of elevating them to stations of authority without their having to take "the oath of supremacy, in effect an oath to uphold the established Anglican religion."[37]

However, when the King in a letter of mandate on February 9, 1687 attempted to admit a Benedictine Monk named Alban Francis to the degree of Master of Arts at Cambridge, the vice-chancellor, John Peachell, decided to resist, thereby precipitating a confrontation with the King. In support of Peachell's decision, Newton drafted a letter "apparently intended for someone in authority at the university, urging 'an honest Courage' which would 'save ye University.'' (p. 475) Although he had attained his position as Fellow of Trinity College without being ordained owing to a special royal dispensation, Newton now argued that the letter of mandate should be refused on the grounds that if such appointments violating university oaths and regulations were permitted, then there would be no restraining the King. When a second letter from the King declaring that a refusal would be ''at their peril'' still brought no affirmation, he ''summoned Peachell and representatives of the university to appear before the Court of Ecclesiastical Commission [. . .].'' (p. 477) Probably because of his letter supporting Peachell's decision, Newton was elected one of the eight representatives. When it was proposed to the delegation, as a compromise, that Father Francis be admitted to the degree on condition that this not become a president, Newton persuaded the delegation that such action would be a dishonorable capitulation.

The delegation appeared before the Ecclesiastical Commission four times, the third with disastrous results. Peachell was so intimidated by Lord Jeffreys, the head of the Commission, that he was unable to present a forceful defense of the University's decision. As a consequence, declaring that he was ''guilty of 'an act of great disobedience,' the commissioners deprived him of his office, suspended him from the mastership of Magdalene, and stripped him of the income of his position.'' (p. 478) Peachell having been eliminated, the justification of the University's stand fell to the eight delegates. Newton played a prominent role in helping to draft five letters preceding the final statement of refusal. He even proposed asserting that ''[a] mixture of Papist & Protestants in ye same University can neither subsist happily nor long together'' (p. 479), although the statement was not included in the final document. On May 12, 1687 the delegation appeared before Jeffreys and the Commission without knowing whether they were to be subjected to the same humiliation as Peachell. This time, however, it was the Commission that balked with Jeffreys conceding the opposition with a lecture admonishing the members of the delegation to obey his majesty's command in the future. His majesty, however, was to have a short-lived future because eighteen months later he was deposed by William of Orange and fled to France.

Given Newton's previous reticence to public acclaim, this active involvement in one of the most serious challenges ever to face the University appeared to have a marked effect on his life. His courageous action and wise advice to the delegates did not go unnoticed, so that he was thrust into a position of prominence in the University and duly rewarded. The senate elected him one of the two University representatives to the convention ratifying the revolution and by acts of Parliament he invariably was appointed one of the commissioners to oversee the collection "in Cambridge of aids voted to the government," a lucrative assignment indicative of his increased prestige. After the convention was reconstituted as a Parliament Newton lived in London for a year serving in the new Parliament. It was during his stay in London that he met Christiaan Huygens and his brother Constantyn, along with the philosopher John Locke with whom he maintained extensive correspondence and formed an especially close friendship until Locke's death in 1704.

Following his successful participation in the Glorious Revolution and the international acclaim accompanying the publication of the *Principia*, the years from 1687 to 1693 were a period of "manic euphoria" which transformed Newton from a scholarly recluse to a sociable person admired by his peers and adulated by the younger generation of natural philosophers and mathematicians who sought his patronage. It was also a time of significant achievement in which he published two important papers in mathematics, pursued his alchemical experiments, prepared corrections of the *Principia*, and organized his earlier research in optics into book form. Then suddenly, in the autumn of 1693, the "black year" in Newton's life began due primarily it seems to the break with Fatio de Duillier mentioned previously.

He had met Fatio, a promising Swiss mathematician who was then twenty-five years old, in 1687 and their friendship apparently developed into an intimate relationship.[38] When, as described earlier, Fatio wrote to Newton expressing his desire "to live all my life, or the greatest part of it, with you," and failed to receive a mutual response from Newton, Fatio formed another attachment which led to the termination of their relationship. (cf. p. 533) Plunged into as deep a state of depression as his earlier height of euphoria, Newton suffered despair and a severe mental breakdown during the next eighteen months. Because of the discretion of Newton's friends there is little record of the period, but his letters to Pepys and Locke reveal the degree of his derangement. (cf. p. 524). In some manner he was taken care of by his friends until he regained his mental stability. As in the similar breakdown in 1677-78, he did recover completely and by 1694 had completed the final version of the *Opticks* which Gregory, who saw it in May, declared "would rival the *Principia*." Both the Royal Society and John Wallis were eager to publish the work but Newton declined, as he wrote to Leibniz, "for fear that dispute and controversies may be raised against me by ignoramuses."[39] Since it was Hooke who had provoked the most controversy, he waited until after Hooke's death in 1703 before publishing the *Opticks* in the following year.

WARDEN AND MASTER OF THE MINT

Despite his break with Fatio who had resided mainly in London, Newton still sought a more lucrative position that also might allow him to live in the capital. Locke, because of his influential patrons, was his principal ally in this attempt. Although his efforts to obtain the provostship of King's College or the mastership of the Charterhouse failed, he succeeded through the influence of another friend, Charles Montague, in being appointed Warden of the Mint on March 19, 1696. After a tenure in Trinity College of thirty-five years, Newton seemed eager to turn his back on university life and take up residence in London. Since this work is not intended to be a biography of Newton of which Westfall has provided the definitive account, it is unnecessary to describe Newton's involvement in the Mint.[40] Suffice it to say that while the wardenship could be used as a sinecure under the direction of the Master, Newton decided to exercise serious control. As Westfall says, although Montague looked at the position more as a reward than a challenge, "he did not take Newton's need to escape from intellectual activity into account, or his inability to do anything half way." (p. 558) For a number of reasons, the Mint went through a series of crises that required someone of Newton's inimitable intelligence, knowledge of mathematics, outstanding mechanical skills, and conscientious leadership. Unwittingly, Montague has chosen well. Within two years Newton had, for all practical purposes, taken over the duties of the Master of the Mint to which he acceded on December 26, 1669.

Although the crisis of 1693 and subsequent move to London had practically ended Newton's scholarly research, one episode during this period shows that his mathematical creativity had not been lost. In June 1696 Johann Bernoulli, one of Europe's leading mathematicians, published a challenge problem in Wallis' *Acta eruditorum*, with a limit of six months to meet the challenge. Leibniz responded asserting that he had solved the problem but requested that the time limit be extended to Easter and that it be published in Europe. As a result, receiving no other response Bernoulli added another challenge problem to the original one and had both published in the *Philosophical Transactions* and the *Journal des scavans* to ensure their distribution on the continent as well as the British Isles. When he still had received only Leibniz's reply by December, he sent copies of the problems in January 1697 to both Newton and Wallis. The episode has personal significance because of the bitter dispute between Leibniz and Newton regarding the priority of the discovery of differential calculus that was finally resolved in Newton's favor, though it was agreed that the discoveries were made independently.

When Newton had not taken up the original challenge, apparently Bernoulli (who was a friend of Leibniz) thought Newton was not up to solving it. However, as soon as Newton received the letter posing the problems he could not sleep until he found the answers, immediately sending them anonymously to Bernoulli who, however, clearly identified the author by his technique, "as the lion is recognized from his print." (p. 583) Only three people at the time supplied written solutions, Leibniz, the Marquis de l'Hopital (whose awe of Newton was indicated earlier), and Newton. Needless to say, Bernoulli and Leibniz were mistaken in thinking the old lion (Newton was then 55) has lost his bite.

Settled in a new career remote from his former academic life, honors still continued to be bestowed on Newton. He was offered membership in Louis XIV's Académie Royale des Sciences which would have brought a large pension, but declined the offer. When the mastership of St. Catherine's Hospital fell vacant it was offered to him as was the mastership of Trinity College (the latter if he would take orders), both of which could have supplemented his income at the Mint. Because of his trinitarian views he refused the latter offer, although urged upon him by Tenison, the Archbishop of Canterbury. But with his elevation to Master of the Mint officially in February 1700 (a position he occupied until his death), which brought with it not only an annual salary increase of £100 but also "a set profit on every pound weight troy that was coined" (p. 604), he had no need of additional sinecures. The latter was not an inconsiderable amount considering that the former Master had "earned more than £22,000 during the recoinage." Probably because of this increase in salary, Newton resigned his fellowship at Trinity and Lucasian Chair the following year, in 1701. Perhaps, too, he was influenced by the example of Isaac Barrow who apparently vacated the Lucasian Chair for Newton because at the beginning of 1701 Newton "appointed William Whiston as his deputy in the Lucasian chair with the engagement of its full income [. . .] enabling Whiston to become his successor [. . .]." (p. 607)

Among his other duties as Master of the Mint was membership in the House of Commons. Apparently at the urging of his friend and patron Lord Halifax, he stood for parliament from Cambridge in 1701 and was elected. Defeated the following year he stood once more in 1705 again at the request of Halifax. To promote his candidacy Queen Anne (who succeeded William upon his death) during the customary royal visit to Cambridge University knighted Newton who became Sir Isaac. The latter honor was entirely political, having nothing to do with Newton's scholarly achievements or accomplishments at the Mint. However, even knighthood proved politically futile with Newton coming in last among four candidates, thereby ending his political career for which he had little enthusiasm anyway.

More to his preference was the prospect of becoming President of the Royal Society following the death of Hooke in 1703 who had served as the Secretary for decades. With Hooke's death not only did the Society lose a great natural scientist and ingenious experimenter who had served with distinction since 1662 as Curator of Experiments to the Society,[41] and someone who had devoted much of his life to the direction of the Society, it also was threatened with losing its meeting place at Gresham College since Hooke had provided his chambers for that purpose as professor of geometry at the College. Though to avoid meeting Hooke Newton had not attended frequently the meetings of the Royal Society even when he was in London, Hooke's death in March 1703 provided the opportunity for Newton's being elected president at the next annual meeting. His election was not, as one might expect, a foregone conclusion because he barely received enough votes to be elected to the Council (a precondition for becoming president), and then did not receive enthusiastic support from the members at large, perhaps because of the factional divisions prevalent in the Society. (cf. 629)

Nevertheless, while the preceding presidents were mainly figureheads whose attendance at the meetings was desultory, Newton served with his customary dedication and distinction. The attendance, membership, prestige, and financial viability of the Society improved considerably under his presidency, as well as the quality of discussions at the meetings, although there continued the usual disputes. Moreover, after searching for seven years for a permanent home to replace the Society's intrusive meeting place at Gresham College, Newton, with the help of the Secretary Hans Sloane, maneuvered the membership into purchasing the former house of the late Dr. Edward Browne in Crane Court off Fleet Street which had just come on the market. Despite some opposition, the house was purchased in 1710 and extensively renovated according to the design and supervision of Christopher Wren which must have met with general approval because soon afterwards numerous gifts and bequests were forthcoming, including £100 from Newton. "In less than six years, the society had fully paid for its new home and stood free of debt" so that for "the first time in the fifty years since its establishment, the Royal Society had its own home." (p. 677)

THE *OPTICKS*

One of Newton's first acts on becoming president was to submit his *Opticks* to the Society for publication. As previously indicated, he had organized his earlier research in optics in book form by 1694, but had refused to have it published for fear of reigniting the earlier heated controversies, particularly with Hooke. Now, however, Hooke's death not only removed an impediment to Newton's becoming president of the Royal Society, but also the primary obstacle to having the *Opticks* published. So less than three months after becoming president Newton presented the *Opticks* (as he had the *Principia*) to the Society for publication and, as earlier, Halley was instructed to read it and provide a decision, although this time he did not see to the printing itself. Unlike the dramatic publication of the *Principia* due to Halley's urgent entreaties and meticulous supervision of the printing, little is known about the details of the publication of the *Opticks*. Based on experiments completed thirty years earlier, it contains nothing essentially new regarding optical research as such; yet for reasons to be described, the work had an even greater influence on eighteenth century scientific research than the *Principia*.

While the precise explication of the orbits of the planets with their satellites and explanation of the movements and nature of the comets in the *Principia* can be seen as a culmination of the astronomical and cosmological inquiries begun with the geocentric system of Eudoxus and Aristotle as emended by Apollonius, Hipparchus, and Ptolemy, and then recast along the suggestions of Aristarchus by Copernicus, Kepler, and Galileo, the *Opticks* represents a totally new approach to the possibilities of experimental investigations. Even the strikingly different formats of the two works is indicative of this contrast. While the contents of the *Principia* are presented as rigorous principles and laws derived from geometrical demonstrations and "mechanical reasonings" based on prior definitions and axioms analogous to the works of Euclid and Apollonius, where conjectures and speculative hypotheses usually are kept in abeyance, the *Opticks* is replete with suggestive hypotheses and experimental possibilities for investigating nature. Intended to forestall any possible controversy or criticism, the *Principia* is consciously intimidating in style and preemptive in its conclusions. Aware of his commanding position, Newton conveys his unquestioned authority throughout the work. Although he was not able to define the nature of gravity, accepting its existence allowed him to resolve nearly all of the perplexing astronomical problems of the past, unifying both celestial and terrestrial laws.

In contrast, the *Opticks* introduces and explores conjectures regarding the components and structure of matter, the nature of light and heat along with the phenomenon of radiation, the basis of magnetic attraction and electrical repulsion and affinity, the causes of chemical reactions such as combustion and fermentation, and the manner of transmission of nerve impulses. No longer confined to the astronomical observations of Flamsteed in constructing and testing his deductions, Newton now uses light as an experimental probe in his investigations of the composition of material substances, even attempting to deduce experimentally the actual dimensions of the corpuscles. He speculates as to whether a pervasive subtle, vibratory, aether might not provide a unified explanation for all these diverse phenomena.

The new framework of interpretation that facilitated such speculative inquiries was the corpuscular hypothesis nearly universally adopted throughout the eighteenth century. Whereas Aristotle's framework of explanation in terms of substance and attributes, substantial forms, potentiality and actuality facilitated precise classifications of phenomena by genus and species, it did not encourage an experimental investigation of matter to ascertain its inner composition and organization into particles, corpuscles, or atoms. In contrast, Newton's theoretical schema set the research agenda for all of modern science, including the present. Molecular chemistry, atomic and particle physics, spectroscopic analysis in astronomy, the discovery of electromagnetism, radioactivity, strong and electroweak forces, the explanation of nerve discharges by electrochemical transmitters, and even molecular biology are in a sense culminations of Newton's probing questions and research strategies— although he in no way anticipated or foretold their specific outcome.

Moreover, while the forbidding mathematical demands of the *Principia* made it largely inaccessible except to mathematicians, the less technical, more narrative style (and the fact that it was published in English rather than Latin) of the *Opticks* (particularly Book III) made it attractive to an expanding circle of semi-amateur and professional experimentalists that arose uniquely in the eighteenth century. As I. Bernard Cohen states in his excellent study of Newton and Franklin that inspired this appreciation of the significant difference between the two principle works of Newton and their enduring legacies:

> Not primarily in the *Principia*, then, but in the *Opticks* could the eighteenth-century experimentalists find Newton's methods for studying the properties or behavior of bodies that are due to their special composition. Hence, we need not be surprised to find that in

the age of Newton—which the eighteenth century certainly was!—the experimental natural philosophers should be drawn to the *Opticks* rather than to the *Principia*. Furthermore, the *Opticks* was more than an account of mere optical phenomena, but contained an atomic theory of matter, ideas about electricity and magnetism, heat, fluidity, volatility, sensation, chemistry, and so on, and a theory (or hypothesis) of the actual cause of gravitation.[42]

Ignoring the various editions and modifications of the *Opticks*, the Dover publication now available based on the fourth London edition of 1730 will be the basis of the discussion. Like the *Principia*, the *Opticks* is divided into three Books and while it would be unrealistic to attempt anything like a complete summary of their contents, an endeavor will be made to cite the major discoveries and range of topic covered by each Book, thereby portraying "the mind of the Prince of Natural Philosophers at work [. . .]."[43] The First Book begins with a statement of intent, "not to explain the Properties of Light [in this Book] by Hypotheses, but to propose and prove them by Reason and Experiments [. . .]."[44] Beginning with a definition of the Rays of Light along with their properties of refrangibility (refractivity) and reflexivity and their angles and sines, he then describes or demonstrates their properties in a series of Axioms, followed by descriptive Propositions based on his extensive experiments. He restates his controversial theory presented in 1672 in the *Philosophical Transactions* that ordinary light consists of "primary, Homogeneal and Simple Rays," each having its own specific degree of refrangibility as disclosed in his various experiments. Compounded of these primary or non-resolvable rays, sunlight in contrast is "heterogeneal."
Under Axiom VII he presents a detailed description of how light reflected from all the points on the surface of an object after passing through the pupil and being refracted through the crystalline lens and humors of the eye

converge and meet again [. . .] in the bottom of the Eye [. . .] to paint the Picture of the Object upon [. . .] the *Tunica Retina* [. . . .] And these pictures, propagated by Motion along the Fibres of the optick Nerves into the Brain, are the cause of Vision." (p. 15)

In this explanation Newton distinguishes between the physical rays, which have the "Power and Dispositon" to stimulate the senses conveying motions to the brain, and color itself which exists in the sensorium. This undoubtedly was one of the sources of Locke's distinction between "secondary qualities" defined as the "powers" of the "primary qualities" to affect the senses which then transmit the stimuli to the brain where they are experienced by the mind as sensations or sensory qualities. As Newton says:

> For the Rays to speak properly are not coloured. In them there is nothing else than a certain Power and Dispositon to stir up a Sensation of this or that Colour [. . .] so Colours in the Object are nothing but a Dispositon to reflect this or that sort of Rays [. . .] to propagate this or that Motion into the Sensorium, and in the Sensorium they are Sensations of those Motions under the Forms of Colours. (pp. 124-125)

Having described how the eye functions, Newton then depicts the "Disease of the *Jaundice*" and the causes of near- and farsightedness as "the Humors of the Eye by old Age decay," indicating how these effects are "mended by Spectacles." (pp. 15-16) Explaining the cause of chromatic aberration in refracting telescopes due to the different refrangibility of the rays of light, he defends the superiority of the reflecting telescope he constructed in 1688. Confirming the ancient conjecture of Anaxagoras, he explains rainbows (prismatic-like displays of colors) as caused by the refraction of sunlight by water droplets. (cf. pp. 168-9) These discussions are accompanied by detailed descriptions of the supporting experiments and exact measurements illustrated by numerous diagrams, some of which are quite artistic, demonstrating Newton's unlimited patience for detail.

The Second Book begins with a number of "Observations" on his experiments reflecting and refracting light through different transparent substances such as glass (prisms and convex lenses), air, and water, noting that when sufficiently thick the substances appear clear and colorless but if very thin they display a series of color rings. Describing the intricate variations of these rings of color (since called Newton's rings), he meticulously measured the dimension of the films of air separating the thin plates or "plano-convex glass" along with the diameters of and distances between the successive rings of colors, finding that the squares of the diameters of the lucid colors were in the arithmetical progression of the odd numbers, while those of the less lucid were in the arithmetical progression of the even numbers. It is apparent from these examples that he did not forsake mathematical rigor when he wrote the *Opticks*, as the contrast between it and the *Principia* might suggest. Newton's mathematical and experimental genius are clearly displayed in both works.

Using the previous "Observations" of the measurements of colors produced by reflection and refraction of light through different media, Newton attempted to calculate the structure and magnitudes of the opaque particles within the transparent medium composing different substances. Along with his endeavor to infer the forces among the particles determining the pressure, heat, and dispersion of gases, this is the first attempt to analyze the microstructure of phenomena by optical means (foreshadowing Rutherford's experiments using alpha particles to determine the atomic structure of gold foil). Thus the "Constitutions [of natural Bodies], whereby they reflect some Rays more copiously than others, remain to be discover'd [. . .]."(p. 245) In support of the corpuscular hypothesis that different substances are composed of various tiny particles dispersed in the interstices of a transparent medium, he declares "there are many Reflections made by the internal parts of Bodies, which [. . .] would not happen if the parts of those Bodies were continued without any such Interstices between them [. . .]." (p. 249) Then, having previously correlated the various rings of color with measurements of the film of air or thinness of the plates of glass, he infers the diameters of the interior particles or corpuscles from the color of light they refract:

> [. . .] to determine the sizes of those parts, you need only have recourse to the precedent Tables, in which the thickness of [. . .] Glass exhibiting any Colour is expressed. Thus if it be desired to know the diameter of a Corpuscle, which being of equal density with Glass shall reflect green of the third Order; the Number 16.25 shows it to be 16.25\10000 parts of an Inch. (p. 255)

Yet despite these ingenious experimental inferences to determine the microstructure of substances he concludes: "[b]ut "what is really their inward frame is not yet known to us." (p. 269)

Given this final skepticism as to the "inward frame" of matter, Newton suggests that with the improvement of microscopes one might be able to observe the particles of bodies on which their colors depend. This would involve having the "*microscopical eyes*" envisioned by Locke.[45]

> For if those Instruments are or can be so far improved as with sufficient distinctness to represent Objects five or six hundred times bigger than [. . .] they appear to our naked Eyes, I should hope that we might be able to discover some of the greatest of those Corpuscles. And by one that would magnify three or four thousand times perhaps they might all be discover'd [. . .]. (p. 261)

As a further confirmation of Newton's extraordinary prescience, these discoveries are now being made with the tunneling microscope.

Newton then goes on to present his puzzling theory that in passing through refractive surfaces rays of light are put into certain periodic "transient states" that, as the ray progresses, "*returns at equal Intervals, and disposes the Ray at every return to be easily transmitted through the next refracting Surface, and between the returns to be easily reflected by it.*"(p. 278) It seems that in being refracted a ray of light is put in certain "dispositions," which he terms "Fits of easy Reflection" and "Fits of easy Transmission." (p. 281) These various "fits" apparently signify what we would call diffraction patterns, the "Fits of easy Reflection" corresponding to the light bands in diffraction and the "Fits of easy Transmission" to the dark bands.

> This may be gather'd [. . .] where the Light reflected by thin Plates of Air and Glass, which to the naked Eye appear'd evenly white [. . .] did through a Prism appear waved with many Successions of Light and Darkness made by alternate Fits of easy Reflection and easy Transmission [. . .]. (p. 281)

Since Newton continued to believe in the corpuscular hypothesis of light to explain the sharp edges of shadows and the angles of refraction, these passages are evidence that he also realized that his experiments required a complementary wave aspect to explain what we call the diffraction of light into alternating white and dark bands (indicative of reinforcement and destruction).   Furthermore, he refers to the spaces between the successive returns of these states "the Interval of its Fits," and suggests that the refractive index of different colors are related to the lengths of these intervals, or what we would call their wave lengths.

> *If the Rays which paint the Colour in the Confine of yellow and orange pass perpendicularly out of any Medium into Air, the Intervals of their Fits of easy Reflection [and easy transmission] are the 1/89000th part of an inch.* (p. 285; brackets added)

A century later Thomas Young used Newton's measurements of the distances between the rings and the thickness of the refracting substances (air or glass) to calculate the wave-lengths of the various colors with the results being "in close agreement with present-day accepted value."[46]

Although Newton denies knowing how these fits of dispositions are produced, to satisfy those who "are adverse from assenting to any new Discoveries, but such as they can explain by an Hypothesis" (p. 280), he suggests an analogy between water and sound waves and the vibrations of light, which indicates further his remarkable ability for devising explanatory hypotheses:

> [. . .] as Stones by falling upon Water put the Water into an undulating Motion, and all Bodies by percussion excite vibrations in the Air; so the Rays of Light, by impinging on any refracting or reflecting Surface, excite vibrations in the refracting or reflecting Medium or Substance [. . .] that the vibrations thus excited are propagated [. . .] much after the manner that vibrations are propagated in the Air for causing Sound, and move faster than the Rays so as to overtake them; and that when any Ray is in that part of the vibration which conspires with its motion [reinforcement], it easily breaks through a refracting Surface, but when it is in the contrary part of the vibration [destruction] which impedes its Motion, it is easily reflected; and, by consequence, that every Ray is successively disposed to be easily reflected, or easily transmitted, by every vibration which overtakes it. (p. 280; brackets added)

Because of this recognition of both the corpuscular and undulatory aspects of light (although he apparently did not distinguish between transverse and longitudinal waves) which has been confirmed in the twentieth century, G.P. Thomson declared "this 'guess' of Newton's to be a supreme example of the intuition of genius."[47]

Turning finally to the Third and last Book of the *Opticks* containing the famous "Queries," it is these speculative hypotheses that represent such a striking contrast to the previous books of the *Opticks* and the *Principia* (except for the General Scholium following Book II). Added toward the end of his life, it is as if Newton finally decided it was time to share with the world the depth and extent of his private reflections. As Cohen says, to "the eighteenth-century reader, as to us, these queries reveal the mind of Newton in its innermost thoughts just as the reading of the book of Nature revealed to Newton the mind of the creating God."[48] Originally numbering sixteen, they subsequently were expanded to twenty-four and finally to thirty-one, replacing what had been intended as Book IV. Read extensively, these queries were a primary inspiration for much of the experimental investigations throughout the

eighteenth century. Beginning usually with the words "Do not . . ."or "Is not
. . .", they were intended less as questions than as positive conjectures[49] that
were read as research proposals and investigative strategies by succeeding
generations of scientists.

The scope of these conjectural hypotheses is truly remarkable, the fruit of
years of intense astronomical, optical, and alchemical research (a considerable
portion of the Queries is devoted to the analysis of chemical agents and
reactions, indicative of the many years Newton pursued alchemical
experiments). Here is a natural philosopher who seemed to encompass the
whole domain of nature as his research programme, often anticipating later
discoveries. It is easy to forget how natural it is today for scientists to conduct
experiments with a presumption of success in attempting to explain puzzling
phenomena, but in Newton's time the confidence that such queries could be
answered by future experiments itself was revolutionary. He begins the
Queries with a discussion of Grimaldi's experiments producing what we would
call diffraction patterns, then reports his own investigations using hairs and
knife blades to intercept beams of light passing through a tiny hole in a
darkened room, describing the shadows, colored rings, or parallel fringes
displayed on a sheet of pasteboard. Observing that the broadest fringes were
made by red light while the narrowest were of violet light with the other colors
distributed accordingly, he anticipated the discovery of the light spectrum from
long (red) to short (violet) wave lengths. (cf. 336)

Then turning to the queries themselves, he introduces his general thesis
that "Bodies and Light act mutually upon one another" (p. 339), bodies
refracting, reflecting, and inflecting (diffracting) light while light heats the
bodies. Asserting that black bodies absorb heat more readily than colored
ones, he attributes their change in luminosity and color as they are
progressively heated to "putting their parts into a vibrating motion wherein
heat consists" (p. 339), thus at least partially anticipating one of the
revolutionary developments in the twentieth century pertaining to "blackbody
radiation." Solar heat is explained as due to the progressive interaction of rays
of light (which he considered corpuscular) and "parts" of the sun whose
intensity and duration is attributed to its immense size and density. (cf. pp.
343-4)

Based on an analogy with sound vibrations, he attempts to explain visual
perception as due to vibrations of the rays of light, again assigning the longest
vibrations to red light and the shortest to violate. He describes how these
"vibrations" or "impressions" exciting the retina and "propagated along the
solid Fibres of the optick Nerves into the Brain, cause the Sense of seeing."

(p. 345) Accurately tracing the right and left optic nerves to the right and left sides of the brain respectively, he accounts for the unified visual image by the uniting of both nerves in what we identify as the optic chiasm, although he erroneously concluded that the right and left visual fields were conveyed to the right and left hemispheres of the brain, while we now know that they are reversed. (cf. p. 346)

Discussing Huygens' experiments described in his *Théorie de lumière* of 1690 on the refraction of light in Island Crystal, Newton anticipates the polarization of light which he attributes to different ''sides of light.'' Noting the difference between transverse waves produced when a stone is dropped in water and horizontal waves caused by percussion (cf. p. 348), both of which are symmetric, he contrasts these with light refracted by Island Crystal, conjecturing that the planes in the crystal put the vibrations of light into definite orientations perpendicular to one another, so that if refracted through a second crystal they will either be transmitted or partially deflected depending upon the orientation of the second crystal.

> Have not the Rays of Light several sides, endued with several Properties? [. . .] For one and the same Ray is [. . .] refracted [. . .] according to the Position which its Sides have to the Crystals. If the Sides of the Ray are posited the same way to Both Crystals, it is refracted after the same manner in them both: But if that side of the Ray [. . .] be 90 Degrees from the side of the same Ray [. . .] the Ray shall be refracted after several manners in the several Crystals. (pp. 358-9)

Because of his commitment to the corpuscular theory of light, Newton rejects Huygens wave explanation of this polarization of light, attributing it to the influences of the particles of the crystals on the rays or particles of light.

> And since the Particles of Island-Crystal act all the same way upon the Rays of Light [. . .] may it not be supposed that in the Formation of this Crystal, the Particles not only ranged themselves [. . .] in regular Figures, but also by some kind of polar Virtue [this is the origin of the word 'polarization'] turned their homogeneal Sides the same way. (p. 388; brackets added)

Even though partially incorrect, since today polarized light is explained in terms of waves rather than particles, still this was an ingenious explanation indicative of the powerful scientific intuition of Newton.

But this preference for explanations in term of particles and forces is prevalent throughout the Queries. Thus he suggests that phenomena as diverse as the composition of substances, the cohesion and repelling of particles, electrical attraction and repulsion, gravity and magnetism, chemical interactions, freezing and evaporating, heat and fermentation will eventually be explained by the "Powers, Forces, and Virtues" of particles.

> Have not the small Particles of Bodies certain Powers, Virtues, or Forces, by which they act at a distance, not only upon the Rays of Light for reflecting, refracting, and inflecting them, but also upon one another for producing a great Part of the Phaenomena of Nature? For it's well known, that Bodies act one upon another by the Attractions of Gravity, Magnetism, and Electricity; and these Instances shew the Tenor and Course of Nature, and make it not improbable but that there may be more attractive Powers than these. For Nature is very consonant and conformable to her self. (pp. 375-6)

Whatever these agents and powers are, he says, "it is the Business of experimental Philosophy to find them out." (p. 394) The whole development of science, from Newton's day to ours, has been a confirmation of this belief.

Like his predecessors Descartes and Galileo, the mode of inquiry that Newton espouses is the "Method of Analysis" and the "Method of Composition," claiming that the former should always precede the latter.

> As in Mathematicks, so in Natural Philosophy, the Investigation of difficult Things by the Method of Analysis, ought ever to precede the Method of Composition. This Analysis consists in making Experiments and Observations, and in drawing general Conclusions from them by Induction, and admitting of no Objections against the Conclusions, but such as are taken from Experiments, or other certain Truths. For Hypotheses are not to be regarded in experimental Philosophy. And although the arguing from Experiments and Observations by Induction be no Demonstration of general Conclusions; yet it is the best way of arguing which the Nature of Things admits of [. . .]. (p. 404)

As argued previously, the phrase "Hypotheses are not to be regarded in experimental Philosophy" does not imply a total rejection of hypotheses, but as he emphasized in his previous criticisms of Descartes, the "experimental discovery of properties" must *precede* the use of hypotheses which only then are introduced to explain these experimental discoveries, as his method in the *Opticks* clearly illustrates.

Whereas in the *Principia* previously he had proposed "a certain most subtle spirit"[50] diffused throughout matter and the universe to explain everything from gravity to sensation, he now evokes an "Aether," a "Medium exceedingly more rare and subtile than the Air, and exceedingly more elastick and active" which "pervade[s] all Bodies" and extends "through all the Heavens" (p. 349) to explain the same phenomena. It is this Aether or Medium, becoming progressively denser as it recedes from the celestial bodies, which he suggests "may suffice to impel Bodies from the denser parts of the Medium towards the rarer, with all that power which we call gravity."(p. 351) (Thus for all his criticism of the theory of vortices, this view is not unlike Descartes'.) Despite its increasing density this aether still is so elastic and rare as not to impede the motion of the planets.

There *is* an important difference, however, between the former "subtle spirit" and this "Aether" reflecting his increased preference for explanations in terms of the motion of particles, the latter used to explain the greater rarity and elasticity of the aether over air.

> The exceeding smallness of its Particles may contribute to the greatness of the force by which those Particles may recede from one another, and thereby make that Medium exceedingly more rare and elastick than Air, and by consequence exceedingly less able to resist the motions of Projectiles, and exceedingly more able to press upon gross Bodies, by endeavouring to expand it self. (p. 352)

It would be going too far to suggest that Newton also anticipated the bending of light by gravitational forces as in Einstein's general theory of relativity, yet there is even a remote hint of that: "[d]oth not this Aethereal Medium [. . .] grow denser and denser by degrees, and by that means refract the Rays of Light [. . .] by bending them gradually in curve Lines?" (p. 350)

This later utilization of particles and forces to explain phenomena apparently was not considered by Newton a violation of his injunction against "forming" or "feign hypotheses," convinced that they were "principles" or "laws" whose truth would be manifest from phenomena.

> It seems to me [. . .] that these Particles [. . .] are moved by certain

active Principles, such as is that of Gravity, and that which causes Fermentation, and the Cohesion of Bodies. These Principles I consider, not as occult Qualities, supposed to result from the specifick Forms of Things [as the Aristotelians believed], but as general Laws of Nature, by which the Things themselves are form'd; their Truth appearing to us by Phaenomena, though their Causes be not yet discover'd. For these are manifest Qualities, and their Causes only are occult. (p. 401; brackets added)

Newton had a prophetic vision of later developments in chemistry and atomic physics based on the discovery of various elementary particles and the diverse forces causing their motions. While he was the first to admit that he had not discovered the causes of such forces as gravity, electricity, and magnetism, he nonetheless believed that his fundamental principles of explanation in term of moving particles and forces pointed the way to their discovery, and in this he was essentially correct. As he says,

to derive two or three general Principles of Motion from Phaenonena, and afterwards to tell us how the Properties and Actions of all corporeal Things follow from those manifest Principles, would be a very great step in Philosophy, though the Causes of those Principles were not yet discover'd: And therefore I scruple not to propose the Principles of Motion above-mention'd, they being of very general Extent, and leave their Causes to be found out. (pp. 401-402)

That he embraced the particle or corpuscular theory was not unusual considering that it was the generally accepted alternative to Aristotelianism by the defenders of the new mechanistic conception of the universe. But he was unique in divining the importance of forces, especially as possible explanations of the cohesion of matter, expansion of gases, electrical and magnetic attraction and repulsion, and chemical reactions, even though he could not define these forces or their causes. After rejecting "invented" explanations in terms of "hooked Atoms," "occult Qualities, and "conspiring Motions," he says:

I had rather infer from their Cohesion, that their Particles attract one another by some Force, which in immediate Contact is exceeding strong, at small distances performs the chymical Operations above-mention'd, and reaches not far from the Particles with any sensible

Effect. (p. 389)

There is a slight suggestion in this of the current distinction between strong and weak atomic forces and chemical bonds.

CONCLUSION

When the first edition of the *Opticks* was published in 1704 Newton was to live twenty-three more years, nearly a quarter of a century. Although his mathematical and scientific accomplishments lay in the past, these still were active, fulfilling years for him. Generally in good health and intellectually acute until about five years prior to his death when he began to suffer severe urinary problems, along with loss of memory and mental alertness, he nonetheless retained his positions as president of the Royal Society and Master of the mint, although his effectiveness declined sharply toward the end of his life.[51] For some years he was occupied with correcting and revising editions of the *Principia* and bringing out new editions (such as the Latin translation so that it would be accessible to scholars who did not know English) of the *Opticks*. Of his previous scholarly pursuits, "theology was the primary occupation of his old age." (p. 804) John Conduitt, who married Newton's niece Catherine Barton in 1717, and who succeeded him as Master of the Mint, stated that one of the most prominent characteristics of Newton in his later life, as earlier, was his studiousness. Looking back over his long life of unrivaled achievements, shortly before his death Newton modestly characterized his accomplishments with the following well-known image, itself a touching tribute to his character.

I don't know what I may seem to the world, but, as to myself, I seem to have been only like a boy playing on the sea shore, and diverting myself in now and then finding a smoother peeble or a prittier shell than ordinary, whilst the great ocean of truth lay all undiscovered before me. (p. 863)

He was of course a celebrity. Entertained by King George II and his wife (the former Princess Caroline whom he had known before her marriage), he was sought out by foreign dignitaries and aspiring scholars. And he continued to sit for his portrait. Having become wealthy owing to his position at the Mint and various investments, he was exceedingly generous in his charitable contributions and especially to the numerous members of his family, extending to them outright gifts of money, annuities, and the purchase of property guaranteeing a lifelong source of income. When he realized the end was approaching he carefully provided for the distribution of his estate. After a short illness he died on March 20, 1727 at age eighty-five. Appropriately buried in a prominent location in the nave of Westminster Abbey, his monument bears the concluding inscription: "Let Mortals rejoice That there has existed such and so great an Ornament to the Human Race."

NOTES

1. Edmund Halley, "The Ode Dedicated to Newton," prefixed to Isaac Newton, *Mathematical Principles of Natural Philosophy*, Vol. I, translated by Florian Cajori (Berkeley: Univ. of California Press, 1962), p. xv.

2. J. A. Borelli (1608-1679) developed a model to show that at a certain rotational speed an outward (centrifugal) and inward (centripetal) tendency would balance producing an oval orbit. The fall inward to the sun he described as a "natural tendency," a legacy of Aristotle. Cf. Thomas Kuhn, *The Copernican Revolution* (Cambridge: Harvard University Press, 1957), pp. 248-254.

3. After discussions with Newton and Halley, Sir Christopher Wren became interested in trying to resolve the problem of planetary motions utilizing the inverse square law. In January 1684 "he offered a prize of a book worth forty shillings to the one who would bring him a demonstration within two months" of the laws of planetary motion derived from the inverse-square principle. Richard S. Westfall, *Never at Rest* (Cambridge: Cambridge University Press, 1980), p. 403. As in the previous chapter, the references in the text are to this work until otherwise indicated.

4. Robert Hooke claimed to Wren that he "had the demonstration, but he intended to keep it secret until others, by failing to solve the problem, learned how to value it." Westfall, p. 403. Knowing Hooke's desire for acclaim, if he had the solution he would not have kept it secret for long.

5. More forthright, Edmund Halley admitted to not being able to derive the demonstration and therefore sought the opinion of Newton which led to the publication of the *Principia*.

6. Christiaan Huygens was probably the only one beside Newton with the

mathematical skill to solve the problem, but he was too committed to the Cartesian vortex theory to look for a mathematical demonstration in terms of a gravitational attraction varying with the square of the distance. Shortly after publication of the *Principia*, when Fatio de Duillier wrote to Huygens praising the book, Huygens wrote back "I don't care that he's not a Cartesian as long as he doesn't serve us up conjectures such as attractions." Westfall, p. 464. That is precisely what Newton did "serve up," but for Cartesians "attractions" were equivalent to "occult powers," a relic from medieval philosophy.

7. Joseph Hall Schaffner Collection, University of Chicago Library, MS, 1075-7. Westfall, p. 403.

8. *Corres.* 2, 411. Westfall, p. 444; brackets added.

9. Birch, *History*, 4, 479-80. Westfall, pp. 444-5.

10. *Ibid.*, 4, 484. Westfall, p. 445.

11. *Corres.* 2, 481. Westfall, p. 468.

12. Sir Isaac Newton, *Principia*, Vol. 1 & 2, Motte's translation revised by Cajori (Berkeley: Univ. of California Press, 1934), p. XVIII. From this point on all following page references in the text will be to this work unless otherwise indicated.

13. J. Edleston, *Correspondence of Sir Isaac Newton and Professor Cotes* (London, 1850), pp. 151, 154. *Principia*, Vol. 2, Appendix, p. 629.

14. Edleston, *op. cit.*, pp. 150, 159. *Principia*, Vol. 2, Appendix, p. 635.

15. Newton to Bentley, 10 Dec. 1692; *Corres.* 3, 233. Westfall, p. 441.

16. Cf. Westfall, p. 302.

17. Immanuel Kant, *Critique of Pure Reason*, trans. by Norman Kemp Smith, A 369.

18. *Ibid.*, p. B 47.

19. Immanuel Kant, *Prolegomena to Any Future Metaphysics. FIRST PART OF THE MAIN TRANSCENDENTAL QUESTION*, par. 10.

20. Isaac Newton, *Opticks*, based on the Fourth Edition London, 1730 (New York, Dover Pub., Inc., 1952), p. 370. Brackets added.

21. Cf. George Berkeley, *De Motu*, Par. 60-65 and *Principles of Human Knowledge*, Part I, Par. 111, 117; also Ernest Mach, *The Science of Mechanics*, translated by Thomas J. McCormack, sixth edition (La Salle: The Open Court Pub. Co., 1960), pp. 277-284.

22. H.A. Lorentz, A. Einstein, H. Minkowski, and H. Weyl, *The Principle of Relativity*, translated by W. Perrett and G.B. Jeffery (New York: Dover Pub. Inc., 1923), p. 37. Brackets added.

23. Cf. Richard A. Silverman, *Essential Calculus with Applications* (New York: Dover Pub., Inc., 1977), pp. 101-102.

24. Immanuel Kant, *Critique of Pure Reason*, *op. cit.*, B 106.

25. Cf. Westfall, *op. cit.*, p. 430.

26. Florian Cajori's, "An Historical And Explanatory Appendix" following Book III, "System of the World," Vol. 2 of the *Principia*, p. 630.

27. *Ibid.*, p. 632. Brackets added.

28. Voltaire, *Elements de la philosophie de Newton*, 1783. Brackets added. Quoted by Cajori, *op. cit.*, p. 632.

29. The conception of the atomic theory as constituting the "Metaphysical Foundations of Modern Science" derives from the classic work bearing that title by Edwin A. Burtt (London: Routledge & Kegan Paul Limited, 1924).

30. Cf. Max Jammer, "The Correspondence Principle," in *The Conceptual Development of Quantum Mechanics* (New York: McGraw-Hill Book Co., 1966), pp. 109-118.

31. Newton's letter to Oldenburg, 1672. Isaac Newtoni Opera, Vol. 4, pp. 314-315. Quoted from Cajori, Appendix note 55, p. 673.

32. Cajori, *op. cit.*, p. 673. This argument also constitutes a rebuttal to Popper's claim that the proper method of science is to advance as many conjectural hypotheses as possible and then attempt to find which one survives efforts to refute them. As Newton indicates, this is not the way

science proceeds.

33. Newton's letters to Cotes in J. Edleston, *Correspondence of Sir Isaac Newton and Professor Cotes*, London, 1913. Quoted from Newton's *Philosophy of Nature*, ed. by H. S. Thayer (New York: Hafner Pub. Co., 1953), p. 6.

34. For an extensive discussion of the various uses and meanings of "hypotheses" by Newton see I. Bernard Cohen, *Franklin and Newton* (Cambridge: Harvard University Press, 1966), pp. 138-147.

35. *Keynes* MS 130.5, Sheets 2-3. Westfall, p. 473; brackets added.

36. *Keynes* MSS 130.6, Book 2; 130.5, Sheet. Westfall, p. 468.

37. Westfall, p. 474. The immediately following references are to this work.

38. Although Westfall treats the affair between Fatio and Newton discreetly, when discussing Newton's permissive attitude toward the apparent extra-marital relationship between his niece Catherine Barton and his mentor Charles Montague, elevated to Lord Halifax, he says that Newton "knew what sexual attraction was—and from every indication, its gratification [. . .]." (p. 601)

39. *Corres.* 3, 287. Westfall, p. 524.

40. Cf. Westfall, ch. 12.

41. As mentioned previously, Hooke was a somewhat tragic figure whose scientific achievements and reputation were overshadowed by Newton. His later life was embittered because of the controversy over the discovery of the inverse square law of gravity which he claimed Newton had derived from him or at lest should have acknowledged him as the co-discoverer. Nonetheless, Hooke was an extremely gifted scientist who, though no match for Newton's mathematical, theoretical, and experimental brilliance, still made a number of ingenious experiments and discoveries: for example, he had worked as Boyle's assistant at Oxford developing the air or vacuum pump; he was appointed with Christopher Wren to draw up a plan for London after the Great Fire in 1666 and did much of the practical design and supervision of the rebuilding himself; he invented the balance spring of the modern watch and foresaw the use of the pendulum in clocks; and his *Micrographia* was a classic both for its optical research

and for its drawings of microscopic organisms.

42. I. Bernard Cohen, *Franklin and Newton* (Cambridge: Harvard Univ. Press, 1966), p. 120.

43. *Ibid.*, p. 178.

44. Sir Isaac Newton, *Opticks* (New York: Dover Pub., Inc., 1952), p. 1. The added brackets contain Newton's own words. Unless otherwise indicated, all subsequent page references in the text are to this work.

45. Cf. John Locke, *An Essay Concerning Human Understanding*, Bk. II, Ch. XXIII, Sec. 14.

46. I. Bernard Cohen, Preface to the *Opticks*, *op. cit.*, xli.

47. G.P. Thomson, *The Wave Mechanics of Free Electrons* (New York: McGraw-Hill Publishers, 1930), p. 13. Quoted from I. Bernard Cohen, *Franklin and Newton*, *op. cit.*, p. 114.

48. Cohen, *ibid.*, p. 177.

49. In 1705 Newton declared to David Gregory the firmness of his belief in the assertions of the Queries. Cf. Cohen, *op. cit.*, p. 193.

50. *Principia*, Vol. 2, p. 547.

51. This summary is based on Westfall, *op. cit.*, Ch. 15. The following page references in the text are to this work.

CHAPTER VIII

THE NEWTONIAN LEGACY

The physical sciences of the 18th century were coloured even saturated, by the influence of Newton.[1]

Greenaway

Having solved the ancient problem of the planets and of terrestrial descent in the *Principia* with the universal law of gravitation, in the *Opticks* Newton began investigating more common phenomena such as light, heat, magnetism, and electricity, along with chemical reactions like combustion and fermentation—the very problems that would engage natural philosophers during the succeeding centuries. Just as gravity was believed to be evidence of an invisible affinity among all bodies, magnetic attraction, electrical repulsion, and chemical reactions could be manifestations of similar forces. As Newton said in Query 31 of the *Opticks*: "[h]ave not the small Particles of bodies certain Powers, Virtues, or Forces, by which they act at a distance [. . .] but also upon one another for producing a great Part of the Phaenomena of Nature?" By probing bodies with rays of light to determine the size and structure of the inherent particles, Newton introduced a mode of investigation that would serve as a model for subsequent scientific inquiry.

The present chapter will explore two major scientific advances in the eighteenth and nineteenth centuries illustrating Newton's influence in directing scientific inquiry: first, investigations in electricity culminating in Franklin's one-fluid theory and Coulomb's law, second, experiments in optics leading to the resurgence of the wave theory. Each of these developments show how progress in discovering the underlying causes and basic properties of phenomena was attained during the following two centuries, preparing for the unprecedented breakthroughs in the twentieth century. However, because the character of scientific inquiry itself changed after Newton, it will be useful to investigate the reasons for this change.

THE NEW STIMULUS TO SCIENTIFIC INQUIRY

Unlike the seventeenth century wherein the stimulus to scientific inquiry arose primarily from a long tradition of the investigation of astronomical and mechanistic problems, by the turn of the eighteenth century the questions that evoked the curiosity of natural philosophers more often were due to influences such as the industrial revolution. Contributing to celestial mechanics, terrestrial dynamics, optics, and pneumatics (the major areas of scientific research in the seventeenth century) exacted skill in mathematics, knowledge of Latin still the international language of science, and admission to prestigious scientific societies with access to their publications in order to keep abreast of current experiments and theoretical developments. This in turn usually required admission to the outstanding universities, as Locke and Hooke had studied at Oxford and Barrow and Newton at Cambridge. Moreover, as we have seen, to attain entrance and advancement at Cambridge (which was just as true at Oxford) depended upon social status, family connections, and patronage, along with swearing an oath to uphold the Anglican faith.

All of these requirements usually were beyond the new breed of experimental scientists who did not descend from landed gentry or aristocratic families, had not attended the usual grammar schools where knowledge of Greek and Latin were foundational, had not studied higher mathematics, and whose nonconformist religious backgrounds would have precluded their attending the universities had they been able to qualify in other respects. Often self-taught, they attained their scientific achievements and reputations not as a result so much of academic training or association with famous scholars, but owing to their natural curiosity, self-education, and adeptness at experimentation. This was true of two of the greatest English chemists of the period, the Unitarian minister Joseph Priestley whose father had been a cloth shearer and John Dalton a Quaker whose family earned their living as cottage weavers. (It was true also of Benjamin Franklin who left school at age ten to help his father, a tallow chandler and soap maker.) Nearly all were self-made men either in terms of their scientific reputations or their acquired fortunes. Despite the prominent influence of Newton, they were more Baconians than Newtonians.

Underlying this change in background of the new generation of natural philosophers was the shift of the centers of experimental research from Oxbridge to provincial manufacturing towns like Birmingham and Manchester, the latter with its burgeoning textile industry becoming the leading manufacturing and trading center in the world. The advent of the industrial revolution with its large cotton and woolen mills as well as expanding industries such as coal mining, ironworks, and steel foundries not only attracted huge numbers of workers and created a new middle class of wealthy families, it rewarded manual skills, engineering inventiveness, and entrepreneurial shrewdness—the type of practical intelligence characteristic also of the new breed of natural philosophers. Moreover, the industrial activities themselves provided an incentive to experimental inquiry. The great market for large quantities at the lowest prices of sulfuric acid, alkalis, and chlorine needed for bleaching and dying wool and cotton generated an interest in chemical processes to determine how these substances are produced and react; the demand for more efficient pumps to clear the mines of water and for power to run the machinery in the mills led to the invention and improvement of stream engines along with investigations in pneumatics; the boring of metals producing high temperatures generated research into the exact nature and transmission of heat; and the conversion of coal into coke used to produce steel from iron incited inquiries into the nature of combustion or oxidation and how various oxides and calxes were produced.

It was no accident that these new industrial ventures and experimental inquiries usually were undertaken by individuals with nonconformist religious beliefs (such as Quakers, Presbyterians, and Unitarians) whose practical interests had not been constrained by the traditional classical studies in Greek and Latin literature, Aristotelian philosophy, and Anglican theology. Because of their own unconventional beliefs, they tended to be more tolerant of new ideas and different ways of thinking that emphasized practical results. This new attitude is clearly expressed by the counsel for Richard Arkwright when seeking a patent for one of the latter's inventions.

> It is well known that the most useful discoveries that have been made
> in every branch of art and manufactures have not been made by
> speculative philosophers in their closets, but by ingenious mechanics,
> conversant in the practices in use in their time [. . .].[2]

Not just manufacturing concerns motivated these practical pursuits, but also the necessity of dealing with the problems created by the industrial revolution and growing urban centers, such as city planning, maintaining needed health facilities, constructing adequate means of transportation, providing public education for the workers and more advanced schools for the children of the new class of industrial civic leaders, and establishing libraries like the excellent free Chetham library in Manchester.

Prevented from attending the usual grammar schools and universities whose program of studies in any case was ill suited to their needs, the rising class of industrial intellectuals created their own schools, known as "Dissenting Academies," along with their own prestigious learned societies. In Birmingham, for instance, a group of eminent industrialists, inventors, and natural philosophers that included Josuah Wedgwood (founder of the famous Wedgwood potteries), James Watt (who assisted Joseph Black in his experiments at the University of Glasgow and made a fortune improving the steam engine), Matthew Boulton (Watt's partner), John Wilkinson (an ironmaster who invented a horizontal boring machine to bore the cylinder's for Watt's steam engine and who with Abraham Darby constructed the first iron bridge and then built the first iron boat to sail under it[3]), James Kier (one of the founders of the chemical industry), Dr. William Withering (discoverer of the effects of digitalis), Eramus Darwin (noted scientist and poet who conceived of the evolution of species before his grandson Charles), and Joseph Priestley founded the Warrington Academy in 1757 (the most famous of the dissenting academies) and the Lunar Society about 1775.

Priestley taught English and other languages at the Warrington Academy from 1761-67 and was such a prominent teacher that his methods "revolutionized educational practices and set an educational pattern that would persist in English grammar schools for decades."[4] For a time, these Dissenting Academies provided the best education in England, superior to the tradition-bound grammar schools and lax universities. "Academies sprang up in many localities, often achieving high reputations for the quality of their teaching and reflecting [...] renown upon their founders, their students, and their locales."[5] It was while teaching English at Warrington that Priestley became interested in electricity and chemistry from listening to the lectures and discussions of his colleagues, later becoming so adept at experimentation that he "was the first man to collect gases from chemical reactions systematically over water and over mercury"[6] which led to his discovery of oxygen. Some of these experiments were performed before the Lunar Society, so named because its monthly meetings were scheduled on or near the full moon so that those who came from afar could be guided by the light of the moon on their return.

Manchester in the north mirrored the situation in Birmingham. There, too, men of enormous talent, energy, and civic pride created their own academy and professional society, both of which became well known. Among the founders were Dr. Thomas Barnes (a Unitarian Minister, he had been a student then a tutor at Warrington College and decided, when the latter closed in 1783, to establish a College of Arts and Science in Manchester for teaching science and mechanics which was replaced by Manchester Academy later renamed "New College") who became the first Principal of New College (which eventually was relocated at Oxford University as Manchester College), Thomas Henry (an Anglican who converted to Unitarianism, he became interested in the chemical properties of *magnesia alba* which brought him fame and fortune as "Magnesia Henry"[7]), Samuel Taylor Coleridge, and Dr. Thomas Percival (another graduate of Warrington, he received his medical education at the Universities of Edinburgh and Leyden and became widely known for his public health policies and attempts to improve the abysmal working and living conditions of the factory laborers) who served as the first Chairman of the Board of Trustees of New College and was the principal organizer of the Manchester Literary and Philosophical Society that, like the Lunar Society in Birmingham, was the focus of intellectual activity in Manchester. Founded in 1781 chiefly for the discussion of "experimental philosophy, technology, and literature" it remains "after the Royal Society, the oldest extant scientific body in Britain,"[8] inspiring the formation of many other 'provincial' societies.

The most famous scientist of the community was John Dalton. He was teaching in his own school in Kendal when he was invited in 1793 "to fill the situation of Professor of Mathematics and Natural Philosophy in the new college, Mosley Street, Manchester."[9] Dalton accepted the invitation with alacrity, happily passing the rest of his life in Manchester where he became one of its most celebrated citizens. An active participant in the "Lit. and Phil. Society" for a half-century, he read "one hundred and seventeen papers" to the society, "of which fifty-two were published" in its *Memoires*.[10] In addition, he served as an officer for forty-five years, eight as Secretary, eight as Vice-President, then twenty-even years as President until his death. Although teaching chemistry was one of his duties at New College from the beginning, it was not until he heard a series of talks on natural philosophy and chemistry by Dr. Thomas Garnett in 1796 that he began studying it seriously, a fortuitous occurrence that eventually led to his creating the modern atomic theory for which he will be evermore remembered.

ELECTRICAL INVESTIGATION

Turning now to the actual investigations themselves, we will begin with experiments in electricity since they were prior and directly influenced by Newton. As is true of nearly all scientific phenomena, the earliest known references to electrical attraction occur among the ancient Greeks, Plato in the *Timaeus* (80_c) referring to such "marvels" as "the attraction of amber and the Heraclean stones" (later called loadstones or magnets), although Plato actually rejected the notion of attraction. The word 'electricity' derives from the Greek '*elektron*' meaning amber, the primary substance known to generate attractive forces upon rubbing, though the modern use of 'electric' begins with the reintroduction of the term by Gilbert in *De Magnete*.[11] Despite the general disinterest in natural phenomena during the early middle ages especially, Augustine remarks "that the loadstone has the wonderful power of attracting iron. When I first saw it I was thunderstruck [. . .]."[12] It was not until Jerome Cardan's publication of *De Subtilitate* in 1550 that the distinction between the attractive effects of rubbed amber and the magnetic effects of the loadstone was recognized.[13]

Although Gilbert was concerned primarily with magnetic phenomena in *De Magnete*, he was sufficiently interested in electrification to include a comprehensive review of previous investigations, concluding from his own inquiries that many other substances ('*electrics*') beside amber were capable of attracting straw and chaff. Based on the analogy with a compass whose needle is directed by magnetic forces, he constructed a "*versorium*" (now known as an electroscope) consisting of a pivoting needle that reacts to electric charges. His investigations led him to reject the current theories of electrical attraction (he was not aware of repulsion): namely, that it was identical to the heat of fire, that it involved the absorption of a "fatty humor" (postulated by Cardan), that it was produced by an effluvium from the amber pushing the air in front of it so that when the air rushed back to fill the vacuum it brought the straw or chaff with it, or that it was caused by some quality or form in *electrics* not possessed by *nonelectrics*.

According to his own explanation, when the electric substance is rubbed the heat generated releases a material effluvium which acts directly on the attracted material drawing it to the electrified substance: "electric bodies have their own distinctive effluvia; and each peculiar effluvium has its own individual power of leading to union, its own movement to its origin [. . .] to the body that emits the effuvium."[14] Attempting a more precise explanation, he says:

> The effuvia spread in all directions: they are specific and peculiar, and *sui generis*, different from the common air; generated from humor; called forth by calorific motion and rubbing [. . .] they are as it were material rods—hold and take up straws, chaff, twigs, till their force is spent or vanishes [. . .].[15]

FRANCIS HAUKSBEE

One of the first individuals to perform systematic electric experiments was

Francis Hauksbee. When Newton was elected President of the Royal Society in 1703 following the death of Hooke who had served as the curator of experiments, he was anxious that the position be filled by someone proficient in experimentation to give substance to the weekly meetings. At the very first meeting of the Royal Society at which Newton presided, Hauksbee demonstrated his newly perfected air pump and continued such experiments until his death in 1713.[16] Continuing with demonstrations producing vacuums and capillary action probably suggested by Newton, the curious phenomena of "barometric light"(the flickers of illumination produced in the vacuum above the mercury in an agitated barometric tube) caught his attention. At the time it was believed that this light was due to phosphorus in the mercury, but Hauksbee concluded after a number of ingenious experiments that the flashes were produced by the motion of the droplets of mercury over the glass in the vacuum. Apparently sensing that there might be some similarity between this light and the sparks produced by charged electric bodies, he improvised an experiment in which he caused amber to be rubbed against wool in an evacuated chamber producing similar flashes of light, demonstrating that the intensity of light increased as the rarification of the air in the chamber increased. Because of the difficulty of producing electrification within an evacuated jar, he hit upon the idea of evacuating a sealed globe which he then rotated rapidly between his hands, the rubbing producing an especially bright discharge of light in the evacuated interior of the globe. Further experiments were performed in the usual manner with a rubbed glass tube and then with a nonevacuated spinning globe, the rotary motion of the globe under his hands producing electrification on the surface of the globe.[17] Noting that the charged (the term was borrowed from the usage of loading or "charging" a canon with powder) glass, which he like Gilbert attributed to an "effuvium" generated by rubbing the glass, sometimes attracted and sometimes repelled "leaf-brass," he may have been the first to notice electrical repulsion. Holding an electrified tube to his face he felt a sensation like an "electric wind"which he also attributed to a material effluvium emitted by the electrified body. (cf. 564) Observing that an excited globe can electrify a neutral one close to it, he would have discovered the inducing of electrification from one body to another, called "electrical influence," except that he interpreted the electrification produced on the neutral body as due to the attrition of the material effluvium striking it, rather than to a transfer of electricity.

In another series of clever experiments he encircled a spinning globe with a semicircular wire from which hung threads that did not reach the globe. While the slight breeze produced by the rotating motion of the uncharged globe displaced all the threads in the same direction as the wind, when the globe was charged the attractive force overcame the breeze so that all the threads were aligned circularly around the globe like spokes around an axle. Even more dramatically, when he directed his finger toward the end of the circular band of strings (the ends facing the globe) they were repelled, while if he pointed his finger to the upper part of the strings attached to the semicircular wire they were attracted.   Again Hauksbee came close to discovering opposite or polar charges, but because his effluvium theory only took into account the attractive effect of electrified objects he did not appreciate the significance of the repulsion. Discovering that the electric effect penetrates glass but not muslin, he did not pursue this either.   So while Hauksbee's experiments linked barometric light with electric effects, introduced the triboelectric generator, demonstrated the occurrence of electrical influence, and provided evidence of electrical repulsion as well as attraction, his attempts at explaining the phenomena in terms of a material effluvium were weak, illustrating the importance for scientific progress of theorizing as well as ingenious experimentation.

STEPHEN GRAY

Following in the tradition of Hauksbee was Stephen Gray (1666-1736) who, like Hauksbee, came from a deprived background having lived as a "poor brethren" in the Charterhouse.[18] Performing a series of experiments between 1720 and 1732, these had to do mainly with showing that the electric virtue of a rubbed glass tube could be transmitted at great distances (over 650 feet) to another body if connected by a "packthread." Effectively discovering what is now called "electrical conduction," he also showed that whether the electric fluid was transmitted or not depended upon the nature of the connecting substance, thereby anticipating the distinction between electrical conductors and nonconductors.   But it was Jean Desaguliers, a friend of Newton's and member of the Royal Society, who explicitly made the distinction between "electrical *per se*"and "*non-electrical*," stating that while the former could be made electrical by rubbing the latter could not be electrified by any action done to it but only by coming in contact with an electrified body.[19] According to Cohen, his experiments seem to indicate "that a non-electrical [e.g., glass] can be charged by rubbing because it is not a conductor, while an electrical *per se* [e.g., metal] cannot be so charged because it is a conductor."[20]

Electrifying solid, hollowed out oak cubes, Gray showed that they had the same electric properties, inferring that only the surfaces of electric bodies were involved in the electrification. Probably the most important conclusion derived from his experiments on conduction was that whatever the nature of the electrified substance or "electrick virtue" that is transmitted, once produced it exists independently of the charged source. Gray did not subscribe to the conception of an effluvium, so the notion of an "electric virtue" or "electric fluid" that exists independently of the electrified body and constitutes another reality along with gravity, magnetism, and heat came to be more generally accepted, another illustration of what was emphasized in the first volume, that the development of scientific thought depends upon differentiating phenomena that were indistinct in an earlier stage of syncretic thought.

While investigating electric sparks he also noticed (as Franklin will) that when a metal rod with a pointed end is brought close to an electrified body the transfer of electricity to the pointed rod occurs continuously and silently until all the electricity is discharged, whereas with a metal rod having a blunt end the transfer occurs as a bright flash with a pronounced snap. From this he concluded (again preceding Franklin) that "this electric fire [. . .] seems to be of the same nature with that of thunder and lightning." (p. 590) For his contributions Gray was elected to the Royal Society in 1732.

CHARLES DU FAY

The next major contributor to the understanding of electrical phenomena was Charles Francois de Cisternay du Fay (1698-1739), or as he is more commonly called, simply Dufay. Learning of Gray's experiments in 1733, he began his own investigations with striking success. Being more fortunate than Hauksbee and Gray in having acquired an excellent education, within eight months of learning of Gray's experiments Dufay summarized the results of his own investigations under seven headings that he communicated to the Royal Society. While the first five of his discoveries represent extensions, refinements, or minor emendations of the work of Hauksbee and Gray, the last two contain his most original contributions.

In the sixth section related, he states, to a little known experiment conducted by von Guericke over fifty years earlier, Dufay announces his discovery of a simple but very important principle pertaining to all electrified bodies.

This principle is that an electrified body attracts all those that are not themselves electrified, and repels them as soon as they become electrified by . . . [conduction from] the electrified body. Thus gold leaf is first attracted by the tube. Upon acquiring an electricity. . . [by conduction from the tube], the gold leaf is of consequence immediately repelled by the tube. Nor is it reattracted while it retains its electrical quality. But if . . . the gold leaf chance to light on some other body, it straightway loses its electricity and consequently is reattracted by the tube, while, after having given it a new electricity, repels it a second time. This continues as long as the tube remains electrical. Upon applying this principle to the various experiments on electrification, one will be surprised at the number of obscure and puzzling facts it clears up. . . . (p. 585); brackets and deletions in the original)

While most of the experimental evidence referred to had been noted previously, it was an important accomplishment to generalize and unify it under a single principle, making explicit for the first time the fact, as stated by the Duane Rollers, that "repulsion will occur when both bodies are electrified, provided that the one body has become electrified by conduction from the other." (p. 585)   Following Gray's conception that in conduction the transferred electricity becomes separate from the original electrified body, Dufay conjectures that if the electrical effluvium is self-repulsive, then that part conducted to the second body will repel the part remaining in the first body accounting for the repulsion. (cf. p. 586)

Not satisfied with this discovery, Dufay then asks the important question whether the repelling effect is characteristic of all electrical bodies, even those that have received their electrification from different sources.

"It is than certain that bodies which have become electrical . . . [by conduction] are repelled by those which have rendered them electrical. But are they repelled likewise by other electrified bodies of all kinds? And do electrified bodies differ from one another in no respect save their intensity of electrification? An examination of this matter has led me to a discovery which I should never have foreseen, and of which I believe no one hitherto has had the least idea." (p. 586)

This discovery was of two different kinds (or modes) of electrics, for when a gold leaf that was electrified by coming in contact with a rubbed glass tube, and consequently repelled by it, was brought into contact with a piece of rubbed copal (a resinous substance), it was not, as he anticipated, *repelled* by it but *attracted* to it.[21]

Entirely unexpected, this experimental result, he wrote, "disconcerted me prodigiously." Yet he soon realized its significance, enunciating it as a new principle in section seven of the original publication.

> This principle is that there are two distinct electricites, very different from each other: one of these I call *vitreous electricity*; the other, *resinous electricity*. The first is that of [rubbed] glass, rock crystal, precious stones, hair of animals, wool, and many other bodies. The second is that of [rubbed] amber, copal, gum lac, silk, thread, paper, and a vast number of other substances. (pp. 586-7)

This distinction between two different electrics, named obviously from the two classes of substances involved, '*vitreous*' from glass and '*resinous*' from amber and copal, was one of the important advances in the development of the theory of electricity. According to this new principle, bodies containing the same kind of electricity, either vitreous or resinous, will repel each other while those possessing the opposite kind will attract.

Furthermore, as Dufay adds, an unelectrified or neutral object can be given either a vitreous or a resinous charge depending upon the type of electrified body brought in contact with it, indicating that neutral bodies have a potential for both types of electrification. (Later it was discovered that the type of electrification produced depends not only on the substance rubbed, but also on the kind of material used in the rubbing and the condition of the surface, glass, for example, exhibiting vitreous electricity if rubbed by wool, silk, or cat's fur, but manifesting resinous electricity if rubbed by rabbit's fur. (cf. p. 589) To test which type of electricity a body possesses, Dufay suggested using an electrified silk thread (a primitive electroscope) "which is known to be of the *resinous electricity*" so that if it is repelled the body is resinous and if attracted vitreous.

Although Dufay generally avoids speculating about the nature of electrification and its transmission, he does suggest that bodies are surrounded by an "*atmosphère particulière*" that "retains [. . .] the electric matter diffused around these bodies" by the approach of a charged object, so that when a neutral body is brought into this electric atomosphere "the electric matter with effort, violence and noise, leaves this first atmosphere [. . .] to pass into that which is presented to it."[22] The obscurity of this explanation indicates what little progress had been made in the understanding of the nature and conduction of electricity. However, it does conform to the preferred explanation in the eighteenth century of changes of state as due to a transfer of a fluid substance, the transmission of heat involving a caloric fluid, oxidation and combustion occurring because of the absorption and release of phlogiston, and electric conduction or repulsion dependent upon two types of electric fluid. The theory of electric fluids involved the following assumption:

> (a) there are two, distinct electrical fluids, one of which may be called "vitreous" and the other, "resinous"; (b) any *unelectrified* object possesses equal quantities of these two fluids, which neutralize each other; (c) rubbing electrifies an object by removing from it one or the other kinds of fluid [. . .]; (d) the larger the quantity of a particular fluid removed, the greater the strength of the electrification. Notice that by "equal quantities" of the two kinds of fluid is here meant simply the quantities present in an unelectrified object and, therefore, the quantities that will completely neutralize each other's effects.
> (p. 590)

The concept of electricity as a fluid substance suggested that the gradual loss of electrification when a charged body is left exposed to the air could be explained as an "evaporation" of the electric fluid that might be stored in greater or lesser quantities in an insulated container. At considerable risk to their lives because of the electric shock they experienced, the possibility of collecting electricity in a container was demonstrated by a German clergyman E.G. von Kleist and a Dutch professor Pieter van Musschenbroek. Experimenting with a bottle containing water and blown with a narrow neck enclosing a nail which he electrified by placing in contact with a rubbed globe, withdrawing the bottle from the globe and placing it near an unelectrified object von Kleist produced an intense spark. In addition, when he held the withdrawn bottle with one hand and touched the nail with the other he experienced a shock so severe that it "stuns my arms and shoulders." (p. 594) As long as no object was brought near the nail the bottle retained its charge for many hours, demonstrating that electricity could be stored in a container. However, when he placed the electrified bottle on a table and touched the nail with his finger, no effect was produced, leading him to (the erroneous) inference that the human body contributed some sort of "animal electricity" to the experiment. (cf. p. 594)

Whereas von Kleist described the results of his experiments in privately circulated letters, van Musschenbroek conveyed the results of his directly to the French Academy so that an abstract with a description of his experiments was incorporated in a paper by J.A. Nollet published in the *Memoires* of the Academy in 1746. Beginning with the warning that "I am going to tell you about a new but terrible experiment which I advise you not to try yourself," he then described the experiment. Suspending a gun between two hanging silk threads, he attached to one end of the barrel a brass wire which he then inserted into a glass flask partially filled with water which he held in his left hand. After electrifying the opposite end of the gun barrel and still holding the flask, he extended the fingers of his right hand to the barrel producing a shock so violent "that all my body was affected as if it had been struck by lightning . . . in a terrible way that I cannot describe: in a word, I thought that it was all up with me . . ." (p. 594)

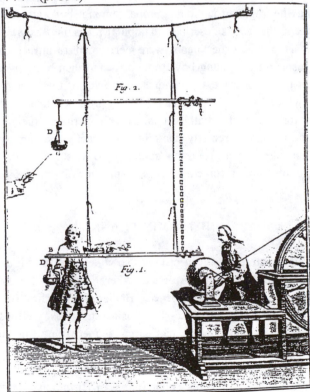

Fig. 1 A lithograph of the Leyden experiment from *Histoire de l'Académie Royale des Science* (Paris). Reprinted by kind permission from *Franklin And Newton*, I. Bernard Cohen (Cambridge: Harvard Univ. Press, 1956), pp. 386-387.

He then reports that placing the flask on a metal support on a table and touching the flask with one hand and the gun barrel with the other produced a similar effect. Because no one was holding the flask, the person's body apparently serving merely as a conductor between the flask and the gun, it was not necessary to assume that the body contributes an additional "animal electricity" to the charge. As the experiment was performed by van Musschenbroek at the University of Leyden, the phial holding the water used to store or "condense" the electricity became known as the "Leyden jar." Other experimenters soon discovered that any conducting material could serve in place of water as long as the outside along with the inside of the vessel was covered with the material (such as metal shot or tin foil), although it was not yet known why the conduction produced an electric spark or shock.

By the middle of the eighteenth century performing electrical experiments was quite the rage throughout Europe, among both amateurs and natural philosophers, the results described in popular magazines as well as in scholarly journals. Dramatic experiments were performed to attract large audiences, such as suspending a young boy from cords and then bringing the rubbed ball to his feet to demonstrate the conducting power of the human body, igniting "spirits" with an electrical discharge, killing by electrification birds (Franklin killed a turkey) and small animals, with perhaps the most humorous demonstration that of secretly charging an attractive young woman and then inviting an eager man from the audience to kiss her who, instead of the anticipated pleasure, received an unpleasant shock. (cf. p. 592)

BENJAMIN FRANKLIN

The public interest in electricity was so widespread that it even reached the English colonies of North America where it came to the attention of "America's first great man of science," Benjamin Franklin. (p. 596) Franklin (1706-1790) was then a successful businessman as well as a prominent publisher and journalist who had already met some of the well-known scientists in England, such as Joseph Priestley, during his visits to Europe (he was very disappointed that a meeting with Newton that Priestly tried to arrange never came about). Like his counterparts in Birmingham and Manchester, Franklin was instrumental in organizing in Philadelphia a club called the "Junto" which evolved into the American Philosophical Society (the first in the colonies organized primarily for the discussion of scientific topics), helped set up with other members of the Junto the Library Company (the earliest circulating or lending library in America), and was one of the founders of the Philadelphia Academy and College (which eventually became the University of Pennsylvania).

Franklin was in his late thirties when he became interested in electrical phenomena because of attending the lectures in Boston in 1743 of Dr. Spencer from Scotland. Fascinated by what he witnessed, Franklin declared that although the experiments on electricity "were imperfectly perform'd" yet "being on a subject quite new to me, they equally surpris'd and pleased me." (p. 596) But the decisive influence probably was due to Peter Collinson, an English manufacturer, naturalist, and Fellow of the Royal Society, who sent to the Library Company an account of recent electrical experiments in Germany along with a glass tube with instructions as to how it could be used to replicate those experiments. As Franklin wrote some years later, this gave him "the opportunity of repeating what I had seen in Boston [. . .]." (p. 596)[23] Becoming progressively intrigued, Franklin in a letter to Collinson in 1747 thanking him for his communication, wrote that "I never was before engaged in any study that so totally engrossed my attention and my time as this has lately done . . ." (p. 597)

When Franklin and his friends in Philadelphia began their experiments the science of electricity, like all sciences in the early stages of development, was in disarray. Considerable experimental data had been accumulated, but no conceptual framework articulated that would account satisfactorily for the data. Dufay had differentiated two modes or kinds of electrification, the vitreous and resinous, to account for attraction and repulsion that gave rise to the two-fluid theory; Desaguliers' distinction between "electrics *per se*"(bodies that can be electrified by rubbing) and "non-electrics"(bodies that could not be electrified by rubbing but could receive an electric charge by contact) led to the conception of nonconductors (like glass and amber in which the electric "*effluvia* or *virtue*" could be generated but not easily transmitted) and conductors (bodies in which the electric fluid could not be generated, such as metals and wood, but readily transmitted); Abbé Nollet explained attraction and repulsion as due to an electric fluid identical to fire and light that circulated among bodies in a vortex passing in ("*afflux*") and out ("*efflux*") of two sets of pores as divergent and convergent rectilinear rays thereby attracting or repelling objects;[24] William Watson (at once mentor and friendly rival of Franklin) developed a theory of an "electrified aether" as a kind of elementary fire "formed by the creator" whose subtlety and elasticity enabled it to pervade all bodies, while its varying densities accounted for their attraction and repulsion;[25] Benjamin Martin (an ardent admirer of Newton) believed he was following Newton when he considered electricity to be a "subtle matter, or spirit" engendered by "the vibratory motion of the parts of an electric body, excited by friction;"[26] and Benjamin Wilson (another follower of Newton) who attempted to demonstrate by experiment that the properties of electricity agree with those of an aether assumed to be the general cause of physical phenomena, concluding "that the aether and electric matter are the same, or productive of the same effects."[27]

Despite the proliferation of these ingenious theories, none provided a satisfactory explanation of the phenomena in the sense of showing how the properties and behavior of electrics could be deduced from the theories, nor did they lead to accurate predictions. Perhaps Franklin succeeded owing not only to his ingenuity, but also because he worked closely with other experimenters in Philadelphia, was informed by the current research in Europe, and yet was sufficiently removed from these latter developments that he would be guided more by experimental results than by theoretical presuppositions. Whatever the cause, Franklin had the unusual trait of being especially critical of his own experimental interpretations and open-minded to the investigations of others. Furthermore, he was frank in admitting his misgivings and mistakes, being quite willing to revise his views as new experimental evidence deemed necessary. The following statement in a letter to Collinson in March 1747 thanking him for his present of the electric tube clearly indicates this attitude.

> On some further experiments [. . .] I have observ'd a phenomenon or two that I cannot at present account for on the principles laid down [. . .] and have therefore become a little diffident of my hypothesis, and asham'd that I have express'd myself in so positive a manner. In going on with these experiments, how many pretty systems do we build, which we soon find ourselves oblig'd to destroy! If there is no other use discover'd of electricity, this, however, is something considerable, that it may *help to make a vain man humble.* (p. 600)

As Franklin's financial condition at the time afforded him ample leisure, he immediately began duplicating the experiments on electrics that he had witnessed in Boston and heard about from Collinson, requesting similar glass tubes to be blown in the local glasshouse to distribute to his friends so they could perform their experiments independently. In the interim between 1743 and his first letter to Collinson in 1747, Franklin had received from Collinson an important publication by William Watson, *A Sequel to the experiments and observations tending to illustrate the nature and properties of electricity,* published in London in 1746. After reading the latter, Franklin felt confident enough of the progress he and his associates had made that he wrote Collinson a second letter in May stating they not only had performed experiments similar to those described by Watson in his *Sequel*, but had discovered "some particulars not hinted in that piece" (p. 598), and even ventured to correct a false conclusion drawn by Watson that the flow of electricity can be bidirectional.   Considering that Watson was regarded as "the leading electrician in England," this was no mean accomplishment.

In the same letter Franklin went on to describe the experiments and state those "particulars" that he claimed went beyond Watson's investigations, introducing the interpretation of electrical charges and conduction in terms of "positive" and "negative" electrification for which he became famous. The major experiment consisted of three individuals, A, B and C, with A and B standing on blocks of wax and therefore insulated so that whatever charge they received was not lost by conduction, while C stood on the floor near them. If, *while* A is rubbing the tube, B extends his finger to the tube a spark will pass between the tube and his finger. *After* this discharge, if C extends his hand to either A or B a spark will occur, but if A and B touch *each other* *while* the tube is being rubbed by A and discharged by B, C will not receive a spark from either of them, indicating they are unelectrified. However, if *after* the tube has been rubbed and B has drawn a spark from it, A and B touch each other, an unusually strong spark occurs between them, following which neither will be electrified.

These experimental results were then analyzed by Franklin as follows. First, he assumed that before the experiment each of the three individuals had an equal share of a common element he calls "electrical fire." Second, by rubbing the glass tube A drew some of this electric fire from his body onto the tube and, because he was insulated by the wax, his body was not resupplied. Third, extending his finger to the tube, B drew the excess charge that had been collected on the tube from A's body and because he too was insulated, he retained this additional charge.   Fourth, C being uncharged when he approached B *received* a spark from B "who has an over-quantity" of the electric fire (having received it from the tube), while when he approaches A he *gives* a charge to A "who has an under-quantity" of the electric fire (A's body having lost some electrification to the tube). (cf. p. 598) Fifth, the reason the spark between A and B was so strong when they touched each other *after* B had received a discharge from the tube was because the *difference* between their respective charges was then the greatest, A's body having lost and B's gained some electrical charge.   Sixth, the reason A and B were not charged if they touched each other *when* B received a spark from the excited tube is that the electric fire was merely circulating between them, leaving A and B neutralized, while the cause of A and B being no longer electrified when they touch each other *after* B had received a charge from the tube is that the excess charge in B was returned to A, leaving them in equilibrium.

Having analyzed the experimental results, Franklin then explains them using the concepts of "positive (plus)" and "negative (minus)" electrification introduced by the Philadelphia experimenters, as follows.[28] (cf. pp. 598-9) (1) All unelectrified bodies contain an "equal share" of a single electric fire or fluid; (2) that electrification is not generated by the vibration of particles caused by the friction of rubbing, as the followers of Newton claimed, but by the transfer of the electric fire from one body to another; (3) that rubbing draws or "collects" the electric fire on the body rubbed from the body doing the rubbing, or in the case of resinous materials draws the electric fire of the body rubbed and gives it to the body doing the rubbing; (4) a neutral conductor brought near a charged body will either draw off the excess electric charge or donate some to the body, depending upon its state of electrification, until equilibrium is reached; (5) electrical conduction consists of an electrified body *giving* its excess of electric charge to a lesser charged body or *receiving* an electric charge from a greater charged body; (6) the transfer of this excess charge is what causes electrical attraction; (7) two bodies each having an equal excess of electric charge (Franklin did not consider the case of two bodies with an equal deficiency of electric charge) will repel each other because their attempt to pass on their electric charges will create an opposition; (8) neutral bodies or those in equilibrium neither attract nor repel because there is no flow of electrification; (9) the electric fire is neither created or destroyed, its total quantity remaining constant, any excess or deficiency in charge ultimately tending to return to equilibrium; (10) not knowing Dufay's terms "vitreous" and "resinous" electrification, the Philadelphia experimenters introduced the terms "positive" or "plus" to designate electrified objects with an excess of electrical fire and "negative" or "minus" to denote those having lost some electric charge, the direction of the flow of electricity (according to this convention) always proceeding from the positive to the negative until equilibrium is reached.

As Franklin expressed this last conclusion:

Hence have arisen some new terms among us. We say *B* (and bodies like circumstanced) is electrified *positively*; *A negatively*. Or rather, *B* is charged *plus*; *A minus*. And we daily in our experiments electrize *plus* or *minus* as we think proper. To electrize *plus* or *minus* no more needs to be known than this: the parts of the tube or sphere which are rubbed do, in the instant of friction, attract the electrical fire, and therefore take it from the thing rubbing; the same parts immediately, as the friction on them ceases, are disposed to give the fire they have received to any body that has less. Thus you may circulate it, as *Mr. Watson* has done. You may also accumulate or subtract it, upon or from any body, as you connect that body with the rubber or with the receiver [if it is insulated], the communication with the common stock being cut off. (pp. 598-9; brackets added)

Even though Franklin and his friends benefited from their knowledge of the research of Watson, still, it was a remarkable achievement to have formulated in less than four years a conceptual framework that accounted for nearly all the experimental phenomena in a consistent explanation. Moreover, a striking advantage of this interpretation is that it lent itself to quantification, the plus and minus charges subject to measurement, as Franklin indicated in a third letter to Collinson in July containing his explanation of the function of the Leyden jar. Because on Franklin's theory the total quantity of electrification in a system must be conserved, when the *inner coating* of the Leyden jar is electricized by *gaining* an external charge through the wire in the cork of the jar, this must be compensated by an equivalent *loss* of electrification on the *outer coating* of the jar which, since it is grounded, is passed on to the earth. The glass separating the inner and outer coatings being a non-conductor, the excess charge on the inner coating somehow must force an equivalent amount of electrification on the outer surface to be discharged to the earth.

This transfer of electric charge through a nonconductor is called "electrification by influence" and its possible quantification suggested as follows.

To understand this, suppose the common quantity of electricity in each part of the bottle, before the operation begins, is equal to 20; and at every stroke of the glass tube [which is connected to the inner coating], suppose a quantity equal to 1 is put in; then, after the first stroke, the quantity contain'd in the inner coating of the bottle will be 21, in the outer coating 19. After the second, the inner coating will be 22, the outer 18, and so one, till, after 20 strokes the inner coating will have a quantity of electricity equal to 40, the outer coating none;

and then the operation ends, for no more can be thrown into the inner
part when no more can be driven from the outer part. If you attempt
to throw more in, it is spued back through the wire, or flies out in
load cracks through the sides of the bottle. (pp. 601-2)

While this example of quantification is an idealization not to be taken
literally, Franklin did devise an experiment to show that when the inner
coating was charged positively the outer coating was equivalently charged
negatively, and that if the two coatings were simultaneously connected
externally by a wire, equilibrium was instantly established. In addition,
Franklin argued that if the jar were insulated rather than grounded the inner
part would not be electrified because an equivalent amount of electric fire
could not be drawn off the outer coating. Finally, in another experiment he
demonstrated that the charge accumulated in the jar when it was disconnected
from the rubber was not stored in the water, as supposed, but contained in the
glass itself.

Thus, the whole force of the bottle, and power of giving a shock, is
in the GLASS ITSELF; the non-electrics [metal coatings] in contact
with the two surfaces, serving only to *give* and *receive* to and from the
several parts of the glass; that is, to give on one side, and take away
on the other.[29]

Not satisfied with this macro-account of the flow of electricity to and from
bodies with a depletion or excess of the fire, Franklin attempted a micro-
explanation in a paper entitled "Opinions and Conjectures concerning the
Properties and Effects of the Electric Matter, arising from Experiments and
Observations made at Philadelphia, 1749."[30] Assuming the electric fire or
matter (as he now calls it), because it can penetrate all substances including
hard metals, consists of very subtle particles, if these particles (like those of
gases) are elastic and repel each other, then the repelling effect of two
positively charged bodies can be attributed to these particles. Furthermore,
although *mutually repellent*, if these particles are *attracted* by those of
ordinary matter, then in a neutral body they will be neutralized because of
being uniformly distributed throughout the body. If a conductor loses electric
particles by their being drawn off, then the material particles will tend to
attract additional electric particles from another body to restore equilibrium.
According to Cohen, Franklin answers Watson's criticism as to how bodies
can acquire an excess of electric matter if they only can retain only a quantity

of electric particles equivalent to their material particles, by claiming that it does "not enter the body but collects on its surface to form an 'electric atmosphere,' in which case the body 'is said to be electrified.'"[31] Bodies vary in their capacity to absorb this electric matter (presumably due to their different structures), electrics *per se* capable of absorbing the greatest quantities. This conception of an "electric atmosphere" was not new (going back at least to Dufay), but Franklin modified it by claiming that it takes the shape of the body it envelops rather than being spherical. Ultimately, the flow of the electric fluid along with the properties of repulsion and attraction were explained in terms of this concept of electric atmosphere composed of electric particles.[32]

Despite its superiority over rival explanations, there was one property of electric phenomena that threatened Franklin's theory because it could not account for it, the well-known fact that negatively as well as positively charged bodies repel each other, a phenomenon Franklin did not encounter until 1748. On Franklin's theory there was no reason two bodies, each retaining a lesser quantity of electric particles than normal, should repulse each other. However, as is usually the case in such instances, if despite an anomaly a theory explains most of the phenomena better than rival theories, then it is retained in the hope that the anomaly later will be removed, either by a new discovery or by some ingenious revision of the theory. The latter proved to be true in this instance when Franz V.T. Aepinus introduced an important new assumption to Franklin's theory.

The revolutionary idea of Aepinus was that in solids, liquids, and gases the particles of what Franklin called "common matter" repel one another just like the particles of the electric fluid in Franklin's theory. Aepinus's revision introduced a complete duality. The particles of common matter and of electric matter each have the property of repelling particles of their own kind while each kind of particle has the additional property of attracting particles of the other kind.[33]

With this assumption Aepinus could remove the anomaly of negatively charged bodies repelling each other because such bodies, retaining fewer electrical particles than required to produce equilibrium, would have an excess of material particles which, repelling each other, explains why negatively charged bodies repulse each other. As often happens, however, this new assumption, as Aepinus realized, contradicted Newton's law that all material particles exert an attractive force (accounting for the solidity of matter) proportional to their masses and inversely proportional to the square of the distances. Attempting to eliminate the contradiction, Aepinus maintained that in unelectrified bodies the attractive force between electric particles and the material particles neutralize the repulsive force of the latter, so that "the universal gravitational attraction of Newton can remain unaffected, even though one admits that there may exist a repulsion of some kind."[34]

That this *ad hoc* effort to save Franklin's one-fluid theory proved unconvincing was pointed out later by Charles Coulomb who wrote:

> It appears to me contradictory to admit at the same time, in the particles of bodies, an attractive force [. . .] demonstrated by universal gravitation, and a repulsive force [. . .]—a force that would necessarily be incomparably larger than that due to gravitation. (p. 622)

Aepinus further emended Franklin's theory by discarding the vague concept of an electric atmosphere, maintaining that two positively charged bodies repel each other because of the excess of electric matter collecting directly on the surface of the body, not in an atmosphere surrounding it.[35] Aepinus thus eliminated the electric atmosphere, retaining the electric particles.

Although Franklin was influenced by Watson's investigations in formulating his own theory, he was correct in asserting that his went beyond Watson's in certain "particulars." Yet when Watson learned of Franklin's explanation he sincerely believed that it was identical to his own, but without resorting to the usual contentious challenges to priority—such as tarnished the luster of Hooke's and Newton's reputations. As Cohen states:

> Although Watson claimed at one point that Franklin's theory of electrical action was the same as his own, it is pleasant to be able to report a complete absence of acrimony between Franklin and Watson. Watson, in fact, referred to Franklin's work in the highest of terms from the very beginning. The first notice in print of Franklin's research was in the articles written by Watson, which included long extracts from Franklin's letters—the first publication of any of his scientific discoveries. When Franklin's book on electricity was published in London in 1751, Watson wrote an enthusiastic review for the *Philosophical Transactions*. [. . .] It was Watson who introduced the motion that Franklin be elected a Fellow of the Royal Society.[36]

There were in fact certain general similarities between the electric theories of Watson and Franklin, such as that all bodies contain a single electric fluid and that the flow of electricity was from "denser" (Watson) or "plus" (Franklin) electric charges to less dense or minus charges; yet the differences were specific enough that experimentally testable implications could be drawn from them demonstrating the superiority of Franklin's conceptual framework.[37] Moreover, the fact that Franklin showed that his conception of positive (plus) and negative (minus) electrification could be quantified, whereas Watson did not, added to the superiority of his theory.

Franklin's originality is additionally disclosed in the practical applications he drew from his theory that brought him international acclaim. While Gray had suggested that electric discharges and lightning were of the same "nature," in an entry in his experimental notebook for November 7, 1749, Franklin indicated twelve ways "the electric fluid agrees with lightning [. . .]." (pp. 604-5) Then in the paper entitled "Opinions and Conjectures" containing his theory of electric particles sent to Collinson in 1750, he included a description of the difference in electric discharges between pointed and blunt objects, along with an account of his belief that clouds were electrified as manifested in bolts of lightning.

Noting that pointed objects draw electric force at a greater distance and with more facility than blunt objects, Franklin wondered whether this effect might also apply to thunder clouds, so that pointed rods could be used to deflect lightning from vulnerable objects. As he stated,

> may not the knowledge of this power of points be of use to mankind, in preserving houses, churches, ships, etc. from the stroke of lightning, by directing us to fix on the highest parts of those edifices, upright rods of iron made sharp as a needle, and gilt to prevent rusting, and from the foot of those rods a wire down the outside of the building into the ground, or down around one of the shrouds of a ship, and down her side until it reaches the water? Would not these pointed rods probably draw the electricity silently out of a cloud before it came nigh enough to strike, and thereby secure us from that most sudden and terrible mischief? (p. 606)

However, before these practical consequences could be put to use Franklin first had to demonstrate that storm clouds were charged. To test this he suggested that if on a high tower or church spire a sentry box were constructed with an iron rod attached to the insulated floor (so the rod would retain any electrification) and then the pointed end extended twenty or thirty feet into the air, when low thunderclouds passed an experimenter in the box could test whether the clouds had discharged any electricity to the rod by observing whether he could draw a charge from the rod to himself. While not foreseeing any danger, Franklin cautioned that it would be safer if one held a grounded conductor by a wax handle and used it to detect any discharge. Although Franklin did not try the experiment himself (perhaps because there were no suitably high promontory in Philadelphia), the experiment was performed at Marly in France in May, 1752, confirming Franklin's suppositions.[38]

Then in the following October he wrote Collinson that he too had verified the results in a different manner, the famous kite experiment. With the help of his son he attached a wire to the top of a kite tied to a kempen cord, while to the end reaching the ground he fastened a metal key and a silk ribbon. At the outbreak of a thunderstorm they raised the kite and then ran into a shed permitting the cord to become wet making it a more effective conductor, but protecting the silk ribbon tied to the cord which they held as an insulation against possible electrification. As Franklin predicted, when the storm broke a discharge of electricity passed from the clouds to the wire on the kite down the moistened cord to the metal key where it collected until they released it into a Leyden jar. (cf. p. 606)

In another variation of the same principle, Franklin caused the electric discharge from a storm cloud to pass down a wire at the side of his house to a metal frame holding two iron bells with metal clappers which, when electrically attracted to the bells, produced a ringing sound. While the experimental tests devised by Franklin should have occurred to anyone, many other experimenters throughout Europe had surmised that it is the electric charge in storm clouds that produces lightning, hence the latter is a bolt of electricity, yet none had suggested an experimental test. That Franklin proposed a confirming experiment is the reason, despite the contribution of other investigators, that "scientists of the eighteenth century, such as Watson, [. . .] referred to the 'verification of Mr. *Franklin's* hypothesis.'"[39]

The success of these experiments made Franklin the preeminent "electrician" of his age spreading his fame throughout Europe. His book, *Experiments and Observations on Electricity* (1752), went through numerous printings and was translated into French and German. In the following year he was awarded the Royal Society's highest distinction, the Copley Gold Medal. Joseph Priestly, in his authoritative *History of Electricity* (1767), wrote that Franklin's proof that lightning is an electrical discharge is "a 'capital discovery'—the greatest, perhaps, since the time of Sir Isaac Newton."[40] Just to be mentioned along with Newton was the highest praise possible. Although

Franklin's conceptual framework attributing two kinds of matter to ordinary objects, particles whose mutual attraction creates an equilibrium, only hinted at the later saturnian conception of the atom composed of positively charged protons and negatively charged electrons (along with neutrally charged neutrons), whose atomic number accounts for the chemical properties of the elements, it served to guide electrical research during the latter half of the eighteenth century. With the kind of prescience characteristic of great scientists, Franklin seemed to foresee that the physical structure and properties of different kinds of substances someday would be explained in terms of their electric constituents, as he suggests in one passage:

> [. . .] if that due quantity of electrical fire so obstinately retained by glass, could be separated from it, it would no longer be glass; it might lose its transparency, or its brittleness, or its elasticity. . . . Experiments may possibly be invented hereafter, to discover this.[41]

COULOMB'S LAW

Given Newton's success in discovering an exact quantitative law that unified terrestrial and celestial mechanics along with Franklin's suggestion that positive (plus) and negative (minus) electric charges could be quantified, a concerted effort was made to discover whether the occurrence of electric phenomena also followed precise quantitative laws—further evidence of the growing confidence that physical phenomena were not capricious or magical, but manifestations of a discoverable underlying causal order. Since Franklin had introduced the principle of the constancy of electric charge, any transfer of electricity should be subject to precise quantitative measurements. Drawing an analogy between Newton's law that gravitational force is a function of mass, distance, and gravitational forces, perhaps electrical forces also could be a function of an electric force, mass, and spatial separation. In 1760 the Swiss physicist, Daniel Bernoulli, devised an electrometer for measuring directly the strength of "the electric force between two charged metal disks when they were at known distances apart" (p. 610), finding in fact that the force varied inversely with the square of the distance.

Priestley (who later would discover oxygen) had begun writing his history of electricity when he met Franklin in London in 1765 and perhaps as a result of his discussions with Franklin began electrical investigations on his own. Replicating one of Franklin's experiments, he confirmed that pitch balls suspended within an electrified vessel, regardless of their distance from the inner surface, were not attracted and thus evinced a net charge of zero. Realizing the similarity between this and Newton's mathematical demonstration, based on the law of gravitation, that the net gravitational force on an object placed anywhere within the hollowed earth would be zero, Priestley inferred that the same inverse square law should apply to the attractive force of electric bodies.

> May we not infer from this experiment that the attraction of electricity is subject to the same laws with that of gravitation, and is therefore according to the [inverse] squares of the distance; since it is easily demonstrated that, were the earth in the form of a shell, a body in the inside of it would not be attracted to one side more than another. (p. 613)

While Priestley deduced his law based on the analogy with gravity, Charles Coulomb (1736-1806) developed an electrical torsion balance so exact that it could measure "with the greatest exactitude the electrical force exerted by a body, however slightly the body is charged" (p. 617), finding that the *repulsive* force between two identically electrified bodies is inversely proportional to the square of the distance. But because electric forces are both attractive and repulsive (unlike gravity which is solely attractive), for a general law to apply, Coulomb had to find whether the *attractive* force between electric bodies also diminished with the square of the distance. To demonstrate this he developed an electric torsion *pendulum* with the same result as previously, thereby justifying a complete generalization of the law, as he claimed.

> We have thus come, by a method completely different from the first, to a similar result. We may therefore conclude that the mutual attraction of the electrical fluid called positive and the electrical fluid ordinarily called negative is inversely proportional to the square of the distance; just as we have found [. . .] that the mutual repulsion of electric fluids of the same sort is proportional to the square of the distance. (pp. 620-21)

If electric forces conform to the same distance law as gravitational forces, do they also agree with the other aspect of Newton's law, that the strength of the gravitational force is proportional to the product of the masses (density per volume)? While an "electric fire" would not seem to possess mass, Franklin's later theory of common and electric matter composed of particles that exert opposite forces among themselves but are mutually attractive suggested an affirmative answer. Such a conclusion must have occurred to Coulomb who applied Newton's formula of gravitational attraction to electrical attraction, substituting "electric mass" for that of ordinary matter: "If two objects, having charges q_1 and q_2, are separated by a distance d, the Coulomb force law tells us that each object will experience a force proportional to $(q_1)(q_2)/d^2$." (p. 621) That electric states and forces could be quantified analogous to gravity, their equations having the same mathematical form, exemplified two major features of the ensuing body of scientific knowledge: that it increasingly would disclose quantifiable relations along with a tendency toward unification. Although the distance law had been affirmed by others, the fact that Coulomb demonstrated experimentally the full generality of the law, and then expressed it in a precise mathematical formula, has resulted in its being called "Coulomb's Law." As the previous long quotation indicates, he did not favor Franklin's one-fluid theory of electricity, preferring Dufay's hypothesis of two electric fluids, one vitreous and the other resinous. But the discovery of the atomic-molecular structure of different kinds of substances in terms of their electrically charged particles and atomic forces would have to await the dawn of the twentieth century.

INVESTIGATIONS OF THE NATURE
AND TRANSMISSION OF LIGHT

As the source of light and heat the sun and fire have long occupied a lofty position in the thought of mankind, *Helios* and *Sol* being the sun gods respectively of the Greeks and the Romans. Believing fire to be of greater significance than the earth, the Pythagoreans replaced the latter's geocentric position by a central fire, calling it the 'Hearth of the World' and the 'Throne of Zeus.' In the *Republic* Plato declared that 'of all the divinities of the skies' the sun is the most glorious because it not only makes things visible and thus gives to the objects of vision their power of being seen, but also their nourishment and existence.[42] Owing to its approach and recession correlated with the changing seasons, Aristotle called the sun the "generator," attributing to it the growth and decay of living things. Plotinus and the Neoplatonists described the three *hypostases* or superfluities of reality analogous to the radiation of the sun and the Good in the *Republic*. Due partially to the influence of these Pythagorean, Platonic or Neoplatonic doctrines, Copernicus and Kepler were willing to cede to the sun the central place in the universe.

Yet despite this glorification of the sun, little was known about the nature of light and its manner of transmission until the seventeenth century investigations into geometric optics (dealing with the geometric properties of light rays) and physical optics (concerned with the composition of light and its manner of propagation). By the time of Newton, Descartes' conception of light as an optical physiological effect caused by the instantaneous ''pression'' of the motionless, contiguous particles comprising the fluid vortices of the universe was the dominant theory Newton attempted to refute in the *Opticks* of 1704.

Earlier in the *Principia*, Newton had rejected Descartes' theory of vortices on the grounds that it could not account for such obvious astronomical phenomena as eclipses and was inconsistent with Kepler's three laws. His criticisms of Descartes' optical theory were based primarily on the fact that if light consisted of an instantaneously transmitted pressure among the vortical particles this would require an infinite force, could not explain how light heated objects, and would imply that it bent around small obstacles like water waves rather than produce the sharp shadows characteristic of rays of light.

> If Light consisted only in Pression propagated without actual Motion, it would not be able to agitate and heat the Bodies which refract and reflect it. If it consisted in Motion propagated to all distances in an instant, it would require an infinite force every moment, in every shining Particle, to generate that Motion. And if it consisted in Pression Motion [. . .] it would bend into the Shadow. For Pression of Motion cannot be propagated in a Fluid in right lines [. . .] but will bend and spread every way into the quiescent Medium which lies beyond the Obstacle.[43]

Believing that these and other optical phenomena such as colored rings (produced when rays striking dense transparent substances are partially reflected and partially refracted due to their ''Fits of easy Reflexion and easy Transmission''), and the double refraction of ''Island-Crystal'' could more satisfactorily be explained by considering light rays to be minuscule particles emitted by luminous bodies, Newton advocated the corpuscular theory.[44] Although he was aware of Huygens alternative explanation of these phenomena in terms of waves, the sharp shadows cast by light and the heuristic success of the particulate theory in other areas of physics led him to believe that the corpuscular theory offered the greatest promise for explaining optical phenomena as well. As he rhetorically asks in Query 29:

> Are not the Rays of Light very small Bodies emitted from shining [luminous] Substances? For such Bodies will pass through uniform Mediums in right [straight] Lines without bending into the Shadow, which is the Nature of Rays of Light. They will also be capable of several Properties, and be able to conserve their Properties unchanged in passing through several Mediums, which is another Condition of the Rays of Light. (Brackets added)

In his earlier prism experiments Newton had demonstrated that ordinary light is composed of colored rays with different refractive powers, their dispersion causes by the sloping surface of the prism, while attributing the different colors and refractive indexes to the various sizes of the corpuscles. Moreover, conceiving rays of light to be composed of particles analogous to material bodies enabled him to utilize attractive and repulsive forces in explaining optical phenomena, a mode of explanation that had proven so successful in accounting for gravitational attraction and the elasticity of gases. Since the wave theory did not countenance forces, it must have seemed to Newton a much less promising theory. Even the phenomenon of double refraction of Iceland Crystal he (erroneously) believed could be explained as due to the "opposite Sides" of the corpuscles, rather than to the polarization of waves. Again as he clearly states in Query 29.

> Nothing more is requisite for producing all the variety of Colours, and degrees of Refrangibility, than that the Rays of Light be Bodies of different Sizes, the least [smallest] of which may take violet [the] weakest and darkest of the Colours, and be more easily diverted by refracting Surfaces from the right Course; and the rest as they are bigger and bigger, may make the stronger and more lucid Colours, blue, green, yellow, and red, and be more and more difficultly diverted. (Brackets added)

Having explained the variety of spectral colors in terms of the sizes of corpuscles, Newton then utilizes "attractive powers" or "Forces" to account for other optical phenomena.

Nothing more is requisite for putting the Rays of Light into Fits of easy Reflexion and easy Transmission, than that they be small Bodies which by their *attractive Powers*, or some other *Force*, stir up Vibrations in what they act upon [. . .] and thereby put them into those Fits. And lastly, the unusual Refraction of Island-Crystal looks very much as if it were perform'd by some kind of *attractive virtue* lodged in certain Sides both of the Rays, and of the Particles of the Crystal. (Italics added)

The predominance of the corpuscular theory of light throughout the eighteenth century usually is attributed to the authority of Newton, but the fact that a particulate theory of light conformed to the progressive application of the atomic theory probably has as much to do with its nearly universal acceptance as the authority of Newton.

The first person to challenge seriously the dominant position of the particle theory was Thomas Young at the beginning of the nineteenth century. In a paper published in 1800 in the *Philosophical Transactions*, entitled "Outlines of Experiments and Inquiries Respecting Sound and Light,"[45] Young highlighted the analogy between light and sound. Unlike the *corpuscular theory* that interpreted *light* as consisting of particles ejected by luminous bodies and propelled through space at tremendous but finite velocities, the *wave theory of sound* invoked a succession of spherical waves consisting of intervals of compression and rarification in some elastic medium (such as air or aether) produced by vibrations or percussions (as by an electronic speaker) in the medium. The expanding concentric waves are not themselves advancing particles but wave configurations or states of motion of the oscillating particles composing the medium.

Thus the properties of particles and waves are just the converse of each other: particles described by mass, momentum, and the energy of motion have a discrete localization in space and interact by deflection with a loss of momentum or energy, while waves characterized by lengths, frequencies, amplitudes, and intensities are diffused in space as wave trains and interact so as to reinforce (if in phase) or destruct (if out of phase). The velocity of a particle is a dynamic state affected by forces that is greatest in a vacuum, while waves are undulations (normally) in a medium produced by a vibratory source with a velocity proportional to the wave length and frequency.

In his initial paper Young attempted to mitigate some of the opposition to the wave theory while raising objections to the particle theory that previously had been overlooked. The first objection pertains to the fact that if light rays were composed of particles, then these particles would be subject to gravitational forces so that their velocities when emitted from luminous bodies would vary with the strength of the gravitation attraction exerted by the bodies. Yet in a uniform medium light travels with an invariant velocity. As Young ironically observes,

> whether the projecting force is the slightest transmission of electricity, the friction of 2 pebbles, the lowest degree of visible ignition, the white heat of a wind furnace, or the intense heat of the sun itself, these wonderful corpuscles are always propelled with one uniform velocity. (p. 17)

This does not pose a similar problem for the wave theory because waves were not thought to be affected by gravity and were propagated in an elastic aether always with the same velocity.

The second objection pertains to Newton's explanation of the partial reflection and transmission of light when directed through two lenses separated by a thin film of air that produces bright rings (Newton's rings) where some of the light is reflected and dark rings where some are transmitted. According to Newton, this phenomenon can be explained as "Fits of easy Reflexion and easy Transmission" caused by the particles producing vibrations in the medium which, having a greater velocity than the particles, overtake them and by agitating them increase or decrease their velocities producing the "fits." (cf. p. 14) Young believed that an explanation in terms of light waves would remove the need for this *ad hoc* hypothesis.

But Young's major contribution to the wave theory resulted from his experiments producing diffraction patterns, clear evidence of waves. He demonstrated that when monochromatic light is directed to a screen which has a circular opening which is large relative to the wave length or color of the light a circular illumination is produced on a second screen behind the first, but that if the diameter of the aperture is reduced to about the dimension of the wave length then alternating light and dark bands are produced on the posterior screen. In another experiment consisting of two holes sufficiently small and close together and a beam of monochromatic light directed at a point midway between the openings, the emerging light again will form alternating bright and dark bands on the posterior screen. A definite indication of diffraction, in a paper published in 1802 entitled "On the Theory of Light and Colours," Young describes these bands in terms of what is known as constructive (in phase) and destructive (out of phase) interference. As he states: "[w]hen two undulations, from different origins, coincide, either perfectly or very nearly in

direction, their joint effect is a combination of the motions belonging to each"
(p. 19), while if they do not coincide they destruct. The intensity of the wave
is established by the number of coincident waves.

Even though Young interpreted these results as due to the interference of
rays (as was customary), his experiments obviously demonstrated diffraction
patterns characteristic of waves. Yet so strongly entrenched was the
corpuscular theory that his demonstrations met with hostility rather than
approbation. Henry Brougham, who ardently adhered to Newton's theory,
described Young's 1802 paper as "destitute of every species of merit [. . .]."
(p. 19) However, the paper did produce a resonance in the thinking of
Augustine Jean Fresnel, a brilliant French engineer, who attacked the
corpuscular explanation of diffraction and repulsion on the grounds that it
depended upon implausible hypotheses that could be experimentally refuted.
For example, according to the corpuscular theory the light and dark bands
produced when homogeneous light is transmitted through a small aperture is
caused by attractive or repelling forces on the light corpuscles due to the
particular shape and mass of the aperture's edges. But when Fresnel tested
this hypothesis by modifying the aperture's mass and shape, no evidence of
any change in the diffraction pattern was observed. Finding that the pattern
only varied with the size of the aperture relative to the monochromatic light
wave, he concluded that we must "reject any hypothesis which assigns these
phenomena to attractive and repulsive forces [. . .]" (p. 20)

Fresnel's own interpretation of diffraction was presented in a "Memoir on
the Diffraction of Light" which was awarded a prize by the Paris Academy in
1819. Unlike Young's qualitative description of his experiments demonstrating
diffraction, Fresnel contributed a mathematical analysis of diffraction based on
the physical properties of waves, such as their lengths, frequencies, amplitudes,
and intensities. Appealing to "Huygen's principle" that at every point where
a light wave strikes a diffracting surface a new secondary, circular wave is
produced, Fresnel attempts, as Achinstein states,

> to determine quantitatively [. . .] the resultant vibration at any point
> behind the diffracting device. His account is much more sophisticated
> than Young's, not only because it is quantitative, but also because in
> determining the resulting vibration it considers wave contributions
> from all points on the wave front [. . .] Fresnel derives mathematical
> expressions for the amplitude of the vibration at any point behind the
> diffractor, and for the light intensity at that point. From these he
> infers the positions and intensities of the diffraction bands—inferences

that were confirmed experimentally. (p. 21)

Nothing convinces modern scientists as much as a mathematical representation of physical properties that leads to experimental confirmation of the magnitudes of those properties, especially when this is accompanied by the prediction of new experimental results. In Fresnel's case, not only were the above interpretations experimentally confirmed, when Simeon-Denis Poisson (a judge on the panel awarding the prize) read Fresnel's essay he inferred that when the diffractor is a circular disk the resultant shadow should contain in its center a bright spot, a prediction subsequently confirmed. (cf. p. 21) Furthermore, the inability to explain the polarization of light rays emerging from Iceland-Spar or crystal based on the assumption that light, as sound, consists of longitudinal waves (which led to Newton's attributing different sides to the corpuscles constituting the rays) was surmounted when Fresnel concluded that light waves were transverse, produced by vibrations perpendicular (up and down) to the light undulations. Because the waves are transverse, when they are beamed on a doubly refracting crystal the internal structure of the crystal divides the vibration into perpendicular directions with two different velocities. Thus the two emerging rays will be polarized at right angles to each other such that if either ray passes into another Iceland spar it will be transmitted or again split into two rays depending on the relative angles of polarization of the ray and the spar. Since some of these phenomena could not be explained on the corpuscular theory, Fresnel's interpretation of polarization vindicated Huygens belief in the wave theory. Fresnel even removed the crucial objection to the wave theory, based on the sharp outline of shadows cast by large objects, by showing that the destruction of light waves at the edges of their propagation accounts for the ray-like appearance, but that if the magnitude of the obstacle is of the order of the wave length then light bends around the obstacle as sound waves do. Finally, when there are just two major competing theories to explain certain phenomena, as is usually the case in science, the most striking instances of confirmation occur when the theories imply contradictory consequences that can be tested (the most dramatic instance of this previously was Galileo's telescopic observation of the phases of Venus predicted on the heliocentric but not the geocentric theory).

Two examples of optical phenomena allowed for these diverse predictions derived from the corpuscular and wave theories. One pertained to predictions related to Newton's rings, because the wave theory implies "that the intervals between the rings produced by the perpendicular incidence of light should be black, whereas this should not be the case for the particle theory." (p. 22) In devising an experiment to test this, Fresnel unequivocally found the results in accord with the wave theory. The second prediction is related to the change of velocity of light in passing from a less dense medium (air) to one of greater density (water or glass). Based on the corpuscular theory Newton had predicted that when passing into a denser medium light not only would be refracted according to Snell's law, but also would have its velocity accelerated due to the greater attractive power on the light corpuscles of the more massive particles comprising the denser medium. The wave theory, in contrast, implied that the secondary waves predicted by Huygens caused by the diffraction of light would be retarded in passing into the denser medium. In what is often cited as an *experimentum crucis,* Jean Leon Foucoult (1819-68) in a series of ingenious experiments begun in 1850 and published in 1862, confirmed that light travels more slowly in water or glass than in air, confirming the wave theory.

From these results Hippolyte Louis Fizeau (1819-96) determined the absolute velocity of light to be 300,000 kilometers per second.[46] Owing to these impressive developments in the mathematical characterization and experimental confirmation of the properties of light, by the middle of the eighteenth century the tide had turned from Newton's corpuscular to Huygen's wave theory of light. As John Herschel wrote in an article as early as 1827 summarizing the developments, while "neither the corpuscular nor the undulatory, nor any other system which had yet been devised, will furnish that complete and satisfactory explanation of *all* the phenomena of light"(p. 22), the wave theory stood out as the superior explanation. Despite Herschel's prescient observation of the limitations of the two theories, after the experiments of Fresnel, Foucoult, Fizeau and others, the wave theory superseded the corpuscular theory until 1905 when Einstein introduced the conception of discrete quanta of light called photons to explain the photoelectric effect.

Before bringing this discussion of the investigation of the nature and transmission of light subsequent to Newton to a close, some mention should be made of the discovery of electromagnetic fields. It was natural for Young and Fresnel, impressed with the similarity between light and sound waves to assume that light, as sound (which is not transmitted in a vacuum), requires a medium to be propagated. Because light, in contrast to sound, is transmitted through a vacuum, it was assumed that there must be an elastic medium, an aether, in which the propagation occurs. This conception of an elastic aether pervading the universe for the transmission of light seemed to support Newton's famous conjecture, at the end of Bk. III: THE SYSTEM OF THE

WORLD, that "a certain most subtle spirit [electrical or ethereal] which pervades and lies hid in all gross bodies"[47] might serve to explain such diverse phenomena as gravitational forces, electrical attraction and repulsion, the various properties of light, along with sensation and muscular control. It came as a considerable surprise, then, when developments late in the nineteenth century displaced the concept of the aether with that of a field.

Hans Christian Oerstead's (1777-1851) experiment on the effects of an electric current on the deflection of a magnetic needle showed that a changing electric current produced a magnetic field, while Michael Faraday's (1791-1867) experiments demonstrated that a changing magnetic field induced an electric current. The interdependence of these phenomena led to the conception of an electromagnetic field which was not the configuration of an underlying aether, but itself a reality. Based on the experimental results of Oerstead and Faraday, James Clerk Maxwell (1831-79) devised the equations describing the structure of the electromagnetic field and how it changes in space with time. Using Maxwell's equations it was demonstrated further that the velocity of the propagation of the waves of an electromagnetic field equals that of light, eventually leading to the conclusion that light too is an electromagnetic phenomenon. Einstein called this "discovery of an electromagnetic wave spreading with the speed of light [. . .] one of the greatest achievements in the history of science."[48]

Toward the end of the nineteenth century Heinrich Hertz (1857-94) experimentally confirmed the existence of electromagnetic waves with a velocity identical to that of light. Since electromagnetism depends upon the interaction of contiguous fields, rather than forces originating in spatially separate bodies acting at a distance, as in Newtonian science, the conceptual framework of electromagnetic fields represented a radical departure from the mechanistic mechanics of Newton. Doubts about the aether began when Michelson and Morely performed their interferometer experiments demonstrating the invariant velocity of light.

Since the experiment was conducted on the assumption that the earth's revolution in its orbit in relation to the stationary aether at rest in absolute space would produce an aether drift affecting differently the velocity of the perpendicularly reflected light rays, the null results of the experiment cast doubt on the existence of the aether, among other presuppositions. The demise of the aether finally occurred when Einstein accepted the invariant velocity of light among different inertial systems in his special theory of relativity and attempted to reduce Newtonian mechanics to electrodynamics in his general theory. As Max Born states:

Concerning the more geometrical laws of optics, reflection, refraction, double refraction, and polarization in crystals and so forth, the electromagnetic theory of light resolves all the difficulties that were quite insuperable for the theories of the elastic ether.[49]

But these developments bring us to the revolutionary changes in science beginning with the dawn of the twentieth century to be discussed in chapter XI.

NOTES

1. Frank Greenaway, *John Dalton And the Atom* (New York: Cornell University Press, 1966), p 26.

2. J. Bronowski and Bruce Mazlish, *The Western Intellectual Tradition* (New York: Harper & Row, Pub., [1960]1975), p. 333.

3. Cf. *ibid.*, pp. 316, 328-29.

4. Elizabeth C. Patterson, *John Dalton And the Atomic Theory* (Garden City: Doubleday & Co., Inc., 1970), p. 45.

5. *Ibid.*, p. 49.

6. Bronowski and Mazlish, *op. cit.*, p. 330.

7. Patterson, *op. cit.*, pp. 50-51.

8. *Ibid.*, p. 58.

9. *Ibid.*, p. 44.

10. *Ibid.*, p. 59.

11. William Gilbert, *De Magnete*, translated by P. Fleury Mottelay (New York: Dover Pub., Inc., 1958), cf. Bk. II, Ch. 2.

12. Augustine, *The City of God*, Bk. XXI, Sec. 4.

13. Cf. "The Development of the Concept of Electrical Charge: Electricity From the Greeks to Coulomb," Duane Roller and Duane H.D. Roller, in James B. Conant and Leonard K. Nash (eds.), *Harvard Case Histories in Experimental Science*, Vol. 2 (Cambridge: Harvard University Press, 1948), pp. 546-7. Unless otherwise indicated, the page references in the text are to this essay. I have found these case histories especially valuable in the present investigation.

14. William Gilbert, *op. cit.*, p. 92.

15. *Ibid.*, pp. 96-7.

16. Cf. Richard S. Westfall, *Never at Rest* (Cambridge: Cambridge University Press, 1980), pp. 632-3.

17. The idea of producing greater electrification by mechanically spinning a globe charged by holding one's hands around it as it turns, called a 'frictional electric' or 'triboelectric generator,' is usually attributed to Otto von Guericke (the inventor of the air pump) who, in 1663, used "a large ball of sulfur mounted on an axle to which was attached a crank" to increase the speed of rotation of the ball under his hands. According to the Duane Rollers, however, "he did not devise it as an electrical generator or use it for investigating electricity," therefore "[s]ince Hauksbee built his generator to study electricity and since it had an immediate and important effect in the area, he should be regarded as the effective inventor of this early electrical machine." (Duane Rollers, p. 566)

18. The Charterhouse was a unique institution founded "to provide schooling for boys who were 'gentlemen by descent and in poverty' and a living for poor brethren who were preferably 'soldiers that had borne arms by sea or land, merchants decayed by piracy or shipwreck, or servants in household to the King or Queen's Magesty.'" (Duane Rollers, p. 571)

19. Cf. Sir Edmund Whittier, *A History of the Theories of Aether & Electricity*, Vol. I (New York: Harper & Brothers, 1960), p. 42 and I. Bernard Cohen, *Franklin and Newton* (Cambridge: Harvard Univ. Press, 1956), p. 377.

20. Cohen, *op. cit.*, p. 378; brackets added. For a more detailed discussion of Desagulier's view see pp. 376-384.

21. Cohen asserts that "the two 'electrics' postulated by Dufay appear to be two modes of electrification, and there is certainly no indication of a belief in two kinds of electrical matter as such." (Cohen, p. 372) While this assertion would appear to be contradicted by Dufay's subsequent reference to "two distinct electricities, very different from each other," and by the fact that the two-fluid theory of electricity became popular after Dufay, Cohen argues that Dufay did not believe that vitreous and resinous substances were endowed with two different kinds of electricities, but that two modes of a single electric was produced from the two different substances. "Thus it is plain that Dufay did not suggest two kinds of electric matter or a two-fluid theory of electricity." (*Ibid.*) I think Dufay's own statement refutes this.

22. Cohen, p. 376.

23. Cf. Cohen, p. 432.

24. *Ibid.*, pp. 388-9.

25. Cf. *ibid.*, p. 390.

26. *Ibid.*, pp. 414-5.

27. *Ibid.*, p. 418.

28. *Ibid.*, pp. 438-40.

29. *Ibid.*, pp. 460-1. Brackets added.

30. *Ibid.*, pp. 467-78.

31. *Ibid.*, p. 468. This account differs from that of the Duane Rollers who assert that Franklin "eventually grows away from the view [. . .] that the attractions and repulsions are due to effuvia in the space around the electrified bodies; instead, he supposes the electric fluid to be confined to the bodies themselves during the attraction or repulsion." (p. 603)

32. Cf. *ibid.*, pp. 469-472.

33. *Ibid.*, p. 540.

34. *Ibid.*, p. 541.

35. *Ibid.*

36. *Ibid.*, p. 390.

37. For a detailed description of Watson's experiments and interpretations along with their contrast with Franklin's see *ibid.*, pp. 398-413; 463-7.

38. Cf. *ibid.*, pp. 486-91.

39. *Ibid.*, p. 488.

40. *Ibid.*, p. 487.

41. *Ibid.*, f.n., p. 463.

42. Cf. Plato, *Republic*, Part III, Ch. XXIII, Sec. VI, 509c.

43. Newton, *Opticks*, Query 28.

44. Huygens discovered the phenomenon of double refraction produced by Iceland Crystal or Spar. When a ray of monochromatic or homogeneous light penetrates Iceland Crystal the single beam is divided into two beams of the same color because of their different refractions when they emerge from the crystal. Since at the time light waves were considered to be propagated longitudinally, this was difficult to explain by the wave theory. Newton thought that because corpuscles have shape, double refraction could be attributed to their having different sides. Still, the fact that crossed beams of light do not interfere or scatter, as one would expect if they were composed of particles, was one reason Huygens advocated the wave theory. Cf. A. D'Abro, *The Rise of the New Physics*, Vol. I (New York: Dover Pub., Inc. [1931]1951), pp. 276-281.

45. *Philosophical Transactions of the Royal Society*, 90 (1800), pp. 106-150. Quoted from Peter Achinstein, *Particles And Waves* (New York: Oxford Univ. Press, 1991), p. 17. Unless otherwise indicated, the page references in the text are to this work.

46. Cf. Charles Singer, *A Short History of Scientific Ideas* (London: Oxford Univ. Press, 1959), p. 374.

47. *Principia*, Vol. 2, *op. cit.*, p. 547. Brackets added.

48. Albert Einstein and Leopold Infeld, *The Evolution of Physics* (New York: Simon and Schuster, 1951), pp. 155-6.

49. Max Born, *Einstein's Theory of Relativity*, revised edition (New York: Dover Pub., Inc. [1924]1962), p. 189.

CHAPTER IX

THE ORIGINS OF CHEMISTRY AND MODERN ATOMISM

The concept of atomism has been the spearhead
of the advance of science. [1]

Whyte

The origin and initial growth of scientific rationalism (recounted in Volume I) began with the endeavor of the Milesian philosophers to attain a better understanding of the origin and nature of the world than that rendered in the antecedent mythopoetic or theogonic accounts. This involved identifying the primal state from which everything in the universe arose, describing how the diversity of nature emerged from this state, and explaining the coming to be, changes, and passing away of ordinary occurrences according to various controlling principles. Positing water, air, or fire as the prime elements or *stoichae*, the Presocratics sought to explain change as due to such familiar processes as "separating out,""condensation and rarefaction," "Love and Strife,"and "Mind" or "Nous."[2]

The speculative attempts to solve these problems that had the most lasting effect were the theories of Empedocles and of the ancient atomists, Leucippus and Democritus. Empedocles' solution consisted of selecting as the four basic elements, fire, earth, air, and water, with change initiated and controlled by the contrasting influences of Love and Strife—the latter an anthropomorphic explanation derived from Hesiod's *Theogony*. Both Plato and Aristotle adopted Empedocles' conception of the four elements, Plato in the *Timaeus* identifying them with the four Pythagorean solids (fire a tetrahedron, air an octahedron, water an icosahedron, and earth a cube) constructed from two kinds of triangles, the cubed-earth from right-angled isosceles triangles and the three other elements formed by dividing an equilateral triangle in half. Transformation among the three elements, along with the breakdown and reconstitution of the earth, was explained as due to the interchange of the triangles, a primitive kind of *a priori* stereometric explanation of the physical elements and their interactions.[3]

Aristotle, in contrast, held that the four elements consisted of an underlying substratum (ultimately prime matter) qualified by pairs of the basic opposite qualities: hotness, coldness, moistness, and dryness with fire consisting of hotness and dryness, air of hotness and moistness, water of moistness and coldness, and earth of dryness and coldness. In accidental change, it was the exchange of opposite qualities inhering actually or potentially in the underlying material substratum that accounted for the orderly transformation of the elements, while in substantial change, the substratum itself was transformed, as when wood burns or food is digested.[4]

The older theory of Leucippus and Democritus, which Aristotle was opposing, described matter as composed of insensible, qualityless, homogeneous atoms defined as solid or indivisible while varying endlessly in shape and size. The observable changes of nature were explained as caused by the motion, impact, and configurational cohesion or deflection of these indestructible particles. Although in the void the atoms possessed mass along with other primary qualities, they lacked weight until Epicurus endowed them with that inherent property as well. The sensory or secondary qualities of objects, such as colors, sounds, and odors, depended upon the impact of the atoms on a sentient organism, thus having no independent existence.[5] These theories of the nature of matter and change—like the older mythopoetic and theogonic accounts—were created because the world as encountered in everyday experience is not self-explanatory but problematic.

While Empedocles' conception of the four elements, as adopted and emended by Aristotle, eclipsed the atomic theory of Leucippus and Democritus until its initial refutation by Robert Boyle, the revival of ancient atomism by Descartes, Mersenne, Gassendi, Galileo, Boyle, Locke, and Newton gave the seventeenth century its fundamental theoretical framework. Still, the alchemical tradition of Paracelsus (1493-1541), claiming as the "*tria prima*" salt, sulfur, and mercury, persisted, along with the theories of van Helmont (1579-1644) based on the view that air and water (he did not consider fire a material substance and believed that earth was formed from water) were the true elements. Although fraught with animistic or anthropomorphic concepts and mystical or magical modes of inquiry, the experimental investigations of the alchemists sometimes led to significant discoveries.

Among those of van Helmont, for example, were the affirmation of the existence of the vacuum based on experimental evidence; the introduction of the term 'gas' (probably from the Greek '*chaos*') to designate the components of air; the identification of various gases now known as nitrogen, carbon dioxide, carbon monoxide, and sulphur dioxide; the conclusion that plants consist entirely of water based on a famous experiment in which he demonstrated that the growth of a large tree depended solely on its consummation of water; the realization that metals dissolved in acids can be recovered and hence his affirmation of the principle of the conservation of matter; and his extensive use of the balance to measure the components in various chemical reactions.

Although alchemy remained a pseudoscience because of its lack of a sound methodology and adequate conceptual framework, still, the extensive research of the alchemists had considerable influence: for example, Boyle's experiments on gases were particularly indebted to the previous investigations of van Helmont "whose works he studied with care and to whom he frequently refers as an authority,"[6] while we noted previously Newton's furtive contact with alchemists and extensive purchase of alchemical texts, equipment, and chemicals in connection with his own extensive experiments. Just as the emancipation of the science of astronomy from the pseudoscience of astrology accompanied Kepler's discovery of the three planetary laws and Newton's universal law of gravitation, so the delivery of the science of chemistry from the pseudoscience of alchemy awaited the discovery that combining gases and elements occur according to exact mathematical ratios.

Given the prevalence of these research programs, it was natural that the earliest chemical experiments involved air (the influential pneumatic tradition beginning with Boyle and Hooke), heat and combustion (Black, Steele, Stahl, Priestley, and Lavoisier), and water (Cavendish, Lavoisier, and Berzelius), along with investigations of the combining volumes of gases and the relative weights of elements forming substances to determine their atomic weights and proportions in molecular compounds (Dalton, Proust, Gay-Lussac, Avogadro, Davy, Berzelius, and Cannizzaro). Not the first to use the balance to measure the exact amounts of the reagents and products of chemical reactions, Lavoisier nonetheless is considered the primary founder of modern chemistry because his meticulous weighing of the components in combustion and oxidation led to the confirmation of the existence of oxygen and overthrow of the phlogiston theory. Similarly, Dalton is regarded as the father of modern atomism because of his theory that gases and chemical compounds are composed of atoms that combine in simple numerical ratios according to their atomic weights.

The realization that the components and structures of common substances like air, water, and salt could be experimentally discovered by exact measurements of the combining volumes or weights of the reagents, and that the interaction and transformation of compound substances (as in the production of metals, acids, and alkalis) occur according to exact laws, was even more important because of the practical consequences, than the discoveries of Galileo, Kepler, and Newton, if not as dramatic. Nearly all our understanding of the natural world—physical, chemical, geological, biological, and physiological—which has transformed our relation to nature in the twentieth century, has utilized this schema of interpretation. That it depended (as did the advances in astronomy and electricity) on the discovery of quantitative relations formulated in precise laws (albeit statistical) has proven so crucial to the development of science that these early *savants* believed (as Einstein) that the intelligibility of nature was evidence of an inherent or underlying rationality.

THE DISCOVERY OF OXYGEN AND DISPROOF OF PHLOGISTON

As the creation of the modern atomic theory followed the chemical revolution that accompanied the discovery of oxygen and its essential role in combustion, oxidation (or calcination as it was then called), and respiration, with the rejection of the phlogiston theory, our account will begin there. The origin of the phlogiston theory began with Johann Joachim Becher (1635-1682) who, in his treatise *Physicae subterraneae* (1669), apparently combined the alchemical elements of van Helmont with those of Paracelsus, claiming that there were five basic elements, air and water along with three earths, sulphur (*terra pinguis*), mercury (*mercurial*), and *salt* (vitreous). Combustion involved the burning off of the "fatty earth."[7] Georg Ernst Stahl (1660-1734), who extolled and refined Becher's views in his own book, *Fundamenta Chymiae* (1723), renamed the latter's inflammable *terra pinguis* "phlogiston," asserting that while it was "the matter and principle of fire," it was not fire as such.

According to this theory substances containing large amounts of this "*in*flammable principle," like charcoal and phosphorus, burn vigorously because they contain and then give off large amounts of phlogiston when heated. A candle burning in a closed vessel will be extinguished when the air becomes saturated with phlogiston, thus air normally contains considerable amounts of this inflammable substance. The conversion of ores to metals occurs because the metallic ores when burned with charcoal absorb the phlogiston released by the charcoal, this "metallizing principle" transforming the ore into a metal. Conversely, burnt metals emit phlogiston leaving calx as a residue which can be restored to its metallic state by being resupplied with phlogiston. Zinc, for example, burns with a bright flame when heated red hot owing to a considerable discharge of phlogiston, leaving a calx in the form of a white substance which returns to zinc when burned with charcoal. Sulphur when heated emits phlogiston reducing to sulfuric acid that converts back to sulphur when heated with a substance containing phlogiston.

While "Stahl inverted the true theory of combustion and calcination" because "adding phlogiston was really removing oxygen, and removing phlogiston was adding oxygen''(p. 88), for a time the theory provided the best explanation qualitatively of a diverse number of chemical reactions. Furthermore, it led to some quantification, Priestley discovering that one-fifth the volume of air is ''dephlogisticated'' (actually containing oxygen), Steele that it is one-fourth to one-third, and Lavoisier finding it to be one-sixth to one-fourth. (cf. p. 120)

The Swedish chemist Carl Wilhelm Scheele (1742-1786) made a number of important discoveries which he reported in a book (1777) translated as a *Chemical Treatise on Air and Fire*. Based on his experiments Scheele divided air into two constituents, one highly flammable and the other inflammable, calling the first ''Fire Air''and the second ''Foul Air.''(p. 105) Later named 'oxygen' and 'nitrogen' respectively, Scheele was the first to isolate a distinct gas which was colorless, odorless, ''in which a taper burned with a dazzling brilliance.'' Although he observed that when air is contained in a flask over water and a candle burned in the air, the water rose as the candle burned filling one-quarter of the flask until the flame went out, implying that the loss of air was due to something having been removed from the gas during the burning, his acceptance of the phlogiston theory prevented him from making the correct inference. Thus while he noticed the presence in the air of what later was called 'oxygen,' he did not realize its true function in combustion.

Similarly, Joseph Priestley (mentioned earlier for his contributions to the development of electrical theory), who is accorded the honor of having discovered oxygen (despite Scheele's having detected it sooner) because he was the first to publish an account of his experiments identifying the properties of the new gas, adamantly adhered to the phlogiston theory even after recognizing the significance of Lavoisier's interpretation of combustion in terms of oxygen. A skilled investigator who designed much of the apparatus used in experiments on gases, Priestley (1733-1804) had obtained oxygen (although it was not yet called that) as early as 1771, independently of and nearly the same time as Scheele. However, at that time he confused it with air so his actual discovery did not occur until August 1774, and because it was published the following year in an article ''Observations on Different Kinds of Air,'' it appeared two years before Scheele's publication. (cf. p. 118)

Having obtained the gas by using a ''burning (magnifying) glass''to heat red oxide of mercury, he clearly was aware of its unique properties, if not its exact status; for example, in the article announcing his discovery he wrote that a candle burned in the gas with a brilliant flame, while a few months later he reported that a mouse lived much longer in this air than in a similar volume of ordinary air, and that when ''he breathed it himself [. . .] his 'breast felt

peculiarly light and easy for some time afterwards [. . .]."'(p. 118) But it was
not until March 1, 1775, owing to tests to distinguish the gas from nitrous
oxide (which he also discovered), that he seemed convinced of his finding. As
Partington states:

> He says himself that he was unaware of the real nature of the new gas
> until this date, and wrote in April, 1775: "I have now discovered an
> air five or six times as good as common air," saying that he had "got
> it first from *mercurius calcinatus, per se*, red lead, etc.; and now, from
> many substances [. . .]. Nothing I ever did has surprised me more, or
> is more satisfactory." (p. 119)

Nevertheless, despite having identified a new gas (oxygen), misled by his
commitment to the phlogiston theory, he called it *"dephlogisticated air."*
According to the phlogiston theory combustion depends upon two variables:
the quantity of phlogiston (the *in*flammable entity causing combustion) in the
burning substance and the amount of phlogiston the enveloping air can receive
when the material is heated. The fact that a candle burned vigorously in a
certain air meant, therefore, that the air must have been *capable of absorbing
a large quantity of phlogiston*, explaining why Priestley called it
"dephlogisticated air"—air devoid of phlogiston and therefore capable of
accepting large amounts of it.

Like Scheele, Priestley noted that when substances are burned in air they
often *gain* weight while the volume of air *decreases*, contrary to the natural
expectation that the release of phlogiston into the air during combustion should
diminish the weight of the burning substance and *increase* the amount of air.
As Priestley says when investigating the transformation of calces to metals:

> For seeing the metal to be actually revived, and that in considerable
> quantity, *at the same time that the air was diminished*, I could not
> doubt, but that the calx was actually *imbibing something* from the air;
> and from its affects in making the calx into metal, it could be no other
> than that to which chemists had unanimously given the name of
> *phlogiston*.[8]

Thus Priestley came within a word of initiating the chemical revolution
fathered by Lavoisier but, like Scheele, was so enmeshed in the conceptual
network of the phlogiston theory that he too failed to realize the significance
of what he observed, despite his own warning that "the force of prejudice

[. . .] biases not only our *judgments* [. . .] but even the perceptions of our senses [. . .]"[9]

Having observed correctly that when calx is converted into a metal something was "imbibed from the air," he misjudged its nature calling it "phlogiston." Even more significantly, although he observed that during combustion the volume of air is reduced (contrary to the phlogiston theory) he did not appreciate its importance, the anomaly apparently removed by the peculiar assumption that "the phlogistication of the air" results in the "diminution in bulk of the air."[10] The person who did recognize the significance of this was Antoine Laurent Lavoisier born in Paris in 1743, who arrived at the correct interpretation of combustion based on the investigations of others supported by his own meticulous quantitative experiments.[11]

ANTOINE LAURENT LAVOISIER

Although others from van Helmont to Black (Lavoisier was especially influenced by Black's quantitative experiments which he repeated) had affirmed the principle of the conservation of matter in chemical reactions, carefully weighing the initial components and byproducts of specific experiments, Lavoisier considered this so important that he insisted that the art of experimentation in chemistry must be founded on this primary axiom or principle:

> [. . .] it can be taken as an axiom that in every operation an equal quantity of matter exists both before and after the operation, that the quality and quantity of the principles remain the same and that only changes and modifications occur. The whole art of making experiments in chemistry is founded on this principle: we must always suppose an exact equality or equation between the principles of the body examined and those of the products of its analysis.[12]

The preeminence of this axiom in his thinking probably accounts for the greater significance Lavoisier gave to the gain in weight of calcinated or burnt materials, accompanied by a loss in volume of the air, than either Scheele or Priestley, and therefore his recognition of the obvious anomaly in the phlogiston theory.

This would seem to be confirmed in the famous sealed note that he deposited with the Secretary of the French Academy on November 1, 1772, which was opened in 1773, for in that note he says that when burnt in air sulphur and phosphorus increase in weight while some of the air is lost or absorbed.

> About eight days ago I discovered that sulfur in burning, far from losing weight, on the contrary, gains it; it is the same with phosphorus; this increase of weight arises from a prodigious quantity of air that is fixed during combustion and combines with the vapors.

> This discovery, which I have established by experiments, that I regard as decisive, has led me to think that what is observed in the combustion of sulfur and phosphorus may well take place in the case of all substances that gain weight by combustion and calcination; and I am persuaded that the increase in weight of metallic calxes is due to the same cause.[13]

While Lavoisier was aware his experiments indicated just the opposite of what was predicted by the phlogiston theory, he did not know yet the cause of these contrary effects. Without going into the details of the experiments, his initial interpretation, as one might expect, proved erroneous, attributing the increase in weight to "fixed air"("carbon dioxide"as it is now called). When an oxide of substances like mercury or phosphorus is heated with charcoal, mercury or phosphorus is formed plus "fixed air:" $2HgO$ (oxide of mercury) + C (charcoal or carbon) → (when heated) yields $2Hg$ (Mercury metal) + CO_2 (carbon dioxide or fixed air).[14] Thus Lavoisier erroneously inferred that what increased the weight of sulphur and phosphorus when heated alone to produce the calx must be carbon dioxide. Failing in his attempt to confirm this, he thought the increase in weight might involve simply common air but was corrected by Priestley.

What misled him was the reduction of the oxide or calx in the presence of charcoal. Once he realized that the calx could be directly reduced to the metal by heating, it was unnecessary to assume that the gas released was carbon dioxide. This he learned from Priestley during the latter's visit to Paris in October 1774 when, in his usual open manner, Priestley

> told Lavoisier at dinner of his discovery of dephlogisticated air [pure air or oxygen], saying he 'had gotten it from *precip* [of *mercurius calcinatus*] *per se* and also *red lead*'; whereupon, he says, 'all the company, and Mr. and Mrs. Lavoisier as much as any, expressed great

surprise.'[15]

The cause of the astonishment was the fact that the "dephlogisticated air" produced by heating mercury oxide had the opposite properties of carbon dioxide: it supported combustion and respiration and did not precipitate lime water nor combine with lime and alkalis. (cf. p. 83) When Lavoisier repeated the experiment he too obtained a "gas purer than common air" which made him realize that while measuring the ingredients of chemical reactions may be the "foundation of the art of chemistry," choosing the right experiments to perform also is crucial. As he stated after considering his earlier mistake:

These reflections have made me feel how essential it is, in order to unravel the mystery of the reduction of metallic calces, that all my experiments be performed on calces which can be reduced without any addition [that is, without the addition of charcoal]. (p. 79)

Two versions of Lavoisier's experiments on the oxide of mercury producing "dephlogisticated" or "pure" or "good air" (oxygen), reported in "On the Nature of the Principle which Combines with Metals during Calcination and Increases their Weight," were read to the French Academy of Sciences, the first on Easter 1775 (and therefore referred to as the Easter Memoir) and the second on August 8, 1778. (cf. p. 77) While there were relatively few revisions in the final paper, those that were made corrected his earlier mistakes. Having repeated Priestley's experiment and tested the gas released finding it was not "fixed air" or nitrogen, Lavoisier thought that because it supported combustion it must be a form of common air, despite describing it as "purer than common air." However, when he learned of Priestley's nitrous air test showing the gas was *not* common air (because in reacting with nitrous oxide it proved more soluble in water than common air), he concluded it must be a new gas that was a constituent of common air but not identical to it; namely, the gas that was *added* in the conversion of metals to calces or oxides when burnt in air and *released* when the oxides themselves were heated.

Based on meticulously weighing the volumes of gases and weights of the reagents involved, this discovery resulted in the eventual overthrow of the phlogiston theory and revolution in chemistry. Though Priestley himself never gave up the theory of phlogiston, he generously conceded the importance of Lavoisier's discovery.

There have been few, if any, revolutions in science so great, so sudden, and so general, as [. . .] what is now usually termed the *new system of chemistry*, or that of the *Anti*phlogistons [. . .]. Though there had been some who occasionally expressed doubts of the existence of such a principle as that of *phlogiston*, nothing had been advanced that could have laid the foundation *of another system* before the labors of Mr. Lavoisier [. . .]. (pp. 69-70)

Lavoisier announced his identification of the new gas accounting for calcination and combustion in his *Mémoire* of 1778, but he did not attack the established theory until 1783 in his *Reflections on Phlogiston*. In fact, as late as 1780 he maintained that combustion and calcination were explained by the phlogiston theory "in a very happy manner," except that it located the inflammable principle in the combustible rather than attributing it to a pure gas in the air. Having identified the new gas, he named it "oxygen."

In 1782 Lavoisier says Condorcet had proposed the name "vital air" for pure air, but in a memoir received in 1777, read in 1779, and published in 1781, entitled "General considerations on the nature of acids and on the principles composing them",Lavoisier called the base of pure air the "acidifying principle" or "oxigine principle"(*principe oxigine*), which he latter changed to "oxygene" [. . .].[16]

Thus while Scheele and Priestley discovered oxygen, it was Lavoisier, as Partington says, who was "the first to understand the consequences of its discovery, to realize its true nature as an element, and by ingenious quantitative experiments to establish the true chemistry of combustion and the calcination of metals [. . .]." (pp. 129-30) Priestley also discovered the gas later called "nitrogen" by Chaptal, but again it was Lavoisier who more precisely identified its properties and named it 'azote,' as it was called at the time, along with establishing that air is composed of 73 parts of nitrogen to 27 parts of oxygen. (cf. p. 128)

A brief revival of the phlogiston theory occurred when Henry Cavendish (1731-1810) who, like Priestley, still adhering to the theory, interpreted the composition of water as consisting of phlogiston (which in the later phlogiston theory was equated with hydrogen) or hydrogen and dephlogisticated air or oxygen. However, as Cavendish acknowledged, because the composition of water could be explained as easily on Lavoisier's theory, and since burning hydrogen in oxygen indicated that water was an oxide of hydrogen with its weight equal to the combined weights of "inflammable air" or hydrogen and "vital air" or oxygen, Lavoisier's theory gained increasing support. Guyton de Morveau suggested the name 'hidrogène' for inflammable air which was changed to 'hydrogène' by Lavoisier. (cf. p. 146)

The similarity between respiration and combustion having long been recognized and accounted for by the phlogiston theory as the expelling of phlogiston during the respiratory process, this also had to be explained by Lavoisier. Although his explanation erroneously attributed the oxidizing process to the lungs, it correctly identified the function of the lungs in inhaling oxygen from the air and exhaling carbon dioxide during respiration:

> Lavoisier believed that the oxygen gas breathed into the lungs oxidizes the carbonaceous materials of the blood, producing carbon dioxide which is exhaled, and the *animal heat* is the result of this chemical process of oxidation. (pp. 133-4)

While a few scientists like Priestley and Cavendish still clung to the phlogiston theory, with the publication of Lavoisier's *Traité de Chimie* in 1789 the superiority of the conceptual framework involving oxygen rather than phlogiston was generally acknowledged. For example, in that year William Higgins (1763-1825) published his highly influential *A Comparative View of the Phlogistic and Antiphlogistic Theories*, in which he not only argued forcefully for the latter theory, but also presented diagrams to illustrate how oxygen might combine with nitrogen to form various oxides. (cf. p. 167)

As the preceding developments clearly illustrate, the revolution in chemistry accompanying the discovery of oxygen and explanation of its role in combustion depended upon carefully measuring the volumes of gases or ratios of chemical ingredients entering into combination. It was proved that air and water were not irreducible elements as formerly believed, but that air is composed mainly of nitrogen and oxygen while water consists of hydrogen and oxygen. Along with the discovery of these new elementary gases, the composition of many compound gases such as nitric oxide (NO), carbon dioxide (CO_2), and mercury oxide (HgO) was determined, as well as acids like nitric acid (HNO_3) and sulfuric acid (H_2SO_4), plus numerous bases, alkalis, and other compounds. Although the apparatus and design of experiments were still primitive yielding imprecise results, the fact that chemical analyses and syntheses indicated that irreducible elements could be identified, and that compound substances were composed of definite multiple ratios of these elements, reinforced the belief that chemical phenomena could be explained in terms of these principles.

THE REBIRTH OF ATOMISM

As this had been the heuristic thesis also of ancient atomism, it was natural that the atomic theory should be reaffirmed at this time. Moreover, as described in preceding chapters, each of the founders of the scientific revolution adopted the atomic theory over Aristotle's explanation of change in terms of an underlying substrate and substantial forms or qualities, Newton proclaiming "that God in the Beginning form'd Matter in solid, massy, hard, impenetrable, movable Particles, of such Sizes and Figures [. . .] as most conduced to the End for which he form'd them [. . .]."[17] Although it would be the Epicurean property of "weight," rather than the Democritean attributes of "sizes and figures," that would prove the crucial factor in the analysis of chemical reactions and structures, Newton's commanding authority is evident in the development of chemistry and rebirth of atomism.

His demonstration of Boyle's law on the mechanistic assumption that gases composed of *static* particles (the kinetic theory would not be developed until over a half-century later), with a repelling force varying inversely with the square of the distance (which Coulomb discovered applied to electrical attraction and repulsion also), caused the pressure to increase as the volume decreases, lent empirical support to what previously had been a purely speculative theory. But while Newton had devised a *physical* atomic theory to explain why the pressure of gases decreases inversely with the volume, given the predominance of alchemy at the time and the belief that all substances are transmutable, it was too early to develop a *chemical* atomic theory to explain chemical reactions and molecular structures. Yet a century later the demise of alchemy, the discovery of new elements along with the determination of their proportions in compounds, and the realization that chemical transformations occur according to definite ratios made the search for chemical laws, along with a conceptual framework incorporating these laws, much more feasible.

One of the early contributors to this effort was Lavoisier himself when he introduced his well-known tentative "definition of an 'element or principle' as "the last point which analysis is capable of reaching,"[18] its tentativeness due to the fact that even when such entities seem to be irreducible and act as simple substances, one can never be certain they are uncompounded. But even before this definition of an element he, Berthollet, de Morveau, and de

Fourcroy published a *Méthode de Nomenclature Chimique* (1787) in which they presented the first modern list of elements based on recent discoveries, giving their traditional equivalents. Then the fact that any sample of a compound substance, such as water, always contains its components (oxygen and hydrogen) in fixed ratios by weight was expressed by Joseph Louis Proust (1754-1826) in 1799 as "the law of constant proportions."

> We must recognize an invisible hand which holds the balance in the formation of compounds. A compound is a substance to which Nature assigns fixed ratios; it is, in short, a being which Nature never creates other than balance in hand, *pondere et mensurâ*.[19]

This conception of "an invisible hand" (whether of Nature or of God) holding a balance in which the fixed ratios of compounds are weighed was invoked also by Adam Smith as a regulating scale between the economic forces of individual self-interest and the common good.[20] Proust went on to say that this "*balance* [. . .] *subject to the decrees of nature, regulates even in our laboratories the ratios of compounds.*"[21] However, this notion that compounds occur in discrete, fixed ratios did not go unchallenged. Based on his experiments with metals heated in air that seemed to oxidize in continuous quantities, Claude Louis Berthollet (1748-1822) argued that compounds are formed in continuous series, dependent upon the physical conditions, up to a fixed limit.

In his rebuttal Proust successfully demonstrated that the *apparent* continuous series of metal oxides really were constituted by a limited number of fixed ratios, and therefore Berthollet's argument involved a confusion between variable compounds and various mixtures of compounds. But while Proust's Law stated "that two elements could combine in more than one proportion," it did not indicate "the ratio of the proportions of one element combining with identical weights of the other."[22] The latter, called the "Law of Equivalent Proportions," was formulated by J.B. Richter (who had been a student of Kant's at Königsberg) in a series of papers between 1792 and 1802. In comparing the weights of different substances when they react completely with other substances, Richter (1762-1807) arrived at the law of equivalences paraphrased by Nash as follows: "*If, for any two substances, there are certain weights that are equivalent in their capacity for reaction with some third substance, the ratio of such weights is the same regardless of what the third substance may be.*"[23]

Although it is apparent from these developments that there was considerable experimental data indicating that compound substances, whether gases, liquids, or solids, are formed in definite and fixed proportions by weights of their constituents, there was no explanation as to how this occurred. Lavoisier had proposed a definition of simple elements, along with a list of those that were then known, while William Higgins attempted to show in diagrams how the forces connecting different oxides of nitrogen might be related,[24] but there was no theory explaining how or why these proportional relations hold because of the volumes or weights involved. Given that oxygen combines in definite proportions by volume or weight with carbon, hydrogen, nitrogen, and mercury, what *in the composition* of these elements accounts for their different densities or weights and why they combine in definite or multiple ratios? While it was believed that gases and substances were composed of particles, how could one infer from the macro-behavior of these substances the properties of the micro-particles that would explain this?

JOHN DALTON AND THE ATOMIC THEORY

Considering all of the accomplished investigators of the period, the person responsible for the theory that initiated the explanation of these chemical properties and reactions, John Dalton (1766-1844), was a most unlikely candidate. Born in a Quaker family living in a tiny rustic village in Cumberland, his father earned his living as a cottage weaver while his mother supplemented the family income by selling writing materials in the second room of their cottage. In 1832, when he was sixty-six years old, Dalton wrote a brief account in the third person of the main features of his life.

The writer of this was born at the Village of Eaglesfield about two miles west of Cockermouth, Cumberland. Attended the Village Schools, there and in the neighbourhood. At 11 years of age, at which period he had gone through a course of Mensuration, Surveying, Navigation, etc.; began about 12 to teach the village school and continued it two years; afterwards was occasionally employed in husbandry for a year or more; removed to Kendal at 15 years of age as assistant in a Boarding School; remained in that capacity for three or four years, then undertook the same school as a principal and continued it for eight years; whilst at Kendal employed his leisure in studying Latin, Greek, French and the Mathematics with Natural Philosophy; removed thence to Manchester in 1793 as Tutor in

Mathematics and Natural Philosophy in the New College: was six years in that engagement: and after was employed as private and public teacher of Mathematics and Chemistry in Manchester, but occasionally by invitation in London, Edinburgh, Glasgow, and Leeds.[25]

As related, Dalton spent most of his life as a teacher and lecturer. What he does not mention is that several people played an important role in shaping his career. While teaching in Eaglesfield he was befriended by a wealthy Quaker named Elihu Robinson, a man of considerable learning especially interested in natural philosophy and meteorology, who corresponded with Benjamin Franklin. Because Dalton had shown an aptitude in mathematics when he won a mathematical dispute, Robinson offered to tutor him in mathematics in the evenings after Dalton had finished his teaching or other labors. For the rest of his life he would recall the kindness of Robinson and his cultured wife, the effect they had on his intellectual awakening, and the wise counsel they provided at crucial junctures when he was considering a change in career and location.[26]

During the twelve years he lived in Kendal he was fortunate again to meet a most unusual and gifted young man, a Quaker by the name of John Gough. Although blind and suffering from epilepsy, thanks to the intellectual and financial resources of his family Gough was able to make "remarkable progress in the study of the classics, languages, mathematics, physics, botany and zoology." (p. 26) Nine years older than Dalton and much more advanced in his study of these fields, nonetheless, when he learned of their common interests and Dalton's aptitudes he became his intellectual mentor. Developing a close friendship, Gough shared his excellent library and fine collection of scientific instruments with Dalton, while the latter served as Gough's reader and amanuensis. As a result of Gough's instruction, Dalton became quite proficient in "mechanics, fluxions, algebra, geometry, chemistry (including some French chemical writings), astronomy and meteorology [. . .]." (p. 21)

In addition to this influence, when Dr. Barnes, Principal of New College in Manchester, wrote in 1793 to Gough (who by then was widely respected as a mathematician) asking his advice in filling a vacancy at New College with a "Professor of Mathematics and Natural Philosophy," Gough unselfishly recommended Dalton for the position, even though this would result in their parting. Dissatisfied with his teaching situation at Kendal, when offered the position as tutor in New College Dalton readily accepted. A wise decision, he spent the remainder of his life in very happy and fulfilling circumstances in

Manchester.

Immediately welcomed by the prominent "Mancunians," he was elected to the prestigious Manchester Literary and Philosophical Society in 1794, soon becoming one of its most active members. As Patterson states:

> The association which Dalton began with the Manchester Literary and Philosophical Society in 1794 was to continue until his death in 1844. During this half century the Society would play a central role in his life and he in its. Before it he read one hundred and seventeen papers, of which fifty-two were printed. For forty-four years he served it as an officer [. . .]. To think of either—the Society or the man—is to think of the other. (pp. 59-60)

Furthermore, although teaching chemistry had been one of his requirements at New College, it was not until he heard the lectures and saw the acclaimed experiments of Dr. Thomas Garnett that his interest in chemistry became fully aroused.

Unfortunately, New College was encountering difficult times with a declining enrollment, so after having taught there for six years Dalton resigned his position as tutor in 1800, supporting himself for the remainder of his life by privately or publicly tutoring and lecturing. When the "Lit. and Phil. Society" moved to new quarters at the beginning of 1800, he was offered rooms for his tutoring along with his experiments which he conducted with diligence until his death in 1844. At one point he considered getting married to a Quaker woman by the name of Hannah Jepson of nearby Lancaster, but his meager income and preoccupation with teaching and lecturing apparently dampened his original ardor.

Perhaps due to the earlier influence of Elihu Robinson who was a meteorologist, Dalton's first investigations and publications had to do with the annual rainfall and whether it was sufficient to replenish the rivers and springs. He also investigated the nature of water vapor in the atmosphere, along with the composition of the air in general and whether its components constituted a mixture, a chemical compound, or some kind of unknown combination. Among his more important inquiries was his confirmation of Lavoisier's determination of the ratios of nitrogen to oxygen in the air. Then, in a series of four essays, he offered important generalizations regarding gases, meteorology, and physical chemistry, indicating in the last essay that he had independently discovered Charles' gas law that at constant pressure all gases will expand equally with the same increase in temperature. Patterson states that the "wealth of material in these four essays is extraordinary. Even today they are hailed as 'epoch-making' and as "laying the foundations for modern physical meteorology." (p. 94)

It was these investigations of the combination of gases, along with their different solubilities in liquids, that redirected his attention from Newton's physical theory of atomic forces to questions regarding the number, weight, and size of the atoms composing interacting gases. Although there have been a number of explanations of the progression of thought by which Dalton arrived at his theory, such as those Thomas Thomson and W.C. Henry gleaned from personal conversations with him, those provided by Dalton himself based on recollections presented in various lectures from 1807 to 1835, and those A.N. Meldrum derived from Dalton's original notebooks (discovered in 1896) chronicling his experiments and reflections, they all contain discrepancies.

His recollections are not consistent with the dates recorded in his notebooks, while some of the experiments mentioned in the papers read in 1802-3 were not performed until 1804 according to citations in the notebooks. This undoubtedly occurred because the papers were not published until 1805 in the *Memoirs of the Literary and Philosophical Society of Manchester*, and since Dalton was Secretary of the Society he would have had ample opportunity to revise them. For these reasons it is not known exactly how or when he arrived at the crucial notion, stated by Greenaway, "that each element had characteristic atoms, of which it might be possible to determine a most important property, namely the relative weight."[27]

The first explicit statement of his theory occurs in a paper he read to an audience of the "Lit. and Phil. Society" on the 21st of October, 1803, entitled "On the Absorption of Gases by Water and Other Liquids." Containing eight sections, the last is the important one.

> The greatest difficulty attending the mechanical hypothesis [of Newton], arises from different gases observing different laws. Why does water not admit its bulk of every kind of gas alike? [i.e., why are not gases equally soluble in water?] This question I have duly considered, and though I am not yet able to satisfy myself completely, I am nearly persuaded that the circumstance depends upon the weight and number of the ultimate particles of the several gases [. . .].[28]

This suggestion that the different solubilities of gases in water can be explained by the weights and numbers of the particles composing the various gases contains the essence of his atomic theory and is "entirely new" as he states.

> An enquiry into the relative weights of the ultimate particles of bodies
> is a subject, as far as I know, entirely new: I have lately been
> prosecuting this enquiry with remarkable success.   The principle
> cannot be entered upon in this paper; but I shall just subjoin the
> results, as far as they appear to be ascertained by my experiments.
> (p. 222)

Scholars have been much vexed as to what the "principle" was that led to the
"remarkable success," but it seems to be lost in the debris of time. Appended
to the paper is a "Table of the relative weights of the ultimate particles of the
gaseous and other bodies," the "first published tabulation of atomic weights,
and the figures cited make it plain that Dalton had by this time formulated all
the essential parts of his theory." (p. 222)

In 1807 he was invited to give a series of lectures in Edinburgh and
Glasgow which, considering his humble origin, must have been extremely
gratifying, especially as he was warmly and admiringly received.   Having
begun writing his great work, a *New System of Chemical Philosoph*y, after his
return from Scotland he repaid the compliment by dedicating the first volume,
published in 1808, to the "Professors of the Universities, and other residents,
of Edinburgh and Glasgow," along with the "Members of the Literary and
Philosophical Society of Manchester."[29]   The chapter "On Chemical
Synthesis" is especially significant because after affirming that every sample
of a homogeneous compound like water, along with its elements hydrogen and
oxygen, contains "*ultimate particles*" that "*are perfectly alike in weight,
figure, etc.*," he sets forth the basic presuppositions and principles underlying
his theory. In contrast to the alchemist's belief in the transmutation of matter,
he affirms its immutability consistent with the view of Democritus.

> Chemical analysis and synthesis go no farther than to the separation
> of particles one from another, and to their reunion. No new creation
> or destruction of matter is within the reach of chemical agency [this
> will be refuted by Rutherford's and Soddy's discovery of radioactive
> nuclear transmutations with the formation of isotopes]. We might as
> well attempt to introduce a new planet into the solar system, or to
> annihilate one already in existence, as to create or destroy a particle
> of hydrogen. All the changes we can produce, consist in separating
> particles that are in a state of cohesion or combination, and joining

those that were previously at a distance. (p. 229; brackets added)

He then maintains that while previous investigators were concerned to ascertain the "relative weights of the simples which constitute a compound" (as in gases or water), no attempt had been made to determine the "relative weights of the ultimate particles or atoms" themselves, nor to use this knowledge to explain why these particles combine in the ratios they do, or, as Proust said, "the means which nature uses to restrict compounds to the ratios in which we find them combined." (p. 240)

> In all chemical investigations, it has justly been considered an important object to ascertain the relative *weights* of the simples which constitute a compound. But unfortunately the enquiry has terminated here; whereas from the relative weights in the mass [of compounds], the relative weights of the ultimate particles or atoms of the bodies might have been inferred, from which their number and weight in various other compounds would appear in order to assist and to guide further investigations, and to correct their results. Now it is one great object of this work, to show the importance and advantage of ascertaining *the relative weights of the ultimate particles, both of simple and compound bodies, the number of simple elementary particles which constitute one compound particle* [by "simple particle" he means an atom and by "compound particle" he means what we call a molecule], *and the number of less compound particles which enter into the formation of one more compound particle* [the combination of compound particles with simple particles or with other compound particles to form more complex compound particles]. (p. 229; brackets added)

Dalton realized that if one could ascertain the relative weights of the ultimate particles or atoms (as Nash states, "relative to hydrogen taken as 1"), along with their combining weights or ratios in compound particles (or molecules), then an atomic explanation of chemical compounds and reactions would be possible. The difficulty consisted in determining in what ratios the ultimate particles combine to form compound particles, for even though Dalton found that "about 6 grams of oxygen united with 1 gram of hydrogen to form 7 grams of water" (p. 230), calculating their relative weights required knowing in what numerical ratio the particles of oxygen and hydrogen combined to form water—that is, finding whether the molecular structure of water is HO,

HO_2 or H_2O in order to conclude that the relative weight of oxygen to hydrogen is 6 to 1 (HO), 3 to 1 (HO_2), or 12 to 1 (H_2O). As Nash states, "[i]t is thus evident that no valid calculation of relative atomic weights can be undertaken until molecular formulas can be determined." (p. 230)

While in hindsight it is easy to see how these molecular structures should be construed, at the time the possibilities were endless. It is a tribute to Dalton's acute physical intuition that he was able to introduce a set of simplifying principles which, though ultimately incorrect, proved extremely useful initially in conceiving how these combinations might occur. These principles, which he called "the rules of greatest simplicity," are the following:

"If there are two bodies, A and B, which are disposed to combine, the following is the order in which the combinations may take place, beginning with the most simple: namely,

1 atom of A + 1 atom of B = 1 [compound] atom of C, binary.
1 atom of A + 2 atoms of B = 1 [compound] atom of D, ternary.
2 atoms of A + 1 atom of B = 1 [compound] atom of E, ternary.
1 atom of A + 2 atoms of B = 1 [compound] atom of F, ternary.
3 atoms of A + 1 atom of B = 1 [compound] atom of G,
    quaternary. etc., etc." (p. 230)

It is evident that these rules reflect Proust's claim that elements combine in definite proportions, rather than Berthollet's position that they form continuous ratios depending upon the physical conditions.

Dalton then lists the "general rules" that will serve "as guides in all our investigations respecting chemical syntheses."

1st.   When only one combination of two bodies can be obtained, it must be assumed to be a *binary* one, unless some cause appear to the contrary.

2d.   When two combinations are observed, they must be presumed to be a *binary* and a *ternary*.

3d.   When three combinations are obtained, we may expect one *binary*, and the other two *ternary*.

4th.   When four combinations are observed, we should expect one *binary*, two *ternary*, and one *quaternary*, etc. . . .

7th.   The above rules and observations equally apply, when two bodies, such as C and D, D and E, etc. are combined. (p. 231)

These rules are ingenious in that when deriving them Dalton must have been guided by the laws of chemical proportions (Constant Composition, Multiple Proportions, and Equivalences), but once formulated they in turn completely account for the Laws. As Greenaway states, "all the rules of chemical proportions follow" from his simplifying principles:

The composition of any substance must be constant (Law of Constant Composition). If two elements A and B combine to form more than two compounds then the various weights of A which combine with a fixed weight of B bear a simple ratio to one another (Law of Multiple Proportions). If two elements A and B combine separately with a third element C, then the weights of A and B which combine with a fixed weight of C bear a simple ratio to each other (Law of Reciprocal Proportions or Law of Equivalents).[30]

Illustrating the applicability of the theory, he refers to a plate (Fig. 1) containing his system of symbols representing the common elements and their atomic weights known at the time.

Fig. 1. One of Dalton's classification of atomic elements derived from a facsimile courtesy of the Science Museum in London.

Although these symbols will be replaced by the conventional system used today that was later introduced by Berzelius, taking the initial letter or letters of the name of the element to stand for the element (for example, H, O, Cl), Dalton provided the major impetus for devising such a convenient notation that directly indicated the number of elements in a molecule by a numerical subscript, such as H_2SO_4.

Dalton thus fulfilled the essential function of a theoretical scientist, that of devising a theory from which experimentally discovered laws can be deduced from the constructs and structural assumptions of the theory. Furthermore, that from his atomic theory of chemical combinations based on atomic numbers and weights *additional predictions* could be derived fulfilled another essential requirement of a scientific framework, as he states.

> Facts and experiments [. . .] relating to any subject are never duly appreciated till [. . .] they are made the foundation of a theory by which we are able to predict the results and foresee the consequences of certain other operations which were never before undertaken. (p. 238)

In an excerpt from the notes for the eighteenth lecture given at the Royal Institution in London in 1810,[31] he provides the rationale for his theory along with his adherence to Greek atomism.

> We endeavoured to show that matter, though divisible in an *extreme degree*, is nevertheless not *infinitely* divisible. That there must be some point beyond which we cannot go in the division of matter. The existence of these ultimate particles of matter can scarcely be doubted, though they are probably much too small ever to be exhibited by microscopic improvements [today they can be "exhibited" using the tunneling microscope]. (p. 228; brackets added)

Thus far Dalton's justification of Atomism is identical to the Greek Atomists response to Zeno's paradoxes regarding the infinite divisibility of matter: namely, that the division must terminate in something that is irreducible otherwise the construction of the world would be impossible.

He then explains why he chose the word 'atom' to denote a basic particle and 'compound atom' to designate the smallest particle of a compound substance having the same properties.

I have chosen the word *atom* to signify these ultimate particles, in preference to *particle, molecule,* or any other diminutive term, because I conceive it is much more expressive; it includes in itself the notion of *indivisible* ['*atmos*' in Greek means full or undivided], which the other terms do not. It may perhaps be said that I extend the application of it too far, when I speak of *compound atoms*; for instance, I call an ultimate particle of *carbonic acid* a *compound atom.* Now, though this atom may be divided, yet it ceases to be carbonic acid, being resolved by such division into charcoal and oxygen. Hence I conceive there is no inconsistency in speaking of compound atoms, and that my meaning cannot be misunderstood. (p. 228; brackets added)

As this quotation indicates, Dalton distinguished between an *element* as the smallest particle of matter having the same properties and the smallest division of a *compound substance* (molecule) having the same properties.

In the same notes to the lectures he gave at the Royal Institution in 1810, he refers to a further aspect of his atomic theory dating back to 1805, namely, that to account for the elasticity and diffusion of gases in terms of the repelling effect of a "layer of heat" or "atmosphere of fire" surrounding the gas particles, he had to acknowledge a difference in the *size* of the particles of different gases due to the combined dimension of the particle and the ring of heat or fire.

Upon reconsidering this subject [of the diffusion of gases], it occurred to me that I had never contemplated the effect of *difference of size* in the particles of elastic fluids. By size I mean the hard particle at the centre and the atmosphere of heat taken together. And if the sizes be different, then, on the supposition that the repulsive power is heat no equilibrium can be established by particles of unequal size pressing against each other. This idea occurred to me in 1805. I soon found that the sizes of the particles of elastic fluids *must* be different [. . .] [so] it became an object to determine the relative sizes and weights, together with the relative number of atoms in a given volume [of gas] . . . . [32]

In addition to inferring that the particles of different gases are different in size, like Newton he attempted to "derive numerical values for the relative diameters of the particles of the different gaseous species." (p. 267) Finding some evidence for the different sizes of particles, this conviction (erroneously) led him to reject Gay-Lussac's law of combining volumes along with Avogadro's law that equal volumes of gases under the same temperature and pressure contain equal number of molecules.

The general reception of Dalton's theory and acknowledgement of its significance was immediate and positive. A year before Dalton's own book was published, Thomas Thomson (1773-1852) visited Manchester to learn directly from Dalton the specifics of his atomic theory which he then summarized in the third edition of his widely circulated *System of Chemistry* published in 1807. Because Thomson's book was accessible and highly respected, it was mainly his version of Dalton's theory, which he presented concisely but accurately and described as "original and extremely interesting," that became known throughout the scientific world.

Although the physical theory of the atom because of Newton's influence was generally accepted, the fact that Dalton's atomic theory as applied to chemical reactions introduced so much order into what had been a mass of empirically disconnected data added considerably to the credibility of atomism. Furthermore, as Nash states, at the time Dalton's theory became known "opinion on the Berthollet-Proust controversy had begun to run quite definitely in the latter's favor—and it was thus an item of credit to the atomic theory that it was in harmony with Proust's finding."(p. 241) When Berzelius, one of the greatest chemists of the early nineteenth century, first learned of Dalton's theory before being able to critically examine it, he wrote in 1811 that "supposing Dalton's hypothesis be found correct, we should have to look upon it as the greatest advance that chemistry has ever yet made in its development into a science." (p. 248) A year later, having read a copy of the *New System of Chemical Philosophy* that Dalton had sent him, he wrote to Dalton that "[t]he theory of multiple proportions is a mystery but for the Atomic Hypothesis, and as far as I have been able to judge, all the results so far obtained have contributed to justify this hypothesis." (p. 249)

Despite its usefulness in portraying the simplest way the particles in compounds might combine, the "rule of greatest simplicity" was *ad hoc* so that the essential weakness of the theory was its "inability to place its molecular formulas (and, thence, its atomic weights) on a rational empirical basis." (p. 288) Ironically, when this basis was provided by Gay-Lussac and Avogadro, it was rejected by Dalton because of his conviction (based, however, on good evidence and sound arguments) that combining gases indicate that the same volume of different gases contains an unequal number of particles of different sizes.

JOSEPH LOUIS GAY-LUSSAC

In 1809 Joseph Louis Gay-Lussac (1778-1850) published a classic paper, "Memoir on the Combination of Gaseous Substances with Each Other," in *Mémoires de la Société d'Arcueil*, announcing his discovery that gases combine in simple integer proportions. Whereas Dalton in formulating his theory had used "parts by weight" in analyzing the composition of gases, Gay-Lussac used "parts by volume," a procedure that yields more exact values!

Analyzing the ratios by which various volumes of gases combine, such as hydrogen and oxygen to form water vapor and nitrogen and oxygen to form nitrous oxide (N_2O), nitrous gas (NO), and nitric acid (HNO_3), converting the combining weights into combining volumes by means of the gas densities, he was able to provide empirical evidence of what he believed to be a strict regularity indicative of the atomic weights of the elements and of the molecular structures of those gases. As he states,

> it appears evident to me that gases always combine in the simplest proportions when they act on one another; and we have seen in reality in all the preceding examples that the ratio of combination is 1 to 1, 1 to 2, or 1 to 3. It is very important to observe that in considering *weights* there is no simple and finite [integral] relation between the elements of any one compound [. . .]. Gases, on the contrary, in whatever proportions they may combine, always give rise to compounds whose elements by *volume* are multiples of each other." (p. 260; italics added)

Furthermore, if there is a contraction in the volume of the gases after the combination, this also occurs according to definite proportions.[33]

Because Dalton's rules of atomic composition were suppositional, whereas Gay-Lussac's law of combining volumes was based on actual measurements of the simple integral ratios of compound gases, the latter, in providing empirical evidence for Dalton's conjectures, was "very favorable" toward it, as Gay-Lussac wrote. One would expect, therefore, that Dalton would have accepted Gay-Lussac's law, but for several reasons he did not. First, he did not believe the experimental evidence for the combining volumes of gases was indicative of precise ratios, but merely represented simplifying approximations of more fundamental combinations that actually were nonintegral (which in fact was true). Secondly, he strongly rejected Gay-Lussac's inference that the reason equal volumes of nitrogen and oxygen combine to form nitrous gas

(NO) is that they each contain equal numbers of atoms, which Gay-Lussac thought might be true for equal volumes of all gases (under the same conditions) As indicated previously, Dalton had concluded from his own analysis of the different solubilities of various gases in water that these gases were composed of particles or atoms of different sizes, implying that the same volume of diverse gases (under the same conditions of temperature and pressure) could not contain the same number of particles because of their variations in size.

Furthermore, this latter conviction was reinforced by the well-known fact that in some instances when different gases combine, the resultant compound is *less heavy* than the *sum of the individual gases*. When oxygen and hydrogen combine the water vapor or steam (H_2O) is *less* dense than the oxygen; ammonia (NH_4) is *less* dense than nitrogen despite its being composed of both nitrogen and hydrogen; and carbon monoxide (CO) is *less* dense than oxygen although it is formed by adding carbon to oxygen. As Dalton realized, these anomalies could be eliminated if the same volume of different gases contained *different* numbers of particles because of their varying sizes. Thus if there are *fewer* particles in a volume of steam, ammonia, or carbon monoxide than in the interacting volumes of oxygen and nitrogen, then the greater *number* of *lighter* particles composing the volumes of oxygen and nitrogen could result in their aggregate being *heavier* than an equal volume of water vapor, ammonia, or carbon monoxide containing *fewer* albeit *heavier* particles of the combined elements. (cf. p. 265)

An even more difficult problem for the equal volumes, equal numbers interpretation pertained to the number of molecules in compound gases, as compared to the number of atoms in one of the original volumes of gases. As Dalton wrote in the *New System* (p. 71):

> It is evident the number of ultimate particles or molecules in a given weight or volume of one gas is not the same as in another; for, if equal measures of azote [nitrogen] and oxygenous gas were mixed, and could be instantly united chemically, they would form nearly two measures of nitrous gas, having the same weight as the two original measures; but the number of ultimate particles could at most be one half of that before the union. No two elastic fluids [gases], probably, therefore, have the same number of particles, either in the same volume or the same weight. (p. 265; brackets added)

Accordingly, if one volume of nitrogen and an equal volume of oxygen combine to form two volumes of nitrous oxide (N_2O), the number of molecules in the nitrous gas (because one molecule of NO contains two atoms) will be half the total number of particles contained in the two original volumes of nitrogen and oxygen. Similarly, if one volume of oxygen combines with two volumes of hydrogen to form two volumes of water vapor, because the number of molecules (H_2O) cannot exceed the original number of oxygen atoms, the *two* volumes of water vapor will contain half the number of molecules *per unit volume* as there were oxygen atoms in the *one* volume of oxygen. As stated by Nash,

> in general, in any case in which the volume of a gaseous reaction product exceeds the volume of one of the reacting gases, there is a strong indication that there are fewer particles in unit volume of the product than there are in an equal volume of the reacting gas. Thus the conclusion that there are different numbers of particles in equal volumes of different gases was powerfully supported by experimental data on gaseous densities and combining volumes in gaseous reactions. (p. 266)

One way the equal volumes, equal numbers generalization could have been maintained was by assuming that when the oxygen atoms interact with hydrogen they split in two allowing the formation of twice the number of H_2O molecules in the water vapor, and hence an equal number of particles per unit volume in both the water vapor and the oxygen. However, this possibility would have been so contrary to the time-honored conception of the atom as indivisible, that it never was considered.

AMEDEO AVOGADRO

Instead, the converse of this solution was proposed by Amedeo Avogadro (1776-1856) in a paper published in 1811 in the *Journal de Physique* entitled, "Essay on a Manner of Determining the Relative Masses of the Elementary Molecules of Bodies, and the Proportions in which They Enter into These Compounds." According to Avogadro's novel proposal, if elementary or simple gases are not composed of single atoms but of combinations of atoms, then one can reconcile Dalton's atomic theory with Gay-Lussac's interpretation that equal volumes of gases contain equal numbers of particles.

Thus if particular gases like oxygen, nitrogen, and hydrogen "*do not consist of* [. . .] *individual atoms* [. . .] *but of groups of atoms* [. . .] *joined in a single molecule* of that element'' (p. 284), then the anomalies can be eliminated. For example, the disparity of water vapor containing half the number of particles as the volume of oxygen can be removed if the particles of oxygen and hydrogen are *binary* rather than *monatomic*, the individual *binary* particles of oxygen *separating*, each combining with a *binary* hydrogen particle so that *double the number* of oxygen particles are available to combine with the hydrogen (without an *individual* atom having to divide in two). As Nash indicates: 1 volume of oxygen (O_2) plus 2 volumes of hydrogen (H_2) combine to form 2 volumes of water vapor [H_4O_2] or $2H_2O$. (cf. p. 285) The H_4O_2 was considered to be an intermediate, unstable formation that divided into two molecules of water.

As Avogadro describes this adopting a terminology that is idiosyncratic, using 'molecule' to mean smallest particle and then adding qualifiers to differentiate the particles, 'elementary molecule' meaning 'atom,' 'constituent molecules' meaning the smallest composite atoms of simple gases, and 'integral molecule' designating the basic molecule of a compound gas or some integral multiple of it:

> We suppose that the constituent molecules [smallest composite particles] of any simple gas [. . .] are not formed of only one elementary molecule [atom], but are made up of a certain number of these molecules [atoms] united by attraction to form a single whole [constituent molecules]. Further, that when such [constituent] molecules [e.g., of oxygen] unite with those of another substance [e.g., hydrogen] to form a compound molecule [e.g., of water], the integral molecule that should result [e.g., H_4O_2] splits up into two or more parts (or integral molecules) [e.g., $2H_2O$], each composed of half, quarter, etc, the number of elementary molecules [atoms] forming the constituent molecule [smallest composite particle] of the first substance [e.g., oxygen] . . . . (p. 283; brackets added)

Therefore a unit volume of water vapor would contain the same number of particles as a unit volume of oxygen.

> This is supposed to occur in such a way that the number of integral molecules of the compound [e.g., H_2O] becomes double, quadruple, etc., what it would have been if there had been no splitting up, and exactly what is necessary to satisfy the volume of the resulting gas.

Thus, for example, the integral molecule of water [H₂O] will be composed of a half-molecule [atom] of oxygen with one molecule [two atoms], or, what is the same thing, two half-molecules [atoms] of hydrogen. (p. 283; brackets added)

By making the ingenious proposal that elementary gases are composed of polyatomic (rather than monatomic) particles that separate into their constituent components or atoms when combining with other gases, Avogadro was able to eliminate the anomalies pointed out by Dalton in opposition to the principle that equal volumes of gases (under the same conditions) contain equal numbers of particles, now known as Avogadro's Law. Moreover, as Avogadro indicates, his explanation of the combining volumes of gases enables him to "confirm or rectify" Dalton's suppositional rules of atomic combination with exact ratios based on more precise experimental data.

Dalton, on arbitrary suppositions that appeared to him most natural [i.e., the rule of greatest simplicity] as to the relative number of molecules in compounds, has endeavored to establish ratios between the masses of the molecules of simple substances. Our hypothesis, supposing it well-founded, puts us in a position to confirm or rectify his results from precise data, and, above all, to assign the size of compound molecules according to the volumes of the gaseous compounds, which depends partly on the division of molecules of which this physicist had no idea. (p. 288; brackets added)

This method of determining molecular formulas and calculating atomic weights from the data on the combining *volumes* and *densities* of gases, led Avogadro to believe that he had obtained more accurate results than Dalton whose calculations were based on the combining *weights* of gases. Still, he graciously acknowledged the importance of Dalton's theory, asserting that his own hypothesis was "at bottom merely Dalton's system furnished with a new means of precision through the connection we have found between it and the general fact [of combining volumes] established by M. Gay-Lussac." (p. 292; brackets added)

Despite these advances, there were three weaknesses in Avogadro's explanation that resulted in considerable uncertainty regarding the correct interpretation. First, although the supposition of simple gases being composed of polyatomic particles rescued the 'law' that equal volumes of gases contain the same number of particles, because the 'law' itself was not yet confirmed nor universally accepted the justification of the supposition was suspect. Secondly, assuming the smallest particles of elementary gases to be polyatomic molecules, how could one determine now many atoms the molecules contain and the nature of the force binding them? Furthermore, since the pressure of gases was believed to depend upon the *repulsive* force of the gas particles, how could one reconcile this force with the *attractive* force required to bind the atoms within the molecules, especially as the atoms were all of the same kind? Thirdly, on what basis could one determine how many of these "integral molecules" combined to form compound gases or substances, such as water vapor, ammonia, and nitric compounds? While considerable progress had been made in measuring more accurately the proportions by volume or weight in which elements combine to form compounds, no reliable method had been found for establishing precisely the number of elements in molecular formulas nor their combined atomic weights. Given a correct measurement of combining weights (densities) or volumes, if either the molecular formulas or the atomic weights were known, then the other could be calculated, but because they were not known the computations varied. (cf. pp. 293-4)

DECOMPOSITION BY ELECTROLYSIS

Much of the research in succeeding years was directed toward solving this problem. When early in 1800 Volta invented the pile for producing an electric current, several investigators who believed that the forces binding the atoms in molecules were electrical, realized that this simple battery might be used to decompose compounds into their elements, thus disclosing their atomic structures. The decomposition of chemical substances by an electric current, known as electrolysis, is caused by the voltaic pile inducing opposite electric charges to two terminals or electrodes which, if strong enough to overcome the binding forces of the particles, attracts the oppositely charged particles within the molecules thereby decomposing them. In 1807 Sir Humphry Davy (1778-1829) wrote that "[i]f chemical union be of the [electrical] nature [. . .] I [. . .] hope that the new [electrical] method of analysis may lead us to the discovery of the *true* elements of bodies." (p. 296) Confirming this supposition within a year, he had decomposed alkali metals by electrolysis, suggesting that the affinity among the particles was due to an electromotive force accounting for the stability of chemical compounds that could be measured. (cf. pp. 295-7)

JÖNS JACOB BERZELIUS

Another investigator attracted to this method of analysis was J.J. Berzelius (1779-1848) who, in experimenting with the electrolysis of water with Hisinger, found that oxygen was attracted to the positive pole of the electrode and hydrogen to the negative. When the electrolysis of other compounds indicated that their components too were attracted to opposite poles, implying that they were oppositely charged, he proposed a dualistic classification of chemical elements into "electopositive and electronegative." Furthermore, since experiments in electricity had indicated that opposite electrical charges attract while like charges repel, he inferred (as Davy had) that the stability of compounds could be explained in terms of the attraction of their oppositely charged particles which, when neutralized, left the substances uncharged. Yet they must retain their electrical charge within the molecular structure because after decomposition by electrolysis they manifest their original charges, the negatively charged elements moving to the positive electrode and the positively charged elements attracted to the negative electrode.

Although this hypothesis was difficult to reconcile with Avogadro's theory of polyatomic particles, since the atoms of these composite particles having the same charge should repel rather than attract each other, Berzelius was able to arrive at "the 'correct' formulas for water, ammonia, nitrous gas and a number of other compounds formed from gaseous elements." (p. 300) Using Gay-Lussac's data on combining volumes, he showed conclusively that H_2O is the correct molecular formula for water. Limited as it was to substances that exist in the gaseous state under the normal conditions of temperature and pressure, his hypothesis was nonetheless an advance because he could deduce more exact values than previously for the atomic weights of these elements based on his determination of the correct molecular structure of the gases. Because calculating the atomic weights depended both on the correctness of the combining weights and the molecular formulas, Berzelius devoted a decade to measuring the combing weights of the elements in compounds to determine their atomic weights, publishing his results in tables (Fig. 2) in 1814, 1818, and 1826.

Fig. 2. (Below) "In this table, columns 2, 4 and 6 give the formulae of the oxides assumed by Berzelius, column 8 the modern formulae of the oxides; columns 3 and 5 give the atomic weights recalculated from Berzelius's values, referred to oxygen = 16; column 7 gives Berzelius's values on his alternative scale of hydrogen = 1."

Partington, *op. cit.*, p. 207. Reprinted with the kind permission of MacMillan and Company, Ltd.

BERZELIUS'S ATOMIC WEIGHT TABLES

1	2	3	4	5	6	7	8
		1814		1818		1826	
Element							
O		16		16		16·03	
S	SO^2, SO^3	32·16	SO^2, SO^3	32·19	SO^2, SO^3	32·24	SO_2, SO_3
P	P^2O^3, P^2O^5	26·80	PO^3, PO^5	62·77	P^2O^3, P^2O^5	31·43	P_2O_3, P_2O_5
Cl		(35·16)		(35·41)	Cl^2O^5	35·47	
C	CO, CO^2	11·986	CO, CO^2	12·05	CO, CO^2	12·25	CO, CO_2
N		(14·36)		(14·05)	N^2O, NO	14·19	N_2O, NO
H	H^2O	1·062	H^2O	0·9948	H^2O	1	H_2O
As	AsO^3, AsO^5	134·38	AsO^3, AsO^5	150·52	As^2O^3, As^2O^5	75·33	As_2O_3, As_2O_5
Cr	CrO^3, CrO^6	113·29	CrO^3, CrO^6	112·58	Cr^2O^3, CrO^3	56·38	Cr_2O_3, CrO_3
Si	SiO^3	48·696	SiO^3	47·43	SiO^3	44·44	SiO_2
Hg	HgO, HgO^2	405·06	HgO, HgO^2	405·06	Hg^2O, HgO	202·86	Hg_2O, HgO
Ag	AgO^2	430·107	AgO^2	432·51	AgO	216·6	Ag_2O
Cu	CuO, CuO^2	129·03	CuO, CuO^2	126·62	Cu^2O, CuO	63·42	Cu_2O, CuO
Bi	BiO^2	283·84	BiO^2	283·81	Bi^2O^2	213·22	Bi_2O_3
Pb	PbO^2, PbO^6	415·58	PbO^2, PbO^3	414·24	PbO, PbO^2	207·46	PbO, Pb_2O_3
Sn	SnO^2, SnO^4	235·29	SnO^2, SnO^4	235·3	SnO, SnO^2	117·84	SnO, SnO_2
Fe	FeO^2, FeO^3	110·98	FeO^2, FeO^3	108·55	FeO, Fe^2O^3	54·36	FeO, Fe_2O_3
Zn	ZnO^2	129·03	ZnO^2	129·03	ZnO	64·62	ZnO
Mn	MnO^2, MnO^3	113·85	MnO^2, MnO^3	113·85	MnO, Mn^2O^3	55·43	MnO, Mn_2O_3
Al	AlO^3	54·88	AlO^3	54·77	Al^2O^3	27·43	Al_2O_3
Mg	MgO^2	50·47	MgO^2	50·68	MgO	25·38	MgO
Ca	CaO^2	81·63	CaO^2	81·93	CaO	41·03	CaO
Na	NaO^2	92·69	NaO^2	93·09	NaO	46·62	Na_2O
K	KO^2	156·48	KO^2	156·77	KO	78·51	K_2O

However, lacking a procedure for deciding the exact molecular structure of compounds, there still was considerable uncertainty as to the true atomic weights of most elements, even though the possibilities had been narrowed. (cf. 301-303)

PETIT'S AND DULONG'S SPECIFIC HEAT METHOD

The next attempt to provide a method for determining accurate molecular formulas and atomic weights was not based on the decomposition of molecules by electrolysis, but related to the thermal properties of the atoms. Devising more precise experimental methods for determining the specific heats (the ratio of the quantity of heat required to raise the temperature of a certain weight of a substance one degree to that required to raise an equal weight of water one degree) of various elements, two French chemists, Alexis Thérèse Petit (1791-1820) and Pierre Louis Dulong (1785-1838), discovered that the product of the specific heats and the relative weights of the atoms of an element is nearly constant for all elements. Utilizing the "law" that "[t]he atoms of all the elements have exactly the same capacity for heat" (p. 307), they discovered that they could calculate the atomic weights of the elements by dividing the constant previously mentioned by the specific heat of the element. Comparing their results with Berzelius' table (1818) of combining atomic weights, they found an agreement between their calculation of the relative weights of the atoms of an element and his.

While this derivation of the relative weights of atoms did not itself provide a conclusive result, by comparing the ratio of an element in a known molecular formula and an element of similar atomic weight they could infer the correct molecular formulas of other substances containing the second element. Also, they could use their computation of the atomic weight of an element to decide which, among several other derivations, was the correct one.

This method served, therefore, as a kind of "control" for selecting correct atomic weights, as they stated:

> Whatever may be the final opinion adopted with regard to this relation [between the weights and the specific heats of atoms], it can henceforth serve as a control of the results of chemical analysis. In certain cases it may even offer the most exact method of arriving at information about the proportions of certain combinations [of atoms]. And if [. . .] no fact arises to impair the probability [. . .] this law will also offer the advantage of establishing in a certain and uniform manner, the relative weights of the atoms of all the elements that can be subjected to direct examination. (p. 307; brackets added)

With this procedure of arriving at approximate atomic weights more correct molecular formulas could be inferred, which in turn allowed the calculation of more precise atomic weights. Judiciously selecting "from among the various possibilities" of these methods, by 1840 Berzelius had arrived at "atomic weights and molecular formulas that are in most cases in excellent agreement with those we now accept as correct." (p. 309)

JEAN BAPTISTE ANDRE DUMAS

Despite these successes, considerable skepticism remained as to whether physical substances actually had the structure posited by the atomic theory. Berzelius' dualistic classification of the particles of the elements into electropositive and electronegative made it difficult to accept Avogadro's theory of polyatomic particles coalescing despite having the same charge. Then, however, Jean Baptiste André Dumas (1800-1884) developed a highly effective procedure (still used today) for determining gas densities at high temperatures, allowing more elements to be studied in the gaseous state. This enabled him to apply Avogadro's suggestion "that the relative weights of the particles of the gaseous elements could be inferred from the corresponding relative gas densities" of many more elements. However, expecting that these results would conform to the relative weights of the atoms established by Petit and Dulong based on specific heats, instead there was considerable divergence in the two results, adding to the uncertainty regarding the validity of the atomic theory.

But while Berzelius in his calculations had rejected the concept of polyatomic particles, Dumas accepted Avogadro's law that equal volumes of gases contain equal numbers of particles, along with his hypothesis that these particles are polyatomic. He then demonstrated that the discrepancies in the atomic weights obtained from using the gas density and specific heat methods could be eliminated if one held, as Nash states, "that the polyatomic molecules of the different elements contain different numbers of the respective atoms." (p. 312) Although promising, this supposition raised additional problems, for if equal volumes of different gases contain the same quantity of particles but with varying numbers of atoms, then the atomic weights of the atoms could not be inferred from the gas densities, only the weights of the molecules containing the atoms.

STANISLAO CANNIZZARO

Yet other developments continued to support the belief that the regularities exhibited by elements forming gaseous or chemical compounds were due to some underlying atomic or molecular proportionality. By the middle of the nineteenth century gas pressure was explained by the kinetic theory, according to which gases were composed of widely dispersed mobile particles, rather than Newton's stratified static particles. In addition, there was new evidence from various sources to support Avogadro's theory of polyatomic particles. Finally, in 1858, fifty years after the publication of Dalton's *A New System of Chemistry*, the resolution of the difficulties was found by the Italian chemist Stanislao Cannizzaro (1826-1910).

Accepting Avogadro's law that equal volumes of gases contain equal numbers of particles, Cannizzaro maintained also that these particles were polyatomic or molecular, hence it was not necessary to assume "that the molecules of all the gaseous elements contain equal numbers of their respective atoms." (pp. 315-6) But if that were true, then the weight of the atoms could not be inferred from the densities of the gases unless it were known how many atoms compose the constituent molecules. To determine this, Cannizzaro suggested a different procedure involving "the comparison of the densities of the gaseous *compounds* of the elements." (p. 316)

By weighing the densities (weights) per unit volume of a number of gaseous compounds containing the desired element and determining what proportion of the compound is constituted by that element, he could calculate what fraction of the weight of the compound is due to the element. Beginning with the minimum quantity of the element contained in the compound, he found that the proportions or ratios of the element are always integral multiples of that amount. Then by comparing the ratios in which these minimal weights of the elements are found in various compounds, he calculated the relative *weights* of the elementary particles. Assuming that the most elementary particle contains one atom, this establishes the atomic weight of that element.

Furthermore, if the unit volume of the pure element is twice the weight that one expected from the atomic weight, it could be inferred that the smallest particle is a binary molecule containing two atoms of the element. Then, by comparing the atomic weights of the elements using hydrogen as a unit of 1, the relative weights of the other elements could be derived: for example, that oxygen is 16, carbon 12, sulfur 32, and so forth. Because these atomic weights agreed with those established by Petit and Dulong and were arrived at by completely different methods, they provided strong independent confirmation of the theory. In 1808 Dalton had emphasized "the importance and advantage of ascertaining *the relative weights of the ultimate particles of both simple and compound bodies*" which, owing to many contributors, was finally achieved by Cannizzaro a half century later. (cf. pp. 318-9)

Thus the prescient conjecture of the ancient atomists, that the inexplicable regularities of nature observed on the macrolevel could be explained by interacting particles existing in the microlevel, which has been *the* fundamental presupposition of science since the overthrow of Aristotelianism, was vindicated. To deny that one is justified in believing in such a domain because it is not directly perceptible is, to say the least, naive, especially since atomic structure is now visible through the tunneling microscope. Today the development of advanced technology often allows one to confirm more directly, by enhanced observation, what there was compelling evidence for believing previously, thereby providing additional vindication of one's former belief.

The determination of accurate atomic weights by Cannizzaro in 1848 culminated slightly more than a decade later in the nearly simultaneous and independent publication of the Periodic Law and Periodic Table by Julius Lothar Meyer (1830-1895) and Dmitri Ivanovich Mendeleev (1834-1907). Mendeleev published his Periodic Table in Russian in April 1869, while Lothar Meyer's paper, although dated December 1869, was not published in Germany until 1870.[34] Mendeleev describes the striking effect Cannizzaro's theory had on the audience at the Karlsruhe world conference of chemists in 1860:

> Many of those present probably remember how vain were the hopes of coming to an understanding, and how much ground was gained at that congress by the followers of the unitary theory so brilliantly represented by Cannizzaro. I vividly remember the impression produced by his speeches, which admitted of no compromise, and seemed to advocate truth itself [. . .] for the ideas of Cannizzaro proved, after a few years, to be the only ones which could stand criticism, and which represented an atom as—'the smallest portion of an element which enters into a molecule of its compound.' Only such real atomic weights—not conventional ones—could afford a basis for generalization.[35]

In his *Principles of Chemistry* published in 1869, as in the first publication, Mendeleev described his "periodic law" as the discovery that "the properties of the elements are in periodic dependence upon their atomic weights."[36] Meyer expressed this correlation in his "well-known atomic volume curve, in which the periodic dependence of a quantitative property was clearly shown as a function of the atomic weight,"[37] the property periodically rising and falling among the elements as the atomic weight increases.

One of the most conclusive instances in the history of science that the regularities found among observable phenomena are caused by properties of elements existing within the microstructure, Mendeleev summarized his conclusions in eight points delivered in a Faraday Lecture to the Fellows of the Chemical Society of the Royal Institution in 1889.

1.   The elements, if arranged according to their atomic weights, exhibit an evident *periodicity* of properties.
2.   Elements which are similar as regards their chemical properties have

atomic weights which are either of nearly the same value (e.g., platinum, iridium, osmium) or which increase regularly (e.g., potassium, rubidium, caesium).

3. The arrangement of the elements, or of groups of elements, in the order of their atomic weights, corresponds to their so-called *valencies* as well as, to some extent, to their distinctive chemical properties—as is apparent, among other series, in that of lithium, beryllium, barium, carbon, nitrogen, oxygen, and iron.

4. The elements which are the most widely diffused have small atomic weights.

5. The *magnitude* of the atomic weight determines the character of the element, just as the magnitude of the molecule determines the character of a compound.

6. We must expect the discovery of many yet *unknown* elements—for example, elements analogous to aluminum and silicon, whose atomic weight would be between 65 and 75.

7. The atomic weight of an element may sometimes be amended by a knowledge of those of the contiguous elements. Thus, the atomic weight of tellurium must lie between 123 and 126, and cannot be 128.

8. Certain characteristic properties of the elements can be foretold from their atomic weights.[38]

In the same lecture Mendeleev gave a more general summary of the import of the periodic law.

Before the promulgation of this [periodic] law the chemical elements were mere fragmentary, incidental facts in nature; there was no special reason to expect the discovery of new elements, and the new ones which were discovered from time to time appeared to be possessed of quite novel properties. The law of periodicity first enabled us to perceive undiscovered elements at a distance which formerly was inaccessible to chemical vision; and long ere they were discovered, new elements appeared before our eyes possessed of a number of well defined properties.[39]

The "foretelling" or "predictive" successes of the Periodic Law and Table contributed significantly to the acceptance of the atomic theory as a description of physical reality, at least at a certain level or domain. Later these chemical properties would be explained more adequately by atomic numbers, but that awaited developments at the turn of the century showing that the atom, rather than being indivisible as believed for two and a half millennia, was composite, the more fundamental subatomic particles accounting for its properties. A whole new world of lilliputian particles had yet to be discovered.

NOTES

1. Lancelot Law Whyte, *Essay on Atomism: From Democritus to 1960* (Middletown: Wesleyan Univ. Press, 1961), p. 3

2. Richard H. Schlagel, *From Myth to the Modern Mind: the Origins and Growth of Scientific Thought*, Vol. I, *Theogony Through Ptolemy*, (New York: Peter Lang Publishing, Inc., 1995), Ch. IV.

3. Cf. *ibid.*, pp. 288-292.

4. Cf. *ibid.*, 327-331.

5. Cf. *ibid.*, p. 227.

6. J.R. Partington, *A Short History of Chemistry*, third edition revised and enlarged (New York: Harper and Brothers, [1937] (1960), p. 69.

7. This account of the history of phlogiston is based on Partington, *op. cit.*, pp. 85-89. Until otherwise indicated, the following page references in the text are to this work.

8. *Experiments on Air*, 1790, Vol. I, p. 248f., 276. Partington, *op. cit.*, p. 137. Italics added except for *Phlogiston*.

9. Cf. James B. Conant, "The Overthrow of the Phlogiston Theory," in James B. Conant and Leonard K. Nash (eds.), *Harvard Case Histories in Experimental Science* (Cambridge: Harvard Univ. Press, 1948), Vol. I, p. 92.

10. *Ibid.*, p. 72.

11. In one of the tragic excesses of the French Revolution, Lavoisier "was tried by Jury, found guilty of conspiracy against the people of France by correspondence with the enemies of France [who were, in fact, English scientists like Priestley], and guillotined on 8th May, 1794." Partington,

op. cit., p. 122; brackets added. Conversely, because of his sympathy for the French Revolution, when a dinner in honor of the fall of the Bastille was given in Priestley's home in Birmingham, his house was sacked and his laboratory pillaged, although he may have been forewarned of the danger and escaped harm by not being present at the dinner.

12. A. Lavoisier, *Traité Élémentaire de Chimie*, 140, 1789. Partington, *op. cit.*, p. 124.

13. Conant, *op. cit.*, pp. 72-3. Cf. Henry Guerlac, *Lavoisier—The Crucial Year* (Ithaca: New York, 1961), for an explanation of the perplexities surrounding this discovery and its publication.

14. Cf. Conant, *op. cit.*, p. 69. Unless otherwise indicated, the immediately following references in the text are to this work.

15. J. Priestley, *The Doctrine of phlogiston Established*, 88, 1800. Partington, *op. cit.*, pp. 126-7. Brackets added. The reference to Mrs. Lavoisier was significant because she worked with Lavoisier in his experiments and drew the diagrams in his famous *Traité de Chimie*.

16. Partington, *op. cit.*, pp. 131-2. Unless otherwise indicated, the immediately following references in the text are to this work.

17. Newton, *Opticks*, Query, 31.

18. *Traité de Chimie*, 140, 1789. Partington, *op. cit.*, p. 134.

19. Partington lists the journals and dates of Proust's publications, but not of the quotation. Cf. pp. 153-154

20. Cf. J. Bronowski and Bruce Mazlish, *The Western Intellectual Tradition* (New York: Harper Torchbooks, 1960), p. 352.

21. Cf. Leonard K. Nash, "The Atomic-Molecular Theory," in James Conant and Leonard K. Nash (eds.), *op. cit.*, p. 239.

22. Partington, *op. cit.*, p. 158.

23. Nash, *op. cit.*, p. 242.

24. Unfortunately, Higgins' attempt to represent atoms by symbols and use the symbols to show how the atoms are related in compounds, connecting them by lines in a kind of primitive valency bond, led him to claim priority in originating the chemical atomic theory and accuse Dalton of plagiarism. However, since Higgins did not attempt to relate the atoms according to their atomic weights, the crucial aspect of Dalton's theory, his claim to priority and charge of plagiarism have been dismissed. Cf. Elizabeth C. Patterson, *John Dalton and the Atomic Theory* (New York: Anchor Books, 1970), pp. 118-19.

25. Frank Greenaway, *John Dalton and the Atom* (Ithaca: Cornell Univ. Press, 1966), p. 57.

26. Cf. Patterson, *op. cit.*, Chapter III for a full description of his early life. The following brief summary is based on her account as are the textual references.

27. Greenaway, *op. cit.*, p. 130.

28. Nash, *op. cit.*, p. 222. The first brackets are added by me and the second by Nash. Unless otherwise indicated, the following references in the text are to this work.

29. Cf. Greenaway, *op. cit.*, p. 132.

30. Greenaway, *op. cit.*, p. 133.

31. The Royal Philosophical Institution of London was founded in 1799 by Count Rumford and members of the English aristocracy. Originally named Benjamin Thompson, he was "a Royalist American in the service of the Elector Palatine of Bavaria, by whom he was created Count Rumford of the Holy Roman Empire [. . .]." Partington, *op. cit.*, p. 181. Humphrey Davy and Michael Faraday contributed to the early reputation of the Institution as one of the most famous scientific organizations in the world.

32. Greenaway, *op. cit.*, pp. 137-8. Brackets added.

33. Gay-Lussac's explanation for why these precise ratios of combination obtain among the *combining volumes of gases*, but not among the *combining weights of substances*, is that the distance among the gas particles preclude the interference of atomic forces, such as attraction and repulsion, that occur in non-gaseous states, allowing the gases to combine

solely in terms of their densities and volumes. As he says, the "attraction of the molecules in solids and liquids is, therefore, the cause that modifies their special properties; and it appears that it is only when the attraction is entirely destroyed, as in gases, that bodies under similar conditions obey simple and regular laws." (p. 253)

34. Cf. Partington, *op. cit.*, pp. 346-349.

35. William C. Dampier and Margaret Dampier (eds.), *Readings In The Literature Of Science* (New York: Harper Torchbooks, 1959), p. 115.

36. Partington, *op. cit.*, p. 349.

37. *Ibid.*

38. I. Mendelyeev, Faraday Lecture, 1889. In *The Principles of Chemistry*, Vol. II. William C. Dampier & Margaret Dampier (eds.), *op. cit.*, pp. 113-114.

39. I. Mendelyeev, *op. cit.*, p. 501; brackets added. Enrico Cantore, *Atomic Order* (Cambridge: The MIT Press, 1969), p. 39, f.n. 54.

CHAPTER X

PROBING THE INTERIOR OF THE ATOM

[. . .] the times in which man has finally seen what
Newton in his Opticks foresaw [. . .].[1]

Pais

However significant the scientific discoveries and theoretical advances of the past centuries, they hardly compare in depth and scope to the developments in science and technology of the twentieth century. This reflects both the fact that there are more scientists engaged in inquiry today than in all its past history and that the cumulative achievements in this century have proven so remarkable. In 1918 Rutherford declared that "[t]he two decades, 1895 to 1915, will always be recognized as a period of remarkable scientific activity which has no counterpart in the history of Physical Science . . ."[2] But as momentous as these accomplishments may have seemed to Rutherford, they represent just the beginning of a tidal wave of experimental and theoretical developments that would sweep through and transform civilization.

Rutherford died in 1937 from an operation for a strangulated hernia that today would be routine. He did not live to witness nuclear fission and fusion, the development of radio telescopes, tunneling microscopes, nuclear reactors and particle accelerators, genetic engineering, computer technology, not to mention the lunar landing and controlled interplanetary space flights. Such extraordinary achievements were beyond even the imaginations of visionaries like Leonardo da Vinci and Jules Verne. Perhaps the most momentous of the developments is the fact that the destiny of our species no longer depends solely on accidental genetic changes, but also on deciphering and rewriting the genetic code.

One indication of the magnitude of the changes that were to come is illustrated in the conception of the atom in 1895. As had been true for nearly two millennia and a half, the atom retained its original meaning of a homogeneous indivisible particle—although Epicurus as early as the fourth century B.C. had conjectured that the various sizes and shapes of atoms might be due to internal "minima" which, like quarks, cannot exist separately.[3] Maxwell (1831-1879) similarly believed that even though spectroscopic emissions produced by the vibration of atoms were indicative of "a very considerable degree of complexity," they nevertheless were unalterable and indivisible, affirming that "an atom is a body that cannot be cut in two"[4]and that despite the cataclysmic changes in the universe throughout the past "the foundation stones of the material universe [atoms] remain unbroken and unworn [. . .] as they were created—perfect in number and measure and weight . . ."[5]

The considerable progress during the early nineteenth century in identifying elements like oxygen, hydrogen, and carbon according to their relative atomic weights, along with analyzing the chemical composition of substances like water and carbon dioxide into their atomic components H_2O and CO_2, lent considerable credibility to the atomic theory—the experimental discovery of atomic weights and molecular compounds implying the prior existence of these physical structures. Nonetheless, a number of distinguished scientists, including the famous chemist Wilhelm Ostwald (1853-1932) and influential physicist Ernest Mach (1838-1916), continued to deny the existence of atoms (until the evidence became compelling) on the grounds that while the concept of atoms serves a heuristic purpose in organizing and predicting data and in imagining the composition of compounds, in reality they are more like the variables in algebraic equations that can be given various numerical values for computational purposes without representing anything actual.

It was not until J.J. Thomson identified (1898) the electron and conceived of ionization as "broken atoms," Einstein explained (1905) Brownian motion deriving an independent value for Avogadro's number and molecular diameters, and Rutherford conducted (1908) his scattering experiments directing *alpha* particles on gold foil, that the conversion to atomic realism occurred. Persuaded finally by J.J. Thomson and S.A. Arrhenius, Ostwald "recanted in the 1912 edition of his *Allgemeine Chemie*,"[6] while the evidence of the scintillating effects of the *alpha* particles may have convinced Mach at the end of his life, although the evidence is not conclusive. In any event, by 1914 the great French experimentalist, Jean Perrin (1870-1942), who confirmed Einstein's Brownian motion calculations, wrote in a book that presents the extensive evidence at the time supporting the atomic theory that

> [t]he atomic theory has triumphed. Its opponents, which until recently were numerous, have been convinced and have abandoned one after the other the sceptical position that was for a long time legitimate and no doubt useful.[7]

But while the question of the existence of atoms may have been settled, the problem of whether they were internally compact and therefore indivisible or structurally composite and hence decomposable, was not. Moreover, if the latter were true, as new experimental discoveries seemed to indicate, then how was this structure to be determined? As the previous reference to Maxwell indicated, spectroscopic analysis provided not only one of the earliest and most reliable methods of identifying elements, it also presented clues for determining atomic and nuclear structures. As with most modern discoveries, the origins of spectroscopy occur in Newton's prism experiments demonstrating that when a beam of sunlight is refracted through a prism a spectrum of colors is formed, indicating that ordinary light is not homogeneous but composed of discretely colored rays. Furthermore, Newton anticipated the modern procedure of spectroscopic analysis and the mechanism producing it when he conjectured in Query 8 of the *Opticks*: "[d]o not all fix'd Bodies, when heated beyond a certain degree, emit Light and shine; and is not this Emission perform'd by the vibrating motion of its parts?"

SPECTRAL EMISSIONS AND BALMER'S SERIES

Perhaps taking his cue from Newton, Thomas Melville (1726-1753) may have been the first to observe discrete spectral lines when he found that burning ordinary salt in a flame produced monochromatic yellow light (actually the heated sodium atoms in the salt molecule produce the yellow D-line). Then William Wollaston (1766-1828) and Joseph von Fraunhofer (1787-1826) detected the lines of the solar spectrum, the colored lines representing the emission and the dark lines the absorption spectrum. Because basic gases as well as elements have a signature spectrum, spectroscopic analysis was used also to identify gases. For example, in 1853 Ångström (1814-1874) observed the spectrum of hydrogen (which would play such a crucial role later in Bohr's model of the atom), detecting red, blue-green, and two violet emission lines (later called the Balmer series). Since Newton's interpretation of colored rays in terms of variously sized corpuscles had been replaced by the wave theory of Young and Fresnel comprising wavelengths and frequencies, Ångström (along with Julius Plücker) computed the wavelengths of the four spectral emissions of hydrogen which agree remarkably with modern values, indicating how precise experimental measurements were becoming.

Gustav Kirchhoff (1824-1887) then investigated the functional relation between emission and absorption spectra, formulating

what is now known as Kirchhoff's law of blackbody radiation, according to which [. . .] the ratio [stated loosely] of emissive to

absorptive power of a body in thermal equilibrium with radiation is a
universal function of frequency ν and temperature T.[8]

This functional correlation between the spectral density and blackbody
radiation will provide Planck the essential clue to his famous equation and
constant. Because spectral analysis requires heating the element, exact results
depend upon a non-luminous flame which does not contaminate the sample.
To this day chemistry laboratories are equipped with Bunsen burners because
the burner perfected by Robert Bunsen (1811-1899) produces a purified flame.
This invention led to Kirchhoff and Bunsen collaborating to identify elements
because spectral emissions are more accurate than atomic weights for
discovering the chemical properties of elements.

> In spectrum analysis . . . the colored lines [. . .] determine a chemical
> property of a similar unchangeable and fundamental nature as the
> atomic weight . . . and they can be determined with an almost
> astronomical accuracy. What gives the spectrum-analytic method a
> quite special significance is the circumstance that it extends in an
> almost unlimited way the limits imposed up till now on the chemical
> characterization of matter.[9]

Although the situation was more complex than Kirchhoff and Bunsen
originally believed, with Plücker and Johann Hittorf (1824-1914) discovering
that even elementary substances produce different line spectra under different
temperatures, they nonetheless realized that the technique could be used to
discover new elements and to analyze the chemical composition of the sun and
distant planets. Thus gaps in the Periodic Table were filled with new
discoveries, while solar and stellar spectra still provide our main information
about the chemical composition of planets, comets, and the nearest stars.
Moreover, because substances contain fixed amounts of elements with their
particular spectrum, they also produce characteristic band spectra consisting of
closely packed lines which serve as labels for their components.[10]

At the time it was believed that heating the atoms or molecules increase
their vibrations or oscillations which in turn cause the emissions, the
temperature correlated with the frequencies of the emission according to
Kirchhoff's law. Temperature variations would, of course, affect the
vibrational or oscillatory frequencies of the atoms and molecules, but how does
that produce the emissions? Until the electron was discovered and more was
known about the internal structure of the atom such explanations were not

possible, so instead a search began for a mathematical expression correlating the series of emissions.

In two physics papers published when he was sixty years old that brought him lasting fame, Johann Balmer (1825-1898) discovered a harmonic relation among the wavelengths measured by Ångström of the series of four hydrogen spectra which he expressed in the following formula (using modern notation): "$v = R(1 \backslash n^2 - 1 \backslash m^2)$ where $n = 1, 2, 3. . ., m > n$ and integer."[11] In the formula n and m represent the wavelengths of succeeding spectral lines, R a constant, v the frequency. Although originally applied to the wavelengths of the hydrogen series, when Balmer was told of additional wavelengths he found that these too fitted his formula so that he was able to predict an infinite number of new frequency lines from those found earlier, while also discovering a new constant. This constant R is known as the Rydberg-Ritz constant because Johannes Rydberg (1854-1919) and Walter Ritz (1878-1909) each produced more general formulas containing the constant R of which Balmer's is a special case.

Again, however, the formula as a correlation among measurable data had no physical significance regarding the structures and processes that produced the correlations. Antirealist scientists or philosophers of science, who restrict their interpretation of physics to the search for predictable correlations among measurable phenomena, *do not realize how crucial the search for the mechanisms producing these correlations have been for the progress of science.* Each subsequent step, as Pais clearly illustrates in his three superb books, depends upon discovering the elements, structures, or interactions that produce the observable mathematical correlations. The antirealist interpretation of science is as inadequate as an explanation of the movement of an automobile would be limited to descriptions of the external operations of the driver and the vehicle without any reference to how the motor, electrical system, transmission, and differential work. As we now realize, although Balmer's formula does not reveal the underlying causes of the correlations, it nonetheless does have an essential significance which will be apparent to Bohr when he formulates the quantum theory of spectra.

Four other developments between 1895 and 1915 were, like emission spectra, indicative of an internal atomic transformation without, however, disclosing the nature of this transformation: Röntgen's discovery of X-rays, Becquerel's and the Curies' detection of radiation, J.J. Thomson's identification of the electron, and Rutherford's discovery of *alpha* (α) and *beta* (β) rays. The reason these discoveries were interpreted as evidence of internal atomic structures and transformations is that while the emissions undoubtedly originated from the atoms of the substances, no adequate account of the emission was possible based merely on the vibration or oscillation of *solid* atoms.

RÖNTGEN'S DISCOVERY OF X-RAYS

The discovery in 1895 by Wilhelm Conrad Röntgen (1845-1923), when he was fifty years old, of an unknown ray with startling properties is often described as accidental, as if being unrelated to any background circumstances. Yet as is true probably of all discoveries, this one occurred due to an extensive history of related research on cathode rays (so named by Eugen Goldstein), illustrating a feature of scientific inquiry that will become increasingly important from this time forward, the dependence of scientific advances on improved apparatus. Ever since Michael Faraday's investigation of electrical discharges in gases (1833-38) using a vacuum tube in which a current is passed through rarified gases from a negative electrode or cathode to a positive electrode or anode, producing a glow on the inner surface of the opposite end of the tube, scientists were curious as to the nature of the electrical discharges causing the glow, as well as to the glow itself. Since the luminosity resembled that produced by phosphorescent substances, it was thought that it was a kind of phosphorescent phenomena, while various experiments passing the cathode rays through electrical and magnetic fields were performed to determine if the effects disclosed something about the nature of the rays.

Because the effectiveness of the experimental investigations depended on the degree of the vacuum produced in the tube along with the strength of the current, considerable effort was made to increase the vacuum and the induction. About the middle of the nineteenth century Johann Geissler (1815-1879) perfected a mercury vacuum pump used by Faraday that produced a greater and more stable vacuum. Later Johann Hittorf, Philipp Lenard (1862-1947), and Sir William Crookes (1832-1919) performed numerous experiments with cathode rays in evacuated tubes much improved with the new vacuum pumps and tubes.

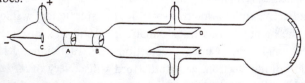

Fig. 1. A drawing of a cathode ray tube in Philosophical Magazine. 1897. 44:293.

In addition, Heinrich Rühmkorff (1803-1874) devised a new type of induction coil or transformer generating high voltage differences that produced sparks in the air or induced stronger currents in the vacuum tube. Faraday used this Rümkorff coil in his later experiments, as did all subsequent investigators.

Intrigued by previous experiments with cathode rays, particularly those of Lenard on rays extracted from the tube, Röntgen was repeating these experiments when he made his famous discovery of a mysterious new kind of ray with remarkable penetrating power. Working in a dark room to enhance the observability of the cathode rays on the evening of November 8, 1895, he had completely covered a Hittorf vacuum tube with black cardboard to shut out any rays. The accidental discovery occurred when unexpectedly he noticed that a sheet of paper coated with barium platinum-cyanide placed a short distance from the cathode tube fluoresced, indicating that some rays must have interacted with the coating producing light. Investigating further, he found that even when he reversed the screen so the uncoated side faced the tube or when he moved the screen farther away, the effect continued.

But the most startling result occurred when he placed various objects between the tube and the screen which did not project an image, appearing to be transparent unless, like his hand, the bones or a metal ring obstructed the rays producing a dramatic picture of the skeletal structure of his hand.

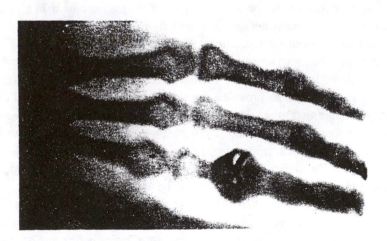

Fig. 2. Röntgen's X-ray of his wife's hand taken in 1895.

As familiar as we are today with X-ray machines as well as radio, television, and microwaves, it is difficult to appreciate the extraordinary novelty of this discovery. Röntgen was so astonished at his experimental findings that he had difficulty accepting what he witnessed, delaying publishing his discovery until he had replaced the screen with photographic plates that recorded what he observed.

When he finally felt confident enough of his discovery to submit the results for publication the following month, he described them as follows:

> If we pass the discharge from a large Rühmkorff coil through a Hittorf or a sufficiently exhausted Lenard, Crookes, or similar apparatus and cover the tube with a somewhat closely-fitting mantle of thin black cardboard, we observe in a completely darkened room that a paper screen covered with barium-platino-cyanide lights up brilliantly and fluoresces equally well whether the treated side or the other be turned towards the discharge tube.[12]

He added that "the fluorescence is still visible at a distance of two meters from the apparatus" and that it "is easy to prove that the cause of the fluorescence emanates from the discharge apparatus and not from any other point in the conducting circuit."[13] Referring to the unknown rays as "X-rays," he confirmed his discovery by including "photographs . . . of the shadows of the bones of the hand; . . . of a set of weights enclosed in a small box; of a compass in which the needle is entirely closed by metal; . . . and so on."[14] To ensure scientific recognition, he sent preprints of his article to prominent scientists such as Boltzmann, Lord Kelvin, Stokes, and Poincaré.

The reaction throughout the world was stunning. While initially incredulous, the photographs provided nearly incontrovertible evidence, as did the fact that scientists the world over readily reproduced the effects. Moreover, the significance of these X-ray photographs for medical diagnosis was immediately apparent, increasing their importance. For his discovery Röntgen received the Nobel Prize in physics in 1901, the first to be awarded. In the original article reporting his discovery, he naturally speculated as to the nature of the rays, concluding that although the term 'rays' was appropriate to designate the transmissions because they produced shadows, these extracted rays (occurring outside the cathode tube) could not be cathode rays because they are much less absorbent in air than cathode rays.[15]

Performing the usual experiments to detect the properties of electrical discharges, he found that the rays were not deflected by strong magnetic fields, nor did he detect any significant refraction, reflection, or polarization despite the fact that the intensity of the rays decreased inversely with the square of the distance, just as electromagnetic waves. He thus concluded that the rays were a form of electromagnetic vibration but that unlike light, they were not transverse vibrations in the ether but longitudinal vibrations.

> May not the new rays be due to longitudinal vibrations in the ether? I must admit that I have put more and more faith in this idea in the course of my research, and it now behooves me therefore to announce my suspicion, although I know well that this explanation requires further corroboration.[16]

Although this conclusion violates a fundamental principle of electromagnetism that light rays vibrate "only in directions transverse to its motion," as Pais points out, this was not as well established at the time, so that a number of physicists such as FitzGerald, Boltzmann, and Oliver Lodge supported Röntgen's interpretation of these rays as longitudinal vibrations in the ether. Other physicists noted that the absence of appreciable refraction, reflection, and polarization would not be indicative of a different direction of vibration if the wavelength of X-rays were small, making these effects difficult to detect. It was not until 1912 when Max von Laue (1879-1960) suggested using crystals whose regular molecular structure would serve as a grid, that diffraction was experimentally confirmed by Walter Friedrich (1883-1968) and Paul Knipping (1883-1935). That meant that beyond the solar spectrum in the upper range there exist much smaller wavelengths, extending the range of the unobservable.

As word of Röntgen's discovery of a mysterious new ray spread throughout the world, physicists took up the challenge of determining precisely the origin and nature of these rays. As indicated earlier, the resemblance of the glow on the inner surface of the cathode tube to phosphorescence led physicists initially to assume that they were related. Having learned from his colleague Poincaré (one of the recipients of Röntgen's preprints) that Röntgen was convinced that the fluorescent glow on the inner surface of the cathode tube was the source of the X-rays, Henri Becquerel (1852-1908) decided to determine if all phosphorescent substances emitted X-rays.

BECQUEREL'S DISCOVERY OF RADIATION

The third generation of a distinguished family of physicists to have investigated luminescence among other subjects, after experimenting with various phosphorescent bodies without detecting any rays, Becquerel turned to a sample of uranium salt which he knew to be fluorescent: uranyle potassium sulfate which had been studied by his father. Proceeding like Röntgen but substituting uranium salt for the cathode tube, he wrapped a photographic plate in black paper placing the uranium salt on top. Assuming that like other phosphorescent material, light or heat was required to produce the effect, he placed the arrangement in the sun for several hours and found that after being developed the photographic plate did have an image of the uranium salt, even though enveloped by the black paper. When he placed a coin or pieces of metal between the salt and the paper, an outline of these objects appeared on the negative, indicating that the rays were obstructed by the metal but had penetrated the ordinarily opaque paper, analogous to Röntgen's experimental results.

Then, however, the unexpected happened. Intending to perform a similar experiment with a thin copper cross inserted between the paper and the uranium but finding the Paris sky overcast (as it usually is in March), he placed the sample in a dark cupboard until he could repeat the experiment in the sunlight. Whether by chance or premonition, after the cloud banks persisted for several days he decided to develop the photograph even though there had been no sun to activate the uranium and produce an image. As his son Jean (the fourth generation of physicists to occupy successively the same chair of physics at the Paris *Musée d'Histoire Naturelle*) reported, his father "was stupefied . . . when he found that his silhouette pictures were even more intense than the ones he had obtained the week before."[17] This discovery was made on March 1, 1896, the year following Röntgen's similar unexpected discovery. The reason for his astonishment is that he thought that uranium salts like phosphorescent materials would not emit rays unless activated by the sun. The fact that they did so independently of the effects of the sun or of any external cause seemed to imply that the rays were generated *spontaneously* within the uranium compound itself.

THE CURIES' DISCOVERY OF RADIOACTIVE SUBSTANCES

Unlike Röntgen's X-rays that were internationally acclaimed, Becquerel's discovery was unheralded even by scientists. It was not until Marie and Pierre Curie took up the inquiry of radioactivity, as it was named by Marie Curie, two years later that it became of paramount importance. Born in Warsaw Poland, Marya Sklodowska (1867-1934) emigrated to Paris when she was twenty-four years old to study physics, enrolling in the Faculty of Sciences. In 1894 she met Pierre Curie (1859-1906) who was then director of the laboratory in the School of Industrial Physics and Chemistry in Paris. Married the following year, they began the most famous husband and wife collaboration in the history of science. They had two children, Irène and Eve, the latter known for her excellent biography of her mother while the elder Irène (1897-1956), following her mother's example, married Jean Frédérick Joliot (1900-1958), a physicist, with whom she shared the Nobel Prize in physics in 1935 for their work in radioactivity.

In 1897 at Pierre's suggestion, Marie (as she then was called) decided to investigate "Becquerel rays" as the subject of her doctoral dissertation, repeating Becquerel's experiments using an electrometer improved by Pierre in place of Becquerel's electroscope to measure more precisely the degree of radiation. Determining "that the intensity of the uranium radiation was proportional to the amount of uranium in the compound and independent of its chemical form,"[18] she confirmed Berquerel's suspicion that the source of the rays was the uranium atoms, not the molecular compound. In a paper coauthored by Marie, Pierre, and Gustave Bémont, the authors state that "[o]ne of us [Marie] has shown that radioactivity is an atomic property,"[19] affirming for the first time that radioactivity was an inherent property of atoms. Analyzing the known elements, Marie discovered that only thorium emits rays similar to uranium, introducing the term 'radioactive substance' in the title of her second paper to describe the spontaneous radiation, the first use of the term.[20] Deciding to examine natural radioactive ores, she found that some were considerably more radioactive than uranium or thorium, inferring that the more intense radiation must be indicative of a new element. As Pais states, "[w]ith this conjecture she introduced another novelty into physics: *radioactive properties are a diagnostic for the discovery of the new substances* [. . .]."[21]

Because isolating an element from an ore by chemical analysis is an extremely arduous and time-consuming task, Marie enlisted the help of Pierre who thereafter discontinued his own research to devote all his time to their collaborative investigation of radioactive materials. Together they extracted from pitchblende (containing uranium oxide) and calcite (containing uranyl phosphate) a residue so highly radioactive that they concluded it must be another new element, naming it "polonium" in honor of Marie's natal country. They announced their discovery in a paper presented jointly to the *Académie des Sciences* in 1898, which was published in the issue of *Comptes Rendus* previously cited. They also found that polonium spontaneously discharges half its radioactivity in a characteristic time, called "half-life." Continuing in their task of isolating radioactive elements, they discovered another new residue which they named "radium," the atomic weight of which was determined by Marie in 1902 to be 225.   While it was known that the newly discovered radioactive elements spontaneously emit radiation having a certain energy or heat, the source of the energy was unknown at the time.   Although those explanations were yet to come, the discovery of radioactivity by Becquerel and the isolation of radioactive elements by the Curies was a major accomplishment for which they shared the Nobel Prize in 1903, while Madame Curie after the death of Pierre received a second Nobel Prize in 1911, this time in chemistry.

Pierre Curie had been killed in April 1906 at age 46 when he was struck by a vehicle in Paris as he was crossing the rue Dauphine on the left bank near the Pont Neuf.   In 1900 he had been appointed assistant professor at the Sorbonne, a distinction long overdue.   Shortly after his death Marie was appointed his successor, "the first time in the venerable institution's [the "mother of universities"] more than six-hundred-year-long history that a women was appointed to a professorship."[22]   In her inaugural address the following November, Marie began reading at precisely the place Pierre had stopped in his last lecture.

Later, during the First World War, she and her eldest daughter Irène "indignant about the lack of radiological equipment in the field hospitals [. . .] personally tried to remedy the situation by organizing an ambulance service equipped with X-ray equipment."[23]   Despite her long exposure to radiation Marie lived to be sixty-seven, although she suffered for many years (as did Pierre) from strange symptoms finally dying in 1934 in a sanitorium from aplastic pernicious anaemia, a deterioration of bone narrow due to overdoses of radiation.

J.J. THOMSON'S DISCOVERY OF THE ELECTRON

In deference to chronological rather than thematic continuity, the account of the investigation of radioactive atomic emissions will be interrupted to describe one of the major events in the history of science, the discovery of a fundamental building block or particle of the universe. As the question of the reality of the atom—regarded as the smallest division of matter—was still very much in doubt, the discovery of a particle even smaller than the atom, one of the basic constituents of physical reality, was "startling." Although a number of individuals contributed to this discovery, Joseph John Thomson (1856-1940) is given credit for its definitive identification.

The term 'electric' derives from the ancient Greeks who observed that when amber (the name of which in Greek is 'electric') is rubbed by wool, some kind of force is generated that attracts chaff or straw. As described in Chapter VIII, much progress was made in the investigation of electricity in the eighteenth century, culminating in the distinction between attractive and repulsive forces or positive and negative charges. But it was not until Geissler developed the mercury vacuum pump and perfected the vacuum tube that sufficiently low gas pressure could be attained, so that the effects of the electrical discharge or cathode rays could be studied. While Röntgen and Becquerel investigated the emissions produced by the supposedly phosphorescent glow caused by the cathode rays, others investigated the rays themselves.

Divided along nationalistic or geographic lines as they had been in Newton's time regarding the nature of light, the English investigators preferred a corpuscular interpretation while the continental physicists, especially the Germans, advocated waves.

> As is well known there are two opposing views on the nature of the cathode rays. The earlier one, especially adopted by the English physicists, considers the rays as negatively-charged particles. According to the second one, more representative of the German physicists, especially Goldstein, Wiedemann, Hertz and Lenard, the cathode rays are processes in the ether.[24]

For example, in 1879 Crookes had described the rays as negatively charged gas molecules, "little indivisible particles which with good warrant are supposed to constitute the physical basis of the Universe,"[25] while Röntgen had interpreted them as longitudinal vibrations of the ether.

There the matter stood in 1897 when J.J. Thomson determined that the rays were particles, later named 'electrons.' Having been appointed Cavendish Professor in 1884 at the young age of twenty-eight to succeed Lord Rayleigh (who resigned as intended after serving for five years), who in turn had succeeded Maxwell, the first Cavendish Professor, Thomson was considered extremely clumsy when it came to handling experimental equipment, but a genius at understanding the functioning of apparatus, designing experiments, and interpreting their results. Thus like Rutherford and Bohr he is honored not only for his own discoveries, but also for those produced at the Cavendish Laboratory under his direction: for example, by Rutherford, Wilson, Richardson, etc.

His particular accomplishment did not consist in discovering a new phenomenon, as had been true of Röntgen, Becquerel, and the Curies, but in experimentally determining the nature of the long familiar cathode rays. If these rays were particles, as the English physicists believed rather than vibrations of the ether, then they would exhibit such measurable particle properties as charge, mass, and momentum. Precisely a year prior to Thomson's own initial announcement of his experimental results, Emil Wiechert (1861-1928) at Kant's old University of Königsberg had declared that his experiments led him to conclude not only that cathode rays were particles, but that their mass was many times smaller than the hydrogen atom, the lightest of the known elements. Pais states that it "is the first time ever that a subatomic particle is mentioned in print and sensible bounds for its mass are given."[26]

The following April J.J. Thomson announced to the Royal Institution of London his preliminary determination of the ratio of charge to mass (e/m) of the particles believed to compose the cathode rays. Commenting on Lenard's experiments on the absorption properties of cathode rays, he makes the trenchant statement analogous to Wiechert's:

> [. . .] on the hypothesis that the cathode rays are charged particles moving with high velocities [it follows] that the size of the carriers must be small compared with the dimensions of ordinary atoms or molecules. The assumption of a state of matter more finely subdivided than the atom is a *startling* one . . .[27]

The following August a memoir describing his experimental findings was submitted to the *Philosophical Magazine*. He stated first that the particles were negatively charged, having collected them in a type of Faraday Cage and measured the total charge by an electrometer, as Jean Perrin had done in France. Then experimenting with a cathode tube in which he had inserted two separated parallel electrode plates of opposite charge (see the photograph below), generating an electric field perpendicular to the direction of the cathode rays, he directed the beam of cathode rays through a slit in the anode and between the electrode plates, noting perhaps for the first time their electrical deflection as indicated by a displacement of the glow at the end of the tube.

Fig. 3. One of the cathode ray tubes developed and used in the Cavendish Laboratory by J.J. Thomson. Courtesy of the Cavendish Laboratory, Cambridge University.

Repeating the experiment with a magnetic field perpendicular to the beam generated by a coil outside the tube, he observed their magnetic deflection. From these results he was able to measure the charge to mass ratio as 2.3×10^{17} in *esu/g* (electrostatic units), as well as calculate the velocity of the particles.[28] He also noted the crucial fact that the particles were identical regardless of the material nature of the cathode, anode, or gas, indicating the existence of an invariant component of Nature.

> On this view we have in the cathode rays matter in a new state, a state in which the subdivision of matter is carried much further than in the ordinary gaseous state: a state in which all matter . . . is of one and the same kind; this matter being the substance from which all chemical elements are built up.[29]

The last statement is remarkable in that, as we now know, the chemical properties of the elements is determined by the number of their electrons.

While Thomson's measurement in 1897 of the charge to mass ratio and calculation of the velocity of the cathode particles, along with his positive recognition of a new component of nature, is generally considered sufficient to justify the claim that he was the discoverer of the electron, Pais argues that it was not until 1899 that the issue was actually settled. For it was in that year, using the cloud chamber method developed by his student C.T.R. Wilson (1869-1959), in which charged particles form nuclei for condensed droplets of supersaturated water vapor, that Thomson was able to measure separately the charge and mass of the particles. Finding the charge to be 3×10^{-10} absolute *esu*, he could calculate the mass independently. In 1910 R.A. Millikan (1868-1953) refined this method using an oil drop technique to attain the more accurate value of 4.78×10^{-10} *esu*.

As George Johnstone Stoney (1826-1911) had introduced the term 'electron' in 1894 to designate the unit of electrical charge acquired or lost when atoms become electrified ions, and since it was conjectured that the motion of these particles in atoms might be the source of light, the negatively charged particle discovered by Thomson soon acquired the name 'electron.' In fact, another conclusion in the 1899 article might have contributed to this naming when he discovered that "photoelectrically produced particles [. . .] were electrons" with the m/e for ultraviolet light "the same as for cathode rays."[30]

Here the story might have ended except for one of those fascinating ironies of history. In the same month of April 1897 that J.J. Thomson presented his preliminary findings to the Royal Institution, Walter Kaufmann (1871-1947) at the Physics Institute of the University of Berlin submitted a paper in which he presented his own measurement of the e/m for cathode rays. In addition, he noted that the e/m is a constant for all gases, thus like Thomson detecting some kind of universality.[31] Since Kaufmann's announcement of his determination (which was even more accurate than Thomson's) was practically at the same time and included reference to a constant, why has he not been recognized as a codiscoverer of the electron?

The answer, implied by Pais and explicitly stated by Steven Weinberg, is that while in England there had been a long tradition going back to Newton, Boyle, Dalton, and Proust acknowledging the existence of "insensible particles" or atoms, in Berlin where the antirealist views of the positivist Ernst Mach were prevalent, their existence was denied. Thus when word of the discovery of the electron reached Berlin, no one accepted it. As Weinberg states, it was because Thomson believed he had encountered a new particle and Kaufmann did not, that he is credited with the discovery of the electron.

Like Hertz and other physicists in Germany and Austria, Kaufmann was strongly influenced by the [positivist] [. . .] philosophy of the

Viennese physicist and philosopher Ernest Mach [. . .] who held that it was unscientific to concern oneself with hypothetical entities like atoms that could not be directly observed. It is hard to avoid the conclusion that Thomson discovered the cathode-ray particle that we now call the electron because, unlike Mach and Kaufmann, he thought that it *was* part of the business of physics to discover fundamental particles.[32]

RUTHERFORD'S DISCOVERY OF *ALPHA* AND *BETA* PARTICLES

Returning now to the interrupted account of the investigation of atomic emissions, the next inquirer was to have a dominating influence on physics at the end of the nineteenth and early decades of the twentieth centuries. Asked by a colleague why he was always at the crest of new waves of discoveries in physics, he replied that it is because he created the waves—a truthful if immodest reply. Ernest Rutherford (1871-1937) was born near Nelson on the South Island of New Zealand where he received his early education. An excellent student, on his entrance examination to Nelson College he "scored 580 out of a possible 600 points [. . .] and was first in English, French, Latin, history, mathematics, physics and chemistry."[33]

He received a scholarship to Nelson College, another to Canterbury College where he earned an M.A. degree, and then competed for a scholarship offered by the 1851 London Exhibition for subjects of the British Empire. Although he came in second, fortunately for him and for physics the winner declined the honor enabling Rutherford to go to Cambridge University to further his studies. As Sergè recounts, "[i]t is said that when the announcement of his prize arrived, Rutherford was on the family farm digging potatoes. He read the telegram bringing the news and said, 'This is the last potato I have dug in my life.'" (p. 49) These early successes were a forecast of one of the most brilliant careers ever in experimental physics.

Arriving in England in September 1895 when he was twenty-four years old, there hardly could have been a more auspicious time to begin his research. In the following month Röntgen would discover X-rays, in six months Becquerel would detect uranium radiation, and in about one year and seven months the Curies would report the existence of the new radioactive substances polonium, thorium, and radium. So shortly after arriving in Cambridge, in collaboration with J.J. Thomson (who immediately recognized his remarkable research ability), Rutherford measured the ionization produced by X-rays and, subsequent to its discovery, that produced by uranium. It was during these experiments that he found that uranium radiation, rather than being homogeneous, emits two kinds of rays differentiated by their capacity to be absorbed, *alpha* (α) and *beta* (β), *alpha* being highly absorbable and *beta* very penetrating (it was the *beta* rays that had activated Becquerel's screen while the *alpha* rays were absorbed by the black cardboard wrapper).

These initial discoveries having been made at the Cavendish Laboratory, Rutherford accepted in 1898 a professorship at McGill University in Montreal, Canada. Despite having to leave one of the greatest research centers in physics at the time, the offer of a permanent position with a substantial salary was attractive because it permitted him to marry his fiancé who was in New Zealand. But by then he was confident of his ability to proceed on his own. In his letter of recommendation supporting Rutherford's application to McGill, Thomson graciously wrote "I have never had a student with more enthusiasm or ability for original research than Mr. Rutherford, and I am sure if elected, he would establish a distinguished school of physics at Montreal." (p. 51)

When he arrived at McGill Rutherford "found newly built physics and chemistry laboratories supported and financed by a benefactor of the University, the millionaire William Macdonald." (p. 52) Moreover, John Cox the chairman of the department, after observing Rutherford performing his experiments, decided that "I think I'd better take your classes and do the teaching work. You keep on doing what you have to do." (p. 52) As Sergè remarks, "[h]ere was a demonstration of outstanding intelligence and generosity." So after returning to New Zealand in 1900 to be married and then sailing for Canada with his bride, Rutherford settled in McGill to fulfill Thomson's prophesy. Indeed, the years between 1898 and 1907 when he was at McGill working with such distinguished collaborators as Frederick Soddy (1877-1956) and Otto Hahn (1879-1968) were a period of considerable accomplishment.

Continuing his research on α-rays, contrary to Becquerel's initial claims that the α-rays were neither polarized nor refractive, he demonstrated that they were indeed deflected by electric and magnetic fields indicating they were particles with a positive charge similar to helium. Although his definitive assertion that they were identical to helium ions did not occur until 1908, a year after he had left McGill for Victoria University in Manchester, his discovery that radioactive substances and ores when heated give off helium convinced him as early as 1903 that α-particles were helium ions.

Meanwhile, β-rays, the second radiative emission detected by Rutherford, were being investigated by Becquerel, the Curies, and Walter Kaufmann who found that they too were deflected in electric and magnetic fields, have a negative electric charge, and an *e/m* ratio similar to cathode rays or electrons. In 1902 Kaufmann concluded that β-rays and cathode rays exhibit such similar properties that from "that time on it was considered settled the β-rays are electrons."[34] Two years earlier Paul Villard (1811-1877), at the École Normale in Paris, had discovered a third very penetrating emission of radium, called *gamma* (γ) rays, which resembled X-rays.

In addition to his research on α-rays, while working in close collaboration Rutherford and Soddy between 1900 and 1903 made a startling theoretical discovery regarding the transmutation of radioactive substances—although out of fear of being ridiculed as alchemists they called the process a "transformation." What they discovered is that radioactive emissions alter the internal structure of the radioactive substance turning it into an isotope of the previous element: a new but similar element having the same chemical properties but a different mass. But though there was no doubt these radioactive transmutations occurred, no one could explain why radioactive substances decay into other radioactive elements with characteristic half-lives until stability is reached. When radioactive residues were chemically separated from the original material containing the radioactivity but left in contact with it, the radioactivity seemed to jump from one to the other according to specific but different time scales. In addition, the sum of the curves representing the loss and gain of radioactivity between the two substances over a period of time was constant. (cf. pp. 55-56)

Physicists were as mystified by these occurrences as they were by the source of energy that produced them. No chemical explanation could account for the phenomena without violating fundamental assumptions, along with the law of the conservation of energy, remembering that at the time nothing was known about atomic or nuclear structures. After J.J. Thomson's discovery of the electron it was thought that numerous electrons exist within the atom, including the nucleus, but whether they accounted for the transmutations and how was a mystery. As Marie Curie described the situation in 1900:

> Uranium exhibits no appreciable change of state, no visible chemical transformation, it remains, or so it seems, identical with itself, the source of energy which it emits remains undetectable—and therein lies the profound interest of the phenomenon.[35]

Although Rutherford and Soddy could not throw any light on the internal processes producing the atomic radiation, the fact that they attributed it to subatomic transmutations was a very bold step. In effect they were saying, according to Pais, that "radioactive bodies contain unstable atoms of which a fixed fraction decay per unit time. The rest of the decayed atom is a new radio-element which decays again, and so forth, till a stable element is reached."[36] The crucial aspect of this explanation, as Rutherford realized, is that "the continuous emission of energy from the active bodies is derived from the internal energy inherent in the atom, and does not in any way contradict the law of the conservation of energy."[37]

Thus would begin during the next several decades the search for the clues as to the internal components of the atom and the nature of its structure. Although Rutherford received the Nobel Prize in chemistry in 1908 for his previous research in radioactivity and discovery of transmutation, his major contribution to understanding atomic structure would not occur until later when he had returned to England. In 1913 Soddy introduced the term 'isotope' to designate elements that were identical in their nuclear charge, chemical properties, and place in the periodic chart, but different as to their atomic mass and radioactive properties, such as Ra^{228}, Ra^{226}, and Ra^{224}.[38] In 1921 Soddy received the Nobel Prize in chemistry for his contribution to the recognition of radioactive transmutations and isotopes.

PLANCK'S DISCOVERY OF THE QUANTUM OF ACTION

Quantum mechanics grew out of a common phenomenon familiar to those old enough to remember coal-burning home furnaces. As part of the procedure of stoking the coals one used a black iron poker which, when immersed in the hot coals, would turn a series of colors from red to yellow-green, to violet, to almost white if the heat were intense enough. Typically, such an occurrence, called "blackbody radiation," aroused the curiosity of scientists who are not satisfied with merely observing a phenomenon but want to explain it. It was known by spectroscopic analysis that the various colors corresponded to different wave lengths or frequencies of the electromagnetic emissions, but since nothing was known of the internal structure of atoms, no one understood how this occurred. Nevertheless, because metals generally are good conductors of electricity and the electron had been discovered in 1897 as the unit of electric charge, it was believed that if metals are composed of atoms, the atoms must contain electrons to account for the flow of electric current (as in electrolysis), though how was not yet known. Thus it was conjectured that metals are composed of tiny electronic oscillators which, when heated, are given a sufficient energy jolt to emit some electromagnetic waves with a characteristic wavelength or color.

Furthermore, the equipartition principle that had been applied so successfully to gases, specifying that any addition of heat would be partitioned equally among all the different velocities of the gas particles, was applied to heat radiation. Consequently, since a blackbody absorbs all the incident heat or energy, it was believed that this energy would be distributed equally among all the possible frequencies of the oscillators, the spectral density being the amount of electromagnetism emitted per unit volume of the blackbody. Yet despite the complex interaction of absorption heat and emissive radiation, with all the frequencies and their characteristic intensities represented, at any moment a thermal equilibrium is reached as indicated by the specific color of the poker. Earlier in 1859, as Segrè states, this "crude observation was scientifically formulated in a precise way by Kirchhoff who [. . .] proved by thermodynamics that the ratio of emissivity to absorption coefficient is a function of frequency and temperature only [. . .] independent of the nature of the body." (p. 67) But having demonstrated that the spectral density is a function solely of the radiational frequency and the temperature, Kirchhoff was unable to explain how the variables of frequency and temperature produce this constant function.

Searching for a more precise mathematical specification of the functional relation, Joseph Stefan (1835-1893) deduced from the experimental data that the spectral density or total electromagnetic energy was not simply a function of the temperature, but more precisely was "proportional to the fourth power of the temperature." (p. 67) Then in 1884 Ludwig Boltzmann (1844-1906), one of the founders of statistical mechanics (along with the American Joseph Willard Gibbs), combining thermodynamics with Maxwell's electrodynamics, showed that Stefan's 'law' "holds strictly only for the energy emitted by a blackbody" which "equals the spectral density summed (integrated) over all frequencies times the volume of the blackbody."[39]

Finally, again working with thermodynamics and Maxwell's electromagnetic theory, Wilhelm Wien (1864-1928) stated in 1893 the law that the spectral density "was the product of the cube of the frequency multiplied by a function of the ratio of frequency divided by temperature." (p. 68) Although the exact magnitude of the function was not known at the time, the factor of proportionality was found to be $4\pi/c$, with c the velocity of light. While these mathematical laws contributed to a more precise correlation between the energy or frequency of the spectral emission and the incident temperature, they shed no light on what the subatomic mechanism was that accounted for these correlations. As H.A. Lorentz (1853-1929) stated in 1907, the understanding of blackbody radiation had progressed as far as possible utilizing the laws of thermodynamics and electrodynamics, so "the point had been reached where the special radiation theories had to set in [. . .] based on definite ideas about the mechanism of the phenomena."[40]

In addition, improved experimental techniques that provided more exact data showed that the previous laws were not supported by the new data, applying at best to the limiting conditions of high or low frequencies. Even more serious, the classical predictions expressed in the Rayleigh-Jeans law led to absurd conclusions.   According to this law, although the temperature incident to a blackbody would (on the equipartition principle) be distributed equally among all the frequencies, because the higher frequency oscillators (it was believed) radiate their energy more efficiently, over a period of time the intensity of the high frequency radiations would increase, tending to infinity. Sitting before a fireplace for an extended period of time would be dangerous because of the increasing radiation in the ultraviolet range.

Although this prediction was based on the established laws of electrodynamics and thermodynamics, it not only implied the absurd consequence that the intensity of the high frequency radiations would increase infinitely, it did not conform to the experimental fact that the spectral intensity corresponded to the thermal equilibrium, as indicated by the observed color. Dubbed "the ultraviolet catastrophe," this was one of the "two dark clouds" (the other was the null results of the Michelson-Morley experiment to be discussed shortly) mentioned by Lord Kelvin (1824-1907) as threatening the bright horizon of physics at the end of the nineteenth century.

This was the situation in thermodynamics in 1900 when Max Planck (1858-1947), very conservative by nature, introduced his famous equation describing blackbody radiation that at the very beginning of the twentieth century issued in an entirely new era of physics. In a felicitous continuity of events, when Kirchhoff died in 1899 Planck succeeded to his position at the University of Berlin after Boltzmann, to whom the offer was first extended, finally declined after initially accepting. Not only was this a very prestigious position at one of the greatest German Universities, it had the added advantage of access to the latest experimental data on blackbody radiation provided by the *Physikalisch Technische Reichsanstadt* of Berlin. Asserting that "I had always regarded the search for the absolute as the loftiest goal of all scientific activity,"[41] Planck took up Kirchhoff's challenge of finding the exact functional relation between the spectral frequency and the incident energy or temperature.

His solution proved revolutionary because it indicated that thermodynamic or radiational processes, rather than being continuous as previously assumed, were discrete or discontinuous. Examples of continuous processes are the flow of water as long as it forms a constant stream and an analogue volume adjustment that can be gradually increased or decreased; discontinuous processes are the bullets fired from a gun which are individually separate and digital settings of fixed intervals. In devising a formula that matched blackbody radiation, Planck had to introduce a minimum quantum that would prove to be not only a universal constant, but an inextricable factor in the paradoxes of quantum mechanics.

As previously noted, spectral density or the electromagnetic force had been variously correlated with thermal equilibrium. An alternative conception for equilibrium is entropy, the maximum disorder or randomness of the components of a system which is in equilibrium when it reaches this condition. Because the entropy of a system also is its most probable state, the concepts of entropy, equilibrium, and probability are interrelated. Boltzmann expressed the relation between entropy and probability as $S = k \log W$, where S stands for entropy and "W is the thermodynamic probability and k the universal constant that Planck called Boltzmann's constant."[42] (Like Archimedes whose tomb in ancient Syracuse displayed a drawing of a sphere circumscribed in a cylinder together with the ratio of the cylinder to the sphere, Boltzmann's formula is engraved on his monument in Vienna.) The task facing Planck, who was a master of classical thermodynamics but a novice in statistical mechanics, was to find the exact interpretation, mathematically and physically, of the relation between the energy distribution of the emission density and the entropy distribution of the thermal equilibrium. When asked years later how he had originated the quantum theory he replied:

> It was an act of desperation. For six years I had struggled with the blackbody theory. I knew the problem was fundamental and [. . .] I had to find a theoretical explanation at any cost, except for the inviolability of the two laws of thermodynamics.[43]

Stated simply, the two laws of thermodynamics as introduced in 1885 by R. Clausius (1822-1888) are that "the energy of the universe is constant (first law)" and that "the entropy of the universe tends to a maximum (second law)."[44]

Perhaps the clearest, least technical description of how in October 1900 Planck derived both his formula and its physical significance, is that of Sergè:

At [thermal] equilibrium the entropy has to be maximum, and it can be statistically calculated using the fundamental Boltzmann equation. To calculate the probability by methods of combinatorial analysis, Planck found it convenient to divide the energy of an oscillator into small but finite quantities, so that the energy of the oscillators could be written as $E = P\varepsilon$ where P is an integral number. With this hypothesis Planck could calculate the average energy of an oscillator and thus find the blackbody formula. Planck expected that ε could become arbitrarily small and that the decomposition of E in finite amounts would only be a calculational device. However, for the results to agree with Wien's thermodynamic law, ε had to be finite and proportional to the frequency of the oscillator $\varepsilon = h\nu$ where h is a new universal constant, appropriately called *Planck's constant.*[45]

The physical significance of Planck's discovery is that contrary to classical electrodynamics and thermodynamics where the energy exchange could take any value, the electronic oscillators could not acquire any energy in a continuum, but only in discrete values that were integral multiples of $h\nu$: $\varepsilon = nh\nu$, where n = 1, 2, 3 . . . Planck found the value of h to be 6.55×10^{-27} *erg. per. sec.*

Immediately eliminating the ultraviolet catastrophe, his equation showed in a precise way, exactly agreeing with the experimental data, that the energy distributed among the oscillators did not lead to infinitely high frequencies, but to the frequency corresponding to the incident energy. Agreeing with Kirchhoff's law, the energy exchange in the absorption and emission process corresponds to the available energy, albeit in discrete quantities, the greater the energy the higher the frequency, the less the energy the lower the frequency. Not only did Planck's quantum theory remove the ultraviolet catastrophe, he was able to derive from it a number of constants and empirical values which is the strongest indication of a theory's truth. As Sergè states, even in his first paper "Planck pointed out that from Stefan's law and from Wien's thermodynamical law it is possible to infer the two universal constants h and k [Boltzmann's], and from these the charge of the electron, Avogadro's number, and more."[46] It is these unexpected convergent derivations of an extremely precise nature, obtained from independent phenomena, that provide such convincing evidence that scientific theories must represent, to some degree of approximation, a real domain or context of physical reality, otherwise the derivation would be miraculous or magical.

Although the same evening in October when he presented his quantum formula to a physics seminar at the University of Berlin, Planck was informed by the physicists at the *Reichsanstadt* that it agreed perfectly with the experimental data, he was not at all satisfied with the results. Aware of its significance, having remarked to his son that he had made a discovery whose novelty was perhaps worthy of the great Newton, because his quantum of action (energy times time) violated one of the fundamental principles of classical physics, the continuity of energy exchanges, he labored (fruitlessly) for years attempting to harmonize his results with classical laws. While his search for absolutes was vindicated by the discovery of the fundamental constant h, it did so at the expense of negating a basic assumption of classical physics. Einstein was another physicist who could not reconcile himself to quantum mechanics, asserting that all his "attempts [. . .] to adapt the theoretical foundations of physics to this [new type of] knowledge failed completely. It was as if the ground has been pushed out from under me with no firm foundation to be seen anywhere [. . .]."[47] Planck similarly reported his unsuccessful efforts to assimilate quantum mechanics to classical physics:

> I tried immediately to weld the elementary quantum of action somehow in the framework of classical theory. But in the face of all such attempts this constant showed itself to be obdurate . . . . My futile attempts to put the elementary quantum of action into the classical theory continued for a number of years and they cost me a great deal of effort.[48]

Though he had originated quantum mechanics, like Einstein who made very significant contributions to it, Planck never quite accepted the implications, despite receiving the Nobel Prize in physics in 1920 for his discovery.

EINSTEIN'S THEORIES OF RELATIVITY

No physicist in this century captivated the imagination of people throughout the world as did Einstein. Pais recalls that even among a symposium of physicists at Princeton to mark Einstein's seventieth birthday, an awed hush momentarily pervaded the hall when Einstein entered.[49] While part of the reason stems from his bold revision of Newton's absolute "frames of the universe," dramatically announced to the world in 1919 when A.E. Eddington's eclipse expedition confirmed the bending of light as it passed the gravitational field of the sun, part must be attributed to a certain mystique.

More than any other figure in recent memory, Einstein epitomizes the intense struggle of solitary individuals throughout history to attain a truer and more comprehensive understanding of the universe—an image that perhaps never again will recur now that scientific inquiry has become such a technologically dependent, government sponsored, and team undertaking. According to Pais, his latest and best-informed biographer, even Einstein's continued dissatisfaction with the statistical indeterminism in quantum mechanics did not prevent physicists "from recognizing Einstein as by far the most important scientific figure of this century." (p. 15)

In 1905 when he was just twenty-six years old and employed in the federal patent office in Berne, Switzerland, Einstein (1879-1955) wrote six papers (one his doctoral thesis), five of which were sent to the *Annalen der Physik* between March and December of that year and subsequently published. The first on light radiation contains an explanation of the photoelectric effect and prediction of the existence of light quanta; the second, his doctoral thesis, presents a new calculation of molecular dimensions; the third and sixth on Brownian motion demonstrates the existence of atoms and a new determination of Avogadro's number and Boltzmann's constant k, while the fourth and fifth treat the electrodynamics of moving bodies in the special theory of relativity from which he derived his famous equation $E = mc^2$. (cf. pp. 17-18) Although known primarily for his theory of relativity and resolute opposition to the quantum theory, his first paper dealing with the photoelectric effect was a major contribution to quantum mechanics by introducing light quanta and explicitly raising for the first time the problem of the dual nature of light (it is also for this paper, primarily, that he received the Nobel Prize in 1920, the citation avoiding any reference to his theory of relativity because of its uncertain status at that time).

The contrasting conceptions of light have been described in previous chapters, Newton's corpuscular theory prevailing over Huygen's undulatory interpretation in the seventeenth and eighteenth centuries, while the experiments of Young and Fresnel led to the general acceptance of the wave theory in the nineteenth century. One might suppose that Planck's equation specifying the integral quantification of energy exchanges in blackbody radiation would have given impetus to the particulate conception of light, but since he was dissatisfied with its implications, attempting to harmonize it with classical electrodynamics, it was not fully appreciated until Einstein's interpretation. As Sergè states:

Einstein noted that Planck's derivation, in considering the energy exchanges between oscillators and radiations,"presupposes implicitly that energy can be absorbed and emitted by the individual resonator only in quanta of magnitude *hv*, i.e., that the energy of a mechanical structure capable of oscillations, as well as the energy of radiation, can be transferred only in such quanta, in contradiction to the laws of mechanics and electrodynamics. [50]

Embracing the quantification of radiation, Einstein found an explanation for the photoelectric effect that had eluded classical interpretations. Referring to the illumination produced on the surface of metals when monochromatic light such as ultraviolet radiation is reflected on them, this photoelectric effect was explained analogous to blackbody radiation: the interaction of the radiant (light) energy with the electronic oscillators in the surface of the metal causing an increase in the oscillation producing the ejection of electrons accounting for the illumination. According to the wave theory, monochromatic light of greater intensity (consisting of more superimposed waves) would eject the electrons with a greater velocity and hence greater illumination. Experimentally, however, it was found that the *velocity* of the electrons ejected was dependent upon the color or *frequency* of the homogeneous light, not on its intensity, ultraviolet light with a frequency twice that of red light ejecting the electrons with twice the force. Increasing the *intensity* of light does not increase the velocity of the ejected electrons, but results in a *larger number* of electrons being ejected.

By utilizing Planck's formula $\varepsilon = hv$, Einstein was able to explain the photoelectric effect consistent with the experimental data. If light consists of discrete quanta of energy proportional to the frequency, as Planck's equation stipulates, then this explains why monochromatic light, such as ultraviolet light with a higher *frequency*, ejects the electrons with a greater *velocity* because the interaction involves greater energy. Moreover, increasing the *intensity* of light increases the *number* of light quanta (not the frequency) in the light source, causing more oscillators to be activated ejecting more electrons, but with the same energy. Although this bold explanation accounts perfectly for the experimental data, it replaces the interpretation of light as waves with a return to the particulate theory, introducing a new particle, the photon. As Einstein stated:

If [. . .] monochromatic radiation of sufficiently small density behaves like a discontinuous medium consisting of energy quanta of magnitude *hv* it is reasonable to inquire if the laws of emission and transformation of light are so constituted as though light were composed of these same energy quanta [photons].[51]

Despite the reasonableness of Einstein's explanation, the theoretical introduction of a strange new particle met with considerable resistance, especially from Niels Bohr, surprisingly, one of the founders of quantum mechanics. It was not until Arthur Compton's (1892-1962) demonstration in 1923 of the scattering of X-rays by electrons showing that the X-rays followed the same conservation laws of deflection and momentum as colliding particles, with the energy $h\nu$ predicted by Einstein, that the reality of photons was finally accepted. Having discovered photons, Einstein was acutely aware of the paradox introduced by the contrasting evidence for the dual nature of light, although he expected that a new theory would be developed that would fuse the wave and particle theories.

The third and sixth articles written in Einstein's *annus mirabilis* grew out of his doctoral thesis. Pais states that "[i]t is not sufficiently realized that Einstein's thesis is one of his fundamental papers," cited more frequently than the others following its publication as an article in 1906. (p. 89) His first article on Brownian motion was submitted just eleven days after he completed his thesis, while the latter was submitted three weeks later, although not published until 1906. As indicated previously, the significance of Brownian motion lies in the fact that for nearly a century it provided the most convincing evidence—although not without some opposition—of the existence of molecules since Robert Brown (1773-1858) suspended pollen grains in water in 1827, attributing their observed random motion to the impact of the water molecules in the liquid.

Because the motion of the particles is a function of their size and density along with the viscosity and temperature of the water, Einstein was able to provide a theory of Brownian motion utilizing the kinetic theory of gases, deriving new values for Avogadro's number and Boltzmann's constant k. When Einstein's third calculation of Avogadro's number was confirmed by Jean Perrin in 1909, it agreed so closely with other determinations that the question of the existence of molecules could be considered settled. As Perrin wrote:

I think it is impossible that a mind free from all preconception can reflect upon the diversity of the phenomena which thus converge to the same result without experiencing a strong impression, and I think that it will henceforth be difficult to defend by rational arguments a hostile attitude to molecular hypotheses. [52]

This was a further example of the continuing affirmation of scientific realism.

Einstein's fourth and fifth articles dealing with"the electrodynamics of moving bodies"contain his special theory of relativity. Unlike his first article on the photoelectric effect that contributed to the most revolutionary development in physics in the twentieth century, quantum mechanics, his articles on the special theory of relativity, although radically revising Newton's conception of the basic spatial and temporal frames of the universe, should be seen as"the natural completion of the work of Faraday, Maxwell, and Lorentz."[53] Interpreted this way, his general theory of relativity is the culmination of the two classical theories coexisting at the end of the nineteenth century, Newtonian mechanics and Maxwell's theory of electromagnetism.

For over two centuries following Newton's definitions in the *Principia*, space and time had been considered "absolute frames of the universe" to account for absolute rest and motion. With the success of the wave theory of light and Maxwell's electromagnetic theory in the nineteenth century, it was believed that Newton's absolute space was filled with a stationary ether necessary for the propagation of electromagnetic waves considered to be vibrations of the ether. Not content with merely assuming the existence of entities like absolute rest and motion or with postulating an ether, scientists devise experiments to test the validity of such concepts. So between 1881 and 1929 Albert A. Michelson (1852-1931) and Edward W. Morley (1838-1923), both independently and in collaboration, attempted to confirm the existence of absolute motion with respect to the ether at rest in absolute space, thereby confirming three assumptions: the existence of the ether, absolute motion, and absolute space.

Because absolute motion could not be detected mechanically, Michelson developed an interferometer to confirm it by optical methods. Assuming that as the earth revolved in its orbit through the stationary ether it would create an ether wind or drift opposite to its motion, a source of light divided into two beams traveling the same distance back and forth but at right angles to one another, one running parallel to the ether drift and the other transverse to it, the diverse effects of the ether drift on the velocity of the separate light beams would lead to their being slightly out of phase on their return. Specifically, the time difference in the return of the two beams was predicted as"about an extra 1/25 of a wavelength" for the beam running parallel to the either drift. (p. 112) This added 1/25th of a wavelength for the parallel beam (coinciding with the slightly longer time to complete its passage) would be indicated by an interference of the light beams at the moment of their return.

Fig. 4. Below is a schematic diagram of an interferometer.

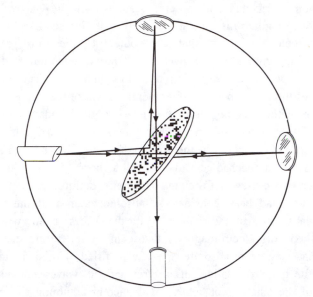

But no interference was detected, however precisely the experiment was conducted to eliminate any vibratory perturbation or compensating factor due to the earth's orbital position at the time of the experiment. So in 1881 Michelson announced that there was no evidence of an effect of an ether drift on the velocity of light: "'[t]he result of the hypothesis of a stationary aether is thus shown to be incorrect, and the necessary conclusion follows that the hypothesis is erroneous."[54] When Michelson repeated the experiment with Morley in 1887 they found the same null results indicating the non-existence of an ether effect, along with the invariance of the velocity of light as measured by the interferometer. In 1907 Michelson was the first American scientist to be awarded the Nobel Prize, not for the ether drift experiments which were not mentioned in the citation, but for his invention of ingenious optical instruments and experiments.

Despite the significance of these experimental results constituting one of the "two dark clouds" on the frontiers of physics, with the important exception of Lord Kelvin, Lord Rayleigh, and Lorentz, little attention was paid to it at the time. Though the null results of the experiment often are cited as one of the important sources of Einstein's special theory of relativity, because the latter's postulation of the constant velocity of light agreed with the experimental results, this was not the case. (cf. pp. 114-134). While Einstein was aware of Michelson's conclusion, he stated that it did not play a "decisive role" in the creation of the special theory (although it might have added to his conviction that the velocity of light is constant). In fact, when he was just sixteen years old he had raised the question of how light would appear if he could attain the same speed—would it seem to be at rest or would it appear to have the usual velocity?

It was not the null result of the Michelson-Morley experiments, but reflections on stellar aberration, Fizeau's measurements of the velocity of light in moving water, and especially the 1895 article by Lorentz on the electrodynamics of moving bodies (the title of Einstein's first article on relativity theory) in which he stated, "*[a]ccording to our theory the motion of the earth will never have any* [. . .] *influence whatever on experiments with terrestrial light sources*,"[55] that directly influenced Einstein. As he recalled later in a talk given in Japan, what convinced him of the invariant velocity of light were the Maxwell-Lorentz equations in electrodynamics.

> I took into consideration Fizeau's experiment, and [. . . .] the truth of the Maxwell-Lorentz equations in electrodynamics [. . .] [which] showed [. . .] the so-called invariance of the velocity of light [. . .] should hold also in the moving frame of reference. This invariance of the velocity of light was, however, in conflict with the rule of addition of velocities we knew of well in mechanics.[56]

Given the two postulates affirmed in his original paper, Galileo's principle of the indistinguishability of moving inertial systems (because the laws applying to bodies within the systems are the same) and the constancy of the speed of light, Einstein's revision of Newton's "absolute frames of the universe" follows with stunning simplicity. In fact, the assumptions are just the reverse. According to Newtonian mechanics, because the length of measuring rods and the rhythm of clocks are unaffected by velocities, the measurement of a moving body by two systems in relative motion must differ by their relative velocities: the measurement by the system in relative motion necessarily being *less* than by the system at rest. For example, if an automobile has a velocity of fifty miles per hour measured by a person at rest relative to the earth, then the same automobile will have a velocity of ten miles per hour measured by a person in a second automobile traveling forty miles per hour in the same direction. This is the rule of "addition of velocities" (or of the Galilean transformation) referred to by Einstein at the end of the previously quoted passage.

Because the velocity of light is constant or invariant regardless of the relative velocities of the measuring systems, the simplest way of accounting for this is by assuming that the instruments of measurement, the rods and clocks (since velocity is distance traveled per time), are somehow affected in the system moving relative to the stationary one. More precisely, because the velocity of light as measured by the system moving uniformly relative to the one at rest is *not less* (as in the automobile example) but the same, this can be explained if one assumes that within that moving system the measuring rod contracts and the clock slows down just enough to give the added value for the velocity of light. Since v = d/t, if the distance measurement is greater due to using shorter measuring rods and the time measurement is less because of the slowing down of the clocks, then the fraction d/t will give a larger value for v, the velocity.

Thus Einstein's conclusion is the converse of Newtonian mechanics. In the latter, because measuring rods and clocks are invariant within systems in relative (inertial) motion, their measurement of an independent velocity must be different from the system at rest. However, as regards light or electromagnetic phenomena, because the velocity of light is constant as measured by systems in relative motion, the rods must contract and time dilate in the system moving relative to the one assumed to be at rest to account for this constancy. Einstein therefore affirms what Newton explicitly denied in the Scholium of the *Principia* regarding the invariance of absolute time (and space) in relation to motion: "[a]ll motions may be accelerated and retarded, but the flowing of absolute time is not liable to any change."

The new equations replacing the Galilean transformation equations for correlating the distance and time measurements from the system at rest to the one in motion, given the latter's velocity, are the Lorentz transformation equations which preserve the invariance of Maxwell's equations. The factor of contraction or dilation is:

$$\sqrt{1-\frac{v^2}{c^2}},$$

thus the equation correlating the distance measurement x by the system at rest with the distance measurement x' by the system moving with the velocity v relative to x, is

$$x' = \frac{x - vt}{\sqrt{1 - \dfrac{v^2}{c^2}}}.$$

Analogously, the correlation of the time measurement is

$$t' = \frac{t - \dfrac{vx}{c^2}}{\sqrt{1 - \dfrac{v^2}{c^2}}}.$$

In the transformation equations the minus sign indicates the effect of the velocity on the contraction of the measuring rod and the slowing down of the clock in relation to the system at rest. It is apparent that as the velocity approaches the velocity of light the magnitude of the fraction v^2/c^2 increases so that the factor of contraction and dilation increases. Conversely, if the velocity of the system is minuscule compared to the velocity of light, as is true for mechanical velocities, then the fraction v^2/c^2 is so minimal that the factor is negligible, reducing to the Galilean transformation equations x' = x-vt and t' = t.

The same effect applies to mass which, according to Newton's equation F = ma, is the ratio between force and acceleration, and therefore varies with the velocity according to the formula

$$m' = \frac{m}{\sqrt{1 - \dfrac{v^2}{c^2}}}.$$

Again, when the velocity of the system is slight the equation reduces to the Galilean transformation m' = m, but as the system approaches the velocity of light the mass tends to increase infinitely which is why the velocity of light is a limiting velocity that no material entity can reach. As indicated in Einstein's second article on the special theory of relativity, this also implies that energy and mass are equivalent according to his famous equation $E = mc^2$. For the first time physicists could answer the ancient question of why the sun has not burnt out, given its massive radiation throughout history, because the enormous mass of the sun, comprising about 98 per cent of the mass of our solar system, is equivalent to energy.

While the Lorentz transformation equations correlate the spatial, temporal, and mass measurements from a system at rest to one in uniform motion, in 1908 Hermann Minkowski (1864-1909), one of Einstein's former professors at the Polytechnical School in Zurich (ETH), devised a formula $\sqrt{(cT)^2 - R^2}$ that gives the *same* value for the duration between two events as measured by systems in relative motion. As described by G.J. Whitrow:

> If, according to a particular observer, the difference in time between any two events is T, this associated spatial interval is cT. Then, if R is the space-distance between these two events, Minkowski showed that the difference of the squares of cT and R has the same value for all observers in uniform motion. The square root of this quantity is called the *space-time interval* between the two events. Hence, although time and three-dimensional space depend on the observer, this new concept of space-time is the same for all observers.[57]

It is Minkowski's formula, especially, that gave rise to the conception of the universe as a four-dimensional continuum of events, three of space and one of time.

Because the systems are kinematically equivalent in the special theory due to their being inertial, it is important to realize that the modifications *attributed* to the rods, clocks, and mass in the moving system by the system at rest are reciprocal, either system being equivalent as the reference point. Thus in the special—in contrast to the general—theory the effects are *apparent* rather than *actual*. As this effect is analogous to the apparent reciprocal reduction in the size of objects seen from a distance owing to the laws of perspective, it has been called the "perspective of velocity."[58]

It should be remembered also that what has been described applies only to electromagnetic phenomena, not to mechanical or acoustical. In the latter cases, the Galilean addition of velocities principle holds, but in the case of light the velocity is independent of the motion of its source, as well as of any moving observer. The wavelength and frequency *are* affected by the velocity of the source, but in such a way that the product of the two (accounting for the velocity of light) always remains constant. As a result the measurement of distant events will necessarily vary among moving systems, the duration among events or whether they are simultaneous being relative to the system of reference. But since any information about distant events requires some causally transmitted effect such as a light signal, no effect can appear before its cause in any system of reference, contrary to some science fiction accounts.

Although Minkowski's formula relates these measurements to a common four-dimensional continuum, it does not constitute a return to Newton's absolute space and time.

In contrast to the special theory according to which the contraction of measuring rods (now called "the FitzGerald-Lorentz contraction" because George F. FitzGerald (1851-1901) was the first to propose it in 1889), retardation of clocks, and increase in mass are only reciprocal and apparent because of the theory's restriction to uniform inertial motions without forces, in the general theory completed in 1915 the effects are inherent and actual because of nonuniform accelerated motions that generate forces. Although it is not known what the physical process is that produces the effects, the contraction of the length of physical rods, the slowing down of all natural processes, and the increase of mass actually occur in systems in which either the accelerating forces or strength of the gravitational field is strong.

As the classic example of the twins paradox introduced by Paul Langevin (1872-1946) under the name of *voyage au boulet* illustrates, if one twin remains on earth and the other boards a spaceship that accelerates just less than 1/20,000th the velocity of light, because of the intense gravitational effect generated by the enormous acceleration, the twin on the spacecraft will have aged two years during the two year round trip flight as indicated by the clocks and other changes on the ship, while the other twin will have died years before because of the two centuries that had elapsed on the earth.[59] These effects (which initially sound like science fiction) have been confirmed in delicate experiments with clocks placed in jet aircraft that circled the earth and especially by radioactive particles from outer space whose decay lifetimes were extended because of their great velocities. Consequently, these effects are now incorporated into relativistic quantum field theory, as required by the velocities of the subatomic particles.

As indicated previously, because the special theory applies to the restricted conditions of uniform motions or inertial systems, Einstein was concerned to extend or generalize his theory to nonuniform accelerated motions involving noninertial systems and forces.[60] But as in the special theory, his aim in the general theory was to arrive at a simpler conception of nature based on universal laws. Using ingenious thought experiments comparing investigators in elevators falling freely in a gravitational field (so that the free fall cancels the effects of gravity) with those suspended in a gravity free environment in outer space who are trying to determine what state they are in, he was able to demonstrate the inertial equivalence of the two systems.

Similarly, comparing the experimental effects of being in a stationary elevator in the gravitational field of the earth with that of being in a gravity free elevator in outer space but accelerated upward at the same rate as the earth's gravitational force, he was able to show the equivalence of gravitational and accelerated effects. Because the same effect could be achieved merely by shifting one's frame of reference, he concluded that, like inertia, the effects of gravity and acceleration are neither independent nor irreducible—just as he had shown that mass and energy are equivalent in the special theory. The realization that the "gravitational field has only a relative existence," the key to the general theory, as he asserted in an unpublished paper, was "the happiest thought of my life [. . .]."[61]

This driving belief in the possible reductive unification of concepts based on generalized laws motivated his research throughout his career, especially his lonely premature search in later life for a unified field theory. In 1931 he wrote:

> Since Maxwell's time, Physical Reality has been thought of as represented by continuous fields . . . not capable of any mechanical interpretation. This change in the conception of Reality is the most profound and the most fruitful that physics has experienced since the time of Newton.[62]

Just as Maxwell had shown that the propagation of electromagnetic phenomena did not require an underlying ether but could be described as the dynamic structure of a field of space, and had inquired whether Newton's gravitational force acting at a distance might not also be reduced to the effects of a dynamic field of space, Einstein proposed a reduction of matter or energy to a condensation of a gravitational field which in turn could be reduced to a Riemannian curvature of space-time. As Pais states:

> The scientific task which Einstein set himself in his later years is based on three desiderata, all of them vitally important to him: to unify gravitation and electromagnetism, to derive quantum physics from an underlying causal theory, and to describe particles as singularity-free solutions of continuous fields. [. . .] As Einstein saw it, Maxwell's introduction of the field concept was a revolutionary advance which, however, did not go far enough. It was his belief that, also, in the description of the sources of the electromagnetic field, and other fields, all reference to the Newtonian mechanical world picture should be eradicated.[63]

Although his search for a unified field theory that would combine electromagnetic and gravitational fields (as Maxwell had unified electrical, magnetic, and optical waves) still has not been attained, the tremendous progress since his day in unifying electromagnetic with the strong and weak (nuclear) forces in the so-called Grand Unified Theory (GUTs) has vindicated his undaunted belief in the possibility of such unifications. Moreover, his emphasis on simplicity, elegance, and generality in the formulation of theories has been supported by the crucial role of symmetries in recent physics. The few but significant testable implications of his general theory specified at the end of his 1916 article, the precession of Mercury, the bending of light in the gravitational field of the sun, and the red shift due to the recession of stellar bodies, have been confirmed. His theory of a finite-infinite spherical universe (finite in configuration but boundless in extent), based on a general relativistic cosmology, provides the theoretical framework for the modern conception of the universe.

On the other hand, his unyielding conviction that quantum mechanics is incomplete and that it is possible to construct a more fundamental theory (usually called "a hidden variable theory"), retaining strict causality and the objective reality of conjugate properties (position and momentum, energy and time) that would eliminate the probabilities and paradoxes of quantum mechanics has not been realized, despite the best efforts of a few physicists like David Bohm.[64] Moreover, the amazing progress in particle physics, along with the alternative explanation of fields of force in terms of the exchange of (virtual) particles such as photons, gluons, and vector bosons has not confirmed his expectation that fields, apart from particles or singularities, are the basic reality. Nonetheless, just the breadth of these speculations reveals the extraordinary sweep of his thought, unsurpassed except by Newton.

As outstanding as were the scientific advances just described, they were prologue to what will be presented in the following, concluding chapter. Yet just as prologue is prophesy, these advances forecast what was to follow. Without the various investigations of spectral lines, discoveries of X-rays, radiation, radioactive elements, electrons, and *alpha* and *beta* rays along with nuclear transmutations forming isotopes, there would have been no justification for proposing subatomic structures and interactions. Without Planck's unexpected explanation of blackbody radiation as absorptive and emissive exchanges in units of discrete quanta of energy correlated with the frequencies, the essential key for interpreting these interactions would be missing. If Einstein had not introduced light quanta to account for the photoelectric effect, confirmed by the scattering experiments of Compton, the existence of discrete units of energy might have remained a mere aberration, while the wave-particle duality would not have taken on the importance it did. And though relativity theory applied to the cosmic rather than the atomic domain, the necessity of including relativistic effects along with Einstein's advocation of fields led to quantum electrodynamics, one of the most successful theories ever developed. But this will be the subject of the next chapter, along with the various attempts to model the interior structure of the atom. The stage is now set for the discoveries portrayed in this chapter to reach their dénouement in the next.

NOTES

1. Abraham Pais, *Inward Bound* (New York: Oxford Univ. Press, 1986), p. v. The title of this book henceforth will be abbreviated as IB.

2. E. Rutherford, *J. Röntgen Soc.* 14 (1918): 81. Pais, IB, p. 217.

3. Cf. Richard H. Schlagel, *From Myth to Modern Mind: the Origins and Growth of Scientific Thought*, Vol. I., *Theogony through Ptolemy* (New York: Peter Lang Publishers, Inc., 1995), pp. 398-399.

4. J.C. Maxwell, *The Scientific Papers of J.C. Maxwell*, edited by W.P. Niven, Vol. 2 (New York: Dover Pub.), p. 376. Pais, *Niels Bohr's Times* (New York: Oxford Univ. Press, 1991), p. 103. This title henceforth will be abbreviated to NBT.

5. *Ibid.*, p. 361. Pais, IB, p. 73. Brackets added.

6. Emilio Segrè, *From X-Rays to Quarks* (San Francisco: W.H. Freeman and Co., 1980), p. 7.

7. Jean Perrin, *Atoms*, trans. of *Les Atomes* by M.A. Hammick (Woodbridge, Conn.: Ox Bow Press, [1913] 1990), p. 216.

8. Pais, IB, p. 167. Brackets added. This discussion is based largely on Pais' account.

9. G. Kirchhoff and R. Bunsen, *Ann. der Phys. und Chem.*, 110 (1860): 160; trans. in *Phil. Mag.* 20 (1860): 89. Pais, IB, p. 168.

10. Cf. Pais, IB, p. 169.

11. *Ibid.*, p. 170.

12. W. Röntgen, "Über eine neue Art von Stahlen,"*Sitzungsberichte der Phys. Mediz. Gesellschaft zu Würzburg*, 137 (1895): 132. Trans. in *Nature* 53 (1896): 274. Serge, *op. cit.*, p. 22.

13. Pais, IB, p. 38.

14. *Ibid.*

15. This summary is based on Pais, IB, pp. 40-41.

16. Segrè, *op. cit.*, p. 23.

17. Pais, IB, English translation, p. 46.

18. Serge, *op. cit.*, p. 35.

19. *Comptes Rendus* 127 (1898): 1215. Pais, IB, p. 55. Brackets added.

20. Pierre and Sklodowska Curie, *ibid.*, 127 (1898): 175. *Ibid.*, p. 54.

21. Pais, IB, p. 55.

22. *Ibid.*, p. 57. Brackets added.

23. Serge, *op. cit.*, p. 43.

24. W. Wien, *Verh. Phys. Ges. Berlin* 16 (1897): 165. Pais, IB, pp. 81-82.

25. W. Crookes, *Chem. News* 40 (1879): 127. *Ibid.*, p. 80.

26. Pais, IB, p. 82.

27. J.J. Thomson, *The Royal Institution Library of Science*, Vol. 5, p. 36. *Ibid.*, p. 85. Italics added.

28. Cf. Serge, *op. cit.*, pp. 15-19 and Pais, IB, pp. 84-86.

29. J.J. Thomson, *Phil. Mag.* 44 (1897): 311. Pais, IB, pp. 85-86.

30. *Ibid.*, 48 (1899): 547. *Ibid.*, p. 86.

31. W. Kaufmann, *Ann. der Phys. und Chem.* 61 (1897): 544. *Ibid.*, p. 83.

32. Steven Weinberg, *The Discovery of Subatomic Particles* (New York: Scientific American Books, Inc., 1983), p. 71.

33. Sergè, *op. cit.*, p. 47. The account of Rutherford is based on Sergè and Pais, IB, pp. 58-63. The immediately following references in the text are to Segrè.

34. Pais, IB, p. 87.

35. M. Curie, *Rev. Sci.* 14 (1900): 65. Pais, IB, p. 112.

36. *Ibid.*, p. 113.

37. E. Rutherford, *Radioactivity* (Cambridge: Cambridge Univ. Press, 1904), pp. 2-4. Pais, IB, p. 113.

38. F. Soddy, *Nature* 92 (1912): 400. Cf. Pais, IB, p. 224. Also cf. Yuval Ne'eman and Yoram Kirsh, *The Particle Hunters* (Cambridge: Cambridge Univ. Press, 1986), pp. 13-15.

39. Pais, NBT, p. 77.

40. H.A. Lorentz, *Verh. Deutsch. Phys. Ges.* 9 (1907): 206. Pais, NBT, p. 78.

41. M. Planck, *Scientific Autobiography and Other papers*, trans. by F. Gaynor (London: William and Norgate, 1950), p. 7. Pais, NBT, p. 83.

42. Sergè, *op. cit.*, p 73.

43. Armin Hermann, *The Genesis of Quantum Theory* (Cambridge: MIT Press, 1971), p. 23. Sergè, *op. cit.*, p. 76.

44. Pais, NBT, p. 81.

45. Sergè, *op. cit.*, p. 73. Brackets added.

46. *Ibid.* Brackets added.

47. A. Einstein, "Autobiographical Notes," in *Albert Einstein: Philosopher-Scientist*, edited by Paul Schilpp (Evanston, Ill.: Library of Living Philosophers, Inc.), p. 45.

48. M. Planck, *Scientific Autobiography and Other Papers, op. cit.*, p. 7. Pais, NBT, p. 86.

49. Cf. Abraham Pais, '*Subtle is the Lord. . .*' (Oxford: Oxford Univ. Press, 1982), pp. 7-8. Unless otherwise indicated, the following page references in this section of the text are to this work. Henceforth the title of this book will be abbreviated as SIL.

50. Sergè, *op. cit.*, p. 86.

51. A. Einstein, *Ann. der Phys.* 19 (l905): 143. Brackets added. Sergè, *op. cit.*, p. 87.

52. Jean Perrin, *Brownian Movement and Molecular Reality*, trans. by F. Soddy (London: Taylor and Francis, 1910), concluding paragraph. Pais, SIL, p. 95.

53. Pais, IB, p. 250.

54. A.A. Michelson, *Am. J. Sci.* 22 (1881): 120. Pais, SIL, p. 112.

55. H.A. Lorentz, *Versuch Einer Theorie der Electrischen and Optischen Erscheinungen in Bewegten Körper*, *Collected Paper*, Vol. 5 (Leiden: Brill Pub., 1895), p. 1. Pais, SIL, p. 117.

56. T. Ogawa, *Jap. St. Hist. Sci.* 18 (l979): 73. Pais, SIL, p. 139.

57. G.J. Whitrow, *The Structure and Evolution of the Universe* (New York: Harper Torchbooks, 1959), p. 85.

58. M. Čapek, *The Philosophical Impact of Contemporary Physics* (New York: Van Nostrand, 1961), p. 195.

59. Cf. *Ibid.*, p. 201.

60. A. Einstein, "Die Grundlage der allgemeinen Relativitätstheorie,"*Ann. der Phys.* 49 (1916). The English edition, A. Einstein, H.A. Lorentz, H. Weyl, H. Minkowski, *The Principle of Relativity*, trans. by W. Perrett and G.B.

Jeffery (New York: Dover Pub. Inc., 1923), pp. 111-164.

61. Pais, SIL, p. 178.

62. A. Einstein, *James Clerk Maxwell* (Cambridge: Cambridge Univ. Press, 1931), p. 66. Pais, IB, p. 244.

63. Pais, SIL, p. 289.

64. Cf. David Bohm, *Wholeness and the Implicate Order* (London: Routledge & Kegan Paul, Ltd., 1980).

CHAPTER XI

ATOMIC STRUCTURE AND QUANTUM MECHANICS

Never in the history of science has there been a theory which has had such a profound impact on thinking as quantum mechanics [. . .].[1]

Jammer

Having described the origins of quantum mechanics and the creation of the theory of relativity, we return to investigations of atomic and nuclear structure, with Rutherford initially playing the dominant role. In 1907 he left McGill to become Langsworthy Professor of Physics at the Victoria University in Manchester, England, resuming his *alpha* and *beta* scattering experiments in the city where Dalton, a century earlier, had developed his atomic theory. It was while he was in Manchester (before accepting in 1919 the position as head of the Cavendish Laboratory succeeding his former teacher J.J. Thomson), and after he had received the Nobel Prize in chemistry in 1908 for his investigations of *alpha* and *beta* emissions, that he undertook his most important experimental investigations of atomic composition, culminating in his discovery of the atomic nucleus.

Spurred on by the numerous discoveries and theoretical developments at the end of the nineteenth and first decades of the twentieth centuries, including the discovery of X-rays, radioactivity, electrons, α and β particles, ions and isotopes, and gamma rays, there was a burst of enthusiasm for atomic modeling. Among those involved were James Jeans, Philipp Lenard, J.J. Thomson, Lord Kelvin, Jean Perrin, Alfred Mayer (whose experiments with magnetized corks floating on water served as a useful guide for picturing electron orbits, because he found that as the number of magnetized corks were increased they spontaneously organized into successive shells according to specific numbers[2]), and the Japanese physicist Hantaro Nagaoka.

Given the evidence of radioactive transmutations, the discovery of the electron, along with the emission of particles and rays, it became increasingly evident that the ancient conception of a solid indivisible atom as the smallest particle of matter no longer was tenable. In 1901 Perrin, among others, conjectured that the structure of the atom might resemble that of the solar system.

Each atom might consist . . . of one or more positive suns . . . and small negative planets . . . If the atom is quite heavy, the corpuscle farthest from the center [. . .] will be poorly held by the electron attraction . . . The slightest cause will detach it; the formation of cathode rays [electrons] will become so easy that [such] matter will appear spontaneously radioactive [. . .]."[3]

In England, however, the preeminent version was the "plum pudding" model of J.J. Thomson (an ardent atomic model builder) consisting of a positively charged mushy sphere of fixed radius on which electrons were embedded like plums in a pudding, the negative charge of the electrons balancing the diffuse positive charge surrounding the central sphere, producing a neutrally charged atom. He also believed that the mass of the atom was not due to the nucleus, but depended upon the electrons which, therefore, should be exceedingly numerous—a conception of atomic mass just the reverse of the actual case.

RUTHERFORD'S DISCOVERY OF THE PROTON

Yet despite all the diverse experimental evidence, the data were insufficient for determining which model was correct until Rutherford uncovered new clues with his scattering experiments in Manchester. Once installed in the excellent laboratory that had been equipped by his predecessor and sponsor, Sir Arthur Schuster, he resumed his α-scattering investigations with the help of two able assistants, Hans Geiger (who had been trained by Schuster and later would invent the Geiger counter for detecting radiation) and twenty-year old Ernest Marsden (who emigrated from New Zealand to work with his famous compatriot).

One of Rutherford's first accomplishments at Manchester was the confirmation, based on spectroscopic evidence, of his earlier belief that α-particles were ionized helium atoms, their positive charge, large mass, and great velocity making them ideal as atomic probes. Then, in the hope of uncovering new evidence of atomic structure, he had his assistants direct α-particles at thin gold foil measuring the percentage of deflections striking the scintillating screen (coated with zinc sulfide and capable of being rotated through 360°) at various angles. Geiger (1882-1945) and Marsden (1889-1970) were assigned the boring task of counting the scattered scintillations as they flashed on the screen.

While expecting that most of the α-particles, being heavy and fast-moving, would pass directly through the atoms composing the metal foil, it was thought that a few might be deflected at slight angles. Perhaps on a whim or a hunch, Rutherford asked Marsden if he could observe (by changing the angle of the screen) any particles deflected at larger angles and was amazed a week later when Marsden reported that a few had actually been deflected straight backwards—directly towards the eyepiece through which he was observing the scintillations—as if repelled by some massive body or force within the interior atoms composing the metal foil.

Rutherford's initial astonishment had a lasting effect as he reported in one of his final lectures: "'[i]t was quite the most incredible event that has ever happened to me in my life. It was almost as incredible as if you fired a 15-inch shell at a piece of tissue paper and it came back and hit you."'[4] The "as if"comparison was due to the fact that, according to J.J. Thomson's model of the atom, the metal foil being packed with identical mushy atoms it should have had the same density throughout, making it difficult to understand what could have caused some particles to be deflected directly backward. Though amazed, Rutherford was not deterred in seeking an explanation, writing a year later to his friend Professor Boltwood at Yale that "'I think I can devise an atom much superior to J.J.'s, for the explanation of and stopping of α- and β-particles, and at the same time I think it will fit in extraordinarily well with the experimental numbers."'[5]

Based on Geiger's and Marsden's measurements of the percentages of deflections at various angles, Rutherford devised a formula for correlating the number of α-particles deflected at specific angles, given the number of atoms per unit volume of the metal foil and its thickness.[6] According to his formula, this number depends on the velocity of the α-particles, the angle of deflection, and the charge of whatever was causing the deflection.[7] From this he inferred that the atom consists of a constricted "nucleus" (his term) possessing the atomic mass and having a positive charge calculated by his formula, indicating the atomic number of the element. The later was independently confirmed by J.J. Thomson and H.G.J. Moseley (1887-1915) based on X-ray emissions of the atom. Thus Rutherford was able to determine the two defining properties of the nucleus, the atomic mass and atomic number.

Surrounding this nucleus are the negatively charged electrons which are relatively massless (because they had no effect on the trajectories of the incoming α-particles), but whose orbits compose most of the volume of the atom. The electrostatic attraction between the positively charged nucleus and the negatively charged electrons accounts for the size of their orbits, analogous to the gravitational attraction between the sun and the planets determining the orbital dimensions of the planetary system as described by Kepler's three laws.

While the orbital velocities of the electrons in the outer atomic shells cause the visible spectra, X-ray spectra are produced by the electrons in the inner shells. Thus the X-ray spectra are evidence of electron orbits not revealed by optical spectra. Moreover, Moseley was able to show that the latter are determined by the nuclear charge, thus providing independent evidence of the atomic number. As Segrè states:

> The new science of X-ray spectroscopy not only allows the study of deep electron shells and elementary chemical analysis on an unprecedented level of sensitivity and certainty; it also opens the way to the exploration of crystalline lattices and, more generally, the architecture of solids and of molecules.[8]

Once he was convinced that the experimental evidence supported his calculations, Rutherford presented his results initially to the Manchester Literary and Philosophical Society in March 1911—the very society to which Dalton had submitted his atomic theory and had served as officer for so many years. A more detailed account was sent in May to the *Philosophical Magazine* followed by an article entitled "The Structure of the Atom" in the same journal in February 1914. Although he still did not know enough about the structure of the atom to explain either normal atomic stability or radioactive instability, he did conjecture about the latter in his book published in 1913.

> The instability of the atom may be [. . .] considered to be due to two causes . . . the instability of the central mass and the instability of the electronic distribution. The former . . . leads to the expulsion of an α-particle, the latter to the appearance of β- and γ-rays. [9]

While not completely correct, this was an astute conjecture. In the February 1914 article on the structure of the atom, he refers to the recent atomic theory of Niels Bohr (who by then was working with Rutherford in Manchester) which will be discussed in the next section.

But while a more detailed description of atomic structure and explanation of spectral emissions eluded Rutherford, his contribution to a better understanding of atomic (particularly nuclear) composition was crucial. Moreover, his experimental results produced independent confirmation of a number of constants, along with compelling evidence for the existence of atoms, as Serge states:

By counting atoms, Rutherford and Geiger had a means of determining Avogadro's number, the charge of the electron, and other universal constants that could also be found by entirely different experiments, for instance, by studying the blackbody radiation. The numbers derived from both methods corresponded very well, and these experiments convinced even the most skeptical physicists of the real existence of atoms, overthrowing the most obstinate, conservative rear guard.[10]

Rutherford's conception of the composition of the nucleus and electron orbits, though still incomplete, did enable physicists to formulate a much clearer notational representation of the nuclear composition and properties of the atom. For example, if the *charge* is designated as plus or minus e and Z stands for the *number* of charged units, then $+Ze$ represents the total charge of the nucleus with $-Ze$ standing for the total charge or number of electrons in a particular atomic element. In a neutral atom the number of $+Ze_s$ equals the number of $-Ze_s$, while ionization represents a loss or gain of electrons and radioactive transmutations a change in nuclear number due to the emission of α, β, or γ rays. It was concluded finally that all *radioactive* emissions originate in the nucleus because only changes of the nucleus, of the nuclear number, could transform one element into another, as uranium when emitting an α-particle transmutes into thorium: $_{92}U^{238} \rightarrow {}_{90}Th^{234} + {}_2He^4$.[11]

Because the number of $-Ze_s$ determines the chemical properties of the elements, which in turn normally corresponds to the number of $+Ze_s$, it indicates the place of the element in Mendeleev's periodic chart. While the previous organization of the elements according to their atomic weights did not explain the consequent regularity of chemical properties, it was now evident that "the ordinal numbers of each element in the periodic table is the same as its atomic number $Z!$"[12] Isotopes are atoms with identical nuclear numbers, hence the same chemical properties, but different atomic weights, the three isotopes of hydrogen symbolized as $_1H^1$, $_1H^2$, $_1H^3$.

Yet while the nuclear number and weight were the crucial properties, the question remained what they were properties of. Rutherford had already discovered (1919) that a hydrogen nucleus is emitted when an α-particle interacts with a nitrogen nucleus, but did this mean that hydrogen nuclei were constituents of all atomic nuclei? The answer was obtained several years later when Rutherford and others found that bombarding the nuclei of other elements also produced the ejection of a hydrogen nucleus. Physicists called this first nuclear particle to be identified the 'proton,' after the Greek word '*protos*' meaning first.[13] But not all the puzzles were solved by the discovery of the proton, especially the fact that the combined mass of the protons did not match the atomic weight of the atom.

Again the interaction of α-particles with nuclei, this time the nuclei of lighter elements such as beryllium, provided the answer when a new particle was ejected that was neutral in charge but quite massive. In 1932 Rutherford's colleague at the Cavendish, James Chadwich (1891-1974), was able to determine the mass of the new particle which he found to be nearly that of the proton. Because of its neutral charge, Chadwich named the new particle the 'neutron,' earning the Noble Prize in 1935 for his effort. So another piece of the puzzle was added, the neutron, a nuclear particle or nucleon that did not contribute to the nuclear charge (nuclear number) but, when combined with the proton, constituted the mass number.

As will prove to be true with the ensuing proliferation of particles, their introduction seemed to resolve many problems at a stroke, as Ne'eman and Kirsh affirm.

> The discovery of the neutron is a classic example of the way in which the addition of a new building block clarifies as if by magic previously inexplicable facts. For example, it became clear that the mass number A is just the total number of protons and neutrons in the nucleus. The fact that the atomic mass is always quite close to an integral number of amu [atomic mass unit] found a simple explanation: the masses of both the proton and the neutron are close to 1 amu. Different isotopes of an element are atoms the nuclei of which have the same number of protons but not the same number of neutrons.[14]

While the prediction of new particles such as the neutrino, positron, muon, and omega minus with specific properties is based on theoretical or mathematical deductions to solve paradoxes within current theories, their existence is not accepted until confirmed by experimental evidence. Yet the fact that when once admitted they resolve so many theoretical problems is a decisive factor in their acceptance.

Following the discovery of the proton, Rutherford also induced nuclear *disintegration* by ejecting α-particles into the air. In June 1919 he published an article entitled "Collision of Alpha Particles with Light Atoms," describing the effects of α-particles in disintegrating nitrogen nuclei producing oxygen and hydrogen: $_7N^{14} + _2He^4 = _8O^{17} + _1H^1$.[15]

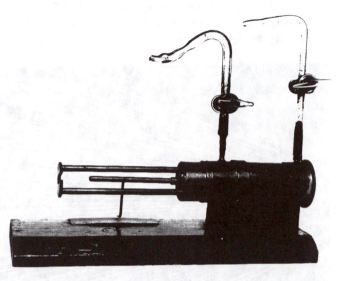

Fig. 1.   A photograph of Rutherford's nuclear disintegration chamber. Courtesy of the Cavendish Laboratory, Cambridge University.

Consistent with the laws of conservation, the atomic numbers and masses remain equal on each side of the equation. Thus was the alchemist's dream of transmuting elements realized in nuclear physics. As Rutherford describes his experimental results:

> We must conclude that the nitrogen atom is disintegrated under the intense forces developed in a close collision with a swift alpha particle, and that the hydrogen atom which is liberated formed a constituent part of the nitrogen nucleus . . . . The results as a whole suggest that if α-particles—or similar projectiles—of still greater energy were available for experiment, we might expect to break down the nuclear structure of many of the lighter atoms.[16]

As the last sentence indicates, the remarkable progress in particle physics during the second half of the twentieth century due to the development of increasingly powerful particle accelerators would not have surprised Rutherford.[17]

While the experimental evidence as theoretically interpreted implied the disintegration of the nitrogen nucleus, this effect was more directly observed by P.M.S. Blackett and D. Lea in the Wilson cloud chamber image of cascading particles as shown below.[18]

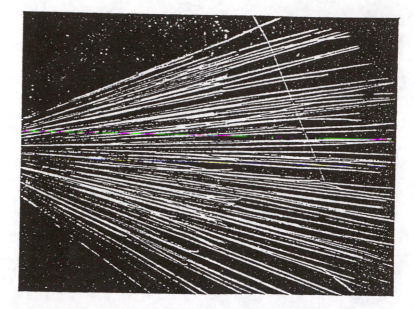

Fig. 2.   The cloud chamber image of the paths of different particles due to the disintegration of the nitrogen nucleus.

Although it is customary for scientists familiar with these detectors (the bubble chamber invented by Donald Glaser came into common use in the later 1950s) to describe their experience as 'seeing' the interaction of particles, the antirealist philosopher of science Bas C. van Fraassen objects to this usage. Calling attention to the similarity between the vapor trail of a jet and that of a particle, he condones saying "there is a jet" on the evidence of seeing its vapor trail because the jet is independently observable, but not of the particle because one cannot directly observe it under any conditions. Based on this distinction, he concludes that "while the particle is detected by means of the cloud chamber, and the detection is based on observation, it is clearly not a case of the [p]article's being observed."[19]

Although this verbal distinction is literally correct, it has little evidential or epistemic significance, which is an illustration of why scientists pay no attention to what philosophers of science say (I have yet to come across any reference to a philosopher of science by a contemporary scientist). Sergè reports that when Rutherford was talking to a famous philosopher (who probably would have been Bertrand Russell) about their respective disciplines, "'Rutherford proclaimed that philosophy was nothing but hot air."' [20] Einstein's assessment was hardly more flattering: "'[i]s not all of philosophy as if written in honey? It looks wonderful when one contemplates it, but when one looks again it is all gone. Only mush remains.'"[21]

Van Fraassen's position is based on the recently *discarded* positivist assumption that the evidence presented in ordinary experience is relatively theory-neutral, therefore constituting a more certain or secure evidential basis than the experimental evidence of science. One would have thought, however, that developments in science such as the Copernican revolution, relativity theory, and the genome project would have disabused one of this naivety. The restriction of 'observable' to what manifests itself directly in a visual image overlooks the fact that *all* visual observation itself is mediated by complex physical processes: atomic, radiational, optical, and physiological. Our perceptual image of the sun surely is not an exact replica of the sun's independent existence, yet it would be supercilious to claim that we never 'observe' the sun. With such technological advances as the optical and radio telescopes, optical, electron, and tunneling microscopes, PET and CAT scanners, and so forth, the distinction between the experimental detection of something in contrast to enhanced sensory observation has been blurred. As Ne'eman and Kirsh state in opposition to van Fraassen: "[n]ot even the most powerful microscope will enable us to see sub-atomic particles. But there are certain instruments which so unmistakenly reveal the presence of these particles and trace their paths that we can indeed claim to be able to 'see' them."[22]

If all observation is theory laden or dependent, as is now generally held, then ordinary observation statements are merely a subclass of experimentally derived observation statements—our bodies serving as one among innumerable instruments facilitating data gathering. That ordinary observation statements are more familiar and more representative of everyday experience, while most scientific statements are based on more theoretical interpretations and sophisticated apparatus, does not endow the former with any epistemic superiority, which the Copernican revolution clearly illustrated. As Paul Churchland states:

Our perceptual judgments can no longer be assigned any privileged status as independent and theory-neutral arbiters of what there is in the world. Excellence of theory emerges as the fundamental measure of all ontology. The function of science, therefore, is to provide us with a superior and (in the long run) perhaps profoundly different conception of the world, *even at the perceptual level.*[23]

As will be true now that scientific theories have become more dependent upon the experimental evidence, as well as more representative of the infrastructures of nature, each theoretical advance, while resolving some problems, opens up new ones that were not apparent previously because the understanding then was insufficient to bring them to light. Although critics of science point to theory change as a liability to any claim to scientific truth—as if there were evidence of some alternative permanent universal knowledge—in fact this self-generating, self-corrective aspect of science is its major strength ensuring its continuing improvement and development.

NIELS BOHR'S SOLAR MODEL OF THE ATOM

Returning to the early attempts to construct a viable model of the atom, as we have seen Rutherford provided half of the answer with his conception of the nucleus composed of positively charged massive protons and the postulated neutron, but there still was no consensus regarding the arrangement within the atom of the electrons, the other half of the problem. This answer was provided mainly by Niels Bohr (1885-1962), the great Danish physicist from Copenhagen, whose contribution to the structure of the atom along with the early development of quantum mechanics was unsurpassed. Together with Einstein, he was a dominant influence on the development of theoretical physics in the second decade of the twentieth century by his own theories, and later through the extraordinary influence of his famous Institute of Theoretical Physics in Copenhagen to which all the younger generation of physicists, such as Kramer, Heisenberg, Pauli, Schrödinger, and Dirac were attracted.

Bohr's interest in electrons began with his doctoral dissertation written on the electronic theory of metals. Having read of J.J. Thomson's atomic model which he referred to in his dissertation, when he received a stipend from the Carlesberg Foundation (which later would contribute so generously to the construction and support of his Institute) to study abroad, he decided to go to Cambridge to do postgraduate work under the supervision of Thomson. Unfortunately, however, their initial meeting in the fall of 1911 was not too satisfactory. Although very respectful and courteous, Bohr was an exceedingly earnest person very much caught up and driven by his own ideas, with the result that during their very first meeting he pointed to a passage in one of Thomson's books that he had brought with him, declaring that it was "wrong." Probably not accustomed to being corrected by a twenty-six year old student who barely spoke English, the relationship between the two, though cordial, did not flourish. This is indicated in a letter Bohr wrote to his younger brother Harald (who was to become a famous mathematician in his own right):

> Thomson [. . .] is an excellent man, incredibly clever and full of imagination . . . extremely friendly, but . . . it is very difficult to talk to him. He has not yet had time to read my paper [the doctoral dissertation] and I do not know if he will accept my criticism.[24]

Then in early November Bohr had the good fortune to meet Rutherford in Manchester through a friend of his father and later hear him lecture in Cambridge on his theory of the atom (a theory to which Thomson strongly objected). These encounters with Rutherford apparently led him to decide (after discussing the situation with Thomson) to leave Cambridge to spend part of his year abroad working in Rutherford's laboratory in Manchester. In contrast to his relation with Thomson, Bohr's association with Rutherford flourished, developing into a deep friendship based on mutual admiration that lasted until Rutherford's death in 1937. Bohr later said of Rutherford that "[t]o me he had almost been like a second father," especially as Bohr had lost his own father earlier. When Bohr was married the following August, before continuing their honeymoon in Scotland he took his bride to visit Rutherford and his wife in Manchester.

Arriving in Manchester by March of 1912, Bohr took a course in radioactivity and then, at the suggestion of Rutherford, conducted experiments on α-absorption. Soon realizing these investigations were not conducive to his main interest in atomic composition, he discontinued his experiments to concentrate on a theoretical determination of the arrangement of electrons within the atom. In this endeavor he was influenced by two other research associates in Rutherford's laboratory, Georg von Hevesy (1885-1966) and Charles Galton Darwin (1887-1962). Hevesy, a young Hungarian nobleman who was to become famous for his ingenious applications of radioactivity, told Bohr of his creation of many new isotopes due to induced nuclear transmutations. Darwin, the grandson of the famous evolutionist, discussed his experiments involving the interaction of α-particles, not as Rutherford with the nucleus but with electrons, noting the loss of velocity of the α-particles when they interacted with a cluster of electrons and the occasional ejection of the latter. The discussion with Darwin, particularly, led Bohr to consider the status of the electrons surrounding the nucleus, initially believing them to be "atomic vibrators" bound to the nucleus by electrostatic attraction. More importantly, he thought the vibrators must radiate according to Planck's quantum of action, as he later wrote in one of his famous articles published in 1913: "'[a]ccording to Planck's theory of radiation . . . the smallest quantity of energy which can be radiated out from an atomic vibrator is equal to v [times] k,'"[25]with v standing for the number of vibrations per second and k representing what we know to be Planck's constant h. As Pais says, "'[t]hus *did the quantum theory enter the interior of the atom for the first time in Bohr's writings*." (p. 128)

In the summer of 1912 when he was married, Bohr prepared a draft article "On the constitution of atoms and molecules" which he sent to Rutherford for his comments. While it is not known which passage in Thomson's book Bohr objected to, in the "Rutherford memorandum," as it is called, he raised a number of critical questions pertaining to Thomson's conception of the arrangement of electrons in his model, centering on the problems of atomic stability and radius. Essentially, the criticisms reflect his realization (already indicated in his doctoral dissertation which he had hoped Thomson would read) that the principles of classical mechanics were insufficient for solving these problems.

First, the kind of static arrangement of electrons (like plums in a pudding) in Thomson's model would prove unstable, yet if the electrons revolved in orbits, according to classical electrodynamics they would continuously radiate energy eventually spiraling into the nucleus. Secondly, all the electrons could not rotate in the same orbit because that too would prove unstable on classical principles, implying they must form successive shells or orbits. Thirdly, according to Thomson's model the radius of the atom was determined by the size of the spherical nucleus, but not only was there no evidence to support this, Rutherford's experiments indicated that the mass and charge of the nucleus were concentrated in a point-like particle in the center, the proton.

Concluding that it would be "hopeless" to try to resolve these problems solely in terms of classical mechanics, Bohr was aware that the solution must incorporate the quantification of radiation introduced by Planck and Einstein. As early as 1906 Einstein had declared that Planck's radiation theory implied that

the energy of a [linear material oscillator] can take on only those values that are integral multiples of hv; in emission and absorption of energy the energy of [this oscillator] changes by *jumps* which are integer multiples of *hv*."[26]

But the problem, as usual, was finding the empirical data that would provide clues for a viable solution. While Bohr was in Cambridge he very likely met John William Nicholson (1881-1955), who in 1911 "associated spectral lines with various modes of vibration of electrons around their equilibrium orbits in the field of a central charge." (p. 198) Moreover, Nicholson had attempted to determine the number of electrons of the simplest and lightest atoms, such as hydrogen, while in a paper published in 1912 he had proposed that if one knew the mass, velocity, and radius of a revolving electron, then its angular momentum *L* would be equal to their product, *mvr*. He also noted, as Pais, states, that this product

just equals the ratio of the particle's energy to its frequency. This ratio, Planck had proposed in another context, should equal *h*. "If, therefore, the constant *h* of Planck has . . . an atomic significance, it may mean that *the angular momentum of a particle can only rise or fall by discrete amounts when electrons leave or return.*" In modern terms, Nicholson had quantized angular momentum. (p. 145; italics added)

Whether it was due to his having read Einstein, talked with Nicholson, or his own speculations, Bohr also realized that the angular momentum of the electrons was an important factor in determining their orbits, noting "a relation between the kinetic energy *W* ($W = \frac{1}{2}mv^2$, *m* = mass, v = velocity) of an electron running around in a circle within the atom and its frequency *v* [. . .] given by $W = Kv$." (p. 138) The similarity between this formula and Planck's equation $\varepsilon = hv$, correlating the energy of an oscillator with its frequency, must have reinforced Bohr's belief that the new quantum discoveries should play a role in deciphering the enigma of electron orbits.

But according to his own recollection, it was when a student friend who had experimented with spectra at Göttingen, Hans Marius Hansen, asked him whether his speculations of possible electron orbits implied anything about spectral emissions, with Bohr forced to admit they did not, that was the decisive influence on his thinking. Advised by Hansen to consider Balmer's formula, Bohr recalled that "'[a]s soon as I saw Balmer's formula the whole thing was immediately clear to me.'"[27] So early in 1913 following his conversation with Hansen, Bohr looked up Balmer's formula in Vol. II of J.

Stark's *Prinzipien der Atomdynamik.*

What Bohr might have realized when he saw Balmer's formula:

$$\nu = R(\frac{1}{n^2} - \frac{1}{m^2}) \ ,$$

which predicted among the spectral lines of hydrogen a definite regularity of frequencies where n and m are positive integral numbers with $n < m$, was its formal resemblance to Planck's formula describing the relation between different energy states, $E_1 - E_2 = h\nu$, also incorporating positive integral numbers. In any case, even in the introduction to his doctoral dissertation Bohr had conjectured that the forces involved in interatomic processes were not solely mechanical:

> The assumption [of mechanical forces] is not a priori self-evident, for one must assume that there are forces in nature of a kind completely different from the usual mechanical sort [. . . .] [because] there are [. . .] many properties of bodies impossible to explain if one assumes that the forces which act within the individual molecules . . . are mechanical [. . .] for instance [. . .] the radiation law for high frequencies [. . .]." (pp. 137-138; brackets added)

Thus like Einstein and Nicholson, Bohr apparently concluded that the angular momentum of electrons can change only by discrete amounts, in contrast to classical mechanics, but saw in Balmer's formula the crucial correlation between the spectral emissions of hydrogen occurring in integral numbers of discrete frequencies and the discontinuous frequencies of the orbiting electrons also occurring by integral numbers. As Ne'eman and Kirsh state,

> if one assumes that the angular momentum of the electron is an integral multiple of $h/2\pi$ [. . .] the model accounted very accurately for the wavelengths of light that the hydrogen atom was observed to emit or absorb. This 'quantization rule' fitted nicely into the photon model: just as light energy can be delivered only in integral multiples of hf, the angular momentum of a system must be an integral multiple of a 'natural unit' which equals $h/2\pi$ (this unit is denoted $\hbar$).[28]

So rather than the possibility of an infinite succession of electron orbits, Bohr introduced the novel conception of a series of privileged orbits which he called "stationary states," their fixed status depending upon the electron's angular momentum and frequency or energy. Moreover, he now was in a position to explain that not all atomic instability originates in transmutations in the nucleus, some emissions originating in transitions or "jumps" of electrons from one energy level to a another, accompanied by the radiation or absorption of a quantum of energy according to Planck's equation:

$$E_1 - E_2 = hv.$$

Thus the discreteness of electron spectra is a consequence of the discreteness of orbital states, the transitions of which produce the emissions.

The jump of an electron from a higher energy, less stable state to a lower energy, more stable one produces the emission of a photon whose energy equals the difference of the two energy states; conversely, when energy is absorbed by the atom it will be in discrete integral quanta as Planck showed, sufficient to propel an electron to a higher stationary state. This explanation of line spectra underlies all spectroscopic analysis to this day. The classical prediction of an electron in the lowest orbital state radiating its energy until its angular momentum was overcome by the electrostatic force, causing it to be drawn into the nucleus, was solved by postulating that the "ground state" was "stable." As Pais indicates, Bohr eliminated the difficulty by "introducing one of the most audacious postulates ever seen in physics," namely, "that the ground state *is* stable, thereby contravening all knowledge about radiation available up to then!" (p. 147)

This preliminary explanation of spectra based on orbital frequencies, stationary states, and transitions of the electrons was "audacious" also because it combined both classical and quantum mechanics in an extremely unorthodox way—the *mechanical* frequencies of the stationary orbits described in terms of *classical* mechanics while the *optical* frequencies of the photons emitted during the transitional states were described in terms of *quantum* mechanics. Thus Bohr's solution incorporated two contradictory principles of mechanics, as he states.

1. That the dynamical equilibrium of the systems in the stationary states can be discussed by the help of ordinary mechanics, while the passing of the system between different stationary states cannot be treated on this basis.

2. That the latter process is followed by the emission of

> *homogeneous* radiation, for which the relation between
> frequency and the amount of energy emitted is the one
> given by Planck's theory (i.e. , $E_1 - E_2 = h\nu$).[29]

Although Emerson claimed that "simple consistency is the hobgoblin of little minds," in science the rule of consistency, as the principle of simplicity depicted in Occam's Razor (hypotheses should not be multiplied beyond necessity), plays such a crucial role in scientific thought that Bohr's ability to adopt two contradictory scientific principles, albeit applied to different electron states, was quite remarkable. In this mode of thinking one finds the first indication of two guiding principles that later would influence so significantly Bohr's interpretation of quantum mechanics: the "correspondence principle" and the "principle of complementarity." The first principle is indicated in his assertion that

> the frequencies calculated [. . .] in the limit where the motions in
> successive stationary states differ comparatively very little from each
> other, will tend to coincide with the frequencies to be expected on the
> ordinary theory of radiation from the motion of the system in the
> stationary states.[30]

Thus in the limit where the magnitudes of the frequencies merge with classical dimensions, the calculations will tend to correspond (as in relativity theory). On the other hand, his willingness to use two principles of physics that would be contradictory if referred to the same experimental phenomena, but which are "complementary" when applied to different experimental conditions, illustrates his second principle.

As the saying goes, "the proof is in the pudding," but in this case not the plum pudding concoction of Thomson. The consequences of Bohr's theoretical conception of electron orbits published in 1913 were striking. Without going into the mathematical calculations,[31] Bohr was able to derive Balmer's formula from his own formulas and obtain precise numerical values for the Rydberg constant R ($R = 3.1 \times 10^{15}$), along with the radius of the bound state of the stable hydrogen atom, called the "Bohr radius" ($r_1 = 0.55 \times 10^{-8}$ cm.). As impressive as these calculations were, his primary achievement was in demonstrating that a series of stellar spectral lines discovered earlier by Charles Pickering in 1896 and attributed to hydrogen, which then were rediscovered in 1912 by Alfred Fowler, were in fact the spectral lines of ionized helium, consisting of two protons and one electron.

spectral lines of ionized helium, consisting of two protons and one electron. (cf. p. 149) But when Bohr's formula for R gave the value as $4R$, Fowler objected that the correct value was not 4, but 4.0016 (another indication of how precise scientific computations were becoming). Bohr replied that his calculation had been based on approximate values for the hydrogen and helium nuclei, but that when the true masses are used the quantity 4.00163 is obtained "''in exact agreement with the experimental value.''"[32] As Pais declares, "[u]p to that time no one had ever produced anything like it in the realm of spectroscopy, agreement between theory and experiment to five significant figures.'' (p. 149)

In addition to these computational achievements, Bohr was able to provide a number of new theoretical explanations of spectral emissions utilizing the theories of blackbody radiation, the photoelectric effect, nuclear radioactivity, electron radiation, and spectroscopy. In particular, he was able to give convincing explanations of X-ray and *beta* ray spectra. Dividing the electron orbits into inner and outer shells, he attributed the origin of visible spectra to the radiation of the outer electrons while X-rays originate when an electron from an inner shell is ejected, the replacing of the ejected electron by one from an outer orbit causing an additional radiation of a photon. As a result, X-ray spectra show regularities pertaining to nuclear charge or atomic number not revealed by visible spectra.[33] *Beta* rays, later identified as electrons, he correctly attributed to radioactive processes in the nucleus. Rutherford and Royds had proved in 1909 that α-particles were helium nuclei; gamma rays it was found carry no electrical charge or mass but have very short wavelengths like X-rays.[34] According to Bohr's conception of atomic structure, the number of electrons (which in stable elements equals the number of protons) determines the chemical properties of the atoms. He even attempted to explain magnetism in terms of electrons moving with a certain angular momentum in closed orbits. (cf. p. 151)

Like Einstein's five publications in 1905 when he was twenty-six, Bohr's three publications on ''the constitution of atoms''in 1913 when he was twenty-eight revolutionized physics. As Pais summarizes his achievements:

The very existence of line (and band) spectra suggests, he noted, that electrons move in discrete stationary orbits inside atoms and molecules. Spectra (including X-ray spectra) arise because of quantum jumps between these states. (It would take until the 1980s before such individual jumps were directly observed.[35]) The quantitative confirmation of these ideas by his treatment of hydrogen and ionized helium mark a turning point in the physics of the twentieth century and the high point in Bohr's creative career. The insistence on the role of the outermost ring of electrons as the seat of most chemical properties of the elements, in particular their valencies, constitutes the first step toward quantum chemistry. The sharp distinction between atomic/molecular and nuclear physics begins with his realization that β-rays emanate from the nucleus. (p. 152)

The reaction to these amazing achievements, as one would expect, were diverse. Rutherford, to whom he had sent the early memorandum and later an article on "the constitution of atoms" to be forwarded to the *Philosophical Magazine*, was generally favorable, asserting that "'[w]hile it is too early to say whether the theories of Bohr are valid, his contributions . . . are of great importance and interest.'"[36] His major objection focused on how the electrons know which privileged orbits to select in their transitions. But the strongest opposition came from Bohr's use of conflicting principles from classical and quantum mechanics, which seemed to depend upon mere expediency to account for the diverse phenomena.

Perhaps the most extreme negative reaction (although later they became converts) was by Otto Stern and Max von Laue who declared of Bohr's theory "that if by chance it should prove correct, they would quit physics."[37] But most responses were more positive, if somewhat cautious. Sommerfeld wrote to Bohr from Munich that "'[a]lthough I am for the present still a little skeptical about atomic models, your calculation of the constant [in the Balmer formula] is nevertheless a great achievement.'"[38] Moseley, the brilliant young spectroscopist who was killed tragically in battle during the first world war, was very affirmative: "'[y]our theory is having a splendid effect on Physics, and I believe when we really know what an atom is, as we must within a few years, your theory even if wrong in detail will deserve much of the credit.'"[39]

Fifty years later Alfred Landé recalled that after Bohr gave seminars in 1914 at the University of Göttingen to leading German physicists on his views of electron orbits, some said "'[i]f its not nonsense, at least it doesn't make sense,'" while Max Born (the preeminent originator of the statistical interpretation of quantum mechanics) asserted "'[a]ll this is absolutely queer and incredible, but this Danish physicist looks so like an original genius that I cannot deny there must be something to it . . .'"[40]

But the most eloquent tribute was paid by Einstein who, although a severe critic of quantum mechanics in later life, was a genuine admirer and close friend of Bohr.

That this insecure and contradictory foundation was sufficient to enable a man of Bohr's unique instinct and tact to discover the major laws of the spectral lines and the electron shells of the atoms together with their significance for chemistry appeared to me like a miracle—and appears to me as a miracle even today. This is the highest form of musicality in the sphere of thought.[41]

Bohr, if anything, was as critical and as skeptical of his explanation of the hydrogen spectra as anyone, very much aware of its *ad hoc* makeshift foundation. Yet he had introduced considerable order and clarification of the problem which seemed to have some factual foundation and truth because of its precise agreement with the empirical evidence and consistency with other quantitative derivations. At least now there was a theory sufficiently developed that could be used in evaluating new experimental data and revised as required, the prerequisite for any progress in science! As Pais accesses his achievement:

Atoms had been postulated in ancient times. As the year 1913 began, almost unanimous consensus had been reached, after much struggle, that atoms are real. Even before that year it had become evident that atoms have substructure, but no one yet knew by what rules their parts moved. During that year, Bohr, fully conscious that these motions could not possibly be described in terms of classical physics, but that it nevertheless was essential to establish a link between classical and quantum physics, gave the first firm and lasting direction toward an understanding of atomic structure and atomic dynamics. In that sense he may be considered the father of the atom. (p. 152)

THE END OF THE OLD AND CREATION OF THE NEW QUANTUM MECHANICS

What has since come to be called "the old quantum theory" had its apogee in 1913 with Bohr's partially successful orbital explanation of the hydrogen spectra. But this success was achieved at the cost of using two incompatible principles, one from classical and the other from quantum mechanics. Moreover, Bohr could not explain why the electrons in the hydrogen atom were restricted to particular orbits in which their angular momentum was an integral multiple of Planck's constant h, nor could he derive or predict the spectra of atoms with an electronic structure more complex than hydrogen. The solutions to these problems would not occur until the years 1925-27 as a result of the construction of "the new quantum theory," or quantum mechanics as it came to be called, due to the contributions essentially of de Broglie, Heisenberg, Dirac, and Schrödinger, along with Pauli, Jordan, and Max Born.

The turning point began in 1923 with a most unlikely development from an even more unlikely contributor. It will be recalled that one of Einstein's five papers published in 1905 dealt with the photoelectric effect concerning the ejection of electrons when monochromatic light of sufficient frequency is directed to the clean surface of an "alkali metal like sodium in a vacuum."[42] This was the origin of the modern paradoxical wave-particle duality because instead of explaining the ejection of the electrons as the effect of monochromatic waves of a certain intensity (reinforced waves), Einstein attributed their ejection to the impact of minute quanta of energy (later named photons) within the light source defined by Planck's equation $\varepsilon = h\nu$. Because the ejection of the electrons by the light quanta presupposes an exchange of momentum or energy characteristic of particle interactions, while the energy of the light quanta is defined by its frequency ν, a characteristic of waves, this injects dual properties into the conception of light.

Yet there was considerable opposition (especially on the part of Bohr) to accepting the reality of light quanta until Compton's scattering experiments of 1922 demonstrated that when light or X-rays interact with an electron the "scattered rays" behave as if there had been an exchange of energy or momentum among *particles*. Because momentum is a product of mass and velocity and photons do not have mass, the photon's momentum (p) was attributed to its wavelength (λ), according to the formula $p = h/\lambda$. Yet there was indisputable evidence, extending back to Newton and Huygens and confirmed experimentally by Young and Fresnel, that light produces diffraction patterns owing to its *waves* being in or out of phase and therefore reinforcing or destructing. Thus light exhibits both wave and particle attributes depending upon the experimental arrangements.

LOUIS DE BROGLIE'S ATTRIBUTION OF WAVES TO PARTICLES

Although his previous training was as an historian, Prince Louis de Broglie (1892-1987) became fascinated by the physical investigations of his older brother, Duke Maurice, an accomplished physicist, carried out in the laboratory of their home in Paris. Aiding his brother in experiments that demonstrated the dual properties of light, Louis de Broglie was intrigued by this dualism, wondering whether the inverse of Einstein's thesis also was not true: that just as light manifests particle characteristics, perhaps particles such as electrons have wave characteristics. Attempting to apply Einstein's relativistic principles to the subatomic particles because of their high velocities, he derived formulas describing the waves associated with particles such as electrons and photons.

> Every particle, every electron, proton and so on was to have an associated wave, of frequency v_0 given by $m_0c_2 = hv_0$ when at rest, where m_0 is the rest mass of the particle. When moving a particle with momentum p has a de Broglie wavelength λ such that $p = h/\lambda$ [. . .] the wave length of a monochromatic [. . .] pure sine wave.[43]

When he submitted his derivations as a doctoral thesis, the examining committee at the Sorbonne did not know what to make of them, so one member of the committee, Paul Langevin, sent the thesis to Einstein for his evaluation. Einstein responded very favorably and so de Broglie received his *Doctorat ès Sciences* in 1924.[44] The confirmation that electrons display wave characteristics when radiated through a diffraction grating was confirmed by Clinton Davisson (1881-1958) and Lester Germer (1896-1971) in 1927. In terms of its subsequent influence on Schrödinger, the importance of de Broglie's work was the localization of 'particles' by means of a wave train or wave packet with their velocities determined by the properties of the wave packet.[45] In addition, interpreting electrons as waves enabled him to explain why Bohr's orbiting electrons were limited to specific stationary shells. Because the number of wavelengths in an orbit must be integral if they are not to interfere or destruct ($2\pi r$, the circumference, equals $n\lambda$, where n is an integer and λ the wavelength), this restricts the size of the orbit so that their angular momentum is a multiple of Planck's constant, $n\hbar$. De Broglie won the Nobel Prize in 1929 and Davisson and George P. Thomson (1892-1975), the son of J.J. Thomson, shared the prize in 1937 for their independent confirmation of his theory.

WERNER HEISENBERG'S MATRIX MECHANICS

The next contributor to this development was Werner Heisenberg (1901-1976), a multifaceted genius whose father was a professor of Greek at the

University of Munich. Personifying the Nazi ideal of a superior Aryan race, he was blond, handsome, athletic with a mystical love of nature, a gifted pianist, well versed in the Greek classics (which he read in the original), and fond of quoting passages from the German romantic poets such as Goethe. Undoubtedly the only mathematical physicist ever to have been attracted to atomic physics because of reading Plato's *Timaeus* in Greek (in preparation for an examination when he was not quite seventeen), he was intrigued by Plato's attempt to equate the four elements, fire, earth, air, and water (along with the cosmos) with the four of the five Pythagorean geometric solids, explaining their breakdown and recombination due to the interaction of imperceptible right-angled isosceles or half-equilateral triangles. Although "the whole thing seemed to be wild speculation" that had "no explanatory value at all," Heisenberg nonetheless "was enthralled by the idea that the smallest particles of matter must reduce to some mathematical form."[46]

Earning his doctorate in physics in 1923 at the University of Munich at age twenty-two, he studied mainly with Sommerfeld whose name is often linked with Bohr as coauthor of the Bohr-Sommerfeld model of the atom. It was with Sommerfeld that Heisenberg traveled to Göttingen in 1922 to hear Bohr lecture and where they met for the first time. Impressed by the precocious young scholar, Bohr invited him to Copenhagen, but first Heisenberg decided to go to Göttingen to work with Max Born where he remained until the fall of 1924. At Munich Heisenberg had been taught the latest atomic theories which were called quantum mechanics, but he found them very unsatisfactory. Attributing the deficiencies to the attempt to accommodate the experimental data to the conjectured electron shells and spontaneous transitions, he decided to see if more sense could be made of the data if confined to the measurable phenomena, discarding the visual pictures or mechanisms.

Suffering from an acute attack of hay fever in May 1925 while working in Göttingen with Born, he decided to seek refuge in a small island called Heligoland on the North Sea where the sea breeze could be counted on to disperse any pollen-laden air. There he not only regained his health, but began writing a paper that would initiate a true quantum mechanics. Replacing the fictitious "orbits" with measured "states," he organized the series of frequencies correlated with the electron states in arrays of horizontal and vertical volumes, as depicted below by Crease and Mann. According to the table "S_1 stands for 'state $\lambda 1$,' S_2 for 'state $\lambda 2$,' and so on, and v, again, is [. . .] 'frequency.' When an electron goes from S_1 to S_2, it produces light of frequency v_{2-1}."[47]

$$
\begin{array}{c|cccc}
 & S_1 & S_2 & S_3 & \cdots \\
\hline
S_1 & v_{1\text{-}1} & v_{2\text{-}1} & v_{3\text{-}1} & \cdots \\
S_2 & v_{1\text{-}2} & v_{2\text{-}2} & v_{3\text{-}2} & \cdots \\
S_3 & v_{1\text{-}3} & v_{2\text{-}3} & v_{3\text{-}3} & \cdots \\
 & & & & \\
\cdot & \quad\cdot & \quad\cdot & \quad\cdot & \\
\cdot & \quad\cdot & \quad\cdot & \quad\cdot & \\
\end{array}
$$

Despite the extreme formalism of the approach, precluding any intuitive representation of the quantum processes, Heisenberg seemed to find in this array of numbers an abstract reflection of the interior of the atom—just as Plato had seen the geometric structure of the four elements along with the universe itself depicted in the five Pythagorean solids. As Heisenberg vividly describes this feeling:

> Within a few days [. . .] it had become clear to me what precisely had to take the place of Bohr-Sommerfeld quantum conditions in an atomic physics working with none but observable magnitudes. [. . .] I had the feeling that, through the surface of atomic phenomena, I was looking at a strangely beautiful interior, and felt almost giddy at the thought that I now had to probe this wealth of mathematical structures nature had so generously spread out before me.[48]

Although heady with this vision, he had little understanding of what it meant. Yet he completed the paper in July which was published in the *Zeitschrift für Physik* in September 1925. In the paper he noted that when he performed the usual mathematical functions between the array of matrix numbers, such as multiplication, the results were unlike those of traditional mathematics. It was not until he returned to Göttingen in the fall of 1925 that this peculiar mathematical relation was recognized by Born when he read the paper.

Unlike the University of Munich where the approach to quantum mechanics emphasized the physical interpretation (with Sommerfeld contributing to the construction of the atom) or Bohr's Institute at Copenhagen where the emphasis was on the conceptual interpretation, the University of Göttingen was famous for its mathematicians David Hilbert and Richard

Courant whose focus was on the mathematical formalism of physics. Steeped in this mathematical background, Born was able to discern in Heisenberg's array of numerical frequencies a little known branch of mathematics called matrix theory. The mathematician who originally organized numbers into these rectangular matrices was Augustin Cauchy, while Arthur Caley was the first to explore their mathematical properties when the matrices are added, subtracted, or multiplied.[49]

It is when multiplying matrices that the most surprising result occurs, violating one of the fundamental laws of mathematics, the commutative law. That law states that when multiplying two numbers the order of numbers multiplied makes no difference: $7 \times 9 = 9 \times 7$. Multiplying matrices, however, is noncommutative: 7×9 does not equal 9×7. When Born began rewriting Heisenberg's equations based on frequency matrices he realized

that the matrix q for position and the matrix p for momentum are noncommutative in a very special way: that is, pq is not only different from qp, but the difference between pq and qp is always the same amount, no matter what p or q you choose. Mathematically, he wrote this [as] $pq - qp = \hbar/i$ where $\hbar$ as usual is Planck's constant divided by twice *pi* [2π], and i is the special symbol mathematicians use for the square root of minus one [$\sqrt{-1}$].[50]

Once he understood what Heisenberg's paper implied, Born enlisted the help of a student also gifted in mathematics, Pascal Jordan (1902-1980), to help write a paper that clarified the basic principles of matrix mechanics. Written mostly by Jordan, the paper was completed in August 1925 and published in the *Zeitschrift für Physics* the following November. Like Bohr who was always concerned to show that quantum theory presupposed *classical* mechanics, Born and Jordan were able to demonstrate that the spectral matrices were related to classical physics in the way that Bohr's explanation of hydrogen spectra was related to classical mechanics by using a mathematical operator, the *Hamiltonian*, which stands for the measured energy of the system. Thus Born and Jordan replaced Bohr's insertion of Planck's quantum of energy into the *Hamiltonian* with the matrix frequencies.[51]

When Heisenberg read their paper it was decided that the three of them should collaborate in writing another paper expressing their combined views. This third paper written in October 1925 was published in February 1926 in the same journal as the two previous articles. This new mechanics was called *quantenmechanik*, and while it produced some results—Pauli, for example, was able (with considerable effort) to derive the hydrogen spectra from it that agreed with Bohr's derivation—the mathematics of matrices was so unfamiliar to physicists that it attracted few advocates. Moreover, the physical significance of the noncommutative parameters of position q and momentum p was not clarified until Heisenberg showed later that it imposed a limitation on the exact measurement of such conjugate parameters, introducing a reciprocal "uncertainty," or more accurately, "indeterminacy" on their joint measurements. Yet matrix mechanics was a crucial contribution to the development of quantum mechanics for which Heisenberg received the Nobel Prize in 1932.

PAUL DIRAC'S "TRANSFORMATION THEORY"

In between his visit to Heligoland in May and his return to Göttingen in the fall of 1926, Heisenberg made trips to Berlin, Leiden, and the Cavendish Laboratory at Cambridge. Apparently he had left copies of his original paper at the Cavendish because Paul Dirac (1902-1984), another mathematical prodigy who was studying mathematics at St. John's College, Cambridge, first became acquainted with quantum mechanics through reading Heisenberg's paper.[52] So while the trio in Göttingen was writing their formulation of matrix mechanics, Dirac alone and at age twenty-four produced a more general and rigorous version of quantum mechanics that he called "transformation theory" which quite unsettled Heisenberg when he read it. As described by Crease and Mann:

A lengthy letter in Dirac's minute, fussy handwriting arrived in Göttingen on November 20, 1925. Written in English, it explained to the astonished Heisenberg how in a few concise steps his version of quantum mechanics could be reformulated in classical terms using a mathematical device [the Poisson bracket, a probability density function], he had never heard of. Moreover, working alone, Dirac had come up with a version of quantum mechanics much more general and complete than that produced by Heisenberg, Born, and Jordan in their just-completed joint paper.[53]

Although taken aback by this *tour de force*, Heisenberg graciously wrote Dirac complimenting him on the superiority of "your extraordinarily beautiful paper on quantum mechanics.'' As it turned out, the two formalisms were demonstrated later to be mathematically equivalent.

ERWIN SCHRÖDINGER'S WAVE MECHANICS

The years 1925-6 were seminal in the development of quantum mechanics. In the same fall and winter in 1925 that Heisenberg, Born, and Jordan were formulating matrix mechanics and Dirac was creating his independent system of quantum mechanics, a fourth entrant was formulating still another version of the new mechanics, called wave mechanics. Born in Vienna but working at the time in Zürich, Erwin Schrödinger (1887-1961), already a well-known physicist who was a friend of Planck and Einstein, was at thirty-eight relatively old compared to the *wunderkinder* Heisenberg, Pauli, Jordan, and Dirac, who were barely in their mid-twenties.

Informed by Einstein of de Broglie's doctoral thesis, Schrödinger was aware that the latter had shown that mass and momentum, previously considered exclusive properties of particles, could be depicted as functions of waves. As regards mass, Einstein had shown the equivalence of mass and energy ($E = mc^2$) while Planck had equated energy with frequency ($\varepsilon = hv$), previously thought to be a property only of particles. The sequence of these equivalences could be interpreted as meaning that waves were basic while particles were derivative, their apparent existence due to a constricted wave packet. An added motivation for this preference for waves over particles was Einstein's belief that Maxwell's equations for describing the structure and propagation of electromagnetic fields could be extended to electrostatic and gravitational attractions as well.

Schrödinger shared Einstein's belief that waves or fields should replace material particles as the basic reality and that an explanation of emission spectra (which after all are waves) consistent with classical electrodynamics could be formulated that would eliminate electron orbits and especially the detested quantum jumps. Rather than the obscure mathematics of matrices, he would use the familiar formalism of wave theory to explain not only electromagnetic and acoustic phenomena, but also subatomic structures and interactions. Ignoring relativistic effects as a simplification, Schrödinger devised a formula using wave functions for Bohr's angular momenta of the orbiting electrons that produced images resembling various smeared or cloudy Rorschach images.

Initially it was believed that these figures, based on solutions to his wave equation, were actually "electron clouds," a kind of diffuse condensed electric charge similar to Einstein's *"Gespensterfeld "* or ghost field guiding the path of light quanta.[54]

It was these "electron clouds" or "wavefields" that Max Born would interpret as a probability field propagating in phase or configuration space.

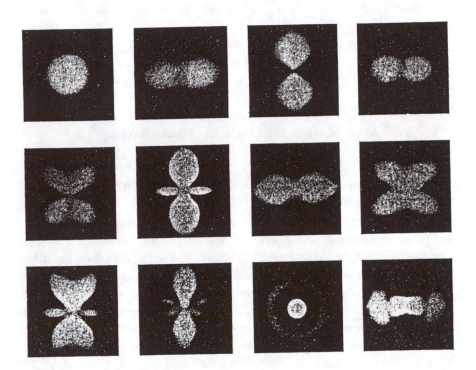

Fig. 3.   Schrödinger's electron clouds representing the stationary states of a hydrogen atom.

Schrödinger presented the new wave mechanics in four papers under the title "Quantization as a Eigenvalue [single value] Problem" that appeared in *Annalen der Physik* from January to April 1926. Because the theory was an extension of classical electrodynamics, provided a physical interpretation in terms of waves or fields, and utilized the more familiar formalism of wave mechanics in place of the obscure matrix mechanics, it was nearly universally acclaimed by physicists who were relieved by the more traditional approach.

Even Born, one of the formulators of matrix mechanics, wrote to Schrödinger after reading his first paper that

> I want to defect—or better, return—with flying colors to the camp of continuum physics. After my whole course [through quantum mechanics], I feel myself drawn to the place from where I set out, namely, the crisp, clear conceptual formulations of classical physics.[55]

Such is the appeal of traditional physics even for someone as innovative as Born.

MAX BORN'S STATISTICAL FORMULATION
OF WAVE MECHANICS

Ironically, considering the above statement, it was Born who introduced a radical probability interpretation of Schrödinger's wave mechanics in two papers entitled (in translation) "Quantum mechanics of collision phenomena," published in June and July of 1926.[56] The first paper deals with what later came to be called the "measurement problem," the uncertainty introduced into the measurement of the position and momentum of a particle due to the momentum exchange or scattering caused by the impact of the ray used to measure the particle. According to Pais, it *"is the first paper to contain the quantum mechanical probability concept."*[57] Born interpreted the effect of the collision as introducing an essential probability in the measurement, thus eliminating from quantum mechanics the kind of strict causality and determinism that prevails in classical mechanics.

It is in the second paper that Born reinterprets Schrödinger's absolute square of the wave function $|\psi|^2$ as the probability distribution for locating the particle where the density is greatest, rather than as a description of an actual wave packet of a certain intensity. He thus added to the probability *measurements* the probability of *states*. Although attracted to Schrödinger's formalism, he rejected the physical interpretation because, as he says, Schrödinger

> believed . . . that he had accomplished a return to classical thinking; he regarded the electron not as a particle but as a density distribution given by the square of his wavefunction $|\psi|^2$. He argued that the idea

of particles and of quantum jumps be given up altogether; he never faltered in this conviction . . . I, however, was witnessing the fertility of the particle concept every day [. . .] and was convinced that particles could not simply be abolished. A way had to be found for reconciling particles and waves.[58]

Born was awarded the Nobel Prize in 1954 "for his fundamental research, especially for his statistical interpretation of the wave function."

According to Born's probabilistic version and the subsequent interpretation of Schrödinger's wave mechanics, the *possible* states of the electron are indicated by the scalar wave function psi (ψ), while the *probability* of actualizing the various possibilities during measurement is given by the wave function squared $|\psi|^2$. This was Born's statistical interpretation of Schrödinger's wave function, which replaced the latter's wave packets with probability waves. The simplest modern version of Schrödinger's equation is $i\hbar\partial/\partial t|\psi\rangle = H|\psi\rangle$ which depicts the continuous, deterministic, dynamical progression of the quantum system until it is disturbed by an external act of measurement, whereby the superposition of probabilities composing the wave function squared collapses into a determinate measurement or *eigenvalue*. As Polkinghorne states, from whom the equation is taken:

> The left side is $i\hbar$ times the rate of change with time of a state vector. The right hand side equates this with the effect of an operator, the *Hamiltonian*, which is simply the observable corresponding to the energy of the system under consideration. [. . .] The symbol ψ reminds us that it is a generalization of Schrödinger's wavefunction [. . .] [or] 'state vector' [. . .].[59]

Measurement involves the interaction of a macroscopic instrument with the evolving quantum system, collapsing what is called the superposition of possible states of the wave packet into a definite quantity. As described by Polkinghorne:

> The dynamical development of a quantum system is, therefore, made up of two elements. In between measurements its state vector (wavefunction) propagates in the smooth and orderly way prescribed by the Schrödinger equation. In this respect things are not qualitatively different from the picture afforded by classical physics. At least there is continuity of development. However when a

measurement is made the state vector undergoes a discontinuous
change, collapsing onto that particular eigenvalue which corresponds
to the result actually observed on that occasion. At this point is
located all that is capricious and probabilistic, all that is
quintessentially quantum mechanical and alien to classical
mechanics.[60]

Although the response of most physicists to Schrödinger's wave mechanics
was very enthusiastic for the reasons previously indicated, this was not true of
Heisenberg who believed that all his intense effort to create matrix mechanics
with the express purpose of limiting the formalism to measurable quantities,
thereby precluding a physical interpretation such as Schrödinger's, was being
undermined.   Like Heisenberg, Born too rejected Schrödinger's physical
interpretation while focusing on the crucial probabilistic values of the
quantitative measurements in the formalism, but at first Born's articles were
largely ignored while Schrödinger's were in the forefront of discussion.   The
negative reaction of Heisenberg is vividly described by Crease and Mann, who
state that when

> Schrödinger's wave equation appeared, Heisenberg reacted in a fury;
> he must have envisioned all his work being consigned to oblivion. He
> berated Born for deserting matrices [when he originally praised
> Schrödinger] and told Pauli that the wave business was so much
> 'crap.'[61]

As it turned out, just as the formalism of Dirac's quantum mechanics was
found to be equivalent to matrix mechanics, first Pauli and then Schrödinger
himself proved that the formalism of wave mechanics was equivalent to the
previous formulations.   As Sergè states:

> A big hurdle was successfully overcome when Schrödinger [. . .] and
> others independently recognized that Heisenberg's and Schrödinger's
> theories were mathematically equivalent.   If one knew how to solve
> Schrödinger's equation for a certain problem, one could calculate
> Heisenberg's matrices, and vice versa.[. . .]

Dirac's theory, too, is equivalent to Heisenberg's and Schrödinger's
theories.   For all three the essential relation that produces the quantization
is $pq - qp = h/2\pi i$. For Heisenberg p and q are matrices; for Schrödinger

q is a number and p is a differential operator $p = (h/2\pi i) \times (d/dq)$. For Dirac p and q are special numbers obeying a noncommutative algebra. The results of any calculation on a concrete problem done by any of the other three methods are identical.[62]

What today is called quantum mechanics is a formalism that John von Neumann derived from both theories and presented in his classic book translated into English as the *Mathematical Foundations of Quantum Mechanics*.

Although Bohr was more willing than Heisenberg to acknowledge the significance of Schrödinger's contribution, he also disliked his attempt to return to the formalism of classical electrodynamics and eliminate such quantum mechanical features as Planck's constant of action and Bohr's own explanation of spectral lines in terms of quantum transitions or jumps. So to try to come to some theoretical accommodation, Bohr invited Schrödinger to visit his Institute on 27 October where they met for the first time. Although Bohr was by nature a considerate and friendly person, when it was a question of clarifying the conceptual foundations of quantum mechanics he could be relentless in his questioning. Heisenberg, also in residence at the Institute at the time, vividly describes the severity of their discussions.

> The discussions between Bohr and Schrödinger began already at the railway station in Copenhagen and were continued each day from early morning until late at night. Schrödinger stayed in Bohr's house and so for this reason alone there could hardly be an interruption in the conversations. And although Bohr was otherwise most considerate and amiable in his dealings with people, he now appeared to me almost an unrelenting fanatic, who was not prepared to make a single concession to his discussion partner or to tolerate the slightest obscurity. It will hardly be possible to convey the intensity of passion with which the discussions were conducted on both sides, or the deep-rooted convictions which one could perceive equally with Bohr and with Schrödinger in every spoken sentence . . .[63]

Perhaps as a result of the intensity of the discussions Schrödinger, who was not as robust as Bohr, fell ill with a feverish cold. Confined to bed he was gently nursed by Bohr's wife Margrethe, but even at his bedside Bohr persisted with his questioning. Yet as Crease and Mann indicate, it was not a question of ego, pride, or obstinacy, but of the very nature of physical reality.

The intensity of the debate at the birth of quantum mechanics was more than a matter of careers, temperaments, and prejudices; the participants were gripped by the conviction, endemic to the science, that they were arguing about the shape of the Universe itself, and that the picture they were forming had profound philosophical resonances. In some respects, the belief that discerning the laws of the quantum world is equivalent to deciphering the most primary code of nature is naïve and reductionistic; but in other ways it is exactly what they were doing, and the physicists of the time—as well as their successors today—have rightly been caught up in the breathtaking implications of their quest.[64]

Under the intense barrage Schrödinger might have conceded that wave mechanics was insufficient for taking into account quantum effects, but like Planck, Einstein, and de Broglie he continued to believe that it was possible to devise a physical framework based on waves or fields that would maintain continuity and causal determinism. In desperation during one point in his debate with Bohr he made the now famous remark that "'[i]f all this damned quantum jumping were really to stay then I should be sorry I ever got involved with quantum theory.'"[65] Yet despite being pushed to illness by the constant badgering, Schrödinger retained the highest regard for both Bohr and Heisenberg, as he says in a letter to Wien.

In spite of everything I had already heard, the impression of Bohr's personality from a purely human point of view was quite unexpected. There will hardly again be a man who will achieve such enormous external and internal success, who in his sphere of work is honored almost like a demigod by the whole world, and who yet remains—I would not say modest and free of conceit—but rather shy and diffident like a theology student [. . .]

In spite of all [our] theoretical points of dispute, the relationship with Bohr, and especially Heisenberg, both of whom behaved towards me in a touchingly kind, nice, caring and attentive manner, was totally, cloudlessly, amiable and cordial [. . .].[66]

Even after Schrödinger left Copenhagen Bohr and Heisenberg carried on the discussion with the same intellectual combativeness trying to resolve the paradoxical wave-particle duality brought to the fore by Einstein, Planck, de Broglie, and Schrödinger, along with the puzzling noncommutative relations.

The basis of the conflict was Heisenberg's belief that the resolutions would be found in the mathematical formalism, while Bohr believed it depended on a deep clarification of the underlying conceptual framework and the language in which it was expressed (it turned out that both were correct). This continued through the end of 1926 until each was on the verge of nervous exhaustion. Realizing that they had reached an impasse and that their frayed nerves could jeopardize their close friendship, Bohr decided to take a skiing vacation to Norway (he was an excellent skier even into his sixties) in February, leaving Heisenberg in Copenhagen to work on the problems.

During this same period in October Pauli had written Heisenberg that he too was troubled by the meaning embedded in $pq - qp = \hbar/i$. In the letter he wrote that "'[o]ne cannot simultaneously hook together both the p-numbers and the q-numbers with ordinary c-numbers [that is, regular classical variables]. You can look at the world with p-eyes or with q-eyes, but open both eyes together and you go wrong.'"[67] What did it all mean? Pascal Jordan, Heisenberg's friend and former collaborator, also was puzzled by the same question, called the measurement problem by Born and others—which involves the difficulty of measuring the position and momentum of a particle like an electron using an instrument such as a microscope. For the detection to occur there must be an interaction between the electron and a light ray, but for the most exact position determination the ray must have the shortest possible wavelength, like a gamma ray, but such a short wavelength has a high frequency or energy according to Planck's formula $\varepsilon = h\nu$. So to reduce the momentum displacement a particle with a longer wavelength is required, but this results in a less accurate position determination. These were the questions that preoccupied Heisenberg when he was left alone by Bohr. The answers came within a week of Bohr's departure. By 23 February he had formulated the famous uncertainty or indeterminacy relations which appear in a letter to Pauli, after which he wrote Bohr in Norway on 10 March that "'I believe that I have succeeded in treating the case where [the momentum] p and [the coordinate] q are given to a certain accuracy [. . .].'"[68]

Before presenting Heisenberg's uncertainty or indeterminacy relations, their significance will be clearer if compared to two fundamental presuppositions of classical or Newtonian mechanics. Keeping in mind that the primary purpose of a mechanical explanation is to predict precisely the future trajectory of a projectile or a system of particles, the first assumption was best expressed by Laplace.

An intellect which at a given instant knew all the forces acting in

nature, and the position of all things of which the world
consists—supposing the said intellect were vast enough to subject
these data to analysis—would embrace in the same formula the
motions of the greatest bodies in the universe and those of the
slightest atoms; nothing would be *uncertain* for it, and the future, like
the past would be present to its eyes.[69]

Simply stated, the *first* presupposition is that of an isolated or closed
system in which the future trajectories of the particles are determined
completely by the initial conditions of the system: the space-time coordinates,
the momentum, and whatever forces are involved. The *second* presupposition
required to make the prediction assumes that it is possible to ascertain the
parameters of the initial conditions either without disturbing them or by
calculating and taking into account the effects of the disturbance. These
presuppositions are what Heisenberg's indeterminacy relations preclude
regarding the position and the momentum coordinates, as well as the time and
energy coordinates.

According to Heisenberg's equations, although either the position or the
momentum or the time or the energy of a particle can be measured with
unlimited precision, the conditions necessary for measuring these parameters
conjointly limit their combined accuracy: that is, the conditions for measuring
the correct position will limit the accuracy of the momentum measurement,
while the conditions for measuring correctly the momentum will limit the
precision of the position measurement. The same is true of time and energy.
Thus if the degree or increment of indeterminacy or uncertainty of the
conjugate measurement is represented by the delta symbol Δ, then the product
of the conjugate indeterminacies of the momentum p and position q or time t
and energy ε measurements cannot be reduced to less than Planck's constant
barred: $\Delta p \times \Delta q \cong \hbar$ or $\Delta t \times \Delta \varepsilon \cong \hbar$. This is the physical consequence of
Heisenberg's interpretation of the noncommutivity relations.

Later theoretical developments showed that the wave-particle duality
provides a more fundamental physical explanation of this inherent limitation
of the accuracy of these joint measurements. Because on this interpretation the
particle's position and momentum or energy and time are determined by the
wave properties of the wave packet, it is the inherent opposition of these
properties that limits the accuracy of the conjugate measurements. The
position of the particle, for example, is located most precisely where the
converging amplitudes (the height of the crests) of the waves composing the
wave packet is greatest. But for such a converging amplitude to occur the

wavelengths of the lesser amplitudes must have a maximum variation to destruct at other areas than the amplitude. However, according to de Broglie's momentum formula for waves $p = h\backslash\lambda$, this variation of wavelengths will cause an uncertainty or indeterminacy in the momentum. To minimize this uncertainty the variation in wavelengths must be restricted which in turn will decrease the amplitude, thus reducing the accuracy of the position coordinate.

Analogously, to determine accurately the time coordinate the wavelengths must be shortest at the moment when they are measured, but such short wavelengths produce a variation in the wave's frequencies. Again according to Planck's equation $\varepsilon = h\nu$, any uncertainty in the frequency will result in an indeterminacy of the energy. To decrease the variations in the frequencies the differences in wavelengths must be reduced, but this will introduce a spread in the time coordinate of the particle. As this interpretation indicates, the uncertainties or indeterminacies are not a result of the imprecision of the measuring apparatus but due to the inherent conflicting properties of the waves composing the wave packets that provide the evidence for the parameters of the particle. No improvement of the apparatus or refinement of the measuring procedure can eliminate the irreducible indeterminacies. This is what is so crucial regarding these uncertainty relations (which are better described as indeterminacies than uncertainties because the latter suggests a limitation of knowledge that could possibly be removed).

When Bohr returned around the middle of March from his skiing trip to Norway, Heisenberg showed him the paper with his equations. At first Bohr was impressed, but when he read the paper more carefully (which illustrated the noncummutative or indeterminacy relations with the measurement problem involving the electron and the gamma ray microscope) he had a crucial objection: given the conservation of momentum it should be possible in principle to compute the momentum transfer between the ray and the particle eliminating the indeterminacy in the position measurement. Bohr even advised Heisenberg not to submit the paper for publication unless he took account of the objection, which he did.

After reflection, however, the indeterminacy of position was reaffirmed, but attributed to the diffraction of the gamma rays as they passed through the lens of the microscope producing a slightly indeterminate location. According to Pais, classical optics indicates that the light rays are diffracted by the lens, called the "finite aperture effect," which makes "its direction imprecise, hence makes the electron's position imprecise. A quantitative analysis of this imprecision shows that it is exactly in accord with the uncertainty relations."[70] The improved version of the article was published under the title (English translation) ''Quantum theory and measurement'' in the *Zeitschrift für Physik* in April 1927. Bohr sent a copy of the proofs of the paper to Einstein along with a letter stating the paper '''represents a most significant . . . exceptionally brilliant . . . contribution to the discussion of the general problems of quantum theory.'''[71] Despite their often heated disagreements about the correct interpretation of certain aspects of quantum mechanics, Bohr always had the highest regard for Heisenberg (except when Heisenberg visited Bohr during the German occupation of Denmark in World War II and told him that Europe would be better off if Germany won the war).[72]

As indicated previously, the intense arguments between Bohr and Heisenberg following Schrödinger's visit were based on their contrasting beliefs as to how the paradoxes of the incommensurate relations and wave-particle duality could be resolved—Heisenberg insisting that the solution would come from the mathematical formalism while Bohr thought a clarification of the underlying conceptual framework and its linguistic expression would resolve the problems. Heisenberg's equations describing the indeterminacy relations were a vindication of his point of view, the essence of which is stated in a famous passage:

> Instead of asking: How can one in the known mathematical scheme express a given experimental situation? the other question was put: Is it true, perhaps, that only such experimental situations can arise in nature as can be expressed in the mathematical formalism. The assumption that this was actually true led to limitations in the use of those concepts that had been the basis of classical physics since Newton.[73]

This is precisely what his equations showed: that the possible experimental measurements were limited to those not proscribed by the equations.

Coincidentally, while Heisenberg was demonstrating the fruitfulness of his approach, ''the complementary argument [although not the term] first dawned on''[74] Bohr during his trip to Norway. In the letter mentioned previously accompanying the proofs of Heisenberg's article that he sent to Einstein in April, Bohr included an indication of his own approach:

> It has of course long been recognized how intimately the difficulties of the quantum theory are connected with the concepts, or rather with the words that are used in the customary description of nature, and which always have their origin in the classical theories. . .[75]

A further example of Bohr's position occurs in his reply to the article by Einstein, Poldolsky, and Rosen (called the EPR article) in which the authors argue that though the quantum mechanical formalism was consistent with all the known data, it was incomplete because it did not provide precise conjugate values for the position-momentum, time-energy measurements.[76] Bohr replied in the next issue of the *Physical Review* that

> we are not dealing with an incomplete description characterized by the arbitrary picking out of different elements of physical reality at the cost of sacrificing other elements, but [. . . .] [with] the *impossibility*, in the field of quantum theory, of accurately controlling the reaction of the object on the measuring instruments [. . . .] Indeed we have [. . .] not merely to do with an *ignorance* of the value of certain physical quantities, but with the *impossibility* of defining these quantities in an unambiguous way.[77]

While after sixty years this interpretation seems obvious, it was not that apparent at the time, as the charge of incompleteness by the authors of the EPR article indicates.

But Bohr's crucial conceptual contribution was his notion of "complementarity," the term appearing "for the first time in a draft 10 July 1927."[78] This is the conception that he introduced, as a result of the wave-particle duality and the indeterminacies of measurement, to clarify the difference between the expectations regarding possible scientific knowledge in classical mechanics as compared to quantum mechanics.

> Within the scope of classical physics, all characteristic properties of a given object can in principle be ascertained by a single experimental arrangement, although in practice various arrangements are often convenient for the study of different aspects of the phenomena. In fact, data obtained in such a way simply supplement each other and can be combined into a consistent picture of the behaviour of the object under investigation.[79]

As he goes on to say, investigations at the atomic or subatomic level in quantum mechanics do not confirm these classical expectations (any more than Einstein's investigations of the electrodynamics of moving bodies confirmed the principles of classical mechanics at high velocities).

In quantum physics, however, evidence about atomic objects obtained by different experimental arrangements exhibits a novel kind of complementary relationship. Indeed, it must be recognized that such evidence which appears contradictory when combination into a single picture is attempted [such as the wave-particle duality], exhausts all conceivable knowledge about the object. Far from restricting our efforts to put questions to nature in the form of experiments, the notion of *complementarity* simply characterizes the answers we can receive by such inquiry, whenever the interaction between the measuring instruments and the objects forms an integral part of the phenomena.[80]

According to this "Copenhagen interpretation," as it has come to be called, in the quantum domain we cannot assume that the scientist is a spectator of the physical world whose knowledge can be acquired without interacting with and consequently disturbing it, as our ordinary experience and classical science presupposed. When we observe the ordinary macroscopic world, it is as if it were disclosed to us as it is unaffected or unmodified by any conditions, because the conditions (radiational, optical, and neurophysiological) are for the most part hidden. What we experience is the *outcome* of a very extensive and complex series of physical processes, not the *processes* that produce the experience. As Kant forcefully argued, the world we experience is not the world "as it is in itself," but the world "as it appears to us" owing to our human sensory and cognitive structures. When the invention of telescopes and microscopes demonstrated that the direct awareness assumption was false regarding ordinary perception which does not disclose these more extensive domains, classical physics merely usurped this direct awareness assumption into its world view. Nor is the older conception of experimentation as a means mainly for testing hypotheses any longer sufficient. The remarkable discoveries and progress of science in the twentieth century are due largely to the use of experimentation for probing deeper domains of physical reality to acquire new information about the more basic causes of phenomena, with the apparent consequence that inquiry at that level imposes limitations on the information attainable.

Physical investigations do not simply disclose the world "as it is in itself" or in terms of its independently existing inherent properties (as Einstein and the EPR article argued). Like ordinary perception, what properties the world reveals depends partially upon what instruments are used (for humans they are our sense organs and central nervous system) or how the experiment is designed or conducted. Furthermore, Heisenberg's indeterminacy relations and Bohr's complementary interpretation indicate that the structure of physical reality itself at the subatomic level precludes experiments that will give the kind of unconditional, unlimited measurement values presupposed by classical physics. The experimental conditions or investigative apparatus seem to be an integral component of whatever is disclosed, as Bohr insisted. But this does not support Kant's absolute distinction between the world and it is in itself and as it appears to us, because the conception of the world as "it is in itself" would seem to make little sense from the standpoint of the human investigator.[81] What we can know about it presupposes an interaction with it to disclose its properties, although even its existence apart from us appears always to be relative to certain conditions. However, this does not imply that a realist interpretation of science is no longer justified—it means, rather, that the conception of scientific realism is more complicated and conditional than previously believed.

Yet there is a sense in which Bohr's conclusion is similar to Kant's in that if we can attribute properties to things only relative to some experimental condition, then this implies that we do not know anything about them, cannot "say" anything meaningfully about them, as they exist apart from these conditions. Yet this Copenhagen interpretation, which seems so initially plausible when applied to such puzzling phenomena as the wave-particle duality, negates the usual scientific belief that particles do possess properties, such as mass, charge, spin, and decay characteristics, independently of the experimental detection. This was the position that Einstein defended and it is one that is paradoxical to deny completely, just as Bohr's interpretation cannot be rejected completely.

The imposition of physical reality on the experimental conditions, as Bohr always emphasized, is a necessary but not sufficient condition of scientific inquiry because the conditions play a crucial role in what is 'observed,' 'detected,' or 'reduced.' Yet the precision, convergence, and interrelatedness of scientific discoveries are too striking to be a mere coincidence or function of a collective scientific imagination or illusion, without any grounding in physical reality. Unlike earlier mythologies (as in the Old Testament account of creation) which were subject to little or no external constraints (or even internal ones like the laws of contradiction), physical reality does exert a constraining influence on scientific inquiry which accounts for its self-corrective, progressive, consensual results. That we cannot know everything about the world does not mean that we do not know anything about it! Like Kant's distinction, this too must be rejected on the basis of the incontrovertible achievements or progress of science. Any adequate conception of science must be based on its actual accomplishments, as well as its failures and limitations—not on *a priori* conditions or intuitive expectations based on past experience. As the method of inquiry of science along with its theoretical framework evolves as scientists probe deeper into physical reality, so must our understanding and conception of science evolve to match its development and achievements.

ELECTRON SPIN

Before concluding this phase in the development of science, two discoveries regarding the properties of electrons and other particles will be mentioned, followed by a brief description of a major achievement in quantum theory climaxing this stage of its development. Like macroscopic objects, particles are defined by basic properties, but in their case the basic properties are mass, charge, energy, and momentum which, though more difficult to detect, explain the behavior and causal effects of the particles. In 1924 two physics students also in their mid-twenties from the University of Leyden in Holland proposed an additional, unusual property of electrons. Samual A. Goudsmith (1902-1978) and George E. Uhlenbeck (1900-1988) suggested that like planets, which have both an orbital revolution and an axial rotation, electrons have an axial rotation in addition to their orbital angular momentum. This "spin," as they called it, has an invariant axial angular momentum, $\frac{1}{2} \times h/2\pi$.

The relation of the direction of the axial rotation (westward or eastward) to the spin vector or advance motion of the particle is given by "the right hand rule." If the palm of your right hand faces you with your fingers curled inward, then the direction of the spin is shown by the direction of the fingers while the upward thrust of the thumb indicates the spin vector or advancing movement of the spinning electron. Conversely, if the spin rotation is in the reverse direction, then this is shown by the direction of your curled fingers with the back of your right hand facing you, the spin vector or progression indicated now by the downward thrust of the thumb. Not only are the possible spin vectors always opposite to one another, the orientation of the spin can occur only in certain discrete directions, as described by Ne'eman and Kirsh:

The projection of the spin on a defined axis can take only certain discrete values, in steps of $h/2\pi$. A particle of spin 1/2 has two possible orientations relative to any defined direction in space, spin 1 particles have three allowed orientations and spin 3/2 particles—four.[82]

Measurement seems to indicate that in general "for a spin equal to s (in units of $h/2\pi$) there are $2s+1$ possible positions." (p. 55)

Along with the electron having a spin with possible opposite orientations, the fact that it is electrically charged as it rotates means that it acts as a tiny magnet with a measurable magnetic moment. Not based simply on an analogy with planets, electron spin had explanatory as well as empirical consequences that could be experimentally tested. The two possible spin orientations with their opposite vectors implied two energy states which offered an explanation for the puzzling pattern of close lines or doublets found in the Balmer series of the hydrogen spectrum. Moreover, Otto Stern and W. Gerlach in an ingenious experiment found that when a beam of particles with random magnetic orientations is passed through a magnetic field, their orientations align so that the beam divides into narrower beams whose direction is opposite to each other proving "that the spin [. . .] can take up only two orientations regarding a defined direction in space." (p. 56) Finally, when physicists measured the magnetic moment of the electron in "a unit called the Bohr magneton, denoted μ_e," they attained a remarkable accuracy up to ten digits: 1.001 159 652 μ_e. (p. 58) Although the concept of spin as an actual rotary motion is no longer taken literally, the property is considered another important defining characteristic of particles, although the explanation of such properties awaited the development of a new formulation of quantum mechanics, called quantum electrodynamics.

PAULI'S EXCLUSION PRINCIPLE

The second discovery regarding additional properties of electrons was made by Wolfgang Pauli (1900-1958), an Austrian physicist of unusual temperament and bearing, who became well known at age twenty-one for writing an authoritative article on relativity theory for the *Encyklopädie der Mathematischen Wissenschaften* that Einstein himself praised very highly. His unusual bearing appeared in an uncontrolled rocking motion when he was concentrating intensely on what someone was saying, while his acerbic, insulting manner was legendary, evident in his occasionally signing his letters "The Wrath of God." Fortunately, scientists acquired sufficient respect for

Pauli's analytical acuteness that they learned to overlook his rudeness. In addition to the excellent article on relativity theory, he later wrote one of the best expositions of quantum mechanics. Possessing an exceptionally critical mind, physicists of his generation, like Heisenberg, often would use him as a sounding board for their new ideas before submitting them to paper or for publication. But he too made original contributions, as described by Sergè: "his discoveries were the exclusion principle [. . .], the hypothesis of the neutrino, and the unraveling of the connection between spin and statistics of a particle."[83]

It is Pauli's exclusion principle formulated in 1924 that helped explain the limitation of the number of electrons permitted in the successive stationary orbits of Bohr's solar model of the atom. Within the atom the state of an electron is described by four quantum numbers: (n) represents the orbital position of the electron, (l) its angular momentum, (m) the axial inclination of its angular momentum, and (m_s) its having one of the two possible spin orientations. Pauli's exclusion principle states that no two electrons can have identical quantum numbers which helps explain why different electrons occupy different orbits according to Bohr's model.

Later it was found that Pauli's principle is valid for electrons whose spin is not integral or fractional, but does not apply to those with integral spin. The former particles are called 'fermions' and obey laws described by the Fermi-Dirac statistics, while the latter are named 'bosons' (for the Indian physicist S.N. Bose) which follow laws described by the Bose-Einstein statistics. Thus no fermions with the same identical quantum numbers can occupy the same orbital states while any number of bosons with the same number can occur in the same region of space, "the difference between the fermions and bosons [. . .] related to the connection between the spin and the symmetry of the wave function of the particles"[84]—further evidence of the inherent wave-particle duality. Pauli was awarded the Nobel Prize in 1945 mainly for his discovery of this principle.

DIRAC'S QUANTUM ELECTRODNAMICS

In another coincidence that seems to have been typical of that remarkably creative time, during the period that Schrödinger was visiting Copenhagen, Heisenberg formulating his indeterminacy equations, and Bohr in Norway conceiving his idea of complementarity, Dirac also was in Copenhagen doing post-doctoral research from September 1926 to February 1927. Following his earlier success in devising a more elegant, axiomatized formalism for quantum mechanics than the matrix mathematics presented in the article by Heisenberg, Born, and Jordan, Dirac realized the necessity of incorporating relativistic effects into quantum mechanics, since the latter describes the behavior of particles like electrons with velocities close to that of light. Schrödinger had tried to take into account relativistic effects in his wave equations, but without much success.

Turning to the concept of field introduced by Maxwell and adopted by Einstein as the foundation of his general theory of relativity, Dirac decided like Schrödinger to consider the particle a component of the field. As Crease and Mann state:

Using Heisenberg's quantum mechanics, Dirac was able to come up with a Hamiltonian [the operator standing for the energy of the system] for the field that was fully compatible with the Hamiltonian for the atom from quantum mechanics. Dirac was thus able to say that the Hamiltonian for the entire process could be found by adding up the separate Hamiltonians for the atom, field, and the interaction. Moreover, Dirac showed that by juggling the Hamiltonians through an appropriate mathematical procedure, he could prove a law that Einstein had discovered, which gave the probability that a given atom in a given state that sat in a particular field in a particular configuration would absorb or release a photon.[85]

Having combined electrodynamics with quantum mechanics in a new quantum field theory, Dirac called it "quantum electrodynamics," which later was abbreviated to QED. The paper with these results was completed in Copenhagen at the end of January 1927 and submitted to the *Proceedings of the Royal Society* where it appeared the following March. This initial paper was followed by two others published in 1928, also in the *Proceedings of the Royal Society*. They contain the well-known relativistic wave equation of the electron, or what has come to be known as the "Dirac equation," which Pais says "ranks among the highest achievements of twentieth-century science."[86] It did prove remarkably fruitful in that Dirac was able to calculate from it the value of Bohr's magnetron along with the magnitudes of the electron's spin beginning with $h/4\pi$ and its magnetic moment of $eh/4\pi mc$.[87]

Completely unexpected, these mathematical derivations of spin and magnetic moment were no longer *ad hoc* but predictable properties following from the equation. Like Schrödinger's wave equation given a probabilistic interpretation, Dirac's equation predicts the probability of the position of a particle with the lesser probabilities clustered around the maximum, but rotating due to the electron's spin.[88]

For his outstanding achievement, Dirac was appointed in 1932 to Newton's old chair of Lucasian Professor of Mathematics (now occupied by Stephen Hawking) at Cambridge University and shared the Nobel Prize with Schrödinger in 1933.

But like medicines which alleviate certain problems while often having peculiar side effects, Dirac's equation predicted very puzzling physical conditions. For example, the formalism suggested that when the electromagnetic field was quantized and interpreted according to the uncertainty principle, space no longer was an empty vacuum but filled with oscillators and photons that at zero state could not be detected but still possessed a vast amount of energy or, according to Einstein's equation equating mass and energy, a huge quantity of undetectable matter. As described by Crease and Mann:

> The spaces around and within atoms, previously thought to be empty, were now supposed to be filled with a boiling soup of ghostly particles. From the perspective of the quantum field theory, the vacuum contains random eddies in space-time: tidal whirlpools that occasionally hurl up bits of matter, only to suck them down again. Like the strange virtual images produced by lenses, these particles are present, but out of sight; they have been named *virtual particles*.[89]

Yet as weird as these implications were, there was another just as strange. When his equation was solved for the Hamiltonian of a single electron Dirac obtained two possible values, one negative and one positive. While positive energy is well known, the existence of negative energy, and by implication negative matter, was unheard of. It was not until 1930 when Carl D. Anderson (1905-1991) built an improved version of Wilson's cloud chamber to detect cosmic rays that tracks began appearing of unusual light particles which could be either negatively or positively charged. When a special experiment was designed to detect either an upward or downward direction of the particle, indicative of a negative or positive charge respectively, the curvature swung downward. Thus the particle, with a mass similar to an electron, had a positive charge: "Anderson called the new particle a 'positive electron'; *positron* was the name that stuck."[90] Thus a new form of matter called 'antimatter' was discovered so that when an electron and a positron interact they annihilate one another producing two photons. Anderson received the Nobel Prize for his experimental discovery of positrons or antimatter in 1936.

Fig. 4. The interaction of a high-energy gamma ray with an atomic electron producing an electron-positron track. Because the interaction occurred within a strong magnetic field, the electron curves to the right and the positron to the left due to their opposite charges.

In the following decades quantum electrodynamics (QED) was developed into what is now called "the standard model," one of the most successful physical theories ever formulated. Based on Dirac's initial quantum electrodynamics introduced in 1927-28, it was completed by the Japanese physicist Sin-itero Tomonaga and the Americans Richard Feynman and Julian Schwinger, the three men sharing the Novel Prize for their achievement in 1965. According to Chris Quigg at the Fermi National Accelerator Laboratory

(Fermilab), QED

is the most successful of physical theories. Using calculation methods developed in the 1940s by Richard P. Feynman and others, it has achieved predictions of enormous accuracy, such as the infinitesimal effect of the photons radiated and absorbed by the electron on the magnetic moment generated by the electron's innate spin. Moreover, QED's descriptions of the electromagnetic interaction have been verified over an extraordinary range of distances, varying from less than 10^{-18} meter to more than 10^8 meters.[91]

LOOKING AHEAD

Here the attempt to reconstruct the rationale underlying past major developments in physics will end, with a brief summary of the highlights of subsequent discoveries to indicate the direction that progress in physics will take in the remainder of the century. The succeeding decades, especially after the second world war with the development of increasingly powerful particle accelerators, witnessed the transmutation of subatomic particles into new ones with unforeseen properties. These particles predicted by theorists such as Wigner, Yukawa, Gell-Mann, Schwinger, Weinberg, Glashow, Ting, and Richter are created out of mass-energy transformations according to Einstein formula $E = mc^2$ and have been experimentally confirmed. Such a plethora of particles composing the nucleons and complementing the electron has been discovered (often compared to a zoo), that a new kind of periodic table of elementary particles has been drawn up composed of hadrons and leptons, with the former further divided into baryons and mesons.[92]

Along with the discovery of this new world of particles and their associated antiparticles with similar properties but opposite charge, two new forces in addition to electromagnetism and gravity were posited: a strong force binding the nucleons (the protons and neutrons) and a weak force controlling radioactivity within the nucleus. Unlike gravity and electromagnetism, the two new forces are effective only within extremely short distances. In addition, the traditional notion of forces acting at a distance was superceded by the conception of an exchange of 'virtual' particles, photons exchanged in electromagnetism, gluons in strong interactions, and the vector bosons W^-, W^+, and Z^0 in weak interactions. While leptons respond only to the weak force consisting of the exchange of photons and the three bosons, the hadrons react to both strong and weak forces.

It was believed initially that the leptons and hadrons (in addition to the photons and postulated gravitons) exhausted the basic classification of particles, but with the proliferation of the hadrons (baryons and mesons) it seemed natural to infer that they too must be composed of a simpler structure of components. So in 1964 Gell-Mann and George Zweig independently proposed theories accounting for the composition of the hadrons, Gell-Mann whimsically naming these particles "quarks" from a passage in James Joyce's *Finnegan's Wake* ("Three quarks for Muster Mark!"), and the term caught on. Unlike previous particles that have integral charges, the quarks have fractional charges of plus two-thirds or minus one-third. Like Epicurus' minima, they never exist separately but are joined as pairs or triplets to form the hadrons, a quark and anti-quark pair composing a meson and three quarks comprising a baryon. Although the theory was entirely inferential or deductive to account for the hadronic interactions, their possible combinations into hadrons have been experimentally verified.

Beginning with the property or charge of "strangeness" postulated by Gell-Mann and then "charm" suggested by Sheldon Glashow, physicists now account for the hadrons and their interactions as due to combinations of quarks, classified as "flavors:" up (u), down (d), charm (c), strange (s), bottom/beauty (b), and top/truth (t). According to this schema, matter consists of the two groups of six leptons and six quarks, plus the elementary particle forces. Based on the Yang-Mills Gauge Theory (a mathematical theory that maintains symmetry under certain variations of properties) and group theory developed by the mathematicians Marius Sophus Lie and Élie-Joseph Cartan, a new quantum theory analogous to quantum electrodynamics (QED) was formulated, baptized "quantum chromodynamics" (QCD) by Gell-Mann. The name was chosen because chromodynamics (unlike electrodynamics that was based on electric charges) consists of a strong force or charge called "color" that binds the quarks within the hadrons.

However, not satisfied with two separate categories of basic particles, the quarks and the leptons, as well as three (ignoring the graviton) independent exchange particles accounting for the electromagnetic, strong, and weak forces, a search began for a unified theory, such as had eluded Einstein. The first stage in this unification was the integration by Glashow of weak and electromagnetic interactions into an "electroweak theory." Then Stephen Weinberg added the important concept of symmetry breaking by means of the Higgs-boson, explaining how Glashow's W and Z particles acquired mass, a crucial link in the search for unification. The following year Abdus Salem contributed further to the explanation. Then in 1969 the Dutch physicist 't Hooft showed in two excellent papers how Cartan's group theory could be applied to gauge theories, enabling Weinberg in 1973 to formulate a successful gauge field theory of strong forces involving color charge, the basis of QCD.

But while the theory of quarks and QCD explained the strong forces, they did not account for electroweak forces. So Glashow, in a paper written with James Bjorken, proposed a new quark called "charm" that provided a bridge between QCD and the electroweak theory, adding theoretical support to both theories, and paving the way for a grand unified theory. But the task of confirming the existence of charm proved unusually difficult because quarks, as indicated earlier, are never found in a independent state, existing in self-enclosed couplets or triplets within the hadrons. Any attempt to isolate and confirm the existence of quarks results in a new combination of quarks concealed in the hadrons. Finally, however, evidence of charmed particles was found by investigators in Japan and at Brookhaven.

Then Samuel Ting at Brookhaven and Burton Richter at the Stanford Linear Accelerator (SLAC) confirmed the existence of a new particle (called "J" by Ting and "psi" by Richter) which is now known as the J/ψ particle. Considered to be a new meson composed of a charmed quark and anti-quark, its discovery confirmed the existence of charmed quarks. Ting and Richter received the Nobel Prize in 1976 for their discovery, and Glashow, Weinberg, and Salem shared the Prize in 1979 "for their contributions to the theory of the unified weak and electromagnetic interaction between elementary particles [. . .]." To climax these results, Carlo Rubbia and Simon van der Meer were awarded the Nobel Prize in 1984 for their confirmation at CERN (the European Nuclear Center near Geneva) of the existence of the W^-, W^+, and Z^o particles.

But the search for a grand unified theory combining both strong and electroweak forces had barely begun. A bold step towards unification was made by Glashow and Howard Georgi in a series of four papers published in 1973 and 1974, one of which had the imposing title, "Unity of All Elementary-Particle Forces." According to their Grand Unified Theory (GUTs), quarks and leptons would be combined into one family on the grounds that they decay into one another. In addition, a "superweak force" was proposed unifying strong and electroweak interactions. Later in 1974 Georgi wrote a paper with Weinberg and Helen Quinn claiming that while at low energies the three forces remain distinct, at very high temperatures or energies, such as existed at the birth of the universe with the Big Bang, the three forces were united. Although not verified, at least the framework of a

Grand Unified Theory has been introduced. As Crease and Mann summarize these achievements:

> The result is a ladder of theories. Firmly on the bottom is SU(3) × SU(2) × U(1) [the SU stands for special unity group based on Cartan's group theory], whose predictions have been confirmed ("to the point of boredom," Georgi says) [. . .]. The W and Z particles were discovered at CERN [. . .] last year [1983], but the theory was so well established by then the event was—for theorists at least—an anticlimax. The GUTs proposed by Georgi and Glashaw and other physicists, which fully unite the strong, weak, and electromagnetic forces, are the next rung on the ladder. Although as yet unconfirmed, these theories are considered compelling by most physicists. Finally, at the top of the ladder, in the theoretical stratosphere, are supersymmetry and its cousins, which are organized according to a principle somewhat different from SU(5), though, like that model, they put apparently different particles together in groups. Supersymmetry groups are large enough to include gravity, but are so speculative that many experimenters doubt that they can ever be tested.[93]

As the summary of these developments illustrate, the recent advances in physics are so abstract because of their dependence on the mathematical formalism that it is nearly impossible to provide any explication in terms of more familiar concepts. This, perhaps, is one of the reasons that some philosophers of science believe that contemporary physics lacks any realistic representation of physical reality. But the history of science, as this study vividly illustrates, shows a continuous discarding of common sense concepts, yet the necessity of experimentally confirming theories ensures that they are anchored in the physical world to some extent, however indirectly.

The striking experimental confirmations of the brilliant theorizing of the last several decades, which has led to a general theory unifying what seems to some investigators to be the ultimate particles and forces of the universe, has left physicists in a highly excited and optimistic state. It appears as if the basic components of the universe have been discovered, so that a complete and final explanation of the cosmos is within reach. In words reminiscent of John Trowbrige, the head of the physics department at Harvard at the turn of the century, who discouraged students from pursuing graduate work in physics in the belief that everything of importance had been explained, Harold Fritzsch, a co-worker of Gell-Mann's who contributed to QCD, says:

> Today we can state unequivocally that the physics of the atom is understood. A few details need to be cleared up, but that is all [. . .]. Important and fascinating discoveries have been made in high-energy physics, especially since 1969, and today it appears that physicists are about to take the important step towards a complete understanding of matter.[94]

This extreme optimism was expressed also by Stephen Hawking, probably the world's foremost cosmologist, in his inaugural lecture when he assumed the Lucasian chair in physics in April 1980 (because he is suffering from amyotrophic lateral sclerosis (a nerve degeneration) a student had to read the lecture for him).

> In this lecture I want to discuss the possibility that the goal of theoretical physics might be achieved in the not-too-distant future, say by the end of the century. By this I mean that we might have a complete, consistent, and unified theory of the physical interactions which would describe all possible observations. Of course one has to be very cautious about making such predictions [. . .]. Nevertheless, we have made a lot of progress in recent years and, as I shall describe, there are grounds for cautious optimism that we may see a complete theory within the lifetime of those present here."[95]

In my opinion there are considerably more grounds for caution than for optimism. Given the vastness of the universe and the acknowledged limitations or impasses in human knowledge, it is very unlikely that we are reaching an end even of our understanding of "physical interactions." Just as earlier physicists knew nothing of atomic radiation, antimatter, or cosmic rays, how much more lies hidden in the physical universe than we have any inkling of? It is still possible to ask innumerable questions that even defy any foreseeable answer: how did the original state of the universe described in the big bang theory originate? Where is the mysterious matter located that is required by cosmic theory? What is the significance of the violation of Bell's inequality theorem which implies a denial of local causality and a phase entanglement unifying physical processes in a completely inexplicable way?[96] How do neuronal discharges which are chemical-electrical processes involving ions give rise to conscious states such as perception of sensory qualities, sensations and feeling, thoughts and intentions, and experiences of free will or choice? If they have some validity, which on purely statistical grounds seems to be the case, how are we to account for paranormal experiences, especially precognition?

Near the conclusion of his book, *A Brief History of Time*, Hawking presents three views that can be taken regarding the possible outcome of scientific inquiry:

1) There really is a complete unified theory, which we will someday discovery if we are smart enough.

2) There is no ultimate theory of the universe, just an infinite sequence of theories that describe the universe more and more accurately.

3) There is no theory of the universe; events cannot be predicted beyond a certain extent but occur in a random and arbitrary manner.[97]

It is the second view that I defended in my book, *Contextual Realism: A Metaphysical Framework for Modern Science*, although it was published before Hawking's book. I cannot describe the position more clearly than stated there. The history of science up to the present—and we are just beginning to see the potentiality of science—seems to indicate, in my opinion,

that physical reality consists of a series of [inexhaustible] levels, each composed of distinct layers of entities with unique properties that account, to some extent, for the kinds of structures and interactions one finds on the succeeding higher levels. That they account only partially for the higher domains implies that new features emerge that are not fully explicable. The discovery of each of these levels depends upon modes of investigation correlated with increased intensities of energy. It is as if we were gazing into an enormous sphere, the interior structures of which changed as, aided by various instruments, we penetrated more deeply into its interior. The outer level is the most painterly, consisting of the richest diversity of qualities and forms, as well as the greatest variety of interrelations, while each successive level becomes less intricate and varied, though disclosing new substructures and interactions. This progressive decline in complexity is compensated for by an evident increase in simplicity, unity, and coherence among the elements, contributing to their greater intelligibility [unless we have reached the end of our capacity to understand, as more pessimistic physicists believe].

Yet it seems to be a fundamental feature of this magnificent sphere that complete, continuous transitions from one level to another are neither perceptually nor conceptually feasible, new levels of entities emerging into prominence as we penetrate further with the aid of our instruments. Thus while deeper levels account in some ways for the higher levels, in the absence of a continuous transition we cannot fully explain how or why the higher contexts acquire their distinctive qualities, properties, and forms. [Nor can we foresee what remarkably unexpected discoveries will be uncovered when nature is probed at still deeper and more extensive domains.] This is the meta-physical picture of contextual realism, a conception that seems [to me] to be more consistent with the achievements of contemporary science than Kant's notion of a[n absolute] cognitive curtain separating phenomena from noumena, or the reduction of other levels to one basic level [as is the usual aim of physicists].[98]

Although an unending quest for knowledge might seem unfulfilling from one perspective, the actual attainment of a final theory of the universe would appear less satisfying from another, at least from the point of view of future investigators. Would it really be more desirable to have nothing further to inquire into, losing the challenge and excitement of new discoveries, experimental as well as theoretical? Or is it not the case, as Lessing stated, that "the aspiration to truth is more precious than its assured possession."[99] At any rate it seems presumptuous to conclude that at just this juncture in history mankind has fathomed the deepest domains of physical reality, dispelling its enduring mysteries as if by some piercing light, when in actuality the journey may have barely begun.

NOTES

1. Max Jammer, *The Philosophy of Quantum Mechanics* (New York: John Wiley & Sons, 1974), p. v.

2. Cf. Abraham Pais, *Inward Bound* (Oxford: Clarendon Press, 1986), p. 184. Hereafter abbreviated as IB.

3. Jean Perrin, *Rev. Scientifique* 15 (1901): 447. Pais, IB, p. 183.

4. E.N. da C. Andrade, *Rutherford and the Nature of the Atom* (New York: Doubleday, 1964), p. 111. Pais, IB, p. 189.

5. L. Badash, *Rutherford and Boltwood* (New Haven: Yale Univ. Press, 1969), p. 235. Pais, IB, p. 188.

6. Cf. Emilio Sergè, *From X-Rays to Quarks* (Berkeley: Univ. of California Press, 1980), pp. 105-6.

7. Cf. Yuval Ne'eman and Yoran Kirsh, *The Particle Hunters* (Cambridge: Cambridge Univ. Press, 1986), p. 7.

8. Sergè, *op. cit.*, p. 136.

9. Ernest Rutherford, *Radioactive Substances and Their Radiations* (Cambridge: Cambridge Univ. Press, 1913), p. 184. Pais, IB, p. 193.

10. Sergè, *op. cit.*, p. 102.

11. Cf. Ne'eman and Kirsh, *op. cit.*, p. 14.

12. *Ibid.*, p. 10.

13. *Ibid.*, p. 16.

14. *Ibid.*, p. 18. Brackets added.

15. Cf. Sergè, *op. cit.*, pp. 110-111.

16. Ernest Rutherford, *Philosophical Magazine* 37 (1919): 581. Sergè, *op. cit.*, p. 110.

17. Cf. Leon Lederman with Dick Teresi, *The God Particle* (New York: A Delta Book, 1993).

18. P.M.S. Blackett and D. Lea, *Proceedings of the Royal Society* 136 (1932):225.

19. Bas C. van Fraassen, *The Scientific Image* (Oxford: Clarendon Press, 1980), p. 17. Brackets added.

20. Sergè, *op. cit.*, p. 115.

21. Rosenthal-Schneider, *Reality and Scientific Truth* (Detroit: Wayne State Univ. Press, 1980), p. 62. Pais, '*Subtle is the Lord. . .*' (Oxford: Oxford Univ. Press, 1982), p. 318. Hereafter this title will be abbreviated as SIL.

22. Ne'eman and Kirsh, *op. cit.*, p. 21.

23. Paul. M Churchland, *Scientific Realism and the Plasticity of Mind* (Cambridge: Cambridge Univ. Press, 1979), p. 2.

24. Niels Bohr, letter to Harald Bohr, 23 October 1911, *Collected Works*, Vol. I, p. 527. Pais, *Niels Bohr's Times* (Oxford: Clarendon Press, 1991), p. 120. Brackets added. Hereafter this title will be abbreviated as NBT.

25. Niels Bohr, *Phil. Mag.* 25 (1913): 10, reprinted in *Collected Works*, Vol. 2, p. 18. Pais, NBT, p. 128. The immediately following references in the text are to this work unless otherwise indicated.

26. Albert Einstein, *Ann. der Phys.* 20 (1906): 199. Pais, *IB*, p. 193.

27. Sergè, *op. cit.*, p. 121.

28. Ne'eman and Kirsh, *op. cit.*, p. 39. Brackets added.

29. Niels Bohr, *Collected Works*, Vol. 2, p. 136. Sergè, *op. cit.*, pp. 122-123.

30. Sergè, *op. cit.*, p. 125.

31. Cf. *ibid.*, p. 126 or Pais, NBT, pp. 147-152.

32. Niels Bohr, *Nature* 92 (1913): 231. Pais, NBT, p. 149.

33. Cf. Sergè, *op. cit.*, p. 133.

34. Cf. Ne'eman and Kirsh, *op. cit.*, p. 14.

35. Cf. A.L. Robinson, *Science* 234(1986):24.

36. Ernst Rutherford, *Proc. Roy. Soc.* A (90): 1914, insert after p. 462. Pais, NBT, p. 153.

37. Sergè, *op. cit.*, 129.

38. Arnold Sommerfeld, letter to Niels Bohr, 4 September 1913, *Collected Works*, Vol. w, p. 603. Pais, NBT, p. 154.

39. H.G. Moseley, letter to Niels Bohr, 16 November 1913, *Collected Works*, Vol. 2, p. 544. Pais, NBT, p. 152.

40. Alfred Landé, interview by T.S. Kuhn and J.L. Heibron, 5 March 1962, *Niels Bohr Archives*. *Ibid.*, p. 155.

41. Albert Einstein, "Autobiographical Notes," *Albert Einstein: Philosopher-Scientist*, ed. by Paul A. Schilpp (Evanston, Ill.: The Library of Living Philosophers, Inc. 1949), pp. 45-46.

42. Peter Gibbins, *Particles and Paradoxes*, (Cambridge: Cambridge Univ. Press, 1987), p. 21.

43. *Ibid.*, pp. 23-24.

44. Pais, SIL, p. 438.

45. Cf. Gibbins, *op. cit.*, p. 24.

46. Werner Heisenberg, *Physics and Beyond* (New York: Harper Torchbook, 1972), p. 8.

47. Robert P. Crease and Charles C. Mann, *The Second Creation* (New York: Macmillan Pub. Co., 1986), p.47.

48. Heisenberg, *op. cit.*, p. 61.

49. Cf. Crease and Mann, *op. cit.*, p. 47-51.

50. *Ibid.*, p. 50. Brackets added.

51. *Ibid.*, p. 51.

52. *Ibid.*, p. 50.

53. *Ibid.*, p. 79. Brackets added.

54. Cf. Pais, SIL, p. 443.

55. Letter, Max Born to Erwin Schrödinger, 6 November 1926, *Archives for the History of Quantum Mechanics*, American Institute of Physics, New York. Crease and Mann, *op. cit.*, p. 56.

56. Cf. Max Born, *Zeitschr. Phy.* 37 (1926): 863, and 38 (1926): 803, 1926. Pais, NBT, pp. 286-7.

57. *Ibid.*, p. 286.

58. Max Born, *My life and my views* (New York: Charles Scribners and Sons, 1968), p. 55. *Ibid.*, p. 288.

59. J.C. Polkinghorne, *The Quantum World* (Princeton: Princeton Univ. Press, 1985), p. 30.

60. *Ibid.*, pp. 32-3.

61. Reprinted in Max Born, *My life: Recollections of a Nobel Laureate* (New York: Charles Scribners & Sons, 1975), p. 233. The letter to Pauli was on 8 June (*LET*), vol. 1). Crease and Mann, *op. cit.*, p. 57. Brackets added.

62. Sergé, *op. cit.*, pp. 164-5.

63. Werner Heisenberg, *op. cit.*, pp. 73-76. Pais, NBT, pp. 298-9. The quotation is from the latter source because it is a better translation.

64. Crease and Mann, *op. cit.*, p. 59.

65. Pais, NBT, p. 299.

66. Erwin Schrödinger, letter to Wilhelm Wien, 21 October 1926, *Niels Bohr Archives*. Pais, NBT, p. 299.

67. Letter, Pauli to Heisenberg, 19 October 1926. LET. Crease and Mann, *op. cit.*, p. 62.

68. Werner Heisenberg, letter to N. Bohr, 9 March 1927, *Niels Bohr Archives*. Pais, NBT, 304.

69. P.S. Laplace, *Introduction à la théorie analytique des probabilités* (Paris: Oeuvres Complètes, 1886, p. VI. Brackets added.

70. Pais, NBT, p. 313.

71. Niels Bohr, letter to Einstein, 13 April 1927, *Collected Works*, Vol. 6, p. 418. Pais, NBT, p. 309.

72. Cf. Pais, NBT, p. 483.

73. Werner Heisenberg, *Physics and Philosophy* (New York: Harper Torchbooks, 1958), p. 42.

74. Pais, NBT, p. 310. Brackets added.

75. See footnote 71. Pais, NBT, p. 311.

76. Cf. A. Einstein, B. Podolsky, and H. Rosen, "Can Quantum Mechanical Descriptions of Physical Reality be Considered Complete?", *Physical Review*, No. 47, 1935, pp. 777-780.

77. Niels Bohr, "Can Quantum-Mechanical Description of Physical Reality Be Considered Complete?", *Physical Review*, 48, 1935, pp. 696-702. Brackets and italics added.

78. *Niels Bohr's Collected Works*, Vol. 6, p. 27. Pais, NBT, p. 311.

79. Niels Bohr, *The Philosophical Writings of Niels Bohr*, Vol. III, *Essays 1958-62 on Atomic Physics and Human Knowledge* (Woodbridge Conn.: Ox Bow Press, 1987), p. 4.

80. *Ibid.* Brackets added.

81. Cf. Richard H. Schlagel, *Contextual Realism: A Meta-physical Framework for Modern Science* (New York: Paragon House, 1956), pp. 170-173.

82. Ne'eman and Kirsh, *op. cit.*, p. 54, Fig. 2.10. The immediately following references in the text are to this work.

83. Sergè, *op. cit.*, p. 155. Brackets added.

84. Ne'eman and Kirsh, *op. cit.*, p. 60. This summary is based on their excellent exposition.

85. Crease and Mann, *op. cit.*, p. 82. Brackets added.

86. Pais, IB, p. 290. For those with the mathematical background, Pais presents the equation along with its derivation on pp. 290-92.

87. Cf. Sergè, *op. cit.*, p. 171.

88. Cf. Crease and Mann, *op. cit.*, p. 84.

89. *Ibid.*, p. 83. This description is based on that given by Crease and Mann.

90. *Ibid.*, p 90.

91. Chris Quigg, "Elementary Particles and Forces,"*Scientific American*, April 1985, p. 89.

92. This and the following account are based on my book, *Contextual Realism: A Meta-physical Framework for Modern Science*, *op. cit.*, pp. 226-230. This discussion in turn is based largely on Crease and Mann's excellent account, *op. cit.*, chs. 15, 16.

93. Robert P. Crease and Charles C. Mann, "How The Universe Works," *The Atlantic Monthly*, August 1984, p. 91. Brackets added.

94. Harold Fritzsch, *Quarks*, trans. by M. Roloff and the author (New York: Basic Books, 1983), p. 10. Also Steven Weinberg, *Dreams of a Final Theory* (New York, Vintage Books, 1992), p. 90.

95. Stephen Hawking, "Is the End in Sight for Theoretical Physics?", in J. Boslough, *Stephen Hawking's Universe* (New York: Morrow Pub., 1985). Crease and Mann, *op. cit.*, p. 410.

96. Cf. Nick Herbert, *Quantum Reality* (Garden City: Anchor Book, 1985), p. 223.

97. Stephen Hawking, *A Brief History of Time* (New York: Bantam Books, 1988), p. 166.

98. Schlagel, *op. cit.*, p. 294. Brackets added.

99. Gotthold Lessing, *Helle Zeit, dunkle Zeit*, ed. by C. Seelig (Zürich: Europa Verlag, 1956). Pais, SIL, p. 468.

Having rendered an overview of the growth of scientific rationalism from its origin in mytho-theogonic thought to roughly the present, it now is the moment to reflect on the deeper meaning of this cognitive development. Though concerned with the underlying thought processes that generated the scientific world view, it is natural to ask what this portends for the other ideological shaper of Western civilization, the religious outlook. For human beings the world over and throughout history have developed two radically diverse conceptions of the kinds of forces influencing human destiny and producing natural phenomena, the religious and the scientific. According to the oldest interpretation, the history of mankind along with natural occurrences are the intentional creations of a spiritual reality, whether that reality be conceived as polytheistic, monotheistic, deistic, or pantheistic.

The Old Testament, for example, is a narrative account of the divine creation of the universe, of man and woman, and of the origin of the tribes of Israel. It relates the destiny of the Jewish people dependent on the intentions of El or Jahweh as revealed to prophets like Abraham, Moses, and Isaiah, as well as manifested in direct interventions on behalf of the Jews in their historical conflicts. Similarly, the early Christians and Church Fathers found in the life and teachings of Jesus, as portrayed in the Gospels of the New Testament (written about forty years after Jesus' death), a metaphor for mankind's fundamental relation to a Transcendent Being. Existence on earth was a mere prelude to the possibility of an eternal life in the Heavenly Kingdom of God. Investigation of the physical universe was inconsequential compared to what the holy scriptures taught concerning a beatific afterlife. The only significant knowledge was that contained in the Bible whose authenticity was guaranteed by the authority of the Holy Spirit or God as revealed to Old Testament Prophets or the testimony of the Apostles and writings of the Evangelists. Although it is doubtful whether Jesus claimed to be God, he later was interpreted as the 'Son of God' or Christ sent to redeem mankind from its sins, the Messiah or Savior of humanity.

The Qur'an or Koran (as it is known in English) is the sacred book of Islam believed by Muslims to be the word of God revealed to Muhammad ibn Abdullah (the prophet). In contrast to the Hebraic-Christian religions, the Arabs had no dominant mythology nor previous history of prophesy until Muhammad, at age forty in the seventh century, was awakened from sleep by a formidable divine presence and commanded by the Archangel Gabriel to recite in Arabic a new scripture. At first resisting, he was forced by a series of terrifying embraces by the Archangel to recite the words of al-Lah (Allah) which later was called the Qur'an or Recitation. Initially horrified by the experience, it was not until several years later that Muhammad acknowledged receiving a divine revelation indicating he had been selected to be the Prophet of Allah to the Arabs.

As a result of successive wrenching revelations by Gabriel, the scriptures composing the Qur'an were gradually revealed over a twenty year period to Muhammad who, because he could neither read nor write, recited then to others who memorized them and wrote them down. Thus unlike the revelations in the Old and New Testaments, those of Muhammad were directly recorded. Finally accepting his role as religious leader, by the time he died he had been able to unify nearly all the Bedouin tribes of the Arabian peninsula within the new Muslim religion, a tribute to his unusual organizational powers. While the sacred truth in the Qur'an represents the highest form of knowledge, unlike the prophets of the Old and New Testaments, Muhammad insisted that investigation of nature along with the contemplation and recitation of the verses of the Qur'an reveals the "Face of Allah." This is the reason for Islam's significant contribution to scientific knowledge, from the ninth to the twelfth centuries, based on the earlier investigations of the Greeks, whose manuscripts they preserved, translated, and studied.

As this brief account illustrates, whole civilizations have been galvanized and guided by the revelations and divine directives experienced by select individuals who believed they came from God. Unlike visions of grandeur or self-promoting prophesies which could be attributed to egotistical or selfish motives, the Prophets frequently proclaimed their unworthiness or unsuitability to be the chosen agents of God, as Moses had protested that his slowness of speech disqualified him as a spokesman for Yahweh and as Muhammad had vigorously resisted Gabriel's command to recite the scripture. Sometimes they were appalled, as Isaiah, at the proclamation of doom or imminent catastrophe they were directed by God to convey. Yet these religious utterances, so beautifully rendered in the Bible and Qur'an, carried such moral authority and commanding prophesy that they could owe their origin, it seemed, to nothing less than divine revelation. Yet is should not be ignored that the biblical revelations, preserved and transmitted in the oral tradition, were interpreted and transcribed according to individual religious and political needs, accounting for the variations, discrepancies, and inconsistencies among the Old Testament texts, such as Genesis, and the New Testament Gospels.

It is a fascinating question as to how it came about, especially if one does not believe that a god could have appeared in human form, a burning bush, a blinding light from heaven, or through the agency of an angel. What made it possible for people of that time and culture to have these terrifying yet transforming experiences? What was the origin of these extraordinary visions, revelations, and directives with epic consequences? For it is epiphanies and revelations, such as occurred to Moses on Mount Horeb, to Saul on the road to Damascus, and to Muhammad on Mount Hira, that lie at the core of these religions. Even in our current secular age driven by science and technology, the persistent vitality of fundamentalism among some Protestants and Muslims who accept the literal and exclusive truth of scripture—as fundamentalists believe the story of Adam and Eve—despite the overwhelming contrary evidence of geology, paleontology, evolution, and genetics, is astonishing.

We know that animism, the natural tendency to apprehend all movement as due to some inner psychic force or mana, was prevalent in all primitive cultures. So, too, was the inherent disposition to anthropomorphize or personify objects and events, investing them with supernatural or occult powers and mysterious intentions or meanings. Not experienced as projections onto the world of affective qualities, nature was seen as manifesting an aura of numinous or occult powers. Living in a world where the supernatural was omnipresent, these inherent cognitive dispositions generated witchcraft, sorcery, magic, and mystery rites, while sanctioning the casting of spells, charms, and omens. Children's stories are replete with instances of fabulous episodes, but so are the mythical explanations of early man, such as the Enuma Elish myth.

Freud claimed that the incredible condensations and transpositions of dream images are due to the relaxation of a super sensor or reality principle permitting the unconscious (or brain) to project into consciousness these lifelike inner experiences when the mechanisms of repression are weakened. Are the exotic myths and religious parables of early man similarly due to the natural propensity under intense psychic duress, when the influence of external reality is diminished, to fabricated stories based on dreams as to how things came to pass? Often extraordinarily vivid and seeming to convey a hidden meaning, dreams must have appeared to primitive man to be evidence of unseen powers communicating an inner message, especially as they are not under the control of the dreamer. Not surprisingly, a large number of epiphanies and revelations, like those of Muhammad, occurred while the individuals were asleep or just awakening at a time in their lives when they were struggling with deep religious conflicts, hence the dream-revelations could be interpreted as a resolution of that inner struggle. Lacking culturally established conventions later developed by scientists for testing and matching beliefs against objective states of affairs, the criteria of acceptability at that time was their striking vividness and whether they could be integrated with one's life so as to make the latter more meaningful and purposeful.

As for the current acceptance of these historical accounts, there is the curious fact that people are much more susceptible to accepting miraculous occurrences if they are attributed to persons or events remote in time and space, their very remoteness disarming criticisms based on realistic criteria. How many people today who believe that Christ was the son of God, born of a virgin, walked on water, and raised a man from the dead would accept these attributions if claimed by a living person? Nor can one justify them without circularity on the grounds that they are believable because they were performed by a divine being, since the reason for accepting the divinity of Jesus is largely based on the claim that he performed these 'miracles'—just as the Catholic Church requires evidence of 'miracles' in conveying beatitude and sainthood on individuals.

Still, how do we explain the experience of actually seeing and being spoken to by an angel, holy spirit, or a god? We are aware that psychedelic drugs can cause hallucinations so vivid that they are confused with normal perceptions or even override them. Sensory depravation experiments have shown that when normal sensory stimuli are lacking, the brain will project an image of a three-dimensional world very similar to the real one. People suffering from epileptic seizures or migraine headaches have had experiences which they describe in terms similar to those used by mystics to describe their mystical experiences. There also are the fascinating cases of out-of-the-body experiences, multiple personalities, and mentally disturbed individuals who hear voices. Some children have imaginary playmates they interact with, while street people occasionally can be observed in animated conversation with an unseen person. It is not unusual for someone who has lost a loved one to have that person appear in dreams or communicate to the bereaved when awake. Thus the experience of sensing the presence of an unseen being and of having been spoken to is not that uncommon. Perhaps it is the frequency of such experiences that has led to the prevalent religious claim that God is to be found within the person, rather than in the outer world.

It is possible, therefore, that the brain of early man under extreme emotional stress or as a result of traumatic historical circumstances projected images and created voices, either in dreams or in trancelike wakeful states, which understandably were interpreted as revelations of a divine reality, there being no alternative explanation for their occurrence. How else are we to account for the common reports during the Middle Ages of individuals perceiving demons, seraphim, unicorns, and centaurs? Unlike dinosaurs which became extinct, there are no fossil remains as evidence that these fabulous creatures once existed. Perhaps the reason for mankind's predisposition for mythical, mystical, or theogonic explanations is that all perceptions are mediated by cognitive structures or preconceptions, and that until the advent of scientific rationalism these structures or preconceptions were not formed as much by what we call objective, external stimuli as by subjective, internal experiences.

Because any interpretation of experienced phenomena depends upon a preexistent conceptual framework unconsciously acquired through education from one's particular culture, how events are conceptualized, understood, and explained will be a function of this framework. Thus people are Jews, Buddhists, Hindus, Christians, or Muslims depending upon the religious culture into which they are born. Beliefs, sacraments, and rites will be meaningful and acceptable in so far as they can be assimilated into the framework, otherwise they are experienced as unbelievable or unreal. But since we now know, contrary to Kant, that the basic categories and conceptual implications of the framework change (consider the difference between the Aristotelian, Newtonian, and Einsteinian concepts of space and time, or the concepts of soul or mind in the philosophies of Aristotle, Descartes, and Daniel Dennett), the criteria of intelligibility along with that of reality will change with the modification of the framework. Whereas the conceptual system of medieval people countenanced spirits and souls, griffins and unicorns, cherubs and angels, along with heaven and hell, ours admits atoms and molecules, subatomic particles and cosmic radiation, neurons and quarks, as well as supernova and black holes.

Moreover, because of biblical and medieval reports (along with those of current fundamentalists like Billy Graham) of actually seeing or conversing with supernatural beings, the conceptual frameworks not only must be a precondition of what is conceived and believed, they also must influence what is experienced or perceived. It is as if a higher level of integrated neurons interpret and reconstruct the sensory signals conveyed by our more basic perceptual systems, projecting in consciousness data of its own creation (analogous to dreams). On the other hand, when individuals (like Buddha, Moses, Saint Paul, and Muhammad) have transforming perceptual experiences, these apparently can realign the higher neuronal network producing radically different beliefs and redirected lives. While this is conjecture, unless we are willing to concede that we have lost access to a reality experienced by early man (which is what some religionists claim), some kind of interpretation in terms of neuronal projections and cerebral constructs is required.

Whether the Greeks conversed with their gods, they certainly believed in the intervention in human affairs of Zeus, Apollo, and Athena, yet no one today assumes such gods must have existed to account for these beliefs. Why, then, should we continue to believe that Yahweh, Allah, or God exists to explain current religious beliefs? Considering the brain's capacity to produce hallucinations, delusions, and fabulous beliefs, it seems more reasonable to attribute the appearances and revelations of angels, spirits, and gods to subjective causes, than to the reality of these beings. Moreover, within certain historical or cultural milieu these objects of belief can acquire an objective reality, but as the supporting rationale wanes, the actuality of these beings begins to fade, as is true today.

As stated at the beginning, the second of the two conceptions of the forces controlling natural events is due to scientific rationalism which attributes all occurrences to physical causes discoverable by empirical investigation. In contrast to nature being manifestations of numinous powers or divine intentions, a radically new outlook emerged ascribing ordinary phenomena to natural causes that could be discovered empirically and explained rationally. This momentous departure changing the way we think about the world was initiated in sixth century Greece before the Christian era by the Milesian philosophers. While the attempt by Anaximander to derive the world from an original "chaos" by the mythical process of "separation" due to a "conflict of opposites" controlled by a "a retributive justice" shows that he still was thinking within the framework of Hesiod's *Theogony*, nonetheless his use of empirical analogies and the principle of sufficient reason was an attempt to penetrate the veil of myth to attain a clearer understanding of the real world. *Logos* was replacing *Mythos*.

Although not influenced by the Theogony, the static monism of Parmenides and the arithmogeometric system of the Pythagoreans also manifest a primitive form of concrete, syncretic thought, Parmenides confounding the formal proscriptions of logic with ontological constraints while the Pythagoreans conflated the formal properties of numbers, such as oddness and evenness, with their spatial representation. Still, the logical principles articulated by Parmenides, the baffling paradoxes of Zeno, and the daring astronomical conjectures of Pythagoreans like Philolaus (who claimed the earth revolved around a central fire) and Heraclides (who attributed the apparent diurnal revolution of the universe to the axial rotation of the earth) directly influenced later scientific speculation. In fact, what is most significant about the inquiries of these ancient Greeks is that they represent a *continuous* tradition of *critical* evaluation of previous theories creating a *progressive* articulation of thought involving a *differentiation* and *refinement* of concepts that culminated eventually in our present stage of scientific knowledge. There is no evidence that a similar tradition of successive criticism of previous theories occurred elsewhere in the world, which is one of the reasons (along with their tremendous creativity in all areas of culture) that the ancient Greeks have been so justly venerated in the West.

Two of these Presocratics so transcended their epoch that their speculations about the world would not be matched until two millennia later. It was not until Galileo's telescopic observations of 1609 disclosed the mountainous and cavernous surface of the moon that Anaxagoras' bold speculation that the moon and the earth were similar was confirmed. The atomic theory of Leucippus and Democritus not only eliminated any vestige of the older animistic, theogonic explanations, it was adopted as the basic physical framework by the founders of modern science, remaining relatively unchanged until Bohr introduced his planetary conception of the atom in 1913. Even Empedocles made a major contribution with his theory of the four elements and conjecture that man evolved from lower species.

Perhaps because of his soaring literary imagination, from the scientific point of view Plato's conception of the soul, theory of Forms, and "likely story" in the *Timaeus*, of the construction of the universe by the Divine Craftsman or Demiurge, was too anthropocentric and fanciful to be a forwarding influence, despite his contribution to astronomy and stereometric attempt to equate the four elements of Empedocles with four of the Pythagorean solids, explaining their interactions as due to the exchange and regrouping of the triangles composing them. Moreover, his view that mathematics was a discipline intended to free the soul from dependence on the senses in the ascent to knowledge of the Forms, disparaging its applied use by the Pythagoreans to solve astronomical or physical problems, had an adverse effect on the notion of the role of mathematics in scientific inquiry.

Aristotle's contribution is much more difficult to assess. On the one hand his organismic conception of science based on a biological model did not prove correct for physics or cosmology, nor did his view of scientific method as a logical demonstration based on inductively discovered generic classifications of phenomena. Moreover, his animistic explanation of the motion of the celestial spheres in terms of prime movers was regressive, but his exhortations to philosophers to use their senses to examine the world, strikingly illustrated in his own acute biological observations and empirical approach to psychology, physics, and political theory, especially in contrast to the *a priori* theorizing of Parmenides, the Pythagoreans, and Plato, had a sobering influence on later thinkers.

It is because he grounded his scientific inquiries on empirical observations and inductions, provided astute analyses of natural occurrences, and formulated some of the basic concepts used initially in interpreting many phenomena (such as the conception of uniform motion) that he can be considered the grandfather of scientific inquiry, as Galileo is considered the father of modern science. While chided by Galileo for his uncritical reliance on direct observations and lack of experimental tests, the awareness that sensory observations can be misleading and thus must be tested, which underlies the use of experimentation, could not occur until the necessary relevance of empirical observation itself was recognized, which we owe to Aristotle.

The transition from the Hellenic speculative systems of the fifth and fourth centuries BCE in Athens to the state supported Hellenistic research in the Library and Museum of Alexandria in the succeeding centuries was a remarkable development. Here we find in the contributions to pure and applied mathematics by Euclid, Archimedes, Eratosthenes, and Apollonius, in the biological investigations of Herophilus and Erasistratus, and in the astronomical innovations of Heraclides, Apollonius, Aristarchus, and Hipparchus not only some of the greatest intellectual achievements and scientific advances of all time, but the forerunners of the creators of modern classical science. The geometry of Euclid, Archimedes' solution of intricate mathematical problems, formulation of the basic principles of statics and hydrostatics, and refinement of the method of exhaustion for approximating infinitesimal magnitudes, Apollonius' investigations of conic sections, Erasistratus' anticipation of Harvey in proposing the circulation of the blood through the arteries and veins, and Aristarchus' conception of a heliocentric universe were extraordinary achievements. These, in turn, culminated in the first evidence of the use of experiments by Strato and Hero along with the anatomical investigations of Galen and astronomical system and tables of Ptolemy, the latter the basis of all subsequent investigations in biology and astronomy by Muslim and Renaissance scientists.

Then this great surge of mathematical and scientific creativity declined with the rise and fall of the Roman civilization, finally ceasing altogether during the Middle or Dark Ages when the earlier religious outlook gained ascendence casting a shadow over the West. The veneer of disciplined thought is so thin that given the least provocation it is easily overcome by ignorance, superstition, and fantasy which seem to come more naturally to mankind. Whatever the political, cultural, and institutional structures necessary for motivating and sustaining scientific inquiry were destroyed. All the hard-won techniques for investigating nature, applying empirical criteria in evaluating theories, and utilizing mathematics to quantify empirical laws and express functional correlations were dissipated in the mists of theological debates where only logic had any disciplining effect.

Although much of the great legacy of Greek scholarship was tragically lost when the papyrus scrolls were destroyed in the great fire that consumed the Library of Alexandria, fortunately some were preserved in other libraries in Perganum, Antioch, Constantinople, and Damascus, as well as in isolated monasteries such as St. Galle. It was the Arabs who mainly retained, translated, and wrote commentaries on the ancient Greek manuscripts, while also renewing in the ninth century scientific investigations in astronomy, biology, mathematics, medicine, optics, and physics: investigators such as Al-Kindi, Al-Khwarizmi, Al-Battani, Al-Razi, Abu'l-Wafa, Al-Farabi, Al-Birumi, Ibn Sina (Avicenna) and Ibn Rushd (Averroës). As a result of the Arabic conquest of southern Spain in the thirteenth century, Greek manuscripts were reintroduced to the West where they were translated from Arabic into Latin. Other important manuscripts were recovered from Constantinople and various monasteries by the Humanists who translated them directly from the Greek. The availability of more exact translations of the scientific works of the Pythagoreans, Aristotle, Archimedes, Galen, and Ptolemy had much to do with the scientific renewal in the West as part of the general Renaissance.

The establishment of universities throughout the West, especially in Paris, Oxford, Bologna, and Padua, was another important factor. It was natural philosophers in the thirteenth and fourteenth centuries inquiring into Aristotle's cosmology and mechanics, with such unlikely names as Robert Grosseteste at Oxford, Thomas Bradwardine, William Heytesbury, Richard Swineshead, and John Dumbleton at Merton College, and scholastics like Nicole Oresme and John Buridan at the University of Paris, who reestablished the tradition of successive criticism, although they themselves refrained from revising Aristotle's system. Their critical analysis of Aristotle's conception of the diurnal rotation of the universe (citing the relativity of uniform motion to suggest that the same effect could be achieved by the earth rotating on its axis in the opposite direction), explanation of projectile motion (introducing the concept of impetus), and analysis of gravitational fall (demonstrating graphically that the spatial increments increase with the odd numbers beginning with 1) eventually led to Galileo's confirmation of these views. Moreover, the partial translation, commentary, and critical examination of Ptolemy's system by Georg Peuerbach and his pupil Regiomantus (Johannes

Müller) in the fifteenth century, along with the renewed interest in heliocentrism and Aristarchus' system by Copernicus' teacher Domenico Maria de Novara, set the stage for Copernicus' revolutionary heliocentric theory of the universe, *De Revolutionibus*, published in 1543.

No scientific theory has had as profound an effect eventually on reshaping the conception of the universe and our place in it, as the heliocentric system advanced by Copernicus. Although his own revision was conservative, maintaining the ancient model of the finite spherical universe with the central earth replaced by the sun, the conceptual disruption due to that change reverberated throughout the framework dislocating its conceptual implications. The rejection of a homocentric universe was as intellectually liberating, although equally traumatic, as the child's cognitive development beyond an egocentric perspective, as Jean Piaget pointed out. It was the beginning of the rending of the elaborately woven scheme of the universe bequeathed by Aristotle. The effect not only reshaped astronomy and cosmology, it transformed philosophy, physics, and theology. While theism fitted into a simplistic universe with man at the center enveloped by a heavenly realm where Christ could ascend to the Kingdom of God, the conception of a vastly expanded universe containing innumerable other worlds possibly with life made the appearance of a god-like figure on the earth seem quaint, while also allowing God to vanish in the infinite void of outer space. So, too, the elaborate organismic philosophy of the scholastics would prove sterile when confronted with the new mechanistic conception of the universe.

Originally attracted to heliocentrism by the "monstrous" disconnectedness or ad hoc nature of the Ptolemaic system whose astronomical tables based on geocentrism precluded calendar reform, Copernicus' objections were amply justified by Kepler's discovery of his three planetary laws based on heliocentrism along with Galileo's telescopic observations. Assuming the sun to be the central body in the planetary system and finally discarding the ancient presuppositions of uniform circular motion, Kepler derived his first two laws of planetary motion from Tycho Brahe's improved astronomical observations of Mars: that the orbits are elliptical and that a line connecting the sun to the planet describes equal areas in equal times. Completely eliminating the necessity for such previous astronomical artifices as epicycles, eccentrics, and equants, these laws finally solved the ancient "problem of the planets." Inferring that the central position of the sun indicates it as the source of two dynamic forces, one propelling the planets in their various spheres at their respective distances, and another pulling them into their elliptical orbits, Kepler set about describing these forces and deriving his third law that the planetary distances cubed are proportional to their orbital periods squared. Although the principle of inertia would eliminate the need for a propelling force, his eventual conception of a physical force drawing the planets into elliptical paths (and explaining the tides) was a lasting contribution along with his three laws.

But it was Galileo's introduction of entirely new astronomical evidence for the first time in history, owing to his improved construction of the telescope, that was the decisive factor in establishing the truth of the Copernican system. Though his telescopic discoveries could not directly confirm the heliocentric hypothesis, his observations of the mountainous surface of the moon, disclosure of innumerable new stars wherever he looked implying a greatly enlarged universe (eliminating the crucial objection of the absence of stellar parallax), discovery of the four satellites of Jupiter, detection of sun spots and the ears of Saturn, and the verification of the phases of Venus predicted by the heliocentric but not the geocentric system, eventually swept away all theoretical objections to heliocentrism grounded, as they were, on the qualitative distinction between the celestial and terrestrial realms and their particular natural motions.

There still remained, however, the objections based on the terrestrial implications of attributing two motions to the earth, an annual revolution and diurnal rotation. In one of the most brilliant dialectical works ever written, *The Dialogues Concerning the Two Chief World Systems*, Galileo deconstructed the Aristotelian system showing that the ordinary observations, qualitative distinctions, and definitions of natural motions on which it was based were only initial approximations that from a deeper understanding lose their force. In discovering what Einstein would call the "restricted principle of relativity," that the inertial states of uniform motion and rest are physically equivalent, explaining why an object thrown straight upward would fall back to its original position (rather than west of it because of the earth's eastward rotation), Galileo inadvertently revealed the important principle that conceptual revolutions in science are often counterintuitive. Thus while the initial objections to a radical conceptual revision based on previously established assumptions and conceptual implications can appear incontrovertible, within a revised framework these objections often lose their intuitive import, one of the most significant lessons learned from the development of science.

Galileo's achievements were not without their ironies, however. His belief that the compelling evidence for the Copernican system, that the tides were caused by the two motions of the earth required by heliocentrism, was false. More tragically, his attempt to persuade the authorities of the Catholic church not to proscribe the Copernican system knowing that this eventually would prove a lasting disgrace had just the opposite effect. Forced under threat of torture to abjure his belief in heliocentrism and kept under house arrest until his death in his villa in Arcetri, he wrote his scientific masterpiece, *Dialogues Concerning Two New Sciences*, when he had turned seventy and was becoming blind. It is that work containing his experimental proof of the law of free fall (that falling objects accelerate according to the square of the times), along with his demonstration that if the motion of a projectile is the combination of uniform horizontal motion and vertical descent, then the path described will be parabolic, that established him as the father of modern science. Just as we are indebted to the Milesian philosophers for the transition from the mytho-theogonic outlook to that of scientific rationalism, so we owe the conceptual transition from the ancient to the modern world to Galileo.

But there were other giants in what Whitehead called "the century of genius" who contributed to this transformation. While Descartes did not make the usual scientific contributions in terms of discovered mathematical laws to astronomy and physics (although his optical and physiological investigations were very detailed and sophisticated), he was the first to state the law of inertia in its full generality. More importantly, discarding Aristotle's organismic cosmology he presented the first completely mechanistic system of the universe, a system of contiguous vortices that eliminated the need for forces acting at a distance. In addition, by basing all knowledge on self-evident principles analogous to mathematics, he introduced two crucial reversions into modern philosophy: the epistemic and ontological priority of consciousness and its contents over the external world, along with the consequent Cartesian dualism of mind and body. These reversions, in relation particularly to Aristotelian realism, set the epistemological problems for all of modern philosophy and much of science from whose grip we are just beginning to free ourselves. The primary assumption (only recently challenged) of modern thought that knowledge as such must be based on some indubitable foundation, whether rational or empirical, we owe largely to Descartes.

Francis Bacon was another savant who helped usher in the modern world without making actual scientific contributions to it. While his investigations were considerably less accomplished than Descartes', and though he was naive in believing that scientific inquiry consisted of a mechanical application of specific inductive rules, his curiosity in natural history and project for the Great Instauration, or Renewal, that emphasized the utility of science for improving human prosperity, helped generate institutional support for the new discipline. Furthermore, the realization fostered by the new science that its method of inquiry was freeing mankind from the bonds of ancient illusions and misconceptions, opening up a whole new world of interpretation, was nowhere as vividly expressed as in Bacon's "Idols of the Mind." But the new science needed more than inspired support for "the advancement of learning;" it also required a new theoretical framework to replace Aristotle's or the Alchemist's for interpreting the behavior of gases and other physical phenomena. On the continent this framework, a revival of ancient atomism, was championed by Descartes, Mersenne, and Gassendi, but in England it was Robert Boyle who embraced "the corpuscular or mechanical philosophy" in rejecting Aristotle's explanation of change in terms of substrata, substantial forms, and potentiality and actuality, along with the Alchemist's principles of sulphur, salt, and mercury and project of transmuting the elements.

In his investigation of gases Boyle discovered the first gas law, that under constant temperature the pressure of a gas varies inversely with the volume, attributing the variation in pressure to the changing force of the corpuscles striking the inner surface of the vessel as its volume is reduced or increased. Rejecting the "obscure" views of the Aristotelians and the alchemists, he embraced the "clear principles" of the new mechanistic philosophy incorporating "insensible particles" or "corpuscles" interacting according to mechanical laws. These principles, he believed, would provide explanations of the causes of phenomena as well as the "textures" of compound substances. It was this new corpuscular-mechanistic framework of interpretation that posed the epistemological problems addressed by Locke, Berkeley, and Hume, Locke especially clarifying the distinction between the primary, secondary, and tertiary qualities or powers of the insensible particles along lines suggested by Boyle.

But if the seventeenth century produced extraordinary giants, the greatest of these was Newton. Although scientists have excelled in one or two of the three facets of scientific genius, experimental, theoretical, and mathematical, no one has embodied all three to the extent of Newton who made outstanding contributions to each: experimental discovery of the spectrum of light, formulation of the universal law of gravitation, and discovery of the calculus (independent of Leibniz). Naming his monumental work (in contrast to Descartes'), *The Mathematical Principles of Natural Philosophy* because he was unable to explain the nature or cause of gravity, his universal law of gravitation nonetheless finally provided an exact mathematical description and prediction of how the force of the sun determines the orbital motion of the planets.

Based on Kepler's third law that the sizes of the planetary orbits vary with the 3/2nd power of their distances from the sun, Newton was able to demonstrate that the distances and sizes of the orbits were determined by the gravitational force of the sun diminishing with the square of the distance. Furthermore, he formulated the essential features of the mechanistic framework that would guide research in the physical sciences for the ensuing two centuries. Declaring "that God in the beginning form'd Matter in solid, massy, hard, impenetrable, moveable Particles," he devised the laws of motion and defined the forces determining the trajectories of the particles, along with the absolute "frames of the universe," space and time, which he thought supported absolute motion. Assuming that the initial conditions, parameters, and forces acting on a physical system could be ascertained without disturbing it, Laplace boasted that all future or past states could be predicted with certainty, a presupposition shattered by Heisenberg's indeterminacy principles.

While Newton's achievement in the *Principia* was the culmination of previous astronomical inquiries not challenged until Michelson and Morely failed to confirm the existence of absolute motion and Einstein reduced Newton's absolute frames of space and time to a variable four-dimensional continuum of events, Newton's *Opticks* opened up whole new areas of inquiry that set the problems for scientists in the following two centuries. Based on his earlier prism experiments showing that ordinary sunlight is not homogeneous but composed of a spectrum of independent colors, he tried to explain the nature of these colors and other optical phenomena such as reflection, refraction, and diffraction by the corpuscular theory, attributing the different colors to the different sizes of the corpuscles. He also made the prescient suggestion that the heat generated and light reflected when intense rays of light strike metallic objects are caused by the light particles increasing the motion of the interior corpuscles of the object, anticipating Einstein's explanation of the photoelectric effect.

His extensive alchemical experiments reflecting his tremendously creative imagination can be seen as the background for his attempted explanations of chemical properties and reactions, of gravitational attraction along with magnetic and electrical repulsion and attraction, as well as the vibration of animal spirits through the nerves, attributing all of these processes to "a certain most subtle spirit which pervades and lies hid in all gross bodies [. . .]." As he claims at the end of "The System of the World" appended to the *Principia*, it is "by the force and action" of this spirit that the "particles of bodies" attract, cohere, and repel, that light is emitted, reflected, diffracted, and heats bodies, and that sensations are propagated as vibrations of this spirit from the sense organs to the brain. What an extraordinary range of inquiries and possible explanations are anticipated by this farsighted statement!

Before turning to the subsequent investigations inspired by Newton's Queries in the *Opticks*, something should be said about the modification of religious beliefs brought about by the scientific revolution in astronomy and physics. While the new framework of interpretation was the corpuscular-mechanistic system, all the scientists and most of the philosophers (Hobbes and Hume being possible exceptions) of the period maintained strong religious convictions. The Bible generally continued to be the primary source of religious beliefs, supported by the pervasive institutionalization of Christianity, whether Catholic, Anglican, Lutheran, or Calvinistic, among the western nations, but scientists and philosophers increasingly referred to the order of nature to justify their belief in God—if the universe were a vast mechanism, then there had to be a divine mechanic to create and maintain it. Thus the underlying assumption, as Hume put it, was *"that the cause or causes of order in the universe probably bear some remote analogy to human intelligence."*

When opponents of the heliocentric system pointed to scriptural passages indicating the earth was stationary and that the sun moved, Galileo argued that their significance should be judged in relation to the state of knowledge at the time they were written and in view of the fact that "the great book of nature" as interpreted by natural philosophers also is a manifestation of God's creative powers: "nor does God less admirably discover himself to us in Nature's actions, than in the Scripture's sacred dictions." Believing that the delicate balance of planetary motions could not have occurred by chance, he maintained that the planets must have been placed in their respective orbits with their exact motions by God. Yet despite this recourse to God in explaining the origin of the planetary system, Galileo fought for the independence of natural philosophy from the control of theology, acknowledging the authority of scripture and the Church concerning questions of Christian doctrine, faith, and morality, but maintaining the autonomy of experimental inquiry regarding questions of nature.

Knowing that in adopting the atomistic view of Democritus and Epicurus they could be charged with atheism, the defenders of the new mechanistic world order were anxious, therefore, to preserve a role for God in their system. Thus while Descartes grounded his mechanistic theory on clear and distinct ideas or self-evident principles, he appealed ultimately to the veracity or goodness of God as the guarantor of these criteria. Moreover, in reasserting the Neoplatonic view that the essence of man is thinking, a function of the soul substance, he identified man with this spiritual reality, rather than with the material machine constituting the body. In his work on *The Excellency And Grounds Of The Corpuscular Or Mechanistic Philosophy*, Boyle explicitly denies that the origin of the universe could have occurred by "atoms accidentally meeting in an infinite vacuum," declaring that God not only originally endowed the particles with motion, but also devised the mechanical properties and laws to produce the universe he intended. Newton, too, was an ardent believer in God as the creator, declaring that "[b]lind metaphysical necessity [. . .] could produce no variety of things," therefore the wonderful diversity of nature "could arise from nothing but the ideas and will of a Being necessarily existing."

Because the mechanistic framework itself could not account for the delicate balance and purposeful design observed in nature, especially among organic creatures, the corpuscularians attributed this teleological organization to God. The Archdeacon William Paley became famous in the nineteenth century for his argument from design, citing the marvelous intricacy of the eye as an example of what could not have been produced by mechanical necessity or blind chance—which had been Aristotle's major objection also to the deterministic atomic theory of Democritus. It was not until Darwin introduced the theory of evolution that a naturalistic explanation was possible of the origin and development of progressively complex organic structures that function with the purpose of sustaining the organism, although the idea that this could have occurred as a result of an accumulation of accidental genetic changes that enhanced the organism's competition for survival and reproduction still appears counterintuitive to many people.

Returning to the diverse research projects identified by Newton in the *Opticks*, the investigations in the following two centuries were a vindication of and tribute to his foresight. For example, it was Francis Hauksbee, whom Newton had engaged to conduct experiments at the meetings of the Royal Society, who began exploring electrical conduction after noting the similarity between barometric light and electrification. Among his experiments he discovered that rotating an evacuated globe between one's hands produced a spark in the interior of the globe, while rotating an unevacuated sphere between one's hands produced a charge on its surface. This manner of generating electric charges was so much more efficient than rubbing glass tubes that it considerably enhanced electrical experimentation, which by then was becoming very popular.

While Hauksbee noted the difference between electrical attraction and repulsion and that the electricity conducted from one object to another acquires a separate existence, it was Charles du Fay who first described the phenomena precisely. Using a gold leaf as an electroscope, he noted that though initially attracted to a charged body, if it came in contact with the body (drawing off some of the electricity) it was repelled unless it lost its electrical charge by giving it to a neutral body, after which it again was attracted to the charged body unless coming in contact with it, and so forth. Thus he noted that bodies will repel provided the second body is electrified by the first, the repulsion apparently caused by the opposition between the two identical but separate electrical charges. He then asked if other electrified bodies would react in a similar manner, even if they received their electrification from another source. In pursuing this question he discovered two kinds or modes of "electrics," finding that if a gold leaf repelled by coming in contact with a rubbed glass tube is then brought near rubbed copal (a resinous substance), it will not be repelled as he expected but attracted, indicating a contrast in electrical charges.

Observing that this difference occurred among a number of substances, he distinguished two kinds of electrics, naming one "vitreous" for glass and the other "resinous" from amber and copal. Substances containing the same kind of electricity, either vitreous or resinous, will repel each other while those possessing the opposite kind will attract. An unelectrified or neutral object capable of receiving an electric charge can be given either a vitreous or resinous charge depending upon which type of electric body is brought in contact with it (although what kind of electrification is produced depends upon many aspects). Despite the fact that Dufay was not able to explain the nature of the electrification, this classification made the phenomena considerably more intelligible.

It was Benjamin Franklin who attempted a theoretical interpretation of Dufay's experimental distinctions in terms of an electrical fiery matter. According to his theory, all unelectrified bodies contain an "equal share" of a single electric fire or fluid, the action of rubbing causing some of the electric fire to pass from the body doing the rubbing to the body rubbed, where it is collected. When a neutral conductor is brought near a body with an excess of electricity it will draw off this excess until equilibrium is reached, the total amount of electrical charge being conserved. Thus electrical conduction is the transfer of an excess of electric charge to a lesser charged body or, looking at the process in reverse, a body with a lesser charge drawing an additional charge from another body having an excess of electricity. It is this capacity to receive an excess charge that causes electrical attraction while the conduction of electricity from one body to another, so that they both have the same charge, explains the repulsion. Two bodies with an excess (or deficiency) of electrical charge will repel each other because the attempt to pass on the electricity is opposed. Neutral bodies neither attract nor repel because there is no flow of electricity due to the equilibrium of the charge. Franklin and his Philadelphia friends introduced the terms 'positive' or 'plus' to refer to an excess of electric charge and 'negative' or 'minus' to refer to a deficiency of electric charge, the flow always occurring from positive to negative, as from a higher fluid pressure or temperature to a lower one. This classification had the advantage of being quantified. Franklin, with the help of his son, also proved with his famous kite experiment that lightning is an electrical discharge.

Like other admirers of Newton, Franklin attempted to provide a corpuscular interpretation of the electrical reactions by supposing that the attractive fire or matter, because it can penetrate solid objects, consists of "very subtle elastic particles" (like those of gases) which repel each other, the repulsion of two positively charged bodies due to the repelling effect of their particles. In neutral bodies their repelling effect is diffused by their being distributed equally among the atoms of the body. How the repelling effects of the electric particles could be harmonized with the attractive forces of the atoms composing the neutral body posed a problem which at the time was nearly impossible to resolve. Charles Coulomb made the important discovery that the strength of the attractive or repulsive force among charged bodies is the same as Newton's law of gravitation, being inversely proportional to the square of the distance between the bodies and directly proportional to the product of their charges. This was as far as the explanation could be developed before the discovery of the electron, a negatively charged particle, as the element of electrical conduction.

In optics Newton's preference for the emission theory of light, wherein a luminous body emits rays of light in the form of minute corpuscles propelled in straight lines, as indicated by the sharp boundaries of shadows, ensured its dominance over the wave theory throughout the eighteenth century. Then at the very beginning of the nineteenth century Thomas Young was attracted to the wave theory based on the analogy with sound waves, along with his discovery of the general law of the interference of light. Dissatisfied with Newton's corpuscular explanation via "easy fits of reflection and transmission" of the well-known diffraction patterns produced when waves are propagated through small apertures, Young proposed his own interpretation based on his theory of interference. According to this theory, the illuminated bands of the diffraction pattern are produced by light waves being in phase and therefore reinforcing, the dark bands caused by the light waves being out of phase and therefore destructing, these constructive and destructive effects readily observable in water waves.

Initially Young's explanation was strongly opposed by the supporters of Newton's corpuscular theory, but when Fresnel several years later provided a more convincing explication (than Newton's corpuscular interpretation) by means of waves of the polarization of light produced by Iceland spar, explained why light appears to travel in straight lines, and then demonstrated that light waves (as water waves) are propagated at right angles or transverse to the direction of the motion of their source, the tide began to change. When he performed interference experiments that enabled him to measure the wavelengths and amplitudes of the diffracted light, still more scientists were converted.

Then in what is often referred to as an *experimentum crusis*, performing a series of ingenious experiments in mid-century Foucoult confirmed that light travels more slowly in water or glass than in air. Because Newton had predicted that the stronger attractive force of the particles composing the denser medium not only produced the angle of refraction, but would cause an acceleration of the light particles in the denser medium, while the wave theory predicted a retarding effect on the velocity of the light waves, Foucoult's proof that light travels more slowly in denser media was considered a decisive confirmation of the wave theory. From mid-century, when Fizeau determined the velocity of light to be 300,000 kilometers per second, the wave theory was universally accepted until Einstein's explanation of the photoelectric effect in 1905 reintroduced discrete quanta or corpuscles of light, again raising the problem of its dual nature.

But though Newton's corpuscular theory of light did not fare well under the experimental investigations of Young, Fresnel, and Foucoult, his atomic conception of matter received brilliant support from the atomic theory of Dalton and subsequent investigators. Although from a poor family of Quakers who conducted his experiments in the provincial city of Manchester rather than Cambridge or Oxford, and thus was not in the privileged tradition of scientists such as Boyle, Hooke, and Newton, Dalton nonetheless was an ardent admirer of Newton and inheritor of the English receptivity toward atomism or corpuscularianism. Furthermore, he was preceded by developments in pneumatic chemistry by Boyle, Cavendish, and Priestley that culminated in the chemical revolution involving the overthrow of the phlogiston theory and confirmation of the role of oxygen in combustion by Lavoisier. Owing to this revolution, a number of other elements were identified such as carbon, nitrogen, and hydrogen along with compound gases like carbon dioxide (CO_2) and nitrous oxide (NO), as well as the components of water, hydrogen and oxygen, although not in their exact proportion. In addition to these discoveries, the analysis of chemical reactions was begun with an attempt made to identify, weigh, and assign symbols to the initial elements and byproducts of the reactions.

In light of these previous developments it was natural to ask what the underlying principles were on the basis of which these elements combined, which is exactly what Dalton did. Yet as he indicates in his first paper "On the Absorption of Gases by Water and Other Liquids" in which he announced his atomic theory, it was not chemical reactions, but the different solubilities of gases in water that he believed provided the clues to a solution. Attributing the differences to "the weight and number of the ultimate particles of the several gases," he appended to the article a table of "the relative weights of the ultimate particles of the gaseous and other bodies." Quoting Newton's *Principia* and "Dr. Priestley," he indicated that he was influenced also by the question of how compound gases can mingle to form a uniform mixture in the atmosphere, notwithstanding their different specific gravities and the various repulsive forces of their particles. He says that in attempting to relate what was known about the gaseous composition of the atmosphere to "the Newtonian doctrine of repulsive atoms or particles, I set to work to combine my atoms on paper."

This led to his formulation of "the postulates of atomism" plus "simplifying rules" as guides for combining atoms into compounds. The postulates were that all matter is composed of indivisible atoms; that all the atoms of an element are alike in weight and all other properties; that the atoms of different elements have different weights; and that because the atoms are indivisible and indestructible they retain their identities in all chemical interactions—still the fundamental principles underlying molecular chemistry. Weight being the essential property of the atoms for explaining their combination, Dalton attempted to calculate their atomic weights relative to hydrogen taken as 1, but without knowing the actual atomic composition or chemical formula of substances he had to guess the rules governing their combination.

Devising symbols to represent the various elements, he combined the symbols on paper to see how the elements might actually unite to form compound substances. While Dalton's atomic theory was only a provisional schema for interpreting the composition of substances or gases, compared to the previous lack of any explanatory principles, his was an enormous step forward. Moreover, his simplifying rules of combination took account of the three laws of chemical combination recognized at the time: the law of definite proportions, the law of equivalent proportions, and the law of multiple proportions. As frequently emphasized, an initial conceptual framework, however provisional or approximate, is indispensable for any further progress because without a framework of interpretation the phenomena are unintelligible, but having one makes it possible to examine the data more closely to determine the fit and make whatever revisions are necessary.

As previously indicated, the basic weakness of Dalton's theory was that his simplifying rules for deciding how elements were combined to form (molecular) compounds was not based on an exact knowledge of the chemical structures or formulas of the compounds, hence he did not know the exact number of the elements forming a compound which precluded determining precisely the atomic weights. This was partially remedied when Gay-Lussac and von Humbolt devised a more reliable method based on the proportions by volume that gases combine to form compound gases, known as "the law of combining volumes." By substituting "parts by volume" for Dalton's "parts by weight," Gay-Lussac was able to establish more accurate laws of combination because, unlike elements which do not seem to combine in simple integral proportions by *weight*, gases form compounds whose elements by *volume* are integer multiples of each other. Although relying on volumes rather than weights to measure the proportional combinations, Gay-Lussac believed he was confirming Dalton's "rules of greatest simplicity" by demonstrating that "gases always combine in the simplest proportions."

But Dalton did not accept Gay-Lussac's support because he believed it implied that equal volumes of different gases contain the same number of basic gas particles (either atomic or molecular). This he thought could not be true because sometimes when *two* gases combine the density of the compound gas is less than *one* of the original gases, despite a second gas having been added. Moreover, when two volumes of hydrogen are combined with one volume of oxygen they form two volumes of water vapor ($2H_2O$). Since the number of water vapor particles cannot exceed the number of oxygen particles in the original one volume of oxygen, when these H_2O particles are dispersed in the *two* volumes of water vapor any unit volume of the latter will contain only half the number of particles contained in either of the original gas volumes, further supporting Dalton's objection. Finally, he also believed that the sizes of the atomic particles (surrounded by a ring of heat) vary, thus the same volume of gases could not contain the same number of particles if they differed in size.

However, suppose one postulates, a Avogadro did, that instead of the original gas particles being monatomic some are polyatomic, so that the original oxygen particles can be composed of two atoms of oxygen (O_2) instead of one. If each of these binary particles divide when the oxygen particles combine with the hydrogen, one oxygen atom combining with two hydrogen atoms (because the two volumes of hydrogen contain twice the number of particles as the one volume of oxygen), then the result will be $2H_2O$: two volumes of water vapor. So if the two atoms of hydrogen that replace the one atom of oxygen in the binary oxygen particle *weigh less* than the oxygen atom (as is the case), the density of the water vapor will be *less* than that of the original oxygen, eliminating the first objection.

Furthermore, if when interacting with the hydrogen the binary oxygen particle *divides in two* there will be twice as many oxygen atoms available to combine with the H_2 in forming the two volumes of water vapor, maintaining an equal number of particles, removing Dalton's second objection. In this way both anomalies are eliminated and "the equal volumes-equal numbers principle"preserved. If, in addition, the particles composing the original gases are not limited to just binary atoms but can be composed of additional numbers, then more complex compounds can be formed, such as ammonia (NH_3), without violating Avogadro's principle. This is another example of an objection to a theory being reasonable in relation to certain intuitions or assumptions, but losing its force when these assumptions are revised or discarded.

Avogadro's principle that equal volumes of gases contain equal numbers of particles is now an established law. Using this principle, Avogadro derived more accurate formulas for molecular compounds and therefore more precise calculations of atomic weights (relative to hydrogen) than Dalton. Based on Gay-Lussac's law of combining volumes, by 1830 Berzelius constructed a table of atomic weights which are practically identical to those used today. When later investigators, such as Einstein, were able to deduce numerical values for Avogadro's number (the number of particles in a mole of a substance), this was considered an important justification of their theories. But it was Stanislao Cannizzaro, introducing a new procedure involving "the comparison of the densities of the gaseous compounds of the elements," who finally was able to calculate accurately the atomic weights. His method was so reliable that Meyer and Mendeleev could organize their Periodic Tables of the elements based on his precise determination of their atomic weights. This was perhaps the most impressive instance yet in the history of science of explaining macroscopic regularities in terms of microscopic elements and their recurring properties.

But as important as these developments were in providing considerably more exact empirical evidence for the atomic conjectures of Leucippus, Democritus, and Epicurus, they still did not represent an essential emendation of the ancient atomic theory which awaited the early decades of the twentieth century. Despite Avogadro's conception of polyatomic particles of some elements, the atoms composing these compound particles still were considered to be indivisible, unalterable, and to interact according to the mechanical principles of attraction and repulsion. Franklin had conjectured that similarly charged bodies repel because of the repulsive force of the identically charged particles composing them. The corpuscularians or atomists had attributed the repelling force of elastic fluids or gases to the repulsion of the particles, while explaining the formation of gaseous and chemical compounds by the attractive force of the atoms. Davy and Berzelius, using Volta's electric pile, had shown that compound substances, such as water, could be decomposed by an electric current with the atoms of hydrogen and oxygen attracted to opposite electrodes, classifying the elements into "electropositive" and "electronegative." Given what was known about the attraction of oppositely charged bodies, it appeared that the elements were bound in molecular compounds by some kind of electrical force, yet there was no awareness that the atoms themselves might be composed of charged particles and electrical forces that could account for these reactions.

As early as 1820 Oersted had demonstrated that a wire carrying an electric current deflects a magnetic needle if placed parallel to it, but not if aligned at right angles, while the position of the wire above or below the needle determined the direction of its deflection. Soon afterward Ampère formulated the laws describing this deflection, along with the mutual attraction and repulsion of the electric currents themselves, those flowing in the same direction attracting and those in the opposite direction repelling. Aware of Ampère's discovery that when a current is passed through a coil it behaves like a magnet, Faraday designed experiments showing that a magnetic "field of force" is created concentric to the current passing through the wire. He then found that the converse effect could be created if a wire were wound around a magnet whose magnetic field was altered by coming in contract with another magnet, the change in magnetic contact producing a momentary electric current in the wire.

What these experiments revealed is that the electromagnetic effects were produced either by the movement of the coil or magnet, or by the disruption of the contact or current which somehow produces "fields of force," magnetic or electrical. Maxwell later (1862) formulated equations (which Einstein described as one of the greatest achievements in physics) depicting the structure and propagation of the electromagnetic fields, showing that they are propagated in a direction transverse to their cause and with the same velocity as light, thereby establishing the identity of the two. The demonstration of these electromagnetic fields produced a breach in the accepted mechanistic view of the universe because fields, as a structure of space, are different from forces transmitted in space, establishing the new science of electrodynamics along with the older sciences of kinematics, dynamics, and thermodynamics.

Yet even more remarkable investigations occurred toward the end of the nineteenth and early decades of the twentieth century, indicating that the atom has an internal structure capable of transformation, accounting for the various atomic emissions then being discovered. Cathode rays were demonstrated to be electrically charged particles by J.J. Thomson that came to be called 'electrons.' Röntgen discovered X-rays, Becquerel radioactivity, while the Curies identified radioactive substances like radium, thorium, and polonium. The spectral emissions of various gases were investigated with Balmer devising a formula predicting the hydrogen spectrum. Rutherford discovered *alpha* and *beta* rays while Villard identified *gamma* rays.

Using the *alpha* particles as a probe to investigate the interior structure of the atoms composing gold foil, Rutherford and his assistants detected the existence of a relatively massive, positively charged nuclear particle subsequently named the 'proton,' while postulating another massive, uncharged particle called the 'neutron' to account for the total atomic mass without adding to the charge. Inferring that these two particles plus the electron in some manner constituted the interior elements of atomic structure held together perhaps by the familiar electrostatic force, there was no convincing model of this arrangement until Bohr introduced his planetary conception of the atom: the proton and neutron occupying the nucleus with the electrons revolving in the surrounding orbits. Utilizing Planck's explanation of blackbody radiation along with his quantum equation, but finding the key in Balmer's formula, Bohr displayed tremendous ingenuity in constructing the first provisional model of the atom.

With his postulated "electron jumps" explaining spectral emissions and Rutherford's and Soddy's discovery of "nuclear transmutations" accounting for atomic radiation, the age of atomic and nuclear physics had begun. Moreover, the realization that properties of the elements could be accounted for by means of the number and organization of the electrons or nuclear protons (which in a neutral atom are numerically the same) provided a deeper explanation of the Periodic Table utilizing atomic numbers in place of weights. This conception also allowed for the explanation of ions and isotopes, as well as chemical reactions and bonds in terms of shared electrons with their electrical charges. Skepticism regarding the reality of atoms all but disappeared.

In a succession of remarkable developments between 1925 and 1927, investigators like Bohr, Heisenberg, Jordan, Dirac, de Broglie, Schrödinger, Pauli, and Born established the new quantum mechanics which, when developed into quantum electrodynamics and quantum chromodynamics, has served as the fundamental theoretical framework of scientific inquiry in the physical sciences. Creating increasingly more powerful particle accelerators for discovering new particles, along with the modes of disintegration of previous ones, particle physics has been one of the most productive areas of scientific research in the twentieth century.

Despite paradoxical aspects of quantum mechanics, such as Heisenberg's principles of indeterminacy and the wave-particle duality of matter introduced by Einstein, which Bohr attempted to mitigate with his principles of correspondence and complementarity, the progress made in the physical and biological sciences in the twentieth century exceeds that of all previous centuries. We know more about the early state, development, and structure of the physical universe, the chemical bonds and composition of molecular substances, the particles and forces composing the subatomic or subnuclear structure of matter, the chemical-electrical discharges of the central nervous system, and the biomolecular coding of our genes directing embryological development and physiological processes than previous scientists ever dreamed of.

Yet notwithstanding these extraordinary developments that have had so many amazing beneficial applications in the latter half of the twentieth century, not all the consequences have been favorable. On the positive side, there have been remarkable improvements in agricultural yield and industrial productivity that have raised the standard of living in most areas throughout the world. Dramatic advances in medicine and pharmacology, along with more extensive health benefits and coverage, have eliminated many diseases, reduced infant mortality, and produced healthier life spans for most people. Amazing developments in transportation, communication, and information technology have provided instant access to the data essential for dealing effectively with the complex problems of modern life, offered immediate visual coverage of world events, and brought peoples throughout the globe much closer. Increased prosperity helped to reduce illiteracy, allow more people the advantages of higher education, created more challenging and rewarding employment, and provided greater opportunity for travel and cultural enrichment. All of these benefits have contributed to a much fuller and satisfying life which it is easy to take for granted.

On the other hand, these advances have been accompanied by devastation of the natural environment, especially the rain forests; depletion of natural resources and elimination of many species of flora and fauna; pollution of rivers, lakes, and oceans along with the atmosphere; and a calamitous overpopulation in some parts of the world that is projected to increase disastrously in the future, unless family planning becomes more widespread. Moreover, the greater prosperity due to advances in technology has led to radical changes and fluctuations in the job market producing considerable employment insecurity and less demand for unskilled labor, disrupting family life and condemning segments of society to a life of unemployment and poverty. These unfortunate economic consequences in turn have contributed to alcoholism, drug addiction, abusive behavior, decline in social responsibility, along with a surge in violent crime that seems so out of place at this stage of civilization. In addition, there is the degrading effect of television which exerts such a strong influence on contemporary mores, at least in the United States, replacing religion as "the opiate of the people." Despite its artistic and educational potential, television projects the worst model of human behavior: glamorized materialism, base sexuality, voyeurism, mindless brutality, and stupefying superficiality.

That we have not yet learned to control the consequences of technology in the most advantageous way can be attributed to at least three possible reasons. First is the fact that the benefits of these developments have not been distributed equally throughout the world, or even in individual countries, so that groups of people still live in a state similar to primitive man, in tribal clans or urban gangs constantly preying on one another. Illiteracy, poverty, famine, overpopulation, and tribal warfare continue to be widespread in certain countries, so people are desperate to immigrate posing a threat to the economic and social stability of more developed societies. Attempts to meliorate these conditions have proved frustrating because the methods devised for resolving problems in more advanced countries do not work as well, if at all, in these primitive conditions.

A second reason is that while science and technology, at least in industrialized countries, have to an increasing extent displaced religion as the dominant intellectual, social, and cultural influence, the crucial role religions traditionally played in instilling higher values, sanctioning ethical principles, and reinforcing a sense of community spirit has not been replaced by humanistically inspired values and behavior. Previously community life was centered around the temple, church, or mosque where religious leaders decried excessive materialism, premarital sexual relations, infidelity, and moral corruption, encouraging more spiritual values, self-discipline, unselfishness, family cohesiveness, and social responsibility. Earlier in the century teenage sex, unwed mothers, uncaring fathers, divorce, child abuse, and homicides were exceptional, not prevalent as they are today. Yet as important as religions have been in promoting moral values, teaching ethical responsibility, and providing consolation in times of crisis and tragedy, if the *intellectual* justification of religion is no longer credible, then some other means has to be found for fulfilling these functions. It is not possible to say, as one did previously, that if God did not exist he would have to be invented, using the threat of divine punishment to keep mankind in check. One cannot feel threatened by something that one does not believe exists.

A third reason the advances in knowledge and technology have not had a greater effect on improving the human condition is that despite the raised standards of living, higher levels of education, and enhanced opportunities for personal growth, the other crucial element influencing the quality of life, *human nature*, has remained essentially unchanged. It is common knowledge that there are two independent variables, nature (one's genetic makeup) and nurture (one's environmental circumstances) that constitute the limiting conditions within which personal growth occurs. These variables are independent for any particular individual because the genetic factor depends upon one's accidental chromosomal endowment at conception, while the nurture factor depends upon the accidental environmental circumstances at birth. Previously it was believed that the impact of nurture was much more important than nature in a person's self-development, but now we recognize the equal importance of both. Moreover, in the past only the nurturing or environmental factor could be improved because the nature or genetic component was outside of human control, a limitation that no longer exists.

If these are three major causes of the adverse effects of applying our recently acquired technological knowledge, then it is possible that as we come to know more about these consequences we can learn to control them to better advantage. Regarding the current unequal distribution of the world's wealth, we should be able to devise a more equitable sharing of the earth's productivity that would raise all people to a similar higher standard of living with all the advantages that this brings, especially in terms of improved educational and employment opportunities, along with greater social harmony and stability.

As for the second reason, despite the present decline of academic standards in many secondary schools, we should be able to create an educational system that eventually will replace traditional religions in instilling moral values, justifying ethical principles, and inculcating civic virtues in our youth. Providing we can reduce the underlying socioeconomic causes of immoral conduct, such as poverty, the breakup of the family, teenage pregnancies where the mother herself is underdeveloped morally and where there is no adequate paternal role model, neighborhoods infested with drug traffic and crime, and the corrupting influence of television, young people can be taught that being a person of good character, able to exert moral responsibility over one's life, is necessary for any personal fulfillment. But that presupposes the individual is not genetically flawed.

This brings us to the third reason for the present state of mankind because any ultimate improvement of the human condition requires not only meliorating the nurturing influences, but also nature—mankind's genetic makeup —which implies that human nature is perfectible. Although this was not possible in the past, having used science and technology to lessen the first cause of being personally disadvantaged by improving the environmental conditions, we now have the power to use genetic engineering to reduce the second cause of being disadvantaged by improving an individual's genetic endowment. Just as we can by genetic engineering eliminate birth defects and other inherited biological weaknesses that cause so much physical suffering, so we can begin to eliminate the genetic or physiological basis of alcoholism, drug addiction, violent behavior, pedophilia, and other forms of antisocial conduct that cause so much personal suffering. Despite the dangers that always accompany such an undertaking, when one considers the brutality and inhumanity of mankind in the past—the devastation of previous wars, the holocaust, or the current genocide in Bosnia or Rwanda—the risk appears well worth taking. It is not without warrant that Hegel described mankind's past as the "slaughter bench of history."

Would trying to exert some compassionate control over the adverse genetic determinants of human nature, and therefore human destiny, be any worse than leaving it to purely fortuitous natural processes? We have not balked at using our enhanced capabilities to provide an environment more conducive to personal growth and well being, so why should we refrain from using what we know about genetic engineering to improve the other crucial aspect determining the human condition. How much better off mankind would be if we could cease producing alcoholics, drug addicts, rapists, violent individuals, child abusers, serial killers, sadistic torturers, and brutal despots, replacing these with people with a greater disposition for kindness, appreciation of the simpler things in life, reasonable conduct, aesthetic sensitivity, curiosity for learning, and respect for the common good. Education, self-discipline, and moral or character development still would be essential for personal realization, but they would occur in much more favorable circumstances. Even if there are no simple isolated genetic causes for these behavioral predispositions, which undoubtedly is the case, we are finding that they are considerably more dependent upon physiological conditions than we thought —conditions that can be modified and over which we can exert some control. The recent discovery that low levels of serotonin are correlated with highly aggressive behavior is a promising example.

It is undeniable that there always has been more suffering and misery in the world than personal fulfillment and happiness, so if this can be reversed by population control and *very carefully supervised, strictly controlled genetic engineering sensitive to the rights of individuals as well as society*, then not to proceed because of religious scruples or fear of the unforeseen shows a weakness of nerve and want of self-determination. Most endeavors to improve society have usually involved some risk, but given the deplorable natural conditions in which most humans have lived in the past, the risk has been justified.

Opposing population control, Pope John Paul II refers to the "sacredness of human life," but how sacred is life when one is facing debilitating starvation, hopeless poverty, or ruthless genocide? Does the sacredness of life prevent babies from being born with AIDS or drug addiction, or entering into an unloving family of sexual or physical abuse, or having a genetic defect that makes life a continuous struggle with severe depression or addiction, or with a genetic marker that turns one into a monster? Whether life is sacred is not a god-given fact, but a question of what circumstances one is fortunate enough to be born into, both genetic and environmental. How many lives in the past have been diminished or destroyed by the deplorable effects of one or the other of these "disadvantages"? If one objects that by genetic engineering humans would be "playing God," then one can reply, as Hume did, that the plight of mankind has not been a great tribute to God's foresight, love, or wisdom. Nor is it very persuasive to argue that the present condition of mankind is so perfectly adjusted, producing the maximum happiness possible, that it would be foolhardy to attempt to improve it.

Like the scientific revolution of the seventeenth century that transformed mankind's conception of the universe and man's place in it, along with the methodology used to attain knowledge and resolve problems, so the twentieth century has been a watershed in the advance of human knowledge and development of technology. Extending the use of experimentation from a method primarily for testing hypotheses to a means for probing nature to discover the deeper or more extensive domains of physical reality causing natural phenomena accounts for the extraordinary advances in science in this century, from atomic fission and fusion, molecular biology and pharmacology, to space flights and the lunar landing. While the seventeenth century saw the dismantling of the geocentric, homocentric universe and introduction of a mechanistic framework of interpretation, the twentieth century has witnessed the demise of religion as an intellectual and moral force owing to a better understanding of the universe and ourselves. Einstein could still speak of the "the old one," reference to a God that is "subtle but not malicious" and who "does not play dice," but utterances such as these have all but disappeared among the present generation of physicists.

For many people the demise of God may be difficult to acknowledge, but we have seen profound enough intellectual, cultural, and political changes in the past to accept the vanquishing of religion by science as another historical reality. If the intellectual and technological changes that lie ahead are anywhere near as remarkable as those of the past four centuries, particularly the present century, it is impossible to imagine what the future transformation in human thinking and in the human condition will be like. Compare, for example, someone from the seventeenth century peering into the twilight of the twentieth century with someone from the dawn of the twenty-first century peering into the twenty-fourth century. Are the changes apt to be any less astonishing or unforeseeable? Entering a new millennium, we are approaching a threshold of possibilities perhaps never encountered previously by mankind since the emergence of scientific rationalism. That we have reached this point is some assurance that we can persevere on our own in the future.

SELECT BIBLIOGRAPHY

Achinstein, Peter. *Particles And Waves*. New York: Oxford University Press, 1991.

Andrade, E.N. da C. *Rutherford and the nature of the atom*. New York: Doubleday, 1964.

Aristotle. *De Caelo*. Translated by J.L. Stocks.
———. *Physica* . Book VII, Ch.5. Translated by R.P. Hardie and P.K. Gaye.

Augustine. *The City of God*.

Bacon, Francis. *The New Organon*. Edited with introduction by Fulton H. Anderson. Indianapolis: The Bobbs-Merrill Co., 1960.

Badash, L. *Rutherford and Boltwood*. New Haven: Yale Univ. Press, 1969.

Berkeley, George. *De Motu*.
———. *Principles of Human Knowledge*.

Blackett, P.M.S., and D. Lea, *Proceedings of The Royal Society*. 136 (1932): 225.

Boas, Marie. *The Scientific Renaissance, 1450-1630*. New York: Harper & Row, 1962.

Bohm, David. *Wholeness and the implicate order*. London: Routledge & Kegan Paul, Ltd., 1980.

Bohr, Neils, Letter to Harald Bohr, 23 October 1911. In *Collected Works*. Vol. 1, 527. In *Niels Bohr's Times*, by A. Pais. Oxford: Clarendon Press, 1991.
———. Letter to Harald Bohr, 13 April 1927. In *Collected Works*. Vol. 6, 418. In *Niels Bohr's Times*, by A. Pais. Oxford: Clarendon Press, 1991.
———. *Phil. Mag.* 25 (1913): 10.
———. "Can Quantum Mechanical Descriptions of Physical Reality be Considered Complete?". *Physical Review*. 47 (1935): 777-780.

————. *Philosophical Writings*, Vols. I, II, III. Woodbridge, Conn.: Ox Bow Press, 1987.

Born, Max. *Einstein's Theory of Relativity.* Revised edition. New York: Dover Pub. Inc., 1962.
————. *Zeitschr. Phy.* 37 (1926): 863.
————. *Zeitschr. Phy.* 38 (1926): 803.
————. Letter to Erwin Schrödinger, 6 November 1926. In *Archives for the History of Quantum Mechanics.* New York: American Institute of Physics.
————. *My life and my views.* New York: Charles Scribners and Sons, 1968.
————. *My life: Recollections of a Nobel Laureate.* New York: Charles Scribners and Sons, 1975.

Boyle, Robert. *The Sceptical Chymist.* London: J.M. Dent & Sons, Ltd., n.d.

Bricker, Philip and Hughes, R.I.G. *Philosophical Perspectives on Newtonian Science.* Cambridge: The MIT Press, 1990.

Bronowski, J. and Mazlish, Bruce. *The Western Intellectual Tradition.* New York: Harper & Row, Pub., 1975.

Bruno, Giordano. *Cause, Principle, and Unity.* Translated by Jack Lindsey. New York: International Pub., Inc., 1962.

Buridan, Jean. *Questions on the Four Books on the Heavens and the World of Aristotle.* Translated by E.A. Moody. In *The Science of Mechanics in the Middle Ages,* by Marshall Clagett. Wisconsin: The University of Wisconsin Press, 1959.
————. *Questions on the Eight Books of the Physics of Aristotle.* Translated by Marshall Clagett. In *The Science of Mechanics in the Middle Ages,* by Marshall Clagett. Wisconsin: The University of Wisconsin Press, 1959.

Burtt, E.A. *The Metaphysical Foundations of Modern Science.* Garden CIty, New York: Doubleday & Co., 1954.

Butterfield, Herbert. *The Origins of Modern Science.* New York: Collier Books, 1962.

Cajori, Florian. "An Historical and Explanatory Appendix." In *Principia* by Isaac Newton. Book III, Vol. 2. Translated by Andrew Motte. Revised by Florian Cajori. Berkeley: University of California Press, 1934.

Cantore, Enrico. *Atomic Order*. Cambridge: The MIT Press, 1969.

Čapek, Milič. *The Philosophical Impact of Contemporary Physics*. New York: Van Nostrand, 1961.

Casper, Max. *Kepler*. Translated and edited by C. Doris Hellman. London: Abelard-Schuman, 1959.

Churchland, Paul M. *Scientific realism and the plasticity of the mind*. Cambridge: Cambridge Univ. Press, 1979

Clagett, Marshall. *The Science of Mechanics in The Middle Ages*. Wisconsin: University of Wisconsin Press, 1959.

Clark, Ronald W. *Einstein: The Life and Times*. New York: The World Publishing Co., 1971.

Clavelin, Maurice. *The Natural Philosophy of Galileo*. Translated by A.J. Pomerans. Cambridge: The MIT Press, 1974.

Cohen, I. Bernard. *Franklin and Newton*. Cambridge: Harvard University Press, 1966.
————. Edited *Isaac Newton's Papers and Letters on Natural Philosophy*. Cambridge, Mass., 1958.

Conant, James B. "The Overthrow of the Phlogiston Theory." In *Harvard Case Histories in Experimental Science*. Edited by James B. Conant and Leonard K. Nash. Cambridge: Harvard University Press, 1948.

Crease, Robert P., and Charles C. Mann. "How The Universe Works". *The Atlantic Monthly*. August, 1984: 91.
————. *The Second Creation*. New York: Macmillan Pub. Co., 1986

Crookes, W. *Chem. News* 40 (1879): 129.

Curie, M. *Rev. Sci.* 14 (1900): 65.

Curie, Pierre and Sklodowska, Marie. *Comptes Rendus* 127 (1898): 175, 1215.

D'Abro, A. *The Rise of the New Physics.* Vol I. New York: Dover Pub., Inc., 1951.

Dampier, William C. and Margaret, ed., *Readings In the Literature of Science.* New York: Harper Torchbooks, 1959.

de Santillana, Giorgio. *The Crime of Galileo.* Chicago: University of Chicago Press, 1955.

Descartes, René. *The Philosophical Works.* Vol. I. Translated by Haldane and Ross. Cambridge: At the University Press, 1967.
————. *Principles of Philosophy.* Translated by V.R. Miller and R.P. Miller. Dordrecht: D. Reidel Pub. Co., 1983.
————. *Traité du monde.*

Dijksterhuis, E.J. *The Mechanization of the World Picture.* Translated by C. Dikshoon. Princeton: Princeton University press, 1986.

Drake, Stillman. *Galileo: Pioneer Scientist.* Toronto: University of Toronto Press, 1990.
————. *Galileo At Work: His Scientific Biography.* Chicago: University of Chicago Press, 1978.

Drake, Stillman and Drabkin, I.E. *Mechanics in the Sixteenth-Century Italy.* Madison: The University of Wisconsin Press, 1969.

Duncan, A.M., trans. *Copernicus: on the Revolutions of The Heavenly Spheres.* Newton Abbot: David & Charles Limited, 1976.

Edleston, J. *Correspondence of Sir Isaac Newton and Professor Cotes.* London: 1913.

Einstein, A. *Ann. der Phys.* 19 (1905) 143.
————. *Ann. der Phys.* 20 (1906) 199.
————. ''Die Grundlage der allgeneinen Relativitäts theorie.'' *Ann. der Phys.*

49 (1916).

———. "Autobiographical Notes." In *Albert Einstein: Philosopher-Scientist.* Edited by Paul Schlipp. Evanston, Ill.: Library of Living Philosophers, Inc., 1949.

———. *James Clerk Maxwell.* Cambridge: Cambridge University Press, 1931.

———. *Relativity.* New York: Crown Pub. Inc., 1961.

Einstein, Albert, H. A. Lorentz, H. Minkowski and H. Weyl. *The Principle of Relativity.* Translated by W. Perret and G.B. Jeffrey. New York: Dover Pub. Inc., 1923.

Einstein, Albert and Infeld, Leopold. *The Evolution of Physics.* New York: Simon and Schuster, 1951.

Einstein, Albert, B. Podolsky, and H. Rosen, "Can Quantum Mechanical Descriptions of Physical Reality be Considered Complete?". *Physical Review.* 48 (1935): 696-702.

Favaro, Antonio. *Le Opere di Galileo Galilei.* Vol. 10. Florence: 1890-1909.

Feyerabend, Paul. *Against Method.* London: Verso, 1975.

Fine, Arthur. *The Shaky Game.* Chicago: University of Chicago Press, 1970.

Fritzsch, Harold. *Quarks.* Translated by M. Roloff and the author. New York: Basic Books, 1983.

Galilei, Galileo. *Dialogue Concerning the Two Chief World Systems-Ptolemaic and Copernican.* 2d ed. Translated by Stillman Drake. Berkeley: University of California Press, 1967.

———. *Il Saggiatore (The Assayer).* Reprinted in *The Controversy On The Comets.* Translated by Stillman Drake and C.D. O'Malley. Philadelphia: University of Pennsylvania Press, 1960.

———. *Dialogues Concerning Two New Sciences.* Translated by H. Crew and A. de Salvio. New York: McGraw-Hill Book Company, 1963.

———. *Sidereus Nuncius.* Translated by Albert Van Helden. Chicago: The University of Chicago Press, 1989.

Gilbert, William. *De Magente*. Translated by P. Fleurty Motteley. New York: Dover Pub. Inc., 1958.
———. *De Mundo Nostro Sublunari Philosophia Nova*. N.p., 1651.

Gibbins, Peter, *Particles and Paradoxes*. Cambridge: Cambridge Univ. Press, 1987.

Greenaway, Frank. *John Dalton and the Atom*. Ithaca: Cornell University Press, 1966.

Guerlac, Henry. *Lavoisier-The Crucial Year*. Ithaca: New York, 1961.

Halley, Edmond. "The Ode Dedicated to Newton." In *Principia Mathematica*, Vol. I, by Isaac Newton. Translated by Andrew Motte. Revised by Florian Cajori. Berkeley: University of California Press, 1962.

Hawking, Stephen. "Is the End in Sight for Theoretical Physics?" In *Stephen Hawking's Universe*, by J. Boslough. New York: Morrow Pub., 1985.
———. *A Brief History of Time*. New York: Bantam Books, 1988.

Heisenberg, Walter. *Physics and Beyond*. New York: Harper Torchbooks, 1972.
———. *Physics and Philosophy*. New York: Harper Torchbooks, 1958.

Herbert, Nick. *Quantum Reality*. Garden City: Anchor Book, 1985.

Hermann, Armin. *The Genesis of Quantum Theory*. Cambridge: The MIT Press, 1971.

Hutchins, R.M., ed. *Great Books of The Western World*. Vol. 16. Chicago: The University of Chicago, 1952.

Huygens, Christian. *Oeuvres complètes de Christiaan Huygens*. In Société hollandaise des Sciences. Vol. I. Lattaye: Martinus Nijoff, 1888.

Jammer, Max. "The Correspondence Principle." In *The Conceptual Development of Quantum Mechanics*. New York: McGraw-Hill Book Co., 1966.
———. *The Philosophy of Quantum Mechanics*. New York: John Wiley &

Sons, 1974.

Kant, Immanuel. *Critique of Pure Reason*. Translated by Norman Kemp Smith. New York: The Humanities Press, 1950.
————. *Prolegomena to Any Future Metaphysics*. Translated by James W. Ellington, newly revised. Indianapolis: Hackett Pub. Co., 1977.

Kaplan. Morton. *Homage to Galileo*. Cambridge: The MIT Press, 1965.

Kaufman, W. *Ann. der Phys. und Chem.* 61 (1897): 544.

Kearney, Hugh. *Science and Change, 1500-1700*. New York: McGraw-Hill Book Co., 1971.

Kepler, Johannes. *Mysterium Cosmographicum*. Translated by A.M. Duncan. New York: Abaris Books, 1987.
————. *Astronomia Nova*. In *The Sleepwalkers*. By Arthur Koestler. New York: Grossett's Universal Library, 1959.
————. *Harmonice Mundi, Gesmmelte Werle*. Vol. II. Lib. IV: I. In *The Sleepwalkers*. By Arthur Koestler. New York: Grossett's Universal Library, 1959.
————. Letter to D. Fabricius. 4.7.1603. *Gesmmelte Werle*. Vol. XIV. p. 409.

Kirchoff, G. and Bunsen, R. *Ann. der Phys. und Chem.* 110 (1860): 160. Translated in *Phil. Mag.* 20 (1860): 89.

Koestler, Arthur. *The Sleepwalkers*. New York: Grosset's Universal Library, 1959.

Koyré, Alexander. *Galileo Studies*. Translated by John Mepham. New Jersey: Humanities Press, 1978.

Kuhn, Thomas S. *The Copernican Revolution*. Cambridge: Harvard University press, 1957.
————. *The Structure of Scientific Revolutions*. 2d ed. enlarged. Chicago: The University of Chicago Press, 1970.
————. *The Structure of Scientific Revolutions*. In *International Encyclopedia of the United Sciences*. Vol. II, No. 2. Chicago: The University of Chicago

Press, 1962.

Laplace, P.S., *Introduction à la théorie analytique des probabilités*. Paris: Oeuvres Complètes, 1886.

Lavoisier, A. *Traité Élémentaire de Chemie*. 1789.

Lederman, Leon, with Dick Teresi. *The God Particle*. New York: A Delta Book, 1993.

Lessing, Gotthold. *Helle Zeit, dunkle Zeit*. Edited by C. Seelig. Zürich: Europa Verlag, 1956

Locke, John. *An Essay Concerning Human Understanding*.

Lorentz, H.A. *Versuch Einer Theorie der Electrischen und Optischen Erscheinungen in Bewegten Körper, Collected Paper*. Vol. 5. Leiden: Brill Pub., 1895.
————. *Verh. Deutsch. Phys. Ges.* 9 (1907): 206.

Mach, Ernest. *The Science of Mechanics*. 6th ed. Translated by Thomas J. McCormack. LaSalle Court Pub. Co., 1960.

Matthews, Michael R., ed. *The Scientific Background to Modern Philosophy*. Indianapolis: Hackett Pub. Co., 1989.

Maxwell, J.C. *The Scientific Papers of J.C. Maxwell*. Vol. 2. Edited by W.P. Niven. New York: Dover Pub., n.d.

Mendeleev, I. "Faraday Lecture, 1889." In *The Principles of Chemistry*. Vol. II. Edited by William C. Dampier and Margaret Dampier. N.p., n.d.

Michelson, A.A. *Am. J. Sci.* 22 (1881): 120.

Mill, John Stuart. "Of the Four Methods of Experimental Inquiry." In *A System of Logic*. Bk. I:VIII.

Moseley, H.G., Letter to Niels Bohr, 16 November 1913. In *Collected Works*. Vol. 2, 544.

Ne'eman, Yuval and Yoram Kirsh. *The Particle Hunters*. Cambridge: Cambridge University press, 1986.

Newton, Isaac. *Opticks*. Based on London 4th ed. (1730). New York: Dover Publications, Inc., 1952.
————. *Principia Mathematica*. Vol. 1 & 2. Translated by Andrew Motte. Revised by Florian Cajori. Berkeley: University of California Press, 1934.
————. *Philosophy of Nature*. Edited by H.S. Thayer. New York: Hafner Pub. Co., 1953.

Ogawa, T. *Jap. St. Hist. Sci.* 18 (1979): 73.

Oresme, Nicole. *On the Book of the Heavens and the World of Aristotle*. In *The Science of Mechanics in the Middle Ages* by Marshall Clagett. Wisconsin: University of Wisconsin Press, 1959.

Pais, Abraham. *Inward Bound*. New York: Oxford University Press, 1986.
————. *Neils Bohr's Times*. Oxford: Clarendon Press, 1991.
————. *'Subtle is the Lord...'*. Oxford: Oxford University Press, 1982.

Partington, J.R. *A Short History of Chemistry*. 3rd ed. rev'd. and enlarged. New York: Harper & Brothers, 1960.

Patterson, Elizabeth C. *John Dalton And The Atomic Theory*. New York: Anchor Books, 1970.

Perrin, Jean. *Atoms*. Translation of *Les Atomes* by M.A. Hammick. 1913. Woodbridge, Conn.: Ox Bow Press, 1990.
————. *Brownian Movement and Molecular Reality*. Translated by F. Soddy. London: Taylor and Francis, 1910.
————. *Rev. Scientifique*. 15 (1901): 447
Philosophical Transactions of the Royal Society. 90 (1800): 106-150.

Planck, M. *Scientific Autobiography and Other Papers*. Translated by F. Graynor. London: William and Norgate, 1950.

Plato. *The Republic*. Translated by F.M. Cornford.
————. *Timaeus*. Translated by F. M. Cornford.

Polkinghorne, J.C., *The Quantum World*. Princeton: Princeton Univ. Press, 1985.

Priestly, J. *The Doctrine of Phlogiston Established*. N.p., 1800.

Prigogine, Ilya and Isabelle Stengers. *Order Out of Chaos*. New York: Bantam Books, 1984.

Quig, Chris. "Elementary Particles and Forces." *Scientific American*. April, 1985: 89.

Roller, Duane and Duane H.D. Roller. "The Development of the Concept of Electrical Charge: Electricity From the Greeks to Coulomb." In *Harvard Case Histories in Experimental Science*. Vol. 2. edited by James B. Conant and Leonard K. Nash. Cambridge: Harvard University Press, 1948.

Röntgen, W. "Über eine neue Art von Stahlen." In *Sitzungsberichte der Phys. Mediz. Gesellschaft zu Würzburg*. 137 (1895): 132. Translated in *Nature*. 53 (1896): 274.

Rosen, E. *Kepler's Conversation with Galileo's Sideral Messenger*. New York: Johnson Reprint Corp., 1965.
―――. *The Naming of the Telescope*. New York: Henry Shuman, 1947.

Rosenthal-Schneider, *Reality and Scientific Truth*. Detroit: Wayne State Univ. Press, 1980.

Rutherford, E. *Radioactivity*. Cambridge: Cambridge University Press, 1904.
―――. *J. Röntgen Soc.* 14 (1918): 81.
―――. *Radioactive substances and their radiations*. Cambridge: Cambridge University Press, 1913.
―――. *Philosophical Magazine*. 37 (1919): 581.
―――. *Proc. Roy. Soc.* A90 (1914): 462.

Sambursky, S. *The Physical World of the Greeks*. Translated by Merton Dagut. New York; Collier Books, 1962.

Schlagel, Richard H. *Contextual Realism: A Meta-physical Framework for*

Modern Science. New York: Paragon House, 1968.

———. *From Myth to Modern Mind: the Origins and Growth of Scientific Thought.* Vol. I. New York: Peter Lang Pub., Inc., 1995.

———. "Critical Notice: Fine's 'Shaky Game' (and Why NOA is no Ark for Science)". Vol. 58, No. 2 *Philosophy of Science* (June 1991): 307-323

———. "Experimental Realism: A Critique of Bas van Fraassen's 'Constructive Empiricism.'" In *Review of Metaphysics.* 41 (June, 1988): 789-814.

Schrödinger, Erwin. Letter to Wilhelm Wien, 21 October 1926. In *Niels Bohr Archives.* In *Neils Bohr's Times*, by A. Pais. New York: Oxford University Press, 1991.

Segrè, Emilio. *From X-Rays to Quark.* San Francisco: W.H. Freeman and Co., 1980.

Silverman, Richard A. *Essential Calculus with Applications.* New York: Dover Pub. Inc., 1977.

Singer, Charles. *A Short History of Scientific Ideas.* London: Oxford University Press, 1959.

Small, Robert. *An Account of the Astronomical Discoveries of Kepler.* 1804. Reprint, Madison: The University of Wisconsin Press, 1963.

Soddy, F. *Nature.* 92 (1912): 400.

Sommerfeld, Arnold. Letter to Niels Bohr, 16 November 1913. In *Collected Works.* Vol. 2, 603.

Stein, Howard. "On Locke, 'the Great Huygenius, and the incomparable Mr. Newton,'" Ch. 2, Philip Bricker and R.I.G. Hughes, *Philosophical Perspectives on Newtonian Science.* Cambridge: The MIT Press, 1990.

Thomson, G.P. *The Wave Mechanics of Free Electrons.* New York: McGraw-Hill Publishers, 1930.

———. *Phil. Mag.* 44 (1897): 311.

———. *Phil. Mag.* 48 (1899): 547.

————. *The Royal Institution Library of Science*. Vol.5.

Toulmin, Stephen and June Goodfield. *The Fabric of the Heavens*. New York; Harper & Row, 1961.

van Fraassen, Bas C. *The Scientific Image*. Oxford: Clarendon Press, 1980.

Voltaire. *Elements de la philosophie de Newton*.

Weinberg, Steven. *The Discovery of Subatomic Particles*. New York: Scientific American Books, Inc., 1983.
————. *Dreams of a Final Theory*. New York: Vintage Books, 1992.

Westfall, Robert S. *Never at Rest*. Cambridge: Cambridge University Press, 1980.

White, Andrew D. *A History of the Warfare of Science with Theology in Christendom*. New York; Appleton, 1896.

Whitehead, Alfred N. *Science and the Modern World*. New York: A Mentor Book, 1925.

Whitrow, G.J. *The Structure and Evolution of the Universe*. New York: Harper Torchbooks, 1959.

Whittier, Sir Edmund. *A History of the Theories of Aether and Electricity*. Vol. I. Harper Torchbooks, 1960.

Whyte, L.L. *Essay on Atomism: From Democritus to 1960*. Middletown: Wesleyan University Press, 1961.

Wien, W. *Verh. Phys. Ges. Berlin* 16 (1897): 165.